D1260490

CHRISTIANITY IN CRISIS

21st CENTURY

HANK HANEGRAAFF

THOMAS NELSON
Since 1798

NASHVILLE   DALLAS   MEXICO CITY   RIO DE JANEIRO   BEIJING

Published in Nashville, Tennessee, by Thomas Nelson. Thomas Nelson is a registered trademark of Thomas Nelson, Inc.

Thomas Nelson, Inc. titles may be purchased in bulk for educational, business, fund-raising, or sales promotional use. For information, please e-mail SpecialMarkets@ThomasNelson.com.

Unless otherwise noted, Scripture quotations are taken from the Holy Bible: New International Version®. © 1973, 1978, 1984 by International Bible Society. Used by permission of Zondervan Publishing House. All rights reserved.

Scripture quotations marked NASB are taken from the New American Standard Bible®. © The Lockman Foundation 1960, 1962, 1963, 1968, 1971, 1972, 1973, 1975, 1977. Used by permission.

Scripture quotations marked NKJV are taken from the New King James Version®. © 1982 by Thomas Nelson, Inc. Used by permission. All rights reserved.

Scripture quotations marked KJV are taken from the Holy Bible, King James Version.

Library of Congress Cataloging-in-Publication Data

Hanegraaff, Hank.
  Christianity in crisis : 21st century / Hank Hanegraaff.
      p. cm.
  Includes bibliographical references (p. 356) and indexes.
  ISBN 978-0-8499-0006-8 (hardcover)
  1. Faith movement (Hagin) I. Title.
  BR1643.5.H37 2009
  289.9'4—dc22

                                    2008050180

              Printed in the United States of America
              09 10 11 12 13 QW 7 6 5 4 3 2 1

To Erwin de Castro—who continues to be an inspiration to my family
as a faithful friend and co-laborer in Christ

CONTENTS

ACKNOWLEDGMENTS

First, I want to thank my heavenly Father for giving me health, strength, and everything necessary to complete *Christianity in Crisis: 21st Century*. May He use this volume for His glory and for the extension of His kingdom—not by might, nor by power, but by His Spirit.

Furthermore, I wish to acknowledge the staff and support network of the Christian Research Institute. God has blessed me with a wonderful board and co-laborers whose prayers and encouragement are crucial to this and every project in which I engage. Also, I want to acknowledge Kathy and the kids. As always, their patience and support during the writing process were deeply appreciated.

Finally, a word of thanks to Matt Baugher and his team. When I think of them, the word *professional* comes to mind. Their input and suggestions were extraordinarily helpful!

PREFACE

Even from your own number men will arise and distort the truth in order to draw away disciples after them. So be on your guard! Remember that for three years I never stopped warning each one of you night and day with tears[1]

—THE APOSTLE PAUL

Twenty years ago, I began working on a book that would become a runaway bestseller and winner of the prestigious Gold Medallion Book Award for excellence in evangelical Christian literature. That book, titled *Christianity in Crisis*, unmasked the fatal flaws of a movement that threatens to undermine the very foundation of the faith once and for all delivered to the saints. In those days, Kenneth Hagin was the prime mover behind the message. While his platform was enormous and his influences global, a new breed of prosperity preachers have taken his preaching and practices to unimaginable heights (depths). Indeed, those who followed in his train—men such as Joel Osteen, and women like Joyce Meyer—are living proof that error begets error and heresy begets heresy. As such, they have taken the crisis in Christianity spawned by Hagin and popularized by disciples such as Kenneth Copeland and Benny Hinn to levels that I could have scarcely imagined when I was writing in the twentieth century. And that is why I have now released *Christianity in Crisis: 21ˢᵗ Century*. While *Christianity in Crisis: 21ˢᵗ Century* has similarities with its predecessor, it has remarkable differences as well.

To begin with, I have retained the core of the original. As such, this volume, like its predecessor, is formulated around the acronym F-L-A-W-S. While the nub remains, it is interspersed with quotations from current stars in the faith constellation. Indeed, each of the relevant chapters begins with an epigraph from a mega-faith star that epitomizes the crisis—whether a prostitution of the biblical concept of faith, a critical compromise respecting the nature of God, or a current con and cover-up. Moreover, each of these chapters ends with a summary titled "Error Begets Error," which demonstrates that the heresies of original faith proliferators have been not only perpetuated but often exacerbated by the new breed. E. W. Kenyon's original deviations from orthodox Christianity were minor compared to those that characterized the later stages of his ministry. And with each of Kenyon's successive disciples, the errors become more pronounced. Hagin, who popularized Kenyon, not only expanded his errors but added to them as well. The progression from bad to worse has continued with purveyors such as Kenneth Copeland and Benny Hinn and has now sunk to new depths through the proliferation and practices of faith luminaries such as T. D. Jakes and Joyce Meyer.

Furthermore, this volume is complemented by a new introduction that not only provides a compelling overview of the issues addressed in the body of the book but documents the eerie similarities between pop sensations such as Rhonda Byrne's *The Secret* and Joel Osteen's *Your Best Life Now*. Such similarities are indicative of a slide within Christianity as a whole. Having lost the ability to think biblically, postmodern Christians are being systematically transformed from cultural change agents and initiators into cultural conformists and imitators. Pop culture beckons, and postmodern Christians are taking the bait. As a result the biblical model of faith has given way to an increasingly bizarre array of fads and formulas. Put another way, the biblical passion for exercising spiritual disciplines (see Part Seven: Back to Basics) is giving ground to the fast formulas of Faith theology. As such, I have taken pains to enhance the "Back to Basics" section of this volume in order to erect a lighthouse in the midst of the gathering storm.

Finally, *Christianity in Crisis: 21ˢᵗ Century* has been augmented with a "Cast of Characters" section that provides comprehensive information as well as biblical evaluation of the newest and most prolific stars in the faith galaxy—virtual rock stars who command the attention of presidential candidates and media moguls. While this cast of characters is far from a monolith, they uniformly traffic in twisted texts, make-believe miracles, urban legends, and counterfeit Christs. What you will discover in the new "Cast of Characters" section is so horrifying that your first reaction may be utter disbelief or outright denial. But I assure you that what I have written is carefully documented and contextually defensible. As a case in point, as hard as it may be to believe, John Hagee not only shamelessly promotes the pretext of a prosperous Jesus—who lives in a big house and wears designer clothes—but brazenly depicts a sectarian Christ who "refused to be Messiah to the Jews."

In all, *Christianity in Crisis: 21st Century*, like its predecessor, is a book that needed to be written. In the end, it is not as much about the Faith teachers themselves but about Faith followers who inevitably become distracted, disillusioned, and discouraged. My heart aches for the parent who put his dead baby on ice and in the midst of tears and desperation drove 350 miles to a Counterfeit Revival center because he trusted the testimonies of Faith preachers who were touting resurrections from the dead.[2] I equally grieve for the millions who have left Faith churches in the midst of failed Faith formulas. Some conclude that God must not love them; others question the integrity of the whole Christian enterprise.

The tragedy is that too often we look for God in all the wrong places. The real experience is found not in counterfeit formulas but in Christian fundamentals. Think for a moment about prayer. Rather than seeking formulas through which we can get things from God, we must be ever mindful that prayer is an opportunity for developing intimacy with the Lover of our souls. If we are honest with ourselves, most of us have learned to pray backward. We hurry into God's presence with techniques and incessant babblings and in the process drown out the sound of the very One whose voice we so long to hear. All too often we want God to move the fence posts and enlarge our houses and lands. God wants something far better for us. He wants us to be still so that He can enlarge the territories of our hearts. He has sent us sixty-six love letters etched in heavenly handwriting. And the more we meditate upon those words, the clearer His voice will resonate in the sounds of our silence.

As *Christianity in Crisis* has impacted the lives of literally thousands of people from Nairobi, Kenya, to Seoul, Korea; and from Beijing, China, to Los Angeles, California, it is my prayer that *Christianity in Crisis: 21st Century* will likewise turn the hearts of millions toward home.

—Hank Hanegraaff
Charlotte, North Carolina
September 2008

INTRODUCTION

Our words are vital in bringing our dreams to pass. It's not enough to simply see it by faith or in your imagination. You have to begin speaking words of faith over your life. Your words have enormous creative power. The moment you speak something out, you give birth to it. This is a spiritual principle, and it works whether what you are saying is good or bad, positive or negative.[1]

—JOEL OSTEEN

Everyone wants to know the secret—you know, the secret to health; the secret to wealth; the secret to successful relationships; the secret to making a fortune on Wall Street; the secret to maintaining your perfect weight. The list is endless. Thus, when Rhonda Byrne informed the world she had discovered "the Secret to life"— a secret harnessed by "the greatest people in history: Plato, Shakespeare, Newton, Hugo, Beethoven, Lincoln, Emerson, Edison, Einstein"[2]—the world took notice. Within weeks *The Secret* topped bestseller lists and morphed into a cultural phenomenon.[3] Oprah dubbed *The Secret* "life changing." According to Oprah, "The thoughts and the feelings that you put out into the world, both good and bad, are exactly what is always coming back to you, *so you have the life that you have created.* I've been talking about this for years on my show. I just never called it *The Secret*."[4]

What is the secret? It is "the law of attraction." Says Byrne: "The greatest teachers who have ever lived have told us that the law of attraction is the most powerful law in the Universe."[5] As Byrne goes on to explain, "The law of attraction is the law of creation. Quantum physicists tell us that the entire Universe emerged from thought! You create your life through your thoughts and the law of attraction, and every single person does the same. It doesn't just work if you know about it. It has always been working in your life and every other person's life throughout history."[6]

While the science of quantum physics is complex, it is allegedly simple to apply. Says Byrne, "The Creative Process used in *The Secret*, which was taken from the New Testament in the Bible, is an easy guideline for you to create what you want in three simple steps"[7]: *Ask*, *Believe*, and *Receive*.[8] Byrne points to herself as a prime example. To transform herself from fat to thin, she thought thin thoughts and did not so much as look at fat people: "If you see people who are overweight, do not observe them, but immediately switch your mind to the picture of you in your perfect body and *feel* it."[9] As a result she says, "I now maintain my perfect weight of 116 pounds and I can eat whatever I want."[10] According to *The Secret*, the error is to think that food is responsible for weight gain:

> The most common thought that people hold, and I held it too, is that food was responsible for my weight gain. That is a belief that does not serve you, and in my mind now it is complete balderdash! Food is not responsible for putting on weight. It is your *thought* that food is responsible for putting on weight that actually has food put on weight. Remember, thoughts are primary cause of everything, and the rest is effects from those thoughts. Think perfect thoughts and the result must be perfect weight.[11]

While at first blush Byrne's rhetoric may seem merely silly, there is a clear and present danger in her reasoning. Just as her followers must avoid fat people for fear of becoming fat, so they, too, must avoid cancer victims for fear of contracting cancer. Or poor people for fear of becoming poor. In other words, you should avoid the very people Jesus exhorts us to care for—do not so much as look at them!

Byrne and her contributors are remarkably open with respect to the many dangerous hues of "the secret's" dark underbelly. As such, she points out events in history "where masses of lives were lost." While some might find it incomprehensible that multitudes could have attracted the same massacre, Byrne does not. "If people believe they can be in the wrong place at the wrong time, and they have no control over outside circumstances, those thoughts of fear, separation, and powerlessness, if persistent, can attract them to being in the wrong place at the wrong time." Says Byrne: "*Nothing* can come into your experience unless you summon it through persistent thoughts."[12]

Indeed, as contributing authors of *The Secret* have made plain, victims of suffering and tragedy attracted those circumstances to their lives. When asked by Larry King whether Jessica Lunsford, a nine-year-old Florida girl who was brutally raped and murdered, attracted this horror to herself, contributing author Joe Vitale responded, "We are attracting everything to ourselves *and there is no exception.*"[13]

In short, thoughts are the primary cause of everything—whether good or bad. On one hand, thin thoughts produce thin bodies; on the other, six million Jews brought the horrors of the Holocaust upon themselves. As *The Secret* makes clear, "The law of attraction never slips up . . . There are no exclusions to the law of attraction. If something came to you, you drew it, with prolonged thought."[14] Says Byrne, "You are the Master of the Universe, and the Genie is there to serve you."[15]

For Rhonda Byrne, the Genie is the law of attraction. For Joel Osteen, another cultural phenomenon, it is the Word of Faith. As such, he is committed to the notion that faith is a force, that words are the containers of the force, and that through the force of faith, people can create their own realities. As he explains in his mega-bestseller *Your Best Life Now*, "You have to begin speaking words of faith over your life. Your words have enormous creative power. The moment you speak something out, you give birth to it. This is a spiritual principle, and it works whether what you are saying is good or bad, positive or negative."[16]

According to Osteen—who influences the lives of "tens of millions of people in more than a hundred nations worldwide . . . through his weekly television broadcasts, his *New York Times* best-selling books, his sold-out international speaking tours, and his weekly top-ten podcasts"[17]—"It's not enough to merely think positively: You need to speak positively about yourself. You need to hear it over and over again."[18]

While Osteen and Byrne have noteworthy differences, they are united in the belief that the force of faith is so powerful that even God (however you define Him) is bound by its irrevocable reality. In evidence, Osteen cites the birth of John the Baptist. Zechariah doubted that his wife could give birth to a son, thus God rendered him speechless during the entirety of Elizabeth's pregnancy. "Why did God take away his speech?" asks Osteen. "It's because God knew that Zechariah's negative words would cancel out His plan . . . See, God knows the power of our words. He knows we prophesy our future. And He knew Zechariah's own negative words would stop His plan."[19]

Osteen is so convinced that words create reality that he transforms an unfortunate paralytic from a hero to a heel. In Osteen's twist of the text, Jesus encounters a man by the pool of Bethesda just "lying around feeling sorry" for himself. In response to Jesus' "simple, straightforward question," the paralytic begins "listing all of his excuses. 'I'm all alone. I don't have anyone to help me. Other people have let me down. Other people always seem to get ahead of me. I don't have a chance in life.'" With nary a hint of mercy, Osteen continues: "Is it any wonder that he remained in that condition for thirty-eight years?"[20] In sharp contrast, Osteen says his sister Lisa arose from the ashes of a painful divorce and remarried. Unlike the paralytic, she "wasn't going to sit around by the pool for thirty-eight years feeling sorry for herself."[21]

"Positively or negatively," reiterates Osteen, "creative power resides in your words."[22] In making his point, Osteen cites the story of Abraham and Sarah. The moment God told Sarah she was going to have a child, Sarah—who "saw herself as an older, barren woman"—began making negative confessions. Indeed, says Osteen, "God had to change the image Abraham and Sarah had of themselves before they could ever have that child. How did God do that? He changed their names; *He changed the words they were hearing.* He changed Sarai to Sarah, which means 'princess.' . . . [Thus] every time somebody said, 'Hello, Sarah,' they were saying, 'Hello, princess.' Over time, that changed her self-image. Now, she no longer saw herself as an older, barren woman; she began to see herself as a princess." As a result, writes Osteen, "she gave birth to a child."[23]

For Osteen, words are downright magical. "In the physical realm, you have to see it to believe it, but God says you have to believe it, and then you'll see it."[24] "Think about it," exhorts Osteen. "Your words go out of your mouth and they come right back into your own ears. If you hear those comments long enough, they will drop down into your spirit, and those words will produce exactly what you're saying."[25] As proof, Osteen invokes the Bible: "The Scripture tells us that *we* are to 'call the things that are not as if they already were.'"[26]

Not only does Osteen rashly reason that God's purpose in changing Sarai to Sarah was to affect her self-image and alter her negative confessions, but he makes a morally reckless application to the present. He tells the story of a friend named Joe whose wife had five miscarriages before "something clicked inside of him." He realized that his given name was *Joseph*, meaning "God will add." Joe then required everyone to call him Joseph, believing that in doing so "they were speaking faith into his life" and as a result God would add to him a son. Writes

Osteen: "Several months after Joseph began believing his name, his wife became pregnant again. And for the first time in ten years, she carried the child to full term, and gave birth to a healthy baby boy." The moral of the story, concludes Osteen, is that "with our words, we can prophesy our own future."[27]

The implication is hard to miss. Had Joe listened to "God speaking to him"[28] ten years earlier, the lives of five children would have been saved, and he and his wife would have been spared a world of hurt. Not only so, but with millions of Osteen books in print, one can only imagine the numbers of people who must even now be superstitiously fretting over the spiritual implications of their names.

Osteen's methods are remarkably similar to those used by Byrne. In pulpit and in print, he communicates an endless string of undocumented anecdotes and urban legends. Sometimes the stories seem singularly silly. In seeking to buttress his belief in generational curses, Osteen chronicles "an interesting study done in 1993 by the United States military. They were curious about what traits get passed down from one generation to the next." As Osteen tells the story:

> The researchers extracted some white blood cells from a volunteer and they carefully placed them in a test tube. They then put a probe from a lie-detector machine down in that test tube, to measure the person's emotional response. Next, they instructed this same volunteer to go a couple of doors down and watch some violent scenes from an old war movie on television. When this man watched the scenes, even though the blood that was being tested was in another room, when he got all uptight and tense, that lie detector test shot off the page. It was detecting his emotional response even though the blood was no longer in his body.[29]

Osteen adds that this was not an isolated experiment. The United States "experimenters did this with person after person with the same results. They concluded that the blood cells seem to 'remember' where they came from."[30] While this tale is obviously bizarre on many different levels, Osteen employs it to convince his readers that the problems they encounter in the present can be pawned off on proclivities of parents and grandparents in the past.

Where Byrne primarily abuses science in sanitizing her stories, Osteen principally abuses Scripture. While his misinterpretations might be rationalized on the basis of limited theological acumen, his misquotations cannot. Again and again he alters the text to conform to Word/Faith proclivities. As noted, to buttress the belief that words create reality, Osteen writes, "The Scripture tells us that we are to 'call the things that are not as if they already were.'" As Osteen surely knows, Scripture says nothing of the sort. Indeed, the very passage Osteen references (Romans 4:17) clearly communicates that it is "the God who gives life"—*not we*—who "calls things that are not as though they were."

Osteen's stories and Scriptorture are not unique. A host of prominent Word of Faith teachers have employed similar techniques and as a result are plunging Christianity into an ever-deepening crisis. In the late twentieth century, Word of Faith teachers like Kenneth Hagin, Robert Tilton, Marilyn Hickey, John Avanzini, and Morris Cerullo were at the fore. In the early twenty-first they are being overshadowed by a new breed of prosperity preachers (Creflo Dollar, Rod Parsley, Joyce Meyer, John Hagee, T. D. Jakes, and Paula White) who have increasingly become mainstream. Paula White is lauded by Donald Trump as "an amazing woman" with "a significant message,"[31] and T. D. Jakes is trumpeted by *Time* as perhaps "the next Billy Graham."[32]

If occult sources such as those referenced in *The Secret* pose the greatest threat to the body of Christ from without, the deadly doctrines disseminated by prosperity preachers pose the greatest threat to Christianity from within. To avert this crisis, a paradigm shift of major proportions is desperately needed—a shift from perceiving God as a means to an end, to the recognition that He *is* the end.

And while change must come, it clearly will not come easily. Those who are dispensing spiritual cyanide by the megadose occupy powerful platforms within evangelical Christianity. They control vast resources and stand to lose multiplied millions if they are exposed. The stakes are so high that those who are plunging Christianity into crisis are willing to do and say virtually anything to silence opposition.

Paul Crouch, founder of the Trinity Broadcasting Network (TBN), went so far as to suggest that if God does not kill "heresy hunters," he will.[33] Benny Hinn took it a step further. On TBN's *Praise the Lord* program, he said, "You have attacked me. Your children will pay for it."[34] On another occasion Hinn shouted, "If you care for your kids, stop attacking Benny Hinn; you're attacking on the radio all the time. You will pay, and your children will. Hear this from the lips of God's servant. You are in danger."[35] Other threats could be cited, including the time Hinn ominously snarled, "I'm not exactly the normal kind of guy, you know. I'm from Israel. Sometimes I wish God would give me a Holy Ghost machine gun. I'd blow your head off."[36]

Additionally, because of my stance on the Word/Faith tenets outlined in this book, I have experienced censorship on Christian radio and television. Moreover, churches that once welcomed me with open arms now shut me out. While this has been extremely discouraging, what has been even more disheartening is that credible Christian leaders, some of whom might otherwise be considered Christian statesmen, are shamefully silent when it comes to identifying wolves among us, camouflaged in sheep's clothing.

While they do not hesitate to blast the secular media and the Hollywood entertainment industry, when it comes to exposing darkness on Christian television and radio, they cower in fear of losing their platforms and the millions of dollars these forums provide. In exchange for free programming or publicity on networks such as TBN, some of these Christian leaders have gone so far as to provide uncritical, unqualified endorsements for preachers and programming that clearly confuse, compromise, and contradict essential Christian doctrine.

Despite the consequences, I am absolutely convinced that *Christianity in Crisis: 21st Century* is a book that needed to be written—a book that I pray will serve not only to expose the cancer that is ravaging the body of Christ from within but also to effect enduring changes among those who dare to take the sacred name "Christian" upon their lips.

This cancer has now reached the epidemic stage, and is spreading with such speed as to genuinely warrant the words "Christianity in Crisis." It has so disfigured the face of Christianity that pagans looking on from without either smile with condescension and cynicism, or, with CNN founder Ted Turner, caricature Christians as "bozos" and "idiots."[37]

As unfortunate as this sort of stereotyping is, one can hardly blame those who have never seen the real face of Christianity for their smug characterizations. They suppose that the distorted image of Christianity—which can be viewed daily in the comfort of their living rooms—is in fact the real thing.

Because these self-styled "prophets" start with a distorted concept of the Creator, they end up with aberrant doctrines that literally boggle the mind. Their so-called revelations reduce God to the status of a "cosmic gofer," while simultaneously exalting man to the position of "sovereign of the universe."

Camouflaged as shepherds, they present a Christ who is remarkably unlike the Jesus of the Bible. Their Jesus wears designer clothes, lives in a palatial mansion, and is surrounded by a band of very wealthy disciples. In concert with New Thought gurus such as Dr. Catherine Ponder, author of *Dynamic Laws of Prosperity*, they laud "the millionaires of the Bible." As *The Secret's* Rhonda Byrne further states, "If you have been brought up to believe that being wealthy is not spiritual, then I highly recommend you read The Millionaires of the Bible Series by Catherine Ponder. In these glorious books you will discover that Abraham, Isaac, Jacob, Joseph, Moses, and Jesus were not only prosperity teachers, but also millionaires themselves, with more affluent lifestyles than many present-day millionaires could conceive of."[38]

What you will discover as you continue is so horrifying that your natural inclination may be disbelief or denial. But I assure you that what I am communicating is painstakingly accurate and assiduously documented. The organization I head has built a solid reputation of handling issues with a high degree of accuracy and integrity. Even those who do not share the Christian Research Institute's (CRI) worldview would affirm our commitment to careful research, devoid of hype and sensationalism.

Because Faith teachers are part of a movement and not a monolithic organization, not every Faith teacher holds to every doctrine examined in this book. However, the spectrum of false teachings I analyze does accurately represent the entire Faith movement. In other words, not all Faith teachers subscribe to exactly the same beliefs on every point of doctrine, but they do hold to an aberrant core of doctrine that rightly places them within the broad outlines of the Faith movement.

I had three categories of readers in mind as I sat down to pen this book. First, my heart goes out to those people who have been misled into joining the Faith movement. These dear people are sincere in their desire to serve the Lord, but they have been directed into a pathway that leads inevitably to the kingdom of the cults. I desperately desire that these precious people see the truth of the gospel and exchange a counterfeit faith for a real one—one that has encouraged, nurtured, and strengthened men and women throughout the two-thousand-year history of orthodox Christianity.

Furthermore, I write to committed Christians who may be either concerned or confused about the Faith movement. I pray this book forever settles whatever questions you may have about the true nature of the movement and where it fits on the Christian spectrum. The answer is: it doesn't. The Faith movement is every bit as cultic as the teachings of the Mormons, the Jehovah's Witnesses, and Christian Science. And as such, it is not worthy of Christian support.

Finally, I want to clearly demonstrate to outside observers that the Faith movement does not represent biblical Christianity. In the past few months multiple Faith teachers have been exposed in the national media for questionable beliefs and practices, and I want to cogently communicate that the Faith movement does not represent the historic Christian faith. Perhaps the burden I felt in writing *Christianity in Crisis* is best characterized by the warnings codified by the prophet Jeremiah and the apostles Peter and Paul. Consider their words as they ring down through the ages with prophetic poignancy.

> *This is what the LORD Almighty says: "Do not listen to what the prophets are prophesying to you; they fill you with false hopes. They speak visions from their own minds, not from the mouth of the LORD . . . I did not send these prophets, yet they have run with their message; I did not speak to them, yet they have prophesied . . . How long will this continue in the hearts of these lying prophets, who prophecy the delusions of their own minds?" (Jeremiah 23:16, 21, 26)*

> *But there were also false prophets among the people, just as there will be false teachers among you. They will secretly introduce destructive heresies, even denying the sovereign Lord who bought them . . . Many will follow their shameful ways and will bring the way of truth into disrepute. In their greed these teachers will exploit you with stories they have made up. (2 Peter 2:1–3)*

> *Even from your own number men will arise and distort the truth in order to draw away disciples after them. So be on your guard! Remember that for three years I never stopped warning each of you night and day with tears. (Acts 20:30–31)*

May God be pleased to use the pages that follow to expose the skin of truth stuffed with a lie and prescribe solutions for *Christianity in Crisis*.

part one

TURNING TRUTH INTO MYTHOLOGY

The following tale is a composite of the erroneous teachings of individuals such as Joel Osteen, Joyce Meyer, Creflo Dollar, Benny Hinn, Kenneth Copeland, Kenneth Hagin, Frederick Price, Myles Munroe, T. D. Jakes, Paula White, Juanita Bynum, John Hagee, and many others. While not all the Faith teachers hold to every aspect of this tale, they have all made substantial contributions to both the production and proliferation of these aberrations and heresies.

Once upon a time, long, long ago on a faraway planet,[1] there lived a good God. This God was very much like you and me—a Being who stands about six feet two inches to six feet three inches tall, weighs a couple of hundred pounds, and has a hand span of about nine inches.[2]

This God's wisdom and power were so great that He literally had the ability to speak things into existence. In fact, this God could actually visualize beautiful images in His mind and then turn them into reality[3] by utilizing a special power called the "force of faith."[4]

One day, this God had a cosmic brainstorm. He decided to use the force of His faith to create something superb and special.[5] He decided to bring a whole new world into existence.[6] This was not going to be just any old world; it was going to be the most fantastic world imaginable. In fact, this world would become so wonderful that it would actually feature an exact duplicate of the mother planet where God lived.[7]

After carefully visualizing every detail of this wonderful, wonderful world, God went into action. Releasing the force of His faith like a whirlwind, God

1

spoke into existence the planet He saw in His mind's eye.[8] And boy, was God excited! Looking down with fondness on this classic new creation, He named the planet "Earth."

And this was only the beginning. Suddenly, a host of brilliant new ideas began to flood into God's creative consciousness. He began to visualize vast oceans and springs abounding with water. He saw magnificent mountains and fertile fields. His mind produced flashes of thunder and lightning. Plants, flowers, and trees blazed in rapid succession through His thoughts. Now on a roll, God began to visualize life replete with beautiful birds and creatures of every size and shape imaginable.

Yet this was merely the beginning. For after five days of vivid visualizations, God's mind moved into yet another dimension. On day six, His imagination went wild and, in His mind's eye, God saw the crowning jewel of His creation. As the details developed within His fertile mind, God suddenly found Himself focused on an exact duplicate of Himself.[9]

Throwing all caution to the wind, God spoke, and suddenly, out of the pristine soil of planet Earth, there arose another god—a god spelled with a small "g" but a god nonetheless.[10] As the image of this little god[11] took form, God saw that He had literally outdone Himself. For there, before His very own eyes, stood another god—an exact duplicate of Himself, including size and shape.[12]

God had finally done it! He had thought the unthinkable and, by His word of faith, God had created a creature that was not even subordinate to Himself.[13]

And boy, was God ever glad. For now He had a colleague whose nature was identical to His own—a god who could think like Him, be like Him, and do almost but not quite everything that He could do. God called His carbon copy "Adam," and He gave him dominion and authority over the entire creation.[14] As a matter of fact, this creature had so much power that his Creator could do nothing in the earth realm without first obtaining his permission.[15]

Adam was truly a super being! He could fly like the birds and swim underwater like a fish. And that's not all. Without a space suit Adam could literally fly through the universe. In fact, with just one thought, he could literally transport himself to the moon![16]

Yet even after creating a super being like Adam, God was not fully satisfied with His accomplishments. Somehow, He just knew that a piece of the puzzle was still missing. So putting His mind into overdrive, God began brainstorming once more.

And then, in a flash, it dawned on God! Why hadn't He thought of it before? Adam was made in His image, so obviously he was as much female as he was male, right? So, why not double His pleasure and double His fun? Why not separate the male part from the female part?

Not wanting to waste a single moment, God charged into action! Causing a deep sleep to fall upon Adam, God opened him up, removed the female part from the male part, and made a being of surpassing beauty. He made woman—man with a womb—and He called the womb-man "Eve."[17]

This time God had clearly gone too far: He had actually brought into existence the very beings that would one day get Him kicked off of the very planet He had created. As incredible as it may seem, these super beings would one day turn on their Creator and relegate Him to the status of the greatest failure of all time.

You see, long before God had visualized planet Earth into existence, He had also created a whole other world full of beings called angels. One of these angles was a being of such breathtaking beauty and brilliance that he was named "Lucifer," the Morning Star.

Lucifer had great ambitions. In fact, he wanted to take control of everything God had ever visualized into existence; he wanted to become exactly like the Most High. Well, because of his treason, Lucifer was cast out of heaven and renamed "Satan," the deceiver.

Tumbling down from the mother planet where God lived, Satan landed on the replica that God had spoken into existence. He landed on planet Earth, the very planet on which Adam and Eve would one day live. There, he lay in wait for the opportunity of the ages, the opportunity to get back at God.

And then, one day, opportunity came knocking. Not long after God had spoken Adam and Eve into existence, Satan spied them standing naked in the middle of the garden of Eden.

Satan instantly transformed himself into a serpent and cunningly tricked the two little gods into committing cosmic treason. For just the price of an apple, Adam and Eve sold their godhood to Satan. The devil, through Adam, became the god of this world.[18]

Alas, not only did Adam and Eve lose their nature as gods, but they were actually infused with the very nature of Satan himself.[19] Adam had become the first person to be born again; he was "born" with the nature of God and "born again" with the nature of Satan.[20]

In one blinding instant, the first man and woman who had ever lived were transformed from divine to demonic. Immediately, they became susceptible to sin, sickness, suffering, and, more importantly, spiritual death. In fact, Eve's body, which like Adam's was originally made to give birth out of her side, underwent a radical transformation—from that moment on, she and her female offspring would bring forth children from the lower region of their anatomies.[21]

In that fateful moment, Adam and Eve were summarily barred from Eden, and God was banished from the earth. Satan now had legal rights to the earth and all her inhabitants,[22] and God was left on the outside desperately searching for a way to get back in.[23]

God, in a flash, had become the greatest failure of all time. Not only had He lost his top-ranking angel, as well as at least a third of His other angels, but now, in addition, He had lost the first man He had ever created, the first woman He had created, and the whole earth and the fullness therein![24]

But as they say in baseball, "It ain't over till it's over!" God was not yet ready to throw in the towel. He had that winning attitude and refused to let go. Realizing that He needed man's invitation to get back into the earth, God immediately went to work. And after thousands of years God finally found an "old boy," named Abraham, who took the bait and became the vehicle through which God, if He was lucky, may one day win back the universe He had lost.[25]

You see, through Abraham would eventually come a Second Adam who would reverse the consequences of Satan's deception. This Adam, if all went according to plan, would return to man his godhood and to God His good earth.

Well, in time, God got Abraham to strike a deal with him. In fact, God and Abraham became blood brothers[26] and forged a covenant that would gain Abraham health and wealth, and regain for God a foothold in the world He had created.[27] God's plan was to make Abraham the father of all nations and to produce from his seed another Adam who would regain the turf that was lost by the first Adam.

In keeping with His Word, God made Abraham very, very wealthy. And then, once again, He proceeded to visualize. Through God's mind raced images of a brand-new Adam—a man who would one day restore to Him His rightful place in the universe, and who would forever banish His archrival, Satan, from the kingdom.

And then it happened! One fine day, the image of this Savior coalesced in

God's mind. Without hesitation, God began speaking into existence the picture of the redeemer He had painted on the canvas of His consciousness.[28] Excitedly, God positively confessed, "The Messiah is coming, the Messiah is coming!"[29]

As God's Spirit hovered over a little woman named Mary, the confession began to take shape before His very eyes.[30] The spoken Word became legs, arms, eyes, and hair. And then, presto! There, before God's very own eyes, emerged the body of the Second Adam.[31]

The Second Adam was named Jesus. And as Abraham's descendent, Jesus was wealthy and prosperous. He lived in a big house,[32] handled big money,[33] and even wore designer clothes.[34] In fact, Jesus was so wealthy that He actually needed a treasurer to keep track of all His money.[35]

Jesus, who was a whiz at speaking things into existence, showed His disciples how to master the art of positive confession.[36] Thus, they, too, experienced unlimited health and unlimited wealth. The fact is that some of His followers caught on so well that they became rich beyond comprehension. The apostle Paul, for example, had so much money that government officials would work feverishly to try to get a bribe out of him.[37]

Jesus also overcame every trick and temptation that Satan could throw His way. Despite the fact that He never claimed to be God, Jesus succeeded in living a life of sinless perfection.[38] When all was said and done, Jesus passed the test that the first Adam had failed.

And then, at the prime of His life, Jesus entered a garden—a garden much like Eden, where the first Adam had lost his godhood. In this garden, called Gethsemane, Jesus moved into the final stages of a process that would transform Him from an immortal man to a satanic being[39] and would, in turn, re-create men as little gods[40] who would no longer be subject to the scourge of sin, sickness, and suffering.[41]

As part of the process, Jesus would have to die a double death on the cross. He would have to die spiritually as well as physically. If physical death had been enough, the two thieves on the cross could have atoned for the sins of mankind.[42] No, the real key was spiritual death and suffering in hell.

And then, one day, upon a cruel cross, the crystal Christ—the paragon of virtue—was transformed into a defiled demoniac. The lamb became a serpent[43] and was ushered into the very bowels of the earth. There, Christ was tortured by Satan and his minions.[44] And all hell laughed.[45]

Little did Satan know, however, that the last laugh would be on him. For just as Adam had fallen for Satan's trap in Eden, now Satan had fallen for God's trap in hell.[46]

You see, Satan had blown it on a technicality. He had dragged Jesus into hell illegally.[47] The truth is that Satan had completely forgotten to take into consideration the fact that Jesus had not actually sinned. You see, Jesus had merely become sin as a result of the sin of others. Alas, Satan and his demonic hosts had tortured the emaciated, poured out, little wormy spirit of Christ without legal rights.[48]

And this was exactly the opening God had been looking for. So seizing the moment, God spoke His faith-filled words into the bowels of the earth. Suddenly, the twisted, death-wracked spirit of Jesus began to fill out and come back to life.[49] He began to look like something the devil had never seen before.

There, in the sinister presence of the evil one himself, Jesus began to flex His spiritual muscles. As a horde of whimpering demons looked on, Jesus whipped the devil in his own backyard. He snatched Satan's keys and emerged from hell as a born-again man.[50]

God had pulled off the coup of the ages. Not only had He tricked Satan out of his lordship, using Jesus as the bait, but He had also caught Satan on a technicality through which Jesus could be born again.

But that's not all! You see, because Jesus was re-created from a satanic being to an incarnation of God, you, too, can become an incarnation—as much an incarnation as Jesus Christ of Nazareth![51] And, as an incarnation of God, you can have unlimited health and unlimited wealth—a palace like the Taj Mahal with a Rolls Royce in your driveway.[52] And if I could shock you (and maybe I should), you, my friend, are a little messiah running around on earth![53]

All it takes now is to recognize your own divinity. You, too, can harness the force of faith. Never again will you have to pray, "Thy will be done."[54] Rather, your word is God's command.[55] By simply using your tongue, you can literally speak whatsoever you desire into existence;[56] and then you can live happily ever after on this planet of prosperity.

𝔗𝔥𝔢 𝔈𝔫𝔡

What you have read is a composite of the writings and ramblings of some of the most powerful and prolific prosperity preachers operating within the church today—"teachers" who are systematically turning the truth into mythology.

1

CULT OR CULTIC?

The word *cult* may be defined from both a sociological and theological perspective. From a sociological perspective it describes a group of people who are controlled by their leader(s) in virtually every dimension of their lives, potentially resulting in illegal, immoral, and antisocial consequences. From a theological perspective, a cult may be defined as a modern-day movement that claims to be Christian but compromises, confuses, and contradicts essential Christian doctrine, such as Christ's atonement upon the cross.

While the Faith movement is undeniably cultic—and particular groups within the movement are clearly cults—it should be pointed out that *there are many sincere, born-again believers within the movement.* I cannot overemphasize this crucial point. These believers, for the most part, seem to be wholly unaware of the movement's cultic theology.

I have personally met several dear people who fall into this category. I question neither their faith nor their devotion to Christ. They represent that segment of the movement that, for whatever reason, has not comprehended or internalized the heretical teachings set forth by the leadership of their respective groups. In many instances, they are new converts to Christianity who have not yet been grounded in their faith. But this is not always the case.

For example, I remember with great fondness the kindred spirit I shared with two ladies who participated in my Personal Witness Training class in Atlanta, Georgia. Year in and year out, these ladies would diligently and faithfully work to equip church members to effectively communicate the good news of the gospel. They were as committed to Christ as any two people I have ever met; yet they were both staunch supporters of Kenneth Copeland and Kenneth Hagin. I can still recall the conversations we had in 1985 concerning this topic.

What stands out most vividly in my mind was their honest conviction that these men did not teach what I claimed they did.

Over the years I have received hundreds of letters from people immersed in the Faith movement who were completely oblivious to the rank heresy they were being fed—individuals who have said, "Until I saw the evidence with my very own eyes, I was not willing to accept it." For this reason, we must take care to judge the *theology* of the Faith movement rather than those being seduced by it.

WHAT MAKES A CULT?

Christ Himself, in His magnificent Sermon on the Mount, taught us to not judge self-righteously or hypocritically. As frail mortals, we can only look on the outside; it is God who discerns the intent of the heart (1 Chronicles 28:9; Jeremiah 17:10).

Having said that, let me reiterate that those who knowingly accept Faith theology are clearly embracing a different gospel, which is in reality no gospel at all. Let us never forget that Scripture admonishes us in the strongest of terms to test all things by the Word of God and to hold fast to that which is good (1 Thessalonians 5:21; cf. Acts 17:11). As Jude exhorts us, we must contend earnestly for the faith (Jude 3).

By the time you finish reading this book, you will have come face-to-face with detailed documentation that conclusively demonstrates that many of the groups within the Faith movement are cults. Therefore, we need to understand exactly what is meant by the term *cult*. For the purposes of this writing, I will focus on two primary ways in which a cult may be defined.

First, a cult may be defined from a sociological perspective. According to sociologist J. Milton Yinger, "The term cult is used in many different ways, usually with the connotations of small size, search for a mystical experience, lack of an organizational structure, and presence of a charismatic leader."[1] For the most part, sociologists have tried to avoid negative overtones in their descriptions of cults. The same cannot be said, however, for the media-driven public at large.

According to religion observer J. Gordon Melton, the 1970s saw the emergence of "secular anti-cultists" who "began to speak of 'destructive cults,' groups which hypnotized or brainwashed recruits, destroyed their ability to make rational judgments and turned them into slaves of the group's leader."[2] Cults of this variety are viewed as both deceptive and manipulative, with the groups' leadership exercising control over virtually every aspect of the members' lives. Furthermore, converts are typically cut off from all former associations—including relatives and friends—and are expected to give their complete devotion, loyalty, and commitment to the cult.[3] Examples of cults labeled as sociologically destructive range from the Hare Krishnas to Reverend Sun Myung Moon's Unification Church to the Family of Love led by "Moses" David Berg.

A second way to define a cult is from a theological perspective. A cult, in this sense, is deemed a pseudo-Christian group. As such, it claims to be Christian but denies one or more of the essential doctrines of historic Christianity; these doctrines focus on such matters as the meaning of faith, the nature of God, and the person and work of Jesus Christ. Years ago, Denver Seminary professor Gordon Lewis succinctly summarized it this way:

> A cult, then, is any religious movement which claims the backing of Christ
> or the Bible, but distorts the central message of Christianity by 1) an addi-
> tional revelation, and 2) by displacing a fundamental tenet of the faith with
> a secondary matter.[4]

Christian Research Institute founder Walter Martin adds that "a cult might also be defined as a group of people gathered about a specific person or person's misinterpretation of the Bible."[5] From a theological perspective, cults include organizations such as the Church of Jesus Christ of Latter-day Saints, the Watchtower Bible and Tract Society, and the Church of Religious Science.

A primary characteristic of cults in general is the practice of taking biblical texts out of context in order to develop pretexts for their theological perversions.[6] In addition, cults have virtually made an art form out of using Christian termi- nology, all the while pouring their own meanings into the words.[7] For example, while practically all cults laud the name "Jesus," they preach a Jesus vastly differ- ent from the Jesus of the historic Christian faith. As Jesus Christ Himself put it, the real litmus test is "Who do you say I am?" (Matthew 16:15).

Mormons answer the question by saying that Jesus is merely the spirit- brother of Lucifer. Jehovah's Witnesses assert that Jesus is Michael the Archangel. New Thought practitioners refer to Jesus as an avatar or mystical messenger. As blasphemous as all of this is, however, many Faith adherents actually reduce

Jesus to an even lower level. For them, He is no more an incarnation of God than is any believer.

THE DIFFERENCE BETWEEN "CULTIC" AND A "CULT"

Given these definitions of a cult, it is completely justified to characterize *particular* groups within the Faith movement as cults—either theologically or sociologically or, in some cases, both. However, in classifying the Faith movement in general, it is more precise to use the term *cultic*, which essentially means "cult-like." This distinction clarifies that cults (from a theological perspective) refer to groups with uniform sets of doctrines and rigidly defined organizational structures; they are monolithic. "Movements," on the other hand, are multifaceted and diverse in their beliefs, teachings, and practices. Thus, while certain groups within the Faith movement can be properly classified as cults, the word *cultic* more aptly describes the movement as a whole. To put it another way, the Faith phenomena collectively reflects the sort of diversity found in movements (such as the New Age movement), as opposed to mirroring the homogeneous and relatively static character of cults such as the Mormon church and the Watchtower organization. The Faith movement, as all other movements, is composed of various groups, each with its own distinctives, but which share a common theme, vision, and goal.[8] For this reason, the numerous Faith churches, teachers, and adherents should be judged on an individual basis. Each should rise or fall on his or her own merits. Kenneth Copeland Ministries, headed by Kenneth and Gloria Copeland, for example, bears all the marks of a cult. First, it has a formalized hierarchical structure; it boasts a centralized organizational facility; and it is equipped with a publishing arm complete with a distribution mechanism. Additionally, as will be fully documented, the Copelands bludgeon many of the essentials of historic Christianity, preaching their own deviant brand of antibiblical theology that the vast majority of their devotees accept without question. Furthermore, fervent followers consider the Copelands to be the final authority in matters of faith and practice. Thus we can legitimately characterize the Copelands as being cult leaders who, in the vernacular of the apostle Paul, represent "a different gospel—which is really no gospel at all" (Galatians 1:6–7).

THE ERROR CONTINUUM

In combating the errors that confront Christianity, it is important to understand that *all errors are not created equal*; some are clearly more damaging than others. It may be helpful to picture these errors as resting on a continuum that stretches from the outright silly to the gravely serious. Benny Hinn's comment about women originally giving birth out of their sides, for example, can be considered a *silly* statement—which, while nonbiblical, poses no direct threat to essential Christian doctrine.[9]

On the other hand, such teachings as God possessing a physical body, humans created as exact duplicates of God, and Christ's transformation into a satanic being fall squarely on the other end of the "error spectrum." They are *heretical*, which is another way of saying that they directly oppose the clear teaching of Scripture on matters of essential importance as highlighted in the creeds and councils of the church.

Classifying errors can oftentimes be a tricky business, as a sizable gray area exists between the serious and the not-so-serious type of error. Nevertheless, such difficulties should not discourage us from judging whether certain teachings and practices are faithful to the Word of God and the doctrines of historic Christianity. If anything, they ought to move us to spend more time in carefully thinking about the things we hear daily and hold dearly.[10]

You, the reader, will inevitably need to decide whether you think the Faith movement is cultic or Christian. You must decide whether these doctrines are true or false or some muddy mixture of both.

If you decide that this movement is a valid expression of Christianity, then in all fairness you should also embrace as fellow believers the Mormons, the Jehovah's Witnesses, the Christian Scientists, and a host of other groups normally thought of as cults.

That is the choice before you.

2

CHARISMATIC OR CULTIC?

In essentials, unity; in nonessentials, liberty; and in all things, charity.[1]

I have become both weary and wary of those who use the perversions of the Faith movement to drive a wedge between charismatic and noncharismatic Christians.[2] Frankly, this is both counterproductive and divisive, for the Faith movement is not charismatic; it is cultic.

I want to make it crystal clear that the issues discussed in this book do not involve an "in-house" debate among committed Christians over such matters as the perpetuity of spiritual gifts. This book is not about whether you speak in tongues or whether God still heals today. It is not about the way you were baptized. It is not about the timing of the tribulation or the meaning of the millennium.

I want to stress that sincere and dedicated believers can differ in good conscience when it comes to such secondary issues. They cannot do so, however, when it comes to the primary doctrines that separate Christianity from the kingdom of the cults. When it comes to such matters as the fabric of faith, the nature of God, and the atonement of Christ upon the cross, there must be unity. In the words of the time-tested dictum noted above: *In essentials, unity; in nonessentials, liberty; and in all things, charity.*

For the most part, charismatics and noncharismatics are unified when it comes to the essentials of the historic Christian faith. Their primary differences involve nonessential Christian doctrine. Therefore, while we may vigorously debate secondary matters within the faith, we must never divide over them.

Not so, however, when it comes to the Faith movement; there we must draw the line. The Faith movement has systematically subverted the very essence of Christianity so as to present us with a counterfeit Christ and a counterfeit Christianity. As such, standing against the false theology of the Faith movement does *not* divide; rather, it unites believers.

It would be a grave error to equate the Faith movement with the charismatic movement. It is indeed a travesty that the Faith teachers have been able to cleverly disguise themselves as charismatics, thereby tarnishing the reputation of a legitimate movement within Christianity.

Furthermore, it is tragic that a number of noncharismatics have attempted to use the Faith teachers to prove that the charismatic movement is in chaos. In fact, some have used the statements of Faith teachers to label charismatics as having zeal without knowledge and enthusiasm without enlightenment—in short, being keen but clueless. This, of course, is clearly untrue.

Are we prepared to call a man like Dr. Gordon Fee, one of the foremost Bible scholars today, "keen but clueless"? Are we going to say that Dr. Walter Martin, father of the modern-day countercult revolution, had zeal but not in accordance with knowledge? Some of today's clearest thinkers are charismatic Christians. Moreover, some of the most scholarly rebuttals of Faith theology have come from within the charismatic movement itself. Notable examples include the works of Walter Martin,[3] Gordon Fee,[4] Dan McConnell,[5] Charles Farah,[6] Elliot Miller,[7] H. Terris Neuman,[8] and Dale H. Simmons.[9]

What is especially tragic is that a wide assortment of Christian men and women (both charismatic and noncharismatic) are endorsing leaders within the Faith movement. It is incredible to think that this cultic system has become so powerful that otherwise credible Christians have given it carte blanche to proliferate its poisonous doctrinal perversions to an unsuspecting public.

Perhaps even worse, Christian broadcasters are all too eager to bring some of these men and women, live and in color, into the homes of millions of viewers every day. If Christians are going to promote such teachings, they might as well begin broadcasting programs produced by the Unity School of Christianity or the Church of Religious Science.

Years ago, when Moody Press realized that one of its authors had traded Christianity for the kingdom of the cults, they immediately pulled his book from circulation. They prudently refused to promote a man whose teachings were at least indirectly responsible for tragic physical consequences toward as many as ninety men, women, and children.[10]

In sharp contrast, when certain publishers and producers are warned about the cultic theology of people like Benny Hinn, they immediately come to their defense.

One is left to wonder where the heroes of the faith are. Where are those who are willing to stand for integrity? Where are those men and women who, like the saints of old, are willing to face "the tyrant's brandished steel, the lion's gory mane, and the fires of a thousand deaths" to preserve the faith once and for all delivered to the saints? If Christians were willing to give their very lives in days gone by, shouldn't we be willing to sacrifice our positions, platforms, and popularity in order to preserve the faith?

We are currently faced with a crisis within Christianity. But this crisis is not the fault of the charismatic renewal. Rather, it is focused on a life-and-death struggle between orthodoxy and heresy—between the kingdom of Christ and the kingdom of the cults.

3

CAST OF CHARACTERS

Many will say to me on that day, "Lord, Lord, did we not prophesy in your name, and in your name drive out demons and perform many miracles?" Then I will tell them plainly, "I never knew you. Away from me, you evildoers!"[1]

—JESUS THE CHRIST

ong before the Faith movement became a dominant force within the Christian church, Phineas Parkhurst Quimby (1802–1866), the father of New Thought, popularized the notion that sickness and suffering have their origin in incorrect thinking.[2] Quimby's followers held that man could create his own reality through the power of positive affirmation (confession).[3] As such, metaphysical practitioners taught adherents to visualize health and wealth and then to affirm or confess them with their mouths so that the intangible images may be transformed into tangible realities.[4]

The similarities between Word/Faith theology and the teachings inherent in New Thought metaphysics are significant. Mike Dooley, New Thought entrepreneur and contributor to *The Secret*, summed up the most striking of such similarities in three words—"Thoughts become things!"[5] Or as Rhonda Byrne put it, "Your current thoughts are creating your future life. What you think about the most or focus on the most will appear as your life."[6] Likewise, many of the notions espoused by these prosperity teachers can also be found in Religious Science, Christian Science, and the Unity School of Christianity.

Although proponents of Faith theology have attempted to sanitize the metaphysical concept of the "power of mind" by substituting in its stead the "force of faith," for all practical purposes they have made a distinction without a true difference. New Thought writer Warren Felt Evans, for example, wrote that "faith is the most intense form of mental action."[7] In treating a patient, Evans commented that "the effect of the suggestion [or positive affirmation that the patient is well]

15

is the result of the faith of the subject, for it is always proportioned to the degree in which the patient *believes* what you say."[8] Likewise, H. Emilie Cady, a well-known writer for Charles and Myrtle Fillmore's Unity School of Christianity, explained that "our affirming, backed by faith, is the link that connects our conscious human need with His power and supply."[9] Cady also claimed that "there is power in our word of faith to bring all good things right into our everyday life."[10] Such statements demonstrate that the distinction between the "mind" of metaphysics and the "faith" of Faith theology is little more than cosmetic.

While New Thought metaphysics and Word of Faith theology have notable similarities (as well as obvious dissimilarities), the substance, style, and scams endemic to the movement are traceable to teachings and practices expressed primarily by certain post–World War II faith healers and Counterfeit Revivalists operating within Pentecostal circles.[11] Kenneth Copeland and Kenneth Hagin point to T. L. Osborn and William Branham as true men of God who greatly influenced their lives and ministries. This despite the fact that Osborn himself consistently followed E. W. Kenyon's Scripture-twisting practices[12] and Branham denounced the doctrine of the Trinity as coming directly from the devil.[13]

Unfortunately, Hagin and Copeland are not alone in affirming Branham; Faith proponent Benny Hinn gives him hearty approval as well.[14] When it comes to *style*, however, Hinn gravitates more toward such Faith healers as Aimee Semple McPherson and Kathryn Kuhlman. The influence of these women on Hinn's life and ministry is so great that he still visits their grave sites and experiences "the anointing," which he claims emanates from Aimee's bones.[15] In addition, Hinn has given his endorsement to notorious revivalist A. A. Allen,[16] a huckster if ever there was one. Faith teachers such as Robert Tilton and Marilyn Hickey have embraced many of the practices pioneered by A. A. Allen and Oral Roberts as well.

Oral Roberts, you may recall, is the prosperity preacher who claimed Jesus told him God had called him to find an effective treatment for cancer. In a lengthy appeal, Roberts avowed that the Lord told him, "I would not have had you and your partners build the 20-story research tower unless I was going to give you a plan that will attack cancer." Roberts then said that Jesus instructed him to tell his partners that "this is not Oral Roberts asking [for the money] but their Lord."[17] (The project was completed, but has since been "shut down and sold to a group of investors for commercial development."[18] And no cure for cancer was found.)

In like fashion, Allen scammed his followers by asserting that he could command God to "turn dollar bills into twenties."[19] He also was known to have urged his followers to send for his "prayer cloths anointed with the Miracle Oil"[20] and offered "Miracle tent shavings" as points of contact for personal miracles.[21] Allen even "launched a brief 'raise the dead' program."[22] Of course, it died.

Allen was eventually expelled from the Assemblies of God denomination when he jumped bail after being arrested for drunk driving.[23] In 1970 he died from what "news accounts report [as] sclerosis of the liver."[24] Notwithstanding Allen's well-documented frauds and fabrications, teachers like Benny Hinn continue to extol him as a great man of God.

As we examine the primary purveyors of Faith theology, you will see living proof of the maxim that "error begets error and heresy begets heresy." If, for example, you examine the cultic progression of E. W. Kenyon's theology, you will discover that his original deviations from orthodox Christianity were minor compared to those that characterized the later stages of his ministry. And with each of Kenyon's successive disciples, the errors become ever more pronounced.

Hagin, who popularized Kenyon, not only expanded Kenyon's errors but added to them as well. The progression from bad to worse has continued with people like Kenneth Copeland and Charles Capps, and is now sinking to new depths through ministry leaders such as Creflo Dollar, Frederick Price, and Benny Hinn.

Twisted texts, make-believe miracles, and counterfeit Christs are common denominators of the Faith movement's cast of characters. We continue by taking a closer look at Essek William Kenyon, who represents the genesis of the modern-day Word of Faith movement.

Essek William Kenyon

The believer is as much an incarnation as was Jesus of Nazareth.[25]

—E. W. KENYON

Ask those familiar with Faith theology who the father of the Faith movement is and they will invariably point to "Dad" Hagin. In truth, Essek William Kenyon is the father of the Faith movement and Dad Hagin is the man initially responsible for popularizing his material.

Born on April 24, 1867, E. W. Kenyon began his public ministry in the

Methodist Church. In the early 1900s Kenyon established the Bethel Bible Institute, but in 1923 resigned his position as the school's superintendent under a cloud of controversy. A true pioneer of religious broadcasting, Kenyon started a radio program in 1931 called *Kenyon's Church of the Air*. The taped transcripts of this broadcast eventually became the basis for many of his writings, which have proven to be his most lasting legacy. Many of the phrases popularized by present-day prosperity preachers, such as "What I confess, I possess,"[26] were first coined by Kenyon.

There is little doubt that New Thought metaphysics had an enormous impact on Kenyon. The evidence from his works, from eyewitnesses, and from external sources provides ample testimony to his cultic connections. Since a number of scholars have established the cultic influence of the Faith movement via Kenyon, I will not belabor the point here.[27] It is worth mentioning that Kenyon was influenced by a variety of New Thought practitioners and that he attended Emerson College of Oratory—a virtual hotbed of New Thought metaphysics.[28]

It should also be noted that Kenyon's influence within Pentecostal circles was not confined to Kenneth Hagin. He was widely read and quoted by post–World War II healing revivalists, including William Branham and T. L. Osborn.[29] Kenyon is also said to have visited the meetings of Pentecostal leaders such as F. F. Bosworth and Aimee Semple McPherson.[30]

Although Kenyon was mild by comparison to some of the more outrageous Faith teachers today, he did communicate both the bizarre and the blasphemous throughout his lifetime. For example, Kenyon said that if Jesus' physical death was sufficient to pay for sin, then every Christian should be able to pay the penalty for their sin with their own deaths. He went so far as to say that the physical death of our Lord did not touch the sin issue at all:

> If Jesus' physical death could pay the penalty of sin as some contend, then why is it necessary that a Christian die? If a Christian dies physically, does he not pay the penalty of his own sin? If physical death is the penalty for sin, then why do not the whole human race pay their own penalty and save themselves, for all die? But we hold that the physical death of Jesus did not touch the sin issue at all.[31]

As blasphemous as this is, Kenyon constantly outdid himself. For example, in a book titled *The Father and His Family*, Kenyon states that "every man who has been 'born again' is an incarnation, and Christianity is a miracle. The believer is as much an incarnation as was Jesus of Nazareth."[32] Kenneth Hagin used this and other statements to forward the notion that the "believer is called Christ." Says Hagin, "That's who we are; we're Christ!"[33]

Kenneth Hagin

Man was created on terms of equality with God, and he could stand in God's presence without any consciousness of inferiority.[34]

—KENNETH HAGIN

Kenneth Hagin ("Dad Hagin") is best known as the father of the modern-day Faith movement. Hagin was largely responsible for popularizing and proliferating Kenyon's preaching and publications among Pentecostals. Hagin's claim that "the Holy Spirit gave him the *same* words as Kenyon without his having prior knowledge of the sources"[35] is dubious at best. Despite evidence to the contrary, Hagin insists: "Kenyon's influence on my ministry has been minute. Only his teachings on the name of Jesus have much to do with my theology. I absolutely deny any metaphysical influences from Kenyon. I teach not Christian Science, but Christian sense."[36]

What Hagin claims to be "Christian sense," might better be characterized as *non*sense. In evidence Hagin told a "visionary" tale involving a "demon monkey."[37] According to Hagin, he and Jesus were discussing demons when suddenly a "demon monkey"[38] jumped between them and began to drown out Jesus' words, yelling, "Yackety, yack, yack, yack" in a shrill voice. After some time had passed, Hagin took control of the situation by telling the demon to "shut up in the name of Jesus." Jesus responded with the words, "If you hadn't done something about that, I couldn't have."[39] Surprised and shocked, Hagin suggested that the Savior might well have stumbled over His own words. Rather than saying He "couldn't have," Jesus meant to say He "wouldn't have."[40] Jesus, however, assured Hagin that He had not misspoken. Hagin was not convinced. Hagin told Jesus that he would not believe Him unless He could produce two or three proof texts. After telling Hagin "sometimes your theology needs upending,"[41] Jesus smiled sweetly and proceeded to accommodate him with four proof texts.[42] What is particularly ironic about Hagin's demon-monkey story is that Jesus was personally instructing Hagin on the finer points of spiritual warfare and yet was

19

unable to practice what He preached. Indeed, without Hagin, Christ was impotent in the presence of a demonic monkey.

Despite being "excommunicated" by the Southern Baptists in 1937[43]—Hagin's span of influence has been nothing short of sensational. Virtually every major prosperity preacher has been influenced by Hagin. His disciples include such luminaries as Frederick K. C. Price and Kenneth Copeland. As Hagin popularized Kenyon, so Copeland and company popularized Hagin. Hagin Jr. put it this way: "Other people have gotten started because of my Dad's ministry. They'll even admit it. They have preached his sermons *almost verbatim* from his tapes. Ken Copeland did."[44] Additionally, Hagin helped his son-in-law, Doyle "Buddy" Harrison, organize an International Convention of Faith Churches and Ministers, which has ordained such men as Charles Capps and Benny Hinn.[45]

Hagin's syndicated radio show is currently carried by some 249 stations,[46] and his Rhema Bible Training Center (located near Tulsa, Oklahoma) continues to produce graduates at a hefty rate. In 1992 alone, Hagin's *The Word of Faith* magazine recorded 777 enthusiastic Rhema graduates, making a total of more than twelve thousand graduates since the school opened in 1974. Two of these, Paul and Nikki, were specially featured because they were the first Russians to graduate from Rhema and were poised to spread Hagin's heresies in their homeland.[47] In addition to on-site training, Rhema offers correspondence courses that boasted sixteen thousand students during its first dozen years of existence.[48]

Hagin's *The Word of Faith* magazine now reaches close to four hundred thousand homes,[49] and as of 1992 the ministry had sold more than 47 million copies of the various books and publications, with translations of many into twenty-six foreign languages.[50] More than one hundred books, pamphlets, and tapes are listed in Hagin's most recent catalog.[51] Hagin's ministry reported a total of 290 full- and part-time employees, and his annual camp meetings boast an attendance of upwards of twenty thousand participants.[52]

Hagin's popularity can be attributed, at least in part, to his claim to be an authority on spiritual matters. In turn, Hagin's "authority" appears to be derived largely from so-called personal contacts with Jesus. During a contact chronicled in *I Believe in Visions*, Jesus supposedly took Hagin on a whirlwind tour of heaven and hell. Hagin devotes page after page to the details of his apocalyptic journeys to the place of the "damned."[53]

Not only did Hagin boast of alleged visits to heaven and hell, but in his writings he recounts numerous out-of-body experiences in vivid detail.[54] In describing his conversion in 1933, Hagin reported a near-death out-of-body experience in which "I slipped back into my body as a man slips into his trousers in the morning, the same way in which I had gone out—through my mouth."[55] In all, Hagin claimed to have died and been resurrected on three separate occasions. The first time he "died" (1933) Hagin described experiencing heat from the very "fires of hell."[56] Seventy years later, in 2003, Hagin died a fourth and final time without benefit of a subsequent resurrection. In the interval between his first and final deaths, Hagin's life was a series of mind-blowing experiences.

On one memorable occasion, Hagin was in the middle of a sermon when he was transported back in time to a little town fifteen miles from the church where he was preaching. Leaning up against a building, he watched a woman walking down the street. Suddenly a car pulled up to the curb and honked the horn, and she got in. Just as suddenly Hagin found himself in the backseat. Upon reaching a spot away from the town, the driver committed adultery with the woman under Hagin's watchful eyes. The entire experience lasted about fifteen minutes, after which Hagin abruptly found himself back in church, summoning his parishioners to prayer.[57] This, by the way, was not an isolated experience.

Hagin also recalled walking home from a church he was pastoring at the time. He was taking a shortcut through an alley overgrown with trees. Suddenly he noticed a car backed into the shadows. Instantly the inside of the car was illuminated with supernatural light so that he could see everything. And there in the car he saw this same woman (a woman someone had tried to get him interested in, no less) sitting in another man's lap. Fortunately, Hagin spared his readers the detailed documentation of what he observed taking place. As Hagin puts it, "He had his arm around her and that's not all they were doing, but that's as much as I'll describe."[58]

Hagin claimed that Jesus appeared to him in 1950 and gave him a special anointing to minister to the sick. As Hagin puts it:

[Jesus] went on to instruct me that when I would pray and lay hands upon the sick I was to lay one hand on each side of the body. If I felt the fire jump from hand to hand, an evil spirit or demon was present in the body causing the affliction . . . If the fire, or anointing, in my hand does not jump from hand to hand, it is a case of healing only. I should pray for the person in His name, and if he will believe and accept it, the anointing will leave my hands

21

and go into his body, driving out the disease and bringing healing. When the fire, or the anointing, leaves my hands and goes into his body, I will know he is healed.[59]

During this incredible encounter, Christ, in King James English, told Hagin to "stretch forth thine hand." Jesus then stretched out His own hands so that Hagin could look into them. "For some reason," remarks Hagin, "I expected to see a scar where the nail had pierced His flesh and had since grown together. I should have known better, but many times we get ideas that are not really Scriptural, yet they are accepted beliefs. I saw in the palms of His hands the wounds of the crucifixion—three-cornered, jagged holes. Each hole was large enough so that I could put my finger in it. I could see light on the other side of the hole."[60]

What is noteworthy about this story is that after criticizing "ideas that are not really Scriptural," Hagin himself proceeded to narrate a story that has little basis in reality. Jesus could never have shown Hagin the alleged holes in His palms. As any student of Scripture and history knows, the nails were driven through Christ's *wrists* as opposed to His palms. The Greek word used in the text (*cheir*) actually refers to the entire forearm, including the hand.[61]

In addition to Scripture, archaeology and medicine provide strong evidence that crucified individuals could not have been nailed through the palms of their hands: the weight of the body would have ripped the nails right through the fingers of the hands.[62] Hagin's fanciful story conclusively demonstrates that the Jesus who supposedly anointed him "to minister to the sick" could not have been the Jesus of the Bible (cf. 2 Corinthians 11:4).

Despite glaring distortions in his stories, Hagin still had the temerity to pronounce divine judgment on those who dare to question his so-called prophetic ministry. He even sneered at fellow prophets, saying, "I've drawn back from the prophet's ministry because I don't want to be classed with all those idiots and half-wits."[63]

Hagin ominously claimed that God Himself told him that if individuals, churches, and pastors do not accept his message, they may well pay the ultimate price. Says Hagin: "There will be ministers who don't accept it and will fall dead in the pulpit."[64] In evidence Hagin chronicles the account of a pastor who paid the ultimate price for disbelieving. "The pastor fell dead in the pulpit," says Hagin, "because he didn't accept the message that God gave me to give him from the Holy Spirit."[65]

Hagin's wife, Oretha, allegedly experienced the devastating impact of such divine judgment firsthand. During one of Hagin's meetings, a woman levitated from an altar and "stood in mid-air dancing."[66] Several people, including Oretha, questioned whether this was of God. As a result of doubt, she was "slain" by the Spirit of God. Reeling backward, as though struck with a "ball bat," Oretha was knocked flat and, as it were, "glued to the floor."[67] It wasn't until she acknowledged that what was going on in the meeting was of God that God permitted Hagin to release his wife. With a touch of his finger, Oretha was restored.

Many of today's Faith teachers have taken Hagin's sinister pronouncements to new extremes. Benny Hinn, for example, boldly declared on national television that he wished he could blow the heads off his "stink[ing]" enemies with a "Holy Ghost machine gun."[68] After apologizing for this remark, Hinn came back a year later with a vengeance.[69] During a rally (which I personally attended) of some seventeen thousand people, Hinn made the following chilling pronouncement:

> The Holy Ghost is upon me . . . The day is coming when those that attack us will drop dead. You say, "What did you say?" I speak this under the anointing of the Spirit. Can I tell you something? Don't touch God's servants; it's deadly . . . Woe to you that touch God's servants. You're going to pay. "And the day will come," the Lord said that to me. He said, "The day will come when I will punish instantly. Woe to those who touch My chosen." They will fear us. Hear this: today they mock us; tomorrow they will fear us.[70]

In similar fashion, Paul Crouch stated that if God did not kill his enemies, he would.[71] Kenneth Copeland, to whom we now turn, claimed not only that "Faith critics" would go to an early grave but that they would experience the dreaded disease of cancer.[72] Lest you suppose that Copeland is just blowing off steam, allow me to assert what will be documented later—Faith teachers are absolutely convinced that their words can literally bring death into the lives of their critics.

Kenneth Copeland

I was shocked when I found out who the biggest failure in the Bible actually is . . . The biggest one is God . . . I mean, He lost His top-ranking, most anointed angel; the first man He ever

created; the first woman He ever created; the whole earth and all the fullness therein; a third of the angels, at least—that's a big loss, man . . . Now, the reason you don't think of God as a failure is He never said He's a failure. And you're not a failure till you say you're one.[73]
—KENNETH COPELAND

Kenneth Copeland got his start in ministry as a direct result of memorizing his mentor Hagin's messages.[74] Although he once worked as a pilot for Oral Roberts, it was Hagin who ultimately revolutionized Copeland's life.[75] Hagin's impact was first felt in 1967, when former Hagin manager (and later son-in-law) Doyle "Buddy" Harrison took pity on young Copeland and gave him a selection of Hagin's tapes, which Copeland at the time was too poor to purchase.[76]

Within a year of this acquisition, the husband-and-wife team of Kenneth and Gloria Copeland felt they had gleaned enough from Hagin's tapes to establish their own evangelistic association. The small home studies initially conducted by the Copelands would soon be transformed into mass revivals in internationally famous arenas.[77] Yet, this was only the beginning.

In 1973 Copeland began publishing a newsletter called the *Believer's Voice of Victory* and three years later launched his *Believer's Voice of Victory* radio program.[78] Copeland says that on March 23, 1979, God "spoke" to him, giving him a "broadcasting . . . commission to expand into television."[79] In 1981 he advanced into the high-tech world of satellite communications and by August of the following year "made history by initiating the first *global* religious broadcast," linking a reported two hundred cities across the United States and more than twenty countries around the world by satellite.[80]

With offices in such distant locations as England, the Philippines, South Africa, Australia, Canada, and Hong Kong, Copeland's organization today truly can be regarded as international in scope and significance. In fact, I recently experienced firsthand Copeland's far-reaching influence. I had the privilege of delivering the keynote address at the National Day of Prayer in the Kingdom of Tonga, located in the South Pacific. During my stay I learned there was only one Christian bookstore on the island. Thinking it might be interesting to see what items were available, I decided to pay the store a visit, and quickly discovered that they were vigorously promoting Copeland materials. Since Tonga can be described as being the "last place in time" (when it is midday in Jerusalem, it is midnight in Tonga), it may well be said that Copeland's destructive doctrines have now reached the uttermost parts of the earth.

Not only does Copeland espouse concepts common to cultists, but he often throws around reckless remarks that make even the deviant doctrine of the cults seem tame by comparison. Consider for a moment the striking similarity between Copeland's assertion that "Adam, in the Garden of Eden, was God manifested in the flesh"[81] and Mormon prophet Brigham Young's teaching that "Adam is our father and our God."[82]

Or compare Copeland's teaching that God is six feet two inches to six feet three inches tall, weighs around two hundred pounds, and has a hand span of about nine inches[83] with Mormon founder Joseph Smith's statement that if you were to see God today, "you would see him like a man in form—like yourselves in all the person, image, and very form as a man."[84] If that doesn't shock you, consider how Copeland's claim—that Adam was an exact duplicate of God, and not even subordinate to Him[85]—parallels Joseph Smith's statement that "God himself was once as we are now, and is an exalted man."[86] Not only does Copeland teach that Adam and God were exact duplicates, but he also perpetuates the myth that earth is an exact replica of the mother planet on which God lives.[87]

All this, however, is but the tip of the iceberg. As will be duly noted, Copeland blatantly pronounces God to be the greatest failure of all time,[88] boldly pontificates that "Satan *conquered* Jesus on the Cross,"[89] and brashly proclaims that Christ went to hell as an "emaciated, poured out, little wormy spirit."[90]

Copeland appears to be as at home in the world of the occult as he is in the kingdom of the cults. As a case in point, he is clearly committed to the magical concept that intangible words, imbued with the force of faith, can take on tangible reality. As documented in chapter 6, he insists that a believer can speak an eighty-two-foot yacht into existence.[91] That Copeland advocates a method of occult visualization is incontrovertible. Says Copeland, "Any image that you get down on the inside of you that is so vivid when you close your eyes you see it, it'll come to pass."[92] He is well aware of the fact that occultists do similar things, going so far as to say, "The visualization they do in meditation and metaphysical practices . . . is the perverted form of the real thing."[93] Referring to creative visualization and positive confession, Copeland claims that "New Age is trying to do this; and they'd get somewhat results out of it because this is spiritual law, brother."[94]

In addition to tantalizing his converts with the possibility of creating wealth through occult practices, Copeland also tempts them with the dangerous doctrine that they can create health as well. He suggests to scores of suffering saints that when "you get to the place where you take the Word of God and build an image on the inside of you of not having crippled legs and not having blind eyes, but when you close your eyes you just see yourself just leap out of that wheelchair, it will picture that in the Holy of Holies and you will come out of there. You will come out."[95]

As though this is not bad enough, Copeland's wife, Gloria, attacks the reputation of the Apostle to the Gentiles. With shrill voice she claims that the apostle Paul did not receive the healing he asked for in 2 Corinthians 12:8 because he asked God to heal him when in reality he could have done it himself![96]

If the Copelands are anything, it is brassy. In a November 6, 2007 letter, Senator Grassley (R-Iowa) asked the Copelands "to provide detailed accounting of their compensation, housing allowances, credit card statements and a list of bank accounts, the tax-exempt purpose of layovers in Hawaii and Fiji on the church's Citation X jet and information on a 40th anniversary 'gift' of $2 million from other ministers."[97] In a minister's conference broadcast January 22, 2008, Copeland shot back, "You can go get a subpoena, and I won't give it to you . . . It's not yours, it's God's and you're not going to get it and that's something I'll go to prison over. So, just get over it . . . And if there's a death penalty that applies well just go for it!" With Bible in hand, Copeland added, "You wanna get in a fight with me? Why, just come on. But, I'm gonna warn you, I fight dirty."[98]

Long before Grassley's probe into Copeland's finances, Benny Hinn, to whom we now turn, ominously warned an international audience, "Those who attack Kenneth Copeland are attacking the very presence of God."[99]

Benny Hinn

When you were born again the Word was made flesh in you. And you became flesh of His flesh and bone of His bone. Don't tell me you have Jesus. You are everything He was and everything He is and ever He shall be . . . It [the new man] says, "I am as He is." That's what it says. As He is, so are we in this world. Jesus said, "Go in My name, go in My stead." Don't say, "I have." Say, "I am, I am, I am, I am, I am." That's why you never ever, ever, ever ought to say, "I'm sick." How can you be sick if you're the new creation? Say, "I'm healed!" Don't say, "I'm a sinner." The new creature is no sinner. I'm the righteousness of God in Christ.[100]

—BENNY HINN

26

"The very presence of God" is exactly what thousands of people clamor for when they attend one of Benny Hinn's "Miracle Crusades." They hope to see God move in a mighty way through an outpouring of miraculous healing power.

After personally attending a number of Hinn crusades, I can say from experience that the likelihood of being hurt is vastly greater than that of being healed. I observed with great anguish scores of men, women, and children who could not even get near the stage to be healed by Hinn. The scenario might best be described as a vulgar display of "survival of the fittest," with people stampeding madly to get on stage so they can experience falling at Hinn's feet.

In Houston, Texas, a woman attending a Hinn crusade crushed a fellow crusader when her fall was not checked by a catcher. The woman she landed on pleaded with her, "Get up, get up," but to no avail. All she could say in response was, "I can't, I can't."[101] In Oklahoma City a woman attending a Hinn crusade was not merely crushed; she was killed. Ella Peppard died from complications she suffered after someone was slain in the Spirit right on top of her. The ensuing lawsuit was settled out of court.[102]

Tragically, those who attended the meeting in wheelchairs ended up leaving in the same physical condition. Some departed in tears. Others told me they left feeling that God neither cared for them nor had the time to consider their needs. To assuage disillusionment, Hinn promises, "The day is coming, I tell you this, I know it like I know my name, the day is coming there will not be one sick saint in the body of Christ. Nobody will be, nobody's gonna be, no one will be raptured up out of a wheelchair. No one will be raptured out of a hospital bed. You're all gonna be healed before the rapture."[103]

Hinn claims that God directed him to begin monthly crusades in 1990.[104] Says Hinn, "I immediately began to receive power to drive out devils of sickness and affliction and to receive specific direction as to what the Holy Spirit was doing among the crowds of twelve to fifteen thousand that attended each night. Hundreds of verified healings and thousands of conversions have occurred, including people rising from wheelchairs and leaving crutches. Several blind eyes and deaf ears have been opened and verified."[105]

Not only does Hinn claim to have raised people out of wheelchairs, given blind eyes sight, and opened the ears of the deaf, but he also claims he has healed at least four people of AIDS.[106] When pressed for verification, Susan Smith, who helps document such healings for Hinn, becomes strangely elusive.[107]

Regarding AIDS, her response was that the final tests are not yet in. When queried about an Orlando woman who was allegedly cured of blindness due to diabetes, Susan would not divulge the name of the woman. She subsequently stated that the woman's vision may still be cloudy and that she still has diabetes, which ironically enough precipitated the problem in the first place. "I wish she would get off insulin," says Susan. "That's what makes them blind."[108]

To make matters worse, Hinn heaps guilt upon the heads of those who are either not healed or lose their healing. In *Lord, I Need a Miracle*, Hinn blames believers for their lack of faith;[109] their wrong thinking;[110] and for not consistently following his three principles,[111] four laws of healing,[112] and seven guidelines.[113] His book is not only replete with twisted texts and dogmatic declarations, but it is also full of tantalizing testimonies camouflaged by a thin veneer of scientific substantiation. While the foreword written by Dr. Donald Colbert appears to provide medical authentication for Hinn's claims, in reality virtually no real documentation is provided. According to Dr. Colbert, two cases were extremely impressive. The first involves David Lane, who was allegedly healed of colon cancer.[114] A careful examination of the medical records, however, indicates that the malignant tumor had apparently been surgically removed (prior to an appendectomy), rather than miraculously healed.[115]

The second case concerns lupus patient Marsha Brantley, who Dr. Colbert claims experienced a dramatic healing that can only be explained as a miraculous touch from God.[116] In reality, this case is difficult to verify in that lupus is well known for going into spontaneous remission. What can be verified, however, are the effects of lupus, which in this case involved damage to the sacroiliac joint—a condition that was definitively *not* healed.[117] This critical piece of information in the medical report was conveniently omitted.

Out of the hundreds of healings Hinn claims, he provided me with proof of one additional case involving a spinal tumor and various cancers. According to medical consultant Preston Simpson, MD, this case, like the others, was poorly documented and confused.[118] First, the tapes of the CAT scan of the spine were "erased before the bones could be evaluated."[119] Furthermore, the records reveal that the spinal tumor began shrinking some three months *prior* to Hinn's Miracle Invasion Rally. Finally, the tumor was still present—and not healed—months after the alleged "healing."[120]

Make no mistake: I believe in God's power to heal. But if God is healing through Hinn, the evidence is conspicuous by its absence. If "evidence" like this is the best Hinn can muster after years of "miracle rallies"—with a staff working to document cases of healing—then there is no credible evidence that he has ever been involved in a bona fide miracle. Not a single war veteran who has lost an arm or a leg has ever stepped forward to show the world that Hinn represents the real power of the Spirit.

Instead, like hypnotists and Hindu gurus, Hinn uses the power of suggestion to create placebos for psychosomatic symptoms and sickness. In truth there is nothing supernatural about this kind of "healing." Hinn can "heal" asthma, allergies, and arthritis, but then, so can mesmerists and medicine men. Indeed, the difference between the "magic" of mental manipulations and genuine miracles is dramatic. When Jesus and the apostles healed people, the miracles were always 100 percent successful and immediate, and there were no relapses.[121]

While Hinn can create the illusion of "lengthening" legs, he can't re-create an amputated limb; while Hinn can create the illusion of slaying subjects in the Spirit, he can't resurrect the slain; and while Hinn can create the illusion that someone's vision has been restored, he can't replace a missing orb. In the end he creates disillusionment and self-deception. The power of the Spirit creates life and limb. Hinn's power of suggestion only creates a lamentable lie.[122]

The illusion that Hinn's miracle-working power comes from God is one thing; the delusion that his theology is given him via the Holy Spirit is quite another. While claiming to be "under the anointing," Hinn has uttered some of the most off-the-wall statements imaginable. Recall, for instance, that Hinn claims the Holy Spirit revealed to him that women were originally designed to give birth out of their sides.[123] Hinn also admits he frequents the grave sites of both Kathryn Kuhlman and Aimee Semple McPherson to get the "anointing" from their bones.[124] On one occasion Hinn got more than he could reasonably handle. Said Hinn, "Oh, I was drunk, still drunk."[125] In this instance, Hinn was so "intoxicated" that he could not even remember the prophecy he had just uttered. Sadly, he had to ask his audience to tell him what he had just been saying under the "anointing."

Despite all this and more, Hinn has managed to gain broad acceptance in the evangelical community. He reaches millions via television and millions more with blockbuster bestsellers such as *Good Morning, Holy Spirit* and *The Anointing*.[126] In pulpit and in print, he creates the illusion that special mystical powers have been given him from on high. In *Good Morning, Holy Spirit*, he recalls a scene in which his mother was cleaning the hallway outside his room while he was inside having a customary chat with the Holy Spirit. (If Hinn is to be believed, these chats are so meaningful that the Spirit of God begged him for "'five more minutes. Just five more minutes.' The Holy Spirit longed for my fellowship.")[127] When Hinn stepped into the hallway, the presence of the Lord was so strong that his mother was thrown back against the wall. Hinn adds that his "brothers will tell you of the times they came near me and didn't know what was happening—but they felt something unusual."[128]

Scores of illustrations can be cited to document Hinn's methods for creating the illusion of a special anointing from God. The following is a classic case in point. The date was December 7, 1974. The place was Oshawa, Ontario. The occasion was the very first time Hinn had ever stood behind a pulpit.[129] After preaching a message replete with insights that continue to amaze him even to this day, Hinn lifted his hands and summoned the Holy Spirit. "Instantly the power of God hit the place," Hinn writes. "People began to cry and many fell to the floor." The power was reportedly so incredible that Hinn ended up crying, "Oh, dear God, what do I do now?"

Hinn tried to turn the service over to "the fellow who was leading the meeting, hoping he would come and take the service out of my hands. But as I turned and pointed toward him, he fell backward several feet. I was trying to get him to come close and suddenly he was farther away."[130] The raw power emanating from young Benny was allegedly so potent that each time the leader would struggle to get near him, he would be hurled against the wall. This was but the beginning of a ministry characterized by Holy Ghost anointing and powerful preaching. Says Hinn, "Miraculously my ministry began and instantly mushroomed."[131]

Hinn's book *The Anointing* might best be characterized as overpromising and underperforming.[132] His message to charismatic Christians is: if all you have experienced to date is "the baptism of the Holy Spirit" and speaking in tongues, then you haven't had much. As he puts it, "If this is all there is, I'm not sure there's much to it."[133] His solution is "the anointing." Hinn tells story after story of how that power (allegedly from God) is displayed through him, all the while reinforcing the theme that without it you have nothing. "I am not overstating the case," says Hinn. "The anointing is mandatory if you are called to serve the Lord. Without it there will be no growth, no blessing, no victory in your ministry."[134] Notice that Hinn does not qualify his statement. He does not say, "Without it your growth will be limited." He says, "Without it there will be *no* growth."

The anointing has so permeated Hinn that he has lost all earthly desires. "In my case," says Hinn, "I know I have lost complete desire for anything to do with the world. My worldly desires are gone . . . I no longer have any rebellion in me."[135] On another occasion, however, Hinn exclaimed:

> I'm sick and tired of hearing about streets of gold. I don't need gold in heaven, I gotta have it now! I mean, when I get to glory, all my bills will be paid, brother. I won't have bills in glory! I won't need to worry about bills in glory! I gotta have it here! You say, "Well, Benny Hinn, isn't it wonderful to have streets of gold in heaven?" Well, of course, but if I hear the thing one more time of how it will be and how it was, I'm gonna kick somebody![136]

Despite errors and extravagances, I was cautiously optimistic that Hinn would reject some of his more egregious doctrines and practices after my initial meeting with him December 5, 1990. Hinn pledged to remove doctrinal errors from *Good Morning, Holy Spirit* and promised to refrain from throwing his coat at devotees clamoring to be "slain in the Spirit." In a 1991 interview with *Christianity Today*, he admitted his assertion that there were "nine of them" in the Trinity (because the Father, the Son, and the Holy Spirit each had His own personal spirit, soul, and body) was "a very dumb statement."[137] Hinn also expressed regret for wishing he had "a Holy Ghost machine gun" so he could blow the heads off his critics.[138] The icing on the cake came when Hinn commented, "I really no longer believe the Faith message. I don't think it adds up."[139]

Was Hinn sincere, or was this just damage control? The answer appears to be the latter. Within weeks he was back to his old ways. At the World Charismatic Conference in Anaheim, California on August 7, 1992, he unleashed his most chilling threat to date. "I'm pointing my finger with the mighty power of God on me," said Hinn, "You hear this: There are men and women in Southern California attacking me. I will tell you under the anointing now; you'll reap it in your children unless you stop . . . You attacking me on the radio every night—you'll pay and *your children will*. Hear this from the lips of God's servant. *You are in danger*. Repent! Or God Almighty will move His hand. Touch not my Anointed."[140] On October 23, 1992, in a TBN-sponsored marathon of televised attacks on "heresy hunters," Hinn issued yet another threat: "You have attacked me, *your children will pay for it*."

As for Hinn giving up his Faith teaching, that, too, can be discounted. Hinn has completely flip-flopped. Not only has he continued teaching his own brand of Faith theology, but he has gone out of his way to defend such Faith teachers as Hagin and Copeland—whose International Convention of Faith Churches and Ministers ordained him in the first place.[141] Within months, Hinn warned, "Those who attack confession are on the devil's side."[142] Soon thereafter, Hinn dogmatically declared, "Words create reality."[143] Hinn came completely out of the closet when he proclaimed, "Faith is released when I speak the *Word of Faith*."[144]

Over the past fifteen years Hinn has continued to add to his litany of spurious prophecies and pronouncements. On October 19, 1999, he predicted that instead of burying the dead, people around the world would line up caskets around television sets, place the hands of the dead on TV screens, and marvel as their loved ones arose from the dead. Said Hinn:

> Here's first what I see for TBN. You're going to have people raised from the dead watching this network. You're going to have people raised from the dead watching TBN . . . I'm telling you, I see this in the Spirit. It's going to be so awesome—Jesus, I give you praise for this—that people around the world—maybe not so much in America—people around the world who will lose loved ones, will say to undertakers, "Not yet. I want to take my dead loved one and place him in front of that TV set for twenty-four hours." . . . I see rows of caskets lining up in front of this TV set, and I see them bringing them closer to the TV set, and as people are coming closer, I actually see loved ones picking up the hands of the dead and letting them touch the screen, and people are getting raised as their hands are touching that screen.[145]

On January 1, 1990, Hinn attempted to delude devotees into believing that God spoke to him and revealed the fate of Castro in Cuba and homosexuals in America: "The Spirit tells me Fidel Castro will die in the '90s." Not only so, asserted Hinn, but "he will not stay in power."[146] (As of this writing Fidel is alive and his repressive regime continues unabated.) Regarding the homosexual community in America, Hinn alleged the Almighty revealed to him both the timing and the means of their demise. Said Hinn, "The Lord also tells me to tell you in the mid-90s, about '94, '95, no later than that, God will destroy the homosexual community of America. But He will not destroy it with what many minds have thought Him to be [*sic*]. He will destroy it with fire."[147]

In 1993, Hinn pontificated that because Jesus promised that He would return within a generation of Israel's restoration in 1948 and because a generation was "51.4" years—six years remained before Christ would come back to rapture His saints.[148] Seven years later, on March 29, 2000, Hinn predicted Jesus would "appear physically in one of our crusades in the next few months." According to Hinn, the Lord had spoken audibly to the now-deceased Ruth Heflin, saying, "Tell Benny I'm going to appear physically on the platform in his meeting."[149] A month later Hinn reiterated his assertion that Jesus was going to make physical appearances prior to His second coming. Said Hinn, "I'm prophesying this, 'Jesus Christ, the Son of God, is about to appear physically in some churches and some meetings and to many of His people for one reason: to tell you He's about to show up.'"[150]

What is particularly noteworthy about this prophecy is that Hinn here is prophesying that "Jesus, God's Son, is about to appear physically in meetings" and that this supernatural event was to take place in Nairobi, Kenya.

> I'm careful in how I am saying it now because I know that people in Kenya are listening. I know deep in my soul something supernatural is going to happen in Nairobi, Kenya. I feel that I may very well come back—and you [Paul] and Jan are coming; Paul and Jan are coming to Nairobi with me—but Paul, *we may very well come back with footage of Jesus on the platform.*[151]

Why is this worthy of particular note? Because scarcely weeks before Hinn's prophecy, a Florida newspaper drew attention to New Age guru Benjamin Creme's prediction that the second coming of Christ had taken place in Nairobi, Kenya, in 1988. *Florida Today* reported that in a photograph utilized by Creme, "a dark-skinned, heavily bearded man in a white head dress and white robe seems to float above a crowd of worshippers" at a healing service in Nairobi. *Florida Today* not only noted the mass healings that allegedly took place but reported that even though Christians present "firmly believe that Jesus Christ appeared to them that day," Creme held that Maitreya—the fifth and final incarnation of Buddha—had materialized.[152]

In any case, another seven years have come and gone since the prophet

Hinn predicted that Jesus would appear physically in churches and crusades. As 2008 fades into history, his prophecy remains unfulfilled. As the apostle Peter wrote two thousand years ago, "[Jesus] must remain in heaven until the time comes for God to restore everything" (Acts 3:21).

As the Master Teacher tarries in heaven, misguided teachers continue to proliferate on earth. Among the most noteworthy is a man named Joel Osteen.

Joel Osteen

It's not enough to simply see it by faith or in your imagination. You have to begin speaking words of faith over your life. Your words have enormous creative power. The moment you speak something out, you give birth to it. This is a spiritual principle, and it works whether what you are saying is good or bad, positive or negative.[153]

—JOEL OSTEEN

Joel Osteen today has eclipsed Benny Hinn's star status as the preeminent prosperity preacher on the planet. *People* magazine describes Osteen as the "pastor of Lakewood Church, with a weekly attendance of 47,000[154] (twice as big as the nearest competitor); the main attraction of Sunday services broadcast in 100 countries; an author of two bestselling books (his first, in 2006, outsold Billy Graham's latest); and the headliner of touring motivational-meets-worship shows that sell out venues like New York City's Madison Square Garden."[155] The subhead to this major spread reads, "He Lives in a Mansion, Travels by Private Jet And, with His Latest Bestseller, Has Already Reportedly Earned $13 Million."

Despite stupendous successes, Joel Osteen's sermons, in concert with other Faith teachers, consist of an endless string of undocumented anecdotes and urban legends buttressed by misquotations and misinterpretations of the Bible. As a case in point, Joel alters Jesus' account of a paralytic lying by the pool of Bethesda, in order to prove the premise that by our words and actions we create reality. In Osteen's version of the story, this paralytic lay around the pool of Bethesda for thirty-eight years, feeling sorry for himself. To alter his reality all he had to do was pick up his mat and walk. Instead, for thirty-eight years he made excuses. Exhorts Osteen: "If you're serious about being well, if you really want to be made physically and emotionally whole, you must get up and get moving with your life. No more lying around feeling sorry for yourself."[156] Tragically, Osteen has turned Jesus' rendition of the story on its head. According to Jesus, the paralytic was first cured and then picked up his mat and walked. Put another way, both logically and linguistically the paralytic was cured prior to walking.[157] In Joel's revision of the text, the paralytic picked up the mat and walked prior to being cured.

Urban legends and legendary stories are standard fare in Osteen's books and sermons. Ironically, even points well taken are buttressed by baloney. In *Your Best Life Now*, Osteen recounts a common urban legend regarding codfish. "Many years ago," writes Osteen, "fishing for codfish up in the Northeast had become a lucrative commercial business. The fishing industry recognized that a great market for codfish existed all over America, but they had a major problem in the distribution." The problem, according to Osteen, is that the owners could not freeze the codfish because "after the codfish was frozen, it lost its taste." Further, shipping codfish across the country in huge tanks of saltwater just made matters worse. "Because the fish were inactive in the tank, they became soft and mushy, and once again they lost their taste." The owners finally solved the problem by putting catfish in the tanks. Says Osteen, "Catfish are a natural enemy of codfish, so as the tank traveled across the country, the codfish had to stay alert and active and be on the lookout for catfish."[158]

If this was the only urban legend circulated by Osteen it would be one thing. But Osteen follows up his fish story with one suspicious story after the other. While spinning legends about bees dying in outer space because of a failure to use their wings[159] or about monkeys captured with their hands in the proverbial banana bin[160] is forgivable, what is not is the spin Osteen places on essential Christian doctrine.

During Easter messages, for example, Osteen is fond of telling his devotees that Jesus did not finish the work of redemption on the cross. While Jesus says it is finished, Joel says it is far from finished. While Scripture says Jesus made "a public spectacle" of the devil and his demons, "triumphing over them by the cross" (Colossians 2:15), Joel says Jesus triumphed over the demonic hordes in hell. While the Bible tells us that our Savior has always had control of death and hell, Joel says Jesus had to rip the keys of death and hell out of Satan's hands. And against the whole counsel of Scripture, Osteen pontificates that in hell "the two most powerful forces in the universe have come together to do battle for *the first time in history.*"[161]

In an imaginative reconstruction that has no basis in the Bible, Osteen transitions the triumph of the Cross to the corridors of hell. There Jesus "did battle with Satan face to face." In direct contradiction of the biblical text, "when Jesus bowed his head and died on the cross," Osteen says, "Satan and all those demons they gathered in Hell for a great victory celebration. I can imagine it looked something like the victory party in the locker room after the Super Bowl." In the end, however, the Savior overwhelmed Satan and "ripped the keys of death and hell out of Satan's hands. And he grabbed Satan by the nap [*sic*] of his neck and He began to slowly drag him down through the corridors of Hell. All beat up and bruised because He wanted to make sure that every single demon saw very clearly that Jesus was indeed the undisputed Champion of all time!"[162]

It is almost inconceivable that anyone—particularly someone who takes the sacred name of Christ upon his lips—would so blatantly reconstruct the centrality of Christ's atonement upon the cross. Yet in the face of Scripture, which plainly tells us that *"by his death"* Jesus destroyed him "who holds the power of death—that is the devil" (Hebrews 2:14, emphasis added), Osteen has Christ in the cauldron of hell, finishing the work of redemption. I will not belabor the horrors of such *atonement atrocities* here, in that I do so in Part Four, but suffice it to say that this is among the most egregious of Osteen's doctrinal perversions.

Incredibly, in Osteen's revision of Scripture, even Christ's victory in hell was insufficient to atone for our sins. After the Resurrection, "there still had to be a blood sacrifice for our sins. There still had to be a price paid." That is why Jesus "presented his own blood in the high court of heaven as a sacrifice for all our sins, past, present, and future." Indeed, according to Osteen that is precisely the reason that Jesus commanded Mary to not touch Him after the Resurrection. "Why didn't Jesus want Mary to touch her [*sic*]?" asks Osteen. "I'll tell you what it was. Jesus had just risen from the grave, and He still had His Holy blood on Him. It was this blood He was going to use as a sacrifice for our sins."[163]

In reality, nothing could be further from the truth. Far from having some sort of magical efficacy, *the blood of Jesus Christ* is emblematic of *the death of Jesus Christ*.[164] Nor is there any warrant for suggesting that sometime between His encounter with Mary and His encounter with Thomas, Jesus went to heaven to sprinkle His blood upon the mercy seat. Instead, believers throughout the ages have celebrated the precious sacrament of communion as the broken body and shed blood of Jesus Christ for the *complete* remission of sins. Again, it was not Christ's triumph over Satan in the cauldron of hell that atoned for sin—Jesus said, "Father, into your hands I commit my spirit (Luke 23: 46; cf. John 19:30) not "Satan, into your clutches I submit My spirit"—nor did the debt remain unpaid until Christ ascended into heaven. The debt for all sin past, present, and future was paid by Christ's passion upon the cross. When His passion on the cross was complete, Christ uttered the word *tetelestai*—meaning "the debt has been paid in full!" No further debt remained to be discharged in this world or the next.

As serious as Osteen's atonement atrocities are, his contention that the force of faith is so potent that even the Sovereign of the universe is bound by it is equally troublesome. As noted in the introduction, Osteen goes so far as to say that God knew that Zechariah's negative confessions—"Are you really sure this is going to happen? Do you see how old we are? I just don't think this could be possible"—would stop His plan.[165] As such, God had to take away Zechariah's speech. Once again, however, we have entered the spin zone. Not only has Osteen added spin to the biblical text, but he has left out significant portions of the biblical narrative.

First, even though Zechariah "was startled and was gripped with fear" at the presence of an angel (Luke 1:12), God personified Zechariah as "upright" and "blameless" (v. 6).

Furthermore, Gabriel specifically said to Zechariah, "Your prayer *has been heard*. Your wife Elizabeth *will* bear you a son" (v. 13, emphasis added). In response Zechariah asked, "How can I be sure of this?" (v. 18). The angel Gabriel responded by giving him a sign: "You will be silent and not able to speak until the day this happens, because you did not believe my words, which *will* come true at their proper time" (v. 20, emphasis added).

Finally, nowhere in the text is there any indication that God had to take away Zechariah's speech because He knew that Zechariah's negative words would cancel out His plan. On the contrary, if the Bible teaches us anything, it is that God is supreme in His authority and power. As Daniel reminded Belshazzar, immediately prior to the fall of the Babylonian Empire, his father Nebuchadnezzar had come to believe in the sovereignty of his personal rule and command; thus, God gave him "the mind of an animal; he lived with the wild donkeys and ate grass like cattle; and his body was drenched with the dew of heaven, until he acknowledged that the Most High God is sovereign over the kingdoms of men and sets over them anyone he wishes" (Daniel 5:21).

As the mighty Nebuchadnezzar acknowledged after being reduced to eating grass like a cow, God's dominion (not Nebuchadnezzar's) "is an eternal dominion; his kingdom endures from generation to generation. All the peoples of the earth are regarded as nothing. *He does as he pleases with the powers of heaven and the peoples of the earth.* No one can hold back his hand or say to him: 'What have you done?'" (Daniel 4:34–35, emphasis added).

Another of Osteen's core convictions is that both generational curses and generational blessings are passed down via "the bloodline being formed in your DNA."[166] This despite the reality that there is no biblical basis for believing in either generational blessings or generational curses. Scripture communicates that consequences—not curses—are passed on through the generations. In this sense, the Bible says children are punished for the sins of their fathers "to the third and fourth generation" (Exodus 20:5). The children of alcoholic fathers frequently suffer neglect and abuse as a direct consequence of their father's sinful behavior. Furthermore, Scripture explicitly tells us that "the son will *not* share the guilt of the father, nor will the father share the guilt of the son" (Ezekiel 18:20, emphasis added). Finally, when ancient Israel quoted the proverb, "The fathers eat sour grapes, and the children's teeth are set on edge" (v. 2), God responded in no uncertain terms: "As surely as I live, declares the Sovereign LORD, you will no longer quote this proverb in Israel, . . . *The soul who sins is the one who will die*" (vv. 3–4, emphasis added).

Yet in contradiction of the clear communication of Scripture, Osteen offers up an urban legend in support of generational curses (see introduction), and in support of generational blessings he offers up the story of a friend who pastors several thousand people but desperately wants to pastor "thousands and thousands more." Additionally, the pastor covets the realization of his "dream of writing books that will affect the world."

Despite the reality that the average church has fewer than a hundred members, every time this pastor drives by a church that is larger than his own, he feels "as though salt were being rubbed in a wound." As a result, he begins to speak out words of fear rather than words of faith—"God, it's just not fair. I poured my heart and soul into the dream that You gave me, but I don't think I'll ever measure up to this man's success . . . I feel like I'm being laughed at. I don't even know if I should stay in the race."[167]

One might think that God would chide this pastor for seeing success from a worldly perspective or for succumbing to the sins of envy and covetousness. Instead the Almighty apparently affirmed the pastor's materialistic proclivities by suggesting he take solace in the possibility that he was "laying the groundwork" for the future success of his grandchildren. In other words, the Almighty allegedly held out the hope that, like generational curses, generational blessings "may be harvested by your sons and your daughters."[168]

Osteen writes about a circumstance in his own life where, like this pastor friend, he uttered negative confessions. He and and his wife, Victoria, were living in a "crooked" little house when one day they came upon a beautiful home in the final stages of construction. Joel was so convinced that owning such a home was beyond the realm of possibility, that he continuously spoke words of fear. Victoria, however, did not. "Over the next several months, she kept speaking words of faith and victory." Eventually Joel rid himself of "limited thinking" and started agreeing with her. "We kept on believing it, seeing it, and speaking it," writes Joel, and "we saw it come to pass."[169]

The faith of Joel is apparently being "harvested" by his son, Jonathan, as well. "One day as we were riding down the freeway," writes Joel, "we came upon the Compaq Center, the sixteen-thousand-seat arena that was the former home of the Houston Rockets . . . I slowed down and pointed. 'Jonathan, look over there. One day, that's where you're going to be preaching. He said, 'Oh no. Daddy. When I get old enough, I'm going to preach in Reliant Stadium!' (Reliant Stadium is Houston's seventy-thousand-seat home of the Houston Texans football team.)"[170] This is precisely how Joel's father, John, had taught his son to think. Says Osteen, "Whenever people asked me, 'Joel, do you think that you will be able to do as much as your dad?'" I would always say, 'I believe I'm going to do more than my dad.'"[171]

While there is certainly nothing inappropriate in dreaming big dreams for ourselves or for our children, there is no biblical warrant for supposing generational blessings are passed down via "the bloodline being formed in our DNA."[172] Nor is there any reason to believe that Osteen's acquisition of a big house is the result of his effectively wielding the inexorable force of faith any more than Rhonda Byrne's acquisition of a big house resulted from her "placing an order with the catalogue of the universe."[173] It is far more likely that they have what they have as a result of telling people what they want to hear (i.e., the moment you speak something out, you give birth to it). Not only so, but big is not always better. I have been privileged to have a much bigger platform than my father had during his earthly ministry, but it may be that in God's economy my father will have a greater reward in eternity due to faithful service, self-sacrifice, and suffering. Such enduring rewards are not often the subject of contemporary sermons; they were, however, a constant theme in the sermons of Christ.

Joyce Meyer

There is no hope of anyone going to heaven unless they believe this truth I am presenting. You cannot go to heaven unless you believe with all your heart that Jesus took your place in hell.[174]

—JOYCE MEYER

Like Joel Osteen, Joyce Meyer is a rising star in the Faith galaxy. As noted on her Web site, Meyer "has authored over 80 books," and as of 2008, "more than 12 million of her books have been distributed worldwide." Moreover, her Web site claims, "Joyce also has a television and radio program, *Enjoying Everyday Life*, that is broadcast worldwide to a potential audience of 3 billion people."[175] Though she boasts "an earned PhD in theology from Life Christian University,"[176] her teachings lack in scriptural credibility in much the same way that LCU lacks in scholastic accreditation. (Other notable faith luminaries who have received "earned" PhDs from LCU include Dr. Benny Hinn, Drs. Kenneth and Gloria Copeland, and Drs. Adonica and Rodney Howard-Browne—aka the Holy Ghost Bartender.)[177]

In lockstep with Joel, Joyce twists the biblical text in order to portray a helpless paralytic lying by the pool of Bethesda for thirty-eight years as faithless and foolish. In Joyce's revision of Jesus' words, the paralytic invokes one pathetic excuse after the other. Without so much as a hint of compassion, she responds, "I would think that after thirty-eight years a diligent, determined person could have crawled over to the edge of that pool. Even if that man had only moved an inch a year, it seems that in thirty-eight years, he ought to have been able to get close enough to the edge to just roll over into the water when it was stirred up."[178] (Given her disgust for a paralytic in the past, one can scarcely imagine the disdain she feels for the paralytics she encounters in the present.)

Meyer makes a sharp distinction between her own faith and that of the paralytic. Says Meyer, "Thirty-eight years is a long time to lie somewhere, waiting for somebody to do something for you. I would have been on the edge of that pool, and next year when the angel came around, when that water started bubbling, I would have fallen in and said, 'Either I'm going to get healed or I'm going to die, but I'm not staying like this.'"[179] Meyer concludes her excoriation of the paralytic with virtually the identical words used by Osteen: "Sometimes we have to get up, get going and just keep moving forward."[180] Meyer's moral is this: if you are a paralytic or a paraplegic, *you* are the problem! Instead of

40

feeling sorry for yourself, just "Get up!" Put another way, the key to health and prosperity is to have faith in your faith rather than faith in your God. Says Meyer, "Faith is not just some little, 'Well, you know, I believe in Jesus.' Faith is a force that will change your life and change your destiny."[181]

Meyer made this explicit, saying, "Words are containers for power. They carry creative or destructive power, positive or negative power. And so we need to be speaking right things over our lives and about our futures if we expect to have good things happen. Because what you say today is what you'll probably end up having tomorrow."[182] In other words, the words we speak will create the future realities we experience.

According to Meyer, the words you speak not only create future realities but are the means by which you "keep the Devil under your feet."[183] In sharp contrast to the archangel Michael—who "did not dare to bring a slanderous accusation against [the devil], but said, 'The Lord rebuke you!'" (Jude 9)—Meyer is quite comfortable rebuking the devil. In person and in print, she teaches devotees to "talk back to the devil."[184] For the apostle Paul, exercising spiritual disciplines is the key to becoming Christlike. For Meyer "speaking forth the truth to the devil . . . is the only way to see a mindset changed."[185] As such, she habitually rebukes demons, ranging from the spirit of accidents to the spirit of lust.[186]

Like Osteen, Meyer believes in generational curses. As such, she confides that "a spirit of incest" has been passed down through her family bloodline. In a sermon titled "Trophies of God's Grace," she explains what she believes to be the spirit of incest passed from her grandparents to her father. Thus, her father abused her sexually and opened the door for the spirit to be passed on to her children. Meyer confessed that she does not know why God would allow a spirit to be passed down through the generations but is nonetheless confident that He does.[187]

As such, she employs personal anecdotes to convince followers that the problems they encounter in the present may be pawned off on proclivities of past generations. As previously noted, however, Scripture clearly communicates that consequences—not curses—are passed down through the generations.[188] Thus, Meyer suffered the horrors of sexual abuse solely as a consequence of her father's incestuous behavior, not as the result of "a spirit of incest" that passed down through her family bloodline.

In a publication titled *The Most Important Decision You Will Ever Make*, Meyer proliferates another hallmark of Faith theology—namely, Jesus not only had to suffer on the cross, but He had to suffer in hell in order for you and me to be born again. Says Meyer, Jesus "was in the grave three days. During that time, He entered hell, where you and I deserved to go (legally) because of our sin. He paid the price there."[189]

After three days of torment, continues Meyer:

God rose up from His throne and said to demon powers tormenting the sinless Son of God, "Let Him go." Then the resurrection power of Almighty God went through hell and filled Jesus. On the earth, His grave, the tomb where they had buried Him, filled with light as the power of God filled His body, and He was resurrected from the dead—*the first born-again man.* The Bible calls Him "the first-born among many brethren" (Romans 8:29). He was the first so that now *you* can be one of the many brethren.[190]

In sharp contrast to Meyer's assertion, the Bible *never* says that Jesus Christ was born again. Indeed, the biblical concept of being born again (John 3:3) applies solely to sinful humanity. While the Bible says that Jesus was begotten, it does not say He was born again. When John refers to Christ as "the One and Only, who came from the Father" (John 1:14), he was emphasizing the unique nature of our Lord. As such, Jesus alone is fully God and fully man, the unique and eternal Son of the Father. Jesus had no need to be born again in hell, for Jesus is and always has been the eternal Son of God.

So strident is Meyer in her contention that Jesus suffered and was born again in hell that in subsequent revisions of her original publication, she reiterates the notion that apart from believing that Jesus suffered in hell, we have absolutely no hope of going to heaven. Says Meyer, "There is no hope of anyone going to heaven unless they believe this truth I am presenting. You cannot go to heaven unless you believe with all your heart that Jesus took your place in hell."[191] Thus while Jesus said, "Father, into your hands I commit my spirit" (Luke 23:46), Joyce says, the spirit of Christ "went to hell because that is where we deserve to go."[192] If we are to take the words of the Savior seriously, however, He committed His spirit to His Father; He did not commit His spirit to Satan. Paul put it ever so plainly: "Having disarmed the powers and authorities, he made a public spectacle of them, triumphing over them *by the cross*" (Colossians 2:15, emphasis added).

Ironically, Meyer has a habit of denying what she affirms. As previously mentioned, in *The Most Important Decision You Will Ever Make: A Complete and Thorough Understanding of What It Means to Be Born Again*, Meyer dogmatically affirms the notion that after suffering in hell for three days, Jesus emerged as the first born-again man. Yet, in an interview with *Charisma* magazine, she denied teaching the born-again Jesus theory, contending it was "a doctrine she does not believe and has never taught."[193]

Likewise, while Meyer readily affirms that she sins all the time,[194] she also emphatically denies that she is a sinner. Says Meyer, "I didn't stop sinning until I finally got it through my thick head I wasn't a sinner anymore. And the religious world thinks that's heresy and they want to hang you for it. But the Bible says that I'm righteous, and I can't be righteous and a sinner at the same time."[195] If she was a sinner, contends Meyer, it would nullify the very death of Christ upon the cross: "I am not poor, I am not miserable, and I am not a sinner. *That is a lie from the pit of hell.* That is what I were *and if I still was, then Jesus died in vain.*"[196]

Not only does Meyer contradict herself in this regard, but she also contradicts Scripture. While *positionally* we are righteous before God, on account of the righteousness of Christ, *practically* we are yet sinners. Said the apostle John, "If we claim we have not sinned, we make him out to be a liar and his word has no place in our lives" (1 John 1:10). Far from suggesting that he was not a sinner, the very apostle who wrote two-thirds of the New Testament epistles cried out, "I know that nothing good lives in me, that is, in my sinful nature. For I have the desire to do what is good, but I cannot carry it out. For what I do is not the good I want to do; no, the evil I do not want to do—this I keep on doing" (Romans 7:18–19). While believers are covered by the righteousness of Christ, they are yet sinners and will be until the day they are glorified. Luther graphically portrayed this reality when he referred to Christians as "snow covered dung."[197]

Sometimes Meyer's teachings seem somewhat silly. "When we are praising and worshipping God," she says, "there's actually an odor that comes off of us that is offensive to the enemy. And I don't know if you've ever had the opportunity to smell a demon-possessed person but I have and I tell you it is a stench . . . people that are demon-possessed have an offensive odor to me and I'm glad that because I am Holy-Ghost-possessed that I've got an offensive odor to the devil."[198]

At other times, Meyer's doctrinal aberrations are singularly serious. This is particularly so with respect to her contention that God created men as "little gods." As Meyer explains, "If you as a human being have a baby, you call it a human kind. If cattle have another cattle, they call it cattle-kind. I mean, what's God supposed to call us? Doesn't the Bible say we're created in His image? Now, you understand, I'm not saying you are God with a capital 'G.'" Meyer seems acutely aware of the fact that she is on tenuous grounds. Thus, she adds, "Don't go trying to stone me or yell blasphemy at me!"[199]

While it would certainly seem that Meyer's contention borders on blasphemy, one thing is certain—it is anything but biblical. Though we are "sons" of the Most High, we are not sons by *nature*; we are sons by *adoption* (Galatians 4:5–8). Only Christ Himself can be said to have the nature of God. As such, Christ alone is the only begotten (*monogenes*) Son of the Father. That humans are created in God's image simply means that they share, in a finite and imperfect way, the *incommunicable* attributes of God. Again, I will not belabor the point here as I do so in Part Three, titled "Little Gods." Suffice it to say for now, nowhere does the Bible teach Meyer's "little gods" doctrine.

One final word concerning Meyer's subjectivism before we move on: Meyer is convinced that God would not allow her to lapse into error without first sounding an alarm. In her words, "If I'm accidentally, or any other way, getting into error, I'm going to have a bell go off in the inside of me that is going to be so loud that not only am I going to hear it, but so is everyone else."[200] If Meyer had been truly tethered to the text of Scripture, she would most certainly have heard the tolling of the bell.

John Hagee

Let us put an end to this Christian chatter that *"all the Jews are lost"* and can't be in the will of God until they convert to Christianity![201]

—JOHN HAGEE

Another Faith teacher who, like Meyer, routinely embarks upon subjective flights of fancy is the bombastic televangelist John Hagee. While Hagee is increasingly recognizable as a militant Zionist—who routinely castigates pastors as anti-Semitic if they do not embrace the notion of a secret coming of Christ followed by a Holy Land Holocaust in which a vast majority of Jews perish—the hallmark of his preaching remains prosperity. As such, Hagee shamelessly promotes the pretext of a prosperous Jesus. To begin with, Jesus allegedly lived in a mansion. Says Hagee, "John 1:38 says that Jesus turned to those who were following and said, 'come with me,' and they said, 'where dwellest thou?' He said, 'come and see,' and Jesus took the crowd home with Him to stay in His house. That meant it was a big house."[202] Furthermore, Jesus wore designer clothes. As Hagee puts it, "Jesus had a seamless robe so valuable that Roman soldiers gambled for it at the cross. It was a designer robe."[203] Moreover, says Hagee, "When you have to have a secretary-treasurer to carry the excess money, you're not poor."[204]

As I demonstrate later on, the notion of "Jesus with a Rolex" is the stuff of myths and fables. Indeed "the crowd" Jesus allegedly invited to stay with Him in His mansion is the mere figment of Hagee's overactive imagination. The very passage cited by Hagee makes it clear that far from inviting a *crowd* to join Him in His mansion, Jesus invited *two* people to see "where he was staying" (v. 39). Likewise the notion that the soldiers gambled for Christ's garment because it was "so valuable" is completely ad hoc. In reality, they cast lots for the garment of Christ not only "that the scripture might be fulfilled" (John 19:24) but because, as common sense dictates, one garment divided into four rags would have been of little value to them.[205] Even if we suppose that this was an expensive undergarment, there is no warrant to presume that the closet of Christ's mansion was replete with more of the same. Nor can we presume that because the disciples had a money bag that Jesus was a multimillion-dollar Messiah. Instead the message of Jesus was consistent and clear. "It is easier for a camel to go though the eye of a needle than for a rich man to enter the kingdom of God" (Mark 10:25).

Ironically, Hagee recognizes the force of these words and goes to great lengths to strip them of their meaning. In his book *The Seven Secrets*, he makes light of those who use Christ's words as a corrective to his Word of Faith theology. As such, he refers readers to the archeological discovery of a "needle gate" five feet from a main gate leading into Jerusalem. After midnight, he contends, camel riders were resigned to squeezing their camels through a "needle gate" into the city.[206] What he doesn't divulge to devotees is that this gate did not even exist in Jesus' day. In point of fact, it did not come into existence until the medieval period.[207]

In concert with other Word of Faith preachers, Hagee says that our prosperity is predicated on our thoughts, on our tongues, and on our tithes. As a result of his thoughts, opines Hagee, the disciple Thomas "accomplished virtually nothing."[208] In the same book Hagee advances several stories to buttress his belief that thoughts can create reality. One such story involves Nick, whom

45

Hagee describes as "a strong, healthy rail yardman." Though Nick was a consistently reliable worker, he "had a deep fear that he would be locked in an isolated, refrigerated boxcar." One night Nick's fears became reality. "Nick was accidently locked in a refrigerated boxcar, which was in the yard for repairs." Believing that the temperature in the boxcar was zero degrees, "Nick thought, *If I don't get out of here I'll freeze to death.* Shivering uncontrollably, he scrawled a message to his wife. 'So cold, body's getting numb. If I could just go to sleep . . . These may be my last words.'" The moral of the story, according to Hagee, is that though "the temperature inside was never lower than 61 degrees, Nick's fear became a self-fulfilling prophecy."[209] Does Hagee's story have any basis in reality? Of course not! As you have no doubt already guessed, in concert with his assertions regarding Thomas, Hagee is repeating a commonly communicated urban legend.[210]

As with thoughts, Hagee believes that our tongues are at the root of our realities: "I believe that when a person says, 'I wish I were dead,' he or she invites the spirit of death to invade his or her life. When an unhappy wife says, 'My marriage is a failure,' she has pronounced the doom of this relationship. When a pregnant mother says, 'I don't want this baby,' she is pronouncing the termination of her pregnancy or a curse upon the life of a child yet to be born. Speech is that powerful."[211] In evidence he writes, "'Death and life are in the power of the tongue' (Proverbs 18:21). What you say has a strange and powerful way of becoming reality."[212] As noted elsewhere, this is a perversion of Proverbs. While it is true that our tongues can have a devastating impact on ourselves and on others, nowhere is there any biblical support for the idea that what we say can invite the spirit of death into our lives or put a curse on someone yet unborn. If this were the case, the common cliché "I'll be a monkey's uncle" would pose a dramatic threat to one's pregnant sister.

For Hagee our tithe is yet another piece of the faith puzzle. From his perspective, a reluctant two-dollar donation he made to a missionary was the key to his spiritual well-being and financial wealth. In his words, "I knew as certainly as I know my name is John Hagee that giving is the secret to financial and spiritual wealth. My two-dollar gift to the kingdom of God changed the destiny of my life."[213] The formula is simple. "When you tithe, God gives to you. When you don't tithe, God takes it away from you." Or put more bluntly: "Why tithe? Because you live under the financial curse of God when you don't."[214] Once again, however, Hagee's perspective is seriously skewed. Tithing should never be viewed as a means through which we can accumulate wealth. Rather, we tithe so that we might learn to lean more heavily on the arm of our heavenly Father than upon the arm of flesh. We tithe so that we might catch the joy of contagious giving—or as Moses communicated to the children of Israel, we tithe "so that [we] may learn to revere the LORD [our] God always" (Deuteronomy 14:23).

There is no telling what can be accomplished in our generation if we, too, may but catch the joy of contagious giving. Not only would we be empowered to spread the gospel around the globe, but we also would be enabled to feed the hungry, clothe the naked, and care for the sick. Like our forefathers, who founded great centers of Christian education, established countless hospitals, and funded myriad relief organizations, we might yet leave an indelible mark on our generation. As with our thoughts and our tongues, our perspective regarding the tithe can make all the difference in the world.

As noted at the outset, Hagee's text-twisting tactics extend far beyond his Word of Faith message. As a leading Christian Zionist, he routinely castigates those who do not share his "two-people of God" theory as "Replacement theologians" who are "carrying Hitler's anointing and his message."[215] This despite the fact that it is he—not those he impugns—who holds that Israel will soon *replace* the church as the focus of God's plans. Indeed, in his view in the not-too-distant future, two-thirds of the Jews he is now helping to herd into the Holy Land will suffer a holocaust that will make the Nazi atrocities pale by comparison. Not only so, but it also is truly tragic that Hagee places far greater emphasis on returning Jews to the land than turning Jewish people to the Lord. Says Hagee, "Let us put an end to this Christian chatter that *'all the Jews are lost'* and can't be in the will of God until they convert to Christianity!"[216] Incredibly, Hagee goes so far as to take the onus off of the Jewish community and place it squarely on the Jewish Christ: "If Jesus refused by his words or actions to claim to be the Messiah to the Jews," asks Hagee, "then HOW CAN THE JEWS BE BLAMED FOR REJECTING WHAT WAS NEVER OFFERED?"[217] Hagee goes so far as to say that the Jewish people "wanted [Jesus] to be their Messiah but he absolutely refused . . . the Jews were not rejecting Jesus as Messiah, it was Jesus who was refusing to be Messiah to the Jews!"[218]

Anyone who has read through the Gospels even once knows full well that Jesus emphatically contradicted such sentiments. Who can forget the emotionally charged words uttered by Jesus as He was leaving the temple: "O Jerusalem, Jerusalem, you who kill the prophets and stone those sent to you, how often I have *longed to gather your children* together, as a hen gathers her chicks under her wings, but *you* were not willing" (Matthew 23:37, emphasis added). Or as the apostle John explains: "He came to that which was his own, but his own did not receive him" (John 1:11). It was the Jews who rejected Jesus, not the other way round (Mark 12:1–12). Plainly put, Hagee's spin is historical revisionism pure and simple.

To suggest as Hagee does that the Jews are somehow entitled to building settlements in Gaza and yet excluded from the blessed salvation of the gospel might well be the height of anti-Semitism. Worse still, the notion that Jews in the twenty-first century will endure a holocaust for the first-century sins of their fathers is as unbiblical as it is unthinkable. Indeed only a gospel of peace and justice through faith in the one who died for both Jew and Gentile is potent enough to break the stranglehold of anti-Semitism fueled in large part by bad theology.

Creflo Dollar

Because you came from God you are gods—you're not just human.[219]
—CREFLO DOLLAR

Another Word of Faith televangelist who is the very embodiment of bad theology is Dr. Creflo A. Dollar, founder and senior pastor of World Changers Church International (WCCI). Despite heresy that strikes at the very core of Christianity, he has been awarded an honorary doctor of divinity from Oral Roberts University.[220] Lest one think that the word *heresy* is a bit much, consider the fact that Dollar not only denies the deity of Christ but also denigrates pastors who proclaim that Christ is fully God as "fantasy preachers." He further chides followers for falling for such fantasies:

> And somebody said, well, Jesus came as God! Well, how many of you know the Bible says God never sleeps nor slumbers? And yet in the book of Mark we see Jesus asleep in the back of the boat. Please listen to me. Please listen to me. This ain't no heresy. I'm not some false prophet. I'm just reading this thing out to you of the Bible. I'm just telling you, all these fantasy preachers have been preaching all of this stuff for all of these years and we bought the package![221]

And this is not an isolated incident. Dollar has gone so far as to say that because Jesus got tired, He could not have been God. As rationale for this deviation from essential Christian doctrine, Dollar simply says, "If he [Jesus] came as God and he got tired—he says he sat down by the well because he was tired— boy, we're in trouble."[222] Moreover, "If Jesus came as God, then why did God have to anoint him?" He answers his own question, saying, "Jesus came as a man, that's why it was legal to anoint him—God doesn't need anointing. He is anointed. Jesus came as a man, and at age thirty God is now getting ready to demonstrate to us and give us an example of what a man with the anointing can do."[223]

Dollar's departure from orthodoxy cuts to the heart of Christ's passion on the cross. While it is true to say that Christ set aside the prerogative for independently using His divine attributes when He took on the limitations of humanity—it is false to say that Christ was divested of a single attribute of deity. Indeed, the historic Christian church has consistently maintained that in the Incarnation, Christ was undiminished deity! If Christ was not fully God, His passion on the cross would have been insufficient to atone for sin. As man, Christ is our representative—the Second Adam; as God, His death was sufficient to provide redemption for the sins of the world. To suggest, as Dollar does, that those who teach that "Jesus came as God" are fantasy preachers is to say that a whole host of credible pastors from Charles Spurgeon to Charles Stanley have missed the answer to Christ's most basic question—namely, "Who do you say that I am?"

Not only does Dollar demote Christ, but he also deifies Christians. On one occasion he went so far as to pour water from a bottle into a glass as evidence for his contention that "the same stuff that God is, man is." Says Dollar, "Notice the substance didn't change just because it was moved from one vessel to the other. Listen to what I am saying. When God poured of himself into man, the stuff that man came from didn't change."[224]

On yet another occasion, Dollar cleverly coerced his congregation into saying that they were gods. He began with the declaration that "everything produces after its own kind." As such, he asked, "If horses get together, they produce what?" His congregation responded, "Horses." He continued asking, "If dogs get together, they produce what?" Again, his audience responded, "Dogs." Next he asked, "If cats get together, they produce what?" Everyone shouted, "Cats!" And then came the clincher: "If the Godhead gets together and says 'Let us make man,' then what are they producing?" With one accord they all cried out, "Gods." For Dollar the point was self-evident. Just as dogs beget dogs, so God begets gods. Said Dollar, "Because you came from God you are gods—you're not just human."[225]

Having seen Dollar up close and personal, I easily understand how people can get caught up in his rhetoric. Upon reflection, however, it is equally easy to spot Dollar's sleight of mind. While it is true to say that cats beget cats or that humans beget humans, there is nothing to suggest that the Creator begets in the manner of His creation such that God begets little gods. Scripture reveals precisely the opposite. As the gospel of John makes clear, Jesus is "the only begotten Son" (John 1:18 NKJV). In other words, Jesus is the only human who ever walked the planet who is "in very nature God" (Philippians 2:6). The Almighty Himself emphatically made the point: "Before me no god was formed, nor will there be one after me" (Isaiah 43:10). Lest one miss the message, God reiterates the self-same sentiment, one chapter later: "I am the first and I am the last; apart from me there is *no* God" (Isaiah 44:6, emphasis added).

Incredibly, God's message seems completely lost on Dollar. As such, he takes the Spirit-inspired words of Philippians 2:5–6 and uses them as a pretext for urging his followers to talk themselves into believing that they have equality with God. The essence of his argument is this: if Jesus "thought it not robbery to be equal with God . . . then my whole attitude should be, I have equality with God." Dollar then begins to urge devotees to believe in their equality with God. Says Dollar: "Well, keep saying it, *I have equality with God*. Talk yourself into it; you've talked yourself into other things. Talk yourself into this attitude. Talk yourself into this way of thinking. Talk yourself into it until you build a confidence on the inside of you that I have equality with God."[226] In truth, the point of the passage is not that we should exalt ourselves by supposing we have equality with God but that we should humble ourselves as Christ—who is "in very nature God"—humbled himself by "taking the very nature of a servant."

While it is hard to imagine a greater example of twisting the text, Dollar has proven more than equal to the task. Indeed, Dollar takes the words of Isaiah and turns them completely on their head. When the divine Creator asks, "How dare you tell Me what to do with the work of My hands," Creflo Dollar responds, "Who do you think you are going around commanding God around? Well, that's what the Bible said to do in the book of Isaiah. Command ye Me!"[227] Therefore Dollar is perfectly content to command God to do a healing.

Says Dollar, "It is not, 'Oh God, will You do it?' No, You got to!" To those who would say, "Well, God ain't got to do nothing for you!" Dollar retorts, "Yes, He does! You've got to understand. He does! It wasn't my idea to say, "By Your stripes you're healed. He said it!"[228] Again, Dollar prostitutes the point of the passage. As I will demonstrate in greater detail later on, Isaiah could hardly make it clearer that he had spiritual—not physical—healing in mind when he wrote, "He was wounded for our *transgressions*, He was bruised for our *iniquities* . . . by His stripes we are healed" (Isaiah 53:5 NKJV).

Dollar seems as comfortable commanding God as he is in predicting the time of Christ's return: "Around 2003–2005, Jesus will break through the sky, and those of us who remain shall be changed and caught up to meet Him in the air." To those who would say, "Brother Dollar, you got real bold, you calling dates," he responds "You wait 'til you hear what I got to teach you . . . Jesus said, 'I'm coming back for a church without spot or wrinkle,' and I'm telling you debt is a wrinkle."[229] In point of fact, Jesus made no such statement. The apostle Paul uses the phrase "spot or wrinkle" (Ephesians 5:27 NKJV) with respect to the church, not as an assurance that she will be perfect when Christ returns but in the sense that even now His bride is covered with the spotless robes of His own righteousness. Nor is there any warrant for supposing that the church must be out of debt before the Lord returns. Indeed Jesus can return at any moment regardless of whether or not we have a mortgage—besides that, the year 2005 is now a distant memory.

Perhaps most dangerous of all is Dollar's assertion that the King James translation of Psalm 8:5 "is the work of a gutless translator." Why? Because in Dollar's view man is assumed to be a little god; in the King James Version, he is "a little lower than the angels." Thus, if the translator had guts, he would have interpreted man to be a little lower than the Almighty, not a little lower than the angels.[230] To hear Dollar cash this out is frightening—not merely because of his reckless interpretation of the text but because if he is right, the Holy Spirit who inspired the New Testament commentary on Psalm 8:5 is wrong—dare we say, "gutless." Truth is, Hebrews 2:7 specifically employs the Greek word *angelous* from which the English word *angel* is derived. Moreover, what Dollar dubs gutless is not unique to the King James Version of the Bible. One would be hard-pressed to find a single credible Bible translation or Bible teacher that would say otherwise.

While a complete litany of Dollar's doctrinal deviations would comprise a book in itself, it is sufficient to say here that Dollar, in concert with other Faith teachers, misses the main message of Messiah. Jesus said: "Do not store up for yourselves treasures on earth, where moth and rust destroy, and where thieves break in and steal. But store up for yourselves treasures in heaven, where moth and rust do not destroy, and where thieves do not break in and steal. For where your treasure is, there your heart will be also" (Matthew 6:19–21). In stark contrast, Dollar declares: "The Bible speaks more about money than it does about heaven."[231]

T. D. Jakes

As long as Jesus was talking on the cross he couldn't die. It was only when he shut his mouth and hung his head in the locks of his shoulder that death could come and take him because he had so much life in his mouth that as long as he was talking, death couldn't get near him.[232]

—T. D. JAKES

When talk turns to money, Theodore Dexter Jakes has few peers. "Somebody take out your wallet," he adjures. "Get it out right now, get it out right now, get it out right now, get it out right now, get it in your hand and hold it up in the air. Hallelujah. Your wallet, your billfold, your checkbook, God said I will heal your money."[233]

Question is, *how?* Answer: Just get out your wallet. Just give your seed. Jakes "will pray over your seed," and says Jakes, you will "experience *increase!*" According to Jakes, "There are certain truths that transcend all principles,"[234] and giving to get is one of them: "It would be ridiculous for me to pray that God would give it [your money] back to you because if all He was going to do was give it back to you, you ought to keep it . . . *That's ridiculous!* If you got a hundred dollars or a thousand dollars and you were going to get a thousand dollars, I tell you what, you just broke even. You could have kept the thousand dollars and not gone through the trouble."[235] This, however, is far from what Jakes dubs a "certain truth." As Moses communicated to the children of Israel, we give "so that [we] may learn to revere the LORD [our] God always" (Deuteronomy 14:23). We give so that we might meet the physical needs of those less fortunate. Ultimately, we give so that we might extend His kingdom. In short, to suggest that it is "ridiculous" to give for the sake of giving, as opposed to giving for the sake of getting, is in itself ridiculous.

Despite running the gamut from the ridiculous to the bizarre, *Bishop* Jakes—he is vice-prelate of the National Executive Board of Senior Bishops in a Oneness Pentecostal organization of churches known as Higher Ground Always Abounding Assembly[236]—has managed to gain international acclaim. An article in the *New York Times* went so far as to list him as one of five possible candidates to succeed Billy Graham as America's "national evangelist."[237] He was the subject of a *Christian Research Journal* cover story in 1999 as well as 2007.[238] And an article in *Time* dubbed him "one of religion's most prodigious polymaths." The article went on to note that "his books, starting with his breakthrough inspirational volume, *Woman, Thou Art Loosed!*, have sold millions. His 26,000-member Potter's House megachurch in South Dallas drew George W. Bush and Al Gore prior to the 2000 election. Jakes is a Grammy-nominated gospel singer and has a deal with Hallmark for a line of 'Loose Your Spirit' inspirational greeting cards. He preaches regularly to millions on both Black Entertainment Television and the Trinity Broadcasting Network."[239]

Jakes is equally prolific in proclamations regarding the power of the tongue. Says Jakes, "You gotta be careful what you speak to, because the power of life and death is in your tongue."[240] As such, blind Bartimaeus was healed not by the power of Christ but by the power of confession. In fact, according to Jakes, "Jesus was saying, 'My hands are tied because I can't do any more for you than what you say.'"[241] Conversely, says Jakes, "If the power of life and death is in the tongue and you can have whatever you say," it's time for you to "Declare it! Speak it! Confess it! Get your list out!"[242] Even Jakes's Jesus seems subject to the power of the tongue: "As long as Jesus was talking on the cross, He couldn't die. It was only when He shut His mouth and hung His head in the locks of His shoulder that death could come and take Him because He had so much life in His mouth that as long as He was talking, death couldn't get near Him."[243] In other words, Jesus did not stop talking because He died; He died because He stopped talking.

Despite his convictions regarding the power of words, Jakes reduces differences between Trinitarians and Oneness Pentecostals to a mere "matter of semantics."[244] This despite the Oneness Pentecostal belief that unless you are baptized using the correct formula, you are not even saved. Their conviction that one must be baptized in the name of *Jesus only* has not only led them to distance themselves from orthodox Pentecostalism but has led to the further error that Jesus is Himself the Father, the Son, and the Holy Spirit—or as Jakes is wont to say—one God in three "manifestations." Indeed, Oneness adherents routinely dismiss the doctrine of the Trinity as a pagan polytheistic philosophy.

In truth, the Trinity is neither pagan polytheism nor pagan philosophy. Rather, it is biblically based. Scripture plainly reveals personal self-distinctions within the Godhead. As such, the Father says of the Son, "Your throne, O God, will last for ever and ever" (Hebrews 1:8); and the Son says of the Father, "I am one who testifies for myself; my other witness is the Father, who sent me" (John 8:18). Moreover, the very fact that Jesus prays to the Father demonstrates that Jesus cannot merely be reduced to a manifestation of the Father. While I am frequently told by Oneness adherents that this is explained by the notion that Jesus' human nature prays to His divine nature, this is clearly not the case—natures can't pray; only persons can.

Jakes is quick to point out that his belief in one God, who manifests Himself as Father in creation, Son in redemption, and Holy Spirit in regeneration (as opposed to one God revealed in three Persons who are eternally distinct) does not derive from his Oneness associations but rather is derived from the text of Scripture. As such, he contends, "The Apostle Paul himself used this term ["manifestations"] referring to the Godhead in 1 Timothy 3:15 [*sic*], 1 Corinthians 12:7, and 1 John 3:5–8 [*sic*]. Peter also used the term in 1 Peter 1:20."[245] This, however, is a clear case of obfuscation. At first blush it may sound plausible, but upon examination it becomes clear that Jakes has taken the texts in question out of context and used them as pretexts for his Oneness proclivities. Indeed, none of these texts relates to unpacking the nature of the Godhead. Three of the four deal with Christ's manifestation in bodily form, and the fourth (1 Corinthians 12:7) deals with the Spirit's manifestation through spiritual gifts.

Jakes not only believes that God manifests Himself as Father, Son, and Holy Spirit, but contends that God "manifests himself in many different ways." Says Jakes, "He just kept turning into stuff . . . He became quail and started flying through the air . . . He became water, came gushing out of a rock . . . He became a tree and turned the bitter water sweet. I mean, He just kept turning into stuff! One God manifesting in a multiplicity of ways!"[246]

In sum, Jakes—in lockstep with most Faith teachers—fosters a give-to-get mentality, makes a habit of distorting the plain meanings of passages, and considers the spoken word to be even more powerful than the Word made flesh. As noted previously, he goes so far as to put the following words in the mouth of the Messiah: "My hands are tied because I can't do any more for you than what you say." Perhaps his greatest error, however, is to use Trinitarian language all the while pouring decidedly unbiblical meanings into the words.

Rod Parsley

There is not one place in the Bible where Jesus ever denied healing to someone who came to Him in faith.[247]

—ROD PARSLEY

Another Word of Faith preacher consistently guilty of text abuse is Rod Parsley. In lockstep with Jakes, he is committed to the notion that God cannot do anything in the earth realm apart from the word of man. Like Jakes, Parsley is emphatic: "Why does God say, 'Ask of me?' [Psalm 2:8] Why does He say that? Because He can't do it on His own! He can't get what He wants on His own because He placed you in authority on this earth. Did you hear me?"[248] Ironically, the very passage Parsley abuses, in his attempt to prove that God can't get what He wants apart from the authority of man, makes precisely the opposite point. Indeed, God laughs at the vain notion that mere men can supplant His wisdom and authority upon the earth (Psalm 2:1–7). As the psalmist underscores elsewhere, "The LORD has established his throne in heaven, and his kingdom rules over *all*" (Psalm 103:19, emphasis added). The words of the pagan Nebuchadnezzar provide an apt rebuke to Parsley's pretext. After a first-hand encounter with the power of God, he humbly confessed, "All the peoples of the earth are regarded as nothing. He does as he pleases with the powers of heaven and the peoples of the earth. No one can hold back his hand or say to him: 'What have you done?'" (Daniel 4:35).

As a prominent televangelist, best-selling author, and founder of World Harvest Church in Ohio, Parsley convinces followers they are on their way to owning houses they didn't build, full of good things they didn't buy. On one occasion, Parsley exhorted followers to experience abundance and luxury as a means of producing its reality: "Some of you better get ready to drive around in neighborhoods where you never thought you'd be able to afford to live. Some of you better go down to that Lexus and Mercedes dealership and just sit down in one of those things with that leather all over it." If asked to give a reason for the hope of the luxury that lies within them, Parsley simply instructs followers to say, "Well, I'm just feeling out what my Father is going to give me

. . . I heard a word from the man of God, and when I obeyed that word, it unleashed that anointing into my life, and I'm on my way to houses I didn't build, full of good things I didn't have to buy."[249]

On another occasion Parsley cried out, "I don't know how big a miracle you need, but let your seed represent your need. Some of you need to do that four thousand dollars right now; some of you need to do five thousand dollars, or ten thousand dollars. Some of you need to do a hundred thousand dollars tonight." From Parsley's perspective, the size of your miracle corresponds directly to the size of your donation. Says Parsley, "There's a miracle attached to your seed."[250]

On yet another occasion Parsley touted prayer cloths as the means to manufacturing miracles. "I'll be laying my hands on them [prayer cloths]. Juanita Bynum, Dwight Thompson, Bishop Eddie Long, Benny Hinn, we'll all be laying our hands on them, and then at the end of Camp Meeting I'm gonna send that prayer cloth back to you as your point of contact for your miracle."[251] No less a luminary than Jan Crouch, cofounder of TBN, procured a perspired-on Parsley prayer patch during a TBN fund-raiser as the means to her miracle. As Parsley explains it, "I didn't know it, but Jan had had a sickness or pain in her throat for three years without saying anything to me. She took that handkerchief [a handkerchief he says was soaked in his sweat], took it home with her, and slept with it on her neck. She said within days that pain left; it has never been back again."[252]

Despite Parsley's persuasive proclivities, there is no biblical warrant for suggesting that Christians should fixate on luxury cars or homes. Instead, our Lord continually exhorted followers to elevate their gazes from earthly vanities to eternal verities. Likewise, Parsley's prayer cloths are little more than cheap parlor tricks that serve to separate devotees from their dollars. Indeed, in Acts 19 the Holy Spirit highlights the stark difference between magic/superstition and the genuine power of God. As I will demonstrate later on, the fact that Paul met the Ephesians at the point of their superstition in order to highlight the supernatural power of God is hardly a precedent for manipulating people in the present. Moreover, nowhere in the text does Paul use prayer cloths as "points of contact" by which to effect healings. Parsley's superstitions are not limited to prayer cloths. He regularly promotes the notion that devils ranging from pornography to headaches are at the root of personal problems:

I came in here tonight to set you free. I'm going to set some of you free. You don't even know you're bound. You think you just got a problem and you got a devil. You think you got a headache and you got a devil. You think you just got a problem with your bank account and you got a devil. You think you've got a problem with your temper and you've got a devil. You think you've got a problem with depression and you've got a devil. I'm live. There ain't nothing they can do about it. It don't matter to me. I'm not here to win friends and influence people.[253]

A partial consequence of preachers like Parsley is that a broad range of people from across the sociological spectrum have become convinced they house demons and that deliverance is the cure. As anthropologist Michael Cuneo points out, one would be hard-pressed to come up with a better scheme. "Whatever one's personal problem—depression, anxiety, substance addiction, or even a runaway sexual appetite—there are exorcism ministries available today that will happily claim expertise for dealing with it. With the significant bonus, moreover, that one is not, for the most part, held personally responsible for the problem. Indwelling demons are mainly to blame, and getting rid of them is the key to moral and psychological redemption."[254] The result is that the discipleship model of spiritual warfare once championed by Christians has given way to a deliverance motif. Put another way, the passion for exercising spiritual disciplines in order to become like Christ has given way to Parsley's quick fix ("I came in here tonight to set you free") of exorcising demons.

Other demonic spirits supposedly bound by Parsley include AIDS, alcoholism, arthritis, back problems, deafness, homosexuality, incest, leukemia, and ringing in the ears.[255] He contends that he himself was miraculously healed of a cancerous growth diagnosed by the devil. When Satan tried reminding him that he had a family history of cancer, Parsley says he stayed focused on God's promises. As a result, he says he woke up one morning to find a cancerous growth: "fingerlike tentacles protruded out of the heart of that growth, tentacles that had come right out of my body," lying next to him on his bed.[256] Says Parsley, "There is not one place in the Bible where Jesus ever denied healing to someone who came to Him in faith. You won't find a single place in the Gospels of Matthew, Mark, Luke or John where He refused to perform a miracle! The idea that God won't heal today is just a man-made doctrine thought up by religious people who didn't have any faith."[257]

As a father and husband, it is hard for me to imagine a crueler contention than that family members suffer as a result of faithlessness. Indeed, according to Parsley's theology, his own son, Austin, is plagued by the demon of Asperger's syndrome and has been denied healing due to a lack of faith.[258]

Frederick K. C. Price

Do you think that the punishment for our sin was to die on a cross? If that were the case, the two thieves could have paid your price. No, the punishment was [for Jesus] to go to hell itself and to serve time in hell separated from God.[259]

—FREDERICK K. C. PRICE

Another Word of Faith preacher who proclaims that people struggle with death and disease due to a lack of faith is Frederick K. C. Price. Dr. Price boldly asserts, "We don't allow sickness in our home."[260] He also discourages the use of medication, saying, "When you have developed your faith to such an extent that you can stand on the promises of God, then you won't need medicine."[261] Despite such contentions, his wife contracted cancer ("inoperable malignant tumor in her pelvic area") and underwent an "ordeal of pain, chemotherapy, and radiation treatments."[262]

Price, who claims, "Kenneth Hagin has had the greatest influence upon my life of any living man"[263] is an increasingly prominent prosperity preacher. His Crenshaw Christian Center in south-central Los Angeles claims more than seventeen thousand "fellowshipped members;"[264] he heads a national television ministry; and he is a frequent guest on TBN's *Praise the Lord* broadcast. Price's first brush with the kingdom of the cults came as a result of being reared in a Jehovah's Witness family.[265] After his conversion Price experimented with a wide range of denominations, including Baptist, African Methodist Episcopal, Presbyterian, and Christian and Missionary Alliance.[266] As his wife puts it, they were "in all kinds of trouble going nowhere!"[267] That is, until a friend gave him a booklet titled "Authority of the Believer" by Kenneth Hagin.[268] Since becoming a Faith teacher, Price has called himself the "chief exponent of Name It and Claim It."[269] He has also referred to his organization as a "Star Wars program for the Lord" and as a "Stealth bomber for Jesus."[270] Referring to his own wealth, Price once said, "That's the reason why I drive a Rolls Royce—I'm following Jesus' steps."[271]

Not only has Price become an able communicator of the Faith teachings he learned from Hagin, but he has also added his own personal stamp. For example, Price made the following remark concerning praying in accordance with God's will: "If you have to say, 'If it be thy will' or 'Thy will be done'—if you have to say that, then you're calling God a fool."[272] This, of course, directly contradicts such passages as James 4:15 and Matthew 6:9–10. The implications of Price's comment pose serious problems for the biblical doctrine of God's sovereignty (Psalms 115:3; 135:6; Daniel 4:35; Romans 9:20). Unfortunately, Price's rhetoric does not end there. Like other prosperity preachers, Price mis-defines the biblical concept of dominion and sneers at those who believe God has dominion over this earth. Commenting on Genesis 1:20, Price says:

> If them animals belonged to, if those animals belonged to God, how come God didn't give them their names? Why did he leave it up to a puny man to give them the names to the animal kingdom, the plant kingdom, and the vegetable kingdom? Because they belonged under the control of Adam and not of God . . . Why? He had dominion. Not God, Adam.[273]

Price has made a habit of calling into question God's overarching author-ity. His theological errors, however, touch on other crucial areas as well. For example, Price believes that Jesus died spiritually, thereby taking on the nature of Satan before His crucifixion. Referring to Christ, Price states, "Somewhere between the time He was nailed to the cross and when He was in the Garden of Gethsemane—somewhere in there—He died spiritually. Personally, I believe it was while He was in the Garden."[274] On an equally sobering note, Price mocks the sufficiency of Christ's atonement at Calvary: "Do you think that the punishment for our sin was [for Jesus] to die on a cross? If that were the case, the two thieves could have paid your price. No, the punishment was [for Jesus] to go to hell itself and to serve time in hell separated from God."[275] Tragically, Price is not content to wreak havoc upon the centrality of Christ's work upon the cross.

Price also portrays a completely different Christ during His earthly minis-try. Consider, for example, Price's argument that Jesus "must have had a whole lot" of money: [276]

> The Bible says that He [Jesus] had a treasurer . . . named Judas Iscariot; and the rascal was stealing out of the bag for three and a half years and nobody knew that he was stealing. You know why? Because there was so

much in it . . . If He had three oranges in the bottom of the bag and he stole two of them, don't tell me He wouldn't know that some was missing. Beside that, if Jesus didn't have anything, what do you need a treasury for?[277]

Upon such a flawed foundation rests a fundamental Faith fantasy—namely, that Jesus was wealthy, that He wore expensive clothing, and that His disciples lived in luxury.

John Avanzini

If Jesus was poor, I want to be poor. If Jesus slept under a bridge, I want to sleep under the bridge. But if Jesus was rich, I, too, want to be rich! [278]

—JOHN AVANZINI

Dr. John Avanzini bills himself as a noted Bible teacher and recognized authority on biblical economics. "Brother John," as he likes to call himself, claims to have studied the life of Christ to the extent that he is now prepared to dispel the popular misconception that our Lord was poor. Contrary to "tradition" (and in concert with John Hagee), John Avanzini asserts that Jesus was so wealthy that He wore custom-made designer clothes.[279]

Avanzini uses John 19:23 in an attempt to make his point. What Avanzini doesn't seem to realize is that what he describes as a seamless custom-made designer coat is what competent Bible scholars refer to as an undergarment.[280] Thus, if we are to take Avanzini seriously, he has built the case that Jesus wore custom-made designer underwear!

Avanzini continues his attempt to demonstrate that Christ was wealthy by pointing out that, contrary to what people have been taught, "Jesus had a nice house, a big house."[281] Anticipating a rebuttal, Avanzini offered this response to Matthew 8:20:

Foxes have holes and the birds in the air have nests, but the Son of man hath nowhere to lay His head is not a declaration that Jesus didn't have a house . . . It meant that [the] Samaritans canceled the meeting that He was going to, if you remember the account. And in those days, there wasn't a Holiday Inn on every corner . . . If your advance men got canceled, then you walked to the next meeting and take up there. It's very clear that He had a house . . . The Bible states He had a house.[282]

This is no mere academic point, for according to Avanzini, "until you know that Jesus was prosperous, you won't be either." Elsewhere, as previously noted, he says, "If Jesus was poor, I want to be poor. If Jesus slept under a bridge, I want to sleep under the bridge. But if Jesus was rich, I, too, want to be rich."

Armed with a bundle of biblical texts taken out of context, Avanzini teaches people that they should give to get. Avanzini has even suggested that "a greater than a lottery has come. His name is Jesus!"[283] For those who have failed to get what they paid for, Avanzini has written a book titled *It's Not Working, Brother John*.[284] Avanzini lists no fewer than twenty-five reasons why his techniques for personal prosperity may not be working for some people. He puts the blame on virtually everyone and everything—not tithing, no faith, no patience, not trusting God's man, hidden sin, tradition, and much more—but not himself.

What is particularly noteworthy is that Avanzini begins virtually all of his arguments by mounting a diatribe against theologians and apologists. Claiming that he once was an apologist himself, Avanzini said, "I'm not impressed with the apologists any longer, and I may as well get it out—I used to be one, and God forgave me, and I promised not to ever do it again."[285]

Avanzini is quick to point out that "theologians don't get their prayers answered" and that "they deal with an impersonal God." He also has lodged the following criticism against "heresy hunters":

You know what the problem is with all those heresy hunters? They do not believe in a personal God. They believe in a general God that laid down some rules, then went on vacation and said, "You operate by these rules."[286]

What makes Avanzini's remark so interesting is that the God he erroneously ascribes to theologians and heresy hunters sounds remarkably like the false god of the Faith movement—a God who Himself is caught up in a universe governed by spiritual laws. Perhaps that is why Avanzini has now exchanged his former "apologetic" role for that of a self-proclaimed prophet. Avanzini has made full use of his newfound office. He misquotes and misapplies to himself the words contained in 2 Chronicles 20:20: You say, "Brother John, can I believe you?" He answers, "Believe the prophet, and you will prosper."

Perhaps the saddest fact of all is that Avanzini takes the Word of God—which was designed to bring light to men—and reduces it to a means to bring in funds. In the words of Benny Hinn, "The wicked are piling up the funds, and I love the way John teaches on this. He's the best there is when it comes to teaching you on how to get the wealth of the wicked. Man, I like it!"[287]

Robert Tilton

If I'm going to go to the cross, I'm going to go in a pretty place. Not some dusty place like Jerusalem. That's gravel is all that place is.[288]

—ROBERT TILTON

Just as McDonald's has popularized fast food, Robert Tilton's ministry has propagated "fast faith." Boiled down to its irreducible minimum, Tilton's message is simple: God wants you to flourish financially and physically. But you need faith. To prove your faith you need to make a vow of faith, and all vows should be sent in care of Brother Bob.

Although the material Tilton uses for his sermons has been adapted largely from Hagin and Kenyon, the marketing techniques appear to have been adapted directly from a real-estate marketer named Dave Del Dotto.[289] As Tilton tells the story, the successful current format of his show—the "infomercial"—emerged from his heartache over repeated failures with his television show.[290] So he went into the wilderness to hear from God. (When Tilton says "wilderness," he doesn't mean self-denial and deprivation. What he means is Hawaii. As Tilton puts it, "If I'm going to go to the cross, I'm going to go in a pretty place. Not some dusty place like Jerusalem. That's gravel is all that place is.")[291]

After his "wilderness" experience, Tilton turned to TV and found Dave Del Dotto.[292] Inspired by Del Dotto's real-estate "infomercials," Tilton came up with a religious infomercial called *Success-N-Life*.[293] Tilton's program has been ranked as high as twelfth in the national religious Arbitron ratings. Before scandal sapped his audience share, it was viewed by an estimated 6 million households over 212 stations.[294] Add to that his cable television audience, his mailing list of 880,000, and his full-time staff of more than 850 employees,[295] and Tilton truly once was a megastar in the Faith movement's constellation of prosperity preachers. According to former wife Marte's testimony during a federal court hearing, their 8,000-member Word of Faith Family Church and World Outreach Center in the north Dallas suburb of Farmers Branch once took in an amazing $65 million per year.[296]

Network television has sounded its own warnings about Tilton. The prayer requests that Tilton promises he will personally pray over all too often end up in garbage dumpsters, as ABC's *PrimeTime Live* cameras have demonstrated.[297] Regrettably, after his financial indiscretions were aired, Tilton went on the offensive with an attack video titled *PrimeTime Lies*, which attempted to investigate the investigators, complete with a newscast-type studio set and a reporter who looked like ABC's Diane Sawyer.[298]

Tilton tells his followers he is being persecuted for the cause of Christ.[299] Assuring them that ABC was wrong and that he personally prayed over each of the thousands of prayer requests that came into his ministry daily, Tilton provided the following incredible rebuttal:

> Those prayer request forms have ink on them and all kinds of chemicals. I laid on top of those prayer requests so much that the chemicals actually got into my bloodstream and began to swell my capillaries . . . It got into my immune system, and I had two small strokes in my brain that brought about some numbness in my body.[300]

As a result, Tilton said he had to undergo plastic surgery to remove the bags from under his eyes.[301]

"If you want to find Robert Tilton these days," writes Sean Rowe in a *Dallas Observer* piece titled "Second Coming," "a good place to start looking is at a South Florida television studio . . . The old studios in Dallas and San Diego were lugubrious dens lined with leather bound books. The new set looks like a Sunday-school vision of ancient Palestine, complete with Styrofoam "stone" walls and a burbling fountain . . . What hasn't changed is Tilton's repetitious message. He quotes a bit of Scripture and speaks in tongues, but mostly he pushes emotional buttons: Cancer. Emphysema. Alcoholism. Credit card addiction. Job layoffs. These ailments can be cured through faith. But faith requires proof, a 'vow.'"[302]

And as it was prior to his "second coming" in the Word of Faith International headquarters in Miami Beach, typical vows begin at a thousand dollars, but the sky is the limit.

Marilyn Hickey

What do you need? Start creating it. Start speaking about it. Start speaking it into being. Speak to your billfold. Say, "You big, thick billfold full of money." Speak to your checkbook. Say, "You, checkbook, you. You've never been so prosperous since I owned you. You're just jammed full of money." [303]

—MARILYN HICKEY

Marilyn Hickey, much like Tilton, uses a wide range of gimmicks to get her followers to send money. Among her many tactics are anointed prayer cloths and ceremonial breastplates that can be used as "points of contact" for miracles.

In one letter, Hickey promised to send a special anointing if the enclosed prayer cloth, along with money, was sent back to her immediately. Hickey promised that if it was returned "right now," she would have it "anointed with an Acts 19 kind of anointing for 'special,' 'unusual' and 'extraordinary' miracles." Hickey assured the reader that the Holy Spirit had been dealing with her about the entire matter and that she was excited about it.

Hickey then suggested that the prayer cloth was the perfect remedy for those who are sick, those who need to sell something, and those who need to break a spirit of rebellion. So that the point would not be missed, Hickey explained that the prayer cloth is so powerful that when a mother slipped it under the pillow of a rebellious child, the spirit of rebellion was broken. Not only that, but with a mere touch of the prayer cloth, a tumor the size of a small grapefruit vanished in just five days.

Hickey then promised that anyone suffering from an extreme financial crisis need only carry the prayer cloth in a purse, wallet, or checkbook to receive a financial breakthrough. There was one small catch: before the cloth could work, it had to be sent back to Hickey. The cloth, according to Hickey, presently "does not carry or contain any special anointing or qualities. It is just a simple piece of plain cloth . . . but in a few days (if you act in faith RIGHT NOW) it can become a miracle prayer cloth."

But Hickey had one more suggestion: when you return the cloth, be sure to send money. As Hickey puts it, *receiving follows giving.*[304]

In another of her appeal letters, Hickey promised that she would slip into a ceremonial breastplate, "press your prayer request to [her] heart," and "place your requests on [her] shoulders" (donation suggested).[305]

Hickey also teaches people to speak to their wallets and checkbooks. Says Hickey:

What do you need? Start creating it. Start speaking about it. Start speaking it into being. Speak to your billfold. Say, "You big, thick billfold full of money." Speak to your checkbook. Say, "You, checkbook, you. You've never been so prosperous since I owned you. You're just jammed full of money."[306]

So that you, too, can experience big miracles, Hickey will send you tiny mustard seeds to remind you to sow a seed in her ministry. Sowing a seed, of course, is another way of saying, "Please send money." When you send the seed, Hickey promises to send you her booklet titled "God's Seven Keys to Make You Rich," and assures you that "God will bless and multiply your gift."[307]

In response to a critic who said that Faith teachers were "always following after prosperity" Hickey retorted, "No, we're not. It's following after us."[308] While prosperity may not be following all of Hickey's followers, success is certainly following Hickey. If you can't see her in person, you can encounter Marilyn and her daughter, Sarah, on scores of television and radio stations. Their teachings are for the most part a blend of the theologies of Tilton, Hagin, Copeland, and other "prosperity personalities." The message is peppered with such Faith jargon as "the God-kind of faith"[309] and "confession brings possession."[310] Hickey's theology has been influenced not only by the kingdom of the cults but by the world of the occult as well.

Charles Capps

This is the key to understanding the virgin birth. God's Word is full of faith and Spirit power. God spoke it. God transmitted that image to Mary. She received the image inside of her . . . The embryo that was in Mary's womb was nothing more than the Word of God . . . She conceived the Word of God." [311]

—CHARLES CAPPS

Charles Capps was ordained as a minister in the International Convention of Faith Churches and Ministers by Kenneth Copeland but derived his teachings directly from Kenneth Hagin. This dangerous elixir has led Capps to make some of the most outrageous statements in Faith lore. Capps claims that when someone exclaims, "I'm just dying to do that" or "That just tickled me to death," he is "buddying up with death." Says Capps, "Adam was smarter than that. It took the devil over 900 years to kill him, but now the devil has programmed his language into the human race until people can kill themselves in about seventy years or less by speaking his words."[312] Capps is so convinced that "the tongue is a creative force" that he contends even Jesus was the product of God's positive confession:

> This is the key to understanding the virgin birth. God's Word is full of faith and Spirit power. God spoke it. God transmitted that image to Mary. She received the image inside of her . . . The embryo that was in Mary's womb was nothing more than the Word of God . . . She conceived the Word of God.[313]

Here Capps takes the concept of visualization and confession to its most heretical extreme. In his book *Authority in Three Worlds*, Capps goes so far as to say that the "pure Word of God" (which he refers to with the impersonal pronoun "it") literally "took flesh upon *itself*."[314] Capps's statement, drawn to its logical conclusion, denies the very personality of the pre-incarnate Christ, who is the Word made flesh (John 1:1, 14).

Ironically, in the same chapter Capps states, "If you continually sit under teaching that is wrong, the spirit of error will be transmitted to you."[315] He makes no doubt about the source of his own peculiar doctrine: "Most of my teaching came from Brother Kenneth Hagin."[316] This spirit of error has now been transmitted to millions of people. Capps's book *God's Creative Power* alone has sold an incredible 3 million copies. And millions more are being impacted by his national television and radio broadcasts.

Let me conclude with Capps's "coon-dog" story. Remember that when Capps tells this story, he is dead serious. The point he is trying to make is that confession must always precede possession:

> I'm going to put in my coon-dog story to make this next point clear. There was a guy who was bragging about having the best coon dog in the country.
>
> "He's the fastest thing on a coon you ever saw. And one thing about this dog, he never lies. When he trees, you'll get a coon."

His friend said, "I want to see that dog hunt."

So they went hunting and, sure enough, that dog treed a coon in ten minutes. But after a while the dog treed up a little sapling that didn't have a leaf on it.

The sapling was 20 feet high, not a hole in it, and there was no coon to be found in that tree.

The friend said, "I thought you said this dog didn't lie."

The guy said, "Well, I forgot to tell you one thing. Not very often but once in a while this dog is so fast that sometimes he gets here before the coon does. Just sit down. That coon will be along any minute!"[317]

Charles caps off the story by pointing out that this is precisely how our faith should work. "If your house payment is due January 1, don't start December 29 confessing that you have abundance," advises Capps. "Start confessing a year before the payment is due."[318]

Through such confessions, Capps continues to plow under Scripture and uproot the faith of many an ungrounded devotee.

Jerry Savelle

Dear God, I can't wait until I get to heaven to be free from sickness and disease and grief and sorrow. I found out I don't have to have any more of that stuff down here, in this world that I'm living in, praise God. Sickness and disease cannot come into my world." [319]

—JERRY SAVELLE

From humble beginnings in 1969, Dr. Jerry Savelle has risen to great prominence as a Faith figure. He has authored forty books, including the bestseller *If Satan Can't Steal Your Joy He Can't Keep Your Goods*, and hosts an international television broadcast that is heard in two hundred countries.[320] Prior to becoming a prosperity preacher, Savelle was an auto body repairman. Today he has fully transitioned from self-characterized "fender bender" to serial Scripture twister. Perhaps more than anyone else, he mirrors the message of his mentor Kenneth Copeland. Copeland describes God as "a Being that stands somewhere around six-two to six-three, that weighs somewhere in the neighborhood of a couple of hundred pounds or little better, has a hand span nine inches across. Glory to God! Hallelujah!"[321] Savelle is similarly convinced. Says Savelle:

I'm convinced that Jesus was—you know—had to look quite a lot like God looked. And He measured out the heavens with a nine-inch span. Now, I don't—my fingers is not quite nine inches. The distance between my thumb and my finger is not quite nine inches. So, I know He's bigger than me, thank God. Amen? But He's not some great, big, old thing that couldn't come through the door there, and you know, when He sat down, would fill every seat in the house. I don't serve the Glob."[322]

Tragically, Savelle's heresies are not limited to redefining the nature of God. Indeed, he repeats virtually every heresy in the Faith arsenal. With respect to health, he pontificates the notion that believers can enjoy perfect health in the present. In his words, "Dear God, I can't wait until I get to heaven to be free from sickness and disease and grief and sorrow. I found out I don't have to have any more of that stuff down here, in this world that I'm living in, praise God. Sickness and disease cannot come into my world."[323] When it comes to wealth, Savelle repeats the well-worn Faith phrase: "You can speak your world into existence."

Your world, first of all, starts on the inside of you, praise God. And then as you begin, begin to speak that world into existence. Now, I'm not talking about that you're gonna be talking a car into existence, necessarily. The car is already out there somewhere, praise God. But what it will do is come into your world. The house is already out there somewhere, but thank God it will come into your world. The clothes you need is already out there some-where, and they'll come into your world, praise God. The finances you need—God's not gonna rain twenty-dollar bills out of heaven, probably. If He wants to, He can. I'll welcome that, but probably that's not the way it will come. They're already in here somewhere. They'll just come into my world, praise God. Amen?[324]

Although Savelle is principally a Copeland clone, he mimics other Faith teachers as well. In the fashion of Price, Capps, and Hinn, Savelle portrays Job as both faithless and foolish—a man who could rightly be blamed for all his troubles. Says Savelle, "Job talked his world into destruction."[325]

Morris Cerullo

Did you know that from the beginning of time the whole purpose of God was to reproduce Himself? . . . Who are you? Come on, who are you? Come on, say it: "Sons of God!" Come on, say it! . . . And when we stand up here, brother, you're not looking at Morris Cerullo; you're looking at God. You're looking at Jesus.[326]

—MORRIS CERULLO

Morris Cerullo claims he first met God when he was eight years old. He was allegedly standing on a ledge, getting ready to end it all, when God miraculously intervened, filling the room behind Morris with His presence and speaking words of assurance to the young Cerullo.[327] As Cerullo tells the story, his life from that point on has been a mind-blowing miracle marathon.

At age fourteen, after being schooled by "the leading rabbis" of a New Jersey town,[328] Cerullo was led out of a Jewish orphanage "by two angelic beings to a refuge that had been prepared for him."[329] Less than a year later, Cerullo was transported to heaven, where he had a face-to-face meeting with God.[330] According to the account, "as Moses beheld the glory of God in the burning bush, Cerullo was taken in the spirit into the heavenlies where he beheld the Presence of God and his life's ministry was clearly detailed before him."[331]

God, who was described by Cerullo as about six feet tall and twice as broad as a human body,[332] took as it were "the lid off Hell and allowed me to see from heaven down into the portals of the underworld."[333] Then, says Cerullo, the Lord spoke to him for the first time. The Creator told Cerullo precisely what He had previously told Isaiah—namely, "Arise and shine, for My light is come upon thee, and the glory of the Lord shall surround thee, for the multitude of the sea of the Gentiles shall be converted unto thee."[334]

Thus, Cerullo became a mouthpiece for God, capable of "revealing things which had not yet come to pass, precisely communicating direct 'Thus saith the Lord' words from God."[335] That's why Cerullo gave up his "driving ambition to one day become governor of my state of New Jersey" to become "a minister of the gospel."[336] Cerullo provides this account as indisputable proof that he is in fact "God's chosen vessel."[337]

But is he really? Consider Cerullo's pontification regarding the purpose of God to reproduce Himself:

Did you know that from the beginning of time the whole purpose of God was to reproduce Himself? . . . Who are you? Come on, who are you? Come on, say it: "Sons of God!" Come on, say it! . . . And when we stand up here, brother, you're not looking at Morris Cerullo you're looking at God. You're looking at Jesus.[338]

In a promotional piece, Cerullo acknowledges that "the true test of a prophet is—what he speaks will come to pass."[339] Yet even a cursory examination of his predictions demonstrates that Cerullo's batting average when it comes to prophecy is little better than that of the Watchtower organization. In 1972, Cerullo claimed God told him "the U.S. is about to witness a great revival."[340] It is now three and a half decades later, and the "great revival" has not occurred.

In September 1991, the Holy Spirit allegedly spoke to Cerullo and said, "Son, the world *will* be reached with the gospel by the year 2000!"[341] As I write, 2009 looms on the horizon, and the prophecy Cerullo attributed to God remains unfulfilled.

Paul Crouch

Get out of God's way. Quit blocking God's bridges, or God's gonna shoot you if I don't! [342]
—PAUL CROUCH

To say that Paul and Jan Crouch are influential in Christian circles may well be the understatement of the year. With an estimated net worth in excess of half a billion dollars and revenues of 190 million annually,[343] Crouch's Trinity Broadcasting Network "reaches every major continent via 70 satellites and more than 12,500 television and cable affiliates worldwide."[344] As Paul Crouch puts it, "God has, indeed, given us the MOST POWERFUL VOICE in the history of the WORLD."[345] Tragically, that voice is being used as a primary vehicle to promote and proliferate both the false teachings and false teachers of the Faith movement.[346]

John Avanzini's financial principles, for example, became a staple in Christian broadcasting in large measure because of TBN sponsorship. When Jan Crouch heard about his "hundredfold" concept, she began to beg him to use it during TBN fund-raisers. "Jan Crouch has asked me a dozen times to speak the hundredfold message," says Avanzini, "and I had to say, 'Jan, anything else, but God is just not letting me do it.'"[347] Eventually, Jan's persistence paid off. During TBN *Praise-a-Thon*s, Avanzini prays "the hundredfold," and thousands are led to expect that what they give will be multiplied back to them times a hundred. Today, this give-to-get scheme is standard fare in TBN fund-raisers. Everyone from T. D. Jakes to Juanita Bynum uses variations of it to raise resources on the Trinity Broadcasting Network. During one *Praise-a-Thon* Bynum double-dared devotees to empty out their bank accounts. Said Bynum, "If you got $79.36, empty it out; empty it out at the voice of the prophet. O Jesus, if you got $79.36 I double-dare you to write your last check and declare your bank account empty."[348] During another TBN *Praise-a-Thon*, Bynum allegedly heard "the Holy Ghost saying there are six millionaires that are watching the program right now. God said pledge that seed of $10,000. There's a woman that God is looking [at] right now in the Spirit. You're a Caucasian woman, and God is saying that He wants you to sow that $100,000 seed."[349]

What many of the people who fall for this sort of manipulation do not realize is that their giving supports doctrines that come straight out of the kingdom of the cults. Crouch, for example, has paid for and promoted people like Roy Blizzard[350] and Joseph Good, both of whom openly deny the Trinity.[351] Crouch also gives his staunch support to the United Pentecostal Church (UPC), a cult that claims that the Trinity is a pagan doctrine. [352] It is hard to imagine a greater irony than a broadcasting network named "Trinity" promoting anti-Trinitarian doctrine!

To those who would speak out against this promotion of cultic doctrine, Crouch issues this ominous warning: "Get out of God's way. Quit blocking God's bridges, or God's *gonna shoot* you if I don't!" So that there can be no ambiguity about his opinion of "heresy hunters," Crouch declares, "I think they're damned and on their way to hell, and I don't think there's any redemption for them."[353]

Despite violent outbursts, Crouch maintains that he would never compromise the cardinal truths by which we are saved. He even says, "If you don't believe those [cardinal truths], you are not a Christian."[354] Still, the vast majority of the Faith teachers Crouch promotes overtly deny these cardinal truths. I have personally given Crouch ample evidence to prove that Faith teachers such as Hagin, Copeland, and a host of others compromise the very crux of Christianity: the atonement of Christ upon the cross.

During my personal interactions with Paul, I have found him to be both reasonable and gracious. Publicly, however, he has made remarks that cause me to shudder. On one occasion, Crouch angrily declared, "If you want to criticize Ken Copeland for his preaching on faith, or Dad Hagin, get out of my life! I don't even want to talk to you or hear you. I don't want to see your ugly face. Get out of my face, in Jesus' name."[355]

Sadly, Paul Crouch is now so entrenched in his position that he has publicly proclaimed, "Those who oppose the Faith message have reached me too late."[356] He calls the Faith message a "revival of truth that comes along in the Word of God," restored by "a few precious men" like Kenyon, Hagin, Copeland, and Savelle.[357]

CAST OF CHARACTERS CONTINUES

Tune in to the Trinity Broadcasting Network (TBN) virtually anytime during the day or night and you will find a new star in the Faith movement's cast of characters. The same can be said with respect to a host of other networks including The Inspiration Network, Christian Broadcasting Network (CBN), and God TV. As prosperity preachers continue to proliferate, a growing number are purchasing time on secular broadcasting networks as well. They point to Scripture, produce "miracles," and operate under the banner "Jesus is Lord" but purvey a message that is anything but authentically Christian.

Juanita Bynum

If God's not going to work for you, then why serve Him?[358]

—JUANITA BYNUM

According to Juanita Bynum, one of the new stars in the Faith constellation, we enter into a relationship with God for what we can get. In her words, "If God ain't going to work for you, then what's all the tongues about? If God ain't going to work, what is all the Bible about? If you not going to step out on nothing, and trust God for something, then why are you saved? Are you hearing what I'm saying? Are you hearing God tonight? If God's not going to work for you, then why serve Him?"[359] Put another way, we serve God not for the love of God but for the love of what He can do for us.

Bynum's rants range from the blasphemous to the bizarre. Speaking to

Mark Chironna on TBN's *Praise the Lord* program, she prophesied the birthing of prophets through intercourse in the Spirit. Said Bynum:

> When there's a male and a female, then there's intercourse in the Spirit. And then there can be birth to the nation, and right now as we sit on this broadcast, prophets are being birthed out right now! Their anointings that were once suppressed are being loosed right now! And there will be nothing else that will come against them that will be able to stop what God has predestined for us to be.[360]

Bynum says, "There isn't enough money in Christendom to pay me what God is going to pay me." As such, says Bynum, "people that own Budweiser Company going to buy my stuff. I can't get nobody to shout right there . . . I can't get nobody to shout hallelujah. People that own IBM is going to buy my next house. Come on hear somebody."[361] In reality, believers, not Budweiser, are buying Bynum's "stuff." Likewise, her fame and fortune have more to do with TBN than IBM.

Paula White

Now when God begins to speak to you, you get up and go to the phone, because God is telling you [to give] $68.19 for the next 12 months, which happens to be $818—Deuteronomy 8:18 says that God will give you the power to get wealth.[362]

—PAULA WHITE

Another self-proclaimed prosperity preacher who feeds "faith food" to "millions around the world" is Paula White. White claims "a divine visitation in which God gave her a vision of multitudes of millions of people as far as her eyes could see. In the vision, every time she opened her mouth and began to declare the Word of the Lord, there was a visible manifestation of the power of God—souls were saved, the sick were healed, and the broken were restored. Conversely, when she was silent, people began to fall into utter darkness."[363] The message Paula was commissioned to proclaim is that "God does not want us to live in poverty or lack for he wants you to be prosperous." Indeed, says Paula, "God wants you to have it all."[364]

To have it all God requires the sowing of seeds. "For the next 12 months I am sowing $68.19, based on Psalm 68:19 that daily God will load me up with benefits."[365] The magic in the numbers is breathtaking. As noted by Paula, $68.19 times 12 equals $818, and "Deuteronomy 8:18 says that God will give you the power to get wealth."[366] What is even more astounding than the numerology is how many find merit in White's message. On one occasion White says she "was in prayer and fasting seeking God" when the Almighty spoke to her saying, "Challenge the people to give $66.12 according to Psalm 66:12." White went on to promise devotees, "The Word cannot return void. When you put your faith in the Word, then you have mandated results."[367]

Like other Faith teachers, White's formula for success involves speaking right words and thinking right thoughts. Speaking of the power of words, White says, "Oh come on, Paula . . . are you actually saying that just because my mouth says it, that makes it true? Well I am here to tell you, yes, that's just what I am saying: *Your words create your world*" (emphasis in the original).[368] Paula's justification is that "if God can create something out of nothing, and we are created in his image, then if we can image it, or imagine it, then, so it can be for us."[369]

White garners support not only through claims of revelations, visitations, and prophecies (including the revelatory prophecy that a child would be saved by a thirteen-foot angel) but through specific claims of prophetic healings. Her healing claims rival those of Jesus Christ Himself. According to White she has seen everything from the blind receiving sight to resurrections from the dead.[370] Tragically the devil is in the details. To date White has not provided even basics to buttress her boasts.

Todd Bentley

This is your angel, the angel from John 5 (at the pool of Bethesda). Everywhere you go the angel goes. I want you to be a part of taking healing revival to the nations. I don't want you to have just a gift of healing. I want you to be a part of what has been prophesied, in breaking through and seeing the fulfillment of healing revival.[371]

—TODD BENTLEY

One of the newest prosperity preachers to rise and fall in Faith circles is the well-tattooed biker Todd Bentley. He has been touted by Counterfeit Revivalists ranging from Rick Joyner to John Arnott and by magazine magnates such as Stephen Strang. Strang went so far as to say, "In my 32 years of covering the

charismatic movement, I've never seen any 'revival meeting' get so much attention so fast. Everyone, it seems, is talking about it. A long line of respected
leaders have attended the meetings to see it for themselves. Most have come
away saying it's a genuine move of God."[372]

While Bentley's character and proclivities make it unlikely that he will have
long legs, Christian luminaries continue to sing his praises. Says Counterfeit
Revivalist Che Ahn, "There's a [William] Branham anointing on you. There's a
double portion of it. The Lord is raising you up. I feel like I want to just say that
I must decrease, you must increase."[373] Bentley's own Web site claims that "God
has released an increase of the healing anointing into Todd's life to the point
where the blind see, the deaf hear and growths dissolve as Jesus still heals every
sickness and disease."[374] Two months after being saved, says Bentley, "The heavens opened with a bright flash and a white dove materialized out of thin air and
flew across the lake to a nearby tree. Although it was a single dove, it sounded
as the flapping wings of ten thousand doves. The noise filled the sky and rum-
bled in my spirit; the sound of a ripping, rushing, and mighty wind filled my
ears. As a result," Bentley continues, "I had received not only tongues, but also
an enduement of power from on high for miracles, signs and wonders."[375]

The power is so potent, says Bentley, that "when people visited me at
home, they'd get zapped by an invisible, electrical force field in whatever room
I was in, and then bounce back." One day, says Bentley, "Shonnah my wife
went down under the power as I walked into the kitchen."[376]

The power, however, was not solely divine. During worship, says Bentley,
he was "overcome by a demon. I threw myself at the chairs and knocked them
flying. I screamed, cursed, and writhed on the floor like a snake. Then I rolled
and screamed and tried to avoid the four or five guys who tried to restrain and
deliver me."[377] And that was just the beginning. On another occasion, the Lord
revealed another demon residing within the "born-again" Bentley. During the
ensuing two-hour deliverance session, Bentley again began "flailing, screaming,
and writhing as a snake."[378] During a Vineyard revival, Bentley was supposedly
delivered from a demonic force he identified as "a spirit of death." As Bentley
puts it, "anger, murder, death, suicide, and violence raged inside me." And once
again he "writhed and screamed on the floor."[379]

Despite his demons, Bentley held fast to his dream of "holding crusades
just like the spiritual greats, Reinhardt Bonnke and Benny Hinn."[380] According
to Bentley, dreams of spiritual greatness would eventually turn into tangible

realities. "I would imagine myself preaching in Africa and could picture stadiums filled with multitudes or see people healed and raised from the dead. It was like a sanctified day-dream."[381] Bentley's dreams at times were so grandiose that he would be compelled to pray, "Lord, forgive my pride." Today, he has come to the conclusion that what he once considered pride is in reality a kingdom "principle." As he puts it, "What you see, you be."[382]

Bentley's practice of "marinating and pickling in the Holy Spirit"[383] has led to some amazing encounters with the netherworld. Not only did "the tree of life" appear in his living room, but, says Bentley, "angels also started to appear during my soaking times. They'd come into my bedroom as pillars of shimmering light moving to and fro . . . Once, just before my commissioning into ministry, a huge angel appeared in my living room. He stood about twenty feet tall and towered through the ceiling of the apartment above. His massive chest was level with my ceiling!"[384] After Counterfeit Revivalist John Paul Jackson laid hands on him, Bentley experienced yet another "encounter with an angel." On this occasion, writes Bentley, "the presence of the angel knocked me out of my body." Said Bentley, "I began to wonder, 'How am I going to get back in my body?'"[385] In Albany, Bentley says, he saw an "angel open up a pool on the floor about 30 feet by 30 feet. A portal opened in the heavens and a shaft of light descended. I was under the power of the Spirit and too 'inebriated to minister.'"[386]

Bentley later discovered that this angel was *his* angel. In the words of the Almighty, "This is your angel, the angel from John 5 (at the pool of Bethesda). Everywhere you go the angel goes. I want you to be a part of taking healing revival to the nations. I don't want you to have just a gift of healing. I want you to be a part of what has been prophesied, in breaking through and seeing the fulfillment of healing revival."[387] Says Bentley, "Even warlocks approach me in different services and describe the angel. Countless times people tell me, 'Todd, there's an angel that follows you, and I believe it is the mantle and anointing that was with William Branham.'"[388] None other than the two angels who spoke to Mary after the Lord's resurrection, saying, "The one you are seeking is not here," were commissioned to be part of Bentley's ministry so that he might raise "those dead in spirit, and even those dead in body."[389]

As though it was not sufficient glory to have the very angels who appeared in the biblical account of the empty tomb commissioned as part of his ministry by none other than God Himself, Bentley claims to have had an encounter with Jesus Christ in Redding, California. Says Bentley, "I had a face-to-face encounter with Jesus. It was real." He described Jesus as having "the brownest eyes that I'd ever seen. Kind of reminded me of the movie *Bambi*. Had these big brown eyes. He had long, brownish black curly locks that went down past His shoulders." According to Bentley, "the brightest color that came from the Lord was pink—which is love and emotions."[390]

Indeed, in a prophecy read by Bentley, Jesus was scheduled to physically appear onstage with him June 8, 2008. In the words of Jesus Christ, "I am coming in person." Added Bentley, "Tomorrow, the King of Glory sets foot upon the stage in divine personal one-to-one visitation." But Bentley subsequently hedged his bets, suggesting that Christ's appearance might well be a "spiritual experience" or an "atmosphere" as opposed to an *actual* second coming.[391]

In addition to angels and the Almighty, an apostle appeared to Bentley in order to clear up a conundrum that church fathers and theologians have wrestled with for two thousand years. Bentley describes the apostle Paul as "short, not more than 5'1" or 5'2" . . . He was bald except for a little crown of hair that came around his head. Looking very Jewish with a short, trimmed, white beard, my first thought was of a monk in a monastery! He actually had jolly cheeks and I thought: Paul, you've got a little weight on you! I mean he wasn't fat but he looked a little pudgy!"[392] The pudgy apostle spoke to Bentley, saying, "Abraham taught me, in heaven, and that's how and why I wrote the book of Hebrews. What I heard was from the lips of Abraham himself." Recognizing the full weight of this extraordinary revelation, Bentley continued:

> I know I'm stepping out on theology now; however, I want you to understand that Paul always made it clear when he authored an epistle—"Paul, an apostle of Jesus Christ" or "Paul, a bond-servant of Christ." Always! Yet, for the Book of Hebrews, although most Bible scholars believe that it was authored by Paul, there are those that really can't say it was him because the authorship is never clear. Paul told me why. Here is what he said to me. "Do you know why I know so much about Abraham?" . . . He said, "Abraham himself shared (information) with me and I simply wrote it" (in the Book of Hebrews). "The authorship isn't clear because it was Abraham and I; Abraham shared with me." . . . Paul said, "When I was in the third heaven, Abraham was with me like you are with me now."[393]

In other words, the reason theologians have struggled with the authorship of Hebrews is that—as the apostle explained to Bentley—Hebrews is a hybrid of the writing styles of both Abraham and Paul.

While Bentley marshals credibility for himself through stories of encounters with apostles, angels, and the Almighty, the real story is that his ministry mirrors a host of other Word of Faith luminaries. Indeed, says Bentley, "I copied the models of Oral Roberts, Benny Hinn and T. L. Osborn."[394] As such, when Oral Roberts assigns a guarantee of healing and prosperity to 3 John 2, Bentley follows suit. This despite the obvious reality that John's opening remark to his friend Gaius is simply a standard form of greeting in antiquity (see historical principle, pages 236–37). Likewise, when Benny Hinn, in *Good Morning, Holy Spirit*, writes that the power emanating from him was so great that friends and family would be thrown against the wall,[395] Bentley follows suit by writing that people who encountered him might well be "zapped by an invisible, electrical force field in whatever room I was in, and then bounce back."[396] Bentley goes so far as to revel in the notion that William Branham's mantle and anointing are now his—in full view of the fact that Branham denied such essential Christian doctrines as the Trinity, fancied himself as the end-time angel to the church of Laodicea, and proclaimed that by "1977 all denominations would be consumed by the World Council of Churches under the control of the Roman Catholics, that the rapture would take place, and that the world would be destroyed."[397]

Like Rodney Howard-Browne (aka The Holy Ghost Bartender), Bentley touts "fresh fire" from Florida. In addition to such predictable manifestations as Spirit-induced shaking, laughter, slayings, and drunkenness, Bentley adds Spirit-induced vibrations. As such, he can be heard screeching, "I've got that vibrating again . . . Lord, let everybody vibraa aa aa aa aa aa aate! AHHHH."[398] Howard-Browne says he once slapped a deaf person so hard the person fell flat on the floor. And it worked. The deaf person subsequently got up totally healed.[399] Similarly, Bentley says that God told him "to grab a lady's crippled legs and bang them up and down on the platform like a baseball bat." Says Bentley, "I started banging them up and down on the platform," and "she got healed." On another occasion, Bentley asked God why His power wasn't moving. God allegedly told him, "Because you haven't kicked that woman in the face." Bentley then explained that "there was this older lady worshipping right in front of the platform. And the Holy Spirit spoke to me. The gift of faith came on me. He said, 'Kick her in the face—with your biker boot!' I inched closer and I went like this [Bentley motions a kick]—Bam! And just as my boot made contact with her nose she fell under the power of God."[400]

Bentley's methods are also very similar to those of Smith Wigglesworth who, according to Howard-Browne, once "punched" a man, dying of cancer "so hard he flew through the air and hit the floor, dead! He killed him!" Ten minutes later the man was supposedly resurrected and running around the church.[401] In like fashion, Bentley kicked a man in the gut with his knee in order to heal him of what was reportedly metastatic stage IV colon cancer. When the man bent over in obvious pain, Bentley told him, "I had to be obedient to the Lord, sir, but I believe that colon cancer's comin' right out of your body now . . . Now you're probably feeling a little more pain now. But when we're dealing with cancer sometimes it's a spirit. We're gonna draw that out."[402] And like a host of Faith teachers before him, Bentley claims numerous resurrections from the dead.[403] According to Bentley, a man who had been dead for two days got out of his coffin, leaving the funeral home behind. Conspicuously absent was the man's name, a death certificate, newspaper reports, and eyewitness testimonies.[404]

Ironically, as I was finishing the previous sentence, I received a phone call from a friend. He had just returned from a Todd Bentley tent meeting in Lakeland. He said he had gone to lend moral support to his sister Angela who took what little she had and arranged for the long trek from Michigan to Florida. Like thousands of others, she was desperate. The Christian grapevine from *Charisma* to God TV had provided the hype—thousands had experienced miraculous healings, and some were even being raised from the dead. With faith and expectation she loaded up her wheelchaired daughter and headed to Lakeland.

For two and a half hours, she sang and swayed along with thousands of desperate people. Then came the testimonies. A visiting speaker named Dr. James Malone elevated expectations with stories of dramatic healings. He said that many Hindus who had poured into his meetings in India had been miraculously healed, including a Hindu elder of the village who had been blind for twelve years. Although practically every Hindu who was present came to the front to receive the Lord, not one Muslim professed faith. That is, until a Muslim woman stepped forward and surrendered her crippled child to the Christians. While still in a quandary over why God had moved among the Hindus and not the Muslims, the Spirit of the almighty God demanded that the child be thrown to the ground. Incredibly, the child was healed in midair. Subsequently, practically every Muslim in the meeting came to the saving knowledge of Jesus. Malone went on to speak of other occasions in which a large crowd heard the palpable sounds of hundreds of tumors exploding and of a paraplegic's limbs being restored.[405]

Malone's stories elevated expectations to fever pitch. With tears streaming down her face, Angela wheeled the most precious of her possessions toward the stage. This was her moment. This was the culmination of all her hopes and dreams. Within moments the paralysis of her daughter would be but a distant memory. Suddenly, however, an agony beyond the burden she had carried in her heart for all these years cascaded down upon her consciousness. And in that moment her dreams were dashed. An usher was blocking her entrance to the stage. Only the healed had entry to the healer.

Angela ended up leaving dejected and discouraged. Ironically, my friend Gerry's son Taylor, who suffers from epilepsy, left feeling that he had experienced the miraculous. Had Taylor been interviewed that night, he would no doubt have testified to a complete and total healing. Gerry, however, left in a quandary. If he acknowledged that the healer was a fraud, he risked damaging the fragile faith of his son. If he capitulated to the pressure and threw away the meds, his son might well experience a grand mal seizure.

Gerry's dilemma is not unique. Nor were the expectations of his sister Angela. Just a week prior to their trek to Lakeland, Dr. William Dembski, a leader in the Intelligent Design movement—a man with earned PhDs in both philosophy and mathematics—traveled to a Bentley "impartation service" in Texas. He and his wife were not about to give up on their son's recovery. The organizers of Bentley's meetings urged him to get to the meeting at least four hours early so they could get a seat. And so Dembski and his wife piled the kids into the family minivan and headed off with dreams that this might well be the day that their seven-year-old son would be healed of his autism. Dembski's experience was remarkably similar to that of Gerry's. What follows is his recollection of the event:

> At 7 p.m., Keith Miller, the chief organizer, started things off. After prompting the audience to perform ritualistic acts of worship (stand up, raise your hands, say after me . . .), he passed the baton to a young woman singer and her backup band . . . the music was repetitive in the extreme. In almost two

hours of this "music ministry" only a handful of songs were sung, and many of them seemed to consist of only one or two phrases.

Finally, around 9 p.m. Bentley began to speak. He devoted much of his message to the visions he has received and the miracles he claims have happened in his ministry. Then, almost as an afterthought, he spent a few minutes preaching from the Bible. In fact, he admitted that he was having us open the Bible simply so that it couldn't be said that he didn't preach from the Bible. So much for reverencing the Scriptures. Nowhere in Bentley's message did I see an emphasis on the love and compassion of God—that healing is an expression of God's goodness and care for humanity. Rather, the emphasis throughout was on power—the power to heal and be healed.

Bentley told stories of remarkable healings. In fact, he claims that in his ministry 30 people have now been raised from the dead. Are these stories credible? A common pattern in the accounts of healing was an absence of specificity. Bentley claims that one man, unembalmed, had been dead for 48 hours and was in a coffin. When the family gathered around at a funeral home, the man knocked from inside the coffin to be let out.

But what are the specifics? Who was this man? What was his name? Where's the death certificate? And why not parade the man at Bentley's meetings? If I was ever raised from the dead through anyone's ministry, you can be sure I'll put in a guest appearance. Bentley claims that he is having a team investigate healings performed under his ministry and will soon go public with the evidence. I look forward to seeing it.

After preaching, Bentley took the offering. During the offering he asked "How much anointing do you want to receive?" Thus he linked the blessing we should receive with the amount of money we gave.

After the offering, Bentley said a general prayer for mass healing. People who thought they were healed then came forward. But I saw no obvious or dramatic evidence of healing. After the general prayer for mass healing, Bentley indicated that he would pray for the severest cases.

At this point, a friend who was with us urged that she and my wife take our son with autism down for prayer. Over an hour later my son with autism was still not able to get to the main floor for prayer. Ushers twice prevented that from happening. They noted that he was not in a wheelchair. Wheelchair cases clearly had priority—presumably they provided better opportunities for the cameras, which filmed everything. They also invoked the fire marshals, who, they claimed, prohibited too many people on the floor of the arena. But earlier in the service, during the worship time, they had packed the floor with people singing and whooping it up.

After midnight we were told that it would be an hour and a half before our son could get prayer. At that point, we got up and left. Yet the story doesn't end there. When we got to the minivan, our other son remembered that he had left his Bible in the arena. When my wife went back to retrieve it, everybody, including Bentley, had suddenly cleared out. Staying an hour and a half would not have mattered.

Our son was refused prayer twice because he didn't look the part, and he was told to wait still longer for a prayer that would never have been offered. And even those who looked the part seemed to look no better after Bentley's prayer—the exodus from the arena of people bound in wheelchairs was poignant.

My son's situation was not unique—a man with bone cancer and his wife traveled a long distance, were likewise refused prayer, and left in tears. People with needs were shortchanged. It seemed that power, prestige and money (in that order) were dominating motives behind the meeting. Minimal time was given to healing, though plenty was devoted to assaulting our senses with blaring insipid music and even to Bentley promoting and selling his own products (books and CDs).

Neither my wife nor I regret going. It was an education. Our kids are resilient. But the ride home raised a question. We found ourselves avoiding talking about the event until the children fell asleep. Then, as they drifted off in the early morning, we talked in hushed tones about how easily religion can be abused, in this case to exploit our family. What do we tell our children? I'm still working on that one.[406]

THE ALTERED STATE OF CONSCIOUSNESS

As the years roll on, the names in the cast of characters will continue to change. Old stars like Kenneth Hagin will fade; shooting stars such as Todd Bentley will light the sky for a moment and then crash and burn. Their methods, however, remain remarkably similar.

To begin with, they all work their devotees into altered states of consciousness. Whether in the ashrams of cults or at the altars of churches, the objective of achieving an altered state of consciousness is always the same: *to dull the critical-thinking process because the mind is seen as the obstacle to enlightenment.* As Rodney Howard-Browne once put it, "you can't understand what God is doing with an analytical mind. The only way you're going to understand what God is doing is with your heart."[407]

Sometimes the altered state of consciousness is achieved by singing a song over and over again until one loses touch with reality. As William Dembski experienced for almost two hours, a handful of songs were sung, many of which consisted of only one or two phrases. In other cases devotees are encouraged to jump up and down furiously and chop their hands frantically through the air. Others throw their heads backward and forward violently and bend wildly at the waist. Alternately they laugh and sob uncontrollably. Their frenzied behavior produces a mind-altering form of hyperventilation that dulls the critical-thinking process and empties the mind of coherent thought. And then, as modeled by Todd Bentley, they "marinate" and "pickle" in the Holy Spirit.

The altered state of consciousness can produce powerful psychological and physical manifestations. As such, devotees report seeing angels standing beside Bentley as he ministers. Tragically, many of these devotees are dangerously ignorant of the striking parallels between their experiences and those of Eastern meditators who achieve altered states of consciousness through occult practices. As has been well documented through studies of the occult, such dangerous effects may involve depression, detachment, depersonalization, disillusionment, and many other equally serious disorders. To think that God is obligated to protect people from the consequences of unbiblical behavior is simply misguided. Whether one is a Christian or a cultist, the consequences of swallowing cyanide are identical. Likewise, whether people work themselves into an altered state of consciousness in a cult or in a church, the destructive effects are the same.

THE PSYCHOLOGY OF PEER PRESSURE

As with the altered state of consciousness, peer pressure is a powerful tool in the hands of Word/Faith practitioners. The pressure to be accepted by peers is so potent that devotees often fake a variety of experiences. A classic case in point involves a well-known charismatic leader who participated in a Benny Hinn television extravaganza. Hinn was slaying his subjects in the Spirit when suddenly he moved in this man's direction. He stretched forth his hand and shouted, "In the mighty name of Jesus!" Immediately the man fell backward into the hands of a designated "catcher." Later he confessed that his experience had nothing to do with the power of God. Peer pressure had caused him to fake his fall. Ironically, when he asked a cameraman to edit out the faked fall, the cameraman merely chuckled and told him it was common for people to fake it.

Like Benny, Bentley banks on peer pressure to conform his prospects to predictable patterns. Tragically, those who fall prey to the pressure are not moved in the least when his deceptions are exposed. The peer pressure that caused them to participate in the first place often keeps them from acknowledging that they were willing participants in a spiritual lie.

Bentley carefully crafts his services to enhance the likelihood that participants will cave in to the power of peer pressure. As noted above, he kicks off his meetings with long periods of repetitive music replete with mind-numbing lyrics. On the heels of the music is the time of testimony. During the testimonies pastors and participants routinely pontificate that they once doubted that God could be involved in such bizarre manifestations, but now they "know" experientially that God often moves in mysterious ways. The time of testimony is followed by a time of teaching, cleverly designed to pressure people to participate during the "time of ministry." During the time of ministry, virtually anything goes. The peer pressure to participate is so potent that even otherwise discerning Christians end up casting caution to the wind.

THE EXPLOITATION OF EXPECTATIONS

As proficient as the Bentleys of the world are in using peer pressure as a means of sociopsychological manipulation, they are equally expert at elevating the expectations of followers. The Dr. Malone story described earlier is a classic case in point. Likewise are Bentley's stories of encounters with Jesus, the apostle Paul, and angels. The "evangelastic" stories used to enhance expectations are so bizarre that it is a wonder anyone still takes them seriously.[408] *Charisma* magazine, for example, circulated a story entitled "'Holy Water' Triggers Healing Revival."[409] Readers were informed that plain old bottled water, when "blessed" by a charismatic bishop, was suddenly transformed into "miracle water." Those who drank this miracle water were not only so mightily touched that they "fell down under the power of God," but were also miraculously healed of such ailments as "cancer, tumors, and heart disease." Millions are reportedly hearing about the miracle water from secular sources. Among them are "prominent politicians, celebrities, and doctors," all attempting to acquire some of the miracle water for themselves.

Word of Faith teachers bank on the fact that expectations aroused by stories such as *Charisma's* "miracle water" or Bentley's "resurrections" will initiate a broad range of mystical experiences. When they slay subjects in the Spirit, they bank on the fact that the expectations of their followers will give birth to the experience itself. Almost everyone reading these words can successfully navigate the length of a common wooden plank resting on the ground. Suspend that same wooden plank between the twin spires of a cathedral and you have an entirely different proposition. The very fact that you are now suspended hundreds of feet in the air naturally introduces the expectation of a possible fall. As such, the notion of falling inevitably gives birth to the fall itself. The expectations of Bentley's devotees are now heightened to such a degree that they are "no more capable of resisting the proper hypnotic suggestion than Pavlov's dog was capable of resisting the stimulus to salivate."[410]

THE SEDUCTIVE POWER OF SUGGESTION

Last but not least is the potent power of suggestion. In an altered state of consciousness, this power is magnified such that people become hypersuggestible. Add to this the power of peer pressure and enhanced expectations, and devotees are primed to accept virtually anything that enters their minds no matter how ordinary or how outlandish. As such they are susceptible to spiritual flights of fancy and become unable to differentiate fantasy from reality.

As underscored by author Robert Marks, "people in crowds are more easily influenced than people taken singly. This fact has been capitalized on by stage hypnotists as well as evangelists, political orators, and dictators."[411] In fact as Marks points out, "the effect of suggestion on crowds seems virtually without limit. It can make black appear white. In can obscure realities, enshrine absurdities, and impel men pitilessly to cleave the skulls of their brothers."[412] And as noted by philosopher Charles Baudouin, "In the sphere of movement, suggestion by imitation is common. Immoderate laughter readily spreads through a crowd; yawning is contagious."[413] Once epidemic suggestion contaminates a movement, human beings can "behave like beasts or idiots and be proud of it."[414] No one "is immune to the force of mass suggestion. Once an epidemic of hysteria is in full force it strikes intellectuals as well as morons, rich and poor alike. Its wellsprings are subconscious and biological, not rational."[415]

When Bentley saw Jesus, met with the apostle Paul, and experienced a variety of interactions with angels and the demonic, he may not have been aware that singing a song over and over for hours or "marinating in the Holy Spirit" had caused him to become hypersuggestible. That, however, does not alter the facts. The three-hour repetition of a spiritual song, being slain in the Spirit, or a spiritualistic séance for that matter have at least one thing in common—they cause subjects to become extremely susceptible to suggestion. Charles Baudouin concludes that "in the first place, a condition of mental relaxation is imposed upon the participants. Secondly, an emotional state is invariably aroused by approximation to the mysterious. Thirdly, there exists an expectation that remarkable things will happen."[416]

Pagan religions and pseudo-Christian cults have long capitalized on the power of suggestion to promote their practices. Counterfeit Revivalists from Benny Hinn to Todd Bentley have followed in their train.

While pastors and parishioners are traveling to places like Lakeland looking for quick fixes, the solution to what ails them is found in the fundamentals. While multitudes clamor for a massive revival, what the body of Christ really needs is a mighty reformation. Only as the church is reformed can the culture be revived. Indeed, the tragedy of a Christianity in crisis is that Christians are looking for God in all the wrong places.

4

CHARTING THE COURSE

With every book, either the writer struggles or the reader struggles. I am committed to doing all that I can to ensure the struggle is all mine. As such, my objective is to pen this volume in a way that encourages you to read it from cover to cover, provides you with accurate documentation—in context—and presents the content in memorable fashion.

No pilot worth his stripes would take off without first charting the course. In like fashion it is imperative for you to have a clear understanding of where we are going and of how we are going to get there. As such, I have three basic objectives in mind: (1) to pen *Christianity in Crisis* in a readable style so you not only begin but finish; (2) to provide you with complete and accurate documentation; (3) to present information in a memorable format.

All of memory can be boiled down to the process of making associations. Simply stated, making an association means joining or connecting two pieces of information so that when you think of one, the other also comes to mind. It could be a name and a face, a state and its capital, or a chapter in the Bible and what is contained in it.

There are many ways to make memorable associations. One way is to use acronyms. H-O-M-E-S, for example, can be used in the following way to remind you of the names of the Great Lakes:

Huron
Ontario
Michigan
Erie
Superior

In a similar way I developed the acronym F-L-A-W-S to make the material in *Christianity in Crisis* easy to categorize and remember. As such, in each of the next five parts I will use one letter from F-L-A-W-S to contrast four *spiritual* laws of the Christian faith with four spiritual *flaws* of the Faith movement.

FLAWS

	FAITH IN FAITH	**L**ITTLE GODS	**A**TONEMENT ATROCITIES	**W**EALTH & WANT	**S**ICKNESS & SUFFERING
Force of Faith	Deification of Man	Re-creation on the Cross	Cultural Conformity	Symptoms and Sickness
Formula of Faith	Demotion of God	Redemption in Hell	Cons and Cover-ups	Satan and Sickness
Faith of God	Deification of Satan	Rebirth in Hell	Covenant-Contract	Sin and Sickness
Faith Hall of Fame	Demotion of Christ	Reincarnation	Context, Context, Context	Sovereignty and Sickness

PART 2: FAITH IN FAITH

The "F" in F-L-A-W-S will serve to remind you of the word *Faith*. In chapters 5–8 we will look at the Faith movement's metaphysical concept of faith. The four spiritual flaws in this regard can be summarized as follows:

- *The force of faith.* Faith is a force, and words are the containers of the force. Thus, through the power of words, you create your own reality.

- *The formula of faith.* Formulas are the name of the game in Faith theology. Through them you can literally "write your own ticket with God."
- *The faith of God.* The god of the Faith movement is no god at all. You may be amazed to learn that he is a mere faith being who has to operate in accordance with universal laws of faith.
- *The Faith Hall of Fame.* For the Faith teachers to stand, Job has to fall. Thus they induct Job into the "Faith Hall of Shame" and induct themselves into the "Faith Hall of Fame."

PART 3: LITTLE GODS

The "L" in F-L-A-W-S will remind you of the words *little gods*. In chapters 9–12 we will take a look at the Faith movement's concept of men as little gods. The four spiritual flaws can be summarized as follows:

- *The deification of man.* In Faith theology man was created as an exact duplicate of God, including size and shape.
- *The demotion of God.* The Faith movement not only deifies man but also demotes God to the status of a bumbling bellhop at the beck and call of His creation.
- *The deification of Satan.* Satan is deified as the God of this world and is positioned with so much power that he could manage to "turn the light off in God."
- *The demotion of Christ.* All cults and world religions compromise the deity of the Lord Jesus Christ. The Faith movement is no exception.

PART 4: ATONEMENT ATROCITIES

The "A" in F-L-A-W-S will remind you of *Atonement Atrocities*. In chapters 13–16 you will get a full-orbed perspective of how the Faith movement has tarnished the crux of Christianity—the atonement of the Lord Jesus Christ. The four spiritual flaws can be summarized as follows:

- *Re-creation on the cross.* On the cross, Jesus was re-created from divine to demonic, taking on the very nature of Satan.

- *Redemption in hell.* In the words of one Faith teacher, "Satan *conquered* Jesus on the Cross."[1] In the words of yet another, "If the punishment for sin was to die on a cross . . . the two thieves could have paid your price."[2]
- *Rebirth in hell.* In hell, the "emaciated, poured out, little wormy spirit" of Jesus was born again.[3] "The trap was set for Satan and Jesus was the bait."[4]
- *Reincarnation.* Jesus was reincarnated from demonic to divine and then emerged from hell as an incarnation of God. When you are born again, you, too, are reincarnated from demonic to divine, becoming "as much an incarnation as was Jesus of Nazareth."[5]

PART 5: WEALTH AND WANT

The "W" in F-L-A-W-S will remind you of *Wealth* and *Want*. In chapters 17–20 we will see that Faith theology transforms Christianity from a gospel of grace to a gospel of greed. The four spiritual flaws in this regard are as follows:

- *Cultural conformity.* Rather than transforming our culture to Christ, prosperity preachers feature a Jesus who "wears designer clothes."
- *Cons and cover-ups.* The cons and cover-ups of the Faith movement are so outrageous that you have to read them—and see the documentation—to believe them.
- *Covenant-contract.* The Faith concept of wealth and want finds its genesis in a covenant that God made with Abram. God supposedly told Abram, "I'm making a proposition to you. You can tell Me to bug off if you don't like it."[6]
- *Context, context, context.* Faith teachers are masters at attributing esoteric or mystical meanings to biblical passages. Among other things, they claim to prove that Jesus and the disciples were fabulously wealthy.

PART 6: SICKNESS AND SUFFERING

The "S" in F-L-A-W-S will remind you of *Sickness* and *Suffering*. In chapters 21–24 you will learn that devastation and death have followed in the wake of

90

the false teachings of the Faith movement. The Faith movement's four spiritual flaws on sickness and suffering are as follows:

- *Symptoms and sickness.* Are symptoms merely tricks used by the devil to steal our guarantee of divine health and healing?
- *Satan and sickness.* The cruelty displayed by the Faith movement when it comes to the sick is almost beyond comprehension. Arguably, the most famous of all Faith teachers today writes, "If your body belongs to God, it does not and cannot belong to sickness."[7]
- *Sin and sickness.* It is not enjoyable to read the stories of people who lost their loved ones and were told that it was a direct result of sin, but it may be necessary. Perhaps we will wake up to the fact that the kingdom of the cults has entered the very domain of the church itself.
- *Sovereignty and sickness.* One of our best-selling evangelical authors writes, "Never, ever, ever, go to the Lord and say, 'If it be thy will.' . . . Don't allow such faith-destroying words to be spoken from your mouth."[8] And that's just the beginning. The sovereignty of God is the first casualty in the cultic theology of the Faith movement.

PART 7: BACK TO BASICS

I happen to love the game of golf. Although it has brought me great satisfaction over the years, it has been extremely frustrating as well. After many years of practice and playing, I have stumbled upon a secret: when things go wrong, it is usually not because I am failing to follow some newfangled faddish formula but because I have begun to compromise the essentials. I never cease to be amazed at how quickly things fall into place when I get back to basics.

What's true in golf is applicable to Christianity in crisis as well. Everything can quickly come back into focus by getting back to basics. It may not sound exciting, but this is truly where the real experience of victorious Christian living can be found! In chapters 25–29 we will focus our attention on getting back to basics by following five basic steps. Fortunately, they are as easy to remember as A-B-C-D-E.

A*men.* We begin with the letter "A," which represents the word "Amen." Amen traditionally comes at the end of every prayer, and prayer is our primary way of communicating with God. To help you separate fact from fiction regarding prayer, I've developed the acronym F-A-C-T-S. It will provide you with a good handle on the purpose, the power, and the provision of prayer.

Bible. "B" stands for "Bible." While prayer is our primary way of communicating with God, the Bible is God's primary way of communicating with us. Thus nothing should take precedence over spending time in the Word. If we fail to eat well-balanced meals, we will eventually suffer physically. Likewise, if we do not regularly feed on the Word of God, we will suffer spiritually. The acronym M-E-A-L-S will give you a handle on getting into the Word and getting the Word into you.

Church. "C" stands for "Church." Scripture exhorts us not to neglect the gathering of ourselves together, as is the custom of some (Hebrews 10:25). Today, however, multitudes are turning from the church and tuning into television. We are being conformed to the ways of our culture rather than to the will of God. The acronym G-O-D will give us a good grasp of what it means to get back to the basics of vital church life.

Defense. "D" stands for "Defense." Getting back to basics means equipping yourself for the defense of the faith. The Cold War may be over, but the need to defend the faith is just beginning to heat up. The defense of the faith is not just a suggestion; it is basic training for every Christian. Thankfully, learning to defend your faith is not as difficult as you may think. It all boils down to being able to answer three key questions.

Essentials. "E" stands for "Essentials." Much is being said today about unity. Unity, however, cannot truly exist apart from the essentials on which the Christian faith is founded. The essentials are abiding reference points guiding Christ's body through the storms that have sought to sink it throughout the church age. Christ promised He would be with us always, "to the very end of the age" (Matthew 28:20). In getting back to essential Christianity, we will use the acronym A-G-E as our point of reference.

As you read through the remainder of this book, it is my prayer that you will not just be equipped to spot the skin of the truth stuffed with a lie, but that you will become so familiar with genuine Christianity that when a counterfeit looms on the horizon, you will recognize it instantaneously. With all this in mind, let us press forward by turning our attention to the Faith movement's counterfeit notion of having "faith in faith."

part two

FAITH IN FAITH

Take up the shield of faith, with which you can extinguish all the flaming arrows of the evil one.[1]

—THE APOSTLE PAUL

As the shields of antiquity enveloped a soldier's body, so faith envelopes the entirety of our being. When Satan attacks our heads, the hand of faith holds fast to truth. When Satan attacks our hearts, the hand of faith holds fast to righteousness. Indeed, it might well be said that faith is the apex of a Christian's armor. It is the covering that protects not only the entirety of our bodies but all the other pieces of the full armor of God depicted by the apostle Paul in his letter to the Ephesians. Faith is a defense for all defenses. Every other piece of our armor must inevitably operate in conjunction with faith.

The question is, what is faith? Is faith merely a blind step into the dark, or can faith be considered a leap into the light? Is faith a force? Are words the containers for the force?

And how should I direct my faith? Should it be directed inward—faith in my own faith? Or is God to be the object of my faith?

Speaking of God, is God a faith-being? Would He know of any good faith formulas? While I'm asking, can someone please tell me how to get to the Faith Hall of Fame?

Larry and Lucky Parker thought they knew the way to the Faith Hall of Fame. They had listened to the Faith message for years. They knew the Faith formulas by heart. But this time when a Faith peddler rode through town, they swallowed more of his spiritual cyanide than they could safely digest. They charged in the wrong direction down a one-way street of faith.

Their story, codified in a book titled *We Let Our Son Die*, recounts the tragic details of a misguided trip of faith. In painful detail, Larry and Lucky paint the picture of how they withheld insulin from their diabetic son, Wesley. Predictably, he lapsed into a diabetic coma.

The Parkers, warned about the impropriety of making a "negative confession," continued to "positively confess" Wesley's healing until the time of his death. Even after Wesley's demise, the Parkers, undaunted in their "faith," conducted a resurrection service rather than a funeral. In fact, for more than a year following his death, they refused to abandon their firmly held faith that Wesley would rise from the dead. Eventually, both Larry and Lucky were tried and convicted of manslaughter and child abuse.

A tragic tale? Yes. But this is by no means a singular case. With the dawning of each new day, another gruesome story unfolds. And in each case the plot is always the same: a flawed concept of faith inevitably leads to shipwreck—sometimes spiritually, in other cases physically, and in some cases, both.

Since faith is the thread that weaves Christianity into an exquisite tapestry, it will serve us well to carefully consider the false doctrines that are systematically unraveling the fabric of our faith.

Many people who espouse Faith doctrines have embraced concepts that are so unbiblical they boggle the mind. In some cases these concepts find their genesis in the kingdom of the cults; in other cases they are firmly rooted in the world of the occult.

In the following pages you will come face-to-face with Faith teachers who have completely redefined the biblical concept of faith. They define faith as a force and claim that words are the containers for the force.

You will learn to detect flawed faith formulas that have been virtually canonized by the Faith movement.

You will discover that the "God" of the Faith movement is not the true God at all. He is a pathetic puppet governed by the impersonal force of faith.

It is my hope that you will be equipped to contrast true heroes of the faith, past and present, with the spiritual charlatans who have inducted themselves into what might best be characterized as their own "Faith Hall of Shame."

When it comes to Faith theology, truth is often stranger than fiction. While millions of Faith adherents have not let their children die, they do continue to applaud doctrines that lead to such devastating consequences. Marilyn Hickey, for example, teaches people to speak to their bodies:

Say to your body, "You're whole, body! Why, you just function so beautifully and so well. Why, body, you never have any problems. You're a strong, healthy body." Or speak to your leg, or speak at your foot, or speak to your neck, or speak to your back; and once you have spoken and believe that you have received, and don't go back on it. Speak to your wife, speak to your husband, speak to your circumstances, and speak faith to them to create in them, and God will create what you are speaking.[2]

In like fashion, T. D. Jakes teaches devotees to touch their bodies and decree that they are healed from the crown of their heads to the soles of their feet:

If you got an infection in your body touch that part of your body that's up under attack and in the name of Jesus declare it, and decree that God is healing your body from the crown of your head to the sole of your feet. God is healing your body. You'd been up under attack, but the devil is a liar. Healing is the children's bread. It's promised to us in the Word of God. Doctors have done what they could do, but God can do things that medicine cannot do. I declare a supernatural divine Holy Ghost healing in this house! Healed, be healed; tumors, be healed; cancers, be healed; growths, be healed; legions, be healed; rashes and issues and eye problems, be healed; kidneys and livers and lungs, be healed. Blood disorders, be healed; skin infirmities, be healed; bone marrows, be healed; skin cells, be healed; eye tissue, be healed. In the name of Jesus, somebody praise Him [tongues]. I feel an earthquake in this place. Give the Lord a praise![3]

As we will see, Word of Faith teachers elaborate on such teachings with devastating consequences. It is precisely here that many have taken a dramatic U-turn from Christianity into the world of the occult.

5

FORCE OF FAITH

Words are containers for power. They carry creative or destructive power, positive or negative power. And so we need to be speaking right things over our lives and about our futures if we expect to have good things happen. Because what you say today is what you'll probably end up having tomorrow.[1]

—JOYCE MEYER

I have spent hundreds of hours reading and researching the concepts of Faith teachers who daily parade through our living rooms via the airwaves. Through it all, a significant theme has emerged: faith is a force; words are the containers of the force; and through the force of faith, people can create their own realities.

Kenneth Copeland believes so strongly in this concept that he has made the phrase "force of faith" famous through constant repetition. He even wrote a book titled *The Force of Faith* to propagate this deadly error.

As Copeland puts it, "Faith is a power force. It is a tangible force. It is a conductive force."[2] He further says that in much the same way that the force of gravity makes the law of gravity work, "it is this force of faith which makes the laws of the spirit world function."[3]

According to Copeland, "This force originates from God, out of His unlimited heart."[4] In fact, he says, the world "was born out of the force of faith that was resident inside the being of God."[5]

Copeland goes so far as to say that "God cannot do anything for you apart or separate from faith" because "faith is God's source of power."[6]

Just think of it—God *cannot* do anything for you apart from the force! Without the force of faith, God has no power at all toward you. Already one thing should be clear: Copeland's God is no God at all. The true omnipotent God of Scripture is hardly impotent.

Copeland likens "God's source of power" to a coin. This coin has both a positive and a negative side. The positive side, or "heads," represents faith. Faith activates God. The negative side, or "tails," represents fear. Fear activates Satan. Copeland puts it like this: "Fear activates Satan, the way faith activates God."[7]

To use another analogy, you might picture "God's source of power" as a giant battery in the sky. This battery has both a positive and a negative pole. The positive pole represents "faith" while the negative pole represents "fear."

As Charles Capps puts it, "Job activated Satan by his fear when he said, 'the thing which I greatly feared is come upon me' (Job 3:25 KJV). Active faith in the Word brings God onto the scene. Fear brings Satan on the scene."[8]

So how does God supposedly activate the force of faith? The answer is *through words.*

THE CONTAINERS OF FAITH

In Faith theology, words are the containers that carry the substance of faith. If you speak words of faith, you activate the positive side of the force; if you speak words of fear, you activate the negative side of the force. In Faith vernacular this is called "making positive or negative confessions." The Faith movement would have us believe that everything that happens to us is a direct result of our words: "Words are spiritual containers, and the force of faith is released by words."[9] As Copeland explains: "God used words when He created the heaven and the earth . . . Each time God spoke, He released His faith—the creative power to bring His words to pass."[10]

Copeland claims that words were also the vehicle God used to "paint a picture of a Redeemer, a man who would be the manifestation of His Word in the earth."[11]

It was God's force of faith squeezed into words that saved the day when Jesus was being obliterated by Satan in hell (see chapter 15, "Rebirth in Hell"). From creation to re-creation, according to the proponents of the prosperity message, everything is controlled by words filled with the substance of faith. This is precisely why E. W. Kenyon said, "Faith-filled words brought the universe into being, and faith-filled words are ruling the universe today."[12]

Not only is the Faith movement's concept of faith antibiblical, but it bears striking similarities to New Thought metaphysics. Metaphysical practitioner Rhonda Byrne explains the secret to the universe as being contained in "the law of attraction." Says Byrne: "The greatest teachers who have ever lived have told us that the law of attraction is the most powerful law in the Universe."[13] What is the law of attraction? "The law of attraction is the law of creation. Quantum physicists tell us that the entire Universe emerged from thought! You create your life through your thoughts and the law of attraction, and every single person does the same. It doesn't just work if you know about it. It has always been working in your life and every other person's life throughout history."[14] As New Thought critic Ron Rhodes explains:

> According to New Thought, human beings can experience health, success, and abundant life by using their thoughts to define the condition of their lives. New Thought proponents subscribe to the "law of attraction." This law says that just as like attracts like, so our thoughts can attract the things they want or expect. Negative thoughts are believed to attract dismal circumstances; positive thoughts attract more desirable circumstances. Our thoughts can be either creative or destructive. New Thought sets out to teach people how to use their thoughts creatively.[15]

Parallels to metaphysical cults are by no means a mere coincidence. Kenyon, the real father of the modern-day Faith movement, "majored" in metaphysics. His perversions were embraced and multiplied by Hagin, who regurgitated Kenyon's concepts almost word for word.[16] These distortions have continued to proliferate through men like Frederick Price and Kenneth Copeland. And Price and Copeland have gone on to mentor a host of other Faith teachers, including Creflo Dollar, Jerry Savelle, and Charles Capps.

According to Creflo Dollar, "God used faith substance to make everything that He made . . . God's guts are called faith stuff . . . If you were to cut God open, you'd see nothing but faith." Indeed, says Dollar, "Without faith stuff, you have no stuff, because faith stuff is the stuff of all stuff. Take away the faith stuff, you ain't got no stuff. Get the faith stuff, and you can get some more stuff, because you got the main stuff."[17]

Likewise, Savelle says that "the raw material or the substance that God used to frame this world was His faith and His Word . . . The way that He created the world was, first of all, He conceived something on the inside of Him. He conceived, He had an image, He had a picture. God doesn't just sling things into existence without first of all conceiving it first."[18]

When Savelle was asked if a person can change his world through "the word of faith," he responded that we can talk our world into existence. "That's how you got the one you're living in now," he says. "You talked it in there . . . You talked that one in there, the one you're living in right now, brother. You can't blame it on nobody else. Your words got it there. You framed it. Somebody says, 'You mean the world that I'm living in right now originated by the words of my mouth?' They certainly did, because the Bible says you are snared by the words of your mouth, you are taken by your words. Amen?"[19]

Charles Capps repeats the words of his prosperity peers when he says, "Some think that God made the earth out of nothing, but He didn't. He made it out of something. *The substance God used was faith* . . . He used His words as a carrier of that faith."[20]

Robert Tilton, who pronounced himself the most anointed prosperity pastor on television, also claims that faith is a force. Says Tilton, "If you have a problem, any kind of need, housing, transportation, situation in a marriage, you can release the creative—see, this all works by faith—the creative force of God into existence."[21] Of course, with Tilton it takes more than just words! In his case, it helps to make a vow of faith sealed with a generous donation. In most cases, a thousand dollars is the magic number.

THE ORIGIN OF THE FAITH TEACHING

By now you should be asking yourself, "Where on earth do Faith teachers get this stuff?" As hard as it may be to believe, the standard proof text used by the Faith teachers is Hebrews 11:1, which in King James English reads, "Now faith is the substance of things hoped for, the evidence of things not seen."

"There you have it," say the Faith teachers. "Faith is a substance!"

Imagine: all the perversions just documented are based primarily on one brief passage, in an old translation, wrenched out of context, and presented as a proof text for the Faith message. Like an elephant tottering on the point of a pen, their entire theology rests on the word *substance* in Hebrews 11:1.

The Faith teachers interpret the word *substance* to mean the "basic stuff" out of which the universe is made. As Copeland puts it, "Faith was the raw material substance that the Spirit of God used to form the universe."[22]

Therefore, according to Faith teaching, the book you're reading is made out of molecules, which in turn are made out of atoms, which are composed of subatomic particles, which are comprised of this thing called *faith*. According to Faith theology, virtually everything is made out of faith!

But is this true? Does the word *substance* in Hebrews 11:1 really teach that faith is the tangible stuff out of which the universe is made?

First, remember that *Scripture must always be interpreted in light of Scripture*. As such, faith cannot be rightly understood to mean "the building block of the universe," since it is never used in that sense in the book of Hebrews, much less the entire Bible.

Second, the word translated "substance" in the King James Version is more accurately rendered "assurance" (see NASB). Far from being a tangible material, faith is a *channel of living trust*—an *assurance*—which stretches from man to God. True biblical faith is only as good as the object in whom it is placed. God is both the object and the origin of our faith. Thus, true biblical faith is faith in God as opposed to faith in *substance* (or "faith in faith," as Hagin put it).[23] It is the *object* and the *origin* of faith that renders it effective.

Finally, consulting an interlinear Bible quickly demonstrates that the word translated "substance" in the King James Version is the Greek word *hypostasis*, which in the context of Hebrews 11:1 means "an assured impression, a mental realizing."[24] Other translations, in an effort to offer an accurate rendition, translate *hypostasis* variously as "being sure" (NIV) and "assurance" (NASB). Far from meaning "tangible stuff," it specifically refers to the assurance that God's promises never fail, even if sometimes we do not experience their fulfillment in our mortal existence.

As noted theologian Louis Berkhof so eloquently stated, the writer of Hebrews "exhorts the readers to an attitude of faith which will enable them to rise from the seen to the unseen, from the present to the future, from the temporal to the eternal; and [to that] which will enable them to be patient in the midst of sufferings."[25]

TRUE FAITH

True biblical faith (*pistis* in the Greek) encapsulates three essential elements. The first entails knowledge. The second involves agreement. But it is not until we add the third ingredient, trust, that we end up with a full-orbed, biblical perspective on faith.

Imagine that you currently embrace the cultic teachings of Kenneth

Copeland. You may *know* about a book titled *Christianity in Crisis*; you may even *agree* that it provides an accurate diagnosis of Copeland's teaching; but it isn't until you stop consuming his poison that you demonstrate "faith" that his disastrous teachings have led you from Christianity into the kingdom of the cults.

Likewise, suppose I told you that a candy bar was laced with cyanide and would poison whoever ate it. Then imagine that you responded, "I know! I agree!" *But then you proceeded to take a great big bite of it!* Your action would prove that you had no faith in what I was telling you. (Incidentally, your good intentions would not change the consequences. In the end you would still convulse and die.)

So what difference does a proper definition of faith make? It makes all the difference in the world. Just remember the tragedy of Larry and Lucky Parker, who bought the lie and let their son die. And don't forget that for every example of physical death, there are hundreds of unseen examples of spiritual suicide. For every person sitting in a Faith service, there are thousands more who have sown a similar seed of error and who have reaped the deadly whirlwind. Some, like Larry and Lucky, have found their way back to biblical faith. But countless others have been left reeling, not knowing where to turn or who to trust.

ERROR BEGETS ERROR

While Copeland is a juggernaut in his own right, his influence has been multiplied through Faith megastars such as Joel Osteen and Joyce Meyer. Like Copeland they are expert in twisting the biblical text. As evidence, Osteen tells devotees that the "Scripture tells us that *we* are to 'call the things that are not as if they already were.'"[26] As Osteen must surely know, Scripture says nothing of the sort. Indeed, according to the apostle Paul writing in the book of Romans, it is not *we* but *God* who "calls things that are not as though they were" (4:17). Meyer's prostitution of Scripture is equally bizarre and blasphemous. In compelling fashion she exudes:

> I got fire in my belly tonight, because I know! I know! I know! That there's power and life in right words. That words are containers for power, and I don't care about what kind of mess you got, I am begging you tonight to stop talking about it, and start talking about what the Word says, and what

you can have. Make yourself a list, do some work, do some homework, make sure you got a Scripture to back up every one of your confessions.

We're not talking about some magic goofy, you know, weird New Age thing. I'm talking about doing what the Bible says, calling those things that be not as though they are, prophesying to the dead, dry bones in your life. Oh, you dry bones, hear the Word of the Lord.

Maybe you need to get your checkbook out and say, "Oh you checkbook hear the Word of the Lord, you are not going to stay empty all of your life." Ah, somebody says this is just too weird for me, well then just stay broke. What you're doing's not working! You listen to me, checkbook, the first 10 percent of everything that goes into you is going to God's work, and you are going to be full to overflowing! And I am going to be blessed, and I am going to be a blessing.[27]

As with Osteen, it is inconceivable that Meyer would not be familiar with the biblical text she abuses. Like Osteen, she must surely know that it is the Almighty, not her audience, who can call those things which are not as though they were. Not only so, but taking out one's checkbook and speaking to it is not only weird but decidedly unbiblical. The way one produces wealth is not through speaking words but through sanctified work.

In the end, the entire notion that faith is a force, that words are the containers of the force, and that through the force of faith we can create our own realities is little more than an occult metaphysical concept cleverly packaged for Christian consumption. With this in mind let us now turn to the Faith movement's penchant for formulas.

6

FORMULA OF FAITH

The Creative Process used in *The Secret*, which was taken from
the New Testament in the Bible, is an easy guideline for you to create
what you want in three simple steps . . . Ask . . . Believe . . . Receive.[1]

—RHONDA BYRNE, *THE SECRET*

If Rhonda Byrne's megabestseller is anything, it is formulaic. Attracting
health and wealth is apparently as easy as one, two, three. First, says Byrne,
"you must get clear about what you want" and then "you need to make a
command to the Universe." Second, "you must *believe* that you have received.
You must know that what you want is yours the moment you ask. You must
have complete and utter faith." Third, in order to receive what you believe,
"you have to feel it." If you follow this faith formula, the laws of the spirit world
will give you what you want every time, 100 percent of the time.

What Rhonda Byrne orders from the "Catalogue of the Universe," Faith
teachers order from God—or famously order God for. And as with Byrne,
employing the right formula is the key. Not only do these faith formulas cause
the laws of the spirit world to function, but they also cause the Holy Spirit to
function. As such, God is demoted to the status of a mere bellhop who blindly
responds to the beck and call of formulas uttered by the faithful.

Faith formulas are the name of the game. This is why the Faith movement
has also been called the Positive Confession movement. Faith doctrine teaches
that confessions unlock the formula of faith and activate spiritual law. Positive
confessions activate the positive side of the force; negative confessions activate
the negative side. From a practical perspective, spiritual law is the ultimate
force in the universe. In a book titled *Two Kinds of Faith*, E. W. Kenyon insists
that "it is our confession that rules us."[2]

Kenneth Hagin once complained that unsaved people were getting better results from their faith formulas than were his church members. And then it dawned on him what the unsaved were doing. As he tells the story in his booklet, *Having Faith in Your Faith*, these sinners were "cooperating . . . with the law of faith."[3] Ultimately, according to the formula of faith, the wealth of the world is as close as the word on your tongue.

This is why Hagin teaches people to have faith in their faith as opposed to having faith in their God. "It would help you get faith down in your spirit to say out loud: 'Faith in my faith,'" says Hagin. "Keep saying it until it registers on your heart. I know it sounds strange when you first say it; your mind almost rebels against it. But we are not talking about your head; we're talking about faith in your heart."[4]

Hagin then appeals to Mark 11:23 (KJV), which reads, "For verily I say unto you, that whosoever shall *say* unto this mountain, be thou removed, and be thou cast into the sea; and shall not doubt in his heart, but shall *believe* that those things which he *saith* shall come to pass; he shall have whatsoever he *saith*" (emphasis his). Says Hagin, "Notice two more things about this 23rd verse: (1) He believes in his *heart*; (2) he believes in his *words*. Another way to say this is: *He has faith in his own faith . . . Having faith in your words is having faith in your faith*."[5]

The most basic ingredient in the formula of faith is our words. Words rule! It is through our words that we can learn to activate the force of faith. This is precisely why Faith theology is referred to as "Name it and claim it" or "Blab it and grab it."

WRITING YOUR OWN TICKET

Hagin elaborates on this theme in a booklet titled *How to Write Your Own Ticket with God*. (The name itself should shock you.) Here Hagin claims that Jesus Christ Himself appeared to him and personally gave him the formula for faith. In the opening chapter, titled "Jesus Appears to Me," Hagin claims that while he "was in the Spirit"—just like the apostle John on the Isle of Patmos—a white cloud enveloped him, and he began to speak in tongues.[6]

"Then the Lord Jesus Himself appeared to me," says Hagin. "He stood within three feet of me."[7] After what sounded like a casual conversation about such things as finances, ministry, and even current affairs, Jesus told Hagin to get a pencil and a piece of paper. He then instructed him to "Write down: 1, 2, 3, 4."[8]

Jesus then told Hagin that "if anybody, anywhere, will take these four steps or put these four principles into operation, he will always receive whatever he wants from Me or from God the Father."[9] That includes whatever you want financially.[10] The formula is simply: "Say it, Do it, Receive it, and Tell it."

- Step number one is "Say it." "Positive or negative, it is up to the individual. According to what the individual says, that shall he receive."[11]
- Step number two is "Do it." "Your action defeats you or puts you over. According to your action, you receive or you are kept from receiving."[12]
- Step number three is "Receive it."[13] We are to plug into the "powerhouse of heaven."[14] "*Faith is the plug*, praise God! Just plug in."[15]
- Step number four is "Tell it so others may believe."[16] This final step might be considered the Faith movement's outreach program.

There you have it—the formula of faith, straight from the lips of Hagin's Jesus. According to this Jesus, the formula is to be used by Christians because "it would be a waste of their time to pray for Me [i.e., Jesus] to give them the victory. They have to write their own ticket."[17]

SCRIPTURE "PROOF"

Despite having received this dictation straight from Christ Himself, Hagin had some doubts about the veracity of the formula. Therefore he challenged Christ to "prove it."[18] Without missing a beat, He referred Hagin to the account of David and Goliath (1 Samuel 17). "Now wait a minute," protested Hagin. "You're not going to tell me that is what David did?" Christ promptly responded, "Exactly. Those are the four steps he took."[19]

After going over the account of David and Goliath, Hagin agreed that what Jesus said was true. Says Hagin, "David knew you can have what you say. He knew *you can write your own ticket*."[20]

Any Christian with an open mind who reads Hagin's booklet must conclude that Jesus Christ of Nazareth did *not* appear to Kenneth Hagin. Nor did He say the things Hagin claims He did. Either Hagin is dreadfully deluded or else he had a conversation with another Jesus who presented him another gospel (2 Corinthians 11:3–4).

One thing is certain: Hagin's booklet serves up everything but the clear meaning of Scripture. While at times the things Hagin writes are hilarious, all humor quickly vanishes when you consider that vast numbers of people are swallowing his far-fetched formulas and are wandering far from the Savior.

In a futile attempt to legitimize his faith formula—especially step number one, "Say it"—Hagin points to Proverbs 6:2, "Thou art snared with the words of thy mouth" (KJV). This, according to Hagin, proves that if you speak positively, you will get positive results, but if you speak negatively, you will get negative results.

But this verse has nothing to do with any type of "formula of faith." Nor does it even remotely suggest that words per se have power. Solomon in this passage (cf. verse 1) was simply pointing out that whenever you enter into an agreement with someone, you are bound by that agreement. Affirming yourself as a guarantor for another person makes you liable for that person's debt—which you may end up regretting! You are, in short, getting snared (committed) by your own words (pledge or promise).

Charles Capps takes this same proof text to an even more illogical conclusion. In warning people that they get exactly what they say, Capps explains that people who utter such expressions as "That just tickled me to death" and "I'm just dying to do that" are "buddying up with death." He then adds that "Adam was smarter than that. It took the devil over 900 years to kill him, but now the devil has programmed his language into the human race, until people can kill themselves in about 70 years or less, by speaking his words."[21]

Such reckless reasoning brings up an interesting question: When God said that He covers us with His wings (Psalm 91:4), does Capps believe the Almighty is in danger of becoming a chicken? Does Capps believe Jesus was "buddying up with death" in the Garden of Gethsemane when He said, "My soul is overwhelmed with sorrow to the point of death" (Matthew 26:38)?

CULTIC COPYCATS

Unfortunately, Capps is not the only Faith teacher who has been influenced by Hagin's formulas. Dad Hagin has spawned a host of imitators. One of them is

Norvel Hayes. In one of the most irrational interviews I have ever seen on Christian television, Hayes told Paul and Jan Crouch about a conversation he had with Jesus Christ in which he, too, received the key to the faith formula.[22]

Like Hagin, Hayes claimed to have an out-of-body experience, being transported in a white cloud to the presence of Jesus. No sooner had he arrived than Jesus began to question him about some growths on his daughter's body. Jesus was upset because Hayes had not been able to curse the roots of the growths. As such, Jesus said to Hayes, "You belong to Me the same way as Hagin does." He then told him, "Whatever Kenneth Hagin can do in Jesus' name, you can do." With that, Jesus gave Hayes the faith formula. Although Hayes's version is hazier than Hagin's, the gist is similar.

First, he had to command or curse the sickness. As Hayes learned in "heaven," you don't talk to Jesus about your trouble; you speak directly to the mountains in your life and they will disappear. Second, Jesus told him to believe and never doubt, regardless of what he saw. As Hayes tells the story, he believed and never doubted for forty days and forty nights. After this wilderness experience, Hayes got the breakthrough he was looking for: the growths that had plagued his daughter, Zona, for so long disappeared in an instant.

TBN studios erupted in applause and shrieks of joy as Hayes concluded his story. A little later in the same interview, Hayes told Paul and Jan Crouch a story that Hagin had related to him. In that story, the Lord was said to have healed Hagin's sister of terminal cancer when she was fifty years old. The Lord then supposedly told Hagin's sister that she had five years to build her faith. If she did not, she would die. Five years came and went and Hagin's sister was unable to strengthen her "faith muscle" sufficiently. Thus the cancer came back on her and she died.

Notice the dilemma this creates. On the one hand we are told that we are to claim our healing, even when the physical manifestation has not yet presented itself. On the other hand we are told that when we are healed, disease can appear again if our faith falters. It places you between a rock and a hard place, doesn't it?

Additionally, it lets the Faith teacher off the hook. If you say, "I tried your formula and it didn't work," the prosperity preacher can smugly smile and say, "If you believe and don't doubt, you can have what you say." But if you are supposedly healed and later lose your healing, you are blamed for your own negative confession. Pretty convenient!

WHY BE SO HARSH?

At this point you may be thinking, *Well, maybe Hagin, Hinn, Hickey, Hayes, and a host of other Faith teachers are dead wrong. But do you have to judge their words so harshly?* My answer is a resounding "Yes!" When the core of the Christian faith is imperiled, strong measures are necessary.

The apostle Paul minced no words in calling Elymas the sorcerer "a child of the devil and an enemy of everything that is right!" (Acts 13:10). And he didn't stop there. He went on to describe Elymas as "full of all kinds of deceit and trickery" and as one who was "perverting the right ways of the Lord."[23]

Jesus Christ Himself blistered the false teachers of His day with a scathing denunciation: "Woe to you, scribes and Pharisees, hypocrites, because you travel around on sea and land to make one proselyte; and when he becomes one, you make him twice as much a son of hell as yourselves . . . You serpents, you brood of vipers, how shall you escape the sentence of hell?" (Matthew 23:15, 33 NASB).[24]

It's high time we heeded the words of God as recorded by Jeremiah the prophet:

> *This is what the LORD Almighty says: "Do not listen to what the prophets are prophesying to you; they fill you with false hopes. They speak visions from their own minds, not from the mouth of the LORD." (Jeremiah 23:16)*

There can be little doubt that the visions of Hagin, Hinn, Hayes, and other Faith teachers are delusions of their own minds and do not represent words from the Lord.

> *"I have heard what the prophets say who prophesy lies in my name. They say, 'I had a dream! I had a dream!' How long will this continue in the hearts of these lying prophets, who prophesy the delusions of their own minds?" . . . "Therefore," declares the LORD, "I am against the prophets who steal from one another words supposedly from me." (vv. 25–26, 30)*

One of the frightening aspects of my research into Faith theology is that over and over again I have discovered that the Faith teachers, while claiming to be receiving revelation knowledge from God, are in fact simply repeating stories that they have heard from one another.

"Yes," declares the LORD, "I am against the prophets who wag their own tongues and yet declare, 'The LORD declares.' Indeed, I am against those who prophesy false dreams," declares the LORD. "They tell them and lead my people astray with their reckless lies, yet I did not send or appoint them. They do not benefit these people in the least," declares the LORD. (vv. 31–32)

Tragically, this is precisely what the formulas of the Faith movement do. They "lead [God's] people astray" and "do not benefit these people in the least."

FROM THE CULTS TO THE OCCULT

As damaging as these faith formulas are, it gets even worse. Kenneth Copeland takes Hagin's formulas from the kingdom of the cults into the world of the occult.

In Copeland's version of the faith formula, words of faith actually penetrate what he calls the Holy of Holies and there create the tangible objects they represent. All it takes is: (1) seeing or visualizing whatever you need, whether physical or financial; (2) staking your claim on Scripture; and (3) speaking it into existence.[25]

How would you like a yacht? Copeland's theology tells the believer first to see his eighty-two-foot yacht; then he must stake his claim on Scripture; and finally he is to speak the word of faith. Carried along on the wings of hope (which he says is an "eternal and living substance" residing in every believer),[26] the word mystically penetrates "that veil in the holiest place that exists in heaven" and hovers there in the Holy of Holies. In time, the word that has pierced the veil undergoes a metamorphosis and becomes the very thing it represents.[27]

This, my friends, is nothing but New Thought metaphysics packaged for Christian consumption. Two additional examples confirm such an analysis. First, Copeland discusses a "picture [of a Bible] that came right out of me and went into the Holy of Holies,"[28] and from there developed into an actual physical object. Second, Copeland talks about the application of the same method in the case of physical infirmity:

When you get to the place where you take the Word of God and build an image on the inside of you of not having crippled legs and not having blind eyes, but when you close your eyes you just see yourself just leap out of that wheelchair, it will picture that in the Holy of Holies and you will come out of there. You will come out.[29]

It is striking how closely Copeland's formula parallels three principal beliefs of an occult worldview. First, people in the world of the occult are told that the power to create their own reality lies within themselves. Occultists maintain that they have the inherent capacity to supernaturally change, create, or shape the world around them. Second, these people believe that words are imbued with creative power that directly and dramatically affects the real world in which they live. And finally, occultists believe they can use creative visualization to speak things into existence.

Among the cultic groups that embrace these practices are the metaphysical mind sciences (e.g., Religious Science and Science of Mind), the New Age movement,[30] and various neo-pagan groups, the most familiar being witchcraft.

Copeland is no doubt aware that some people believe he is promoting something that "sounds like that visualization they do in meditation and metaphysical practices."[31] He therefore immediately attempts to turn the tables: "What they're doing sounds like this. The devil is a counterfeiter. He never came up with anything real. That is the perverted form of the real thing. Where do you think he got it? That sucker doesn't know anything on his own. Amen."[32]

On another occasion, Copeland simply affirms that both positive confession and creative visualization are based on the same principle: "Words create pictures, and pictures in your mind create words. And then the words come back out your mouth . . . And when that spiritual force comes out it is going to give substance to the image that's on the inside of you. Aw, that's that visualization stuff! Aw, that's that New Age! No, New Age is trying to do this; and they'd get somewhat results out of it because this is spiritual law, brother."[33]

FURTHER OCCULT CONNECTIONS

Copeland's occult teachings are widely embraced within Christian circles. For example, Paul Yonggi Cho (now known as David), a man who accurately laid claim to pastoring the world's largest church (Yoido Full Gospel Church in Seoul, Korea), has codified these same faith formulas under the label of "fourth-dimensional power" in his best-selling book *The Fourth Dimension*.[34]

Cho is acutely aware that pagan religions harness this power. As such, he claims that God told him that Buddhist and Yoga adherents worked miracle cures because they, unlike their Christian counterparts, had more fully developed their fourth-dimensional powers. Referring to the Buddhist version of a name-it-and-claim-it cult called Soka Gakkai, Cho says that while they belong to Satan, their fourth-dimensional acumen has provided them with dominion over their bodies and circumstances.[35] By "repeating phrases over and over again . . . these people are creating something" and performing "miracles," says Cho.[36] "But if the devil could do these things, why should not the Church of Jesus Christ do all the more?"[37]

What is fourth-dimensional thinking? Cho provides the answer in the form of an illustration. Pastor Cho one day coached a thirty-year-old woman (who had allegedly been praying for a husband for ten years) into "creating" the man of her dreams. When Cho asked her what kind of husband she wanted, she responded, "Well, that's up to God. God knows all."[38] Cho immediately cautioned her that God does not answer vague prayers and that if she wanted to have a husband, she would have to be more specific.[39] Asking her to sit down, he handed her a piece of paper and told her to number it from one to ten.

Number one, Cho asked, "Do you want your husband to be European, Asian, or African?" "European," she answered.[40] Number two, "How tall should he be?" "Six feet," she replied. Number three, "What profession?" "Schoolteacher." (In the first version, question number three asked about desired physical appearance.)[41] Number four, "Hobby?"

On and on they went until she had the ten characteristics of the man of her dreams. Cho then told her to hang the paper by her mirror and to look at it and speak all ten points aloud each day. Cho triumphantly reports that this spinster had the man of her dreams within a short period of time.[42]

Cho summarizes the "law of incubation"[43] as follows: "First make a clear-cut goal, then draw a mental picture, vivid and graphic"[44] to "visualize success."[45] Then "incubate" it into reality, and finally "speak" it into existence through "the creative power of the spoken word."[46]

Unfortunately, Copeland and Cho are not the only Faith teachers whose theology can be traced to the world of the occult.[47] Benny Hinn, during one of his appearances on TBN's *Praise the Lord* program, appealed directly to the story of a witch in discussing the "power of the spoken word":

> I had a witch tell me this . . . She said, "You know that we are taught in witchcraft how to kill birds with words and how to kill people with our mouth . . . We were taught with words to bring disease on—on men . . . by speaking certain words that defeat them." She can actually cause sickness that could very well kill . . . She said, "With words, I used to kill birds. I used to kill birds." She said she would speak to a bird, and the bird would drop dead . . . I said, "Dear God, I didn't know the devil has such power." And the Lord spoke to me, and He said, "The devil can kill with words, then you with your words can bring life." And it just come [*sic*] and clicked inside of me, brother . . . And we Christians don't realize the power in our mouths.[48]

It is precisely because their teachings are unbiblical that Faith teachers are forced to appeal to both witchcraft as well as twisted interpretations of Scripture.

PERVERTING PROVERBS

One of the Faith teachers' favorite tactics is the abuse of Proverbs 18:21 ("Death and life are in the power of *the tongue*: and they that love it shall eat the fruit thereof" [KJV, emphasis added]) to prove that the Bible teaches positive confession.[49] While it is clear from Scripture that the tongue can have a devastating impact on another person, there is no biblical support for the idea that our confessions have the power to create reality.[50] Only God is capable of such a feat.

If God could be controlled through positive confessions, He would be reduced to the status of a cosmic servant subject to the formulas of faith. You would be God and He would be your bellhop! You would sit on the throne of a universe centered around your own ego. And you would wind up with a puny view of God and a bloated view of man.

But Charles Capps claims that God Himself told him, "You are under an attack of the evil one and *I can't do anything about it. You have bound me* by the words of your own mouth."[51]

Frederick Price seemed to be operating on the same wavelength when he hammered home the false teaching that God is a puppet whose strings are controlled by humanity:

> Now this is a shocker! But God has to be given *permission* to work in this earth realm on behalf of man . . . Yes! *You are in control!* So, if man has control, who no longer has it? God . . . When God gave Adam dominion, that meant God no longer had dominion. So, God cannot do anything in this earth unless *we let* Him. And the way we let Him or give Him permission is through prayer.[52]

ERROR BEGETS ERROR

The formulas of faith first popularized in earnest by Hagin and Copeland all fixate on the notion that words create reality. As Creflo Dollar puts it, "There is no such thing as deliverance in this physical, natural realm aside from your mouth. Your mouth is connected to your life. Death and life is in the power of the tongue."[53]

What is increasingly bizarre is the way in which prosperity preachers attempt to biblicize their formulas. Dollar not only instructs his devotees to speak to their debt but uses Scripture as the basis for asserting that "if you don't speak to the debt, debt gonna talk to you." In evidence, Dollar has Jesus speaking to a fig tree and the fig tree speaking back to Jesus:

> Jesus spoke to a thing. He spoke to a fig tree. The Bible says, "He answered it and said," so obviously the fig tree must have been saying something to Him. It had leaves on it, but it didn't have no figs on it. And Jesus showed up hungry, and the fig tree said, "I bet you think I've got some figs on me, but I ain't got no figs on me, and I know you're hungry because I see you shaking, but I ain't got no figs on me. You still going to be hungry." Jesus answered it and said, "Well then, no man will eat fruit of thee hereafter." See, things will talk to you.[54]

Like Dollar, Todd Bentley instructs devotees to take dominion over pain, sickness, and even death through formulaic utterances. Says Bentley, "I want you to put your hand on the part of your body that needs to be healed, and I want you to take dominion in your own body. I want you to take dominion in your own temple right now. I want you to command sickness to leave you right now. I want you to command every disease to come out of your body. I want you to take authority. I want you to speak the word. I want you to speak the healing word."[55]

Like Dollar and Bentley, Joel Osteen attempts to convince followers that the formula of faith is as easy as one, two, three. First, you have to speak it; second, you have to demonstrate that you believe it by repeating what you say again and again; and third, you will receive what you say. Osteen summarizes the formula as follows: "I want to speak to you today about the importance of speaking faith-filled words over your life. Words are like seeds. They have creative power. When we speak something out we give life to what we're saying. It's just like we're planting that seed. And if we say it long enough eventually we're going to reap a harvest."

Like the makers of prescription drugs, Osteen adds a warning with respect to the misuse of the faith formula. Says Osteen, "We're going to get exactly what we're saying. And this can be either *good or it can be bad*."[56]

7

FAITH OF GOD

Now, God used faith substance to make everything that He made . . .
in every one of those words they were filled with faith substance, because
words are nothing but containers . . . every time God speaks, He can't help
but to speak words that are filled with faith . . . God's guts are called
faith stuff . . . Everything in Him is faith . . . What's in His heart is faith . . .
if you were to cut God open you'd see nothing but faith. Every time He opens
His mouth now, He automatically fills those words with His faith material.[1]

—CREFLO DOLLAR

Nothing is more crucial to our concept of faith than a proper understanding of the nature of God. In fact, the very word *theology* is derived from the Greek words *theos*, which means "God," and *logos*, which means "word" or "discourse." Thus, theology is a discourse on God.

In Christian theology, God is portrayed as the Sovereign of the universe. He is described as "spirit," perfectly wise, self-sufficient, omnipotent, and omniscient.

Not so in the cultic theology, of the Faith movement. In these dreary environs, God is nothing but a "faith being."[2] Man, conversely, is deemed to be sovereign. Indeed, God is portrayed as a pathetic puppet at the beck and call of His creatures.

The Faith god has height and weight;[3] he is called a failure;[4] he is bound by the laws of the spirit world and is dependent on the force of faith.[5] This god is impotent rather than omnipotent, limited rather than infinite and omniscient. In other words, the god of the Faith movement is not God at all.

How do the Faith teachers strip God of His omnipotence and rob Him of His omniscience?—by leading the unsuspecting into thinking that the Bible itself substantiates their flawed theology. Showing little originality, Faith teachers pull the same rabbits out of similar hats. The rabbits are Mark and Hebrews; the hats are of varying hues.

MR. HOLMES, I PRESUME?

For just a moment imagine that you are Sherlock Holmes. You have been called upon to solve the mystery of how so many millions of people can be misled into thinking that Mark 11:22 proves that God has faith and is thus a faith being. What will you do?

After carefully considering the options, you decide to begin by paying a visit to Kenneth Copeland, the man dubbed by *Time* magazine as "the chief exponent" of the Faith message.[6] Using all the tools of the trade, you finally succeed in arranging a meeting with Copeland. Upon arrival you get right down to business. You ask him how, in his opinion, Mark 11:22 provides indisputable evidence that God is a faith being. Copeland assures you that it's all really very elementary. Turning to Mark 11:22 in his *Kenneth Copeland Reference Edition of the Holy Bible* (KJV), Copeland, in an authoritative tone, begins to read: "And Jesus answering, saith unto them, 'Have faith in God.'" He looks up from the text and triumphantly says, "There you have it—undeniable proof that God has faith."

"But Reverend Copeland," you ask, "I'm not sure I understand. How do you get from 'have faith in God' to 'God has faith'?"

"Well," says Copeland, "all you need to do is look at this little note I've added to the Bible. See, right here it says, 'Or, Have the faith of God.'[7] Get it?"

"Well, I'm not so sure."

"You don't have to take my word for it," quips Copeland. "You can check the writings of some of the most anointed men alive today. In fact, let me jot down the titles of a few books that will prove beyond a shadow of a doubt that God has faith." Feeling much better, you thank Copeland for the list and bid him farewell.*

On the way back to the office, you stop at your local Christian bookstore

---

* While this conversation with Copeland is imaginary, the substance of everything he is represented as saying is amply documented.

to check out the leads provided by Copeland. Hunting down the books on Copeland's list, you sit down in the back of the store and begin to read. Scarcely two pages into a booklet titled *God's Creative Power*, by Charles Capps, you find just what you are looking for. There you read the words "A more literal translation [of Mark 11:22] is 'Have the God kind of faith, or faith of God . . . God is a *faith* God."[8]

The very next book—*How Faith Works*, by a Frederick K. C. Price— confirms both Copeland and Capps by appealing to the original Greek text.[9] You think, *Maybe Copeland is onto something.* Quickly you open the last book on Copeland's list, *Bible Faith Study Course*, by Kenneth Hagin, and discover that Hagin not only agrees that God has faith but points out that this is precisely what is taught by "Greek scholars."[10]

This is really interesting, you think. Apparently these men have stumbled onto a truth that has escaped the notice of orthodox Christian scholars for the last two thousand years.

While making your way back home, you slowly begin toying with the idea of stopping by the library of a nearby seminary to check out what the Greek scholars have written on the subject. It's only a few blocks away, you reason. But after a brief deliberation, you change your mind.

Surely no one would put his neck on the chopping block by claiming that his position is backed by scholars when it actually isn't. That would be too brazen. Would anyone actually do something as reckless as that?

Upon further thought, however, you decide to check it out. Realizing you may be in the library for quite some time, you breathe an exaggerated sigh and roll up your sleeves. It's one thing to pretend you're Sherlock Holmes; it's quite another to assume the role of a Greek grammarian. Nevertheless, you charge ahead.

Finding a Greek-to-English New Testament,[11] you look up Mark 11:22. There you discover that the original text reads *echete pistin theou* (pronounced "eck-ke-te pis-tin thay-u"). You discover that *echete* means "have," *pistin* means "faith," and *theou* means "of God."

Scratching your head, you think, *Well, perhaps the Faith teachers are correct.* But why then do all the major English versions of Scripture translate this phrase as "have faith in God" and not "have the faith of God"?

Now completely perplexed, you decide it's time to call in the experts. Unlike an amateur, you know your limits!

A. T. ROBERTSON TO THE RESCUE

After some investigation, you decide to start by examining the works of a man named A. T. Robertson, who appears to be almost universally accepted as the final word on Greek grammar. Still nervous about trying to understand Greek, you begin by looking at a book with the friendly title *Word Pictures in the New Testament*.

Flipping through it, you arrive at page 361. There it is, halfway down the page! *Echete pistin theou*, says Robertson, "is translated 'have faith in God.'" Robertson explains that this is the correct translation because *theou* is what he calls an "objective genitive."[12]

But now you're really in hot water. You don't have the foggiest idea what an "objective genitive" is.

And so the search continues.

After several hours you end up in one of Robertson's weightier books, *A New Short Grammar of the Greek Testament*. There, on page 227, he explains what he means by subjective and objective genitives. To your great delight, he even uses Mark 11:22 to illustrate his lesson.

In essence, Robertson says an *objective* genitive means that the noun (in this case, *theou*) is the *object* of the action. So, in Mark 11:22, God is the *object* of faith. This requires that the passage be translated "Have faith in God."

You quickly reason that for the Faith teachers to be correct, a *subjective* genitive is needed. In that case God would be the *subject* of faith and the text should read "the faith of God."

But Robertson insists that such a translation is preposterous. "It is *not* the faith that *God has*," he writes, "but the faith of which *God is the object*."[13]

Because you want to be completely fair, you determine that regardless how much A. T. Robertson is revered as a Greek grammarian, you need a second opinion. Thus you spend days looking through the works of other Greek grammarians. You consult H. E. Dana, Julius R. Mantey, William Douglas Chamberlain, Curtis Vaughan, Virtus E. Gideon, James Hope Moulton, and Nigel Turner, among others.

To your amazement, the conclusion is always the same: The experts who have given their lives to the study of Greek grammar are unanimous in their opinion that Copeland and his cohorts are in error. Contrary to their assertions, their perversions find no basis in the original Greek![14]

This fictitious illustration aside, it doesn't take a detective to determine whether Faith teachers are misleading devotees. In order for their rendering of Mark 11:22 to be accurate, they would have to violate more than one principle of biblical interpretation. A Faith reading of the text dethrones God as Sovereign of the universe and makes Him subject to the impersonal laws of faith.

HACKING APART HEBREWS

As with Mark 11:22, Faith teachers twist Hebrews 11:3 in an attempt to remake God into a faith being. If you've watched Christian television, you have no doubt heard them breezily proclaim that Hebrews 11:3 tells us that God, by His faith, created the world and is thus a faith being.

What do you do when you hear such a thing? You follow the biblical injunction to test everything by the Word of God (Acts 17:11). In doing so, you discover that the text says nothing of the sort. In fact, rather than saying that God *by His faith created the world*, Hebrews 11:3 says that *we by faith understand that God created the world!*

The Faith teachers have absolutely no excuse for their twisting of Hebrews 11:3. The English rendering of the text is so utterly clear that there is no need to consult the Greek. Just look at the sentence construction in Hebrews 11. It says:

By faith Moses . . . chose to be mistreated. (vv. 24–25)
Who chose to be mistreated? Moses chose to be mistreated!

By faith Isaac blessed Jacob. (v. 20)
Who blessed Jacob by faith? Isaac blessed Jacob by faith!

By faith Abraham . . . obeyed. (v. 8)
Who obeyed by faith? Abraham obeyed.

By faith Noah . . . built an ark. (v. 7)
Who built an ark by faith? Noah built an ark by faith.

By faith Abel offered. (v. 4)
Who offered by faith? Abel offered by faith.

By faith we understand. (v. 3)

Who understands by faith? We understand by faith.

Far from teaching us that God, by His faith, created the world, the text clearly states that *we by faith understand that God created the world!* The parallel construction here clearly rules out the spin Faith teachers put on the passage.

Faith disciples believe so strongly that God is a faith being that Zoe College, where such Faith teachers as Drs. Benny Hinn and Ken Copeland got their degrees, actually teaches course MN204, titled "The God Kind of Faith."[15]

The Bible makes it clear, however, that God could never be a faith being. A being who must exercise faith is limited in both knowledge and power, since faith lies in the region of non-absolute certainty and control. If God had to have faith, He would be dependent upon something outside of Himself for knowledge or power. And that is clearly unthinkable.

The Bible portrays God as the One who sees all and knows all from all eternity and who wields supreme and absolute authority. He has no need of faith.

You cannot read very far in the Bible without bumping up against statements such as the one in Psalm 115:3, which obliterates the notion that God is limited in any way: "Our God is in heaven; he does whatever pleases him." *All right*, you answer, *but is His sphere of influence somehow restricted?* Better think again: "The LORD does whatever pleases him, in the heavens and on the earth, in the seas and all their depths" (Psalm 135:6).

Any talk of limiting God not only is antibiblical but also provokes God's wrath! Psalm 50 is one of the strongest statements in Scripture concerning the self-sufficiency and omnipotence of God—and the Lord Himself makes it clear in this psalm what He thinks about those who would shrink His reign: "You thought I was altogether like you. But I will rebuke you and accuse you to your face. Consider this, you who forget God, or I will tear you to pieces, with none to rescue (vv. 21–22)."

A PRISONER OF IMPERSONAL LAWS

Critics of Faith theology have often referred to its God as the impersonal God of the metaphysical cults. The Faith teachers present a personal God in principle, but in practice they teach a metaphysical God. This God cannot operate outside the universal laws by which even He is governed. Copeland, for example, insists that "God cannot do anything for you apart or separate from faith."[16] The reason is that "*faith is God's source of power.*"[17]

In Copeland's theology, even Jesus Christ was produced as a direct result of the faith of God. In unmistakable terms, he portrays God's positive confession as the force that produced Jesus Christ: "God began to release His Word into the earth. He began to paint a picture of a Redeemer, a man who would be the manifestation of His Word in the earth."[18]

Predictably, Copeland is not alone in propagating this perversion. Charles Capps says, "It was an act of the God-kind-of-faith that caused the miraculous conception."[19] Attributing his remarks to the Holy Spirit, he continues: "Mary received the Word sent to her by the angel and conceived *it* in the womb of her spirit. Once *it* was conceived in her spirit [note the repeated use of the word "it"], *it* manifested itself in her physical body."[20] He goes on to say, "The embryo in Mary's womb was nothing but the pure word of God—and it took flesh upon itself."[21] Capps concludes his heretical remarks by saying, "Jesus Christ was born of a virgin through the miraculous conception of faith—the God-kind of faith."[22]

With a single stroke of the pen, Capps corrupts the miraculous *conception* of Jesus Christ into a miraculous *confession*. If this isn't heresy, what is?

But the Faith teachers do not stop here. Not only do they teach that Christ was born of the faith of God, but you, too, are born of this faith! As Copeland puts it, "God is a faith being. You are born of God. You are a faith being. God does not do anything outside of faith. With His faith living in you, you are to operate the same way."[23]

It's all a matter of faith. Faith is the force; words are the containers of the force; faith formulas operate the spiritual laws of the universe. These spiritual laws in turn command and control the pathetic God of the Faith movement.

In Faith theology, it is not God who reigns supreme; the real heroes of the faith are those who learn to work in harmony with the force of faith—and all of this is "sanctified" through the use of the name of Jesus. Jesus is the MasterCard that will allow you to charge to your heart's content. The only credit limit is the extent of your own faith. As Fred Price puts it, "If you have bicycle faith, all you're gonna get is a bicycle."[24] If you have Rolls Royce faith, you, like Price, can drive a Rolls.

Hagin and his imitators loudly proclaim themselves to be the giants of such faith formulas. Hagin actually boasted that he had not *"prayed one prayer in 45 years . . . without getting an answer. I always got an answer—and the answer was always yes."*[25]

So what are we to say of those whose prayers go unanswered? What are we to think of someone such as Joni Eareckson Tada, who for years begged God to raise her from her wheelchair—and yet remains a quadriplegic? And how are we to judge a man like Job, who suffered terribly and yet was called a righteous man?

ERROR BEGETS ERROR

Having researched the rhetoric and writings of Word of Faith proponents for some two decades, I am astounded at how things inevitably go from bad to worse. In a 2008 release titled *8 Steps to Create the Life You Want*, Creflo Dollar blatantly hands humans prerogatives that belong to God alone. As Dollar pontificates, God "has given us the same creative power that He possesses to speak things into existence (Proverbs 18:20–21; Mark 11:23). Just as God's words created the world, His Word spoken from your mouth should also be the starting point for everything you do."

Of course, as we have seen, Mark 11:23 says nothing of the sort. And neither does Proverbs 18:20–21. Our tongues can have a devastating impact on another person, but Solomon does not even hint at the notion that our tongues have the creative power of God.

Nor is there any warrant to suggest, as Dollar does, that God has faith. Yet despite clear biblical evidence to the contrary that has been presented in this chapter, Dollar declares that "God's guts are called faith stuff . . . if you were to cut God open you'd see nothing but faith. Every time He opens His mouth now, He automatically fills those words with His faith material."[26]

While one would hope and pray that Faith preachers would forgo what they must surely know by now is a blatant twist of the text, Mark Chironna peers into the cameras of the largest Christian television conglomerate on the planet and says, "When Jesus says in Mark 11 *have the faith of God*, He's really saying think the way your Father thinks. And then once you hear something in the Spirit, speak it with your mouth as the Father thinks and Son speaks and then the Spirit takes what you say and begins to reorder your world to line up with your faith!"[27]

Regrettably, the television audience responded with thunderous applause.

8

FAITH HALL OF FAME

"For the thing which I greatly fear comes upon me, and that which I am afraid befalls me" (Job 3:25). Fear is a terrible emotion—a self-fulfilling one. Job had fears concerning his children and finally reached a place in his life where he saw his fears coming to pass. The Bible says it will be unto us as we believe (see Matthew 9:29). That principle works in the negative as well as the positive. We can receive by fear as well as by faith.[1]

—JOYCE MEYER

Well, how about it? Who do you think should be inducted into the Faith Hall of Fame? When it's time to cast the ballot, who will you select? I'd like to suggest that you consider Job. The question you must answer is this: Does Job indeed belong in the Faith Hall of Fame along with such luminaries as Abraham, Isaac, and Jacob? Or was Job carnal and faithless, a man whose propensity for negative confessions created his own tragic downfall?

Before you vote, consider what best-selling author Benny Hinn has to say. Hinn claims that Job's troubles came on him because he spoke words of fear and made accusations against God. Hinn describes Job as "carnal" and "bad," asserting that Job's "mouth was his biggest problem." In essence, Hinn says that Job tapped into the negative side of the force through his voluminous negative confessions.[2]

In order for the Faith message to flourish, Job has to fall. And fall he does—but not through some great moral failure of his own doing. Rather, he is tripped up by a smear campaign, a campaign in which Hinn recklessly caricatures Job as one of the great faith failures of all time.

Of course, Hinn must ignore the clear context of Scripture to deliver his diatribe against Job. When God calls Job upright, Hinn calls him carnal. When God calls Job good, Hinn calls Job bad. When God says that Job had spoken right, Hinn says Job made a negative confession. Several times in the first two chapters of Job, God makes it clear that Job was blameless and upright, that he feared God and shunned evil (Job 1:1, 8; 2:3). In fact, the Lord even declared to Satan, "There is no one on earth like" Job (1:8; 2:3).

Despite this divine commendation, Hinn persists in blasting Job. In one of the most horrifying scenes I have ever witnessed on Christian television, Hinn not only vilified Job for his lack of faith but also denounced one of the greatest statements of faith ever uttered in the midst of tragedy.

Despite the somber warning of Proverbs 30:6 ("Do not add to his words, or he will rebuke you and prove you a liar."),[3] Hinn *adds* the word "never" to the text in Job 1:21 and thus completely reverses the meaning of the passage. Encouraged by his audience, Hinn sniggers, "You know what? We've said this a million times, and it's not even scriptural—all because of Job: The Lord giveth, and the Lord taketh away. Blessed be the name of the Lord' [see Job 1:21]. I have news for you: that is not Bible; that's not Bible. The Lord giveth and *never* taketh away. And just because he said, 'Blessed be the name of the Lord,' don't mean that he's right. When he said, 'Blessed be the name,' he was just being religious. And being religious don't mean you're right."[4]

Hinn's outburst is not unique. Long before Hinn bludgeoned Job, men like Copeland,[5] Capps,[6] Savelle,[7] Crouch,[8] and a host of others had done the same thing.

Not only do these Faith teachers alter the passage to read precisely the opposite of what is recorded in the Bible, but they ignore the fact that the very next verse in Scripture commends Job with the following words: "In all this, Job did not sin by charging God with wrongdoing" (v. 22).

Job steadfastly refused to curse his Creator in the midst of some of the most profound pain imaginable. He had been selected as the subject for a stern test of faith because he was indisputably the greatest man of faith alive. God declared that Job's faith was real faith. Satan claimed that Job's faith was fickle. Take away Job's possessions, the evil one suggested, and Job's faith will disappear as well.

As Scripture reveals, Job not only passed the test of faith with flying colors but also demonstrated the remarkable depth of his faith when he uttered these unforgettable words: "Naked I came from my mother's womb, and naked I will depart. The LORD gave and the LORD has taken away; may the name of the LORD be praised" (v. 21). Rather than cursing God, as his wife had goaded him to do (2:9), or blaming his tragedy on secret sin, as his cruel companions urged him to do (11:1–6), Job placed his fate in the hands of a God who is both infinitely just and infinitely merciful.

Job's friends—like their descendants Hinn and the Faith teachers—declare that Job had sinned and thus deserved the calamities that befell him. Eliphaz the Temanite, like Robert Tilton, boasted of having religious authority and mysterious visions; Bildad the Shuhite, like several Faith teachers, was fond of uttering clever clichés; and Zophar the Naamathite, like the modern-day name-it-and-claim-it teachers, believed that Job's calamities were the result of secret sin. All of these "comforters" clung to the belief that sickness and suffering were the result of secret sin or negative confessions. Yet God steadfastly confirmed Job as blameless and upright.

Zophar was the least tactful of those who directly accused Job. He constantly repeated the refrain, "Job, you are being punished because of your own sin." Job knew, however, that his calamities somehow formed a part of God's sovereign plan. Like the apostle Paul, Job believed that "in all things God works for the good of those who love him, who have been called according to his purpose" (Romans 8:28).

The book of Job builds an airtight defense for Job's faith. Who can forget Job's unwavering utterance of faith, "Though he slay me, yet will I hope in him" (13:15)? This singular statement proved the depth of his reliance on God. He cherished his faith above even his life. His eternal perspective is enshrined forever in his words "I know that my Redeemer lives, and that in the end he will stand upon the earth" (19:25).

Indeed, the greatest demonstration of faith is trusting God even when you do not understand. How is it possible for Hinn to miss the central theme of the book of Job? Not only does God make us privy to His conversations with Satan, but He also demonstrates that He permits suffering in the lives of His saints in order to purify and conform them to His will and purpose.

When all is said and done, God commands everyone to cease their ignorant blatherings (chapters 38–41). Speaking out of the storm in a speech dripping with divine sarcasm, God asks Job and his friends if they could comprehend the vast expanses of the earth (38:18). His majestic words sweep across the face of the earth and powerfully proclaim His sovereignty over both His creatures and His creation. At the end of His speech, God condemns Job's friends and instructs them to seek out Job's prayer for their forgiveness (42:8–9).[9] Finally, God commends Job because Job has "spoken of me what is right" (v. 7).

Given this evidence, how do you vote? Does Job make it into the Faith Hall of Fame? Or is he a shameful example of negative confession?

The only verdict can be for the induction of Job into the Faith Hall of Fame. Those who besmirch Job's character—including his friends and the Faith teachers—belong in their own Faith Hall of Shame.

The truth is that the characteristics necessary for induction into the Faith Hall of Fame have little or nothing to do with those being touted by the Faith teachers. Faith, far from being a magical force conjured up through pat formulas, is the sort of confidence in God exemplified by Job as he persevered in the midst of affliction, trusting God despite the whirlwind that blew his life into oblivion. True faith is perseverance in the midst of the storm. True faith is the trait most demonstrated in the life of the apostle Paul, who not only fought the good fight but finished the race and kept his faith. Paul's faith, like that of Job, was fixed not on the temporary circumstances of life but on the Author and Finisher of faith, on Christ Himself (Hebrews 12:2).

The Faith Hall of Fame will surely not be bedecked with the glitz and glamour of those who mock the biblical concept of faith. Rather, it will be filled with the men and women who follow in the train of those who willingly gave their lives in service to the King of kings. Those, who like Gideon, Barak, Samson, Jephthah, David, Samuel, and the prophets, through faith conquered kingdoms; who have been tortured, jeered, and flogged; chained and put in prison; stoned and put to death; destitute; persecuted and mistreated, yet were commended for their faith—because their faith was fixed not on circumstances but on God.

Rest assured that Job was a true hero of faith. In fact, it appears that God thought highly enough of Job's faith to mention it elsewhere, besides in the book bearing his name. Twice in the book of Ezekiel he is lifted up, along with Noah and Daniel, as a man of uncompromised integrity and faith (14:14, 20). And who can forget the words of James, who commended Job for patience and perseverance in the midst of pain and suffering (James 5:11)?

Ironically, Hinn is snared by his own words when he ends his tirade against Job with this statement: "Every wrong confession comes from hell. That's what the Bible says. When you say something that disagrees with the Word of God you are literally being controlled by hell."[10] Thus Hinn is hung on the gallows of his own words. For in disagreeing with the clear teaching of Scripture, he is indeed "literally being controlled by hell."

The biblical Job blazed a trail of faith for all of God's people who would follow—those who, like Joni Eareckson Tada, have learned that true faith does not necessarily equip someone to arise from a wheelchair but rather prepares him or her to use adversity as a means of bringing men and women into the kingdom. The real tragedy is not paraplegia or even dying young. The real tragedy is living a long, robust life and failing to use it for the glory of God. No doubt Joni would rather endure tragedy and pain for a season if, through her suffering, by God's grace she could influence the eternal destiny of millions.

One day soon, health and wealth will matter little. All that will concern you is for the Lord Jesus Christ Himself to turn to you and say, "Well done, good and faithful slave. You were faithful with a few things, I will put you in charge of many things; enter into the joy of your master" (Matthew 25:21 NASB).

ERROR BEGETS ERROR

In recent years, prosperity preachers have continued their unmerciful assault on one of the greatest faith heroes in biblical history. Joyce Meyer, for one, crassly implicates Job in the tragic deaths of his ten beloved children. Without so much as a modicum of compassion, she charges him with bringing about their deaths as a self-fulfilling prophecy. Says Meyer, "Fear is a terrible emotion—a self-fulfilling one. Job had fears concerning his children and finally reached a place in his life where he saw his fears coming to pass." Meyer piles on further by misusing the words of the Master. "The Bible says" she intones, "'It will be unto us as we believe' (Matthew 9:29). That principle works in the negative as well as the positive. We can receive by fear as well as by faith."[11]

Contrary to Meyer, Job, like the blind men in Matthew 9, personified genuine faith. Far from feeling that faith was a force, they understood that it was the object of their faith that rendered faith faithful. Like Hinn, Meyer would be well served to reread stirring biblical accounts of Job's unwavering affirmations of faith—and that in the midst of a storm that threatened to blow his life into oblivion. Perhaps, she should revisit Ezekiel's stirring characterization of Job's faithfulness as a standard bearer for her own faith. Or—why not?—demonstrate compassion and mercy by reflecting on the well-worn words of James, the half brother of Jesus, who—writing to Jewish Christians in the Diaspora—identifies none other than Job as the supreme example of the kind of perseverance that leads to spiritual maturity. Indeed, as James makes clear, it is righteous living in the midst of trials and temptations that ultimately demonstrates genuine trust in the One who holds all things together by His majesty and power.

As much as we may wish otherwise, the scandalizing of biblical saints by prosperity preachers such as Meyer is not relegated to Job. The notorious John Hagee, has gone as far as to impugn Thomas for embracing doubt in place of faith. Incredibly, he pontificates that "the accomplishments of Thomas were very meager because he embraced doubt instead of faith in Jesus Christ." As such, he dubiously places the faith of those who follow his formulas above that of "Doubting Thomas." Hagee's rhetoric in this regard is as revealing as it is revolting:

> Doubting Thomas saw all of these miracles, and yet when Christ went though His trial, Thomas instantly doubted that Jesus was the Son of God. Even after the other disciples had seen the risen Lord, Thomas said, "Unless I see His hands and the print of the nail . . . I will not believe" (John 20:25).
>
> Thomas deserved the nickname "Doubting Thomas," and he's been known by that name throughout the ages. *His accomplishments were very meager because he embraced doubt instead of faith in Jesus Christ. He definitely had an attitude problem . . .*
>
> Doubting Thomas, who lived with Jesus, who ate with Him, who touched Him, and who prayed with Him *accomplished virtually nothing.*[12]

On the face of it, it is simply outrageous to suggest that Thomas accomplished "virtually nothing." The very fact that Hagee castigates Thomas as one who was with Jesus when the Master raised Lazarus from the dead is outrageous. What he conveniently fails to divulge is that in this very passage the apostle John singles out Thomas as a disciple who was willing to die in Judea at the hands of stone throwers (John 11:16). Furthermore, far from accomplishing "virtually nothing," Thomas's confession, "my Lord and my God," is one of the most profound proclamations of Christ's divinity in the whole of Scripture. As such, N. T. Wright rightly identifies Thomas's declaration as "the fullest confession of faith anywhere in the whole Gospel."[13] By it, no doubt, millions, like Thomas, have hailed Christ as Savior and Lord. Moreover, Thomas is almost universally revered as the disciple who brought the gospel to such faraway places as India.[14]

Tragically, as we will now see, the hubris that it took to castigate heroes of the faith like the Old Testament Job and the New Testament Thomas is dwarfed by the propensity of prosperity preachers to see themselves as having the very nature of God.

part three

LITTLE GODS

I said, "You are 'gods;'
you are all sons of the Most High."
But you will die like mere men;
you will fall like every other ruler.[1]

—GOD, PRESIDING IN THE ASSEMBLY OF "GODS"

Years ago I heard the story of a young boy named David who was busily engaged in building the castle of his dreams.[2] This was not going to be just an ordinary castle; this was going to be the most magnificent sand castle ever built.

David labored long and hard. He worked from the early hours of the morning through the heat of the noonday sun. Gradually his sand castle began to take shape. He crafted a magnificent moat to protect the castle from "invaders." He forged huge fortresses with flying buttresses. And he built tall, stately towers, complete with brightly colored flags that fluttered softly in the gentle ocean breeze.

David became so engrossed in his labor that he failed to notice that the sun was slowly sinking. He was oblivious to the dark clouds forming on the horizon and was blinded to the tide moving inexorably closer and closer.

Finally the inevitable occurred. In the growing crescendo of waves there came that mighty torrent of water that crashed over his carefully crafted moat and flattened the castle of his dreams. David stood there, sand and water dripping from his fingers, looking down in utter disbelief as his magnificent sand castle disappeared into the sand around it. The towers had crumbled, the moat had been overwhelmed, and the flags lay muddied in the sand.

A sad story! But not nearly as sad as the fact that this is an accurate illustration for the era in which we live. Like David, we, too, are busily engaged in building our own dream castles. And like David, we seem blithely unaware of the sinking sun, of the dark clouds overhead, and of the inexorable drawing near of the waves.

No doubt the most destructive wave that has crashed upon the already-eroding sands of our culture is the tidal force that swept America out of the "Piscean Age" (the supposed age of Christianity) and into the so-called Age of Aquarius. Without a single shot being fired, America has been converted to a new religion, a religion in which humankind has promoted itself to godhood. One can scarcely forget Shirley MacLaine's bold proclamation in the television movie *Out on a Limb*: with arms thrust skyward along the shores of Malibu she shouted, "I am God!"

Like MacLaine, New Thought guru Eckhart Tolle has no qualms about identifying humanity by the selfsame words God used to identify His transcendent glory as He spoke from the burning bush. Said Tolle, "The ultimate truth of who you are is not I am this or I am that, but I Am."[3] Deepak Chopra is equally convinced that humans are divine: "We remain unfulfilled unless we nurture the seeds of divinity inside us. In reality we are divinity in disguise, and gods and goddesses in embryo that are contained within us seek to be fully materialized."[4]

Over the past few years, Eastern mysticism and the occult, along with multitudes of cultic groups, have gained an alarming level of credibility in the United States. From the mind sciences to the New Age movement, Americans are constantly bombarded by the idea that "all is one, all is God, and man is God."

One would think that people who profess the name of Christ would be loath to mouth such sentiments. But sadly, this is no longer true. The airwaves are rife with a new cluster of religious teachers who take great delight in proclaiming their own deity, all the while naming the name of Christ. Faith teachers joyfully promote all this and more. In their topsy-turvy universe, man is promoted to deity while God is demoted to servitude; Satan is boosted to God's orbit while Christ crashes to the bowels of the earth.

9

DEIFICATION OF MAN

I'm going to say it again! Prayer is man giving God authority, or God license, to interfere in the affairs of man. In fact, God—I'm going to take a deep breath because some of you religious people aren't going to understand me—Are you ready?—God cannot do anything in the earth without a human's permission![1]

—MYLES MUNROE

Ever since the dawn of time, Satan has tried to peddle the lie that mere men can become gods. His seductive hiss "You will be like God," first heard in Genesis 3, has reverberated across the ages with sensuous frequency. He packages and repackages the lie in whatever size or shape is needed to make it sell. In *The Road Less Traveled*, M. Scott Peck, a psychologist popular in both New Age and Christian circles, puts words into the mouth of the Creator when he writes: "God wants us to become Himself (or Herself or Itself). We are growing toward godhood. God is the goal of evolution."[2]

Well-known witch Margot Adler goes one step further. Quoting the *Whole Earth Catalog*, she says: "We are as gods and might as well get good at it."[3]

Notorious cult leader Rajneesh, who in Poona, India, took on the title Bhagwan Shree (meaning "Sir God"), had the temerity to announce, "When you call Jesus, really you have called me. When you call me, really you have called Jesus."[4]

One would surmise that since "Sir God" is now dead, he is well aware that the distance between himself and Jesus is the distance of infinity.

Then there was Maharishi Mahesh Yogi, of Transcendental Meditation fame, who sabotaged Scripture when he slipped in the word "you" for "I," and proudly proclaimed, "Be still and know that you are God."[5]

And who can forget the infamous Jim Jones, who personally led almost a thousand men, women, and children to violent deaths? This deluded cult leader screeched: "It is written that ye are gods. I'm a god and you're a god. And I'm a god, and I'm gonna stay a god until you recognize that you're a god. And when you recognize that you're a god, I shall go back into principle and will not appear as a personality. But until I see all of you knowing who you are, I'm gonna be very much what I am—God, almighty God."[6]

It is no surprise that such blasphemy should spew forth from witches, Yogis, and murderous madmen. What is shocking, however, is that similar statements are now being voiced by some of the biggest names in the church.

MOVE OVER, GOD

The now-deceased Kenneth Hagin asserted that man "was created on terms of equality with God, and he could stand in God's presence without any conscious-ness of inferiority . . . God has made us as much like Himself as possible . . . He made us the same class of being that He is Himself . . . Man lived in the realm of God. He lived on terms equal with God . . . *[T]he believer is called Christ . . . That's who we are; we're Christ!*"[7]

Kenneth Copeland declares that "God's reason for creating Adam was His desire to reproduce Himself . . . He was not a little like God. He was not almost like God. He was not subordinate to God even."[8]

Televangelist John Avanzini claims that the Spirit of God "declared in the earth today what the eternal purpose of God has been through the ages . . . that He is duplicating Himself in the earth."[9]

Morris Cerullo bellows, "Did you know that from the beginning of time the whole purpose of God was to reproduce Himself? . . . Who are you? Come on, who are you? Come on, say it: 'Sons of God!' Come on, say it! And what does work inside us, brother, is that manifestation of the expression of all that God is and all that God has. And when we stand up here, brother, you're not looking at Morris Cerullo; you're looking at God. You're looking at Jesus."[10]

Creflo Dollar is equally dogmatic: "If the Godhead gets together and say let us make man then what are they producing? . . . They're producing gods . . . You are gods because you came from God and you are gods, you're not just human. The only human part about you is this physical body that you live in."[11]

In one of the greatest Scripture-twisting exhibitions I have encountered to date, Dollar marshalled Philippians 2:5–6 as a pretext for exhorting his devotees to talk themselves into equality with God. Said Dollar, "We're not going to shine as lights 'til we accept our equality with God. We're not gonna shine as lights until we stop thinking that being equal with God is a dishonor and a robbery."[12]

Like Dollar, Meyer is convinced that just as a cow produces little calves, so God produces little gods. Says Meyer, "If you as a human being have a baby, you call it a human kind. If cattle have another cattle, they call it cattle-kind. I mean, what's God supposed to call us? Doesn't the Bible say we're created in His image? Now, you understand, I'm not saying you are God with a capital 'G.'"[13]

And that's just for openers! The language used by Faith teachers sounds strikingly similar to that of recognized cults. As a case in point, Charles Capps says, "God duplicated *Himself* in kind! . . . *Adam was an exact duplication of God's kind!*[14]

Capps's sentiments mirror those of cultist Herbert W. Armstrong, founder of the Worldwide Church of God, who said:

> As God repeatedly reveals, his purpose is to *reproduce* himself into what may well become billions of God persons . . . Why did the Creator God put MAN on the earth? For God's ultimate supreme purpose of *reproducing* himself, of recreating himself.[15]

And these are not isolated statements. The terms *duplicate* and *duplication* consistently appear in the Faith teachers' discourses on humanity, as do the terms *reproduce* and *reproduction*.

TOO RADICAL FOR MORMONS

The Faith teachings have now become so blasphemous and bizarre that even cultists are taking issue with them. For example, Mormon scholar and author Stephen E. Robinson, referring to the Faith teachers, says:

> Now, in fact, the Latter-day Saints [the Mormon church] would not agree with the doctrine of deification as understood by most of these evangelists, for in the LDS view we receive the full divine inheritance only through the atonement of Christ and only after a glorious resurrection.[16]

Robinson realizes the absurdity of the Christian church denouncing the Mormon doctrine that men can one day *become* gods while high-profile teachers within the church are consistently proclaiming that we are *already* gods. It is indeed ironic that a scholar from the Mormon cult would find the Faith movement's little gods doctrine too rich for his blood.

In any case, the Faith movement's little gods doctrine is a classic example of how the biblical view of humankind is oftentimes distorted. Faith teachers take the biblical depiction of man in the image of God and twist it into a monstrosity. When Kenneth Copeland proclaims, "You don't have a god in you; you are one,"[17] and Benny Hinn pronounces, "I am a 'little messiah' walking on earth,"[18] they are communicating rank heresy.

Before examining the Scripture-twisting tactics that have produced the little gods doctrine, some significant clarifications are in order.

SCALING THE LANGUAGE BARRIER

First, it should be pointed out that the phrase *little gods* may be unfortunate, but it is not heretical unless it is intended to convey that man is equal with, or a part of, God. The Eastern Orthodox Church, for example, teaches that Christians are deified in the sense that they are adopted as sons of God, indwelt by the Spirit of God, and brought into communion with God, which ultimately leads to glorification.[19] They do *not* teach that mere humans are reproductions or exact duplicates of God. Thus their doctrine of deification falls within the pale of orthodoxy.

By way of contrast, Faith teachers make it clear that by *little gods* they mean a direct departure from orthodox Christianity—or as they like to put it, "traditional church."

I should also draw a clear distinction between the concept of divinity taught by metaphysical cults—such as New Thought, Christian Science, Unity School of Christianity, Mind Science, and Religious Science—and the doctrine of deification taught by the Faith movement. Occult metaphysics does not teach that we are little gods running around on the earth, as do Faith teachers such as Benny Hinn. Rather, they believe that an impersonal principle or substance called "the Christ Consciousness" or "Divine Mind" permeates reality, thus making everything divine.[20] In essence, occult metaphysics is an odd blend of pantheism (all is God) and pan*en*theism (all is part of God). The Faith movement and the metaphysical cults are similar in that they both proclaim the divinity of man. They are distinct in that Faith teachers reject the concept of an impersonal God permeating creation.

Finally, I should clarify that most Faith teachers, like most Mormons, hold to a distinct brand of polytheism. While teaching the unbiblical concept of many gods, as we will see later, they reserve worship for only three (God the Father, Jesus Christ, and the Holy Spirit). Thus it is more accurate to classify Faith teachers as henotheistic rather than polytheistic.[21]

Let us now turn our attention to the Scripture twisting that has enabled Faith teachers to make their doctrines palatable to tens of thousands of unsuspecting people.

A NEW TWIST ON SCRIPTURE

Faith teachers habitually cite John 10:31–39 as proof positive that humans are indeed little gods. This passage finds Jesus about to be stoned for claiming He is God. He responds to His opponents by referring to Psalm 82:6. In ironic fashion Jesus asks, "Is it not written in your Law, 'I have said you are gods'?" (v. 34). To this the Faith teachers exclaim, "Jesus said it, I believe it, and that settles it—we are little gods!" Or as TBN president Paul Crouch puts it, "I am a little god! Critics, be gone!"[22]

But before we capitulate to the Faith movement's little gods doctrine, let us take a closer look at the Old Testament passage to which Jesus was referring. Should it turn out that the Faith teachers are correct in their interpretation of this passage, Christians owe an apology to the kingdom of the cults. But, of course, no such apology is necessary.

The notion of Jesus teaching the little gods doctrine would carry devastating implications. For starters, it would mean that Christ was confused since He previously taught there is only one God (Mark 12:29; cf. Deuteronomy 6:4). Furthermore, it would mean that the Bible is contradictory, on some occasions professing only one God (Isaiah 43:10; 44:6) and on other occasions declaring that there are many, as do the Mormon scriptures.[23] Finally, it would validate the seductive words of the serpent, who said to Eve, "You will be like God" (Genesis 3:5).

So why, in the face of stoning (John 10:31), does Jesus calmly refer the Jews to Psalm 82? Let's take a look.

PSALM 82

In Psalm 82 we find God holding court in the great assembly. He is pronouncing sentence on judges who were supposed to be defending the weak but were instead showing partiality to the wicked. In language so clear that it cannot be easily misunderstood, He ridicules human judges who have the audacity to think of themselves as gods. In other words, God's message is this: "So you think you're gods, do you? Well, the grave will prove you are *mere men*! When you die, you will forever know the infinite difference between Myself and the mightiest of mortals."

One thing is certain: a literal interpretation of the term *god* in Psalm 82:6 is clearly ruled out by the context. It is hard to miss that this passage opens with a strong denunciation of the injustices perpetrated by the judges of Israel (v. 2). As representatives of God (cf. Exodus 4:15–16; 6:28–7:2), they should have been just; instead, they were dishonest. How unlike God men are!

God states: "I said, 'You are "gods"; you are all sons of the Most High.' But you will die like *mere men*; you will fall like every other ruler" (Psalm 82:6–7, emphasis added). These judges are no different from other men. They are subject to the same weaknesses and frailties. They are indeed very far from being gods—however little—in any literal sense.

To interpret the Hebrew judges' designation as "gods" in a literal fashion is ɔ imply that the nation of Israel believed in the existence of more than one ɔod. Yet even a cursory reading of Scripture reveals precisely the opposite.

BUT AREN'T WE SONS OF THE MOST HIGH?

Before moving on, let's take a moment to consider the phrase *sons of the Most High* in verse 6. Isn't it true that offspring take on the nature of their parents? (As Joyce Meyer puts it, "If cattle have another cattle they call it cattle-kind. I mean, what's God supposed to call us?"[24] Or as Earl Paulk puts it, "Dogs have puppies, and cats have kittens, so God has little gods."[25]) And since we are God's "sons," as the verse says, can't we legitimately call ourselves little gods who have our Father's nature?

One place we can test this hypothesis is in the book of Job. In few other portions of Scripture does God go to such lengths to compare Himself with mankind. He spends four complete chapters at the end of that book demonstrating for Job, in spellbinding detail, the vast difference between puny men and their awesome Creator. As Frederick Buechner so eloquently framed it, "God does not explain, He explodes. He asks Job who he thinks he is anyway. Trying to explain the kind of things Job wants explained would be like trying to explain Einstein to a small-necked clam."[26]

This truth is also a recurring theme in the magnificent book of Isaiah. Any number of passages could be cited, but allow me to quote just one:

> *"You are my witnesses," declares the LORD, "and my servant whom I have chosen, so that you may know and believe me and understand that I am he. Before me no god was formed, nor will there be one after me. I, even I, am the LORD, and apart from me there is no savior. I have revealed and saved and proclaimed—I, and not some foreign god among you. You are my witnesses," declares the LORD, "that I am God. Yes, and from ancient days I am he. No one can deliver out of my hand. When I act, who can reverse it?" (Isaiah 43:10–13)*

Despite all attempts to clarify what should be self-evident to those who set themselves up as the very "anointed of God," the Faith teachers persist in propagating their deadly fantasies. In a conversation with Benny Hinn on the meaning of Psalm 82, Paul Crouch put those who disagree with him in league with the devil: "So those that would put that teaching down, want us to have a beginning and an end. That's Satan, isn't it?" Hinn responded, "Those that put us down are a bunch of morons!" to which Crouch exulted, "Glory to God! Glory to God!"[27]

But if Faith proponents want to take Jesus literally when He makes His ironic statement about men being gods, why not take Him literally when He calls the Pharisees "snakes" (Matthew 23:33)? Clearly, not even evil men are literally snakes—and they most certainly are not little gods.

Though we are "sons" of the Most High, we are sons not by *nature* but by *adoption* (Galatians 4:5–8). Only Christ Himself can be said to have the *nature* of God. Christ is the only begotten, unique, one-of-a-kind (Greek *monogenes*, one generation or nature) Son of God (John 1:14). Only He is truly God by nature (Philippians 2:6; cf. John 1:1; Galatians 4:8).

IN SEARCH OF LITTLE GODS

It may be helpful to point out that John 10 and Psalm 82 are not the only passages in which men are referred to as gods. Moses, for example, was to function as a godlike judge over Pharaoh in Exodus 4:16. In addition, the Israelite judges were called *elohim*, or gods, in Exodus 21 and 22 in that they held the power of life and death over men. But both the immediate and the broader context of Scripture make it clear that neither Moses nor Israel's judges were gods by nature.

Satan is also referred to as a "god" in 2 Corinthians 4:4. Yet surely no one assumes that this means that Satan is an exact duplicate of God.

Despite the clear teaching of Scripture, the Faith teachers continue to espouse their little gods doctrine. In fact, they regularly twist the text in a feeble attempt to support the deity of human beings.

PERVERTING PETER

Asking the uninitiated to turn to 2 Peter 1:4, Faith teachers say that the apostle, under the inspiration of the Holy Spirit, espouses their little gods doctrine.

As Copeland puts it, "Now, Peter said by exceeding great and precious promises you become partakers of the divine nature. All right, are we gods? We are a class of gods!"[28]

The following verses (5–11), however, show that Peter is talking not about Christians becoming God or gods, but about undergoing a *moral* transformation of nature from one that emulates the corruption of the world (v. 4) to one that reflects the character of God (vv. 5–11). In no way can this text be twisted to mean that believers actually take on the essence or nature of God. While redeemed man may reflect the moral attributes of God, he in no way qualifies as an exact duplicate of God.

As Faith teachers must surely know, the very first book of the Bible demolishes the myth that mere men are exact duplicates of their Creator. Nevertheless, they continue to perpetuate their blasphemous theories.

If this Faith doctrine were true, can you imagine what would have happened when Satan tried to seduce Eve? Just picture the scene as Satan slithers up to Adam's partner:

"Eat the apple, sweetie pie, and you will become a god!"

Eve, looking perplexed, responds, "Become? Become? What in the world do you think I am now? I am *a little god!* Satan, be gone!"

Not until the Faith fable is stretched to its illogical conclusion can we catch the full-orbed dimensions of just how flawed and fanciful it really is.

JUMBLING GENESIS

As if assaulting Psalm 82 and twisting 2 Peter 1:4 weren't enough, Faith teachers go on to abuse Genesis 1:26–27 in a pathetic attempt to reposition humanity on a level of equality with God.

In Genesis 1:26 God says, "Let us make man in our image, in our likeness." Charles Capps and Jerry Savelle suggest that the Hebrew word for "likeness" (*demuth*) literally means "an exact duplication in kind."[29]

But this is simply wrong. Ironically, the very word Faith teachers abuse to justify their little gods doctrine refutes this erroneous teaching. Hebrew scholars point out that the word "likeness" (Hebrew *demuth*) defines and limits the other word translated as "image" (Hebrew *tselem*) in Genesis 1:26–27 "to avoid the implication that man is a precise copy of God, albeit miniature."[30]

The Hebrew word for "likeness" simply means similarity or resemblance, not identity.[31] The assertion that we are exact duplicates of God is not only deceptive, but it destroys the distinction between Creator and creation.

It is also clear in the broader context of Scripture that humans do not possess the *divine nature* of God.

First, if we are exact duplicates of God—and we, of course, are men—then God must be a man. But the Bible emphatically states that *God is not a man* (Numbers 23:19; 1 Samuel 15:29; Hosea 11:9).

Furthermore, God Himself often makes statements of incomparability.

How can there be any exact duplicates of God if, as God states in Exodus 9:14, "there is no one like me in all the earth"?

Finally, although we were created in the image of God, we possess none of God's nontransferable or incommunicable attributes—such as self-existence, immutability, eternality, omnipotence, omniscience, omnipresence, and absolute sovereignty. God is *eternal* (Psalm 90:2), but man was *created at a point in time* (Genesis 1:26–31; cf. Job 3; 38:4, 21) and has but a brief mortal existence upon the earth (Job 7).[32] God has *life in Himself* (John 5:26), but man is *dependent on God* to sustain him (Acts 17:28). God is *all-powerful* (Job 42:2),[33] but man is *weak* (1 Corinthians 1:25).[34] God is *all-knowing* (Psalm 147:5; Isaiah 40:13–14), but man is *limited in knowledge* (Isaiah 55:8–9).[35] God is everywhere present (Jeremiah 23:23–24),[36] but humans are confined to *a single space at a time* (Psalm 139:1–12).[37]

Far from being a *reproduction* of God, humanity is more correctly portrayed as a *reflection* of God. That humans are created in God's image simply means that they share, in a finite and imperfect way, the *communicable attributes* of God. Among such attributes are personality, spirituality (John 4:24), rationality, including knowledge and wisdom (Colossians 3:10), and morality, including goodness, holiness, righteousness, love, justice, and mercy (Ephesians 4:24ff).

These attributes in turn give us the capacity to enjoy fellowship with God and to develop personal relationships with one another. They also equip us "to carry out God's will . . . that man tend and rule the creation in such a way that it would come to realize its full potential."[38] Theologian Millard Erickson summed it up nicely when he wrote that "the image of God in humanity comprises those qualities of God which, reflected in man, make worship, personal interaction, and work possible."[39]

THE DOMINION DILEMMA

We should note at this juncture that Genesis *never* depicts humanity as an *autonomous sovereign*, but as a *steward* entrusted with the care of his Creator's creation. The cultural mandate makes it crystal clear that while God has given humanity dominion over some of His earthly creation (Genesis 1:26, 28), humans are still mere mortals and are therefore held responsible for how they handle all that God has assigned them to do.

Faith teachers replace the biblical view of dominion with their unbiblical concept of deification. Benny Hinn gets particularly outrageous in waxing eloquent on the Hebrew meaning of the word for dominion:

> Adam was a super being when God created him. I don't know whether people know this, but he was the first Superman that really ever lived. First of all, the Scriptures declare clearly that he had dominion over the fowls of the air, the fish of the sea—which means he used to fly. Of course, how can he have dominion over the birds and not be able to do what they do? The word "dominion" in the Hebrew clearly declares that if you have dominion over a subject, that you do everything that subject does. In other words, that subject, if it does something you cannot do, you don't have dominion over it. I'll prove it further. Adam not only flew, he flew to space. He was—with one thought he would be on the moon.[40]

Truly, not since Brigham Young of Mormon fame claimed that the sun was inhabited[41] have I heard such bizarre biblical exegesis. If one were to draw out Hinn's comments to their illogical conclusions, not only would Adam be able to fly like a bird, but he would also be able to spin webs like a spider, hibernate like a bear, and photosynthesize like an eggplant!

Hinn has a grossly mistaken understanding of the concept of dominion. The Hebrew verb translated "have dominion" (*radah*, Genesis 1:26, 28) also carries the meanings "rule" and "reign."[42] Contrary to Hinn, to rule or reign (to have dominion over someone or something) does not imply that the ruler possesses the unique abilities of his subjects. The fact that a lion trainer exercises dominion over a lion does not mean that the lion trainer is capable of doing everything the lion does. The point is that the trainer has control (i.e., has dominion) over the lion in that he or she can harness the animal's power and capabilities.

Truth is, the Bible nowhere teaches the little gods doctrine. God is infinitely and eternally exalted above humankind. It is the height of arrogance to think that humans can come close to approximating God in His awesome holiness and majesty. Yet this is precisely what proponents of Faith theology are eager to do.

ERROR BEGETS ERROR

One would hope that Word of Faith proponents would have begun to temper their dogmatism with respect to humans having the nature of God, but as we have seen, such is not the case. Paul Crouch, who presides over the TBN juggernaut, depicts those who deny his little god affirmations as being in league with the prince of darkness. Hinn simply dismisses them as "morons."

The new breed is equally dismissive. With typical bravado Joyce Meyer wonders why anyone would be exercised over the notion that God begets little gods in the fashion that cattle beget cattle. "I mean if cattle have another cattle they call it cattle-kind" she exudes![43]

Myles Munroe minces no words: "You have the same nature as God Himself." Indeed, declares Munroe, "You create your own world the same way God creates His. He speaks and things happen, you speak and they happen."[44] Incredibly, according to Munroe, we license God rather than the other way round. Again, he is emphatic and direct. Says Munroe, "I'm going to say it again! Prayer is man giving God authority, or God license, to interfere in the affairs of man. In fact, God—I'm going to take a deep breath because some of you religious people aren't going to understand me—Are you ready?—God cannot do anything in the earth without a human's permission!"[45]

Jesse Duplantis, who dubs himself the "Ragin' Cajun," has deified humanity to the extent that God now has to obey humankind. In one of Duplantis's many two-way conversations with the Almighty, God explicated the conundrum He was experiencing. Jesse's mother wanted to go to heaven. Jesse wanted her to stay. As such, God told Jesse, "You've got me over a barrel here!" After Jesse reminded God that He would cease to be God should He breach His covenant, God responded in exasperated fashion: "'Listen here! You and your momma gotta get together here.' He [God] said, 'I've got to obey somebody around here.'"[46]

While one might be tempted to think that such alleged conversations are little more than humorous attempts at hyperbole, reality is they are common fare in Faith circles. As we will now see, the pattern is painfully persistent: not only is humanity deified; God is demoted.

10

DEMOTION OF GOD

Why does God say, "Ask of Me"? Why does He say that? Because
He can't do it on His own! He can't get what He wants on His own
because He placed you in authority on this earth. Did you hear me?[1]

—ROD PARSLEY

A s prosperity preachers craft human beings in the image of God, so, too,
they create God in the image of humans. When T. D. Jakes gets done
talking, one is left to wonder whether humans look more like God or
God looks more like humans. Of one thing we can be sure, Jakes is convinced
that humans were created directly out of God. So as to leave no doubt, Jakes
provides an exposition directly from the mouth of the Almighty:

> We were made out of God. When God created Adam, He created him from
> the dust of the earth. He put His mouth on him; blew in him the breath of
> life. He became a living soul. *God said,* "I wanted to see what I looked like,
> so I made you to be in My image. You have My DNA. You are created out
> of Me. You are a derivative of Me. You are My picture in the earth.[2]

Creflo Dollar is equally convinced. As he puts it, "When God made Adam,
all He did was make an exact imprint of His self. He duplicated Himself. He
was the image and from His image came His self. Are you following what I'm
saying? You need to understand you're not some second-class something. You
are an exact duplicate of the image of God."

Like Jakes, Dollar puts words in the mouth of the Almighty. As such he has
God saying, "Let us make another speaking Spirit." In answer to the question
"Where'd the body come in?" Dollar opines, "Here's why he had to have a body.
You cannot have dominion in this physical world without a physical suit."[3] In

other words, from Dollar's perspective, without physical bodies humans could not claim sovereignty over the earth realm.

Ironically, according to Kenneth Copeland, the resemblance between God's "physical suit" and his own is downright uncanny. In fact, the span of God's hand is only a quarter of an inch bigger than Copeland's!

A HUSKY POINT-GUARD

Kenneth Copeland claims that "God is not some creature that stands twenty-eight feet tall, and He's got hands, you know, as big as basketballs. That's not the kind of creature He is." Rather, according to Copeland, God is "a being that is very uncanny, the way He's very much like you and me . . . a Being that stands somewhere around six-two to six-three, that weighs somewhere in the neighborhood of a couple of hundred pounds, little better, [and] has a [hand] span of nine inches across."[4]

Where in the world does Copeland derive this monstrosity from? The answer is that he tortures the words of the prophet Isaiah. When Isaiah, using a common figure of speech, says that God marked off the heavens with His span (40:12), Copeland takes out a ruler, measures the span of his hand, finds it to be eight and three-quarter inches, and speculates that God's hand must be about a quarter of an inch larger than his!

Copeland should know that Isaiah 40:12 cannot be interpreted literally. If it were, Isaiah's words would reduce to absurdity: God would not only have body parts, but He would be holding a basket full of dust and would be weighing mountains on a gigantic set of scales.

BOSOM BUDDIES

Copeland is not the only Faith teacher who wrenches Isaiah 40:12 out of context. Other Faith teachers such as Jerry Savelle do so as well. Mirroring the message of his mentor, Savelle exclaims:

> God is not 437 feet tall, weighing four thousand pounds, and got a fist big around as this room. He's big, but He's not a monster. He measured out

heaven with a nine-inch span . . . The distance between my thumb and my finger is not quite nine inches. So, I know He's bigger than me, thank God. Amen? But He's not some great, big old thing that couldn't come through the door there and, you know, when He sat down, would fill every seat in the house. I don't serve The Glob. I serve God, and I've been created in His image and in His likeness.[5]

Savelle seems oblivious to the fact that Isaiah is using figurative language (cf. 40:2, 5–7, 10–11, 22, 24) to convey the supreme majesty and surpassing greatness of our God (vv. 18, 25–26, 28–29). Rather than reducing God to the dimensions of man, Isaiah goes to great lengths to underscore the difference between the Creator and His creation.

Morris Cerullo, in the manner of Copeland and Savelle, demotes God to the stature of a man. Rather than searching for proof texts, however, he takes a more mystical approach. Alluding to one of his out-of-body experiences, Cerullo says:

As I lay there on the floor in this condition, my spirit was taken out of my body and the next thing I knew, I was in the heavens . . . Suddenly, in front of this tremendous multitude of people, *The Glory of God* appeared. The Form that I saw was about the height of a man six feet tall, maybe a little taller, and twice as broad as a human body with no distinguishing features such as eyes, nose, or mouth.[6]

Benny Hinn takes his stories to an even more fanciful extreme. He not only remakes the Holy Spirit in the image of a man, but he claims to know what the Holy Spirit is wearing. Says Hinn, "I could almost visibly see the Lord, and I could tell you what He was wearing." Jan Crouch, giddy about Hinn's statement, asks, "Was that the Holy Spirit?" Acknowledging that he may get in trouble, Hinn resolutely answers, "Yes."[7]

Hinn also embraces a heresy known as tritheism—the false belief in the existence of three gods. During a sermon broadcast to a potential listening audience of millions, Hinn made the following statement, via "revelation knowledge":

Man, I feel revelation knowledge already coming on me here. Lift your hands. Something new is going to happen here today. I felt it just as I walked down here. Holy Spirit, take over in the name of Jesus . . . God the Father, ladies and gentlemen, is a person, and He is a triune being by Himself, separate from the Son and the Holy Ghost. Say, what did you say? Hear it, hear it, hear it. See, God the Father is a person; God the Son is a person; God the Holy Ghost is a person. But *each one* of them is a *triune* being by Himself. If I can shock you—and maybe I should—there's *nine of them*. Huh, what did you say? Let me explain: God the Father, ladies and gentlemen, is a person with His own personal spirit, with His own personal soul, and His own personal spirit body. You say, "Huh, I never heard that." Well, you think you're in this church to hear things you've heard for the last fifty years? You can't argue with the Word, can you? It's all in the Word.[8]

When questioned about this heretical statement, Hinn responded, "That was a very dumb statement . . . I told my church the very next week that the statement was wrong."[9]

After further prodding, Hinn acknowledged that God had nothing to do with his revelation. Rather, says Hinn, it was something he read somewhere.[10] You might hope that after getting caught red-handed, Hinn would drop this distorted declaration from his repertoire.

Instead, two years after his initial revelation, Hinn again voiced virtually the same sentiment. As he put it, "God the Father, God the Son, and God the Holy Ghost—three separate individuals, one in essence, one in work—and, may I add, each one of them possesses His own spirit-body. You don't like it?"[11]

No, I don't! Why? Because it contradicts the clear teaching of the Bible. The assertion that each member of the Trinity has His own distinct spirit-body implies that there are *three separate and distinct beings*—in other words, *three* Gods. This unbiblical view (tritheism) runs contrary to the whole of Scripture, which affirms one God revealed in three Persons who are eternally distinct.[12]

TRUTH OR TRAVESTY?

At this point you may be tempted to say, "So Hinn, Copeland, and company do say some pretty bizarre things, but let's not make a federal case out of it.

After all, we all have our own heresies. Let's allow Jesus to sort it all out in heaven."

Sounds pretty tolerant, doesn't it? But just remember that while tolerance in personal relationships may be a virtue, tolerance when it comes to truth is a travesty. In this case, those who believe that God is made in the image of man do not believe in the God of Scripture.[13]

A doctrine that shrinks God to the status of man destroys an essential of the historic Christian faith. No one who loves truth should simply look the other way and pretend that the travesty of truth is of little consequence. Once the nature of God is twisted to the extent that it has been by the Faith movement, we have departed Christianity and have headed for the kingdom of the cults. The reality is that the Faith god is no god at all. He is in fact more impotent than the god of Mormonism.

If you find this assertion hard to stomach, consider the following statement by Kenneth Copeland:

> I was shocked when I found out who the biggest failure in the Bible actually is . . . The biggest one in the whole Bible is God . . . Now, the reason you don't think of God as a failure is He never said He's a failure. And you're not a failure till you say you're one.[14]

Adding insult to injury, he says:

> Adam committed high treason; and at that point, all the dominion and authority God had given to him was handed over to Satan. Suddenly, God was on the outside looking in . . . After Adam's fall, God found Himself in a peculiar position . . . God needed an avenue back into the earth . . . God laid out His proposition and Abram accepted it. It gave God access to the earth and gave man access to God . . . Technically, if God ever broke the Covenant, He would have to destroy Himself.[15]

The deity of Faith theology bears little resemblance to the God of the Bible. The minute God is assigned physical qualities such as height and weight, He is by definition not the God of Scripture. As Jesus Himself said, God is spirit (John 4:24; cf. Deuteronomy 4:12).

To assert that God is a failure is to question God's omnipotence. If God is all-powerful, can any circumstance be beyond His control? Is it ever possible to frustrate His sovereign will? Clearly, the answer is a resounding NO! Nothing is too hard for the God of all creation (Jeremiah 32:17, 27), with whom all things are possible (Matthew 19:26).

Nebuchadnezzar found this out the hard way. After exalting himself to the level of God, he was treated to a diet of grass for seven years. But at least he learned his lesson. As such, he had this to say after seven years of exile:

> *[God's] dominion is an eternal dominion; his kingdom endures from gen-*
> *eration to generation. All the peoples of the earth are regarded as nothing.*
> *He does as he pleases with the powers of heaven and the peoples of the*
> *earth. No one can hold back his hand or say to him: "What have you*
> *done?" (Daniel 4:34–35)*

God cannot fail, has not failed, and never will fail. God does not have to negotiate with one of His creatures in order to gain access to His own handiwork. Such an idea denies God's unspeakable power.

Furthermore, the thought of God losing control implies that He was caught off guard, that He overlooked some vital factor that caused Him to be ejected from the pilot's seat.

But that cannot happen to the God of Scripture. Our God is omniscient (Psalm 147:5; Romans 11:33; Hebrews 4:13), and nothing catches Him by surprise (cf. Isaiah 42:9). The god of Copeland may well be a failure dependent upon the beneficence of his creation, but his god is purely imaginary. The God of Scripture is self-existent, transcendent, and invincible; and His knowledge is truly perfect (Job 37:16).

What kind of god cannot even maintain a grip on a changing situation? How can he be taken by surprise and lose control of his own creation? What sort of deity can be evicted from a universe that he himself created, and then rely on mere creatures to reenter that same world? Can any such being be seriously equated with the God of the Bible, whose dominion is an eternal dominion, whose kingdom endures from generation to generation, who does as He pleases with the powers of heaven and the peoples of the earth, and whose hand no one can hold back? There is no comparison. The so-called god of the Faith movement may look like the Faith teachers, but he bears no resemblance to the God of the Bible.

ERROR BEGETS ERROR

The demotion of God is seen not only in the Faith notion that God looks remarkably like Copeland but in the pretext that God cannot do anything in the earth realm apart from the permission of people. Prosperity preacher Rod Parsley is resolute in this regard: "Why does God say, 'Ask of Me?' Why does He say that? *Because He can't do it on His own! He can't get what He wants on His own because He placed you in authority on this earth.*"[16]

Does God say, "Ask of me" (Psalm 2:8) because He can't get what He wants on His own? The presumption makes God chuckle! In the very passage invoked by Parsley, God scoffs at the pretention that a mere mortal can thwart His sovereign rule over the affairs of humankind (Psalm 2:1–7). David puts it plainly, "The Lord has established his throne in heaven, and his kingdom rules over *all*" (Psalm 103:19, emphasis added). Or as the prophet Daniel records, "All the peoples of the earth are regarded as nothing. He does as he pleases with the powers of heaven and the peoples of the earth. No one can hold back his hand or say to him: 'What have you done?'" (Daniel 4:35).

Despite Scriptures such as those referenced above, Faith preachers such as Myles Munroe exhort devotees to *reread* their Bible. In doing so, he is certain that they will be utterly persuaded that God can do nothing apart from the permission of His people:

> I want you to read the Bible again. Some of you have never read it before, but try to read the Bible again and find anywhere in the Bible, listen carefully, where God ever did anything on earth without a cooperation of a human. Find it, doesn't exist. When God wanted to free His people free from Egypt, He had to get a man to help Him. When God wanted to burn and destroy Sodom and Gomorrah, He had to get a man to cooperate. When God wanted to do anything in earth, even to save us, He had to send a human being on earth. Therefore, whatever is done on earth, a human must give God permission to do it.[17]

As Munroe must surely know, nothing could be farther from the truth! As demonstrated above, even a cursory reading of Scripture reveals the unilateral power and province of the Almighty. Perhaps Munroe could learn a lesson from the aforementioned Nebuchadnezzar. After seven years of hanging with the heifers, he raised his eyes toward heaven and acknowledged that far from needing the permission of people, "[God] does as he pleases with the powers of heaven and the peoples of the earth" (Daniel 4:35).

The problem with Munroe, as with prosperity preachers in general, is he has little concept of who God really is. With sanity restored, the mighty monarch of Babylon put it all back into perspective: "Those who walk in pride he is able to humble" (v. 37).

11

DEIFICATION OF SATAN

God's on the outside looking in. He doesn't have any legal entrée into the earth. The thing don't belong to Him. You see how sassy the devil was in the presence of God in the book of Job? God said, "Where have you been?" Wasn't any of God's business. He [Satan] didn't even have to answer if he didn't want to . . . God didn't argue with him a bit! You see, this is the position that God's been in . . . Might say, "Well, if God's running things, He's doing a lousy job of it." He hadn't been running 'em, except when He's just got, you know, a little bit of a chance.[1]

—KENNETH COPELAND

So far we have pointed out that the Faith movement not only deifies man but demotes God. Now it is time to explore a new depth of doctrinal distortion as we examine the Faith teaching regarding the deification of Satan.

According to Faith theology, Satan pulled off the coup of the ages when, in the garden of Eden, he tricked Adam into committing cosmic treason. For the price of a piece of fruit, Adam and Eve sold their godhood to Satan.

Not only did Adam and Eve lose their nature as gods, but they were infused with the very nature of Satan. In one blinding instant, the first man and woman were transformed from divine to demonic, and Satan became the god of this world.

In that fateful moment, Adam and Eve were barred from Eden, God was banished from the earth, and Satan acquired the legal rights to all the earth and her inhabitants.

DEADLY DUALISM

This Faith mythology features an implicit form of dualism: two forces fighting it out for control of the universe, and you never know who is finally going to win. If God had not caught Satan on a technicality, Jesus would have been doomed, humans would have been eternally lost, and Satan would have won the universe! In fact, as we saw previously (chapter 10), the condition was so dire at one point that God faced the possibility of literally having to "destroy Himself."

C. S. Lewis described this type of dualism as "the belief that there are two equal and independent powers at the back of everything, one of them good and the other bad, and that this universe is the battlefield in which they fight out an endless war."[2]

This would be an apt description of what is being taught in Faith circles, but for one interesting twist: the powers behind both forces—God and Satan— are *activated* by words spoken by humans. As Copeland articulates it, "Fear activates Satan the way faith activates God."[3]

Ironically, while this concept is foreign to Scripture, it can be found in such pagan belief structures as Zoroastrianism and Gnosticism. Although Faith teachers are not as blatantly dualistic as are Zoroastrians and Gnostics, by implication they teach that God and Satan are positionally peers.

It is truly difficult to overstate the horrifying implications of such a worldview. If embraced, this concept forever destroys the biblical view of God, who is not only omniscient, omnipotent, self-existent, transcendent, eternal, incomprehensible, invisible, immutable, infinite, perfect in wisdom, and holy, but is also the sovereign Being who orders all things according to the counsel of His own divine will (Ephesians 1:11).

DIVINE, DEMONIC, OR DISTINCTLY HUMAN?

What is particularly strange about Faith theology is that man is portrayed as either divine or demonic. From a practical perspective, there is no such thing as a distinct human nature. Benny Hinn made this clear in a message broadcast worldwide via the Trinity Broadcasting Network. Said Hinn:

God came from heaven, became a man, made man into little gods, went back to heaven as a man. He faces the Father as a man. I face devils as the son of God . . . Quit your nonsense! What else are you? If you say, "I am," you're saying I'm a part of Him, right? Is He God? Are you His offspring? Are you His children? You can't be human! You can't! You can't! God didn't give birth to flesh . . . You said, "Well, that's heresy." No, that's your crazy brain saying that.[4]

Incredibly, Hinn prefaced this sermon by saying, "I'm going to be led by the Holy Ghost today."[5] But the Holy Ghost could not have been speaking through Hinn because there is not a shred of biblical evidence that man is anything but distinctly human. Human beings do not have the nature of a fallen angel, and as we have seen in the previous chapter, they most certainly are not little gods.

Adam's fall into a life of sin, terminated by death, did *not transform* his nature from divine to demonic, but rather *tarnished it*. Even after the Fall, the Bible refers to man as being made in the image of God (Genesis 9:6; 1 Corinthians 11:7; James 3:9). As a result of the Fall, human nature was damaged and distorted, but it was definitely not destroyed.

To borrow Calvin's analogy, the image of God was shattered within man, but like reflections of one's face in a broken mirror, distorted images of God's glory can still be seen within fallen man. While the image of God (*imago Dei*) makes man like God, it does not make him a god.

WILL THE REAL SOVEREIGN OF THE UNIVERSE PLEASE STAND UP?

Faith teachers also persist in making both God and Satan subservient to man in their war for the world. In their view, man was directly responsible for causing God to become the most colossal failure of all time. Remember Kenneth Copeland's assertion that God was the biggest failure of all time?[6] It is almost beyond comprehension that, to the applause of devotees, so-called Christian leaders demote God to the status of a failure. Copeland is even willing to deed ownership of the earth to Satan:

God's on the outside looking in. *He doesn't have any legal entrée into the earth. The thing don't belong to Him.* You see how *sassy* the devil was in the presence of God in the book of Job? God said, "Where have you been?" *Wasn't any of God's business.* He [Satan] didn't even have to answer if he didn't want to . . . God didn't argue with him a *bit*! You see, this is the position that God's been in . . . Might say, "Well, if God's running things He's doing a lousy job of it." *He hadn't been running 'em,* except when He's just got, you know, a little bit of a chance.[7]

Like Copeland, Joyce Meyer is convinced that Adam surrendered dominion and authority over the earth realm to Satan. These are her words:

Through listening to Satan rather than God, Adam surrendered to him the authority to rule the earth that God had originally given to man . . . The devil said, "All dominion and authority over the earth has been turned over to me, and it is mine." Adam had been given a lease to the earth by God, and he turned it over to Satan. In 2 Corinthians 4:4 we read that Satan is the god of this world, or we might say, the god of this world system.[8]

How such rhetoric could be tolerated in the Christian community is beyond me. The Bible nowhere gives dominion and authority over the earth to Satan. Far from being a sovereign power, Satan is but a created being (cf. Psalm 148:2, 5; Colossians 1:16). He is an angel—not a god—and a fallen angel at that, who will one day be cast into the lake of burning sulfur for all eternity (Matthew 25:41; Revelation 20:10). The difference between God and Satan is analogous to the difference between a potter and his clay (cf. Isaiah 29:16; 45:9; 64:8; Jeremiah 18:6). Satan may be described as the prince of *this* (not of *the*) world (John 16:11), but orthodoxy has always affirmed that Satan is a finite creature who is ultimately subject to the will of his infinite Creator (Psalm 103:20–21). As such, Satan is the god of this age in the sense that he is the supreme exemplar of evil, *not* in the sense that he is God's equal. Satan is the *de facto* ruler of all who willingly subject themselves to his masterful deceit. Put another way, if we do not belong to the God of the ages, then we are of Satan—"the god of this age" (2 Corinthians 4:4; 11:3; John 8:42–47).

Moreover, if God had no legal right to interfere in a world supposedly under the control of Satan, how could He have banished Adam and Eve from

Eden or subsequently destroyed the world with the Flood? And how could He still have the audacity to claim that "every animal of the forest is mine, and the cattle on a thousand hills. I know every bird in the mountains, and the creatures of the field are mine . . . The world is mine, and all that is in it" (Psalm 50:10–12)? If we are to take seriously what the Faith teachers say, we must inevitably conclude that God issued bold but empty proclamations.

The whole notion of Satan gaining ascendancy over the earth is based on the mistaken notion that human beings were given ownership of the earth, which they transferred to the devil. But this is simply untrue. Human beings are caretakers, not owners, of the earth. Everything belongs to God: "The earth is the Lord's, and everything in it, the world, and all who live in it" (Psalm 24:1).

Even according to the rules of Faith lore, Satan could never have become the legal owner of the earth. Why? Because the person who allegedly gave it to him, Adam, never owned it in the first place!

THE SUPREME COURT OF THE UNIVERSE

It is astonishing to see how glibly Faith teachers reduce God to a failure and elevate Satan to a sovereign. Today you can browse through many Christian bookstores and find a variety of books that make God accountable to "the Supreme Court of the Universe." Here is just one example from Charles Capps's book *Authority in Three Worlds*:

> Adam had revelation knowledge that flowed from God, the Father. But when Adam bowed his knee to Satan, he shut God out. God found Himself on the outside looking in. His man, Adam, had lost his authority. Satan . . . had become the god of the world system . . .
>
> Satan had gained ascendancy in the earth by gaining Adam's authority, and God was left on the outside. God *couldn't* come here in His divine power and wipe them out. He had to move in an area where it would be *ruled legal* by the *Supreme Court of the Universe*.[9]

Just think of it: "God couldn't"! Here we have Adam taking on the nature of Satan, Satan taking on the nature of God, and God getting banished from His universe! The words "God couldn't" alone should be enough to make us shudder. And just who in heaven's name sits on the so-called Supreme Court of the Universe?

The thought of God being accountable to a judicial council is ridiculous in the extreme. Justice itself is a reflection of God's nature (Ezra 9:15; Psalms 119:137; 145:17; Jeremiah 12:1; Daniel 9:14). He delights in exercising kindness, justice, and righteousness (Jeremiah 9:24). If indeed God had to answer to Capps's cosmic committee, He by definition would not really be God.

The God of Scripture is the ultimate Judge of the universe (Genesis 18:25; Psalm 96:13; Ecclesiastes 3:17; Hebrews 12:23; 2 Timothy 4:1); the God of Charles Capps is but the figment of a fertile imagination.

Incredibly, Kenneth Copeland manages to demote God even further. In an audio production titled *What Happened from the Cross to the Throne*, he insists:

> The Bible says that God gave this earth to the sons of men . . . and when [Adam] turned and gave that dominion to Satan, look where it left God. It left Him on the outside looking in . . . He had no legal right to do anything about it, did He? . . . He had injected himself illegally into the earth—what Satan had intended for Him to do was to fall for it—pull off an illegal act and turn the light off in God and subordinate God to himself . . . He intended to get God into such a trap that He couldn't get out.[10]

To suggest that God had no legal right, that Satan might have "turned the light off in God," and that there is a Supreme Court of the Universe to which God is accountable is to promote the most extreme form of heresy. If the Faith teachers do not repent of such blasphemous statements this side of eternity, they will stand condemned before the Supreme Authority of the universe (cf. Matthew 7:21–23; James 3:1). And judgment will be meted out not by some mythological supreme court but by the self-existent, transcendent, all-powerful God who rules all things by the edict of His will.

ERROR BEGETS ERROR

Could it get any worse? Tragically, the answer is yes. One of the most rampant and unbiblical notions popularized in Faith circles—and now in the broader

Christian community as well—is that Satan can possess a person who is indwelt by the Holy Spirit. As such, Christians from across the sociological spectrum are certain they house demons and that exorcism is the cure. Turn on TBN almost any time of the day or night, and you can hear Faith preachers binding devils ranging from the demon of lust to the demon of laryngitis.

Todd Bentley is a classic case in point. Not only has he literally kicked those he believes to be possessed by such forces as the demon of cancer but he professes to be the bearer of demons himself. On one occasion, the born-again Bentley confessed that he was "overcome by a demon. I threw myself at the chairs and knocked them flying. I screamed, cursed, and writhed on the floor like a snake. Then I rolled and screamed and tried to avoid the four or five guys who tried to restrain and deliver me."[11] On another, he was delivered from a demonic force he identified as "a spirit of death." In his words, "anger, murder, death, suicide, and violence raged inside me." As such, he "writhed and screamed on the floor."[12] On yet another occasion he succumbed to the demons of infidelity. According to Rory and Wendy Alec, founders of God TV, the demise of Bentley's Lakeland revival was due in part to the powerful curses placed on him by witches and warlocks. As such, his infidelity is directly traceable to the work of Satan. As the Alecs explain, "the enemy had heard of the great honoring of the Lamb and was determined to destroy it—BY ANY MEANS POSSIBLE AND AT ANY COST." Thus a ferocious wave of attacks "from the covens" and "the warlocks" was launched against Bentley. Indeed, say the Alecs, "we heard firsthand concerning some of these assignments."[13]

Such episodes vastly overrate the power of Satan. Hot-tempered, weak-willed men need to come to grips with the reality that "the devil made me do it" (curse, commit adultery, writhe on the floor like a snake, etc.) is little more than a convenient cop-out for sin. While it has become fashionable to credit the devil with everything from anger to suicide, we must ever be mindful that spiritual warfare involves the world and the flesh as well. As Paul makes clear in his letter to the Ephesians, we are often defeated in spiritual warfare because we follow "the ways of the world" and "the cravings of our sinful nature" (Ephesians 2:2–3). Indeed, to suggest that the temple in which the Holy Spirit dwells can simultaneously be inhabited by demons is the quintessential example of deifying the devil.

Or maybe it gets even worse. Perhaps the quintessential deification of the devil is John Hagee's outrageous assertion that in the end the Antichrist, animated by Satan, will be able to emulate the death and resurrection of Christ. In one of the most horrifying scenes I have ever witnessed on the Trinity Broadcasting Network, Hagee attempted to convince a worldwide audience that the Antichrist will be fatally shot by a Jew and then, like Christ, rise from the dead. Said Hagee: "The Antichrist will be shot in the head, probably by a righteous Jew who figures out who he is by the geometria of the sum of the letters of his last name. He—the Antichrist—*is going to rise miraculously from the dead*, emulating the death and the resurrection of Jesus Christ."[14]

If indeed the Antichrist, like Christ, could rise from the dead, as Hagee contended on TBN, Christianity would lose the basis for believing that Christ's resurrection vindicated His claim to deity. In a biblical paradigm, Satan can parody the resurrection of Christ through "counterfeit miracles, signs and wonders" (2 Thessalonians 2:9), but he hardly possesses power over death and the grave. If Satan were to possess the creative power of God, he could have masqueraded as the resurrected Christ two thousand years ago. Moreover, the notion that Satan can perform acts that are *indistinguishable* from genuine miracles suggests a dualistic worldview in which God and Satan are equal and opposite powers competing for dominance.

One would hope Hagee's outburst was merely an anomaly. Sadly, however, it has become common fare in Christian parlance.

12

DEMOTION OF CHRIST

The Spirit of God spoke to me. And He said, "Son, realize this"—now follow me in this; don't let your tradition trip you up—He said, "Think this way: a twice-born man whipped Satan in his own domain." And I threw my Bible down . . . I said, "What?!" He said, "A born-again man defeated Satan. The firstborn of many brethren defeated him." He said, "You are the very image and the very copy of that one." I said, "Goodness gracious sakes alive." I began to see what had gone on in there [hell], and I said, "Well, now, You don't mean, You couldn't dare mean that I could have done the same thing?" He said, "Oh, yeah. If you'd known . . . had the knowledge of the Word of God that He did, you could have done the same thing because you're a reborn man too!"[1]

—KENNETH COPELAND

So far we have seen Faith teachers re-create man in the image of God, demote God to the status of man, and deify Satan as a god. Now in concert with cults and world religions we will see them go so far as to demote Christ to the status of a mere mortal. Creflo Dollar is particularly dogmatic in this regard. Incredibly, he dismisses those who hold that Christ was divine during His earthly sojourn as mere "fantasy preachers":

> And somebody said, well, Jesus came as God! Well, how many of you know the Bible says God never sleeps nor slumbers? And yet in the book of Mark we see Jesus asleep in the back of the boat. Please listen to me. Please listen to me. This ain't no heresy. I'm not some false prophet. I'm just reading this thing out to you of the Bible. I'm just telling you, all these fantasy preachers have been preaching all of this stuff for all of these years, and we bought the package![2]

Could Dollar and his fellow deity deniers be onto something here? Is the fact that Jesus was "asleep in the back of the boat" proof positive that He came to earth as merely a man? Are the historic creeds and the confessions of Christianity rooted in the ridiculous? Have Christians throughout the ages been misled by fantasy preachers, ranging from the apostles to Athanasius and Augustine? Did we just blindly buy "the package"? Is Dollar onto something in saying, "If he [Jesus] came as God and he got tired—he says he sat down by the well because he was tired—boy, we're in trouble"?[3] Was Dollar insightful in asking, "If Jesus came as God, then why did God have to anoint him?" And what about this Dollar declaration? "Jesus came as a man, that's why it was legal to anoint him—God doesn't need anointing. He is anointed. Jesus came as a man, and at age thirty God is now getting ready to demonstrate to us and give us an example of what a man with the anointing can do."[4]

The answers, as we shall see shortly, are found in the very words of the Word made flesh. Moreover, while it would be true to say that Christ set aside the prerogative for independently using His divine attributes when He took on the limitations of humanity—it would be false to suggest that Christ was divested of a single attribute of deity. If Christ was not fully God, His passion on the cross would have been insufficient to atone for sin. As man, Christ is our representative—the Second Adam; as God, His death was sufficient to provide redemption for the sins of the world. As such, to minimize those who teach that Jesus came as God as mere fantasy preachers is to marginalize Christian orthodoxy and to misunderstand Peter's answer to Christ's most basic question—"Who do you say I am?" (Matthew 16:15).

While Creflo demotes Christ to a mere mortal due to a misunderstanding of the Scriptures, Copeland does so on the basis of a personal prophecy from the lips of Messiah Himself. Here's what Christ supposedly told Copeland:

Don't be disturbed when people put you down and speak harshly and roughly of you. They spoke that way of Me, should they not speak that way of you? The more you get to be like Me, the more they're going to think that way of you. They crucified Me for claiming that I was God. But I didn't claim I was God; I just claimed I walked with Him and that He was in Me. Hallelujah.[5]

When challenged concerning his blasphemy, Copeland retorted, "I didn't say Jesus *wasn't* God, I said He [Jesus] didn't *claim* to be God when He lived on the earth. Search the Gospels for yourself. If you do, you'll find what I say is true."[6]

WILL THE REAL FANTASY PREACHERS PLEASE STAND UP?

If Faith followers would follow the suggestion to search the Gospels, they would discover that they have been horribly misled. Consider the Gospel of John. In John 10:30 Jesus says, "I and the Father are one." Modern readers might misunderstand the significance of His statement, but the ancient Jews most certainly did not. They knew precisely what Jesus meant. They didn't even wait for further clarification. Immediately they picked up stones and denounced Christ for blasphemy, because they said, "You, a mere man, claim to be God" (v. 33).

Here Jesus proclaims Himself to be God; yet Copeland, like the Jews who wanted to stone Jesus, proclaims Him to be *a mere man*. Incredibly, the very next verse of the same chapter (v. 34) is precisely the one used by Faith teachers like Copeland to prove that *men* are gods! In the space of two verses, Faith teachers manage to make Jesus into a little man; and man into a little god. Apparently, almost everyone gets to be God . . . except Jesus.

If John 10:33 is not enough to convince Copeland that Jesus was indeed God in human flesh, how about John 5:18? Here again the Jews try to kill Jesus, not only because He was breaking the Sabbath, but also because "he was even calling God his own father, making himself equal with God."

Or what about John 8:58, where Jesus says, "I tell you the truth . . . before Abraham was born, I am"? Jesus makes His deity so clear in this text that no one should be able to misunderstand the point. By using the phrase "I am," Jesus unequivocally identifies Himself as the everlasting God (cf. Exodus 3:14; Isaiah 43:10). This is no slip of the pen on John's part either. On many other occasions the apostle notes Christ using similar terminology to claim deity (cf. John 1:1, 14; 3:13; 17:5).

Should Faith followers require further evidence, they need only think back to the unmistakable claim to deity that Jesus made before Caiaphas the high priest and the court that condemned Him to death. When Caiaphas asked: "Are you the Christ, the Son of the Blessed One?" Jesus answered: "I am . . . And you will see the Son of Man sitting at the right hand of the Mighty One and coming on the clouds of heaven" (Mark 14:61–62). A biblically illiterate person might have missed the import of Jesus' words. Caiaphas and the council did not. They knew that in saying He was *the* Son of Man who would come *on the clouds of heaven*, He was making an overt reference to the Son of Man in Daniel's prophecy (Daniel 7:13–14). And in doing so, He was not only claiming to be the preexistent Sovereign of the universe but also prophesying that He would vindicate His claim by judging the very court that was now condemning Him. What is more, by combining Daniel's prophecy with David's proclamation in Psalm 110, Jesus was claiming that He would sit upon the throne of Israel's God and share God's very glory. To students of the Old Testament, this was the height of "blasphemy," and "they all condemned him as worthy of death" (Mark 14:64).

Finally, as should be self-evident to Faith folk, Jesus claimed to possess the very attributes of God. For example, He claimed *omniscience* by telling Peter, "This very night, before the rooster crows, you will disown me three times" (Matthew 26:34); declared *omnipotence* not only by resurrecting Lazarus (John 11:43) but by raising Himself from the dead (John 2:19); and professed *omnipresence* by promising He would be with His disciples "to the very end of the age" (Matthew 28:20). Not only so, but Jesus said to the paralytic in Luke 5:20, "Friend, your sins are forgiven." In doing so, He claimed a prerogative reserved for God alone.

After searching the Gospels, we are left on the horns of a dilemma. Either Jesus forgot that He had testified to His deity during His earthly sojourn, *or* conversations such as those claimed by Copeland are mere figments of an overactive imagination.

FROM BAD TO WORSE

If possible, the statements of Benny Hinn negating the deity of Jesus Christ are even more unnerving than those made by Dollar and Copeland. As a case in point, in the first edition of his blockbuster *Good Morning, Holy Spirit*, Hinn penned the following blasphemy:

> Had the Holy Spirit not been with Jesus, He *would have sinned*. That's right, it was the Holy Spirit that was the power that kept Him pure. He was not only sent from heaven, but He was called the *Son of Man*—and as such He

was capable of sinning ... Without the Holy Ghost, Jesus would have never have made it ... Can you imagine Christ headed for the grave, knowing He would remain there forever, if the Holy Ghost would change His mind about raising Him from the dead?[7]

How is it possible that Benny Hinn, who claims to have had frequent communications with God and bills himself as God's anointed, would not have grasped one of the most basic fundamentals of Scripture? When Jesus refers to Himself as the Son of Man (no fewer than eighty-two times), He is using a title that clearly designates Him as the divine Messiah (cf. Daniel 7:13, 14).[8]

Furthermore, every orthodox scholar in the two-thousand-year history of the church has recognized that when Jesus called Himself "the Son of Man" He was indeed claiming to be God. As such, the notion that God could sin is anathema. During the Incarnation, Jesus was 100 percent God as well as 100 percent man. He did not lay aside His divine attributes. To say that Jesus surrendered even one attribute of divinity is to assert that Jesus Christ is less than God and is therefore not God at all.

While Christ voluntarily veiled His divine *glory* (Philippians 2:5–11), Scripture insists that He did not surrender His divine *attributes*. And as God, Jesus *would not* have sinned.

A BILLION INCARNATIONS OF GOD

Faith teachers further diminish the deity of Christ by proclaiming that believers are incarnations of God in the same way that Jesus was an incarnation of God. Copeland, in fact, seems to think he is so much like Christ that if he had the knowledge of the Word of God that Jesus did, he himself could have redeemed mankind:

The Spirit of God spoke to me. And He said, "Son, realize this"—now follow me in this; don't let your tradition trip you up—He said, "Think this way: a twice-born man whipped Satan in his own domain." And I threw my Bible down ... I said, "What?!" He said, "A born-again man defeated Satan. The firstborn of many brethren defeated him." He said, "You are the very image and the very copy of that one." I said, "Goodness gracious sakes alive." I began to see what had gone on in there [hell], and I said, "Well, now, You don't mean, You couldn't dare mean that I could have done the same thing?" He said, "Oh, yeah. If you'd known . . . had the knowledge of the Word of God that He did, you could have done the same thing because you're a reborn man too!"[9]

In saying that he could have redeemed fallen humanity if he had had the knowledge of the Word that Christ had, Copeland clearly underscored the fact that a mere human was sufficient to redeem the sins of humankind. But Copeland goes even further. He emphatically communicates that it would not have been legal for our redeemer to be a God. Says Copeland: "It's got to be a man. He's got to be *all* man. *He cannot be a God* and come storming in here with attributes and dignities that are not common to man. He *can't* do that. It's not legal."[10]

This, of course, is as far from Christian orthodoxy as can be imagined. Indeed, without both natures, Christ's passion on the cross would have been insufficient. As man, Christ is our representative, the Second Adam. As God, Christ's death was sufficient to atone for the sins of all who are fallen in the first Adam.

Yet as outrageous as Copeland's demotion of Christ is, Charles Capps does him one better by asserting that God purposed to make millions and millions of people *exactly like Jesus!*[11] There is no better word than *blasphemy* for a teaching that demotes Jesus Christ to the level of a man and a mere prototype of millions and millions of others who are exactly like Him.

Scripture emphatically declares that Jesus was not merely one of many incarnations of God, but He was *the one and only* incarnation of God—that He is the unique, *monogenes*, the only begotten Son, the Son of God (John 3:16; cf. 1:18).

Tragically, Faith teachers are not content to demote Christ and deify man; they take their heresies to new levels of absurdity by asserting that the incarnate Christ was spoken into being in the same manner in which God spoke the universe into existence. Says Capps, "God spoke it. God transmitted that image to Mary. She received the image inside of her . . . The embryo that was in Mary's womb was nothing more than the Word of God."[12]

Copeland then stretches this heresy to its most ridiculous extreme. He not only has Jesus spoken into existence by God's *Word of Faith*, but has Him coming together piecemeal: "The faith it took to make fingers was loosed, the faith it took to make arms was loosed in the earth, and now God had a way to hover over a little woman by the name of Mary. And there was born of that virgin woman a product of God."[13]

In one of the greatest understatements of his career, Copeland promised, "Here's where we're gonna depart from ordinary church":

> Now, you see, God is injecting His Word into the earth to produce this Jesus—these faith-filled words that framed the image that's in Him . . . He can't just walk onto the earth and say, "Let it be!" because *He doesn't have the right.* He had to sneak it in here around the god of this world that was blockin' every way that he possibly could.[14]

Clearly, Copeland, Capps, and others who teach this heresy have a great deal more in common with the cults than they do with Christianity. With virtually each new utterance, new heresy is brought to the fore. And the consequences are nothing if not devastating.

ERROR BEGETS ERROR

It would be prudent at this point to pause for a moment and reflect on where we are thus far. We began by examining "F" in the acronym F-L-A-W-S and discovered that in the Word of Faith camp, faith is a force, words are the containers of the force, and through the force of faith one creates his own reality. As such, Faith preachers have convinced their followers that what happens in their lives—whether good or bad—is a direct result of what they say. If you, like they, are healthy and prosperous, words created your reality. Conversely, if your baby dies or your wife contracts cancer, you are a prime suspect.

To buttress their biases, prosperity preachers bludgeon some of the greatest heroes of the Bible. You'll recall that Joyce Meyer, not content to merely fault Job for the whirlwind that blew his life into oblivion, went so far as to cruelly implicate him in the deaths of his ten beloved children. With a bravado that boggles the mind, she charged Job with speaking words of fear in bringing about a self-fulfilling prophecy. It doesn't take a rocket scientist to figure out the logical extension of her theology. If calamity befalls you, you need look no farther than your words!

Next we examined the "L" in F-L-A-W-S, which represents the phrase *little gods*. Here we were reminded of the stark reality that virtually every theological heresy begins with a misconception of the nature of God. The ramifications become even more acute when the text of Scripture is taken out of context and abused as a pretext in the process. Indeed, when we as humans lose perspective on the limitless chasm that separates a holy God from a sinful humanity, the essence of Christianity is compromised.

How far we have come from an age in which a fleeting glimpse of the Almighty was enough to cause the holiest man in Israel to cry out, "Woe to me! . . . For I am a man of unclean lips" (Isaiah 6:5), to an epoch in which a man such as Copeland can tell those who take the sacred name of Christ upon their lips that after the Fall, God's prerogatives were so diminished that when He initiated the Abrahamic covenant, "Abram could have turned around and said, 'Forget it, old man, who needs you?'"[15]

We now turn to a further error—an error that is a direct assault on the heart of Christianity. Indeed, as the letter "A" of the acronym F-L-A-W-S is at the center, so, too, the *atonement atrocities* to which we now turn are central to the hope of redemption.

part four

ATONEMENT ATROCITIES

He is the atoning sacrifice for our sins, and not only
for ours but also for the sins of the whole world.[1]

—THE BELOVED APOSTLE JOHN

I shall never forget the first time I heard him tell the story. The impact will live on forever in my heart. I can see it all now in my mind's eye as though it were just yesterday. Dr. D. James Kennedy had just mounted the magnificent pulpit of the Coral Ridge Church in Fort Lauderdale, Florida. Within moments, he was telling the story of a young man named John Griffith.

The time, he said, was the roaring twenties. The place was Oklahoma.

John Griffith was in his early twenties—newly married and full of optimism. Along with his lovely wife, he had been blessed with a beautiful, blue-eyed baby. With delight and excitement, John was dreaming the American dream.

He wanted to be a traveler. He imagined what it would be like to visit faraway places with strange-sounding names. He would read about them and research them. His hopes and dreams were so vivid that at times they seemed more real than reality itself. But then came 1929 and the great stock market crash.

With the shattering of the American economy came the devastation of John's dreams. The winds that howled through Oklahoma were strangely symbolic of the gale force that was sweeping away his hopes. Oklahoma was being systematically ravaged by depression and despair.

And so, brokenhearted, John packed up his few possessions and with his wife and little son, Greg, headed east in an old Model-A Ford. They made their way toward Missouri, to the edge of the Mississippi River, and there he found a job tending one of the great railroad bridges that spanned the massive river.

Day after day John would sit in a control room and direct the enormous gears of an immense bridge over the mighty river. He would look out wistfully as bulky barges and splendid ships glided gracefully under his elevated bridge. Then, mechanically, he would lower the massive structure and stare pensively into the distance as great trains roared by and became little more than specks on the horizon. Each day he looked on sadly as they carried with them his shattered dreams and his visions of far-off places and exotic destinations.

It wasn't until 1937 that a new dream began to be birthed in his heart. His young son was now eight years old, and John had begun to catch a vision for a new life, a life in which Greg would work shoulder-to-shoulder with him, a life of intimate fellowship and friendship. The first day of this new life dawned and brought with it new hope and a fresh purpose. Excitedly they packed their lunches and, arm in arm, headed off toward the immense bridge.

Greg looked on in wide-eyed amazement as his dad pressed down the huge lever that raised and lowered the vast bridge. As he watched, he thought that his father must surely be the greatest man alive. He marveled that his dad could single-handedly control the movements of such a stupendous structure.

Before they knew it, noontime had arrived. John had just elevated the bridge and allowed some scheduled ships to pass through. And then, taking his son by the hand, they headed off for lunch. Hand in hand, they inched their way down a narrow catwalk and out onto an observation deck that projected some fifty feet over the majestic Mississippi. There they sat and watched spellbound as the ships passed by below.

As they ate, John told his son, in vivid detail, stories about the marvelous destinations of the ships that glided below them. Enveloped in a world of thought, he related story after story, his son hanging on every word.

Then, suddenly, in the midst of telling a tale about the time the river had overflowed its banks, he and his son were startled back to reality by the shrieking whistle of a distant train. Looking at his watch in disbelief, John saw that it was already 1:07. Immediately he remembered that the bridge was still raised and that the Memphis Express would be by in just minutes.

Not wanting to alarm his son, he suppressed his panic. In the calmest tone he could muster, he instructed his son to stay put. Quickly leaping to his feet, he jumped onto the catwalk. As the precious seconds flew by, he ran at full tilt to the steel ladder leading into the control house.

Once in, he searched the river to make sure that no ships were in sight. And then, as he had been trained to do, he looked straight down beneath the bridge to make certain nothing was below. As his eyes moved downward, he saw something so horrifying that his heart froze in his chest. For there, below him in the massive gearbox that housed the colossal gears that moved the gigantic bridge, was his beloved son.

Apparently Greg had tried to follow his dad but had fallen off the catwalk. Even now he was wedged between the teeth of two main cogs in the gearbox. Although he appeared to be conscious, John could see that his son's leg had already begun to bleed profusely. Then an even more horrifying thought flashed through his mind: lowering the bridge would mean killing the apple of his eye.

Panicked, his mind probed in every direction, frantically searching for solutions. Suddenly a plan emerged. In his mind's eye he saw himself grabbing a coiled rope, climbing down the ladder, running down the catwalk, securing the rope, sliding down toward his son, and pulling him back up to safety. Then in an instant he would move back down toward the control lever and thrust it down just in time for the oncoming train.

As soon as these thoughts appeared, he realized the futility of his plan. Instantly, he knew that there just wouldn't be enough time. Perspiration began to bead on John's brow, terror written over every inch of his face. His mind darted here and there, vainly searching for yet another solution. What would he do? What could he do?

His agonized mind considered the four hundred people who were moving inexorably closer toward the bridge. Soon the train would come roaring out of the trees with tremendous speed. But this—this was his son . . . his only child . . . his pride . . . his joy.

His mother—he could see her face now. This was their child, their beloved son. He was his father, and this was his boy.

He knew in a moment there was only one thing he could do. He knew he would have to do it. And so, burying his face under his left arm, he plunged down the lever. The cries of his son were quickly drowned out by the relentless sound of the bridge as it ground slowly into position. With only seconds to spare, the Memphis Express—with its four hundred passengers—roared out of the trees and across the mighty bridge.

John Griffith lifted his tearstained face and looked into the windows of the passing train. A businessman was reading the morning newspaper. A uniformed conductor was glancing nonchalantly at his large vest pocket watch. Ladies were already sipping their afternoon tea in the dining cars. A small boy, looking strangely like his own son, pushed a long, thin spoon into a large dish of ice cream. Many of the passengers seemed to be engaged in either idle conversation or careless laughter.

But no one looked his way. No one even cast a glance at the giant gearbox that housed the mangled remains of his hopes and dreams.

In anguish he pounded the glass in the control room and cried out, "What's the matter with you people? Don't you care? Don't you know I've sacrificed my son for you? What's wrong with you?"

No one answered; no one heard. No one even looked. Not one of them seemed to care. And then, as suddenly as it had happened, it was over. The train disappeared, moving rapidly across the bridge and out over the horizon.

Even now as I retell this story, I am moved by emotion. For this is but a faint glimpse of what the Father did in sacrificing His Son, Jesus, to atone for the sins of the world (John 3:16). However, unlike the Memphis Express that caught John Griffith by surprise, God—in His great love and according to His sovereign will and purpose—*determined* to sacrifice His Son so that we might live (1 Peter 1:19–20). Not only so, but the consummate love of Christ is demonstrated in that He was not accidentally "caught" as was John's son. Rather, He willingly sacrificed His life for the sins of humankind (John 10:18; cf. Matthew 26:53).

In light of this most precious gift of salvation, it is almost inconceivable that anyone—particularly someone within the Christian church—would tamper with the atonement. It is astounding that those who set themselves up as the very anointed of God blithely wreak havoc on the centrality of the Cross. And yet that is precisely what Faith teachers do. They nonchalantly exchange the wonder of God's redeeming sacrifice for doctrines that sacrifice redemption.

First, from Hagin to Hinn, they contend that Christ was re-created on the cross from a sinless deity to a Satanic demoniac. Second, they posit that our redemption was secured not on the cross but in the environs of hell. In fact, many Faith teachers claim that Christ's torture by all the demons of hell was a "ransom" God paid to Satan so that He could get back into a universe from which He had been banished.[2] Third, they insist that Jesus was reborn (or born again) in hell. And finally, they hold that Christ was reincarnated through His rebirth in hell—and that those who (like Christ) are born again are likewise "reincarnated."

As you might suppose, the stakes are enormous—no less than the crux of Christianity itself. As such, we now delve deeply into the atonement atrocities of Faith teachers, beginning with Christ's re-creation from divine to demonic upon Calvary's cross.

13

RE-CREATION ON THE CROSS

Spiritual death means something more than separation
from God. Spiritual death also means having Satan's
nature . . . Jesus tasted death—spiritual death—for every man.[1]

—KENNETH HAGIN, FATHER OF THE WORD OF FAITH MOVEMENT

Before we examine the destructive notion that Christ was re-created on the cross, let's take a moment to forge a working definition of *atonement*. Simply put, atonement means that Christ, in His sacrificial death upon the cross, dealt *completely* with the problem of humanity's sin. As such, upon the cross, Christ "redeemed [sinners] from the curse of the law by becoming a curse for us" (Galatians 3:13). Christ, the paragon of virtue, became the sacrificial Lamb upon whom the sins of the world were laid. While *practically* He was perfect and sinless, *positionally* He was accounted as sinful in that all of our sin was laid to His account. Conversely, while we are *practically* sinners, all of His righteousness is imputed to those who place their trust in Him. Thus, through His atoning sacrifice, we are accounted as positionally *righteous before God*.

I cannot emphasize too strongly that the atonement of Christ upon Calvary's cross is crucial to the historic Christian faith. Indeed, the word *crucial* comes from the Latin word *crux* or "cross." Thus in saying that the atonement is the crux of Christianity, I am saying that just as the Cross stands at the center of all history, so our understanding of the atonement is central to the faith once and for all delivered to the saints. Indeed, tampering with the atonement is the most direct pathway from Christianity into the kingdom of the cults. Virtually every cult, in one way or another, denies the doctrine of salvation by grace alone through the sinless sacrifice of Christ upon the cross. The Bible plainly states that your eternal salvation rests on what you personally believe about the blood atonement of Jesus Christ. It is *at the cross*—not in hell—that your salvation is either won or lost. And that is precisely the problem with the most notorious of Faith teachings. These teachings have transferred the saving work of Christ from the cross to the deepest dungeons of hell.

Lest you harbor the illusion that this view is peripheral rather than central to Faith theology, here is what Kenneth Copeland has to say in one of his most provocative messages on the atonement:

> The thing that's necessary for the life of a Christian is knowledge of what happened from the cross to the throne . . . It is the most fascinating thing in the whole Bible. It's very little talked about, almost nonexistent in the traditional church teaching, and I'll never understand why. I guess because it's been covered up and hidden in tradition.[2]

There you have it—not "a" but "the" most fascinating thing in the whole Bible. And, according to Copeland, it has been "covered up and hidden in tradition"! But if this is true—if Copeland is right in suggesting that we have been deceived by church tradition—then we, by the Bible's own standards, will forever remain in our sins and will one day be subject to eternal torment in hell. Only if Jesus were pure and holy, unblemished and without sin, could He have fulfilled the Old Testament concept of the sin offering. That offering redeemed man from the curse of the law and was considered most holy even after death. As such, the sacrifice of Jesus was characterized by the apostle Paul as "a sweet-smelling savour" unto God (Ephesians 5:2 KJV). It is inconceivable that Benny Hinn transforms "a sweetsmelling savour" into a "symbol of Satan." Yet as evidenced below this is precisely what he is wont to do:

> Ladies and gentlemen, the serpent is a symbol of Satan. Jesus Christ knew the only way He would stop Satan is by becoming one in nature with him. You say, "What did you say? What blasphemy is this?" No, you hear this! He did not take my sin; He *became* my sin. Sin is the nature of hell. Sin is what made Satan . . . It was sin that made Satan. Jesus said, "I'll be sin! I'll go to the lowest place! I'll go to the origin of it! I won't just take part in it, I'll be the totality of it!" When Jesus became sin, sir, He took it from A to Z and said, "No more!" Think about this: He became flesh that flesh might become like Him. He became death, so dying man can live. He became sin, so sinners can be righteous in Him. He became one with the nature of

Satan, so all those who had the nature of *Satan* can partake of the nature of God.[3]

Like Hinn, Kenneth Hagin persistently promoted the premise that Jesus took on the nature of Satan during His passion on the cross. Hagin left no doubt with respect to his convictions in this regard: "Spiritual death means something more than separation from God. *Spiritual death also means having Satan's nature* . . . Jesus tasted death—spiritual death—for every man."[4]

One of Hagin's foremost disciples, Frederick K. C. Price, took his mentor's teachings from the blasphemous to the bizarre by supposing that Christ was re-created spiritually—not on the cross but in the Garden of Gethsemane: "Somewhere between the time He was nailed to the cross and when He was in the Garden of Gethsemane—somewhere in there—He died spiritually. Personally, I believe it was while He was in the garden."[5]

If true, the implication of Price's dogmatic declaration would be downright devastating. Indeed, it would mean that a satanic being rather than a sinless Savior was arrested in the Garden of Gethsemane. As such, the Sanhedrin would have been justified in trying and convicting the very personification of sin. Worse yet, a satanic being would have said to the thief on the cross, "I tell you the truth today, you will be with me in paradise."

It is instructive to note here that Price, who was "reared in a Jehovah's Witness environment,"[6] mimics a page right out of the Mormons' playbook! James E. Talmage, who served as an apostle of the Mormon Church, taught precisely the same thing in his book *Jesus the Christ*.[7]

Kenneth Copeland adds his own subjective spin to the subject as a result of an alleged conversation he had with God. In Copeland's version, Jesus became a sign of Satan when He hung upon the cross:

The righteousness of God was made to be sin. He accepted the sin nature of Satan in His own spirit. And at the moment that He did so, He cried, "My God, My God, why hast thou forsaken Me?" You don't know what happened at the cross. Why do you think Moses, upon instruction of God, raised the serpent upon that pole instead of a lamb? That used to bug me. I said, "Why in the world would you want to put a snake up there—the sign of Satan? Why didn't you put a lamb on that pole?" And the Lord said, "Because it was a sign of Satan that was hanging on the cross." He said, "I accepted, in My own spirit, spiritual death; and the light was turned off."[8]

The question is how do such claims square with Scripture? The answer is they don't. In Old Testament days, whenever anyone committed an offense or sin, a sacrifice called a *sin offering* was required in order to "cover" the transgression. And the offering had to be "without defect" (Leviticus 4:3, 28; 9:3). Flawed animals were deemed unacceptable for sacrifice (Deuteronomy 15:21).

Since such sacrifices foreshadowed Christ's ultimate sacrifice on the cross, we can be certain that Christ was offered without spot or blemish, and as such could not have become one in nature with Satan. Indeed, Scripture emphatically communicates that on the cross Christ was "without blemish or defect" (1 Peter 1:19; cf. Hebrews 9:14).

Not only so, but according to Leviticus 6:25–29, the sin offering was "most holy" to God both before *and* after its death. In the same way, Jesus as the sin offering remained holy even after His death on the cross. As such, He was the antitype who fulfilled the types and shadows of the Old Testament sin offerings.

SCRIPTORTURE

As in the kingdom of the cults, Faith teachers conform the text of Scripture to their pet theories. Second Corinthians 5:21 is a classic case in point. Here they seize upon the phrase "God made him who had no sin to be sin for us" as a proof text for the blasphemous notion that Jesus became a satanic being on the cross. But is this really what the apostle had in mind?

To begin with, the word "sin" in this passage is used in an abstract sense. As such the phrase "to become sin" is a *metonym* (a word or phrase substituted for another associated word or phrase) for Christ "bearing the penalty of our sins."[9] Expositor T. J. Crawford maintains that "there can be no doubt that the expression is *metonymical*, since it is impossible that Christ, or any person, could be literally made sin."[10] To interpret this passage as saying that Christ was transformed into sin is to strip the Savior of His personal being and reduce Him to a mere abstraction. Not only is such a notion unbiblical; it is utterly absurd!

Moreover, the Levitical concepts of imputation and substitution are the backdrop for Paul's communication in 2 Corinthians 5:21. As such, Jesus did not literally become sin; sin was *imputed* to Him. Likewise, the Bible clearly communicates that the sacrifice of Christ was a sufficient substitutionary offering *precisely* because it was a sinless sacrifice. One prominent commentator puts it this way:

> But God made Him *sin*: that is to say that God the Father made His innocent, incarnate Son the object of His wrath and judgment, for our sakes, with the result that in Christ on the cross the sin of the world is judged and taken away. In this truth resides the whole logic of reconciliation . . . Not for one moment does He cease to be righteous, else the radical exchange envisaged by the Apostle here, whereby our sin is transferred to Him and His righteousness is transferred to us, would be no more than a fiction or an hallucination.[11]

Faith adherents also frequently cite Numbers 21:8–9 and John 3:14 to "prove" that Jesus took on the nature of Satan on the cross. The argument goes something like this: since Jesus was "lifted up" on the cross in the manner that Moses "lifted up" the bronze serpent in the desert, so must He have taken on the nature of Satan, symbolized by the serpent.

In reality, far from proving that Jesus took on the nature of Satan, these texts, like 2 Corinthians 5:21, refer to the imputation of sin to Christ, rather than to the infusion of sin into Christ. Moreover, these verses speak to *the manner* of His death—namely, *He was lifted up*. This is made particularly clear in John 12:32, where Jesus says, "But I, when I am lifted up from the earth, will draw all men to myself." Verse 33 clarifies the meaning of Christ's words: "He said this to show *the kind of death he was going to die*" (emphasis added). Moreover, one must inevitably ask how Jesus could be a "fragrant offering and sacrifice to God" (Ephesians 5:2) if He truly became a vile serpent upon the cross.

Those who hold that Jesus became a satanic being on the cross must face other difficult questions as well. For example, why does God in Isaiah 53:11 refer to Jesus as His "righteous servant" during the moment of His suffering on the cross? Such a statement would make little sense if Jesus had truly been transformed into a demoniac. It also would be inconsistent for Jesus—after supposedly taking on the nature of Satan—to pray for His enemies, saying, "*Father*, forgive them, for they do not know what they are doing" (Luke 23:34, emphasis added). And if He took on the nature of Satan, then who is this

"Father"? It is hard to imagine that someone with the nature of Satan would pray to God and harder still to envision Satan personifying love and forgiveness toward his enemies.

In sum, it is clear that Christ's re-creation on the cross finds no basis in the biblical text.

THREE THORNY QUESTIONS

Numerous passages attest to the fact that our sins have been dealt with "through the sacrifice of the body of Jesus Christ once for all" (Hebrews 10:10; cf. Romans 7:4; Colossians 1:22; 1 Peter 2:24; 3:18; 4:1). This poses three thorny questions for the Faith movement's view of the atonement.

First, why is there no explicit mention of Christ's "spiritual" death—while the Bible is replete with details on the fact and significance of His physical death—if it was His spiritual death that did away with the curse?

Second, why does the Bible place so much emphasis on Christ's physical death—to the exclusion of His alleged spiritual death—if His physical death was not *the* factor that eradicated sin?

Third, why is it that Christ Himself told us to remember the sacrifice He made with His body and blood (both of which are essentially physical), while saying nothing about any spiritual sacrifice (cf. Luke 22:19–20; 1 Corinthians 11:24–26)?

All the biblical evidence indicates that Jesus did not die spiritually in the Faith sense. Rather, His physical death paid the price for humanity's sin. It would do prosperity preachers well to reacquaint themselves with the precious passage invoked each time we partake of the communion sacrament:

> "This is My *body* which is broken for you; do this in remembrance of Me . . . This cup is the new covenant in My *blood*. This do, as often as you drink it, in remembrance of Me." For as often as you eat this bread and drink this cup, you *proclaim the Lord's death* till He comes. (1 Corinthians 11:24–26 NKJV, emphasis added)

Truly, it was on the cross that we were pardoned through Christ's broken body and shed blood—not through some mythological spiritual death.

ERROR BEGETS ERROR

The error that Christ became a demoniac upon the cross inevitably leads to the further error that His torment upon Calvary's cross was insufficient to atone for the sins of humankind. Joyce Meyer is emphatic: "You cannot go to heaven unless you believe with all your heart that Jesus took your place in hell."[12] As such, when Jesus said, "It is finished!" (John 19:30),[13] Faith teachers say, "It has just begun!" This despite the fact that the Greek word—*tetelestai*—literally means "It is paid; the debt has been paid in full" (cf. Hebrews 9:1–14; 10:19–22).

No one has made this pernicious error more palatable to the masses than has Joel Osteen. Against the whole counsel of Scripture, he pontificates that in hell "the two most powerful forces in the universe have come together to do battle for *the first time in history.*"[14]

As we will now see, Osteen, like his Faith forbearers, transitions the triumph of the cross to the corridors of hell.

14

REDEMPTION IN HELL

Do you think that the punishment for our sin was to die on a cross? If that were the case, the two thieves could have paid your price. No, the punishment was to go into hell itself and to serve time in hell separated from God . . . Satan and all the demons of hell thought that they had Him bound and they threw a net over Jesus and they dragged Him down to the very pit of hell itself to serve our sentence.[1]

—TELEVANGELIST FREDERICK K. C. PRICE

In orthodox theology the end of the atonement took place upon the cross. In Faith theology the cross was "only the beginning." No one is more decisive in this doctrinal deviation than Joel Osteen: "For three days Jesus fought with the enemy. It was the battle of the ages. Light versus darkness. Good versus evil." With great theatre, Osteen tells devotees that their redemption was secured in an epic battle between Satan and the Savior in the very cauldrons of hell:

> The Bible indicates that for three days, Jesus went into the very depths of hell. Right into the enemy's own territory. And He did battle with Satan face to face. Can you imagine what a show down that was? It was good vs. evil. Right vs. wrong. Holiness vs. filth. Here are the two most powerful forces in the universe have come together to do battle for the first time in history. But thank God. The Bible says, "Satan was no match for our Champion." This was no contest.
>
> Jesus crushed Satan's head with His foot. He bruised his head. And He once and for all, forever defeated and dethroned and demoralized our enemy. One translation says, "He paralyzed him and rendered him powerless." But thank God. He didn't even stop there. He went over and ripped the keys of death and hell out of Satan's hands. And He grabbed Satan by

the nap [*sic*] of his neck and He began to slowly drag him down through the corridors of Hell. All beat up and bruised because He wanted to make sure that every single demon saw very clearly that Jesus was indeed the undisputed Champion of all time![2]

It is almost inconceivable that anyone—particularly someone who takes the sacred name of Christ upon his lips—would so blatantly reconstruct the centrality of Christ's atonement upon the cross. Yet in the face of Scripture that plainly tells us that *by his death* Jesus destroyed him "who holds the power of death—that is, the devil" (Hebrews 2:14), Osteen has Christ finishing the work of redemption in hell.

Incredibly, in Osteen's revision of Scripture, even Christ's victory in hell was insufficient to atone for our sins. After the Resurrection, "there still had to be a blood sacrifice for our sins. There still had to be a price paid." That is why Jesus "presented His own blood in the high court of heaven as a sacrifice for all our sins, past, present, and future." According to Osteen that is precisely why Jesus commanded Mary not to touch Him after the Resurrection. "Why didn't Jesus want Mary to touch her [*sic*]?" asks Osteen. "I'll tell you what it was. Jesus had just risen from the grave, and He still had His Holy blood on Him. It was this blood He was going to use as a sacrifice for our sins."[3]

In reality, nothing could be further from the truth. Far from having some sort of magical efficacy, *the blood of Jesus Christ* is emblematic of *the death of Jesus Christ.*[4] Nor is there any warrant for suggesting that sometime between His encounter with Mary and His encounter with Thomas, Jesus went to heaven to sprinkle His blood upon the mercy seat. Instead, believers throughout the ages have celebrated the precious sacrament of communion as the broken body and shed blood of Jesus Christ for the *complete* remission of sins. Again, it was not Christ's triumph over Satan in the cauldron of hell that atoned for sin—Jesus said, "Father into thy hands I commit my spirit" (Luke 23:46; cf. John 19:30) *not* "Satan into your clutches I submit my spirit"—nor did the debt remain unpaid until Christ ascended into heaven. The debt for all sin past, present, and future was paid by Christ's passion upon the cross. When his passion on the cross was complete, Christ uttered the word *tetelestai*—meaning the debt has been paid in full! No further debt remained to be discharged in this world or the next.

Osteen is not alone in his tragic departure from orthodox Christianity. Joyce Meyer is so convinced that Jesus paid for our redemption in hell that she tells devotees, "You cannot go to heaven unless you believe with all your heart that Jesus took your place in hell."[5] In like fashion, Robert Tilton says that, "For three days and three nights He [Jesus] was in the pit of hell, breaking the powers of darkness to set us free."[6] Frederick K. C. Price is even more strident in his declaring that our redemption was purchased in hell:

> Do you think that the punishment for our sin was to die on a cross? If that were the case, the two thieves could have paid your price. No, the punishment was to go into hell itself and to serve time in hell separated from God . . . Satan and all the demons of hell thought that they had Him bound and they threw a net over Jesus and they dragged Him down to the very pit of hell itself to serve our sentence.[7]

Many other Faith teachers could be cited, including Kenneth Hagin, who vociferously proclaimed that the physical death of Christ was insufficient to atone for sin. According to Hagin, Jesus "tasted spiritual death for every man. And His spirit and inner man went to hell in my place. Can't you see that? Physical death wouldn't remove your sins."[8] Copeland is likewise emphatic: "When Jesus cried, 'It is finished!' He was not speaking of the plan of redemption. There were still three days and nights to go through before He went to the throne." As such, intones Copeland, "Jesus' death on the cross was *only the beginning* of the complete work of redemption."[9]

As reprehensible as all these quotes are, perhaps none rivals the remarks of Paul Billheimer in his book *Destined for the Throne*. In full view of the Word of God, which clearly communicates that Jesus "disarmed" the powers of darkness, "triumphing over them by the cross" (Colossians 2:15), Billheimer claims that in hell Jesus was at Satan's mercy. Incredibly, Jan Crouch, the wife of TBN president Paul Crouch, approvingly recited from Billheimer's blasphemous book during a live communion service, which was aired on TBN:

> Because He was "made sin," impregnated with sin, and became the very essence of sin, on the cross He was banished from God's presence as a loathsome thing. He and sin were made synonymous . . . [I]t was not sufficient for Christ to offer up only His physical life on the cross. *His pure human spirit had to "descend" into hell* . . . His spirit must not only descend into hell, but into the lowest hell . . .

The Father turned Him over, not only to the agony and death of Calvary, but to the satanic torturers of His pure spirit as part of the just dessert of the sin of all the race. As long as Christ was "the essence of sin" he was at Satan's mercy in that place of torment . . .

While Christ identified with sin, Satan and the hosts of hell ruled over Him as over any lost sinner. During that seemingly endless age in the nether abyss of death, Satan did with Him as he would, and all hell was "in carnival."[10]

Faith proponents often wrongly argue that the belief that Christ suffered under Satan in hell is consistent with that of the early church fathers. In doing so, they invoke the phrase *he descended into hell* from ancient Christian creeds such as the Apostles' Creed. This, however, is hardly a convincing argument.

First and foremost, we should note that even if the phrase "he descended into hell" was invoked by the early Christian church, the intent was not to communicate that Jesus finished the work of redemption there. If church history tells us anything, it is that the early Christians celebrated the broken body and shed blood of Christ on the cross for the *complete* remission of their sins.

Furthermore, it should be noted that the phrase in question did not even appear in the Apostles' Creed until the fourth century. Thus, it cannot credibly be argued that the notion of redemption in hell was ever countenanced by the early Fathers—much less the apostles.

Finally, as Philip Schaff points out in *The Creeds of Christendom*, the word *hell* with all its connotations was likely inadvertently substituted for the word *hades* in the creeds.[11] As is the case today, Christians have not always been cognizant of the biblical distinction between hades, as depicted by our Lord in Luke 16, and hell, as described by John in passages such as Revelation 20. Put another way, from the perspective of Scripture, hades and gehenna (i.e., hell) are clearly not synonymous. Indeed, as horrifying as hades is, it is but an earnest of gehenna (hell). As such, the apostle John described the time that hades is "thrown into the lake of fire [gehenna]. The lake of fire is the second death" (Revelation 20:14).

In any case, the Canon, not a creed, is the final court of arbitration. How can anyone miss what our Lord said to the thief on the cross: "I tell you the truth, today you will be with me in paradise" (Luke 23:43)? According to the apostle Paul, paradise or Abraham's bosom is in the third heaven (2 Corinthians

12:2). There is simply no way to reconcile this explicit statement by Christ on the cross with the Faith teaching that Jesus purchased our redemption by suffering in hell.[12]

TWO TWISTED TEXTS

In full view of the evidence, Faith teachers seem bent on twisting two passages in particular in an attempt to shore up the notion that Christ suffered under Satan in hell.

In the first of these passages, our Lord prophesied, "As Jonah was three days and three nights in the belly of a huge fish, so the Son of Man will be three days and three nights in the heart of the earth" (Matthew 12:40). As should be painfully obvious to anyone in danger of falling for Faith fabrications, Jesus here clearly alluded to His burial in the tomb of Joseph of Arimathea. Moreover, there is not even a hint in the context that Jesus would experience three days and three nights in mortal combat with the forces of darkness.

In the second passage the apostle Paul writes, "What does 'he ascended' mean except that he also descended to the lower, earthly regions? He who descended is the very one who ascended higher than all the heavens, in order to fill the whole universe" (Ephesians 4:9–10). Again, far from demonstrating that our Lord was incarcerated in hell, this passage contains an idiomatic expression referring to Christ's incarnation on earth. As evidence, David uses this same expression ("lower parts" or "depths of the earth") in exclaiming, "My frame was not hidden from you when I was made in the secret place. When I was woven together *in the depths of the earth*, your eyes saw my unformed body" (Psalm 139:15–16, emphasis added). Surely no Faith follower could possibly conclude that David was born in the underworld! Yet their teachers persist in assigning Jesus to the lowermost regions of that most dreaded place.

ERROR BEGETS ERROR

As we have seen by examining the Scriptures, far from shouting, "Satan into your clutches, I submit my being" Christ cried out, "Father, into your hands I commit my spirit" (Luke 23:46; cf. John 19:30). The apostle Paul put it ever so eloquently: "having disarmed the powers and authorities, he made a public spectacle of them, triumphing over them *by the cross*" (Colossians 2:15, emphasis added). As such, we can be absolutely certain that the hellish "battle of the ages" described by such prosperity peddlers as Joel Osteen is little more than the salacious figment of a fertile imagination.

Yet despite the obvious, Faith preachers such as Joyce Meyer, in lockstep with Osteen, communicate the perversion that Jesus had to suffer in hell in order for you and me to be born again. In a publication titled *The Most Important Decision You Will Ever Make*, Meyer dogmatically declares that Messiah "was in the grave three days. During that time, He entered hell, where you and I deserved to go (legally) because of our sin. *He paid the price there*."[13] After three days of torment, continues Meyer:

> God rose up from His throne and said to demon powers tormenting the sinless Son of God, "Let Him go." Then the resurrection power of Almighty God went through hell and filled Jesus. On the earth, His grave, the tomb where they had buried Him, filled with light as the power of God filled His body, and He was resurrected from the dead—*the first born-again man*. The Bible calls Him "the firstborn among many brethren" (Rom. 8:29). He was the first so that now *you* can be one of the many brethren.[14]

As we turn our attention to the Faith notion of rebirth in hell, we will see that this assertion by Meyer (Jesus was the first born-again man) is anything but true. In point of fact, the biblical concept of being born again (John 3:3) applies solely to sinful humanity. While the Bible says that Jesus was begotten, it does not say He was born again. When John refers to Christ as "the One and Only, who came from the Father" (John 1:14), he was emphasizing the unique nature of our Lord. As such, Jesus alone is fully God and fully man, the unique and eternal Son of the Father. Jesus had no need to be born again in hell, for Jesus is and always has been the eternal Son of God.

15

REBIRTH IN HELL

When you accepted Jesus as your Lord and Savior, you became born again. That simply means that your spirit was transformed from a state of spiritual death to life in a split second of time. But have you ever considered that Jesus went through the exact same thing? Often, in the midst of our religious views of Him, we forget that He was actually the first person to ever become born again.[1]

—CREFLO DOLLAR

Before pressing forward, let's take a moment to retrace our steps. We began this section with Jesus hanging on a cross, where, according to Faith theology, He was re-created from a divine to a demonic being. Thus, the Trinity was destroyed and the deity of Christ demolished. Moreover, according to Faith preachers, Christ's passion on the cross proved insufficient to redeem humankind, and so He had to be savaged by Satan. It is there, in the environs of hell, that we pick up the story. As Adam fell for Satan's trap in Eden, says Copeland, Satan fell for God's trap in hell:

> In hell He [Jesus] suffered for you and for me. The Bible says hell was made for Satan and his angels (Matthew 25:41). It was not made for men. Satan was holding the Son of God there illegally . . . The trap was set for Satan and Jesus was the bait.[2]

The problem, according to Faith theology, was that Satan had blown it on a technicality, in that Jesus had been dragged into hell illegally: "The devil forgot to take into consideration that Jesus hadn't sinned Himself but, rather, had merely become sin as a result of the sin of others."[3] As such, Satan and the demons of hell tortured Christ's "emaciated, poured out, little wormy spirit"[4] without legal right. And this was exactly the opening God had been looking for. Seizing the moment, He spoke His faith-filled words into the bowels of the earth, and suddenly—

> that Word of the living God went down into that pit of destruction and charged the spirit of Jesus with resurrection power! Suddenly His twisted, death-wracked spirit began to fill out and come back to life. He began to look like something the devil had never seen before. He was literally being reborn before the devil's very eyes. He began to flex His spiritual muscles . . . Jesus was born again—the firstborn from the dead.[5]

The fact that Jesus was in hell *illegally* gave God the gotcha He needed. He spoke His faith-filled words into the environs of hell and, as a host of demons looked on, Jesus whipped the devil in his own backyard. He snatched Satan's keys and emerged from hell a born-again man. With His "can do" attitude, God pulled off the coup of the ages. In fact, according to Charles Capps, it was this pivotal event—namely, Jesus becoming born again—that gave rise to the body of Christ:

> Jesus was born again in the pit of hell. He was the firstborn, the firstbegotten, from the dead. *He started the Church of the firstborn in the gates of hell . . . He went down to the gates and started His Church there . . . The Church started when Jesus was born again in the gates of hell.*[6]

Kenneth Hagin was one of the early popularizers of the mythology that "Jesus is the first person ever to be born again."[7] Joyce Meyer, likewise, is emphatic in that declaration that Jesus was "the first born-again man. In a publication titled *The Most Important Decision You'll Ever Make: A Complete and Thorough Understanding of What It Means to Be Born Again*, she details Christ's rebirth in hell as follows:

> He was in the grave three days. During that time, He entered hell, where you and I deserved to go (legally) because of our sin. He paid the price there . . . Then, as God had promised, on the third day Jesus rose from the dead. The scene in the spirit realm went something like this: God rose up from His throne and said to the demon powers tormenting the sinless Son

of God, "Let Him go." Then the resurrection power of Almighty God went through hell and filled Jesus. On the earth, His grave, the tomb where they had buried Him, filled with light as the power of God filled His body, and He was resurrected from the dead—the *first born-again man.* The Bible calls Him "the firstborn among many brethren" (Rom. 8:29). He was the first so that now *you* can be one of the many brethren.[8]

DOCTRINAL PRETZELS

The notion of a born-again Jesus is *so* foreign to "the faith once and for all delivered to the saints" that one wonders how anyone who takes the sacred name of Christ upon his lips could possibly justify teaching it. The answer to the conundrum is found in Colossians 1:18. Here the apostle Paul describes Jesus as "the firstborn from among the dead."[9]

In concert with Jehovah's Witnesses—who through sleight of hand and sleight of mind can seemingly turn the average Christian into a doctrinal pretzel—prosperity preachers twist Paul's words with mind-boggling dexterity. JWs do so by declaring Jesus to be the firstborn creation of God, while Meyer and company do it by saying Jesus was born again in hell.

In reality, as is obvious from the context, "firstborn" (*prototokos*) denotes "primacy," "headship," "preeminence," and "prime position." As a case in point, Ephraim is referred to as God's firstborn (Jeremiah 31:9), not because he was born before Manasseh—he wasn't, Manasseh was firstborn (Genesis 41:51)—but because of his preeminence and prime position. Likewise, in Psalm 89 David is referred to as firstborn despite the fact that he was the youngest of Jesse's sons.[10]

Another text commonly called upon by the Faith movement is 1 Peter 3:18, which says that Jesus "was put to death in the body but made alive by the Spirit." To give you an idea of how severely this passage is mauled, think back to Billheimer's commentary as read by Jan Crouch on TBN:

In order to be made alive unto God and restored to fellowship with His Father, He [Jesus] had to be reborn—for He had become the very essence of sin. Since sin had totally alienated Him from the Father, the only way He could be restored to fellowship with the Father was through a new birth to new life.[11]

In truth, 1 Peter 3:18 is hardly a commentary on Christ's spiritual rebirth. In point of fact, the verse highlights the reality that Christ's sacrifice was physical in character. Indeed, there is not even the slightest hint of "spiritual death." Christ's lifeless body was left hanging on the cross the moment He gave His spirit over to the Father (Luke 23:46). In other words, it was the parting of His spirit that marked Jesus' "death in the body." In the same fashion, it was the return of His spirit into His body that marked His physical resurrection. To use the language of the text, Christ's body was once again "made alive by the Spirit."[12] There is simply no rationale for the text abuse perpetrated by Faith preachers.

REVELATION KNOWLEDGE

Prosperity purveyors seem to implicitly recognize that their Scripture-twisting tactics are less than convincing. As such, they call in a second wave of artillery called "revelation knowledge." This stealth apologetic allegedly bypasses the mind and directly impacts the spirit. Kenneth Copeland calls upon revelation knowledge to buttress the reborn Jesus doctrine and more:

> The Spirit of God spoke to me. And He said, "Son, realize this"—now follow me in this; don't let your tradition trip you up—He said, "Think this way: a twice-born man whipped Satan in his own domain." And I threw my Bible down . . . I said, "What?!" He said, "A born-again man defeated Satan. The firstborn of many brethren defeated him." He said, "You are the very image and the very copy of that one." I said, "Goodness gracious sakes alive!" I began to see what had gone on in there [hell], and I said, "Well, now, You don't mean, You couldn't dare mean that I could have done the same thing?" He said, "Oh yeah. If you'd known . . . had the knowledge of the Word of God that He did, you could have done the same thing because you're a reborn man too!"[13]

It would be hard to overstate the error and arrogance of Copeland's remark. If he is to be believed, no less an authority than almighty God revealed not only the reality of Christ's spiritual rebirth but the reality that Copeland could have done what Christ did if Copeland had the knowledge of the Word of God that Christ had. Just think of it: Copeland could have redeemed you from your sins!

More to the point, he would have us believe that the Creator Himself revealed the potentiality of Copeland's redeeming efficacy.

Benny Hinn's rendition of revelation knowledge is even more *dizzying* than that of Kenneth Copeland. According to Hinn, if Jesus was not reborn spiritually, we ourselves have no hope of being born again:

> My, you know, whoosh! The Holy Ghost is just showing me some stuff. I'm getting dizzy! I'm telling you the truth—it's, it's just heavy right now on me . . . He's [referring to Jesus] in the underworld now. God isn't there, the Holy Ghost isn't there, and the Bible says He was begotten. Do you know what the word "begotten" means? It means reborn. Do you want another shocker? Have you been begotten? So was He. Don't let anyone deceive you. Jesus was reborn. You say, "What are you talking about?" . . . He was reborn. He had to be reborn . . . If He was not reborn, I could not be reborn. Jesus was born again . . . If He was not reborn, I would never be reborn. How can I face Jesus and say, "Jesus, you went through everything I've gone through, except the new birth"?[14]

After claiming that the Holy Ghost showed him all this, Hinn looked into the camera and said, "I'm telling you the truth." And then he appealed to the audience to not let anyone deceive them into doubting the doctrine of the born-again Jesus!

THE SIGNIFICANCE OF "BEGOTTEN"

A crucial question here is, what does the term "begotten" mean? Does it mean "reborn," as Hinn claims? Hardly. The term "begotten" in this context simply means "born." It is in no way synonymous with the word "reborn." Moreover, the biblical concept of being "reborn" (cf. John 3:3) applies solely to sinful humanity and not to the sinless God-man. In fact, John 1:14 (cf. 1:18; 3:16) specifically refers to Christ as "the *only begotten* from the Father" (NASB) or "the *One and Only*, who came from the Father" (NIV), emphasizing the unique nature of the Lord. Jesus alone was fully God and fully man, the unique and eternal Son of the Father. Such a person has no need to be born again, for He is, always has been, and forevermore will be undiminished deity (John 1:1).

Where did this teaching of a "born-again Jesus" originate? Clearly it came *from below* rather than *from above*. There is zero biblical basis for this doctrine of demons. The only conceivable reason for concocting such an outrage was the need of Faith teachers to extricate themselves from the egregious error of contending that Christ had taken on the nature of Satan on the cross. In reality, Jesus never took on the nature of Satan, thus Jesus never needed to be born again.

To say that Jesus' nature underwent radical corruption that needed complete renewal is to turn the divine plan of redemption on its head. If Jesus truly became sin (in the sense the Faith teachers mean), one Person of the Holy Trinity was ripped away from the Godhead. This necessarily implies that the triune God had ceased to exist. It also necessarily requires the destruction of Christ's deity. For how could God, in the Person of Christ, have the nature of Satan? Scripture rejects any such perversion, for God is an unchanging Being (Malachi 3:6; Hebrews 13:8) who has "life in himself" (John 5:26).

The picture of the atonement that Scripture paints is infinitely more majestic, breathtaking, and exhilarating than any fiction the Faith teachers might dream up!

And besides all that, the Bible's version is demonstrably true.

ERROR BEGETS ERROR

Another error implicit in the notion that Christ was the first person to have been born again is that prior to Christ, no one was saved. Creflo Dollar made this explicit when he wrote:

> When you accepted Jesus as your Lord and Savior, you became born again. That simply means that your spirit was transformed from a state of spiritual death to life in a split second of time. But have you ever considered that Jesus went through the exact same thing? Often, *in the midst of our religious views of Him, we forget that He was actually the first person to ever become born again* (emphasis added).[15]

If Dollar is right, everyone from Abraham to Zechariah would have had to be reconciled to God through their works. This, however, is far from the case. The Bible, from first to last, demonstrates that the saved throughout history come to faith in exactly the same way—*by grace alone through faith alone on account of Christ alone.* The apostle Paul quotes the Old Testament extensively to drive home the reality that no one has been, or ever will be, declared righteous by observing the law (Romans 3:20).

Furthermore, Paul points to Abraham, the father of the Jews, to prove that salvation comes through faith apart from works that we perform. In his words, "If, in fact, Abraham was justified by works, he had something to boast about—but not before God. What does the Scripture say? 'Abraham believed God, and it was credited to him as righteousness'" (Romans 4:2–3; cf. Genesis 15:6; Galatians 3:6–9).

Finally, Jesus Christ is the substance that fulfills the types and shadows in the Old Testament (Luke 24:44; Romans 3:21–22; Hebrews 1:1–3). Each year the Jews celebrated the Passover to keep them focused on the One who was to come to die for their sins (1 Corinthians 5:7; cf. Hebrews 11:28, 39–40). As Hebrews says, "The law is only a shadow of the good things that are coming—not the realities themselves" (10:1).

Jesus Christ stands at the apex of history. Just as people today look back in history to Christ's sacrifice on the cross, so people who lived before the time of Christ looked forward to His sacrifice on their behalf.

The ramifications of Christ's rebirth in hell are as maniacal as they are myriad. Indeed, it would be a relief if the madness stopped here. But it doesn't! The error of Christ's rebirth leads inevitably to the error of Christ's reincarnation.

16

REINCARNATION

Every man who has been born again is an incarnation and Christianity is a miracle. The believer is as much an incarnation as was Jesus of Nazareth.[1]

—KENNETH HAGIN, FATHER OF THE WORD OF FAITH MOVEMENT

The reincarnation of Christ is arguably the greatest of all atonement atrocities. Just think about it. According to Faith theology, Jesus came in flesh (incarne) as merely a man. On the cross He was reincarnated as a satanic being. In hell "His emaciated, poured out, little wormy spirit" (Copeland) was reincarnated once again from demonic to divine. As TBN founder Paul Crouch puts it, "That's when His divinity returned."[2]

Of course, to say that Jesus' "divinity returned" presumes the spiritually horrifying notion that there was a point in time when Christ ceased to be divine—when He was no longer God. But any such assertion is as unthinkable as it is unbiblical (Philippians 2:6; cf. Hebrews 13:8).

It would be depressing enough if the Faith crowd would leave it at that. But they don't. Most Faith teachers claim that all Christians, like Jesus, become incarnations of God the moment they are born again. As Hagin puts it, "Every man who has been born again is an incarnation and Christianity is a miracle. The believer is as much an incarnation as was Jesus of Nazareth."[3]

One need only recall the uniqueness of the Incarnation—God the Son, Second Person of the Trinity, condescending to take upon Himself human form (John 1:14)—to recognize the blasphemy of ascribing incarnation to every born-again believer. To assert that such an event is a common-day phenomenon is to trivialize the unique Person and work of the Savior and to rob that glorious occurrence of its surpassingly rich significance.

The word *incarnation* is derived from the Latin word *incarne*, which means "in flesh." According to Christian theology, Christ, who is the Logos, the Second

Person of the Godhead, voluntarily cloaked Himself in human flesh (John 1:18; 14:9–10). Thus, God in the Person of Christ (who is by nature spirit—John 4:24) took on flesh (1:14) and through His incarnation provided redemption for the crowning jewels of His creation (1:29).

The concept of incarnation makes sense only if a person existed prior to having a physical body. And while the Bible clearly declares Christ to be preexistent (John 1:1; 8:58; 17:5), nowhere in Scripture do we find the concept of *human* preexistence. In fact, human preexistence remains a concept relegated largely to such cults as Mormonism.[4] Moreover, the reality that Christians are indwelt by the Father, the Son, and the Holy Spirit (John 14:17, 23) by no means implies that the Bible endorses the concept of incarnation for Christians.

INSURMOUNTABLE OBSTACLES

At least three insurmountable obstacles overwhelm the Faith notion that, as Hagin put it, "the believer is as much an incarnation as was Jesus of Nazareth." First, as noted above, one can only be incarnated if one existed prior to having a body. While preexistence is countenanced in the kingdom of the cults, it is heretofore completely foreign to the kingdom of Christ.

Furthermore, to say that we are as much an incarnation as was Jesus of Nazareth is to forge an unrealistic equality between creature and Creator. If there is one unmistakable truth in Scripture, it is that the distance between an infinite God and a finite creation is the distance of infinity. As such, to say that the believer is as much an incarnation as was Jesus of Nazareth is as untenable as it is blasphemous.

Finally, if men like Copeland are correct in saying, as was noted in chapter 9, that "God's reason for creating Adam was His desire to reproduce Himself," we would inhabit a polytheistic planet. Yet that is precisely what Faith teachers would have us believe. Televangelist Morris Cerullo is unequivocal in this regard. As we have seen, he dares his audience to utter the unthinkable. "Who are you?" he screeches. "Come on, who are you? Come on, say it: 'Sons of God!' Come on say it! And what does work inside us, brother, is that manifestation of the expression of all that God is and all that God has. And when we stand up here brother, you're not looking at Morris Cerullo; you're looking at God. You're looking at Jesus!"[5] This, however, is far from true. In his better moments Cerullo may reflect

God's communicable attributes (spirituality, rationality, morality), but at no time will he, or any other prosperity preacher for that matter, ever be a reproduction of the omnipresent, omnipotent, omniscient I AM! Far from being fashioned as "sons of God," we "live by faith in the Son of God" (Galatians 2:20).

In sum, Jesus never died spiritually, taking on the nature of Satan. He did not finish the work of redemption in hell by suffering under demonic hordes. He did not have to be transformed from demonic to divine and as such emerge from hell as the first born-again man. And born-again individuals are not reincarnated like unto Christ!

The glorious message of atonement is that the unblemished Lamb fully paid for sin through His passion on the cross. As such, each time we take communion, we remember His broken body and His shed blood for the *complete* remission of sin. Whereas the chasm between the nature of the Creator and the nature of created beings cannot be bridged, the relationship between a holy Creator and unholy creatures can be bridged through faith in Christ's atoning sacrifice.

ERROR BEGETS ERROR

Whether it is Paul Crouch alleging that Christ was reincarnated as a divine being at His resurrection, Kenneth Hagin asserting that born-again believers are as much an incarnation as was Jesus Christ of Nazareth, or Morris Cerullo averring that looking at him is tantamount to looking at God, all have moved from Christian essentials to cultic error.

And sadly they have spawned a whole army of imitators. Incredibly, Creflo Dollar goes so far as to say that "after spending three days and nights in the pit of hell, the power of God resurrected Him [Jesus] back to spiritual life with a new spirit and a glorified body." And still he is not done. "The day that Jesus was resurrected" declares Dollar, "He became the first begotten Son of God—born again from spiritual death to life."[6] The outrage here is breathtaking. If Dollar is right, the triune God would have ceased to exist during Christ's sojourn in hell. In biblical theology, the essence of God is indivisible. If the Persons of the Trinity were divided, the essence or nature of God is divided and therefore destroyed. Moreover, the universe that depends on God for its existence would likewise cease to exist.

The point here is to say that ideas have consequences. And in this case the consequences are unthinkable. The error that Jesus was incarnated as merely a man begets the error that on the cross Jesus was reincarnated from divine to demonic, which in turn begets the error that in His resurrection Jesus was reincarnated as a divine being. The errors, however, do not stop here. The hell of it, if I might put it that way, is that Faith preachers go on to teach that when we as believers are born again, we, too, are reincarnated. In the words of Benny Hinn, "you [in your present incarnation] are a little god on earth running around . . . a little messiah walking on earth."[7]

As you will now see, the errors that beget errors and the heresies that beget heresies just keep on coming. Because you have become an incarnation of God, your divine prerogative is a palace like the Taj Mahal with a Rolls Royce in your driveway. All it takes is the recognition of your own divinity. By using your tongue to release the force of faith, you can speak whatsoever you desire into existence. Indeed, your word is God's command.

part five

WEALTH AND WANT

Give me neither poverty nor riches, but give me only my daily bread.
Otherwise, I may have too much and disown you and say, "Who is the LORD?"
Or I may become poor and steal, and so dishonor the name of my God.[1]

—A PROVERB OF AGUR

The year was 1979. I had only recently committed my life to Jesus Christ. Although exhilarated by my relationship with the Lord of the universe, I was also haunted by all the wasted years—years of living by the dictates of my own will. I desperately wanted to make up for lost time.

More than anything else, I wanted to make my life count. I felt that to make up for lost time I had to free myself from financial constraints and considerations. And so I decided to take some of the financial resources I had accumulated and parlay them into what I hoped would be a small fortune.

The silver commodities market seemed to be the quickest route to financial security. I had been watching its rapid ascent and had been hearing about its potential in the financial markets. My research seemed to indicate that silver was grossly undervalued and that it was just a matter of time until it soared to previously unheard-of heights. Even from what I perceived to be a biblical point of view, the ratio between gold and silver should balance at ten to one.

As I continued to consider using silver as the vehicle to achieve financial security, the market began heating up. I decided to wait for a price correction so I could get into the market at a reasonable entry level.

Meanwhile, I planned a visit to my parents, who lived in the Netherlands. My motive was to map out a strategy for financial security: I wanted to serve God from a position of strength as a prosperous Christian. But, as I would soon discover, God had a radically different plan for my life.

After several days in Holland, I looked for something to read to pass the time. Since reading Dutch had become cumbersome for me, I was delighted to find a book printed in English on the coffee table in my parents' den. It was titled *Evangelism Explosion*. Once I began reading, I couldn't put it down. Within a few hours I encountered a whole new world—a world of spiritual multiplication. As I read on, I began to discover how I could become an equipped Christian and live with eternity in mind.

I returned to the States excited about the possibility of spiritual multiplication and immediately enrolled in the evangelism outreach program of my local church. However, my desire for financial security continued to burn brightly.

Silver prices by this time had begun to skyrocket. Anxious to "get on before the train left without me," I jumped into the market at $47.08 per ounce. Often I would look back and kick myself for not having acted sooner. I would calculate exactly how much I lost by not acting when I first began to see silver's meteoric ascent. Leveraged to the hilt, I waited anxiously for silver to continue rising. It did. Within a few days, it hit the fifty-dollar mark, and the predictions were that it wouldn't be long before it would crack the century mark (one hundred dollars per ounce).

Eagerly I waited, fully believing that God would soon allow me to become financially self-sufficient. But within days I received a call that caused my heart to freeze. The voice on the other end of the line merely said, "Hank . . . disaster." Before I could respond he blurted out, "The silver market just crashed." I was told to come over immediately to cover the shortfall (a "margin call") or my position in the market would be liquidated.

Over the next few months this would become a recurring scene. The phone call would come and I would have to cover another shortfall, always wondering how far I should chase the rabbit down the hole. With each passing week I was losing more and more of what had taken me years to accumulate. Yet in seeking advice from the experts, I was consistently counseled to hang in there—that they were just "shaking the amateurs out of the market."

Something else was happening as well. While I was losing financially, I was gaining spiritually. During the on-the-job training portion of *Evangelism Explosion*, I was going into the highways and byways and seeing people come to faith in Christ. On the one hand, I was losing my grip financially. But on the other hand, I was prospering spiritually to a degree I never dreamed possible.

Eventually I lost everything I had worked so long and hard to possess financially. But spiritually, I was gaining an eternal perspective. I was learning to seek first God's kingdom and His righteousness (Matthew 6:33). I was coming to realize that He would take care of my daily needs. Like Agur in Proverbs 30, I was learning to pray, "Give me neither poverty nor riches, but give me only my daily bread. Otherwise, I may have too much and disown you and say, 'Who is the Lord?' Or I may become poor and steal, and so dishonor the name of my God."

While Scripture neither condemns nor commends riches, the goal spiritually is to grow to such an extent in your relationship with Christ that, as the old hymn says, "the things of earth will grow strangely dim, in the light of His glory and grace."[2] The bottom line is to develop an eternal rather than a temporary perspective—eyes that can look beyond time and space into eternity.

Today I can only manage a wry smile as I think back and read the words of the apostle Paul to young Timothy: "People who want to get rich fall into temptation and a trap and into many foolish and harmful desires that plunge men into ruin and destruction" (1 Timothy 6:9).

In the next four chapters, we will see the devastating results of turning Paul's urgent warning on its head.

17

CULTURAL CONFORMITY

The Bible says that He has left us an example that we should follow His steps. That's the reason why I drive a Rolls Royce. I'm following Jesus' steps.[1]

—TELEVANGELIST FREDERICK K. C. PRICE

So why do prosperity preachers redefine faith as a force? Why attempt to talk devotees into believing that Adam was an exact duplicate of God—no difference, no distinction? Why perpetuate the pretext that every born-again person is as much an incarnation as was Jesus Christ of Nazareth? What's the point?

The answer may surprise you. Turning the gospel of grace into a gospel of greed takes a complete revision of what Faith preachers describe as "traditional Christianity." Jesse Duplantis is a classic case in point. Addressing Cornerstone pastor and televangelist John Hagee at a Cornerstone camp meeting, Duplantis explained that God is his comforter "because when you got some stuff it brings you comfort." Jesse's reasoning is remarkable, to put it mildly.

After clarifying that he is not just a millionaire but a multimillionaire, Jesse said to Hagee, "The Lord, I give Him the glory, is my comforter. If He is my comforter, Dr. Hagee, I live in comfort. That's not only spiritually—that's physically too. Because when you've got some stuff it brings you comfort." Jesse went on to pontificate that those who would say otherwise "know nothing about the Bible." With great aplomb he claimed to quote Jesus saying, "The destruction of the poor is their poverty" and challenged those who "know nothing about the Bible" to "explain that!"[2] Talk about biblical revisionism!

First, to say that Jesus is our comforter in that He gives us a comfortable lifestyle might well be said to be the height of cultural conformity. Jesus warned, "Watch out! Be on your guard against all kinds of greed; a man's life does not consist in the abundance of his possessions" (Luke 12:15). The Lord then told

His disciples the parable of the rich fool who was looking to his possessions for security (vv. 16–21). Jesus did not condemn possessions, but instead pointed out the foolishness of a temporary rather than an eternal perspective. Not mincing words, Jesus quoted His Father as saying to the rich man, "You fool! This very night your life will be demanded from you" (v. 20). The Master's command was always the same: "seek first the kingdom of God and His righteousness, and all these things shall be added to you" (Matthew 6:33 NKJV).

How unlike the message of Duplantis and company! They relentlessly hawk the idea that prosperity is the divine right of every believer—a brand of "Christianity" that is little more than baptized greed garbed in a thin veneer of "Christianese." A pitiable conformity to the cultural trends of our day. As Quentin Schultze, author of *Televangelism and American Culture*, astutely notes:

> Televangelists offer their own personalized expressions of the gospel as adapted from and directed to American culture. To put it more strongly, the faith of some televangelists is more American than Christian, more popular than historic, more personal than collective, and more experiential than biblical. As a result, the faith they preach is highly affluent, selfish, and individualistic . . . These three aspects of televangelism's faith system . . . reflect the American Dream, whereby a self-motivated individual supposedly attains great affluence. They also reflect the impact of modernity on the church.[3]

Furthermore, just as Jesus is not our comforter in that He gives us a comfortable lifestyle, Jesus did not, as Jesse declares, say that "the destruction of the poor is their poverty." Nor did He suggest that financial comfort was the destiny of those who place their trust in Him. Instead, Jesus said, "Woe to you who are rich, for you have already received your comfort. Woe to you who are well fed now, for you will go hungry" (Luke 6:24–25). As such, His message is the inverse of that of Duplantis, who pontificates that "poverty is a curse,"[4] or of Hagee, who likewise communicates that "poverty is a curse" and that "it is the result of sin."[5]

Finally, we should note that while Jesus did not say that "the destruction of the poor is their poverty," Solomon did (Proverbs 10:15 NKJV). Indeed, in the book of Proverbs he demonstrated that just as the prosperous are mistaken in considering wealth to be a "fortified city" (NIV) so the poor would be misguided in romanticizing poverty or using it as a pretext for laziness.

In sum, the very perception that Christians who are prosperous by the world's standards are spiritually rich, while the poor are spiritual paupers, is as blasphemous as it is bankrupt. It is more than just ironic that marketers of such drivel are propped up by the dollars sent in by the very poor they exploit. And when riches fail to materialize, the exploited often dejectedly leave what they thought was Christianity and seek safe haven in some other venue within the kingdom of the cults. They, along with their gurus, would do well to heed the words of the apostle Paul when he said, "There will be terrible times in the last days. People will be lovers of themselves, lovers of money, boastful, proud, abusive, disobedient to their parents, ungrateful, unholy, without love, unforgiving, slanderous, without self-control, brutal, not lovers of the good, treacherous, rash, conceited, lovers of pleasure rather than lovers of God—*having a form of godliness but denying its power*" (2 Timothy 3:1–5, emphasis added).

TRANSFORMED BY THE CULTURE

The problem here, of course, is cultural conformity. Far too many Christians are being transformed by our culture rather than by Christ. Seeking the kingdom of God and His righteousness has been perverted into seeking our own kingdom and everything else we can get our hands on.

Nowhere is such cultural conformity more apparent than in the Faith version of the incarnation of Christ. In literature and tape, radio and television, prosperity peddlers present a Jesus who looks remarkably like themselves: He lives in a big house. He is decked out in designer clothes. He has a huge donor base and is said to have so much money that He needs a treasurer.[6]

For some televangelists, the notion of a wealthy Jesus is merely a dogmatic assertion. For Duplantis's Jesus as well as for Hagee's, it's a biblically defensible argument. As such, Hagee points to the gospel of John as proof positive that Jesus had a big house. Says Hagee, "John 1:38 says that Jesus turned to those who were following and said, 'come with me,' and they said, 'where dwellest thou?' He said, 'come and see,' and Jesus took the crowd home with him to stay in His house. *That meant it was a big house.*"[7] Anyone who has read the gospel of John will immediately recognize that "the crowd" Hagee references is pure mythology. Indeed, the very passage cited by Hagee makes it clear that far from inviting a *crowd* to join Him in His mansion, Jesus merely invited *two* people to see "where he was staying" (v. 39).

As noted in my Cast of Characters, Hagee also argues that Jesus wore designer clothes. As he puts it, "Jesus had a seamless robe so valuable that Roman soldiers gambled for it at the cross. It was a designer robe."[8] Again the notion that Roman soldiers gambled for Christ's garment because it was "so valuable" is completely *ad hoc*. Truth is they cast lots for the garment of Christ so "that the Scripture might be fulfilled" (John 19:24). Moreover as plain old common sense dictates, one garment divided into four rags would be of little value to anyone.[9]

John Hagee, of course, is not alone. John Avanzini, for years the star fundraiser for the Trinity Broadcasting Network, tells his vast television audience that if Jesus was poor, he wants to be poor. If Jesus slept under a bridge, he wants to sleep under a bridge. But if Jesus was rich, we, too, should be rich![10]

Prosperity preachers are so committed to presenting a Jesus who wears a Rolex that they are willing to do whatever it takes to sell this myth to their parishioners. Oral Roberts, for example, wrote a book titled *How I Learned Jesus Was Not Poor*. And Frederick Price says he's trying "to get you out of this malaise of thinking that Jesus and the disciples were poor . . . The Bible says that He has left us an example that we should follow His steps. That's the reason why I drive a Rolls Royce. I'm following Jesus' steps."[11]

JESUS WITH A ROLEX

Prosperity gurus are not merely content to preach their pretexts. John Avanzini, for one, goes so far as to attack apologists and theologians for teaching that Jesus was poor. In utter disgust he snorts, "I don't know where these goofy traditions creep in at, but one of the goofiest ones is that Jesus and His disciples were poor. Now there's no Bible to substantiate that."[12]

During one TBN broadcast, Avanzini charged theologians with taking Luke 9:57–58 (cf. Matthew 8:18–20) out of context to prove that Jesus was poor. He then presented what he claims to be the true meaning of the passage—a meaning that has escaped the Christian church for nearly two thousand years.

Avanzini's imaginative recollection of the biblical account finds Jesus on His way to conducting a "seminar" in Samaria. But, alas, His "advance team" had not taken care of business properly, and the "Jesus seminar" got canceled. In replying to a man who wanted to follow Him, Jesus said, "Foxes have holes *in Samaria*, birds of the air have nests *in Samaria*, but I don't have any place to stay tonight *in Samaria*." As Avanzini puts it, "In those days there wasn't a Holiday Inn on every corner," so Jesus was forced to go back home to His nice, big house in Jerusalem.[13]

Like Avanzini, John Hagee makes a mockery out of the words of our Lord as recorded in Luke's Gospel. With reckless abandon he turns the good news of the gospel, as recorded in Luke 4:18, into a perverted prosperity pretext. "What's the good news to the poor?" asks Hagee. "The good news to the poor is this. Christ took your poverty on the cross and gave you the riches of Abraham. Brother, that's enough to make a Baptist to get in the aisles and start dancing. The curse of poverty has been broken at the cross. If you have the anointing, you don't have the curse of poverty." Hagee goes on to promise devotees, "If you practice the principles of prosperity in the Word of God, this [Luke 4:18] says God will make you the head and not the tail."[14]

Is the good news to the poor referenced by Christ in Luke 4:18 really a promise of prosperity for twenty-first-century Christians? Was the curse of earthly poverty really broken at the cross? Are Hagee's followers really going to be the head and not the tail? The answer should be self-evident. Far from a guarantee of riches in the present age, true followers of Christ in every age will experience trial and tribulation. While some may experience material riches, their focus, like every other follower of Christ, is firmly fixed on "a new heaven and a new earth" in which "there will be no more death or mourning or crying or pain, for the old order of things has passed away" (Revelation 21:2, 4).

DISCIPLES WITH DOUGH

Not only do Faith teachers maintain that Jesus was wealthy, they contend that His disciples lived in luxury as well. Avanzini, for instance, argues that the apostle Paul was so rich that he had the financial resources to block up the justice system of his day.[15]

But how can anyone read 1 Corinthians 4:9–13 and contend that the apostle Paul and his companions had the kind of money that could block up justice? How could Scripture more clearly articulate their true condition? "To this very hour we go hungry and thirsty, we are in rags, we are brutally treated, we are homeless" (v. 11). Moreover, would not Paul have been duplicitous were he living in the lap of luxury while teaching Timothy that "people who want to get rich fall into temptation and a trap and into many foolish and harmful desires that plunge men into ruin and destruction" (1 Timothy 6:9)?

And what about Paul's farewell address to the Ephesian elders in which he said that the Holy Spirit personally warned him of impending imprisonment and hardships (Acts 20:23)? Or his immortal words in Philippians 3:7–9: "Whatever was to my profit I now consider loss for the sake of Christ. What is more, I consider everything a loss compared to the surpassing greatness of knowing Christ Jesus my Lord, for whose sake I have lost all things. I consider them rubbish, that I may gain Christ and be found in him"?

JESUS: AN END IN HIMSELF

Following the Resurrection, the disciples of Christ never again considered their Master a means to their ends. To them, He *was* the End. Christ's followers had internalized the message their Lord had preached through His life, His love, and His lips. They rightly understood that their treasure was in another kingdom and that they were simply ambassadors, sojourners, and pilgrims. The disciples knew this was not their final dwelling place. They recognized that their destiny was eternity.

Christ did not come to bring financial prosperity; He came to focus our attention on *eternal* prosperity. Even now the words of the Master ring with divine authority: "Do not store up for yourselves treasures on earth, where moth and rust destroy, and where thieves break in and steal. But store up for yourselves treasures in heaven" (Matthew 6:19–20). How magnificent a sight it must have been to witness the Lord standing on the shore of Galilee, pleading passionately with His followers to labor not for that which perishes but for that which is eternal (John 6:27).

How much Scripture do we need to see the bankruptcy of the Faith movement's teaching on prosperity? Shall we remind ourselves of Christ's account of the rich man and Lazarus in Luke 16:19–31? The rich man, who lived his earthly life in luxury, was not even dignified with a name in eternity. But Lazarus, who lived in poverty, received comfort in the eternal kingdom (v. 25).

Or perhaps we should reread the words of Jesus' half brother, James, when he boldly declared to the rich, "Your wealth has rotted . . . Your gold and silver are corroded . . . You have hoarded wealth in the last days" (James 5:2–3).

The Bible is replete with examples declaring the poverty of the Faith movement's cultural conformity. They have not conformed their teachings to the ancient Scriptures. Instead, they have conformed themselves to American society.

American culture is obsessed with upward mobility and crass materialism, which is precisely what the Faith movement panders toward. It thrives on the idea that "God's kids" can acquire wealth without work and dollars without discipline. Its watchword is not *self-sacrifice* but *self-aggrandizement*. Sadly, a significant portion of contemporary Christianity has bought into the message that we only go around once in this world, so we had better go for all the gusto we can while we're here.[16] They no longer sing "I surrender all." They shout, "I can speak it all into existence through the formula of faith."

We crave rags-to-riches stories and frequently cave in to get-rich-quick schemes. T. L. Osborn, for one, promises people that by learning "7 Simple Secrets in Just 60 Seconds a Day" you can "Get the Best Out of Life in Just 7 Days."[17] As proof he cites, among other stories, the tale of a man who was forced to leave his country and found himself in great financial difficulty. But thanks to Osborn's "fast-faith formula," this man was able to buy "a Rolls Royce and a new home." Predictably, this man goes on to encourage others to "plant $20 or $50" in Osborn's ministry "to see for themselves how God works money MIRACLES."[18]

In sharp distinction, Scripture commands us to not conform to the pattern of this world, but to be transformed by the renewing of our minds. Only then will we be able to "test and approve what God's will is—his good, pleasing and perfect will" (Romans 12:2).

DOES POVERTY EQUAL PIETY?

Having said all this, let me make crystal clear that I do *not* associate poverty with piety (although the poor *do* have a special place in God's heart; see Luke 6:20). The issue is not what you have, but what you do with what you have. Our time, talent, and treasure should be used for God's glory rather than our own gain. I am persuaded that the Bible teaches a form of Christian capitalism—

responsibility associated with wealth. It does not promote the possession of money for the sake of money, but instead encourages us to use money for the sake of the kingdom.

While some Faith teachers assert that they have the same concept in mind, the evidence shows otherwise. Not only do most Faith teachers induce their supporters to give by appealing to their greed, but they indulge themselves in the process. As Frederick Price boasts, "If the Mafia can ride around in Lincoln Continental town cars, why can't the King's Kids?"[19] With bravado, he exudes:

> You can talk about me all you want while I'm driving by in my Rolls Royce that's paid for, and I got the pink slip on it. Talk all you want. Badmouth all you want. Don't hurt me in the least. Doesn't bother me. It's a whole lot easier to be persecuted when I'm riding in my car and I got the pink slip than it is when I'm riding in a car and owe my soul to the company store.[20]

In the end, prosperity proponents teach a lifestyle of self-indulgence and selfishness, as opposed to self-denial and selflessness. The ex-wife of televangelist Richard Roberts summed it up ever so eloquently:

> I know a lot of people were blessed and sincerely ministered to by what we sang on TV, and by what we said—but the overall picture, I'm afraid, seemed to say, "If you follow our formula, you'll be like us," rather than, "If you do what Jesus says, you'll be like Him." It was certainly more exciting to follow us, because to follow us was to identify with success, with glamour, with a theology that made everything good and clean and well-knit together. To identify with Jesus, however, meant to identify with the Cross.[21]

The difference between serving self and serving the Savior is the difference between cultural conformity and conformity to Christ. Jesus said it best: "If anyone would come after me, he must deny himself and take up his cross daily and follow me" (Luke 9:23; cf. Matthew 16:24; Mark 8:34).

A Rolls Royce is certainly more comfortable than a cross, but it is clearly not as enduring.

ERROR BEGETS ERROR

Where Price favors a Lincoln Continental Town Car or a Rolls Royce, Rod Parsley favors a Lexus or Mercedes. The elucidations of their errors, however, are virtually indistinguishable. As such, Parsley has parishioners practicing the preposterous. He instructs them to chant, "I'm on my way to houses I didn't build." Says Parsley, "Some of you better get ready to drive around in neighborhoods where you never thought you'd be able to afford to live." Likewise, if they follow his formulas fastidiously, they are on their way to cars that are beyond their means. "Some of you better go down to that Lexus and Mercedes dealership and just sit down in one of those things with that leather all over it."

If someone inquires about such strange behavior, Parsley has a ready response. "Say, 'Well, I'm just feeling out what my Father is going to give me.'" If the questioner persists, asking, "How?" Parsley programs his devotees to say, "I heard a word from the man of God, and when I obey that word it unleashes that anointing into my life and I'm on my way to houses I didn't build, full of good things I didn't have to buy."[22]

Joel Osteen is similarly disposed. Like sub-prime mortgage lenders of days gone by, he urges followers to reach beyond their means. As documented in the "Cast of Characters" chapter, Osteen offers up himself as a prime example. While living in a "crooked" little house, he and Victoria came upon a beautiful home in the final stages of construction. The home was so far beyond the realm of possibility that Joel uttered words of fear rather than words of faith. As he explains it in *Your Best Life Now*, Victoria saved the day—and with it the dream. "Over the next several months, she kept speaking words of faith and victory." Eventually Joel rid himself of "limited thinking" and started agreeing with her. "We kept on believing it, seeing it, and speaking it," writes Joel, and "we saw it come to pass." Joel now instructs his followers to do what he did. "Conceive it on the inside. Start seeing yourself rising to a new level, doing something of significance, living in that home of your dreams."[23]

All of this, of course, is sanitized with a semblance of Scripture. Says Dollar, "Don't you let them tell you, you can't have a brand-new, a brand-new car, because if Jesus rode in on a donkey that no man had ever sat on, then you and I can ride in an automobile that no man has ever sat on." Even better, according to Dollar, this is a credible way of reaching people for Christ. In his words, there's "a world of people out there that don't know your Jesus. But when they start seeing you with their stuff they're going to want to know how you got it and they'll want you to introduce them to the Jesus that's able to open doors up without the college degree, without kissing up to somebody. They'll want to know the Jesus that opened the doors that no man could shut on your back."[24]

In fact, according to Hagee—"The good news to the poor is this":

Christ took your poverty on the cross and He gave you the riches of Abraham. Brother, that's enough to make a Baptist to get in the aisles and start dancing. The curse of poverty has been broken at the cross. If you have the anointing you don't have the curse of poverty. If you will practice the principles of prosperity in the word of God, this says God will make you the head and not the tail. God will open the windows of heaven and bless you with blessings that you cannot contain. God will give you wells you didn't dig; he will give you vineyards you did not plant. He will give you houses you did not build.[25]

If you listen carefully to the Faith preachers, there is a constant refrain. The way in which one demonstrates that he has faith is by giving. Not traditional giving, however. The kind of giving that ultimately opens up the windows of heaven and pours out a blessing that you cannot receive is the give-to-get kind. With those who have the temerity to respond, "I don't give to get, Brother Jesse, I give because I just love the Lord," Duplantis minces no words. "That's the spirit of stupid on you!" It may sound "churchy," says Jesse, but "that don't mean nothing."[26]

T. D. Jakes is unequivocal in this regard: "There are certain truths that transcend all principles"[27] and, apparently, *giving to get is one of them*. Even the notion of break-even giving would be "ridiculous" in the extreme: "It would be ridiculous for me to pray that God would give it back to you, because if all he was going to do was give it back to you, you ought to keep it . . . *That's ridiculous!* If you got a hundred dollars or a thousand dollars and you were going to get a thousand dollars, I tell you what, you just broke even. *You could have kept the thousand dollars and not gone through the trouble.*"[28]

This, however, is far from true. As Scripture makes plain, we give "so that [we] may learn to revere the LORD our God always" (Deuteronomy 14:23). Moreover, we give so that we might meet the physical needs of the less fortunate. In sum, we give so that we might extend God's kingdom.

The world fuels an unholy trinity—"the cravings of sinful man, the lust of his eyes and the boasting of what he has and does" (1 John 2:16). Genuine biblical faith, however, focuses on the permanent pleasures of paradise rather than the pseudo-pleasures of the present; it blinds the unclean eye that lusts after prosperity and wealth; and it ultimately deadens the pride of life that covets the things of the world.

For the rich man who died and found himself in torment, it is too late. You and I can as yet live with eternity in mind.

18

CONS AND COVER-UPS

You watching me in television land and you saying all I got is $900. But I hear the Lord saying, I double-dare people that are watching me right now, this one is for you, I double-dare you to empty your checking account. If you got $79.36, empty it out. Empty it out, at the voice of the prophet.[1]

—PROPHETESS JUANITA BYNUM

Cons and cover-ups under the guise of Christianity are certainly nothing new. Neither are charlatans.

During a time of spiritual darkness, a crass and carnal monk named Johann Tetzel conned the commoners of his day into buying indulgences (special releases from sin offered by certain Catholic clergy). Tetzel took a complex Catholic creed on purgatory and reduced it to a catchy couplet:

> As soon as the coin in the coffer rings,
> The soul from purgatory springs.

His pitch was intoxicatingly simple. People could purchase a pardon from God that would purge them from a place called purgatory. Unbelievably, thousands fell for the ruse. In fact, the masses—from monks to magistrates—hailed Tetzel as a messenger from heaven. Capitalizing on spiritual insecurity and scriptural illiteracy, he fleeced the flock in order to fund papal projects as well as his own extravagant lifestyle.

Although Tetzel's methods for merchandizing the gospel were outrageous, no one seemed willing to expose him. His popularity, backed by the power of Rome, seemed too formidable a foe. That is, until a monk named Martin Luther came along. Luther could no longer go along with the con. As Philip

Schaff so aptly stated: "As a preacher, a pastor, and a professor, he [Luther] felt it to be his duty to protest . . . To be silent was to betray his theology and his conscience."[2] And so, in 1517, Luther nailed his famous Ninety-Five Theses to the door of the castle church at Wittenberg.

In layman's language, Luther's Ninety-Five Theses protested the pillaging of the poor by the pope. In Theses 27 and 28, Luther labeled the notion that a soul would fly out of purgatory when money fell into the coffers of the church as a perverted prescription for "avarice and gain."[3]

In Theses 45 and 66, Luther expressed outrage that a person would attempt to purchase God's pardon with money. He called the "treasures of indulgences" nets with which the preachers of pardon fished for the "riches of men."[4]

In Theses 50 and 51, Luther stated that the real reason Rome was selling indulgences was not the spiritual well-being of the saints but the financial well-being of the pope and his pet project—the building of the Basilica of Saint Peter's. He wrote with great passion that the mother Church in Rome would be better "burnt to ashes, than that it should be built up with the skin, flesh, and bones" of the pope's sheep.[5]

In Thesis 86, Luther put it all in perspective when he asked why a rich pope, "whose riches are at this day more ample than that of the wealthiest of the wealthy," would not build the Basilica with his own money, rather than taking from the meager resources of the poor.[6]

Rome's reaction was swift and severe. Luther was labeled a "child of the devil" and a "drunken German who when sober will change his mind." But Luther did not change his mind.[7] Under the ban of the Empire and a bull of excommunication, Luther displayed raw courage, rare communication skills, and rich convictions.

When asked to recant, he responded with the famous words "My conscience is captive to the Word of God . . . Here I stand. I cannot do otherwise. May God help me."[8]

Luther's courage established a mighty Reformation that exposed the cons and cover-ups of his day. Today another Reformation is sorely needed. The pillaging of the poor, sanctified by papal bulls in years gone by, is strikingly similar to the appeals of a new generation of "prosperity pope." Tetzel fleeced the poor by promising freedom from purgatory. False teachers today are conning a new generation by promising freedom from poverty and a lifetime of prosperity.

HAVE A NEED, PLANT A SEED

In a book titled *Ashes to Gold*, Patti Roberts compares the "seed-faith" tactic of former father-in-law Oral Roberts to Johann Tetzel's practice of selling indulgences. She points out that she had a "very difficult time distinguishing between the selling of indulgences and the concept of seed-faith inflated to the degree to which we had inflated it."[9]

One distinction Patti did observe was that Oral was more subtle than Tetzel. Rather than offering salvation in exchange for money, Oral appealed to such basic instincts as fear and greed. And he is not alone. Oral's tactics have become standard fare among the Faith teachers. While they may not promise their partners heavenly paradise, they do promise them earthly prosperity. Like Tetzel, many of them have become masters at inventing catchy couplets to make their ideas both understandable and memorable. One seed-faith ditty goes like this: "Have a need, plant a seed."

Says Roberts, "The seed of giving is the seed of faith! And the seed has to be planted BEFORE we can speak to our mountain of need to be removed!"[10] Simply stated, "planting a seed" is synonymous with "mail me money." The seed-faith gimmick is little more than a give-to-get gospel of greed.

Oral Roberts and his son Richard have used both television and the mail to raise millions of dollars. Their methods have been described as "the lowest form of emotional appeal."[11] In their mailings, they appeal to the sympathies of their partners as well as their greed.

On January 4, 1987, Oral Roberts launched his most notorious campaign to date. Roberts told his followers that if he did not raise a total of eight million dollars by March, God was going to take his life.[12] In a follow-up direct-mail letter, Roberts announced that the deadline to raise the remaining 1.5 million dollars was set for March 31. To serve as a reminder to his supporters, a caption, printed in handwritten form at the top of the mass mailing's first page, warned, "Just 30 days left!"[13]

Comparing himself to the apostle Paul, Roberts begged people to not let Satan defeat him. "God," he says, "clearly told me he needs me here on earth. And here's why—because of all the ministries, this ministry is the only one God has on this earth that owns a medical school."[14] Then came the punch line: By sending a "seed" of fifty dollars, Robert's partners can spare his life, save the school, sabotage Satan, and secure lots of money, to boot.[15]

Some time later, Richard Roberts took pen in hand to warn of his father's impending doom. Without "the additional $4,500,000," explained Richard, "God will not extend Dad's life." He then pleaded, "Partner, we cannot let this man of God die. There is no reason for him to die." And this was no idle threat, Richard claimed. As he put it, "When he [Oral] says God speaks to him, he's not bluffing." And just in case someone should doubt or suspect his motives, Richard offered his stirring assurance: "I feel totally called by God to do this . . . I'm writing to you as an anointed servant of God—doing what God has called me to do."[16]

After several pages Richard finally got to the seed-faith solution: take the enclosed birthday card, slip in a seed-faith gift "check," and "then RUSH IT TO ME TODAY."[17]

By the end of the letter, Richard Roberts had done virtually everything to assure his partners that this was a deal they couldn't afford to pass up: send your seed-faith gift and Richard will be proud of you, Oral will pray for you, and God will prosper you.

Like sympathy ploys, fear tactics have proven equally persuasive. Roberts warned partners of impending doom. Supposedly, God supernaturally revealed that 1985 would be a terrible year for Roberts's partners. "Satan is going to bring bad things against you," stated Roberts. "*Worry . . . Fear . . .* stress [that] will be a serious threat against your health. Even worse, I see Satan is going to make his biggest effort to surround you with so many problems you will feel a sense of *hopelessness.*"[18]

There was a silver lining however. Roberts consulted God about "Satan's bad year against you." Supernaturally, "the gift of prophecy came on me," he writes, "and 33 predictions were given to me concerning you."[19] These predictions, Roberts promised, will help you to "avoid TERRIBLE NEW DISEASES" and to "take advantage of the hundredfold return . . . to receive . . . PROSPERITY MIRACLES."[20]

After sternly warning, "IF YOU NEGLECT TO PAY ATTENTION . . . then Satan will take advantage and hit you with bad things and you will wish that 1985 had never come,"[21] Roberts closed his letter with a hard sell. Sending a seed-faith gift will not only enable you to "STOP SATAN IN HIS HATE TO BRING YOU DOWN," it will also "help you get your hundredfold return."[22]

"PROSPERITY MIRACLES . . . are within fingertip reach of your faith," claimed Roberts.[23] Of course, the key was to use your fingertips to send money.

Appealing to greed, Roberts held out the prospect of financial gain to those who would send him the green.

Incidentally, don't ever think of sending Roberts money and then later changing your mind. If you do, saving Roberts's life may be the least of your worries. Consider these chilling words uttered by Roberts:

> Someone will be watching this ministry on the air, who promised a large sum [of money] to God. And you act like you have given it, but you did not pay it. You are so close to lying to the Holy Ghost, that *within days you will be dead* unless you pay the price God said. And somebody here is getting the message. You're on the edge of lying to the Holy Ghost. Don't lie to the Holy Ghost. *The prophet has spoken.*[24]

While Roberts attempts to sanitize his seed-faith theology by surrounding it with scriptural pretexts, his theology is strikingly similar to that of a well-known metaphysical/prosperity cult—the Unity School of Christianity. The reasoning Roberts employs directly reflects the thinking process of Unity's cofounder, Charles Fillmore.[25] Indeed, as acknowledged by Roberts, one of his prosperity devotionals came directly from this cult.[26]

THE HUNDREDFOLD BANDWAGON

Years ago, Roberts promised prosperity to those who would "plant a seed." Today a new breed of prosperity teachers champion even bigger promises of financial reward—the "hundredfold" return.

In a book titled *God's Will Is Prosperity*, Gloria Copeland springs the hundredfold on constituents. Expanding on the promise of Jesus to provide a hundredfold return to those who leave everything behind for the kingdom, Gloria writes, "Give $10 and receive $1,000; give $1,000 and receive $100,000. I know that you can multiply, but I want you to see in black and white how tremendous the hundredfold return is."[27] And just so you don't miss her point, Gloria explains:

> Give one house and receive one hundred houses or one house worth one hundred times as much. Give one airplane and receive one hundred times

the value of the airplane. Give one car and the return would furnish you a lifetime of cars. In short, Mark 10:30 is a very good deal.[28]

Gloria, of course, is not the only Faith teacher to jump on the hundredfold bandwagon. John Avanzini has been used by Faith teachers from Crouch to Cerullo to raise money by using the hundredfold tactic. In fact, it was during a Morris Cerullo convention in Abba, Nigeria, that Avanzini came up with his now-famous hundredfold concept.[29]

It all began when Cerullo's son, David (now chairman and CEO of Inspiration Networks), joined Avanzini's church in Southern California. Avanzini told David that God "dropped in my heart that the wealth of the wicked was laid up for the just." Avanzini then began to beg him, "Please, I want to go with your daddy [Morris] and I want to speak to the nations of the world."[30]

In time, Avanzini gained an audience with Cerullo. His hopes, however, were dashed when Morris rejected him because he did not have "a breakthrough ministry." As Avanzini was to discover later on, a breakthrough ministry was one characterized by "signs and wonders . . . to prove that there is a move of God going on."[31] After waiting patiently for two years, Avanzini finally got the break he was looking for.

Cerullo summoned Avanzini to Abba, Nigeria. There, in a hotel room, God supposedly appeared to Avanzini and said, "I'm gonna have signs and wonders follow your ministry." After giving Avanzini a wordy discourse on fund-raising techniques, God instructed him to take up an offering for Cerullo. As God allegedly put it, "I want you to lay hands on that offering, and I want you to speak hundredfold increase over that offering—that it will be multiplied back to the giver one hundredfold."[32]

Sure enough, the very next day Avanzini had the opportunity to try out the new fund-raising technique. After telling the Nigerian leaders at Cerullo's meeting that they would get a hundred times back whatever they gave in the offering, Avanzini gave the order to pass little collection bowls around the room. Before the bowls had reached the end of the first row, they had already been filled to overflowing. Pillowcases were immediately summoned to take up the rest of the offering. But even that wasn't enough.

By now the crowd was in a frenzy. In fact, as Avanzini put it, "Money was falling out of the balcony." Finally the giving got so out of hand that Cerullo himself had to stand up and shout, "Stop the giving! Stop the giving!"

Eventually order was restored, and once again Avanzini attempted to pray over the offering. But "as I began to pray," said Avanzini, "I felt something hitting me, and I looked up and the people were throwing money. Money was being thrown over the tops of their heads. And I laid hands on that offering and I spoke the hundredfold increase."[33]

According to Avanzini, when Jan Crouch heard about that hundredfold incident, she asked him a dozen times or more to deliver the hundredfold message on TBN. Allegedly, Avanzini answered, "Anything else, but God's just not letting me do it."[34] Nowadays, every time TBN holds a fund-raising drive, God apparently releases John to perform his hundredfold routine.

As in Nigeria, gullible American Christians are now throwing their money to the Faith teachers in the hopes that God will throw back a hundred times as much. Sadly, few seem to notice that the "emperor has no clothes."

If the hundredfold message were fact, prosperity teachers would never again have to ask for money. Instead, they would be in the streets, giving it away as fast as they could so they could get more. All poverty would be gone, and every believer would live in a mansion. The "wealth of the wicked" would indeed be in the hands of the "King's kids." Instead, it is not uncommon to hear appeals like this one from Paul Crouch:

> If you're broke, if you're at your wit's end, if you're out of a job, out of work, let me tell ya. Not only are we gonna bless the world and preach Christ to millions and multitudes around the world, but you can be saved yourself, by planting seed in this fertile soil called TBN.[35]

THE "POINT OF CONTACT" PITCH

Oral Roberts once referred to the "point of contact" as the "greatest discovery" he had ever made.[36] And well he should! In conjunction with the seed-faith strategy, Roberts has used this tactic to raise more money than Tetzel ever dreamed of. Others have done the same.

Robert Tilton, who described the point of contact as a link of faith with his partners, built a financial empire based on this tactic. In mailing after mailing, he claimed the Holy Spirit was directing him in the use of this method. In a 1990 mailout to his partners, Tilton said that God told him to

215

send them a green prayer cloth as a point of contact.[37] He then instructed his partners to

- take the prayer cloth, hold it in their right hand, and pray for a release of "POWER to create wealth";
- fill out a "Power to Create Wealth" personal reply sheet; and
- send lots of money, or as he puts it, "*Sow your very best seed!*"[38]

Next, Tilton urged devotees to "seed out of their need." The greater the sacrifice, the greater the return. Tilton went on to coax people to strike while the iron is hot. As he put it, "Please respond quickly while the anointing is hot and flowing."[39]

When you returned the green prayer cloth with the money, Tilton promised to pray specifically and release his faith for you. The idea was that when you returned the cloth with some cash, this "anointed apostle" would add his faith to your faith and you would experience unbelievable results. Tilton's pitch was plain and simple:

SEND ME YOUR GREEN PRAYER CLOTH AS MY POINT OF CONTACT WITH YOU! . . . WHEN I TOUCH YOUR CLOTH . . . IT WILL BE LIKE TOUCHING YOU! . . . *When you touch this cloth, it will be like taking MY hand and touching me.* I want the anointing that God has put upon my life for miracles of finances and prosperity to come directly from my hand to yours . . . *You can reign in life like a king!* [40]

To help ensure a positive response, Tilton cited an example of a lady who was down-and-out. When she heard his pitch, she took the plunge, sent in the prayer cloth, and started making payments on a vow of faith. Within months she allegedly received the payoff—$286,000 in bonds and $65,000 in cash. As an added bonus, her husband was delivered from alcoholism.[41]

Of course, green prayer cloths are not all you can find in the Faith teachers' tactics. Their points of contact come in various shapes and sizes. They include anointed handkerchiefs, hems from their garments, holy oil, and a host of other gimmicks. There is virtually no end to the variations that could be cited. For a suggested donation of $1,989 or $890 or $89 (for the year 1989), Marilyn Hickey said she would even slip on a ceremonial breastplate, "press *your* 'Breastplate' prayer requests to my heart" and "place your requests on my shoulders."[42]

The Faith teachers inevitably use the Scriptures to make their tactics seem spiritual. Oral Roberts, for example, derived one of his point-of-contact strategies directly from the book of Acts. When Roberts discovered that people were healed by Peter's passing shadow, he decided that people could have their needs met by his passing shadow as well.

As the story goes, at first Oral and his son, Richard, could not figure out how to use their shadows as a point of contact for their partners, since it was impossible to walk by all of them personally. So they began to pray in the Spirit, and God gave them a solution.[43]

God told Roberts to have a photographer take a picture of him and his son praying for the needs of their partners. Then Roberts got some specific instructions "straight from Jesus" to give to his partners.[44]

First, Jesus told the partners to take Oral and Richard seriously as "God's co-evangelists . . . who dream dreams and see visions . . . Write down what you feel led for us to pray for . . . This will help us pray SPECIFICALLY when we bring YOUR NAME to the Lord."[45]

Next, Jesus instructed the partners to "place a love gift of Seed-Faith upon the prayer sheet right on top of your needs."[46]

Then Jesus unveiled an ingenious plan! He instructed Oral's partners to take the picture of Oral and Richard "AND HOLD IT OVER the prayer sheet and your Seed-Faith gift so that the shadow of the picture COVERS THE ENTIRE SHEET." According to Jesus, this "becomes the point of contact for you to loose your faith."[47]

Oral's Jesus saved His most creative instructions for last. He suggested that the partners fold the prayer sheet and the seed-faith gift together to symbolize their union with Oral and Richard. They were then instructed, "Send it back to Richard and me today, if possible, so that he and I can immediately unfold it AND OUR SHADOWS CAN PASS OVER YOUR NAME AND NEEDS ON YOUR PRAYER SHEET."[48]

According to Oral and Richard, Jesus also wanted to make sure that the partners kept "the praying picture" as a "personal reminder that Richard and I [Oral]—co-evangelists of God's healing power—are praying for you daily."[49]

Roberts ended his letter by alerting partners that "skeptics may criticize something scriptural like this."[50] Here Oral is finally correct.

SEED-FAITH IN THE LIGHT OF SCRIPTURE

Despite Roberts's claim that his seed-faith concept came directly from Jesus, it should nonetheless be tested in light of Scripture. As such, it should be more than a passing concern that the Jesus who allegedly dispensed the seed-faith theology in the first place may not be the Jesus of the Bible. This is particularly the case in light of his claim that the core of the Sermon on the Mount is focused on seed-faith![51]

It should likewise be of concern that this Jesus also claimed that Matthew 17:20—"If ye have faith as a grain of mustard seed, ye shall say unto this mountain, Remove hence to yonder place, and it shall remove; and nothing shall be impossible unto you" (KJV)—teaches that the seed-faith principle enables people to move mountains.[52]

If this were the case, Jesus would be seriously confused. As should be obvious to anyone who has read the passage, Jesus does not address the issue of giving in any sense. Conversely, the message of the passage is, had the disciples had faith in their Lord—faith as small as a mustard seed—they would have been able to cast the demon out of a man.

To make matters worse, Roberts's Jesus also claimed that the New Testament, in its entirety, is based on seed-faith, even trying to use Galatians 6:7—"Whatsoever a man soweth, that shall he also reap" (KJV)—to make his point.[53] But as is obvious from the context, the Galatians passage does not appeal to man's greed by formulating a give-to-get scheme (cf. verse 8). Rather, it appeals to people to crucify their selfishness and serve God (Galatians 5:21, 24, 26) and one another (6:9–10) selflessly.

Tragically, Roberts goes on to twist the biblical view of the atonement by claiming that Christ's death was a seed that God sowed, and His resurrection was the harvest that God reaped. As Roberts's Jesus put it, "The cross is the seed of My life, the seed I gave which was multiplied back to Me by the Father raising Me from the dead, increasing My life far more than it was when I was a man." This Jesus also declared, "I fulfilled the old law of tithing by paying the full price on the cross." Giving is no longer a debt I owe but a seed I sow.[54]

The moment Roberts heard this commentary on the precious person and work of our Lord and Savior Jesus Christ, he should have immediately rebuked the demon—or at least his overactive imagination.

HUNDREDFOLD: TOO MUCH OF A GOOD THING?

The hundredfold teaching fares no better in the light of Scripture. We have seen that Faith teachers like Gloria Copeland frequently point to Mark 10:30 ("receive a hundred times") as the basis for this tactic. But the true meaning of Mark 10 is so plain it can hardly be missed. Simply take the time to read the entire chapter in context. The meaning will jump out at you.

Copeland conveniently skips the part in verse 30 about receiving persecutions. She also neglects what is written five verses earlier, where Jesus warns, "It is easier for a camel to go through the eye of a needle than for a rich man to enter the kingdom of God."

Far from being a chapter focused on investment advice for financial prosperity, Mark 10 is clearly designed to portray the deceitfulness of riches. The multiplication envisioned in Mark 10:30 is spiritual rather than physical, metaphorical rather than literal.

In Mark 10, Jesus is using figurative language when He says we will receive a hundred times what we leave behind. David does the same thing in Psalm 50 when he says God owns the cattle on a thousand hills. Clearly he means that God owns everything, and not that God's ownership of hill-grazing cattle extends to exactly one thousand.

To take Jesus literally in Mark 10:30 is to reduce this passage to a logical absurdity. It would be one thing for Christ to promise a 100-to-1 return when it came to houses; it would be quite another to promise a 100-to-1 return on wives and children. I don't know about you, but for me, that may be too much of a good thing!

POINTLESS CONTACTS

Faith teachers frequently cite Acts 19:11–12 to prove that the apostle Paul used points of contact in the manner that they do. Yet even a cursory examination of the text disproves that assertion.

In Acts 19:11–12 we read that "God did extraordinary miracles through Paul . . . handkerchiefs and aprons that had touched him were taken to the sick, and their illnesses were cured and the evil spirits left them."

First, conspicuous by its absence in this text is the mention of finances.

Nowhere does Paul ask for money to be sent back to him with the handkerchief as a point of contact. Conversely, the Bible issues a strong warning to all those who would seek to buy God's miracle-working power with money. As Peter said to Simon the sorcerer in Acts 8:20, "May your money perish with you, because you thought you could buy the gift of God with money!"

Next, there is no suggestion in Acts 19 that those being healed had "released" their faith. There is certainly no indication that they sent Paul their points of contact with a seed-faith gift so that Paul could put an "Acts 19 kind of anointing" on them and pray for them Marilyn Hickey–style.[55]

Quite to the contrary, as the text says, God was manifesting *extraordinary* or *unusual* miracles through Paul. Far from being normative, these miracles were proof that Paul had been uniquely chosen by God as the "apostle to the Gentiles" (Romans 11:13; cf. 2 Timothy 1:11).

Finally, a historical perspective proves that God was demonstrating the difference between magical formulas based on the fraud and deception prevalent in Ephesus (Acts 19:13–19) and the genuine power displayed by Paul in the name of the Lord Jesus Christ. These unprecedented miracles caused "the name of the Lord Jesus [to be] held in high honor" (Acts 19:17; cf. verse 20). Unlike the apostle Paul, today's self-appointed apostles do not bring honor to the name of Jesus. Instead, they cause His name to be dragged through the mud.

TWISTING FACTS

Not only do some Faith teachers victimize the poor and downtrodden by promising what they cannot perform, but they also blame these trusting souls when the results they had expected do not materialize.

In his book *It's Not Working, Brother John!* John Avanzini uses every strategy imaginable to lead hapless followers to believe that a failure to receive means that something is wrong with them. He writes, "The problem is, *something is wrong with the saint* . . . Without fail I find something wrong in their lives."[56]

Avanzini then postulates "twenty-five things that close the windows of heaven."[57] One reason Avanzini cites is double-mindedness.[58] He explains that we each have two minds—a conscious mind and a subconscious mind. The subconscious mind has been conditioned by pastors and teachers to believe that Jesus was poor. Therefore, when the conscious mind is introduced to the prosperity gospel, it is rejected because we believe subconsciously that we ought to be poor.

Avanzini's answer to this dilemma is to have the subconscious mind reprogrammed to believe that Jesus was rich, wore designer clothes, and lived in a big house.[59] And Avanzini has just the ticket to reprogram your mind: for a price he will sell you his videotape *Was Jesus Poor?*[60]

Another reason advanced by the Faith teachers to explain why people are not getting rich is improper thinking. As Avanzini puts it, "You Are What You Think . . . Thoughts Are a Creative Force."[61] Drawing from the false premise that "the way you think in your heart will create what you say,"[62] Avanzini concludes that "Proper Thinking Produces Finances."[63] He sums it up like this: "We can believe and receive, or we can doubt and do without."[64]

Interestingly enough, way back in 1919, Ernest Holmes, the founder of the Church of Religious Science, communicated the same sentiment when he said, "Man is just what he thinks himself to be."[65] Although Avanzini claims that the words in his book were inspired by the Holy Spirit,[66] it is remarkable how closely they mirror the teachings of the metaphysical cults.

Another of Avanzini's explanations for his followers' lack of prosperity is that they do not trust their "man of God." He attempts to use 2 Chronicles 20:20—"Believe his prophets, so shall ye prosper" (KJV)—as a pretext to argue that "if you don't trust God's prophets, *you will not prosper.*"[67] In context, however, this passage does not promise financial prosperity. It is a promise of *military* success to the nation of Israel at a time of great danger from the Moabites and Ammonites.

But Avanzini complains that some people will not even allow their man of God "to have a copy of [*their*] complete financial statement."[68] In an attempt to drum up a biblical precedent for this outrageous demand, Avanzini refers to the account of the widow's oil in 2 Kings 4:1–7:

> When the widow went to Elisha for help with her back-breaking debt, the first thing the prophet asked for was *a financial statement*. He asked, "What do you have in your house?" Thank God this widow was able to trust her man of God . . . Her relationship of trust with him set her *free from debt* as well as funded her retirement![69]

Such an irresponsible handling of the sacred text is by no means uncommon. Nor has it been throughout the church age. Just as the pope used Johann

Tetzel to pillage the poor in order to build St. Peter's, so prosperity teachers mislead the flock in order to build their empires.

ERROR BEGETS ERROR

Just as the cons of Johann Tetzel seem tepid when compared to those of Oral Roberts, so the cons of Oral Roberts seem temperate when compared to a host of those who have followed in his train. As such, the errors just keep on coming.

The error of *giving to receive*, for example, has now metastasized into the error of *giving to receipt*. Joyce Meyer, for one, seems to have learned well at the feet of the master. Says Meyer, "When I talked with Dr. Roberts today and we talked about this seed-faith thing, he said something awesome!" The awesome insight according to Meyer was this: "The word *receiving* means *receipting*." The way it works, explains Meyer, is that "when you give you get a receipt in heaven," and "when you have a need you can then go with your receipt and say, 'You see, God, I have got my receipt from my sowing, and now I have a need, and I'm cashing in my receipt.'"[70]

Meyer's shallowness here is as breathtaking as it is revealing. Instead of gleaning formulas from her mentor, she would have been well served in developing fellowship with her Master. Far from having to go to God with receipt in hand, we go to God as children knowing that He cares for every detail of our lives. While we might want intricate formulas to get things from God—God wants intimate fellowship. Indeed, it is out of this very intimacy and fellowship that everything else flows.

Perhaps the best imitation of Johann Tetzel today is Rod Parsley. Like Tetzel, he effectively assures his devotees that "as soon as the coin in the coffer rings the soul from purgatory springs." If you "really want to know that all of your children are saved," says Parsley, "then sow for it! Sow for it!" To give credence to the con, he says, "I just received that word from the Lord."[71]

Benny Hinn has gone so far as to turn God into a veritable extortionist. Says Hinn, "Every time you hold back your seed, my friend, heaven will charge you 20 percent whether you like it or not. In fact, if you don't give it, God will take it away from you through tragedy. Don't you ever forget that! Yes. That's the Word. If you don't give to God, He'll take it from you whether you like it or not through troubles."[72] This, of course, is far from true. Indeed, everyone who takes the sacred name of Christ upon their lips has *already* given their time, talent, and treasure to God in full. Far from being owners, we are but stewards of God's possessions. As such, we hold what we have with an open hand so that God can take out or put in as He sees fit.

If God can't extort money, as per Benny, He promises miracles in exchange for money, as per Bynum. Indeed, according to Juanita Bynum, the Holy Spirit spoke to her directly during a *Praise the Lord* production on the Trinity Broadcasting Network. Singling out a "Caucasian woman," Bynum said, "God is saying that He wants you to sow that $100,000 seed." The net return for the Caucasian woman would be the restoration of a "tore-up family" and "peace of mind."[73]

This sort of con is common fare for Bynum. God also allegedly challenged an employer to take what little he had left to pay his employees and give it to the ministry of Jan and Paul Crouch. When the employer protested, "God" (Bynum) responded in no uncertain terms. "God said, 'Let me tell you something. In order to get something you ain't never had, you gotta do something that you don't never do.'" In this case, God's requirement was for the unnamed employer to "sow a seed of $20,000."[74]

The theme of giving your last is routine for Bynum. On another *Praise the Lord* broadcast, the command of God spoken through "the voice of the prophet" was simply, "empty it out." Here's Bynum, raw and uncensored:

> You watching me in television land and you saying all I got is $900. But I hear the Lord saying, I double-dare people that are watching me right now, this one is for you, I double-dare you to empty your checking account. If you got $79.36, empty it out. Empty it out, at the voice of the prophet. If you got $736.19, if you're in the audience right now, you all looking at me like I'm crazy, like I done went off. Oh, Jesus, if you got $79.36, I double-dare you to write your last check and declare your back account empty because God said something happens when you give Him your last. He multiplies when you give Him your last.[75]

Think Bynum's bad? Think again! Paula White prostitutes a plethora of biblical passages in her petulant promises of prosperity. Her shtick is to align dollar amounts with biblical addresses. Remember White's plea for $68.19 in the "Cast of Characters" chapter? "God is telling you $68.19 for the next twelve months, which happens to be $818." If the math is lost on you, Paula was not lost for an explanation. "What Deuteronomy 8:18 says," Paula explained, "is that God will give you power to get wealth."[76]

In yet another version of White lies, Paula said she was fasting and praying when God told her to challenge her constituents "to give $66.12, according to Psalm 66:12." The "results," according to White, were "mandated."[77] On another occasion, the amount was $68.19—but in accordance with Psalm 68:19 this time, not Deuteronomy 8:18. In sowing a seed of $68.19 (whatever you do, *do not* round up to $69) you automatically hook up with a vision bigger than yourself. As such, Paula urged prospects to go to the phone and say, "Paula . . . for the next twelve months, I am sowing $68.19, based on Psalm 68:19 (KJV), that daily God will load me up with benefits."[78] As Paula recently explained, "Numbers are important to God. If they weren't important, He wouldn't have taken a whole book out of the Bible to call it Numbers."[79]

While it can be credibly argued that numbers are important to God, the code breaker for numerical values does not reside in "special insight," unbridled speculation, or subjective flights of fancy. It resides in reading Scripture in light of Scripture. When our interpretations are tethered to the hottest sensation rather than to the Holy Scripture, we are apt to grab at anything—and usually miss.

As the cons and cover-ups of ever-increasing numbers of prosperity peddlers continue to proliferate throughout the land, it is crucial that we are so familiar with truth that when such counterfeits appear on the horizon, we can identify them instantaneously.

May God in His mercy save us from the new breed of Johann Tetzels.

19

COVENANT-CONTRACT

The good news to the poor is this. Christ took your poverty on the cross and He gave you the riches of Abraham. Brother, that's enough to make a Baptist to get in the aisles and start dancing. The curse of poverty has been broken at the cross. If you have the anointing, you don't have the curse of poverty. If you will practice the principles of prosperity in the Word of God, this, says God, will make you the head and not the tail.[1]

—JOHN HAGEE

If you still have lingering doubts as to whether the Faith movement is cultic or Christian, its concept of "covenant-contract" should forever settle the issue in your mind. The Faith notion that all Christians have a divine right to wealth and prosperity is rooted in the myth that God is a failure.

Not only is the Faith-God prone to making mistakes, but his failure is so great that he was forced into playing "Let's Make a Deal." That is essentially what the Faith movement's concept of covenant-contract is all about.

Remember that in Faith theology, Adam committed cosmic treason by selling his godhood to Satan for the price of an apple. Satan thereby became the god of this world, and God was left on the outside, desperately searching for a way back in.

But give the Faith-God some credit. He may have been a failure, but he was certainly not a quitter. Rather than throw in the towel, he began to devise a clever comeback—which is precisely where the Faith movement's concept of the covenant enters the picture. Here is how Kenneth Copeland explains it:

> After Adam's fall in the Garden, God needed an avenue back into the earth
> . . . Since man was the key figure in the Fall, man had to be the key figure
> in the redemption, so God approached a man named Abram. He reenacted

with Abram what Satan had done with Adam, except that God did not sneak in and use deception to get what He wanted as Satan had. God offered Abram a proposition and Abram bought it.[2]

According to Benny Hinn, God told Abram He "could not touch this earth till a man gave it back to Him."[3] Or as Copeland commented, "I'm making a proposition to you. You can tell me to bug off if you don't like it."[4] Presumably, the proposition was too posh for Abram to pass up. So rather than telling God to bug off, he took the deal. In exchange for unlimited wealth and prosperity, Abram gave God an avenue back into the earth. Abram and God sealed their deal in blood and became "blood brothers."[5]

COVENANT CONFUSION

Right from the outset, the problem with this doctrine should be apparent. The God of Scripture does not negotiate deals; He issues declarations. God's covenant with Abram was not a bilateral proposition (i.e., arising from the mutual agreement of two equal parties), but a unilateral declaration (initiated by the superior party, who sets nonnegotiable stipulations). Far from having the option to tell God to "bug off," Abram could only bow humbly before the grace and goodness of his Creator (Genesis 17:3).

The difference between the Faith concept of covenant and the Christian concept of covenant is not a peripheral issue; it makes all the difference in the world.[6] At stake is nothing less than the sovereignty of God. Speaking of the Abrahamic Covenant, Kenneth Copeland essentially says God was the lesser party, and Abraham was the greater.[7]

Abraham lived under tremendous pressure because, as Charles Capps puts it, "*if Abraham failed, the Covenant would be void*"[8] and God would not have had a means to get back into the earth realm. Fortunately, Abraham did not fail. As agreed upon, he became the first in a long line of prophets that would act as God's mouthpiece in the earth. Copeland picks up the story by saying, "Through the mouths of His prophets, He kept sending His Word and sending His Word. Finally, the great moment came when that Word was brought forth in human form . . . His name was Jesus."[9]

According to Copeland, Jesus was wealthy and prosperous, just like His forefather Abraham. For thirty-three years He lived the high life. Like Abraham, Jesus appropriated all His rights under the covenant.

The "good news" of Faith theology is that we, like Jesus, are Abraham's seed and, therefore, heirs to the covenant. "Since God's Covenant has been established and prosperity is a provision of this Covenant," reasons Copeland, "you need to realize that prosperity belongs to you *now!*"[10]

Fred Price is similarly emphatic. "Christ has redeemed us from the curse of the Law that the blessing of Abraham might come upon us." In answer to the question, how? Price responds, "With *cattle, gold, manservants, maidservants, camels, and asses. Abraham was blessed materially.*"[11]

Such pretentions, however, are foreign to Scripture! The covenant is not a mere contract we can use to command God. Jesus is not a magic mantra we can use to open Fort Knox. God's covenant with Abram is the proclamation of His sovereign plan to redeem humanity from its sin (Romans 4; Galatians 3:6–9). The overarching message of Scripture is God's redemption of mankind. The covenant is certainly not a contract that guarantees us wealth.

HEADS YOU WIN, TAILS YOU WANT

According to Faith teachers, there are two sides to the covenant coin: heads you *win*, tails you *want*. Put another way, you can live either beneath the umbrella of prosperity or under the curse of poverty. "We have seen that prosperity is a blessing of Abraham and that poverty is under the curse of the law," maintains Copeland. "Jesus bore the curse of the law in our behalf. He beat Satan and took away his power. Consequently, there is no reason for you to live under the curse of the law, no reason for you to live in poverty of any kind."[12]

Faith teachers insist that prosperity signifies spiritual favor while poverty is a sign of spiritual failure. Robert Tilton summed up the sentiments of the Faith movement when he said, "Being poor is a sin."[13] John Hagee was equally decisive: "Poverty is a curse."[14]

Another famous prosperity teacher once preached the same message. And then something happened: he lost it all. The glitz, the glamour, and the gold all vanished. So did the cheering crowds. Almost overnight his riches were replaced with rags. Stripped of his star status, he found himself alone with Scripture. After studying the entire counsel of God's word, he concluded:

There is no way, if you take the whole counsel of God's Word, that you can equate riches or material things as a sign of God's blessing . . . I have asked God to forgive me . . . for preaching earthly prosperity.[15]

Contritely, he confessed that "many today believe that the evidence of God's blessing on them is a new car, a house, a good job, and riches." That, he said, would be far from the truth. "Jesus did not teach riches were a sign of God's blessing . . . Jesus said, 'Narrow is the way that leads to life and few there be that find it.'"

Jim Bakker, who in 1989 was convicted of twenty-four counts of fraud, continued with these stirring words: "It's time the call from the pulpit be changed from 'Who wants a life of pleasure and good things, new homes, cars, material possessions, etc.?' to 'Who will come forward to accept Jesus Christ and the fellowship of his suffering.'

"I believe," concludes Bakker, "the heart of God is grieved when we cannot delay self-gratification for earthly things in exchange for life in eternity with Him." If Bakker was truly weaned from the Faith movement's commitment to earthly prosperity, then his following words from prison say it all: "I wouldn't want to trade places with anyone."[16]

ERROR BEGETS ERROR

Even as Jim Bakker was coming to a true valuation of things in the twentieth century, a new breed was rushing into the void in the twenty-first. And John Hagee has been leading the charge. If there is one theme he is fixated on, it is the covenant-contract that God made with Abraham. As he puts it, "The good news to the poor is this: Christ took your poverty on the cross and gave you the riches of Abraham." As Hagee goes on to explain, "The curse of poverty has been broken at the cross. If you have the anointing you don't have the curse of poverty. If you will practice the principles of prosperity in the Word of God, this says God will make you the head and not the tail." The Abrahamic covenant is so prosperity potent that, according to Hagee, "God will give you wells you didn't dig," and "he will give you vineyards you did not plant," as well as "houses you did not build." Not only so, but "when Satan comes to you and attacks you, God will make the devil give it back to you seven times over."[17]

Hagee would do well to listen to the words of Charles Haddon Spurgeon, who is widely considered to be the prince of preachers. "The old covenant," said Spurgeon, "was a covenant of prosperity. The new covenant is a covenant of adversity whereby we are being weaned from this present world and made meet for the world to come."[18]

If Hagee and company are right, if prosperity is indeed a promise and poverty a curse, the apostle Paul would have been among the most cursed of all men. Yet far from being cursed, Paul was content. As such, he said, "I have learned the secret of being content in any and every situation, whether well fed or hungry, whether living in plenty or in want" (Philippians 4:12).

Sadly, however, Hagee is oblivious to the obvious. Thus, he compounds his previous errors by supposing that God's covenant with Abram is rooted in riches. That, however, is clearly not the case. God's covenant is ultimately rooted in redemption as opposed to riches. The biblical picture is poignant and profound. Adam falls into a life of perpetual sin and is banished from Paradise. He is relegated to restlessness and wandering separated from intimacy and fellowship with his Creator. The very chapter that references the Fall, however, also records the divine plan for the restoration of fellowship (Genesis 3:15). The plan takes on definition with God's promise to make Abram a great nation through which "all peoples on earth will be blessed" (Genesis 12:3). Abram's call, therefore, constitutes the divine antidote to Adam's fall.

God's promise that Abram's children would inherit the promised land was a preliminary step in a progressive plan through which Abram and his heirs would inherit "a better country—a heavenly one" (Hebrews 11:16). The plan comes into sharper focus when we see Moses leading Abram's descendants out of their four-hundred-year bondage in Egypt. For forty years of wilderness wandering, God tabernacled with His people and prepared them for the Land of Promise. Like Abram, however, Moses saw the promise only from afar.

God's plan becomes a tangible reality when Joshua leads the children of Israel into Palestine. The wanderings of Adam, Abram, and Moses finally give way to "rest on every side" (Joshua 21:44). As Joshua exudes, "Not one of all the good promises the LORD your God gave you has failed. Every promise has been fulfilled; not one has failed" (Joshua 23:14).

As Adam had fallen in Paradise, Abram's descendants would fall in Palestine. Thus, Joshua's words in his final farewell take on an ominous reality: "Just as every good promise of the LORD your God has come true, so the LORD will bring on you all the evil he has threatened, until he has destroyed you from this good land he has given you. If you violate the covenant of the LORD your God, which he commanded you . . . you will quickly perish from the good land he has given you" (vv. 15–16).

Though the land promises reached their zenith under Solomon—whose rule encompassed all of the land from the Euphrates River in the north to the River of Egypt in the south (1 Kings 4:20–21; cf. Genesis 15:18)—the land vomited out the children of the promise just as it had vomited out the Canaanites before them. During the Assyrian and Babylonian exiles, the wanderings experienced by Adam were again experienced by the descendants of Abram.

God's promises to Abram, however, were far from exhausted. For Palestine was but a preliminary phase in the patriarchal promise. God would make Abram not just the father of *a* nation but "a father of *many* nations," as his new name, Abraham, would mean (Genesis 17:5, emphasis added). Abraham "would be heir of the world" (Romans 4:13). The climax of the promise would not be Palestine regained but Paradise restored.

As God had promised Abraham real estate, He had also promised him a royal seed. Joshua led the children of Israel into the regions of Palestine; Jesus will one day lead His children into the restoration of Paradise. There they will forever experience rest. From Adam's rebellion to Abraham's Royal Seed, the Scriptures chronicle God's one unfolding plan for the redemption of humanity. Far from a postponement in God's plans because the Jews crucified Jesus, Scripture reveals the fulfillment of God's plans in the Crucifixion. For only through faith in Christ's death and His subsequent resurrection can God's one covenant community find rest from their wanderings (Hebrews 4:1–11). In Christ—"the last Adam" (1 Corinthians 15:45)—God's promises find ultimate fulfillment. As Paul so elegantly put it, "If you belong to Christ, then you are Abraham's seed, and heirs according to the promise" (Galatians 3:29).

The conclusion of the matter is this. All the types and shadows of God's covenant-contract with Abraham have been fulfilled in the holy Christ. It is paradise, not prosperity, for which our hearts yearn. It is the "Holy City, the New Jerusalem, coming down out of heaven from God, prepared as a bride beautifully dressed for her husband" (Revelation 21:2) upon which we fix our gaze.

In the meantime, whether we experience wealth or want, we can endure all things through Christ who strengthens us (Philippians 4:13).

20

CONTEXT, CONTEXT, CONTEXT

If there is not one verse of Scripture in the New Testament that
says Jesus came to be the Messiah . . . And if Jesus refused by
his words or actions to claim to be the Messiah to the Jews, then
how can the Jews be blamed for rejecting what was never offered?[1]

—JOHN HAGEE

I f there is one common characteristic of Faith preachers, it is their failure to
read Scripture within its intended context. As such, they consistently take
texts out of context and use them as pretexts for Faith fantasies. With
respect to immediate context, Joel Osteen and Joyce Meyer misuse Romans
4:17 as a pretext for persuading devotees that through the force of faith they
can "call things that are not as though they were." In other words, from their
perspective of faith, we can create realities by speaking them into existence. An
examination of the immediate context, however, demonstrates that Romans
4:17 says nothing of the sort. To the contrary, Paul says that it is "the God who
gives life"—*not we*—"who calls things that are not as though they were."

What Joel and Joyce do with respect to the immediate context of a verse,
Gloria Copeland does to the broader context of a passage. The gospel of Mark,
chapter 10, is a classic case in point. Rather than read Mark 10 within its intended context, she pulls one verse out of context and uses it as a pretext for her
hundredfold give-to-get hoax. The broader context of the passage, however,
precludes the pretext. Far from being a chapter focused on how one can get a
hundred times what he gives, Mark 10 portrays the deceitfulness of riches. As
such, the multiplication envisioned by Jesus is spiritual rather than physical,
metaphorical rather than literal.

John Hagee takes the texts-out-of-context phenomenon to a whole other
dimension. Not only does he take texts out of their immediate and broader

contexts, but he also perverts the entirety of the biblical message. This is particularly disturbing when Christ is the object of his pretexts. With bravado that quite frankly boggles the mind, Hagee asserts that the Jewish "people wanted him [Jesus] to be their Messiah, but he absolutely refused." Hagee goes on to say, "The Jews were not rejecting Jesus as Messiah, it was Jesus who was refusing to be the Messiah to the Jews!"[2]

A clearer perversion of the overarching context of Messiah's teachings is hard to envision. Anyone who has read through the Gospels even once knows full well that Jesus emphatically contradicted such sentiments throughout the entirety of His earthly ministry. Who can forget His emotionally charged words as He was leaving the temple: "O Jerusalem, Jerusalem, you who kill the prophets and stone those sent to you, how often I have longed to gather your children together, as a hen gathers her chicks under her wings, but *you were not willing*" (Matthew 23:37, emphasis added)? Or what about the words of the apostle John, who wrote: "He came to that which was his own, but *his own did not receive him*" (John 1:11, emphasis added)?

Common decency alone should have been sufficient to absolve Jesus from Hagee's unwarranted implication of self-contradiction. Giving Jesus the benefit of the doubt on a matter of such grave consequences might rightly have been deemed an interpretive imperative. Jesus as the author and finisher of our faith, indeed the author of eternity, does not contradict Himself; neither does He confuse His hearers.

Context, context, context is the antidote to the compromise, confusion, and contradiction of Christ and the Canon.

ATTACK THE CRITICS!

So what happens when somebody speaks out against the compromise of context? You don't have to guess. Just turn on the television.

TBN founder and president Paul Crouch has made it clear that, in his opinion, it is acceptable to judge a man's heart but unacceptable to judge his heresy. In unmistakable terms he judged those who speak out against the Faith movement as being "damned and on their way to hell." He went on to say, "I don't think there's any redemption for them."[3]

Only a few weeks after I spoke out against the deadly doctrines of Faith theology being broadcast on Crouch's internationally syndicated television show, he responded with these ominous words: "To hell with you! Get out of my life! Get out of the way! . . . I say get out of God's way! Quit blocking God's bridges or God's going to shoot you if I don't . . . I don't even want to even talk to you or hear you! I don't want to see your ugly face!" Ironically, in the context of fervently condemning "heresy hunters" to the fires of hell, Crouch consigned reincarnationist General George Patton to a future in heaven.[4]

What did Crouch have to say about judging heresy? His advice was simply to let God "sort out all this doctrinal doo-doo." Elaborating further, he complained, "'We can't have faith preaching.' 'You can't have confession stuff.' 'You can't do this, you can do that.' Who cares? Who cares? Let Jesus sort that all out at the judgment seat of Christ. We'll find out who was right and wrong doctrinally."[5]

Jesus, however, had a totally different perspective. He made it clear that as mere mortals we are incapable of infallibly judging another man's heart (cf. Luke 6:37–42; Revelation 2:23; Jeremiah 17:9–10). When it comes to judging heresy, however, we are to *test all things in the light of Scripture* (1 Thessalonians 5:21; Acts 17:11; 2 Timothy 3:16).

The question immediately arises, "How can I determine whether someone is correctly interpreting God's Word?" Fortunately, with a little help from the acronym L-I-G-H-T-S, you will be equipped to discern between wheat and chaff.

The best antidote to heretical teaching is hermeneutical training. In Greek mythology, the task of the god Hermes was to interpret the will of the gods. In biblical hermeneutics the task is to interpret the Word of God. Simply stated, hermeneutics is the art and science of biblical interpretation. It is a science in that certain rules apply. It is an art in that the more you apply these rules, the better you get at it. The rules can be remembered easily with the help of L-I-G-H-T-S. Just as helmet lights assist miners to discover gold beneath the surface of the earth, so L-I-G-H-T-S will aid you in drawing out of Scripture what the author intends you to understand.

LITERAL PRINCIPLE

The "L" in L-I-G-H-T-S will remind you of what is known as the *literal principle* of biblical interpretation. Simply put, this means we are to interpret the Word of God just as we would interpret other forms of communication—in the most obvious and natural sense. As such, when Scripture uses a metaphor or figure of speech, we should interpret accordingly. Thus, when Jesus says that He is "the door" (John 10:7 KJV), it's clear He isn't talking about wood and hinges.

In a similar sense, when Jesus says that those who leave their families for Him and the gospel will receive a hundredfold return, the natural assumption is that He is speaking metaphorically. Any other interpretation leads to a logical absurdity.

Faith teachers are masters of attributing esoteric or mystical meanings to biblical passages, thereby spawning doctrinal monstrosities.[6] When the *literal principle* of biblical interpretation is compromised or contradicted, truth becomes clouded and the totality of Scripture is confused.

ILLUMINATION PRINCIPLE

The "I" in L-I-G-H-T-S represents the *illumination* that can only come from the Spirit of God. "We have not received the spirit of the world but the Spirit who is from God, that we may understand what God has freely given us" (1 Corinthians 2:12). The Spirit of truth provides not only insights that permeate the mind but also illumination that penetrates the heart. Clearly, however, the Holy Spirit does not supplant the scrupulous study of Scripture. Rather, He provides us with insights that can only be spiritually discerned. Put another way, the Holy Spirit illumines what is *in* the text; illumination does not *go beyond* the text.

This is precisely where virtually all the Faith teachers falter. They claim that the Holy Spirit has given them special illumination and then proceed to read their individual bias into the text. Illumination must always be tested by Scripture. This is particularly significant in that Satan wants us to encounter him and think we are in touch with the living God. Whenever a teaching runs counter to God's revealed truth, you can be sure that the world, the flesh, or the devil, not the Holy Spirit, is behind it (John 16:13).

GRAMMATICAL PRINCIPLE

The "G" in L-I-G-H-T-S represents the *grammatical principle*. As with any literature, a thorough understanding of the Bible cannot be obtained without a grasp of the basic rules that govern the relationships and usages of words. When it comes to interpreting Scripture, we should not suppose that the rules of grammar mysteriously change. As such, it is crucial that students of Scripture have a basic understanding of the grammatical principle of biblical interpretation. It is also helpful to have a basic grasp of the Greek and Hebrew languages.

If you do not know Greek or Hebrew, however, don't panic. Today there are a host of eminently usable tools to aid you in gaining insights from the original biblical languages. Besides commentaries, there are interlinear translations that provide the Hebrew and Greek text of the Bible in parallel with the English text. In addition, there are dictionaries of Old and New Testament words that are keyed to *Strong's Concordance*. Tools such as these make it easy for the layperson to obtain insights on the original Hebrew or Greek of the Bible without being fluent in these languages.[7]

Using tools such as these, along with some common sense, will keep you from being fooled by people who claim a mastery of the biblical languages all the while undermining the grammar of Scripture. For example, one passage that John Avanzini often misuses is Mark 12:44, where Jesus, speaking of a poor widow, says, "They all gave out of their wealth; but she, out of her poverty, put in everything—all she had to live on." Avanzini takes the word "poverty" and changes it to "want," the word used in the King James Version. So far so good.

But then, during a TBN fund-raising drive, Avanzini smiles and tells his audience that this widow did not give out of her poverty, but out of her want. In other words, Avanzini claims that the widow gave "because she wanted something from her God."[8] Simply stated, she gave to get. Avanzini then explains that the church throughout the ages has missed the true meaning of this passage and that he has now presented the world with the deeper meaning of the text.

It's true that the English word *want* can mean "to desire or wish for something." However, the same word can also refer to a state of poverty, lack, or destitution. In order to determine which meaning of *want* is applicable to Mark 12:44, the reader needs simply to look at the context and construction of the text. Closer inspection makes it clear that Christ was contrasting the giving of the "poor widow" (vv. 42–43) with those who were "rich" (v. 41) and had an "abundance" (v. 44 NKJV). Therefore, the word *want* points to the poverty-stricken state of the widow, not her personal desires.

It should also be noted that the parallel account of the poor widow in Luke 21:4 employs the word *penury* in place of *want*. All Avanzini had to do was consult any nearby dictionary to see that *penury* is a fifteenth-century word for extreme poverty. Moreover, had Avanzini bothered to check a Greek lexicon, he would have realized that the word translated *want* in Mark 12:44 is derived from the Greek word *husteresis*, which means "poverty."[9] Hence Avanzini's so-called exposition of the verse is found wanting on the basis of the grammatical principle.

HISTORICAL PRINCIPLE

The "H" in L-I-G-H-T-S represents the *historical principle*. Christianity is historical and evidential (Luke 1:1–4). The biblical text is best understood when one is familiar with the customs, culture, and historical context of biblical times. Such background information is extremely helpful in drawing out the full meaning of any given text. In order to properly evaluate biblical texts, we must take into account their historical legacy. Indeed, the acronym L-E-G-A-C-Y is an apt way of remembering factors historians consider in determining the viability and meaning of ancient manuscripts.

> **L**ocation identifies the geographical setting for the writing and reception of each book of the Bible.
>
> **E**ssence reveals the central message and key themes of each book in a memorable sound bite.
>
> **G**enre provides you with an understanding of the literary form(s) that characterize each book—which is critical to understanding the God-inspired message and meaning.
>
> **A**uthor identifies who wrote a particular book of the Bible and provides insight on the author's life and calling.
>
> **C**ontext reveals the important cultural, spiritual, economic, or political setting in which each one of the books of the Bible was written.
>
> **Y**ear informs you of when the author was writing and the time span covered.
>
> (For further detail, see my *The Legacy Study Bible* and *The Apocalypse Code*.[10])

Unfortunately, Faith teachers often neglect this crucial principle of biblical interpretation. A classic example is Oral Roberts's handling of 3 John 2. The

King James Version of this text reads, "Beloved, I wish above all things that thou mayest prosper and be in health, even as thy soul prospereth." When Oral Roberts first came across this text he excitedly told his wife, "Evelyn, now this means that we're supposed to prosper." Roberts then went on to recount how, after discovering this verse, God gave him a brand-new Buick. According to Roberts, "Everything that has happened to us since that day started with that verse of Scripture." Evelyn enthusiastically agreed with Oral that to prosper "is God's highest wish for us."[11]

Do Oral and Evelyn have an accurate handle on this passage? The answer is an emphatic *no!* Remember, we must take into consideration the passage's historical context. This opening remark in John's letter to his friend Gaius is, as Bible scholar Gordon Fee puts it, "the *standard* form of greeting in a personal letter in antiquity." Fee concludes that "to extend John's wish for Gaius to refer to financial and material prosperity for all Christians of all times is *totally foreign* to the text. John neither intended that, nor could Gaius have so understood it. Thus it cannot be the 'plain meaning' of the text." It may also be instructive to note that, as Fee points out, "the Greek word translated 'prosper' means 'to go well with someone.'"[12]

When it comes to the context and customs of antiquity, there is no need to be led astray by men like Oral Roberts. Unfortunately, however, all kinds of Faith teachers have followed in his train.

TYPOLOGY PRINCIPLE

A "type" (from the Greek word *typos*) is a person, event, or institution in the redemptive history of the Old Testament that prefigures a corresponding but greater reality in the New Testament. It literally refers to a mark or scar. John uses the term *type* in recounting Thomas's doubt concerning the reality of the Resurrection: "Unless I see the nail marks [*typos*] in his hands and put my finger where the nails were, and put my hand into his side, I will not believe it" (John 20:25). A type is thus a copy, a pattern, or a model (for instance, the scars on Christ's hands) that signifies an even greater reality (the actual nails that pierced Christ's hands).

The greater reality to which a type points and in which it finds its fulfillment is referred to as an *antitype* (from the Greek word *antitypos*). As such, the writer of Hebrews specifically employs the word *antitype* to refer to the greatness of the heavenly sanctuary of which the holy land, the holy city, and the holy temple are merely types or shadows: "Christ did not enter a man-made sanctuary that was only a copy of the true one [*antitype*]; he entered heaven itself, now to appear for us in God's presence" (Hebrews 9:24). Indeed, the antitype of the land is found in the Lord; the antitype of Jerusalem is found in Jesus; and the antitype of the majestic temple is found in the Master Teacher.

In Hebrews, as in the rest of the New Testament, the Old Testament history of Israel is interpreted as a succession of types that find ultimate fulfillment in the life, death, and resurrection of our Lord. Thus far from being peripheral, typology is central to the proper interpretation of the infallible Word of God. One cannot fully grasp the meaning of the New Testament apart from familiarity with the redemptive history and literary forms of the Old Testament. Likewise, the New Testament shines its light on the Old Testament and reveals the more complete significance of God's redemptive work in and through the nation of Israel. This relationship between the Testaments is, in essence, typological.[13] Thus, as eschatology is the thread that weaves the tapestry of Scripture into a glorious mosaic; typology is the material out of which that thread is spun.

The New Testament writers' typological interpretation of the Old Testament, though often implicit in allusions to the Hebrew Scriptures, is made explicit in Paul's epistles. The apostle explains to the Corinthian church that the experiences of Israel prefigured the experiences of the believers under the new covenant as "examples [*types*] and were written down as warnings for us, on whom the fulfillment of the ages has come" (1 Corinthians 10:11). In his letter to the Romans, Paul refers to Adam as a "pattern" (literally, *type*) of Jesus Christ (5:14). Similarly, the writer of Hebrews explains that the earthly temple is merely "a copy and shadow of what is in heaven" (8:5) and "the law is only a shadow of the good things that are coming—not the realities themselves" (10:1). Paul, likewise, taught the believers at Colossae that the dietary laws, religious festivals, and Sabbath of the old covenant were "a shadow of the things that were to come; the reality, however, is found in Christ" (Colossians 2:17).

This is precisely where a host of Faith teachers go desperately wrong. Rather than focusing on the finished work of Christ, they focus on Old Testament types and shadows. Joel Osteen is typical in this regard. Far from extolling the finished work of Christ upon the cross as the antitype that fulfills temple, priest, and sacrifice, Joel has Jesus in heaven, sprinkling His blood upon the mercy seat in the literal manner of the Old Testament high priest. Incredibly, in Osteen's revision of Scripture, even after the Resurrection, "there still had to be a blood sacrifice for our sins. There still had to be a price paid." That is why Jesus "presented his own blood in the high court of heaven as a sacrifice for all our sins, past, present, and future." Indeed, according to Osteen, that is the precise reason that Jesus commanded Mary to not touch Him after the Resurrection. "Why didn't Jesus want Mary to touch her [sic]?" asks Osteen. "I'll tell you what it was. Jesus had just risen from the grave, and He still had His Holy blood on Him. It was this blood He was going to use as a sacrifice for our sins."[14]

In reality, nothing could be further from the truth. Far from having some sort of magical efficacy, *the blood of Jesus Christ* is emblematic of *the death of Jesus Christ.*[15] Nor is there any warrant for suggesting that sometime between His encounter with Mary and His encounter with Thomas, Jesus went to heaven to sprinkle His blood upon the mercy seat. Instead, believers throughout the ages have celebrated the precious sacrament of communion as the broken body and shed blood of Jesus Christ for the *complete* remission of sins. The debt for all sin past, present, and future was paid by Christ's passion upon the cross. When His passion on the cross was complete, Christ uttered the word *tetelestai*—meaning the debt has been paid in full! No further debt remained to be discharged in this world or the next.

SCRIPTURAL SYNERGY PRINCIPLE

Finally, the "S" in L-I-G-H-T-S represents *scriptural synergy*. Simply stated, this means the whole of Scripture is greater than the sum of its individual passages. You cannot comprehend the Bible as a whole without comprehending its individual parts, and you cannot comprehend its individual parts without comprehending the Bible as a whole. As such, individual passages of Scripture are synergistic rather than deflective with respect to the whole of Scripture. Scriptural synergy demands that individual Bible passages may never be interpreted in such a way as to conflict with the whole of Scripture. Nor may we assign arbitrary meanings to words or phrases that have their referent in biblical history. The biblical interpreter must keep in mind that all Scripture, though communicated through various human instruments, has one single Author. And that Author does not contradict Himself nor does He confuse His servants.

This principle in and of itself rules out the Faith teachers' misinterpretation of John 10:34. There is no possibility that Scripture is here teaching that the believer is a god, because this would result in the Bible contradicting itself. The Faith view of this verse slanders the Holy Spirit, who reveals that there is only one God (Deuteronomy 6:4; Isaiah 43:10; 44:6).

A final note before we move on to a biblical view of wealth. Each of the hermeneutical principles represented by the L-I-G-H-T-S acronym is a category unto itself but yet is seldom applied in isolation. Carefully considered as a whole, they utterly preclude the ghastly distortions of Scripture that are part and parcel of the Faith message and allow the Scriptures to shine forth in all of their otherworldly brilliance.

A BIBLICAL VIEW OF WEALTH

With the principles of the L-I-G-H-T-S acronym fresh in mind, let us conclude the "Wealth and Want" section by taking a closer look at a biblical view of wealth. It is one thing to rail against the darkness; it is another to light a candle and illuminate the landscape.

The place to begin is Psalm 24:1. Without understanding who owns everything, we are liable to believe all sorts of nonsense. Listen to what David has to say:

> *The earth is the LORD's, and everything in it,*
> *the world, and all who live in it.*

It is crucial that we understand this text. God is the landlord; we are just tenants. The Lord of Glory has title to the universe; we are simply stewards. All the things we acquire in this life are only on loan. We didn't arrive with them, and we won't take them with us; they all belong to God, and He will do with them just as He pleases. Just remembering this basic fact will save us a world of trouble.

It is good for us to periodically answer the apostle Paul's question in 1 Corinthians 4:7: "What do you have that you did not receive?" The answer, of course, is *nothing*. Everything that you have, God gave you. As Paul told the Athenians, "He himself gives all men life and breath and everything else" (Acts

17:25). If you ever start deceiving yourself into believing that by your own strength or godliness you have been able to accumulate great wealth, remember Paul's question.

Second, remember that the accumulation of wealth is not the purpose or the calling of any of God's children. Yes, God prospers some, but He places others in more humble circumstances. Poverty does not equal piety, but neither do riches equal righteousness. If there were a one-to-one ratio between godliness and prosperity, then the godliest people in the world would also be the wealthiest. But any check of the Forbes 500 will quickly dash that illusion.

Third, our attitude toward wealth should mirror the apostle Paul's outlook in the book of Philippians. Several nuggets in that book form a primer for a biblical view of wealth. We might begin by looking at Philippians 4:12–13:

> *I know what it is to be in need, and I know what it is to have plenty. I have learned the secret of being content in any and every situation, whether well fed or hungry, whether living in plenty or in want. I can do everything through him who gives me strength.*

Then we might consider the apostle's words two chapters earlier, where he instructs his friends on the godly use of the resources God entrusts to them:

> *Do nothing out of selfish ambition or vain conceit, but in humility consider others better than yourselves. Each of you should look not only to your own interests, but also to the interests of others. (2:3–4)*

Next we might recall the example that Paul uses to illustrate what happens when God's people use their resources in a way that honors and glorifies their Creator:

> *It was good of you to share in my troubles. Moreover, as you Philippians know, in the early days of your acquaintance with the gospel . . . not one church shared with me in the matter of giving and receiving, except you only; for even when I was in Thessalonica, you sent me aid again and again when I was in need. Not that I am looking for a gift, but I am looking for what may be credited to your account . . . And my God will meet all your needs according to his glorious riches in Christ Jesus. (4:14–17, 19)*

We need to remind ourselves that while we have been promised an *eternal* inheritance far beyond our wildest dreams, God's promise for us *on this earth* sometimes takes on a darker hue:

It has been granted to you on behalf of Christ not only to believe on him, but also to suffer for him. (1:29)

Finally, we need to consider both the warning and the glorious hope that the apostle joyfully lays out for us in Philippians 3:18–4:1:

I have often told you before and now say again even with tears, many live as enemies of the cross of Christ. Their destiny is destruction, their god is their stomach, and their glory is in their shame. Their mind is on earthly things.

But our citizenship is in heaven. And we eagerly await a Savior from there, the Lord Jesus Christ, who, by the power that enables him to bring everything under his control, will transform our lowly bodies so that they will be like his glorious body. Therefore, my brothers, you whom I love and long for, my joy and crown, that is how you should stand firm in the Lord, dear friends!

Wealth comes from the Lord, says Paul. But don't get too attached to it. What you have, use for the furtherance of the gospel and for the betterment of those around you. Expect that hardship will come your way. And never forget that one day Jesus will roll up this earth like a ball of yarn and will bestow upon us a body that will never decay, never hurt, never be in need of food or gold or earthly riches. In other words, lead your life here below as a responsible steward so that one day, at the judgment, God Himself will richly reward you (Matthew 25:21).

I am strongly tempted at this point to quote several passages from the chapter on money in John Piper's book *Desiring God*, but I will content myself with one quotation only. In my opinion, Piper's words in that chapter are among the best I have ever read on the issue of the Christian's use of money. See if you don't agree:

A wealth-and-prosperity doctrine is afoot today, shaped by the half-truth that says, "We glorify God with our money by enjoying thankfully all the things he enables us to buy. Why should a son of the King live like a pauper?" And so on. The true half of this is that we should give thanks for every good thing God enables us to have. That does glorify him. The false half is the subtle implication that God can be glorified in this way by all kinds of luxurious purchases.

If this were true, Jesus would not have said, "Sell your possessions and give alms" (Luke 12:33). He would not have said, "Do not seek what you are to eat and what you are to drink" (Luke 12:29). John the Baptist would not have said, "He who has two coats, let him share with him who has none" (Luke 3:11). The Son of Man would not have walked around with no place to lay his head (Luke 9:58). And Zacchaeus would not have given half his goods to the poor (Luke 19:8).

God is not glorified when we keep for ourselves (no matter how thankfully) what we ought to be using to alleviate the misery of unevangelized, uneducated, unmedicated, and unfed millions. The evidence that many professing Christians have been deceived by this doctrine is how little they give and how much they own. God *has* prospered them. And by an almost irresistible law of consumer culture (baptized by a doctrine of health, wealth, and prosperity) they have bought bigger (and more) houses, newer (and more) cars, fancier (and more) clothes, better (and more) meat, and all manner of trinkets and gadgets and containers and devices and equipment to make life more fun.

They will object: Does not the Old Testament promise that God will prosper his people? Indeed! God increases our yield so that by giving we can prove our yield is not our god. God does not prosper a man's business so that he can move from a Ford to a Cadillac. God prospers a business so that 17,000 unreached peoples can be reached with the gospel. He prospers a business so that twelve percent of the world's population can move a step back from the precipice of starvation . . .

The issue is not how much a person makes. Big industry and big salaries are a fact of our times, and they are not necessarily evil. The evil is in being deceived into thinking a $100,000 salary must be accompanied by a $100,000 lifestyle. God has made us to be conduits of his grace. The danger is in thinking the conduit should be lined with gold. It shouldn't. Copper will do.[16]

It's your choice. You can swallow the Faith preachers' nonsense about your right to wallow in self-indulgence, or you can set your heart on the deep satisfaction that can only come through using your resources generously to further the gospel and improve the lot of those around you. You can live responsibly as a steward of God's resources and expect to hear Him say, "Well done, good and faithful servant," or you can squander His gifts and let these words fall with full force upon your foolish soul: "I tell you the truth, you have your reward in full."

I aim to lay up for myself "a good foundation for the future, so that [I] may take hold of that which is life indeed" (1 Timothy 6: 19 NASB). But I do not intend to lay up for myself "treasures on earth, where moth and rust destroy, and where thieves break in and steal" (Matthew 6:19 NASB).

It's your bank statement in *heaven* that counts. If your hope is fixed on the one you have down here, you're bankrupt no matter how many digits you count next to your name.

part six

SICKNESS AND SUFFERING

Though he slay me, yet will I trust in him.[1]

—JOB, THE QUINTESSENTIAL MAN OF FAITH

I truly did not think I could ever be happy again. In one blinding instant my whole world fell apart. One moment, excitement; the next moment, excruciating pain. If only I could turn back time! Please God, this can't happen. How could You let this happen? Please help me!

With my mind spinning, I gathered up my critically injured son and sped off toward the nearest hospital. I felt as though a knife had been plunged into my heart.

Only hours earlier I had arrived home from a long week of ministry. My son David had slipped quietly into our bedroom in the early morning hours. "Dad," he whispered, "will you help me put my new bike together?" Quietly, so as to not wake anyone in the house, we tiptoed down the stairs. Together we brought the carton containing his new bike into the kitchen and began to undo the packing.

The rest of what happened is still a blur. David pulled a sharp knife out of the kitchen drawer. Impulsively he jabbed the knife into the cardboard box and pulled up with all his might. Unexpectedly, the packing gave way with little resistance. The knife gathered speed as it moved up through the box, and the unimpeded motion of his arm carried the blade upward toward his face. With lightning speed the sharp point of the knife entered through the center of his cornea, pierced deep into the inner chamber, and split open his eye.

As I paced the halls of the hospital that morning, I was sure I could never be happy again. I had lost all perspective. My world plunged into deep darkness and despair. Pain and sorrow had thrust their unwelcome presence into the midst of my family.

But I am not alone. Sooner or later every person experiences sadness and sorrow. It is precisely during those times that each of us, like Job, is put to the test. Job, in fact, was faced with the ultimate test of faith. Even though God acknowledged Job as "blameless and upright," Job suffered unspeakable tragedy. First he lost his financial base; then he lost his family. Finally even his health failed.

Questions and doubts must surely have raced through Job's mind. Was this just a bad dream? Was the sickness but an illusion and the symptoms a satanic ploy to rob him of his faith? Had he indeed given Satan an avenue of attack because he had uttered words of fear rather than words of faith? Were Job's friends correct in suggesting that tragedy had befallen him because he had indulged himself in some secret sin? Or was a sovereign God working all things together for good in the life of a man who loved God and was called according to His purpose?

Job and those closest to him were left in the dark, for Scripture reveals that what was happening in the heavens was hidden from them.

Job's wife impugned the Sovereign of the universe. "Curse God and die," she said (Job 2:9).

Job's *friends* impugned Job. Unanimously they accused him of suffering for some secret sin. "Surely God does not reject a blameless man," they cried.[2]

Job, however, impugned neither himself nor God. Emotionally he was on a roller coaster as his mind searched for answers, but in the end he uttered the ultimate words of faith: "Though he slay me, yet will I hope in him" (Job 13:15).

Today, as each one of us journeys down the road of life, we, like Job, will face the specter of sickness, suffering, and ultimately death. How will you respond? Will you follow in the direction of Job's wife and friends, or will you follow in the footsteps of Job?

Job's wife and friends had an excuse. They were not privy to what was taking place in "the presence of the LORD." But we are! Scripture reveals that all the while Job suffered, God was in control.

As we proceed though the section on *sickness and suffering*, we will draw a clear line between the cultic concepts of the Faith movement and those of the historic Christian faith. As this line becomes blurred, tragedy inevitably ensues.

Sickness and suffering are the common denominator of a fallen world. We all get sick and eventually die—including every single person committed to the

Faith movement. As much as the Faith teachers would have you believe otherwise, there are no exceptions to the rule.

Fred Price may proudly proclaim, "We don't allow sickness in our home,"[3] but the reality is that his wife has been stricken with cancer and has profusely thanked her doctors for the painful radiation and chemotherapy she has received from them.[4] Kenneth Hagin may have bragged that he had not had a headache, the flu, or even "one sick day" in nearly sixty years,[5] yet he suffered at least four cardiovascular crises, including one full-scale heart stoppage and another episode persisting for six weeks.[6] Although Hagin claimed his "rights" and literally stood on his Bible[7] when illness came, his six-week bout with heart trouble defies his "positive confession." In the end, he himself experienced the reality that the death rate is one per person. And absent the descent of our Savior, we are all going to make it.

While still living, Hagin boasted that his confessions of divine healing got results "within just a few seconds," but some of his followers admit it is better "not to insist on seeing a *spectacular* manifestation of healing, but . . . a *progressive* healing," as one cancer victim said who wisely underwent chemotherapy during "the many months" when "we saw no 'spectacular' manifestation [of healing]" during two separate bouts with the disease.[8]

Faith teacher Hobart Freeman may have blamed the death of his grandson on the lack of faith of his son-in-law, but the truth is that a routine medical procedure could have easily saved the boy's life. Ironically, Freeman's own disdain for science and medicine, along with his flawed Faith formulas, led to his own premature death.[9]

Most ironic of all, veteran faith healer Oral Roberts suffered a heart attack just hours after supposedly being healed of chest pains by Paul Crouch on TBN's live broadcast on October 6, 1992—just a few months after Crouch himself suffered from two days of "heart pains," flutters, and "stops."[10]

Sadly, the tragedies of yesterday go unheeded by multitudes of Faith followers today. After one Sunday morning service when I had spoken on the biblical meaning of faith, a woman came to me and tearfully pleaded for help. Her sister in the Lord had tuned in to the Trinity Broadcasting Network and had begun to follow the teachings of Faith preachers such as Marilyn Hickey, Kenneth Copeland, and Benny Hinn. As a result, she had decided to forgo surgery for ovarian cancer. In a letter she wrote, "I'm laying my life on the line of God's Word. He said by his stripes I was healed, am healed, past, present and future. Jesus is real. His Word is real, and it is for me to accept and know, trust as though my very breath depended on it." She concluded her letter with the words, "Believe it and receive it."[11]

I wrote this dear but deceived lady a lengthy letter refuting the fatally flawed teachings of the Faith teachers in hopes it would reach her before it was too late. For some, however, it is already too late!

Some time ago, I received a letter from another woman whose brother-in-law had enrolled in Kenneth Hagin's Rhema Bible Training Center. While there, his wife contracted ovarian cancer. Rather than seeking medical attention, they denied the symptoms of cancer. Predictably, she died.

Unfortunately, Faith follies do not die as quickly as did this dear lady. Not only did these folks attempt to raise her from the dead, but when life did not return, they confessed that she would come back in another body. In the end, they resorted to regurgitating the standard line of the Faith movement: the woman had not been healed due to lack of faith.[12]

Who knows what untold tragedies testify to the devastation that follows in the wake of the false teachings of the Faith crowd. As the perversions continue to expand, it is high time that we carefully consider the utter falsity of their presuppositions.

21

SYMPTOMS AND SICKNESS

People ask me all the time, "Brother Jesse, I've been watching you for years, and I've never seen you sick." Well, ladies and gentlemen, I use the evidence that God has given me against the devil when he tries to put sickness on me. Let me give you a revelation. When the devil tries to put sickness on me, you know what I say? "Jesus, take Your shirt off." He go, "What?" I say, "Take Your shirt off, Jesus." And Jesus takes His shirt off, and I tell the devil, "You see them stripes? By His stripes I am healed. I got evidence that I am healed!" Glory to God, hallelujah! It ain't got nothing to do with feeling it. It got nothing to do with me feeling it. It's got everything to do with Jesus' back. So all you gotta do is stand up and say, "I got evidence that I'm healed before I ever got sick."[1]

—JESSE DUPLANTIS

According to Faith mythology, Adam's sin not only got God thrown off the planet but also resulted in a satanic nature for Adam. Ever since then, mankind has been susceptible to sin, sickness, suffering, and death.

Fortunately, as we have seen, God had a plan. He got a man by the name of Abraham to strike a deal with Him. As part of the deal, Abraham and his seed were promised both tremendous wealth and total health. As Kenneth Copeland puts it, "The basic principle of the Christian life is to know that God put our sin, sickness, disease, sorrow, grief, and poverty on Jesus at Calvary. For Him to put any of this on us now would be a miscarriage of justice. Jesus was made a curse for us so that we can receive the blessing of Abraham."[2]

The Faith teachers hold that those who believe in Christ are Abraham's seed and thus heirs to the Covenant. Says Copeland, "You have a covenant with Almighty God, and one of your covenant rights is the right to a healthy body."[3] Just so you don't miss his point, Copeland adds:

The first step to spiritual maturity is to realize your position before God. You are a child of God and a joint-heir with Jesus. Consequently, you are entitled to all the rights and privileges in the kingdom of God, and one of these rights is health and healing. You will never fully realize or understand healing until you know beyond any doubt that . . . God wants *you* healed . . . Whether or not you accept that and purpose to walk in the reality of the truth is your own decision to make.[4]

Benny Hinn cut directly to the heart of the matter when he wrote, "The Bible declares that the work was done 2,000 years ago. God is not going to heal you now—He healed you 2,000 years ago. All you have to do today is receive your healing by faith."[5]

Hinn believes that Moses should be our example. Moses lived 120 years without his eye growing dim and his natural force abating; therefore we should as well. Says Hinn, "Sickness does not belong to you. It has no part in the Body of Christ. Sickness does not belong to any of us. The Bible declares if the Word of God is in our life, there will be health, there will be healing—divine health and divine healing. There will be no sickness for the saint of God. If Moses could live such a healthy life, so can you."[6]

When Hinn says, "Sickness does not belong to any of us" he really means it. Several pages later he writes, "He promises to heal *all*—every one, any, any whatsoever, everything—all our diseases! That means not even a headache, sinus problem, not even a toothache—nothing! No sickness should come your way."[7]

Don't think for a moment that this is merely a peripheral doctrine for Hinn. He continues by boldly asserting that "God's *greatest* desire for the church of Jesus Christ . . . is that we be in total and perfect health."[8]

Like Hinn, Jerry Savelle believes that "divine health is something we already possess. When symptoms come, it is nothing more than the thief trying to steal the health which is already ours. In other words, divine health is not something we are trying to get from God; it is something the Devil is trying to take away from us!"[9]

SATANIC SUBTERFUGE

Symptoms from the Faith perspective are merely a satanic subterfuge. Says Savelle:

When the Devil tries to put a symptom of sickness or disease on my body, I absolutely refuse to accept it. A short time ago he tried to put symptoms of the flu on me. My nose and eyes started to run. I began to sneeze and ache all over. I haven't had the flu since 1969, and I'm not going to have it now. I'm redeemed from the flu! Immediately I began to confess God's Word that I'm healed by the stripes of Jesus. I rebuked Satan and refused his lying symptoms. I wasn't trying to *get* something I don't have; I was *keeping* something I already have. I *am* healed.[10]

Savelle does not seem troubled in the least by the absurdity of being "healed" of the flu yet continuing to suffer from the symptoms. For Savelle, symptoms are analogous to a satanic stranger attempting to steal your refrigerator:

Suppose a stranger walked into your kitchen, loaded your refrigerator on a dolly, and started wheeling it out the door. What would you do? You would probably stop him . . . No one in his right mind would open the door for a thief, stand there and watch his refrigerator being rolled away . . . He is going to step in front of that thief and say . . . "Where do you think you're going with my refrigerator? Get your hands off my property and get out of here!" He wouldn't be trying to *get* a refrigerator; he would be *keeping* the one he has. So it is with healing. I am healed. When symptoms come, I just brace myself and tell the Devil, "Hold it right there, bud!"[11]

Like Savelle, Kenneth Hagin not only claimed to "have successfully resisted the flu" during his lifetime, but claimed to have successfully resisted sickness period.[12] Tragically, the only sickness he was unable to resist was his last one.

Fred Price has his own twist on symptoms. For Price, symptoms are literally satanic scare tactics:

The devil wanted to scare me into thinking that the pain would kill me. Well, I just let the pain come. My wife can tell you; I crawled around on my bedroom floor, shouting and hollering at the top of my voice. I was in such pain I couldn't stand on my feet . . . I was under attack to that extent. But I refused to give in to it . . . I wanted my faith to work for me. I didn't want to have to call you up and have you pray for me.[13]

251

DEADLY DOCTRINE

Such pronouncements might sound merely silly, but they have a darker hue. Indeed, Copeland is committed to denying symptoms even to the point of death: "I refuse to consider my body, I refuse to be moved by what I see and what I feel . . . I'm going to choose His Word, instead of what my body's trying to say . . . *I've had people die, and me standing there saying, 'Bless God, you ain't going to die!' And they did anyway.* And I'm glad I stood. I ain't never stood for anything in my own life that didn't come to pass. I can only use my faith so far with you."[14] Kenneth Hagin is of similar persuasion:

> *Real faith in God—heart faith—believes the Word of God* regardless of what the physical evidences may be . . . A person seeking healing should look to God's Word, not to his symptoms. He should say, "I know that I am healed because the Word says that by His stripes I am healed."[15]

In his best-selling book *Right and Wrong Thinking*, Hagin tells the story of how during a Full Gospel convention he began to experience "sharp pains" around his heart. Says Hagin, "It seemed to quiver and stop. It even felt as if my breath were being cut off."[16] Hagin then recounts how the devil came to him and suggested that he be prayed for, to which Hagin responded:

> "Why you foul devil, what is the matter with you? Why in the world would I want to be prayed for? God healed me five years ago, and I am still healed." Suddenly, Satan had camouflaged a few symptoms and was trying to make me believe that I was not healed . . . All he could do was to try to get me to believe the symptoms and go by my senses. Nevertheless, I stood my ground. I maintained that God had healed me, and I would not accept anything else. I would not even permit a doubtful thought to enter my mind. The symptoms left me.[17]

As Faith teachers know full well, the dangers of denying symptoms by pawning them off as devilish decoys can hardly be overstated. With diseases like cancer, early detection and diagnosis are crucial to effective treatment and recovery. Far from being satanic subterfuge, symptoms provide testimony to the powerful healing potential that God has designed into our bodies.

Physician Paul Brand summed it up best when he wrote, "The *symptoms that cause patients alarm* are usually spectacular demonstrations of the *body's healing mechanisms* at work (emphasis added)."[18] Not only can symptoms serve as signals that alert us to impending physical peril, but they can also be signs that point to the body's healing processes themselves. Thus symptoms are often a divine demonstration of *God's sovereign healing power* in progress. Dr. Brand notes this reality in the instance of an infected wound that is red and swollen with pus:

> The redness comes from an emergency blood supply rushing white cells and agents of repair to the scene, and the pus, composed of lymph fluids and dead cells, gives stark and beautiful evidence of cellular warfare being fought. Similarly, a fever represents the body's effort to circulate blood more quickly and also create a hostile environment for some bacteria.[19]

Despite such well-documented medical realities, Faith teachers continue to convince devotees that symptoms are tricks of the devil, designed to rob them of divine health and healing. And with each passing day the toll of those who have been victimized by the Faith message continues to grow. All the while thinking they are following the teachings of Christ, Faith followers are being deceived by the doctrines of demons.

CULTIC FAITH HEALING

The Faith movement's teachings concerning symptoms and sickness are virtually indistinguishable from those of notable metaphysical cults such as Christian Science, Religious Science, and the Unity School of Christianity. Like Hagin and company, cult leader Mary Baker Eddy taught adherents to ignore their senses as well as the physical symptoms of sickness. In *Science and Health*, the preeminent text of the Christian Science movement, she writes, "When the first symptoms of disease appear, dispute the testimony of the material senses with divine Science . . . 'Agree to disagree' with approaching symptoms of chronic or acute disease, whether it is cancer, consumption, or smallpox."[20]

Hagin's words and those of New Thought guru Phineas Quimby are also strikingly similar. During his lifetime, Quimby was wont to say, "If I believe I am sick, I am sick, for my feelings are my sickness, and my sickness is my belief, and my belief is my mind. Therefore all disease is in the mind or belief."[21] Hagin echoed Quimby's sentiments in saying:

> It makes a great deal of difference what one thinks. I believe that is why many people are sick . . . The reason they are not getting healed is that they are thinking wrong . . . They simply kept thinking, believing, and talking wrong . . . The thing that makes a believer a success is right thinking, right believing, and right confession.[22]

In point of fact, the cultic concepts of New Thought metaphysics are even more in line with the Faith movement than Christian Science. Unlike Christian Science, New Thought does not deny the reality of physical matter. Rather, New Thought teachers—like Faith teachers—claim that mental confessions can control physical conditions.

Devotees of the Faith movement are so committed to the cultic concept of denying symptoms that they seldom, if ever, admit they are sick. They are convinced that any acknowledgment of sickness opens the door to satanic control. According to Kenneth Copeland:

> When you say, "Every time the flu comes to town, I get it," you are not licensing the angels of God; you are licensing Satan and his agency. Then your actions support your words and give him continuous access to your affairs. When the flu season comes, you go to the drugstore and buy nine boxes of pills and all the cold medicine you can get. Your actions have supported your words.[23]

Fred Price has gone so far as to depict medicine as a crutch for the immature believer: "If you need a crutch or something to help you along, then praise God, hobble along until you get your faith moving to the point where you don't need the crutch."[24] Mature believers, according to Price, can do without such a crutch. "When you have developed your faith to such an extent that you can stand on the promises of God, then you won't need medicine. That's the reason I don't take medicine."[25]

As in New Thought metaphysics, Faith followers are taught that mature believers can dispense with disease, doctors, and drugs. As Hagin put it, "I believe that it is the plan of God our Father that no believer should ever be sick

. . . It is not—I state boldly—it is not the will of God my Father that we should suffer with cancer and other dread diseases which bring pain and anguish. No! It is God's will that we be healed."[26]

WARPING THE WORD

In the manner of their Mind Science counterparts, the Faith teachers use the Bible to snag the unsuspecting. In some cases their interpretation of Scripture seems reasonable; in other cases their interpretations are downright reprehensible.

In the latter category is an outrageous argument codified by Benny Hinn in a book titled *"Rise and be healed!"* Says Hinn, "The Bible says in Ephesians 5:23 that Jesus Christ is the savior of the body . . . If Jesus Christ is the savior of the body, then your body ought to be made whole." Next appears a quotation apparently meant to represent Ephesians 5:23: "You are the savior of my body, Lord Jesus, you are the savior of my soul."[27] A quick check of Ephesians 5:23, however, reveals that Hinn has altered the text to fit his pretext. The actual biblical text has nothing to do with the physical body.

Rather, the "body" referred to in Ephesians 5:23 is clearly identified as "the church." This is so obvious that it simply cannot be missed. Here is what Ephesians 5:23 says: "For the husband is the head of the wife as Christ is head of *the church, his body, of which he is the Savior*" (emphasis added).

Tragically, people often fall for Hinn's sleight of mind because they simply do not know the Scriptures. Instead they blindly follow Hinn in that he claims to be God's anointed. Moreover, they often accept his teachings because high-profile Christian leaders have assured them that what he preaches is in line with the Word of God.

Paul Crouch provided one of his financial partners such assurance: "Leaders at CRI know very well that the people you have mentioned such as Benny Hinn, Dwight Thompson, and others are *not in any sense preaching error.*"[28]

Sadly, Faith devotees often fall for such assurances. Think back to the two ladies I wrote about at the beginning of this section. One has already died. The other tuned in to TBN and subsequently staked her life on the teachings of Hinn, Hickey, and Copeland.

Kenneth Copeland may say that those who do not accept his teaching have fallen for "a lie straight from the pit of hell!"[29] But the Scriptures say otherwise.

He may proclaim that putting "sickness on you after it was put on Jesus would be a miscarriage of justice" and that "any time a believer has a problem receiving healing, he usually suffers from ignorance of God's Word,"[30] but in truth it is the false teachers of the Faith movement who have miscarried justice, righteousness, and equity.

BY HIS WOUNDS WE ARE HEALED

One of the Faith movement's favorite proof texts is the wonderfully true Isaiah 53:5, which says, "He was pierced for our transgressions, he was crushed for our iniquities; the punishment that brought us peace was upon him, and by his wounds we are healed." Contrary to Faith teachings, the Hebrew word *raphah* more often than not refers to spiritual as opposed to physical healing. As such, when the prophet Jeremiah says, "Return, O faithless sons; I will heal [*raphah*] your faithlessness," he is obviously *not* referring to physical healing (Jeremiah 3:22 NASB).[31]

Isaiah could hardly make it clearer that he has spiritual healing in mind when he communicates that Messiah (Christ) was to be pierced for our *transgressions* and crushed for our *iniquities* (Isaiah 53:5).

Peter builds on this understanding by writing, "He himself bore our *sins* in his body on the tree, so that we might die to *sins* and live for righteousness; by his wounds you have been healed. For you were like sheep going *astray*, but now you have returned to the Shepherd and Overseer of your souls" (1 Peter 2:24–25, emphasis added).

Peter's theme here could not be stated more clearly. He says that Christ "bore our sins," *not* "our sicknesses." As such, Peter makes it plain that the healing referred to in Isaiah 53:5 is spiritual, not physical.

But let us suppose, for the sake of argument, that Isaiah 53:5 *did* refer to physical healing. Even so, it wouldn't teach the panacea the Faith teachers claim it does, for such an interpretation carries an unwelcome corollary.

If healing is in the atonement and is accessed by faith, then those who die due to lack of faith must likewise die in their sins. Why? Because if both healing and salvation are included in this passage, they must be accessed in the same way. And if one does not have enough faith to make oneself well, it follows that he cannot have enough faith to be saved. Therefore those who die physically due to lack of faith must also wind up in hell for the same reason. But I doubt you will hear the Faith teachers proclaim this point any time soon. Relatives and friends of the deceased are not likely to applaud teachers of such a melancholy doctrine.

No, it is clear that Isaiah 53:5 does not have physical healing in view. Interestingly, however, the verse immediately preceding it *does* speak of healing for the body. Here Isaiah writes, "Surely he took up our infirmities and carried our sorrows, yet we considered him stricken by God, smitten by him, and afflicted." Not only is physical healing crystal clear here in this context, but it is also affirmed by the Gospels, where it is given an important qualification. Matthew writes, "When evening came, many who were demon-possessed were brought to him, and he drove out the spirits with a word and healed all the sick. This was to *fulfill what was spoken through the prophet Isaiah*: 'He took up our infirmities and carried our diseases'" (8:16–17, emphasis added).

Thus the healing mentioned in Isaiah 53:4 was fulfilled *during the healing ministry of Christ* and consequently does not guarantee our healing today.

ERROR BEGETS ERROR

Make no mistake! This is not an ivory tower debate that has little relevance to the real world. The deadly error of denying symptoms daily produces casualties in lives of friends and family. A caller who identified himself as Kirk from San Marcos, Texas, phoned into the *Bible Answer Man* broadcast. His story left an indescribable lump in my throat. His mother had migrated from Pentecostalism into the Word of Faith movement.

When a lump appeared in her breast, she purposed to deny the symptom and thus rejected medical treatment. So committed was she to the Faith message respecting sickness and symptoms, that even as the tumor continued to grow she stood her ground. It wasn't until the tumor had become a "weeping sore consuming most of her breast" that she finally sought medical attention. By that time, however, it was far too late. As such, she died six months later.

Even at her funeral, Faith folk lauded Kirk's mother for denying her symptoms. I will never forget his anguished words. "It sickened me," he said, "to watch people from her church come to the front and praise her for what she had done and for the tenacity of her faith—it was just mind-boggling."[32]

What is equally mind-boggling is that long after Kenneth Hagin began popularizing the notion that symptoms are simply satanic subterfuge, the new breed continues to perpetuate his errors. Joyce Meyer is a prime example. Her worldview is as convoluted as it is dangerous. "It is vital for us to understand that it is illegal for Satan to put sickness on us, and there is no good reason to let him do it," writes Meyer. "It was illegal for Satan to kill Jesus, but he was able to do it because Jesus *allowed* him. Why? Because Jesus was going to use Satan's illegal action to bring salvation to the world! So it's illegal for Satan to bring sickness on us, and we must stand against it."

Meyer goes on to say, "The moment we begin to recognize the symptoms of sickness, we need to stand against them—we need to resist them in the same way we would resist the temptation to sin." How? By the pretext that by His stripes we are healed. In Meyer's words, "I believe that by the stripes of Jesus, I am healed."[33]

If possible, Jesse Duplantis takes absurdity and blasphemy to a whole new level. "When the devil tries to put sickness on me, you know what I say? 'Jesus, take your shirt off.' He go, 'What?' I say, 'Take your shirt off, Jesus!' And Jesus takes His shirt off, and I tell the devil, "You see them stripes? By His stripes I am healed. I got evidence that I am healed! Glory to God, hallelujah!"[34]

As we have seen, however, this is clearly not the case. Even a cursory look at the context of Isaiah 53 demonstrates beyond the shadow of a doubt that Isaiah had spiritual healing in mind. How could he have made it more obvious? Messiah was pierced for our *transgressions*! He was crushed for our *iniquities*. Even if we were to miss the meaning in Isaiah, the commentaries of the apostles clear up all confusion. In Peter's first epistle he makes plain that the healing referred to in Isaiah 53 is spiritual not physical in nature.[35] While one might credibly argue that healing is provided for in the atonement—particularly in the ultimate sense—there is no credence in saying it is guaranteed prior to the general resurrection and the restoration of all things (John 5:28–29; Romans 8:18–25; 1 Corinthians 15).

Isaiah 53 may be the main pretext the Faith teachers use with respect to healing, but it is hardly the only one. Another example of text abuse is found in their correlation of Galatians 3:13 with Deuteronomy 28. The argument goes something like this: Galatians 3 says that Christ redeemed us from the "curse" of the law. Deuteronomy 28 is part of the "law" and it lists sickness and disease as a "curse." Therefore Jesus died so that believers would not have to suffer from sickness or disease.

This argument can easily be dispensed with. When Paul refers to being redeemed from the "curse" of the law, there is not even the slightest possibility that he is referring to the "curses" described in Deuteronomy 28. The context demonstrates conclusively that the "curse" referred to by Paul is the "curse" of having to live up to God's requirements in our own strength. As Paul points out, "All who rely on observing the law are under a curse, for it is written: 'Cursed is everyone who does not continue to do everything written in the Book of the Law'" (Galatians 3:10). Paul is obviously referring to man's *moral* curse—his inability to observe the requirements of the law apart from Christ—and not to the *physical* curse of sickness and disease.

While it can be argued that Christ's atonement upon the cross extends to redeeming the physical realm (Romans 8), we will continue to suffer the effects of the Fall (such as sickness and disease) until God establishes a new heaven and a new earth wherein dwells righteousness. Paul made this ever so clear when he wrote:

> *The creation itself will be liberated from its bondage to decay . . . Not only so, but we ourselves, who have the firstfruits of the Spirit, groan inwardly as we wait eagerly for our adoption as sons, the redemption of our bodies . . . We hope for what we do not yet have, we wait for it patiently. (Romans 8:21, 23, 25, emphasis added)*

In truth, the Bible is replete with a long list of godly men who suffered sickness and disease:

- Job, who is affirmed by Scripture as a great man of faith, was covered with painful sores from the soles of his feet to the top of his head (Job 2:7).
- The great apostle Paul "confessed" to the Galatians that because of a "bodily illness" he preached the gospel to them for the first time (Galatians 4:13 NASB).
- Timothy was called Paul's "son in the faith," yet suffered from frequent stomach problems. Instead of telling him to "positively confess" his healing, Paul gave him some practical advice: "Stop drinking only water, and use a little wine" (1 Timothy 5:23).
- Elisha was blessed with a "double-portion anointing," yet he suffered and died a sick man (2 Kings 13:14; cf. 2:9).

259

- Many other biblical examples could be cited: Paul left Trophimus sick in Miletus (2 Timothy 4:20); Epaphroditus fell ill and nearly died (Philippians 2:25–30); King Hezekiah became sick and was at the point of death (2 Kings 20:1).

Faith teachers, in candid moments, have to confess that they themselves have experienced the ravages of sickness and disease. And despite their protests, they will in the end be stung by the ultimate sickness: death. Even Kenneth Hagin, who once claimed that he had *never* been sick, died in a cardiac intensive care unit on September 19, 2003.[36] As has been well said, "The death rate is still one per person, and we're all going to make it!"

22

SATAN AND SICKNESS

Everybody healed under the ministry of Jesus was oppressed
of the devil . . . The devil is behind all sickness . . . There is no
such thing as the separation of sickness and disease from Satan.[1]

—KENNETH HAGIN, FATHER OF THE WORD OF FAITH MOVEMENT

The notion that Satan is at the root of all sickness is virtually ubiquitous in Faith circles. As such, those who are sick are said to have only themselves to blame. By speaking words of fear rather than words of faith, they have given Satan the authority to wreak havoc upon their lives. Kenneth Copeland put it this way: *"Your tongue is the deciding factor in your life."*[2] Copeland goes on to assert, "You can control Satan by learning to control your own tongue."[3] And still he is not done. Adding insult to injury, he blames his devotees for using their words to unleash the powers of the evil one:

> You have been trained since birth to speak negative, death-dealing words. Unconsciously in your everyday conversation, you use the words of death, sickness, lack, fear, doubt, and unbelief: *That scared me to death. That tickled me to death. I laughed until I thought I would die. I'm just dying to go. That makes me sick. I'm sick and tired of this mess. I believe I'm taking the flu. We just can't afford it. I doubt it . . .* You say these things without even realizing it. When you do, you set in motion negative forces in your life and the fire blazes . . . Your words loosed the powers of Satan.[4]

Copeland is hardly alone. Long before Copeland was perpetuating Faith pretexts, Finis Dake had gone so far as to relate disease to demons and to dogmatically declare the impotency of medicines. "Disease germs, which are so closely allied to the work of demons" he said, "are really material agents of Satan corrupting the bodies of his victims. No remedy has ever been found that can cure diseases outside of the blood of Jesus Christ. No drug can cure a single disease. Any honest physician will admit that there is no healing power in medicines."[5]

EASY AS PIE

It's as easy as one, two, three! First, if you are sick, it's your own fault. Whether consciously or subconsciously (perhaps even unconsciously) you have spoken "words of fear" instead of speaking "words of faith." Second, the answer is not medicine. "Medicine is not God's highest or best" intones Frederick K. C. Price. "Use your faith, and then you won't need the medication."[6] "Doctors are fighting the same enemies that we are," he adds. "The only difference is they're using *tooth-picks* and we are using *atomic bombs*!"[7] Third, if you don't have enough faith on your own, God has raised up a special class of anointed faith healers who can manifest faith in your stead.

Kenneth Hagin claims to be one of those anointed healers. In his book *I Believe in Visions*, he tells story after story of how he has been miraculously used to heal people of their sicknesses. In each case, the problem was demonic. On one occasion, scarcely a month after Jesus appeared to him, Hagin claims to have healed a young girl of cancer of the left lung.

It all happened while he was in the midst of a healing service. "Suddenly," he says, "the Spirit of God enveloped me like a cloud . . . This young girl and I were standing in the midst of the white cloud. As I looked at her I saw fastened to the outside of her body, over her left lung, an evil spirit, or an imp. He looked very similar to a small monkey."[8]

Hagin healed the girl by casting out the evil spirit. According to Hagin, the demon fell to the floor then ran down the aisle of the church and out the door.

On another occasion God permitted Hagin to peer directly into the realm of the spirit world. This time he saw an evil spirit sitting on a man's shoulder. "The spirit's arms," he said, "were around the man's head in an arm lock."[9] Immediately Hagin sprang into action. He commanded the spirit to leave in the name of Jesus, and the man was miraculously healed.

Such stories make it appear as though demons are not only behind every bush but also behind every disease. As such, you can tune in to "Christian television" on virtually any given day and hear Faith healers screaming at demons. The following is a transcript of Robert Tilton raging at what he believes to be the demonic forces attacking his followers in TV land:

> Satan, you demonic spirits of AIDS, and AIDS virus—I bind you! You demon-spirits of cancer, arthritis, infection, migraine headaches, pain— come out of that body! Come out of that child! Come out of that man . . . Satan, I bind you! You foul demon-spirits of sickness and disease. Infirmities in the inner ear and the lungs and the back. You demon-spirits of arthritis, sickness, and disease. You tormenting infirm-spirits in the stomach. Satan, I bind you! You nicotine spirits—I bind you! In the name of Jesus![10]

DEMONIC BINDING?

One of the most prevalent words in Faith lingo is the word "bind"—as in "I bind you, Satan" or "I bind you, demon of lust." The pretext more often than not is found in Matthew 18:18. The problem, of course, is that the context here is *church discipline*, not a dissertation on *capricious demons*.[11] Not only so, but many of the demons bound by prosperity preachers are clearly identified in Scripture as "the desires of the sinful flesh." (One wonders where the demon of nicotine was before the invention of cigarettes.)

Sadly, because such human vices as lust, selfish ambition, and gluttony are pawned off as demons, believers are prone to pass them off as satanic attacks. When a married man commits adultery, he can conveniently rationalize away his sin, be exorcised of the "demon" of lust, and go his merry way without ever dealing with his root spiritual problem and its true solution—repentance.

Believers with barf bags in hand are herded into "deliverance sessions" to be "exorcised" of demons ranging from alcoholism to zymosis.[12] All the while they seem ignorant of the vast difference between Satan's temptations and satanic possession.

It is deeply troubling that thousands of people standing before their Faith gurus believe they are being healed "from the tops of their heads to the soles of their feet." It is equally troubling that their gurus warn them that to acknowledge their sickness in any way is tantamount to giving Satan the authority to afflict them all over again. The bottom line is this: if you are sick, you have given license to the devil.

Hagin is emphatic: "Jesus plainly taught that sickness is of the devil and not of God . . . *Since Satan is the author of sickness, I ought to walk free from it . . . Divine health is my covenant right!* . . . Everybody healed under the ministry of Jesus was oppressed of the devil . . . The devil is behind all sickness . . . There is no such thing as the separation of sickness and disease from Satan."[13]

Fred Price put it this way: "I don't look at cancer. I don't look at the tumor . . . I can't look at the natural and . . . say . . . 'I'm sick.' Because when I say that, I've signed for the package. I have taken authority for it, and it belongs to me legally. Satan can enforce it upon my body. And he will kill me with it."[14]

The net result of such torturous theology is that the sick in body are further tormented in mind. Imagine the cruelty of telling a quadriplegic or a blind person that his or her condition tarnishes his relationship with God! Imagine hearing Fred Price say:

How can you glorify God in your body, when it doesn't function right? How can you glorify God? How can He get glory when your body doesn't even work? . . . What makes you think the Holy Ghost wants to live inside a body where He can't see out through the windows and He can't hear with the ears? *What makes you think the Holy Spirit wants to live inside of a physical body where the limbs and the organs and the cells do not function right?* . . . And what makes you think He wants to live in a temple where He can't see out of the eyes, and He can't walk with the feet, and He can't move with the hand? . . . The only eyes that He has that are in the earth realm are the eyes that are in the body. If He can't see out of them then God's gonna be limited.[15]

ERROR BEGETS ERROR

Price's psychological error is topped only by those who add physical error to the mix. Even as I write, it is difficult to get the image of mega–Faith star Todd Bentley kneeing a man in the gut—in full view of television lens—out of my mind. What was particularly painful is that the man in question had stage IV metastatic colon cancer. As he doubled over in pain, Bentley opined, "I had to be obedient to the Lord, sir, but I believe that colon cancer's comin' right out of your body now." Bentley proceeded to state the obvious: "You're probably feeling a little more pain now." And then came Bentley's lame rationalization for the physical and psychological outrage he had just perpetrated: "When we're dealing with cancer sometimes it's a spirit."[16] As such, in Bentley's world, force seems an acceptable solution.

While Joyce Meyer and Joel Osteen are arguably more subtle, their errors are equally devastating. As previously noted, Meyer implicates Job for the death of his ten children. His words of fear, she says, produced a self-fulfilling prophecy.[17] The implication for Meyer's followers is anything but subtle: if someone in your family has died in a car accident or is presently dying of cancer, you need look no farther for cause than to your own words of fear.

As you may recall from the "Cast of Characters" chapter, Meyer likewise tortures Scripture in portraying a helpless paralytic lying by the pool of Bethesda for thirty-eight years as both faithless and foolish. In Joyce's revision of Jesus' words, the paralytic invokes one pathetic excuse after the other. With nary a hint of compassion, she bloviates, "I would think that after thirty-eight years a diligent, determined person could have crawled over to the edge of that pool."[18] Instead of lying there feeling sorry for herself, says Meyer, "I would have been on the edge of that pool, and next year when the angel came around, when that water started bubbling, I would have fallen in and said, 'Either I'm going to get healed or I'm going to die, but I'm not staying like this.'"[19]

Osteen is equally caustic and critical. "If you're serious about being well, if you really want to be made physically and emotionally whole," he says, "you must get up and get moving with your life. No more lying around feeling sorry for yourself."[20] Translated: If you are a paralytic, *you* are the problem!

Well, is Bentley warranted in using physical force in order to expel the demon of cancer? Are Meyer and Osteen justified in their psychological torment? Was Hagin correct in declaring that the devil is behind *all* sickness? The answers once again are found in the final court of arbitration. Despite Gloria Copeland's sarcastic assurance that even her three-year-olds were smart enough to figure out that Satan is the author of sickness,[21] an examination of the biblical evidence leads to another conclusion.

To begin with, we live in a cursed creation in which aging is the primary sickness of humanity. As we get older, we all get wrinkles, some of us need glasses, our muscles get shorter, and eventually we all die.

Furthermore, while Scripture makes it clear that Satan is often the agent of sickness; he is not always its author. In Exodus 4:11 God Himself asks the rhetorical question: "Who gave man his mouth? Who makes him deaf or mute?

Who gives him sight or makes him blind? Is it not I, the LORD?" This is no isolated instance. In 2 Kings 15:5 we read the well-known story of the Lord striking King Azariah with a skin disease (presumably leprosy) from which he suffered till the day he died. In Luke we read that the angel of the Lord came directly from God's presence to strike Zechariah with an affliction because he had doubted God's word regarding the birth of John the Baptist (Luke 1:19–20).

Finally, the predilection that Christians are inhabited by demons ranging from lust to lymphoma is biblically indefensible from the outset. Using the illustration of a house, Jesus asks, "How can anyone enter a strong man's house and carry off his possessions unless he first ties up the strong man?" (Matthew 12:29). In the case of a demon-possessed person, the strong man is the devil. In a Spirit-indwelt believer, the strong man is God. The force of Christ's argument leads inexorably to the conclusion that, in order for demons to possess believers, they would first have to bind the One who occupies them—namely God Himself! The point here is pristine and precise: if we are unoccupied by the Holy Spirit, we subject ourselves to the possibility of being inhabited by demons. If, on the other hand, our house is Christ's home, the devil finds no place in us.

The principle is foolproof. If you are a follower of Christ, the King Himself indwells you (John 14:23; Romans 8:9–17). And you can rest assured that "the one who is in you is greater than the one who is in the world" (1 John 4:4).

23

SIN AND SICKNESS

The religious idea that God chastises His own with sickness
and disease and poverty is the very thing that has caused the
church to go 1500 years without the knowledge of the Holy Spirit.[1]

—KENNETH COPELAND

O ver the past two decades, I have received hundreds of letters from people
who have fled the Faith movement. Such letters tell heartrending stories
of the sick being told that their sickness is a direct result of their sin.

One such letter is the personal testimony of a woman who has been blind
from birth. After coming to faith in Christ, she joined a church that had been
infiltrated by the Faith movement. It wasn't long before they were instructing
her to confess perfect sight and commanding God to honor His Word.

When nothing happened, they began to denounce this woman for her lack
of faith. They said there was "something in my life that hindered God's will."
They said, "God was held up because of some point of sin or disobedience that
He just couldn't get around until I straightened up."[2]

This dear lady went on to say, "I spent hours, sleepless nights, agonizing
over the issue. I became depressed and began to lose my joy. I even quit praying. Some Sundays I simply couldn't stand church because I felt like an outsider
in God's family, watching His pet children get 'blessed' because of their 'Faith.'
. . . If I was doing or not doing something that hindered God, I was at a loss
trying to discern what it was. 'God!' I said in utter despair, 'What do You want
me to do?'"

In time she discovered that God had never forsaken her. Her blindness was
not a result of her sin, and the real problem was not her lack of faith but the
Faith followers' lack of understanding. She felt like a "different person." "I
finally recognized that in Jesus' eyes I was whole and that I was still as

important to Him as I had been at the beginning of our relationship. I determined that no one was ever again going to take His joy away from me."

Astutely she observed the real motivation behind the Faith movement: "I've discovered that many people want to see me healed (or pretend to be) because my blindness upsets their theological applecart. It's hard to believe in their beliefs when a disabled person who thanks God for her disability comes along. It's as if their 'faith' won't stand if I don't go along with their agenda. I believe that they want my healing for their own sake, not mine. It might sound harsh, but I don't think they have a thumbnail of faith."

She closes her letter with these words: "I want the staff there at CRI to know that I heartily support your stand concerning this issue. It's a killer, a spiritual cancer. It grieves me that so few in the body of Christ are willing to listen to the truth that you have so diligently exposed. I pray that God will continually encourage you and direct your path through the criticism and denouncements. I almost didn't hear the truth in time."

Another letter chronicles the story of a lady with incurable lupus and fibrosis. Her best friend began listening to Kenneth Copeland, Fred Price, and John Avanzini and immediately started telling the lady her ailments were a result of sin and lack of faith. She closes her letter by saying that she sometimes wishes she could suffer without being punished by her friends too.[3]

Such stories are not the exception; they are the rule. In case after case, Christians with such diseases as cancer or congenital birth defects are condemned for suffering as a result of some unknown sin. The day I wrote these lines, I received a letter that told of a couple who had a stillborn baby. When this grieving couple needed comfort most, they were told their baby died as a result of sin—not the baby's, but the couple's. They were told they had sinned by allowing "fear to set in and did not have enough faith to believe the baby could be risen from the dead."[4]

BACK TO THE WHIPPING BOY

These people do not suffer alone. Remember Job? He was declared by God to be a great man of faith, but when the Faith teachers get done with him, he is accused of bringing disaster upon himself. Kenneth Copeland says, "When are we *all* going to wake up and learn God didn't allow the devil to get on Job. *Job* allowed the devil to get on Job . . . All God did was maintain His confession of faith about that man. He said, 'That man is upright in the earth.' But Job, himself, said he was *not* upright in the earth. He said, 'I'm miserable. My tongue is disobedient.'"[5]

When forced to see that no less an authority than God almighty says Job is upright and blameless, Copeland claims God was simply making a positive confession. If this were true, God would not only be a deceiver but also be self-deluded. Other Faith teachers such as Hinn and Price attack Job even more viciously. Hinn even calls Job a "carnal bad boy" (see chapter 8). Price calls Job "Big Mouth."[6]

And Job is not the only man of faith the false teachers go after. The apostle Paul is also said to be responsible for his sickness. In Paul's case, the sin is said to be a propensity for boasting. Says Fred Price: "Paul was saying in essence, that he interpreted this situation [sickness] to be a part of the plan of Satan, to keep him humble . . . If you read his writings, you will know that there was a peculiarity about the apostle Paul, and that was that he was a man very prone to brag . . . But that was his opinion. That was his opinion."[7]

This is a classic example of Scriptorture. Although the text does not explicitly identify Paul's "thorn in [the] flesh" (2 Corinthians 12:7), it is clear the "thorn" was not a result of a sinful propensity to boast. The text plainly tells us the thorn was given to Paul to *keep him from boasting*—not *because* he boasted.[8]

And consider what this thorn produced in Paul's life. It certainly does not sound like something Satan would be happy to generate:

> *Therefore I will boast all the more gladly about my weaknesses, so that Christ's power may rest on me. That is why, for Christ's sake, I delight in weaknesses, in insults, in hardships, in persecutions, in difficulties. For when I am weak, then I am strong. (2 Corinthians 12:9–10)*

Paul claims that God's power rested on him *precisely because of his affliction.* That is poles apart from Faith preachers who boast that *because they are strong in body*, God's power resides in them. Who do you think is closer to the truth? Charismatic scholar Gordon Fee answers the question in brilliant prose:

> This false theology lay at the very heart of the Corinthian rejection of Paul. His bodily weaknesses did not commend him to their view of apostleship.

An apostle should be "spiritual," . . . living in glory and perfect health. They rejected Paul and his theology of the cross (with its ongoing suffering in the present age), because they saw themselves as "spiritual" redeemed from such weakness . . .

Paul tries everything in his power to get them back to his gospel. In 1 Corinthians 1:18–25, he reminds them that the gospel has as its very base a "crucified Messiah." For the Corinthians that's like saying "fried ice." Messiah means power, glory, miracles; crucifixion means weakness, shame, suffering. Thus they gladly accepted the false apostles, who preached a "different Gospel" with "another Jesus" (2 Corinthians 11:4), and condemned Paul for his bodily weakness (10:10).

In 1 Corinthians 4:8–13 he tried irony. "Already you have all you want! Already you have come into your kingdom—and without us!" he tells them. Then, with absolutely brilliant strokes, he annihilates them with the stark contrasts between himself and them, with himself as the example of what it means to live out the future in the present age.

In 2 Corinthians 4:3–6, he tries to explain the true nature of apostleship, which has a glorious message but is proclaimed by a less-than-glorious messenger. "We have this treasure in jars of clay to show that this all-surpassing power is from God and not from us" he explains (4:7).

Finally in 2 Corinthians 12:10–13, he attacks their false teachers head-on. To do so he plays the role of the "fool" as in the ancient dramas. Paul is forced to boast (because of his opponents), so in what does he boast? In all the very things the Corinthians are against—Paul's weaknesses. In total irony he finally sets himself alongside the boasts of the false apostles, with their great visions and the miracle-stories.

. . . God's strength is perfected *not* in His delivering His Messiah *from* crucifixion, nor in delivering His apostle *from* physical suffering, but is seen *in* the crucifixion *itself*, and *in* the apostle's weaknesses.[9]

Again and again throughout his writings, Paul paints a precise picture of human weakness and suffering. He goes to great lengths to keep us from repeating the error of the Corinthian church. Like the Faith teachers of our day, the Corinthians were convinced that because God heals, every believer should experience perfect health. That was the very reason they shunned the apostle Paul. Jesse Duplantis, who bills himself as the "Ragin' Cajun," makes no bones about it. Says Jesse, "If you start saying you'll never get sick, get ready, because someone will write a book against you and call you a heretic."[10]

Faith teachers continue to propagate the Corinthian error. They fail to realize that death is the universal sickness of mankind. Benny Hinn callously asserts, "If your body belongs to God, it does not and cannot belong to sickness."[11] Such a statement fails to recognize that some of God's choicest saints endure sickness and die young, while some of the most ruthless sinners enjoy soundness of body and live long, robust lives.

Kenneth Copeland says, "The religious idea that God chastises His own with sickness and disease and poverty is the very thing that has caused the church to go 1500 years without the knowledge of the Holy Spirit."[12] Charles Haddon Spurgeon believed otherwise: "I am certain that I never did grow in grace one-half so much anywhere," he said, "as I have upon the bed of pain."[13]

Three thousand years ago, King David gave proof positive that Copeland and his cohorts are dead wrong. God does indeed chastise His own. David was a man after God's own heart, yet he wrote, "It was *good* for me to be afflicted so that I might learn your decrees . . . I know, O LORD, that your laws are righteous, and in faithfulness *you* have afflicted me" (Psalm 119:71, 75, emphasis added).

REASONS FOR SICKNESS

It is tragic indeed that Faith teachers have resorted to the unthinkable horror of accusing sick followers of harboring secret sin. While the Bible teaches that some are sick as a result of sin (1 Corinthians 11:29–30), Jesus made it clear that such is not always the case.

Consider the man born blind mentioned in John 9. Jesus' disciples asked Him, "Master, who did sin, this man, or his parents, that he was born blind? Jesus answered, Neither hath this man sinned, nor his parents, but that the works of God should be made manifest in him" (John 9:2–3 KJV).

Christ's statement speaks for itself. This man was not born blind due to his own sin nor due to the sin of his parents. Instead, his blindness was a sovereign act to display the work of God in his life. This is so obvious that Faith teachers have gone to great lengths to explain away the plain meaning of the text.

Fred Price tries to argue that the phrase "but that the works of God should be made manifest in him" doesn't have anything to do with the blind man but is actually the beginning of another sentence going on to verse 4.[14] As such, Price has to change the punctuation in order to pervert the meaning of the text. When the Bible doesn't agree with Faith preachers, the solution of choice is to simply rewrite it!

Price's pretext directly mirrors George Lamsa's cultic translation of the New Testament.[15] Despite the well-known fact that Lamsa promotes wildly esoteric interpretations—such as that Jesus and Christ are two different people[16]—Price characterizes Lamsa's remarks as "an eye opener."[17] Indeed they are, but not for the reasons Price thinks.

Kenneth Copeland, like Price, is vehemently opposed to biblical passages that point to God as the author of sickness. He denies the effects of the curse on all of creation, asserting instead that we control the universe with our tongue: "Every circumstance—the entire course of nature," says Copeland "is started with *The Tongue*."[18] Then, like other Faith teachers, he is content to put the blame for sickness squarely on the shoulders of the believer. Copeland writes, "*God intends for every believer to live completely free from sickness and disease. It is up to you to decide whether or not you will.*"[19]

Rod Parsley is equally convinced. "Settle the matter once for all," writes Parsley. "God does not want you to be sick."[20] Thus, when the believer continues to suffer with physical ailments, he has only himself to blame.

The biblical writers make plain that sickness and suffering are the lot of all who walk this planet. Since the fall of humankind, both the righteous and the unrighteous have been subject to disease and decay. In the book of Romans we read that "the whole creation has been groaning as in the pains of childbirth . . . Not only so, but we ourselves . . . groan inwardly as we wait eagerly for . . . the redemption of our bodies" (8:22–23). As such, it is Adam and Eve's fall into lives of perpetual sin terminated by death that accounts for the sickness and suffering that plague us in the present. Paul summed up this inviolate truth when he wrote, "The body that is sown is perishable, it is raised imperishable; it is sown in dishonor, it is raised in glory; it is sown in weakness, it is raised in power; it is sown a natural body, it is raised a spiritual body" (1 Corinthians 15:42–44). He makes clear that our frail and fragile bodies will not be changed now but rather when we are resurrected from the dead. "*Then*," says Paul, "the saying that is written will come true: 'Death has been swallowed up in victory'" (v. 54, emphasis added). And for that day we yet wait. Whether we want to or not.

ERROR BEGETS ERROR

The egregious error that sin gives Satan license to inflict sickness is exacerbated by the further error that sin is carried down through the bloodline. Joyce Meyer made this explicit when she confessed to devotees, "There was a spirit of incest in my family bloodline."[21]

John Hagee is equally direct. "America's history is filled with powerful fathers who amass great fortunes by bootlegging and greed and lust for power, destroying the lives of other people as they did that, and the result is that their children and their children's children have lived in a constant state of unexplained tragedy. Why? Because of generational curses—the sins of the father are passed to the sons for 160 years. God said that, I didn't."[22]

Thus if you are sick, it may be directly due to your sins. On the other hand, the root of your sickness may stretch back to your great-great-great-great-grandparents. What that means, says Hagee, is that "a father who is a liar, a drunkard, and a wife beater *will* have a son who is a liar, a drunkard, and a wife beater unless that generational curse is broken."[23]

Christian Broadcasting Network (CBN) founder Pat Robertson is similarly disposed. When a woman named Patti agonized over the unusually large number of deaths in her family and the fact that her grandmother was even now dying of cancer, Robertson responded saying, "Sounds like you have a generational curse." Robertson elaborated as follows:

> I know that sounds a little spooky, but somebody back in your line may have been involved in the occult that may be witches, or they may be fortune-tellers, or they may have been involved in some fashion like that. Or there may be some gross sin back there that has never been atoned for. They may have injured some group, [in a] heinous way, and that thing is being visited on the children. So, what you need to do is to sever the bonds to the past, and you need to bind that spirit that has come upon you, assuming it is satanic; bind Satan and the forces of evil and commanding to leave your family alone. That's what you need.[24]

Do Faith preachers have a point? Can Meyer legitimately pawn off incest as a spirit passed down through her bloodline? Is it true, as Hagee contends, that a father who is a liar *will* have a son who is a liar unless that generational curse is broken"? Did Robertson correctly diagnose the deaths in Patti's family as sins from the past, un-atoned for in the present?

The Scriptures say otherwise. The Canon communicates that consequences —not curses—are passed down through the generations. It is in this sense that children are punished for the sins of their fathers "to the third and fourth generation" (Exodus 20:5). Nowhere is there biblical warrant for the offspring of drunkards or wife beaters to pawn off their ungodly behavior on curses passed down through the generations. Scripture explicitly tells us that "the son will not share the guilt of the father, nor will the father share the guilt of the son" (Ezekiel 18:20). Indeed, when ancient Israel quoted the proverb "The fathers eat sour grapes, and the children's teeth are set on edge" (v. 2), God responded in no uncertain terms: "As surely as I live, declares the Sovereign LORD, you will no longer quote this proverb in Israel . . . *The soul who sins is the one who will die*" (vv. 3–4, emphasis added).

While the notion of generational curses is foreign to Scripture, there is a sense in which the curse of sin has been passed on from generation to generation. Through the first Adam, "all have sinned and fall short of the glory of God" (Romans 3:23). Through the Second Adam—Jesus Christ—atonement is offered to all. Until Jesus returns, however, all will experience the ravages of the Fall. Sickness and suffering are thus the lot of saint and sinner alike.

Charles Spurgeon is a classic case in point. Throughout his exemplary ministry he was severely afflicted with gout, a condition that often brought with it excruciating pain. In a sermon published in 1881 he wrote, "Were you ever in the melting-pot, dear friends? I have been there, and my sermons with me . . . The result of melting is that we arrive at a true valuation of things [and] we are poured out into a new and better fashion. And, oh, we may almost wish for the melting-pot if we may but get rid of the dross, if we may but be pure, if we may but be fashioned more completely like unto our Lord!"[25]

Spurgeon did not live a long, robust life. He died at age fifty-seven. Yet while he lived, he made his life count for time and for eternity. Spurgeon is history's most widely read preacher. His sermon series is the largest set of books by a single author in the history of the Christian church. Spurgeon's life bears eloquent testimony that the tragedy is not in dying young but in living long and never using your life for that which is of eternal significance.

24

SOVEREIGNTY AND SICKNESS

I used to pray the words "if it be Thy will" for healing before I read and believed God's Word. Since I was a good denominational boy, I would get on my knees and pray, "O God! If it is Your will . . ." Do you know what my doubt-filled prayers produced? Seven members of my immediate family died within eighteen months while I faithfully (or faithlessly) prayed, "If it be Your will . . ."[1]

—ROD PARSLEY

In his book *"Rise and be healed!"* Benny Hinn exhorts his followers to "never, ever, ever go to the Lord and say, 'If it be thy will . . .' Don't allow such faith-destroying words to be spoken from your mouth. When you pray 'if it be your will, Lord,' faith will be destroyed. Doubt will billow up and flood your being. Be on guard against words like this which will rob you of your faith and drag you down in despair."[2]

As such, Hinn simply agrees with other Faith preachers. Frederick Price, for example, instructed his followers that praying for the Lord's will to be done is "really stupidity." He calls such prayers a "farce" and "an insult to God's intelligence." In fact, says Price, "If you have to say, 'If it be Thy will,' or 'Thy will be done,' . . . then you're calling God a fool."[3]

In the real world, however, Jesus Christ contradicts these statements in the strongest terms possible. In what is perhaps the greatest literary masterpiece of all time—the majestic Sermon on the Mount—Jesus taught His disciples (and vicariously us) to pray, *"Thy will be done"* (Matthew 6:10 KJV, emphasis added). If Price is right, Jesus Himself would be "stupid," in that in the Garden of Gethsemane He Himself prayed, "My Father, if it is possible, may this cup be taken from me. Yet *not as I will, but as you will*" (Matthew 26:39, emphasis added).

Of course, while Jesus may be our greatest example, He is certainly not our only example. His half brother James also warns those who are prone to "boast and brag" that they ought to pray instead, "*If it is the Lord's will*, we will live and do this or that" (James 4:15, emphasis added).

Christ's closest friend during His earthly ministry, the "beloved" apostle John, echoes the words of the Master when he writes, "This is the confidence we have in approaching God: that if we ask anything *according to his will*, he hears us" (1 John 5:14, emphasis added).

It is sad beyond words that in the face of overwhelming biblical evidence to the contrary (check the eleven additional verses in the endnote),[4] prosperity teachers such as Price can look into the lens of a television camera and assert that it is "stupidity" to pray "Thy will be done." Does Price think the apostle Paul was "stupid" when he earnestly prayed that "*by* God's will" he might have the opportunity to visit the believers in Rome (Romans 1:10, emphasis added)? Can Price seriously suggest that the believers in Rome were "being robbed of their faith" when Paul encouraged them to pray that "*by God's will*" he might join them in Rome (Romans 15:32, emphasis added)?

THE YIELDED LIFE

The sovereignty of God is an overarching principle of Scripture. We ought to be thankful that this world is under His control, not ours. We would be in deep trouble if God gave us everything we asked for! The truth is that we often don't know what is best for us. As noted Pentecostal scholar Gordon Fee has well said, "Our asking is based on our own limited knowledge, and all too often it is colored by our self-interest. We can only praise God that He does not answer every prayer 'prayed in faith.' Hezekiah, after all, had his prayer answered and was granted fifteen more years, but it was during those years that Manasseh was born!"[5]

Had Hezekiah known, as God did, that in those fifteen additional years he would father the most wicked king in the history of Judah, position his kingdom for plunder by the Babylonians, and end up dying with his heart lifted up in pride, he might well have added these words to his prayer: "Nevertheless not my will but *Thy will be done*."

Walter Martin drove the point home with tongue firmly planted in cheek when he told the story of the girl he wanted to marry in high school. He said that he pounded on the gates of heaven until his hands were bloody stumps, but in the end God said, "No!" Twenty years later at his class reunion he encountered the girl again. He quickly took two aspirin and thanked God that the Lord had not paid the slightest bit of attention to his prayers. Billy Graham's wife, Ruth Bell Graham, has a similar story. "If God had answered every prayer of mine," she says, "I would have married the wrong man seven times."

Indeed, one of the most comforting thoughts to a human mind yielded to the will of God is that He who has created us also knows what is best for us. If we walk according to His will rather than trying to command Him according to our own, we will enjoy not a counterfeit panacea, but what He promised: peace in the midst of the storm.

There is great peace in knowing that the One who created us also has every detail of our lives under control. Not only is He the object of our faith, but He is the originator of our faith. Indeed, He is the originator of our salvation and even the originator of our prayers. When we pray the prayer of faith for healing and our will is in harmony with His will, healing will indeed take place—every time, 100 percent of the time.

But when we pray earnestly as Christ did, "Nevertheless not my will but thy will be done," we can rest assured that even in sickness and tragedy all things work together for good to those who love God and are called according to His purpose (Romans 8:28).

LIVING TRUST

Far from being a force through which we can confess into existence divine health and healing, *faith is a channel of living trust between a creature and his Creator.* Think of Job once more. All Job wanted was to hear from God. The question that burned within him was, "Why?!" Job got half his wish, for God revealed Himself majestically. But He did not answer the question *why.* Instead, He asked Job a question: Where were you when the foundations of the earth were laid (Job 38:4)?

In essence, He asked if Job would like to try his hand at running things for a while. "Say, Job—try creating a lightning bolt. How about producing even a tiny drop of dew?" (Job 38:25, 28).

When you reach the end of this ancient literary masterpiece, you finally understand. Like a refreshing drink of water on a dry, dusty day, your thirst for answers is quenched: God is sovereign, and you are not. In this world you will have trouble (John 16:33). Disease, decay, disorder, discouragement, and even death are the natural consequences of a fallen world. In fact, it is the very uncertainty of life that prepares some people to consider their eternal destiny. This explains why Jesus spoke as He did with respect to human suffering:

> *Now there were some present at that time who told Jesus about the Galileans whose blood Pilate had mixed with their sacrifices. Jesus answered, "Do you think that these Galileans were worse sinners than all the other Galileans because they suffered this way? I tell you, no! But unless you repent, you too will perish. Or those eighteen who died when the tower in Siloam fell on them—do you think they were more guilty than all the others living in Jerusalem? I tell you, no! But unless you repent, you too will all perish." (Luke 13:1–5, emphasis added)*

Yes, death comes to all of us in this world. Heartache and suffering naturally accompany a world mired in sin. But as the Master so eloquently put it in John 16:33, "Take heart! I have overcome the world." For the child of God, the hope is not perfect health in this lifetime, but a resurrected body in the life to come. As John the apostle so beautifully put it, "No more death or mourning or crying or pain, for the old order of things has passed away . . . I am making everything new!" (Revelation 21:4–5). True faith consists not in understanding why but in trusting the Sovereign of our souls despite the fact that we do not understand.

ERROR BEGETS ERROR

In full face of biblical evidence to the contrary, Rod Parsley is bent on propagating the error that "faith cannot exist where the will of God is unknown." "Beware!" says Parsley, "The Bible says the traditions of men make God's word void and 'of no effect' (Matthew 15:6)."[6] Parsley goes on to dogmatically declare, "Healing is not a promise; healing is a fact! God didn't promise you anything; He established it by His Word."[7] Parsley mocks the very notion of adding "If it be Thy will" to one's prayers. Says Parsley, "I used to pray the words 'if it be Thy will' for healing before I read and believed God's Word. Since I was a good denominational boy, I would get on my knees and pray, 'O God! If it is Your will . . .' Do you know what my doubt-filled prayers produced?" continues Parsley, "Seven members of my immediate family died within eighteen months while I faithfully (or faithlessly) prayed, 'If it be Your will . . .'"[8]

To suggest, as Parsley does, that to pray "Thy will be done" is to succumb to traditions that make God's Word void and of no effect is a mind-blowing distortion of the words of Jesus Christ. As documented above, Christ contradicted Parsley in unmistakable prose. The very prayer He taught His disciples to pray includes the petition, "Thy will be done." Not only so, but James warned those who were prone to "boast and brag" that they ought to pray instead, "*If it is the Lord's will*, we will live and do this or that" (James 4:15, emphasis added). John, likewise, humbly acknowledged that our confidence in approaching God is that "if we ask anything *according to his will*, he hears us" (1 John 5:14, emphasis added).

Moreover, as a father and husband, it is hard for me to imagine a crueler contention than that doubt-filled prayers produced the death of family members. This is particularly the case in view of the fact that, according to Parsley's theology, his own son Austin is plagued by the demon of Asperger's syndrome and has been denied healing due to doubt or lack of faith.[9]

When my own son, David, suffered his devastating eye injury, the only place I could look was up. All of the positive confession in the world would not put his eye back together again. Truly this was a problem far above my limited human resources. In anguish I cried out to God for help. And almost immediately a friend was there to comfort me rather than condemn me for a lack of faith in praying, "Thy will be done." Scriptures memorized years earlier began to flood my mind, bringing peace, not perplexity. In that moment I felt closer to the Lord than ever before.

I now look back and see how God has used even this tragedy for His glory. I do not have all the answers. I do know from Scripture that sickness and suffering can be the result of a satanic attack. It can also be divine in origin. Moreover, it can be the direct result of sin. Above all, I know God is sovereign and that "All things . . . work together for good to those who love God, to those who are called according to His purpose" (Romans 8:28 NASB).

In God's providence, David did not lose his eyesight. With the use of a contact lens, he can see past the scar that has formed on the surface of his eye.

In the meantime, God provided for all our needs, including a marvelous physician. In full view of Parsley's declaration that "faith cannot exist where the will of God is unknown," I humbly confess that I do not presume to fully know the purposes of God in the midst of such tragedies. Now I see through a glass dimly. In eternity I will fully understand (1 Corinthians 13:12). Better still, in that day David's eye will be completely whole.

In the epilogue to Job's spellbinding story, God commands Job's friends to humbly ask Job for forgiveness and to pray that He will not judge them according to their folly. Job prayed for his friends and God accepted Job's prayer.

May those in the Faith movement, by God's grace, one day soon turn from their foolish notions and place their lives, their fortunes, and their sacred honor into the hands of a sovereign God. And when they do, may those whom they have harmed welcome them back with open arms and forgive them—as they, too, have been forgiven.

part seven

BACK TO BASICS

I tell you the truth, unless a kernel of wheat falls to the ground and dies, it remains only a single seed. But if it dies, it produces many seeds.[1]

—THE MASTER TEACHER

When I first heard the news, I was stunned. Only days before we had been scrunched together in the backseat of a compact car. "Hank," Glenn had said urgently, "don't ever forget! You only have one life. Soon it will be past. Only what you do for Christ will last."

The words had not meant much to me then. But now, with the news that Glenn was dead, they hit me with hurricane force. I just could not believe it. In a flash he had been changed from mortality to immortality.

I met Glenn just days before going into full-time Christian work. He immediately became a role model. Not only was he an equipped Christian who could articulately share his faith, but he was committed to training others to do so as well.

One day he urged me to make my life count; the next his life came to an abrupt end. The newspaper headline "4 Killed When Balloon Hits Wives and Burns" seemed to say it all.[2] The story behind the story, however, provided a completely different perspective.

Glenn's wife, Gail, gave him an early Christmas surprise. It was something he had long dreamed of—the exhilaration of a hot-air balloon ride. And now, early one Saturday morning, he and two of his friends were poised for the thrill of a lifetime.

Glenn and his friends had a zest for living. But they loved the Lord even more than they loved life itself. Before taking off, they told their wives and loved ones they were looking forward to sharing their faith with the pilot of the balloon.

Their families were thrilled as they watched the brightly colored balloon rise magnificently into the air. With great excitement they followed its pristine path through the blue skies over Fort Lauderdale.

Suddenly their ecstasy turned to agony. The gondola struck a high-tension wire and was instantly engulfed in flames. The added heat shot the balloon upward. Then the inevitable occurred. In full view of their loved ones, the men and their pilot plunged from the sky to their deaths on the ground below.

If ever there was a time to test the truth of the verse "Death has been swallowed up in victory" (1 Corinthians 15:54), that time was at hand. The three courageous women who watched their loved ones fall stood fast in the midst of heartrending pain—not because of their own strength, but because God's strength had been made perfect in their weakness.

These women turned tragedy into a tremendous testimony for Christ. Gail, who like Glenn was an equipped Christian, shared her faith with an unbeliever who was badly shaken in the face of death. Not only did she personify the peace that Christ brings in the midst of the tempest, but she also displayed the assurance that her husband leaped from the heat of the flames into the arms of his heavenly Father.

Lois, as her husband, Jack, had committed herself to Christ's Great Commission, sharing her faith with reporters from around the globe. To a journalist in Miami she reportedly said, "Write this down! We know that our loved ones are in heaven, not because of their own good works but because of their faith in the finished work of Jesus Christ." She then spoke of the peace and joy and life that only the Lord can bring to the human heart.

Kathy's faith moved us all. Her fiancé, Rick, died before her eyes. Yet she bore eloquent testimony to the triumph that only Christ can bring out of tragedy. But the testimony of her life that day was not nearly as meaningful to me as the testimony of her lips months earlier. Back then, she had been simply a frightened evangelism trainee who desperately wanted to know how to share her faith effectively. Along with two others, she had knocked on my door while I was still a hardened skeptic. That night I saw the reality of Christ in her life in a way I had never seen. The seeds she planted not only led to my conversion but also had an impact on what I am doing today.

You see, although I had grown up in a Christian home and was the product of a godly heritage, I had never been willing to become a disciple of Christ. Deep down inside I knew that to surrender to Christ meant to submit to His lordship. And that I was not willing to do. I did not want to be deprived of the pleasures this world had to offer. And so for twenty-nine years I chose rebellion rather than repentance.

Yes, you could find me in church from time to time. But I was not there because I wanted to extend God's kingdom; rather, my goal was to extend my own. My eyes were not fixed on things above but focused on things below. I strove for happiness. For moving from one "happening" to another. For grabbing for all the gusto. But I always came up empty. Regardless of my outward successes, I was never inwardly satisfied.

The night Kathy called on me, I was exposed to what it truly means to be a disciple of Christ. While I was padding my life with passing earthly pleasures, Kathy was pursuing eternal heavenly treasures. It wasn't until I caught her eternal perspective that my life was radically transformed.

Jesus warned His followers that He was not merely a means to their ends but that He was the end. "Do not work for food that spoils," He said, "but for food that endures to eternal life" (John 6:27). Paul echoed the warning when he said, "We brought nothing into the world, and we can take nothing out of it." We would do well, said Paul, to lay up treasure for the coming age and in this way take hold of life that is truly life (1 Timothy 6:7, 19).

Are you looking for the real thing? Setting your heart on things above is where you'll find true contentment! This earth is not your dwelling place; you're on your way to another kingdom. Suddenly there will be that crushing pain in your pericardium or the crashing of glass and you will be translated from the temporary to the eternal. In a microsecond, everything will change. The prosperity message will have lost its luster, and some of us will no doubt wonder why we did not spend more time pursuing the eternal.

When tragedy struck, Kathy's faith did not fail. Why not? Because she had been looking for God in all the right places. That's what getting back to basics is all about.

BACK TO BASICS

I happen to love the game of golf. Although it has brought me great satisfaction over the years, it has been extremely frustrating as well. At times I felt I was on the verge of setting new course records. In other instances I wondered why I ever took up the game in the first place.

After many years of practice and playing, however, I have finally stumbled upon a secret: when things go wrong, it is not because I am failing to follow some newfangled faddish formula, but because I have compromised one of the basic fundamentals of the game. I never cease to be amazed at how quickly things fall back into place when I get back to basics.

What's true in the game of golf is applicable to Christianity in crisis. People today run frantically from church to church, looking for a quick fix and getting more and more confused with each passing fancy. From "Miracle Invasion" rallies to "revelation knowledge," hype and sensationalism have become the name of the game. Doctrinal fads proliferate at such breakneck speed that people have become disoriented. Over and over again I hear their frantic cry: "I just don't know what to believe anymore!"

The good news is that everything can come back quickly into focus by getting back to basics. That's where the real excitement is!

We have covered the five basic flaws that led the Faith movement out of the kingdom of Christ and into the kingdom of the cults. They are made memorable through the use of the acronym "F-L-A-W-S." To get back from this counterfeit to the reality of victorious Christian living, we need to follow five basic steps. Fortunately, they are as easy to remember as A-B-C-D-E.

25

A=AMEN

These are the words of the Amen, the faithful and
true witness, the ruler of God's creation.[1]

—THE APOSTLE JOHN

N o relationship can flourish without constant, heartfelt communication.
This is true not only in human relationships but also in our relationship
with God. If we are to nurture a strong walk with our Savior, we must
be in constant touch with Him. The way to do that is through prayer.

"A" represents the word "Amen." Amen traditionally comes at the end of
every prayer, and prayer is our primary way of communicating with God.

"Amen" is a universally recognized word that is far more significant than
simply signing off or saying, "That's all." With the word "Amen" we are in
effect saying, "May it be so in accordance with the will of God." It is significant
that the apostle John saw Jesus as the very personification of the word "Amen":
"These are the words of the Amen," he wrote, "the faithful and true witness,
the ruler of God's creation" (Revelation 3:14).

The word "Amen" is a marvelous reminder that any discussion on prayer
must begin with the understanding that prayer is a means of bringing us into
conformity with God's will, not a magic mantra that ensures God's conformity
to ours.

This is a radical point of departure between true biblical faith and the Faith
movement. As we have seen, Faith teachers such as Benny Hinn, Kenneth
Copeland, and Frederick Price are vehemently opposed to praying, "Thy will
be done." Price, you may recall, said, "If you have to say, 'If it be Thy will' or
'Thy will be done'—if you have to say that then you're calling God a fool."[2]

In one of his pamphlets on prayer, Price boasts that at one time he thought
it was a mark of humility to end his prayers with the words "Lord, if it be Thy

will." He claims he has since come to a true knowledge of the things of God and, thus, no longer ends his petition prayers that way.[3] Says Price, "'If it be Thy will' is a badge of *doubt*."[4] Elsewhere he adds, "If you put, 'If it be,' on the end of a petition prayer, it will not be answered."[5] Price even has the temerity to write, *"I believe the 'Lord's Prayer' is not for Christians today."* [6]

Moreover, Price claims that "there are different kinds of prayers, just like there are different sports, and each kind of prayer, like each sport, has SPECIFIC and DEFINITE rules that govern and control it. If you misapply the rule for a particular kind of prayer, that prayer will not work."[7]

To clarify his point, Price writes: "If I believe I receive at 10:39 A.M., I cannot pray that prayer again at 10:40. If I pray the exact same prayer at 10:40, I am saying I DID NOT receive what I asked for at 10:39. I will CANCEL OUT the prayer I prayed at 10:39."[8]

If this were true, it is hard to imagine what Jesus was driving at in Luke 18:1–8, a passage that is sometimes referred to as the parable of the "persistent widow." Jesus here tells a story about a widow who hounds an unjust judge for a favorable judgment, even though the judge would rather she just go away. The point of the story is not that God is like the judge, but that we should be like the widow. Our persistence in prayer reveals how serious we are. Moreover, that is what Luke says Jesus intended to convey: "Then Jesus told his disciples a parable to show them *that they should always pray and not give up*" (Luke 18:1, emphasis added).

Price does not stop with such comments, however; even worse are his remarks concerning silent prayer: "To pray, you have to SAY something. Some people say, 'Well, I'm praying a silent prayer'—then their 'silent prayers' never get answered! *THERE IS NO SUCH THING AS A SILENT PRAYER. GOD TOLD YOU TO ASK* . . . God has to have permission to operate in this earth realm."[9]

But if silent prayer is unbiblical (Price's statement about God needing "permission" contradicts Daniel 4:35), what did Paul mean in 1 Thessalonians 5:17, where he wrote, "Pray continually"? If he meant "Be in a constant attitude of prayer," as most interpreters think, there is no problem. One can be in an attitude of prayer while remaining silent. But if true prayer is only verbal, Paul either constantly broke his own direction or must have been an extremely annoying neighbor and a horribly messy eater.

And what are we to think of Nehemiah? He tells us he found himself in a terrible dilemma one day as he was attending to the needs of King Artaxerxes.

Chapter 2 of his book explains his predicament. There's a prayer of his between verses 4 and 5, but you'll look in vain for the words he spoke. Not only was his prayer silent, but it was enormously effectual, for it both saved his life and led to the rebuilding of a devastated Jerusalem.

And let's not forget Hannah, the mother of the great prophet Samuel. You can read her full story in 1 Samuel 1:9–20, but for now note especially verse 13: "Hannah was praying in her heart, and her lips were moving but her voice was not heard." You cannot get any more explicitly *silent* than that. Yet her prayer was answered; the proof was the birth of her son, Samuel.

So much for Faith fiction! Let's take a moment to examine the facts. Better yet, let's use the acronym F-A-C-T-S to remind us of the truth concerning prayer.

FAITH

For prayer to be truly meaningful, it must be founded on faith. Since we have previously devoted an entire section to the subject of faith (see Part Two), I will not belabor the point here. I simply want to reemphasize that it is the *object of faith* that renders faith effective. Faith must always be directed upward rather than inward—not faith in *faith* but faith in *God*.

Since God is awesomely revealed in Scripture, the prayer of faith must always be rooted in the Word of God. Prayer becomes truly meaningful only when we enter into a relationship with God through Christ. We can then build on that foundation by saturating ourselves with Scripture. As R. A. Torrey so wonderfully expressed it:

> *To pray the prayer of faith we must*, first of all, *study the Word of God, especially the promises of God, and find out what the will of God is* . . . We cannot believe by just trying to make ourselves believe. Such belief as that is not faith but credulity; it is "make believe." *The great warrant for intelligent faith is God's Word.* As Paul puts it in Romans 10:17, "Faith cometh by hearing, and hearing by the word of God."[10]

Jesus summed up the prayer of faith with these words: "If you remain in me and my words remain in you, ask whatever you wish, and it will be given you" (John 15:7).

ADORATION

Faith in God naturally leads to adoration. Prayer without adoration is like a body without a soul. Not only is it incomplete, it just doesn't work. Through adoration we express our genuine, heartfelt love and longing for God. Adoration inevitably leads to praise and worship, as our thoughts are focused on God's surpassing greatness. The Scriptures are a vast treasury overflowing with descriptions of God's grandeur and glory. The Psalms in particular can be transformed into passionate prayers of adoration. As you commit them to memory, such passages as Psalms 96, 104, and 150 will become marvelous ways to express your adoration to the King of kings and the Lord of lords.

> *Come, let us worship and bow down;*
> *Let us kneel before the Lord our Maker.*
> *For He is our God,*
>   *and we are the people of His pasture,*
> *And the sheep of His hand. (Psalm 95:6–7 NASB)*

CONFESSION

Not only do the Psalms abound with illustrations of adoration, but they are replete with exclamations of confession. Those who are redeemed by the person and work of Jesus are positionally declared righteous. In Psalm 51, for example, King David contritely confesses his sin:

> *Against you, you only, have I sinned*
> *and done what is evil in your sight,*
> *so that you are proved right when you speak*
> *and justified when you judge. (Psalm 51:4)*

The concept of confession carries the acknowledgment that we stand guilty before God's bar of justice. There is no place for self-righteousness before God. We can only develop intimacy with the Lord through prayer when we confess our need for forgiveness and contritely seek His pardon. The apostle John sums it up beautifully when he writes, "If we confess our sins, he is faithful and just and will forgive us our sins and purify us from all unrighteousness" (1 John 1:9).

THANKSGIVING

Nothing is more basic to prayer than thanksgiving. Scripture teaches us to "enter his gates with thanksgiving and his courts with praise" (Psalm 100:4). Failure to do so is the stuff of pagan babblings and carnal Christianity. Pagans, says Paul, know about God, but "they neither glorified him as God *nor gave thanks to him*" (Romans 1:21, emphasis added).

Carnal Christians likewise fail to thank God regularly for His many blessings. They suffer from what might best be described as selective memories and live by their feelings rather than by faith. They are prone to forget the blessings of yesterday as they thanklessly barrage the throne of grace with new requests each day.

That, according to the apostle Paul, is a far cry from how we should pray. Instead we ought to approach God "overflowing with thankfulness" (Colossians 2:7) and "devote yourselves to prayer, being watchful and thankful" (4:2). Such thankfulness is an action that flows from the sure knowledge that our heavenly Father knows exactly what we need and will supply it. Thus, says Paul, we are to "be joyful always; pray continually; give thanks in all circumstances, for this is God's will for you in Christ Jesus" (1 Thessalonians 5:16–18; also Ephesians 5:20).

SUPPLICATION

Before we launch into a discussion of the place and priority of supplication, let's quickly review the aspects of prayer we have covered thus far. We began by noting that prayer begins with a humble faith in the love and resources of our heavenly Father. Thus prayer becomes a means through which we learn to lean more heavily upon Him and less heavily upon ourselves. Such faith inevitably leads to adoration as we express our longing for an even deeper and richer relationship with the One who knit us together in our mothers' wombs. The more we get to know Him in the fullness of His majesty, the more we are inclined to confess our unworthiness and to thank Him not only for His saving and sanctifying grace but also for His goodness in supplying all our needs.

It is in the context of such a relationship that God desires that His children bring their requests—or supplications—before His throne of grace with praise and thanksgiving. After all it was Jesus Himself who taught us to pray, "Give us today our daily bread" (Matthew 6:11). And as we do we must ever be mindful of the fact that the purpose of supplication is not to pressure God into providing us with provisions and pleasures, but rather to conform us to His purposes. As we read in 1 John 5:14–15, "This is the confidence we have in approaching God: that if we ask anything *according to his will*, he hears us. And if we know that he hears us—whatever we ask—we know that we have what we ask of him" (emphasis added).

So there you have it—the F-A-C-T-S on prayer: Faith, Adoration, Confession, Thanksgiving, and Supplication. Don't just memorize these facts, but put them to personal use. The *power* of prayer will become a living reality only as we participate in the *practice* of prayer. And remember, prayer is not merely a means by which we get things from God; it is the means through which we develop a relationship with the Lover of our souls!

B=BIBLE

All Scripture is God-breathed and is useful for teaching, rebuking, correcting and training in righteousness, so that the man of God may be thoroughly equipped for every good work.[1]

—THE APOSTLE TO THE GENTILES

B" stands for "Bible." The Bible not only forms the foundation of an effective prayer life but is foundational to every other aspect of Christian living. While prayer is our primary way of communicating with God, the Bible is God's primary way of communicating with us. Nothing should take precedence over getting into the Word and getting the Word into us.

If we fail to eat well-balanced meals on a regular basis, we will eventually suffer the physical consequences. What is true of the outer man is also true of the inner man. If we do not regularly feed on the Word of God, we will suffer spiritual consequences.

Jesus said, "Man does not live on bread alone, but on every word that comes from the mouth of God" (Matthew 4:4). Great physical meals are one thing; great spiritual meals are quite another. The acronym M-E-A-L-S will serve us well as we get back to basics with regard to the Bible.

MEMORIZE

One of the best things that happened to me as a new believer was being told that all Christians memorize Scripture. By the time I found out that not all of them do, I was already hooked. Now, as I look back, I can truthfully say that nothing compares with the excitement of memorizing Scripture. Charles Swindoll summed up my sentiments in this regard when he wrote:

I know of no other single practice in the Christian life more rewarding, practically speaking, than memorizing Scripture. That's right. No other single discipline is more useful and rewarding than this. No other single exercise pays greater spiritual dividends! Your *prayer life* will be strengthened. Your *witnessing* will be sharper and much more effective. Your *counseling* will be in demand. Your *attitudes* and *outlook* will begin to change. Your *mind* will become alert and observant. Your *confidence* and *assurance* will be enhanced. Your *faith* will be solidified.[2]

Despite such marvelous benefits, far too few Christians have made Scripture memorization a lifestyle. For the most part, it is not because they don't *want* to, but because they have never been taught *how* to. While they may think they have bad memories, the reality is they simply have *untrained* memories.

I am convinced that anyone, regardless of age or acumen, can memorize Scripture. God has called us to write His Word upon the tablet of our hearts (Proverbs 7:1–3; cf. Deuteronomy 6:6), and with the call He has also provided the ability to do so. Your mind is like a muscle. If you exercise it, you will increase its capacity to remember and recall information. If you don't, it will atrophy. Here are a few practical tips to get you started:

- Set goals. He who aims at nothing invariably hits it.
- Make goals attainable. If your goals are unrealistic, you will undoubtedly become discouraged and give up.
- Memorize with a family member or friend. One of my treasured experiences was swinging back and forth on a hammock, memorizing Proverbs 2 with one of my children. Memorizing with someone else is enjoyable and will also make you accountable.
- Use normally unproductive time to review what you have memorized, such as while waiting in lines or falling asleep. Remember, there's no time like the present to get started! A good place to begin is Psalm 119. In fact, committing verse 11 of that passage—"I have hidden your word in my heart that I might not sin against you"—to memory may well encourage you to make Scripture memorization part of your lifestyle.

While you're at it, you may also wish to consider memorizing Joshua 1:8. These wonderful words remind us that memorization facilitates meditation:

"Do not let this Book of the Law depart from your mouth; meditate on it day and night, so that you may be careful to do everything written in it. Then you will be prosperous and successful." If you want the formula for genuine prosperity, there it is![3]

EXAMINE

In Acts 17:11 we read that the Bereans *examined* the Scriptures daily to see if what Paul was teaching was true. For that they were commended as being noble in character.

There is an extremely important lesson to be learned here. The Bereans were not *condemned* for examining what Paul said in light of Scripture. Rather, they were *commended*. Ultimate authority was not placed in the revelation of a man, but in the revelation of the Word.

I cannot overemphasize the importance of examining the Word of God. Examination requires the use of our minds, and the Bible exhorts believers to use their minds to honor God and examine the teachings of men in the light of Scripture. Jesus taught that the first and greatest commandment is to love God with all our heart, soul, and mind (Matthew 22:37). Peter beckoned believers to prepare their minds for action (1 Peter 1:13). Paul urged Christians to test all things (1 Thessalonians 5:21) and to be transformed by the renewing of their minds in order to discern the will of God (Romans 12:2).

Examining the Scriptures may take discipline and dedication, but the dividends are dramatic. The Bereans examined the Bible daily, and so should we. Here's how you can get going:

- *Pray* that Jesus Christ will become ever more real to you through the reading of God's Word.
- *Read thoughtfully.* Ask the Holy Spirit to give you understanding as you carefully reflect upon the meaning of God's words (2 Timothy 2:7). Buried in the texts are all sorts of precious gems. It is up to you to mine their wealth.
- *Read Scripture systematically* rather than using the "scatter-gun" approach. The Bible is one book comprised of sixty-six individual books. To fully understand the big picture presented by God, we must read not merely those individual books or sections of books we find interesting. Rather,

we need to read and carefully consider the entire Word of God in an intelligent and organized manner.

Understanding the science of biblical interpretation will greatly enhance your ability to examine the Scriptures daily. The acronym L-I-G-H-T-S discussed in chapter 20 should prove to be extremely helpful.

APPLY

As wonderful and worthwhile as it is to memorize and examine Scripture, that's simply not enough! We also must take the knowledge we have gleaned from the Word of God and *apply* it to every aspect of our daily lives. Wisdom is the *application* of knowledge.

When Jesus got to the end of His Sermon on the Mount, He concluded with the following words:

> *Therefore everyone who hears these words of mine and puts them into practice [or applies them] is like a wise man who built his house on the rock. The rain came down, the streams rose, and the winds blew and beat against that house; yet it did not fall, because it had its foundation on the rock. But everyone who hears these words of mine and does not put them into practice [or does not apply them] is like a foolish man who built his house on sand. The rain came down, the streams rose, and the winds blew and beat against that house, and it fell with a great crash. (Matthew 7:24–27)*

James used irony to drive home the same point. In essence, he said that anyone who hears the Word and does not apply it is like a man who looks in a mirror and sees that his face is dirty but doesn't wash it (James 1:23–24).

In God's view, obedience is better than sacrifice (1 Samuel 15:22). As James so aptly put it, "Be ye doers of the word, and not hearers only" (James 1:22 KJV).

LISTEN

In order for us to apply God's directions to our everyday lives, we must first *listen* carefully as God speaks to us personally through His Word. Like Samuel, we should say, "Speak, [Lord,] for your servant is *listening*" (1 Samuel 3:10, emphasis added).

One of the most amazing aspects of Scripture is that it is alive and active, not dead and dull. Indeed, God still speaks today through the mystery of His Word. The Holy Spirit illumines our minds to what is revealed in Scripture. The Holy Spirit makes us "wise up to what is written, not beyond it."[4]

While we *listen*, we must also "test the spirits." As John, the apostle of love, warns, "Do not believe every spirit, but test the spirits to see whether they are from God, because many false prophets have gone out into the world" (1 John 4:1). It is particularly important to "test the spirits" because Satan's foremost strategy of spiritual seduction is to disguise himself as an angel of light (cf. 2 Corinthians 11:14). His slickest slogan is "Feel, don't think."

God's Spirit, on the other hand, illumines our minds so that we may understand what He has freely given us (1 Corinthians 2:12). Before I became a Christian, reading the Bible was like reading someone else's mail. Now, however, the Scriptures have become sixty-six love letters from God, addressed specifically to me. As Jesus so wonderfully stated, "My sheep *listen* to my voice; I know them, and they follow me" (John 10:27, emphasis added).

STUDY

Scripture exhorts us to study to show ourselves approved to God, workmen who do not need to blush with embarrassment, correctly handling the word of truth (2 Timothy 2:15).

In *examining* Scripture, it is typically best to start with one good translation and then to stick with it. This will provide you with consistency as well as help you in the process of memorizing Scripture. In *studying*, however, it is best to use a number of good Bible translations.

An example of a good word-for-word translation is the *New American Standard Bible* (NASB). Although it is sometimes stilted, it is excellent for the purpose of study. A great thought-for-thought translation is the *New International Version* (NIV). It is extremely reliable as well as extraordinarily readable. The *New King James Version* (NKJV) is a superior translation in that it preserves the legacy of a common English Bible while taking into consideration manuscripts discovered since the commissioning of the original *King James Version* (KJV) in 1604 and its initial completion in 1611.

There are also a number of paraphrases on the market today, such as the J. B. Phillips paraphrase and *The Living Bible*. While both are readable, I do not recommend them for serious study.

A number of Bible translations should be avoided at all costs. Among them are the *New World Translation*, which reflects the cultic concepts of the Jehovah's Witnesses,[5] and the Lamsa translation, which is doctrinally biased and highly esoteric.[6]

To aid in your study of Scripture, here are some other practical tools.

Study Bibles

There are some excellent study Bibles on the market today, including the *Student Bible* and the *NIV Study Bible* as well as my *The Legacy Study Bible*. The latter's wide margins enable you to chronicle the thoughts and information that touch your heart and inform your mind as you study the Scriptures for yourself; this particular study Bible also contains vital background information for every book of the Old and New Testaments and provides understanding of God's Word in a memorable format. Included is a "Legacy Reading Plan," which equips you to read the Bible as books as opposed to bits.

Study Bibles to avoid include the *Word Study Bible*, with contributions by thirteen leading Faith teachers; the *Holy Bible: Kenneth Copeland Reference Edition Bible*; and the *Dake's Annotated Reference Bible*—perhaps the worst collection of false teachings I have encountered to date. God "goes from place to place in a body like all other persons," says Dake, and is just "an ordinary sized being." "He *wears clothes . . . eats . . . rests . . .* dwells in a *mansion* and *in a city* located *on a material planet* called Heaven."[7]

On the very first page of the New Testament, Dake writes that Jesus "became the Christ or the 'Anointed One' 30 years after He was born of Mary."[8] Even a biblically illiterate person who has only watched the *Charlie Brown Christmas Special* or sung Christmas carols should be familiar with Luke 2:11, which says, "For unto you is *born this day* in the city of David a Saviour, which is *Christ the Lord*" (KJV, emphasis added).

Study Tools

The toolbox of every serious student of Scripture should include:

1. *Commentary*

A Bible commentary serves as a system of checks and balances through which you can evaluate your insights by the insights of others. There are a variety of good commentaries available today, such as the *International Bible Commentary*, edited by F. F. Bruce, which is based on the NIV translation.

2. *Exhaustive concordance*

An exhaustive, or complete, concordance is an indispensable tool. With it you can find every citation of every word used in the Bible, along with a half-sentence excerpt to help you recognize the verse. With most editions, such as *Strong's*, you can also compare English words with the original Hebrew, Aramaic, and Greek.

3. *Bible dictionary*

A good Bible dictionary will give you access to information about the history, culture, people, places, and events in Scripture. One of the best conservative volumes is the *Nelson's New Illustrated Bible Dictionary*, edited by Ronald F. Youngblood; another good choice is the *New Bible Dictionary*, edited by J. D. Douglas.

4. *Systematic theology*

Systematic theology simply refers to systematizing Scripture to provide a clear understanding of the foundational doctrines of the historic Christian faith. A grasp of systematic theology will enable you to understand, defend, and mature in the faith. Bruce Milne's *Know the Truth* is a good introduction to theology and recommends several more comprehensive systematic theologies.

5. *Additional tools*

Some worth considering include my *The Complete Bible Answer Book: Collector's Edition*; language aids, such as *An Expository Dictionary of Biblical Words* by W. E. Vine; and introductions to the science and art of biblical interpretation, such as my book *The Apocalypse Code*, R. C. Sproul's *Knowing Scripture*, or James Sire's *Scripture Twisting*.

Jesus said, "I am the bread of life. He who comes to me will never go hungry, and he who believes in me will never be thirsty" (John 6:35). It is my passionate prayer that the acronym M-E-A-L-S will remind you to nourish yourself daily with the Bread of Life.

27

C=CHURCH

They devoted themselves to the apostles' teaching and to
the fellowship, to the breaking of bread and to prayer.[1]

—DR. LUKE

"stands for "Church." In Scripture, the church is referred to as the body
of Christ. Just as our body is one and yet has many parts, so the body of
Christ is one but is composed of many members. Those who have
received Christ as the Savior and Lord of their lives are already a part of the
church universal. It is crucial, however, that we become vital, reproducing
members of a healthy, well-balanced local body of believers as well.

Scripture exhorts us to not neglect the gathering of ourselves together, as is
the custom of some (Hebrews 10:25). Sadly, multitudes today turn from the
church and tune in to television.

The impact of televangelism on the church has been massive. Worship has
been replaced with entertainment; fellowship has been transformed into indi-
vidualism; and the biblical concept of every believer a witness (Acts 1:8) has been
replaced by the dubious witness of the televangelist. Indeed, the very form and
function of the church is being dramatically altered. Getting back to basics means
returning our focus to the church as the God-ordained vehicle through which
God is worshiped, *oneness* is demonstrated, and we are equipped to be effective
witnesses.

GOD

The first sign of a healthy, well-balanced church is a pastor who is committed
to leading his community of believers in the worship of God through *prayer*,
praise, and the *proclamation* of the Word.

Prayer is so inextricably woven together with worship that it would be unthinkable to have a church service without it. From the very inception of the early Christian church, prayer has been a primary means of worshiping God. Jesus Himself set the pattern for prayer when He taught His disciples to pray:

> *Our Father in heaven, hallowed be your name,*
> *your kingdom come, your will be done on earth as it is in heaven.*
> *Give us today our daily bread.*
> *Forgive us our debts, as we also have forgiven our debtors.*
> *And lead us not into temptation, but deliver us from the evil one.*
> *For yours is the kingdom and the power and the glory forever.*
> *Amen. (Matthew 6:9–13)*

In my book titled *The Prayer of Jesus—Secrets to Real Intimacy with God*, I elaborate on the prayer that Jesus taught His disciples to pray so that you can make the paradigm shift from seeing a prayer as merely a means for obtaining your requests to seeing prayer as an opportunity for developing a relationship with the Lover of your soul.

Praise is another way through which a body of believers worships God. Paul urged the church at Ephesus to "speak to one another with psalms, hymns and spiritual songs" (Ephesians 5:19). In the Psalms, no doubt the hymnbook of the early church, we see a stunning portrayal of a God who is worthy of our praise and adoration. As the psalmist put it:

> *Praise the LORD.*
> *Praise God in his sanctuary; praise him in his mighty heavens.*
> *Praise him for his acts of power; praise him for his surpassing greatness.*
> *Praise him with the sounding of the trumpet, praise him with the harp and lyre, praise him with tambourine and dancing, praise him with the strings and flute, praise him with the clash of cymbals, praise him with resounding cymbals.*
> *Let everything that has breath praise the LORD.*
> *Praise the LORD. (Psalm 150)*

In addition to prayer and praise, the *proclamation* of the Word is a vital aspect of worshiping God. In 1 Timothy 4:13 Paul exhorts Timothy, "Devote yourself to the public reading of Scripture, to preaching and to teaching," and in 2 Timothy 4:2 he writes, "Preach the Word; be prepared in season and out of season; correct, rebuke and encourage—with great patience and careful instruction." Through proclaiming God's Word, believers are edified, educated, and equipped for evangelism.

It is through prayer, praise, and proclamation that we are "being built into a spiritual house to be a holy priesthood, offering spiritual sacrifices acceptable to God through Jesus Christ" (1 Peter 2:5).

ONENESS

The second sign of a healthy, well-balanced church is its oneness. Jesus Christ breaks the barriers of sex, race, and background that divide us and makes us into one body under the banner of love. Communism claimed to turn men into comrades, but Christ turns us into brothers and sisters. The oneness we share as the body of Christ is tangibly manifested through community, confession, and contribution.

Baptism symbolizes our entrance into a *community* of believers who are one in Christ. It is a sign and seal that we have been buried to our old life and raised to newness of life through His resurrection power. Holy communion is the chief expression of the oneness we share as a community of believers, for as we all partake of the same elements, we also partake of that which the elements symbolize: Christ, who binds us together. Our fellowship on earth, celebrated through communion, is a foretaste of the heavenly fellowship we will share when the symbol gives way to what it represents.

The *confession* of our oneness in Christ is based on essential Christian doctrine. These doctrines, which have been codified in the creeds of the Christian church, form the basis of our unity as the body of Christ. They mark the line of demarcation between the kingdom of Christ and the kingdom of the cults. Tragically, this is the very line that has been not only blurred by Faith teachers but virtually obliterated. While we can agree to disagree agreeably on nonessential or secondary doctrines, when it comes to essential Christian doctrine there must be oneness. As has been well said: "In essentials, unity; in nonessentials, liberty; and in all things, charity."

The *contribution* of our time, talent, and treasure also tangibly demonstrates our oneness in Christ. The pastor is not called to do the work of the ministry. Rather, the pastor is called to "prepare God's people for works of service, so that the body of Christ may be built up" (Ephesians 4:12). God has given the individual members of the church spiritual gifts to be used "for the common good" (1 Corinthians 12:7).

Christ called individuals from every tongue and tribe and nation to oneness as the family of God. Remember: no man is an island! Many logs burning together burn brightly, but when a log falls to the side, its embers quickly die out.

DISCIPLES

In the Great Commission, Christ called us not only to make *converts* but to make *disciples* (Matthew 28:19). A disciple is a learner or follower of the Lord Jesus Christ. We are called to the task of making disciples through the testimony of our *love*, the testimony of our *lips*, and the testimony of our *lives*.

One of the secrets of growth in the early church was the testimony of its *love*. The love of Christ not only compelled early Christians to be ambassadors (2 Corinthians 5:20) but constrained the world to take notice of them as well. The love of Christ was so contagious that it swept through the Roman Empire like wildfire. Jesus said, "All men will know that you are my disciples, if you love one another" (John 13:35).

The early Christian church transformed the Roman Empire not only through the testimony of its love but also through the testimony of its *lips*. The book of Acts tells us that on the day Stephen was martyred, a great persecution arose against the church in Jerusalem, and all except the apostles were scattered throughout Judea and Samaria. Those who were scattered preached the Word wherever they went.

Therein lies the second secret of growth in the early church: every believer was a witness for Christ. While it is true that not everyone is called to be an *evangelist*, everyone is called to *evangelize*. This is why the church must take seriously the task of equipping believers. Jesus said, "This is to my Father's glory, that you bear much fruit, showing yourselves to be my disciples" (John 15:8).

Closely related to the testimony of our lips is the testimony of our *lives*. A story is told of a man who was working in a factory in the north of England. While standing on a ladder, he lost his balance and was skewered on a red-hot metal disk. His workmates were frantically scurrying about, looking for a doctor, when the man called out, "Forget the doctor! I'm dying! Can anyone tell me how to get right with God?"

Of the more than three hundred men in the factory, not one stepped forward. Later one of the men confessed that he could have stepped forward, but the testimony of his life had long ago silenced the testimony of his lips.[2]

If we testify only by our lives, we are in danger of testifying only to ourselves. On the other hand, if our lives belie the testimony of our lips, we may well be dragging the name of Christ through the mud. We must testify through both our lives and our lips.

May we, like the early Christian church, come to understand more fully the biblical concept of the priesthood of all believers. Clearly it is not the pastor's calling to do the work of the ministry single-handedly. Rather, the pastor is called to "prepare God's people for works of service, so that the body of Christ may be built up until we all reach unity in the faith and in the knowledge of the Son of God and become mature" (Ephesians 4:12–13).

It is my prayer that you will daily be reminded of your privilege to be vitally connected to a healthy, well-balanced local church: a church in which *God* is worshiped, in which you enjoy *oneness* with fellow believers, and from which you go out to make *disciples* of all nations. Indeed, you are "a chosen people, a royal priesthood, a holy nation, a people belonging to God, that you may declare the praises of him who called you out of darkness into his wonderful light" (1 Peter 2:9).

28

D=DEFENSE

In your hearts set apart Christ as Lord. Always be prepared to give an answer to everyone who asks you to give the reason for the hope that you have. But do this with gentleness and respect, keeping a clear conscience, so that those who speak maliciously against your good behavior in Christ may be ashamed of their slander.[1]

—THE APOSTLE PETER

D" stands for "Defense." The Cold War may be over, but the need to defend the Christian faith is just beginning to heat up. As we move into what has been described as post-Christian America, it is increasingly important for Christians to know *what* they believe as well as *why* they believe it. And that is what the defense of the faith (apologetics) is all about.

The apostle Peter put it this way: "*Always* be prepared to give an answer [*apologia*] to everyone who asks you to give the reason for the hope that you have. But do this with gentleness and respect" (1 Peter 3:15, emphasis added). It is significant to note that apologetics has a dual purpose.

First, the defense of the faith involves *pre-evangelism*. In post-Christian America, few seem to be aware of the fact that Christianity is not a blind leap into the dark but a step into the light. Christianity is historic and evidential in that it is faith squarely founded on fact.

Whenever you are asked "to give the reason for the hope that you have," you have an opportunity to use your well-reasoned answer as a springboard to present the good news of the gospel. In other words, apologetics is not an end in itself but a means to an end. It is not an opportunity to demonstrate mental acumen but a springboard for presenting the claims of Christ. As such it is "the handmaiden of evangelism."

Second, the defense of the faith involves *post-evangelism*. During an age in which Christianity is in crisis, apologetics serves to strengthen our faith. As

Christian leaders fall all around us, it encourages us to know that our faith is based not on the reliability of human beings but on the revelation of God.

In light of the strategic significance of apologetics, it is tragic that apologetics is being mischaracterized and vilified by the Faith movement. Paul Crouch describes apologetics as "apologizing for Scripture,"[2] while John Avanzini asserts that God has forgiven him for being an apologist and promises to never engage in apologetics again.[3]

Apologetics, however, is not optional. Nor is it the exclusive domain of scholars and theologians. The defense of the faith is basic training for *every Christian*. And that means *you*! Thankfully, learning to defend our faith is not nearly as difficult as one might think. In fact, it all boils down to being able to deal effectively with three basic issues:

1. That the universe was intelligently designed by a Creator and thus did not evolve by random or undirected processes. How you view your origins will inevitably determine how you live your life. If you believe that you are a mere function of genetic makeup or brain chemistry, you will live your life differently than if you know you are created in the image of God and are thus accountable to Him.
2. That the God who created the universe is knowable as opposed to merely transcendent. And that He revealed Himself in time and space through the person and work of Jesus Christ—*who demonstrated that He is in fact God through the immutable fact of His resurrection.*
3. That the Bible is divine rather than merely human in origin. If it is merely human, it has little more to commend it than Homer's *Iliad*—the ancient Bible of the Greeks.

A DESIGNED UNIVERSE

First, we must be prepared to demonstrate that the universe was created by God and did not evolve by undirected processes. To do so, it is crucial to be able to communicate the following:

*   The fossil record is an embarrassment to the evolutionary paradigm. Darwin said that the fossil record would bear him out, yet a century and

a half after the publication of his magnum opus, *The Origin of Species*, there is still no credible evidence for vertical transitions in the fossil record (macroevolution).[4]

- The field of paleoanthropology is fraught with ape-men fiction, frauds, and fantasies. In the category of fiction is *Pithecanthropus erectus* (Java man).[5] Nineteen doctrinaire evolutionists who participated in the Selenka expedition—a trek bent on demonstrating that the evolutionary conjectures concerning Java Man were true—produced a 342-page scientific report demonstrating beyond the peradventure of a doubt that *Pithecanthropus erectus* played no part whatsoever in human evolution. Piltdown Man may be factually described as a fraud. While the fraud may have been cleverly conceived, it was crudely carried out. The jaw of an ape was stained to make it appear as though it would match a human skull. Peking Man might best be described as a pure fantasy conceived of by physician Davison Black as he was about to run out of funds for his evolutionary explorations in 1927.

- The idea of chance has no chance in an age of scientific enlightenment. Chance in this sense refers to that which happens without cause. Thus, chance implies the absence of both a design and a designer. Even forming something as basic as a protein molecule by random processes is unthinkable. Ironically, Darwin himself found it hard to swallow the notion that the eye could be the product of blind evolutionary chance, conceding that the intricacies of the human eye gave him "cold shudders."

- Philosophical Naturalism—the worldview undergirding evolutionism—can provide only three explanations for the existence of the universe in which we live: (1) The universe is merely an illusion; (2) the universe sprang from nothing; (3) the universe eternally existed. The only plausible possibility is "In the beginning God created the heavens and the earth." In an age of empirical science, nothing could be more clear, certain, or correct.

JESUS, THE INCARNATE SON OF GOD

Second, we must be equipped to demonstrate that Jesus Christ is God and proved it by demonstrating that He had the power to lay down His life and to take it up again. The resurrection of Jesus Christ is the greatest feat in the annals of recorded history. Through the Resurrection, Jesus demonstrated that He does not stand in a line of peers with Buddha, Muhammad, or any other founder of a world religion. They died and are still dead, but Christ is risen! He is risen indeed!

Resurrection is the capstone in the arch of Christianity; if it is removed, all else crumbles. It is the singular doctrine that elevated Christianity above all the pagan religions of the ancient Mediterranean world. As Paul put it, "If Christ has not been raised, your faith is futile; you are still in your sins . . . If only for this life we have hope in Christ, we are to be pitied more than all men" (1 Corinthians 15:17, 19). It is precisely because of its strategic importance to the Christian faith that each person who takes the sacred name of Christ upon his lips must be prepared to demonstrate:

- The fatal torment of Jesus Christ as recorded in the New Testament is one of the most well-established facts of ancient history. In today's modern age of scientific enlightenment, there is a virtual consensus among New Testament scholars, both conservative and liberal, that Jesus died on the cross, that He was buried in the tomb of Joseph of Arimathea, and that His death drove His disciples to despair.

- On Easter morning some two thousand years ago, the tomb of Jesus Christ was found empty. The bottom line is this: Christianity cannot survive a tomb containing the corpse of Christ. Even the enemies of Christ conceded that the tomb was empty.

- The apostles did not merely propagate Christ's teachings; they were absolutely positive that He had appeared to them in the flesh. Although we are now two thousand years removed from the actual event, we, too, can be absolutely confident in Christ's postresurrection appearances.

- What happened as a result of the Resurrection is unprecedented in human history. In the span of a few hundred years, a small band of seemingly insignificant believers succeeded in turning an entire empire upside down. While it is conceivable that the disciples would have faced torture, vilification, and even cruel deaths for what they fervently believed to be true, it is inconceivable that they would have been willing to die for what they knew to be a lie.

Indeed, the evidence for Christ's resurrection is so overwhelming that no one can examine it with an open mind, desiring to know the truth, without becoming convinced that it really happened.

THE BIBLE IS GOD'S WORD

Third, it is crucial that we be prepared to demonstrate that the Bible is divine rather than merely human in origin. In fact, if you can demonstrate that the Bible was inspired by God rather than merely conspired by men, you can answer a host of objections by referring directly to Scripture as the authority. As such, believers must be equipped to communicate the facts:

- Manuscript evidence gloriously demonstrates that the Almighty has super naturally preserved His Word over time. The manuscript evidence for the authentic preservation of the original biblical text is stronger than that for any other writing of classical literature—including Homer, Plato, Aristotle, Caesar, and Tacitus. Equally amazing is the fact that the Bible has been virtually unaltered since the original writing, as is attested by scholars who have compared the earliest extant manuscripts with manuscripts written centuries later. The accumulation of manuscript fragments for the New Testament is now so great that one can piece together virtually the entire New Testament from manuscripts dated within the first and second centuries. Not only were the manuscripts copied in close proximity to the originals, but the originals were codified in close proximity to the actual events that they record. As such, there is no time for legendary contamination or corruption. The reliability of Scripture is also confirmed through the eyewitness credentials of its authors. We can be confident, therefore, that the text we possess today accurately represents the original text of Scripture.
- Archaeology affirms the historical reliability of the Bible. Over and over again, comprehensive archaeological fieldwork and careful biblical interpretation affirm the reliability of the Bible. For example, recent archaeological finds have corroborated biblical details surrounding the trial that led to the fatal torment of Jesus Christ—including Pontius Pilate, who ordered Christ's crucifixion, as well as Caiaphas, the high

priest who presided over the religious trials of Christ. It is telling when secular scholars must revise their biblical criticism in the light of solid archaeological evidence.

- The Bible records predictions of events that could not be known or predicted by chance or common sense. For example, the book of Daniel (written before 530 B.C.) accurately predicts the progression of kingdoms from Babylon through the Medo-Persian Empire, culminating in the persecution and suffering of the Jews under Antiochus IV Epiphanes, his desecration of the temple, his untimely death, and freedom for the Jews under Judas Maccabeus in 165 B.C. It is statistically preposterous that any or all of the Bible's specific, detailed prophecies could have been fulfilled through good guessing or deliberate deceit.

- Predictions of events recorded in the Bible could not have been anticipated by chance, common sense, or collusion. When you consider some of the more improbable biblical prophecies, it seems incredible that skeptics—knowing the authenticity and historicity of the text—could reject the statistical verdict: the Bible is the Word of God. Careful research *affirms* the predictive accuracy of the Bible. Predictive prophecy is a principle of biblical reliability that often reaches even the hard-boiled skeptic!

- The whole of Scripture is greater than the sum of its individual passages. As such, you cannot comprehend the Bible as a whole without comprehending its individual parts. And you cannot comprehend its individual parts without comprehending the Bible as a whole. In other words, it is synergistic and harmonious. Indeed, the Bible is a collection of sixty-six books, written by forty different human authors in three different languages (Hebrew, Aramaic, and Greek) over a period of fifteen hundred years, on thousands of different subjects, yet it is unified and consistent throughout. How is that possible? The individual writers had no idea that their message would eventually be assembled into one Book, yet each work fits perfectly into place with a unique purpose as a synergistic component of the whole. The synergistic harmony of the Bible is a powerful testimony and an enduring reminder that God has spoken.

For a fuller treatment of the three great apologetic issues that I have outlined, see appendix B. There I provide three memorable acronyms—F-A-C-E,

F-E-A-T, and M-A-P-S—in order to inscribe the information on the tablet of your heart.

If you're looking for a real experience, try using these acronyms in defending "the faith once and for all delivered to the saints." Not only will you experience the power and presence of the Holy Spirit working through you, but you may just find yourself in the midst of an angelic praise gathering when a lost son or daughter of Adam finds his or her way into the kingdom of God.

29

E=ESSENTIALS

Watch your life and doctrine closely. Persevere in them,
because if you do, you will save both yourself and your hearers.[1]

—THE APOSTLE PAUL

Much today is said about unity within the body. But unity at what cost?
Paul Crouch seems to believe in unity at all cost, even if that cost entails
compromising essential Christian doctrine. Not only does Crouch promote the cultic theology of the Faith movement, but he has gone out of his way
to affirm a cult that openly denies the biblical doctrine of the Trinity.

On a worldwide broadcast of *Praise the Lord*, he said he agreed "a million
billion percent" with a former United Pentecostal Church member that to
divide over such a doctrine "is a trick of the devil."[2]

The truth, however, is that unity cannot exist apart from the essentials for
which the martyrs spilled their blood.

Christ warned us to beware of false prophets, and the history of the church
age has borne eloquent testimony to the necessity of the warning. The Bible
throughout warns of false apostles and deceitful workmen who masquerade as
apostles of Christ. Paul concludes that if Satan himself "masquerades as an
angel of light," it should not surprise us that his disciples "masquerade as servants of righteousness" (2 Corinthians 11:13–15).

As the storm clouds gather, these warnings should be heeded as never
before. We must become so familiar with genuine Christianity that when counterfeits loom on the horizon, we recognize them instantaneously.

That is precisely why we now turn our attention to the essentials on which
the faith is founded. These essentials have served the church well through many
perilous times.

Sailors in days gone by fixed their course by the North Star. That star provided an unchanging reference point that guided ships safely toward their destinations. The essentials have likewise guided Christ's body through the doctrinal storms that have sought to sink it. While shooting stars may light the sky for a moment, following them only leads to shipwreck.

Many people today claim that a tidal wave is sweeping us out of the age of the church into a New Age of Aquarius. But this is impossible, for Christ promised that the gates of hell would not prevail against the church. In His final commission He said, "Surely I am with you always, to the very end of the *age*" (Matthew 28:20, emphasis added). Jesus' promise suggests the acronym A-G-E, which serves as a point of reference in getting back to basics.

ATHANASIAN CREED

The Athanasian Creed,[3] widely used throughout the church, is one of the classic creeds of Christianity. It has been said that no other statement of the early church sets forth so incisively and with such clarity the profound theology implicit in the scriptural affirmation that God was in Christ reconciling the world to Himself. Its primary purpose—along with that of the other universally accepted creeds—was to refute heresies that had arisen in the church. One of the obvious functions of the Athanasian Creed was to counter deviant views of the Trinity, including tritheism. The Athanasian Creed is especially meaningful in view of the fact that tritheistic teachings peddled by heretics in the medieval church have resurfaced through the teachings of men such as Benny Hinn and through Bibles such as the popular *Dake's Annotated Reference Bible*.

Other major creeds of the church were used to combat heresy as well. The Nicene Creed was written to combat the dangerous Arian heresy, which denied Christ's full and unqualified deity. The Creed of Chalcedon refuted heresies that challenged the biblical teaching concerning Christ's nature and person. *They all did so by pointing people back to the essentials of historic Christianity.* The Athanasian Creed not only codifies the truth concerning the Trinity but also affirms Christ's incarnation, resurrection, ascension, second coming, and final judgment.

Another important aspect of the creeds is that they help us separate essential from secondary doctrines. The creeds do not discuss disputable areas in eschatology (the study of last things) such as the timing of the Tribulation or the meaning of the Millennium. Instead, they simply state the central issue, which is that "He [Christ] shall come again, with glory, to judge the living and the dead."

It is important to note that the creeds find their basis in Scripture. The Israelites in the Old Testament used the *Shema* (Hear, O Israel: the Lord our God, the Lord is one) as a creedal expression for the unity and uniqueness of Yahweh. The New Testament contains several passages first used as protocredal statements during apostolic times. The most commonly used is found in 1 Corinthians 15:3–4: "For what I received I passed on to you as of first importance: that Christ died for our sins according to the Scriptures, that he was buried, that he was raised on the third day according to the Scriptures."

Because the creeds are a concise expression of biblical truth, they are instructive in affirming doctrinal truth, refuting error, and encouraging doctrinal instruction. However, like all statements written by imperfect men, they are subject to the supreme authority of the written Word of God.

GOSPEL

The gospel is at the heart of the Christian faith. If Christians do not know how to share their faith, they have probably never been to "boot camp." The gospel should be so much a part of you that presenting it becomes second nature.

The first step in communicating the gospel involves learning to develop a *relationship* with an unbeliever. This includes using your personal testimony as a bridge into sharing the good news of the gospel. This is precisely the inverse of grabbing somebody by the lapels and shouting, "Brother, are you saved?"

After a relationship is established, you can move naturally into a presentation of the *gospel*—which essentially involves the words *realize, repent,* and *receive.*

First, according to Scripture, people need to *realize* that they are sinners. If we do not realize that we are sinners, we will not recognize our need for a savior. The Bible says we "all have sinned and fall short of the glory of God" (Romans 3:23).

Furthermore, we must *repent* of our sins. Repentance is an old English word that describes a willingness to turn from sin toward Jesus Christ. It literally means a complete U-turn on the road of life—a change of heart and a change of mind. It means having a willingness to follow Jesus and receive Him as Savior and Lord. Jesus said, "Repent and believe the good news!" (Mark 1:15).

Finally, true belief means a willingness to *receive.* To truly receive is to trust

313

in and depend on Jesus Christ alone to be the Lord of our lives here and now and our Savior for all eternity. It takes more than *knowledge* (the devil knows about Jesus and trembles). It takes more than *agreement* that the knowledge we have is accurate (the devil agrees that Jesus is Lord). What it takes is *trust* in Jesus Christ alone for eternal life. The requirements for eternal life are based not on what *we can do* but on what *Jesus Christ has done*. He stands ready to exchange His perfection for our imperfection.

According to Jesus Christ, those who *realize* they are sinners, *repent* of their sins, and *receive* Him as Savior and Lord are "born again" (John 3:3)—not physically but spiritually. And with this spiritual birth must come growth.

Because we are called to make disciples, not converts, we also need to be equipped to lead those who receive Christ as Savior and Lord through the basic steps of discipleship and growth as new believers.

Consider what would happen if every evangelical Christian led just one person to faith in Christ each year. If we began with only twelve committed Christians and each of them led one person to Christ and discipled that person, next year there would be twenty-four believers. If each of them in turn led one person to Christ and discipled that person the third year there would be forty-eight believers. If this process continued, it would take fewer than thirty years to evangelize the six billion or more people alive today on planet Earth! If in the same time frame the population doubled, it would take only one additional year.[4]

Many people today run from church to church in search of the ultimate experience. No experience, however, can compare with that of the Holy Spirit working through you in the process of bringing someone to a saving knowledge of the Lord Jesus Christ.

ESSENTIAL CHRISTIAN DOCTRINE

The gospel is rendered meaningless if it does not rest on the firm foundation of essential Christian doctrine. The Mormons, for example, proclaim a gospel, and even acknowledge Jesus as Lord. But their Jesus is vastly different from the Jesus of Scripture. Far from being the One who spoke and the universe leapt into existence, He is said to be the spirit brother of Lucifer. The New Age movement also has a gospel. It's called the *Aquarian* gospel. In this gospel, Jesus is reduced to the status of an avatar or a divine messenger. The Faith movement, too, has a gospel—but its Jesus was defeated by Lucifer upon the cross and is now relegated to the status of a cosmic gofer.

All three of these movements have something in common: they have completely redefined essential Christian doctrine. In fact, it is precisely because these essentials have been redefined that millions of people today have a distorted view of what it means to be a Christian.

The Faith movement may use Christian terminology when it comes to essentials, *but the meaning it pours into the words is decidedly unbiblical.* As we have seen, Faith teachers have redefined faith as a force and God as a faith being, and they have completely redefined Christ's substitutionary death upon the cross. Moreover, they have transformed the Christian message from a gospel of grace into a gospel of greed. While the importance of essential Christian doctrine has been trivialized by Faith teaching, it is as important today as ever before.

The importance of essential Christian doctrine can hardly be overstated. These are the very doctrines that form the line of demarcation between the kingdom of Christ and the kingdom of the cults. While believers may debate non-essentials without dividing over them, there must be unity when it comes to essential Christian doctrine. Hence the maxim: In essentials, unity; nonessentials, liberty; and in all things, charity. Essential Christian doctrine is the foundation on which the gospel of Jesus Christ itself rests. From His deity to the certainty that He will appear a second time to judge the living and the dead, essential Christian doctrine is foundational to the gospel. All other religions compromise, confuse, or contradict these essentials. Muslims, for example, dogmatically denounce the doctrine of Christ's unique deity as the unforgivable sin of *shirk*. They readily affirm the sinlessness of Christ, but adamantly deny His sacrifice upon the cross, and His subsequent resurrection as the only hope of salvation.

I am so passionate about inscribing the essentials on the tablet of your heart that I have organized them around the acronym D-O-C-T-R-I-N-E. It is my prayer that you will become so familiar with essential Christian doctrine that when a counterfeit looms on the horizon you will know it instantaneously.

DEITY OF CHRIST

The biblical witness is clear and convincing that Jesus Christ is the eternal Creator God (John 1; Colossians 1; Hebrews 1; Revelation 1). Throughout His earthly ministry, Jesus claimed to be God in word and deed (Mark 14:61–62; John 5:18, 20; 8:58; 10:30–33) and vindicated His claims to deity by living a sinless life (John 8:46; 2 Corinthians 5:21; Hebrews 4:15; 1 John 3:5; 1 Peter 2:22) by manifesting His power over nature (Mark 4:39), over fallen angels (Luke 4:35), over sickness (Matthew 4:23), over death itself (John 4:50; 11:43–44; 1 Corinthians 15), and by accurately prophesying God's judgment on Jerusalem through the destruction of the temple, which occurred in A.D. 70 (Matthew 24:1–2, 32–35).

ORIGINAL SIN

Sin is not just murder, rape, or robbery. *Sin* is a word that describes any thought, word, deed, or state of being that fails to meet God's standard of holiness and perfection. The Bible unambiguously proclaims that "all have sinned and fall short of the glory of God" (Romans 3:23). While the notion of generational curses and spirits is foreign to the text of Scripture, there is a sense in which all people are cursed as a result of an ancestor's sin. Adam's rebellion brought death to us all and tainted every aspect of our being (Genesis 3; 1 Corinthians 15:21–22; Ephesians 2:3). God, however, has provided redemption through the atoning work of the "Second Adam," Jesus Christ (Romans 5:12–21).

CANON

The thirty-nine books of the Hebrew Scriptures along with the twenty-seven books of the Greek New Testament are divine rather than merely human in origin and constitute the entire Christian *canon* (meaning "standard of measurement"). In addition to the internal testimony of the Bible about itself (2 Timothy 3:16), the divine inspiration and preservation of the Bible can be demonstrated by the early dating and consistency of the many available manuscripts, the corroboration of archaeology, and the fulfillment of predictive prophecy.

TRINITY

Though the word "Trinity" is nowhere found in the Bible, it aptly codifies the essential biblical truths that: (1) there is only one God (Deuteronomy 6:4; Isaiah 43:10); (2) the Father is God, the Son is God, and the Holy Spirit is God (Acts 5:3–4; 1 Corinthians 8:6; Hebrews 1:8); and (3) Father, Son, and Holy Spirit are eternally distinct (Matthew 28:19; John 15:26; 17:1–26). It is important to note that when Trinitarians (people who believe in the Trinity) speak of one God, they are referring to the nature or essence of God. Moreover, when they speak of persons, they are referring to personal self-distinctions within the Godhead. Put another way, Trinitarians believe in one *What* and three *Who*s.

RESURRECTION

All four canonical Gospels record the bodily resurrection of Jesus Christ from the dead. The immutable fact of Jesus' resurrection is the cornerstone of Christian faith, because it not only vindicates Jesus' claims to deity but also ensures the future bodily resurrection unto eternal life of all who believe in Jesus Christ as their Savior and proclaim Him as Lord (1 Corinthians 15; 1 Thessalonians 4:13–18). The historical reality of the Resurrection can be demonstrated through the fatal torment of Jesus on the cross, the empty tomb (early Christianity could not have survived an identifiable tomb containing the corpse of Christ), the post-resurrection appearances of Jesus, and the transformation of believers throughout the ages whose lives have been radically altered upon experiencing the resurrected Lord. (For more on the Resurrection, see the F-E-A-T article on pages 332–35.)

INCARNATION

The doctrine of Incarnation is aptly summed up in the words of the apostle John: "In the beginning was the Word, and the Word was with God, and the Word was God . . . And the Word became flesh and dwelt among us, and we beheld His glory, the glory as of the only begotten of the Father, full of grace and truth" (John 1:1, 14 NKJV). The clear testimony of Scripture is that, in the Incarnation, Jesus Christ was fully God and fully man. In other words, Jesus existed as the perfect union of a divine and a human nature in one person (John 1; Colossians 1). As *Theanthropos* ("God-Man"), the spotless "Lamb of God" (John 1:29) lived a perfectly sinless human life and died a sinner's death to sufficiently atone, once for all, for the sins of humanity (Romans 5:1–21; Hebrews 10:11–18).

NEW CREATION

The essential doctrine of New Creation is aptly codified in the words of the apostle Paul: "If anyone *is* in Christ, *he is* a new creation; old things have passed away; behold, all things have become new" (2 Corinthians 5:17, emphasis added). All who believe in the resurrection of Jesus Christ and confess Him as Lord are reconciled to God and inherit eternal life in His glorious presence (John 3:16; Romans 10:9–10). Jesus' resurrection from the dead inaugurates the renewal of all things. The new creation of faithful believers and the new creation of the natural world will be consummated in the Resurrection when Jesus returns bodily to earth as the conquering King (Romans 8:18–25).

ESCHATOLOGY

The word *eschatology* is an intimidating word with a simple meaning—"the study of end times." While the meaning of eschatology is simple to grasp, its importance is difficult to overemphasize. Far from being a mere branch in the theological tree, eschatology is the root that provides life and luster to every fiber of its being. Put another way, eschatology is the thread that weaves the tapestry of Scripture into a harmonious pattern. It is the study of everything we long and hope for. Early in Genesis, Adam and Eve fell into a life of constant sin terminated by death. The rest of Scripture chronicles God's unfolding plan of redemption. While Christians debate secondary aspects of eschatology, such as the timing of the Tribulation or the meaning of the Millennium, we are united in the truth that just as Christ came to earth once to bear the sins of the world, He will return again to gather the elect and to usher in the resurrection of all things (1 Thessalonians 4:13–18; Hebrews 9:27–28). On that day, the just will be resurrected to eternal life and the unjust will be resurrected to eternal conscious torment and separation from the love and grace of God (John 5:28–29). Paradise lost will become Paradise restored, and the problem of sin and Satan will be fully and finally resolved (Revelation 20–22).

Essential Christian doctrine provides the key to successful Christian living. It provides the framework through which we properly relate to God in *prayer*, accurately understand the *Bible*, and actively involve ourselves in vital *church* membership. It is also the way in which we ably defend our faith. *What we believe is demonstrated inevitably in how we live.* That is why the apostle Paul instructed Timothy, "Watch your life and doctrine closely. Persevere in them, because if you do, you will save both yourself and your hearers" (1 Timothy 4:16).

EPILOGUE

Don't fall in love with the gift wrapping, fall in love with Jesus Christ, the Gift of eternal life.

—JIM BAKKER, WRITING FROM A PRISON CELL IN ROCHESTER, MINNESOTA

If there is anyone who personified the dream of the health and wealth gospel, it was Payne Stewart. He had it all. He was handsome, healthy, wealthy, and, above all, a consummate winner. Arnold Palmer aptly noted that he had assured himself a prominent place in the history of golf. Jack Nicklaus called him a devoted family man, a man of strong faith, and a great champion. And Tiger Woods lauded him a true champion—an inspiration.

His legendary win at the U.S. Open contested on North Carolina's famed Pinehurst No. 2 championship golf course on a cool, damp Father's Day in June 1999 forever solidified his memory in the fabled history of golf. For Payne, however, it did much more. It sealed an opportunity to contend in the most prestigious of all golf tournaments—the Ryder Cup. Those who have played in Ryder Cup matches know that there is nothing in the game of golf that quite compares to it. There is the pressure of contending in professional golf tournaments; the pressure of playing in Majors such as the U.S. Open; and then there is the pressure of playing for your country in Ryder Cup matches. Until you have experienced it—say those who have—you simply cannot comprehend it.

The Ryder Cup would be even more intense in 1999. The American team had not won the Cup since 1993 and was desperate to bring it back to American soil. At what is today dubbed "The Miracle at Brookline," team U.S.A did just that. Storming back from a near insurmountable deficit, America regained the Cup in one of the most memorable victories in the storied history of Ryder Cup golf. In the throes of euphoria and victory that day, one could scarcely have imagined that America would not win the Cup again until September 2008.

320

Even more unimaginable is that on October 25, 1999—one month after the U.S.A came from behind to regain the 1999 Ryder Cup in Brookline, Massachusetts, and four months after his U.S. Open victory in Pinehurst, North Carolina—Payne Stewart would lose his life in the depressurized cabin of a private Learjet en route from Orlando, Florida, to Dallas, Texas. Eventually, the plane plummeted from the skies and crashed into a field ten miles west of Aberdeen, South Dakota.

Early that morning Payne had walked out of a dream home near Disney World in Florida. Before day's end, his mansion would be but a distant memory and eternity a dynamic actuality. For Payne, there was a happy ending. The last years of his life were marked by a revitalized faith in his Lord and Savior Jesus Christ. As such, at his funeral, Tracy Stewart characterized her husband as not only the great champion that he was but a devoted husband and above all, a devoted Christian.

While Payne's death was an undeniable tragedy, the real tragedy is not a fabulously handsome, healthy, wealthy, mega-sports-star dying in the prime of his strength; the real tragedy is to live a long, robust life and never use it in the service of the Master.

And that is precisely the problem with Faith theology. In compromising, confusing, and contradicting the crux of Christianity, Faith preachers have focused their messages on earthly vanities rather than eternal verities.

Creflo Dollar is a living personification of the problem. According to Dollar, "The Bible says in Proverbs 11:31 that we're going to be recompensed in the earth. I don't like to hear a lot of songs now about going to heaven, 'cause most people that sing about going to heaven are just so miserable on earth that they want to hurry up and get out. The Bible promises us days of heaven on the earth and I believe that we're right slab dab in the middle of that coming to pass." Dollar went on to say, "I want to know how to live in a mansion *now*! I want to know how to live in a penthouse *now*!"[1]

The Bible, of course, says nothing of the sort. Far from a promise that Faith followers are smack-dab in the middle of a prosperity boom in the here and now, Proverbs 11:31 demonstrates that judgment will begin in the family of faith. Indeed, the apostle Peter quotes the very proverb abused by Dollar in full in order to instruct "those who suffer according to God's will" to "commit themselves to their faithful Creator and continue to do good" (1 Peter 4:17–19).

Jerry Savelle amplified Dollar's remarks when he exclaimed, "Dear God, I can't wait until I get to heaven to be free from sickness and disease and grief and sorrow. I found out I don't have to have any more of that stuff down here."[2]

Benny Hinn aptly summed up the sentiments of fellow Faith preachers during a TBN fund-raiser: "Years ago they used to preach, 'O we are going to walk on streets of gold.' I would say, 'I don't need the gold up there. I've got to have it down here.'"[3]

How unlike the message of Hebrews! In Hebrews 11 we read that Abraham was willing to live like a stranger in a foreign country because he was "looking forward to the city with foundations, whose architect and builder is God" (v. 10). Like the other greats in the Faith Hall of Fame, he realized he was an alien and stranger on earth (v. 13), and so he longed "for a better country—a heavenly one" (v. 16). Like a host of others in the Faith Hall of Fame, he had his eyes firmly fixed on a heavenly reward.

This same perseverance is manifested in the life of the apostle Paul, who not only fought the good fight but finished the race and kept his faith. Paul's faith, like that of Job, was fixed not on the temporary circumstances of life but on the Author and Finisher of his faith—Jesus Christ (Hebrews 12:2). The Faith Hall of Fame is replete with men and women who willingly gave their lives in loving service to the Master. Those like Gideon, Barak, Samson, Jepthah, David, Samuel, and the prophets who through faith conquered kingdoms; who were tortured, jeered, and flogged; who had been chained and put in prison; stoned and put to death; destitute; persecuted and mistreated, yet were commended for their faith—because their faith was fixed not on circumstances but on God. These who were inducted into Hebrews' Faith Hall of Fame blazed a trail of faith for all of us to follow.

Long before Payne Stewart died in the cabin of a Learjet, he had turned his gaze from the temporary to the eternal. He knew that life was but a vapor, here today and gone tomorrow—his WWJD (What Would Jesus Do?) bracelet emblematic of the saying "Only one life, 'twill soon be past, only what's done for Christ will last."

This is the authentic message of hope. When tragedy rears its ugly head, those seduced by the cultic message of Faith theology find themselves empty and confused. Only an eternal perspective, rooted and grounded in biblical faith, brings solace and peace in the midst of the storm.

In the book of Ephesians, the apostle Paul urged Christians to become mature in the faith, attaining to the whole measure of the fullness of Christ.

"Then," he said, "we will no longer be infants, tossed back and forth by the waves, and blown here and there by every wind of teaching and by the cunning and craftiness of men in their deceitful scheming. Instead, speaking the truth in love, we will in all things grow up into him who is the Head, that is, Christ" (4:14–15).

A portion of a letter written from prison by a former prosperity celebrity, who in his heyday raised as much as $170 million in a single year, says it all:

> It is easy to praise God at Heritage U.S.A. with the orchestra playing and the singers and thousands of Christians worshiping God, but those times are not a test of our love for God. It's when everything is going wrong and we still praise God . . . that is the real test . . . True worship has nothing to do with where we are or what is happening. It is who God is and our attitude toward Him.
>
> Job 1:2 tells us of Job's seven sons and three daughters. Job 1:3 tells us what he owned. Then he was totally bankrupt and bereaved of all ten children in one day. The chapter ends by telling us that Job fell down on the ground and WORSHIPED . . .
>
> Yes, in the world's eyes I have lost everything. I have lost Heritage U.S.A., the television network, the daily program, my reputation, our family home, our car, our life savings . . . All is gone, and my wife of 31 years has divorced me, and I am in prison. Some would say to me like Job's wife, "Why don't you curse God and die?" But like Job, I cry out, "Though God slay me, yet will I trust Him." I pray my life will be WORSHIP to God with all self-pity gone. I have learned that happiness is not in things or circumstances, but in knowing God.
>
> Dietrich Bonhoeffer, a Christian theologian who died a martyr's death in a Nazi death camp, in his last letter to his dearest friend said, "What is happiness and unhappiness? It depends so little on the circumstances; it depends really only on that which happens inside a person . . . When Christ calls a man, He bids him, come and die."
>
> I too have learned that happiness is not in things or circumstances, but in knowing God . . . The call to accept Christ should be "Who will come to Christ and be willing to die for Him?" Not "who wants all the good things of life, come to Christ."
>
> We love to read about God's honor roll of faith in Hebrews 11, the great

faith chapter. But many stop reading at verse 35. Let me give you the last part of this great faith chapter from The Living Bible. "But others trusted God and were beaten to death, preferring to die rather than turn from God and be free—trusting that they would rise to a better life afterwards. Some were laughed at and their backs cut open with whips, and others were chained in dungeons. Some died by stoning and some by being sawed in two; others were promised freedom if they would renounce their faith, then were killed with the sword. Some went about in skins of sheep and goats, wandering over deserts and mountains, hiding in dens and caves, they were hungry and sick and ill-treated—too good for this world. And these men of faith, though they trusted God and won His approval, none of them received all that God had promised them; for God wanted them to wait and share the even better rewards that were prepared for us."

After reading these verses, I'm more convinced than ever that what God wants is blind faith—the Job-kind-of-faith, that still stands when material blessings are gone. Even though the Hollywood screen image would somehow make us believe that there are some people who lead a charmed life with no pain or loneliness that the rest of us face, it is simply not true. No one has their lives in total control and pain free. Everyone you meet is fighting their own battles. We need each other.

I can almost hear you ask, "What would you do if you had to do it over?" Oh, there is so much. It would take volumes. But one of the most important things is, I would not emphasize the physical structure, but would work with all my heart to point people to the eternal—helping them to fall in love with our Lord and Savior, Jesus Christ . . . If, by some miracle, I was transported back seven years to P.T.L., I would plead with people to get, and keep, their eyes off the physical and onto Jesus Christ and things eternal. God can still use the buildings at Heritage, or a cathedral, or a cow shed, or people gathered in an open field. Don't fall in love with the gift wrapping, fall in love with Jesus Christ, the Gift of eternal life.

It is time for sackcloth and ashes—it is time to do what God says, "If my people who are called by My Name will humble themselves and pray and seek My Face and turn from their wicked ways, then will I hear from heaven and forgive their sin and heal their land . . ." (2 Chronicles 7:14).

Let me leave you with the words of Jesus found in Mark 8: "What shall it profit a man if he shall gain the whole world and lose his own soul? Or what shall a man give in exchange for his soul?" Keep your eyes on the prize!—on Heaven, on Christ, on things above, "For it has not entered the hearts of men, the things God has prepared for them that love Him." THE BEST IS YET TO COME![4]

While I but gaze at the exterior (only God knows the heart), these words written from a prison cell ring with authenticity. If so, they chronicle a man who has exchanged the love of what is on the Master's table for the love of the Master.

Two thousand years before Jim Bakker wrote from a prison cell in Rochester, Minnesota, the apostle Paul wrote from a prison in Rome. "Whatever you do," said Paul, "work at it with all your heart, as working for the Lord, not for men, since you know that you will receive an inheritance from the Lord as a reward" (Colossians 3:23–24).

Paul's point is that what we do now counts for all eternity. As such, our eyes should be fixed on the paradise of God rather than gold in the present. Indeed, Paul specifically warns "those who are rich in this present world not to be arrogant nor to put their hope in wealth, which is so uncertain, but to put their hope in God, who richly provides us with everything for our enjoyment" (1 Timothy 6:17).

In doing so, says Paul, true believers "will lay up treasure for themselves as a firm foundation for the coming age, so that they may take hold of the life that is truly life" (v. 19).

One day, we, like Payne Stewart will experience transition from this world to the next. On that day the extravaganza begins in earnest.

Appendix A

ARE "GOD'S ANOINTED" BEYOND CRITICISM?

During His Sermon on the Mount, Jesus Christ exhorted His followers to not judge self-righteously or hypocritically. Is this necessarily what Christians do when they question the teachings of "God's anointed" preachers and evangelists? Many teachers who claim such anointing would say so, and many more of their followers commonly reply to all manner of criticism: "Touch not God's anointed."

Some of these teachers even add that such actions carry literally grave consequences. Consider what prominent Faith teacher Kenneth Copeland affirmed in his taped message *Why All Are Not Healed* (#01-4001):

> There are people attempting to sit in judgment right today over the ministry that I'm responsible for, and the ministry that Kenneth E. Hagin is responsible for . . . Several people that I know had criticized and called that Faith bunch out of Tulsa a cult. And some of 'em are dead right today in an early grave because of it, and there's more than one of them got cancer.

In addition to certain Faith teachers, such sentiments may be found among various groups involved with *shepherding* and other forms of authoritarian rule (from diverse "fivefold" ministries to a host of large and small "fringe churches"). The leaders of these groups are commonly regarded by their followers as having a unique gift and calling that entitles them to unconditional authority—sort of a heavenly carte blanche. To dispute any of their teachings or practices is not distinguished from questioning God Himself.

Advocates of such unquestionable authority assume that Scripture supports their view. Their key biblical proof text is Psalm 105:15: "Touch not mine anointed, and do my prophets no harm" (KJV). But a close examination of this passage reveals that it has nothing to do with challenging the teachings and practices of church leaders.

First, it needs to be noted that the Old Testament phrase "the Lord's anointed" is typically used to refer to the *kings of Israel* (1 Samuel 12:3, 5; 24:6, 10; 26:9, 11, 16, 23; 2 Samuel 1:14, 16; 19:21; Psalm 20:6; Lamentations 4:20), at times specifically to the royal line descended from David (Psalms 2:2; 18:50; 89:38, 51), and *not* to especially mighty prophets and teachers. While the text does also mention prophets, in the context of Psalm 105 the reference is undoubtedly to the *patriarchs* in general (vv. 8–15; cf. 1 Chronicles 16:15–22), and to Abraham (whom God called a prophet) in particular (Genesis 20:7). It is therefore debatable whether this passage can be applied to select leaders within the body of Christ.

Even if the text *can* be applied to certain church leaders today, in the context of this passage the words "touch" and "harm" have to do with inflicting *physical* harm upon someone. Psalm 105:15 is therefore wholly irrelevant to the issue of *questioning* the teachings of any self-proclaimed man or woman of God.

Moreover, even if we accepted this misinterpretation of Psalm 105:15, how are we to know who not to "touch"—that is, who God's anointed and prophets are? *Because they and their followers say they are?* On such a basis we would have to accept the claims of Sun Myung Moon, Elizabeth Clare Prophet, and virtually all cult leaders to be prophets. *Because they reputedly perform miracles?* The Antichrist and False Prophet will possess that credential (Revelation 13:13–15; 2 Thessalonians 2:9)! No, God's representatives are known above all by their purity of character *and* doctrine (Titus 1:7–9; 2:7–8; 2 Corinthians 4:2; cf. 1 Timothy 6:3–4). If a would-be spokesperson for God cannot pass the biblical tests of character and doctrine, we have no basis for accepting his or her claim, and no reason to fear that in criticizing his or her teaching, we might also be rejecting God.

Finally, if any individual Christian is to be considered anointed, then every single Christian must be considered anointed as well. For this is the *only* sense in which the term is used (apart from Christ) in the New Testament: "You [referring to *all* believers] have an anointing from the Holy One" (1 John 2:20).

Thus no believer can justifiably claim any sort of *special* status as God's "untouchable anointed" over other believers. With this in mind, it is significant that the apostle John does not use this term with reference to inspired or dynamic preaching or teaching, but to the ability and responsibility of each believer to discern between true and false teachers (vv. 18–24).

Nobody's teachings or practices are beyond biblical evaluation—especially influential leaders. According to the Bible, authority and accountability go hand in hand (e.g., Luke 12:48). The greater the responsibility one holds, the greater the accountability one has before God and His people.

Teachers and other leaders of the Christian community should be extremely careful to not mislead any believer, for their calling carries with it a strict judgment (James 3:1). *They should therefore be grateful* when sincere Christians take the time and effort to correct whatever erroneous doctrine they may be holding and preaching to the masses. And if the criticisms are unfounded or unbiblical, they should respond in the manner prescribed by Scripture, which tells them to correct misguided doctrinal opposition with gentle instruction (2 Timothy 2:25).

There is, of course, another side to this issue: criticism often can be sinful, leading to rebellion and unnecessary division. Christians should respect the leaders that God has given them (Hebrews 13:17). Theirs is the task of assisting the church in its spiritual growth and doctrinal understanding (Ephesians 4:11–16). At the same time, believers should be aware that *false teachers will arise among the Christian fold* (Acts 20:29; 2 Peter 2:1). This makes it imperative for us to test *all* things by Scripture, as the Bereans were commended for doing when they examined the words of even the apostle Paul (Acts 17:11).

Not only is the Bible useful for preaching, teaching, and encouragement, but it is equally valuable for correcting and rebuking (2 Timothy 4:2). In fact, we as Christians are held accountable for proclaiming the whole will of God and warning others of false teachings and those responsible for them (Acts 20:26–28; cf. Ezekiel 33:7–9; 34:1–10).

We need to heed Scripture's repeated warnings to be on guard for false teachings (e.g., Romans 16:17–18; cf. 1 Timothy 1:3–4; 4:16; 2 Timothy 1:13–14; Titus 1:9; 2:1), and to point them out to brothers and sisters in Christ (1 Timothy 4:6). With so much scriptural support, such actions can hardly be considered unbiblical.

Appendix B

APOLOGETICS:
THE DEFENSE OF THE FAITH

There are three major questions all Christians must be prepared to answer in defending the Christian faith. To help make the process of learning these questions more enjoyable, I have developed three easy-to-remember acronyms. From now on, the words F-A-C-E, F-E-A-T, and M-A-P-S may well take on a whole new meaning for you. Let's look at them one by one.

F-A-C-E

We begin with the *FACE* that demonstrates the farce of evolution. Anyone who has gone to school in America has no doubt seen the "face" of *Pithecanthropus erectus*. This is the ape-man you may remember staring at you from the pages of your science textbook. You know—the one with the eyes of a philosopher, his slightly perplexed and preoccupied gaze no doubt designed to give the illusion of intelligence in the making. The truth is, however, that *Pithecanthropus* is little more than the figment of an artist's imagination. But more on that later.

F—Fossils

Let's begin by looking at the first letter in the acronym F-A-C-E, which will remind you that the *fossils* say *no* to evolutionary hypothesis. Colin Patterson, who was senior paleontologist at the prestigious British Museum of

Natural History, which houses the world's largest fossil collection—60 million specimens—confessed, "If I knew of any [evolutionary transitions], fossil or living, I would certainly have included them [in my book *Evolution*]."[1] His statement underscores the fact that the fossil record is an embarrassment to evolutionists. No verifiable transitions from one species to another have as yet been found. Ironically, while the general public seems blithely unaware that no transitions from one species to another (known as *macroevolution*) exist, it is common knowledge among paleontologists.

That is precisely why novel theories such as punctuated equilibrium are constantly evolving. This idea essentially postulates that there were quantum leaps in evolutionary development. For example, in *The Wonderful Egg*, a book written for children, a mother dinosaur lays an egg that hatches into the very first bird. It is indeed tragic that this book earned recommendation from the prestigious American Association for the Advancement of Science, the American Council on Education, and the Association for Childhood Education International.[2]

The problems with this fanciful theory should be self-evident. First, this theory is motivated by the lack of vertical transitional forms in the fossil record. Thus, it is a classic argument from silence. Furthermore, this convoluted concept flies in the face of the science of genetics. Finally, the effects produced by "jumping genes" or chromosomal rearrangements would not produce a hopeful monster but a monstrosity. Even if, as postulated by punctuated equilibrium, the jumps do not go from reptiles to birds but from scales to feathers, the jumps are still too fantastic. Conversely, if the jumps are in reality rather insignificant, then we are right back at square one—gradualism, which predicts that the fossil record would provide abundant evidence of finely graded intermediary life forms as one kind is progressively transformed into another.[3]

A—Ape-Men

Next, you should know that *ape-men* frauds abound. Not only is *Pithecanthropus erectus* a gross mistake (it has since been proved that he was only a gibbon), but so are such notable ape-men as Piltdown man and Peking man. Nebraska man was based on a single tooth found in 1922 by Harold Cook on a farm in Nebraska. With a little creativity, the tooth was imagined to belong to a human skull (it was later proven to belong to a rare pig), the skull was imagined to belong to a skeleton, and the skeleton was drawn to perfection with flesh and features. By the time he hit the London newspapers, Nebraska man was being pictured with Nebraska mom. Imagine that: two people from just one tooth!

At the time of the famous Scopes monkey trial in 1925, Nebraska man was presented as evidence to prove that evolution was a fact. But to say that man evolved from apes because they both have bones is as ridiculous as supposing that a bird and a plane are closely related because they both have wings. The chasm between the smartest ape and the dumbest man simply cannot be bridged.

C—Chance

The letter "C" in the acronym F-A-C-E will serve to remind you of the word *chance*. The idea that the complexity of our universe came about through chance is a statistical impossibility. Even forming something as basic as a protein molecule by random or undirected processes is unthinkable. Despite the evidence, many people seem convinced that, given enough time, even the most improbable events become probable. This argument, however, only seems reasonable when specifics are not considered. We can put it into perspective with the "million monkeys" illustration.[4]

If a million monkeys continually typed on a million typewriters, one of them might eventually pound out a Shakespearean play. Now assume a million monkeys typed twenty-four hours a day at one hundred words a minute on typewriters that had forty keys. Suppose each word of the play contained four letters. How long would it take to get the first four words? About 800 billion years! No one could imagine the amount of time required to produce the first scene.

E—Empirical Science

Finally, "E" in the acronym F-A-C-E will remind you that in light of reason and *empirical science*, the theory of evolution is found wanting. In point of fact, philosophical naturalism—the worldview undergirding evolutionism—can provide only three explanations for the existence of the universe in which we live: (1) The universe is merely an illusion. This notion carries little weight in an age of scientific enlightenment. As has been well said, "Even the full-blown solipsist looks both ways before crossing the street." (2) The universe sprang from nothing. This proposition flies in the face of both the laws of cause and effect and energy conservation. There simply are no free lunches. The conditions that hold true in this universe prevent any possibility of matter springing out of nothing. (3) The universe eternally existed. This hypothesis is devastated by the law of entropy, which predicts that a universe that has eternally existed would have died an "eternity ago" of heat loss. There is, however, one other possibility. It is found in the very first chapter of the first book of the Bible: "In the beginning God created the heavens and the earth." In an age of empirical science, nothing could be more certain, clear, or correct.

While a great deal more could be said, I trust that this brief overview will motivate you to become equipped to defend the faith when it comes to the issue of origins. For a more complete rendition, please see my books, *The Face That Demonstrates the Farce of Evolution* and *Fatal Flaws,* a condensed version of the first book, published by Thomas Nelson.

F-E-A-T

If devotees of the kingdom of the cults, adherents of world religions, or liberal scholars are correct, the biblical account of the Resurrection is fiction, fantasy, or a gargantuan fraud. If, on the other hand, Christianity is factually reliable, the resurrection of Jesus Christ is the greatest *feat* in human history.

The Resurrection is not merely important to the historic Christian faith; without it, there would be no Christianity. Because of its centrality to Christianity, those who take the sacred name of Christ upon their lips must be prepared to defend the historicity of the Resurrection. To make the process memorable, I've developed the acronym F-E-A-T. This acronym should serve as an enduring reminder that, far from being a gargantuan fraud, the Resurrection is the greatest feat in the annals of recorded history.

Each letter in F-E-A-T will serve to remind us of an undeniable fact of the Resurrection.

F—Fatal Torment

The fatal suffering of Jesus Christ as recounted in the New Testament is one of the most well-established facts of ancient history. Even in today's modern age of scientific enlightenment, there is a virtual consensus among New Testament scholars, both conservative and liberal, that Jesus died on the cross, that He was buried in the tomb of Joseph of Arimathea, and that His death drove His disciples to despair.[5] While noteworthy scholars throughout history have suggested that Jesus may have merely swooned, the evidence clearly points in a different direction.

Indeed, believing Jesus merely swooned must surely stretch credulity beyond its breaking point. It would mean that Christ suffered six trials, a lack of sleep, the Roman scourge, being spiked to a cross, and a spear wound in His side; that Jesus survived three days without medical attention, single-handedly rolled away an enormously heavy tombstone, subdued an armed guard, strolled around on pierced feet, and seduced His disciples into communicating the myth that He had conquered death while He lived out the remainder of His pathetic life in obscurity.

According to Gary Habermas, the late Cambridge scholar John A. T. Robinson suggested the swoon theory is so fatally flawed that "if the public were not so interested in virtually anyone who writes on Christianity, it 'would be laughed out of court.'"[6]

E—Empty Tomb

As the historicity of the Resurrection is undermined in the media, it is crucial that Christians are prepared to demonstrate that Jesus was buried and that, on Easter morning some two thousand years ago, the tomb was indeed empty.

First, liberal and conservative scholars alike agree that the body of Jesus was buried in the private tomb of Joseph of Arimathea. Philosopher and theologian William Lane Craig points out that as a member of the Jewish court that condemned Jesus, Joseph of Arimathea is unlikely to be Christian fiction; Jesus' burial in the tomb of Joseph of Arimathea is substantiated by Mark's Gospel and is, therefore, far too early to have been the subject of legendary corruption.[7]

Furthermore, the earliest Jewish response to the resurrection of Christ presupposes the empty tomb;[8] and in the centuries following the Resurrection, the fact of the empty tomb was forwarded by Jesus' friends and foes alike.[9]

Finally, considering the fact that women in ancient Judaism were routinely considered to be little more than chattel, it is remarkable that the Gospel writers highlighted women as the heroes of their empty tomb accounts.[10] This in itself is proof positive that the Gospel writers valued truth over cultural correctness.

In short, early Christianity could not have survived an identifiable tomb containing the corpse of Christ.

A—Appearances

One thing can be stated with iron-clad certainty: the apostles did not merely propagate Christ's teachings; they were absolutely positive that He had appeared to them in the flesh. Although we are now two thousand years removed from the actual event, we, too, can be absolutely confident in Christ's postresurrection appearances.

Paul, for example, points out that Christ "appeared to more than five hundred of the brothers at the same time, most of whom are still living, though some have fallen asleep" (1 Corinthians 15:6). It would have been one thing to attribute these supernatural experiences to people who had already died. It was quite another to attribute them to multitudes who were still alive. As the famed New Testament scholar of Cambridge University C. H. Dodd points out, "There can hardly be any purpose in mentioning the fact that most of the five hundred are still alive, unless Paul is saying, in effect, 'The witnesses are there to be questioned.'"[11]

Moreover, in 1 Corinthians 15:3–7, Paul is reiterating a Christian creed that can be traced all the way back to the formative stages of the Christian church. Incredibly, scholars of all stripes agree this creed can be dated to within three to eight years of the Crucifixion itself.[12] The short duration between Christ's crucifixion and the composition of this early Christian creed precludes the possibility of legendary corruption.[13]

No one summed up the consensus of New Testament scholarship better than Professor Norman Perrin, the late New Testament scholar at the University of Chicago: "The more we study the tradition with regard to the appearances, the firmer the rock begins to appear upon which they are based."[14]

T—Transformation

What happened as a result of the Resurrection is unprecedented in human history. In the span of a few hundred years, a small band of seemingly insignificant believers succeeded in turning an entire empire upside down. While it is conceivable that they would have faced torture, vilification, and even cruel deaths for what they fervently believed to be true, it is inconceivable that they would have been willing to die for what they knew to be a lie. Peter, who was once afraid of being exposed as a follower of Christ, after the Resurrection suffered a martyr's death. James, the half brother of Jesus, who once hated everything his brother stood for, after the Resurrection calls himself "a bond-servant of . . . the Lord Jesus Christ" (James 1:1 NKJV) and, like Peter, was martyred. Paul was likewise transformed; once a ceaseless persecutor of the growing church, he became the chief proselytizer of the Gentiles. As Dr. Simon Greenleaf, the famous Royall professor of law at Harvard, put it, "If it were morally possible for them to have been deceived in this matter, every human motive operated to lead them to discover and avow their error . . . If then their testimony was not true, there was no possible motive for this fabrication."[15]

Not only did the resurrection of Christ transform the disciples from cowards to lions of the faith, but His resurrection continues to transform lives today. Of one thing I am certain—if twenty-first-century Christians would grasp the significance of the Resurrection like their first-century counterparts, their lives will be radically revolutionized. Rather than being microcosms of the culture, they would become change agents. Like a small assortment of seemingly unimportant believers who succeeded in turning an empire upside down, we would leave a lasting mark on society.

In the end, it all depends on whether we *say* we believe in the Resurrection or whether we *really* believe!

M-A-P-S

Finally, to defend the faith we must be equipped to demonstrate that the Bible is divine rather than merely human in origin. If we can successfully accomplish this, we can answer a host of other objections simply by appealing to Scripture. To chart our course I will use the acronym M-A-P-S. Since most Bibles have maps in the back, this should prove to be a memorable association.

M—Manuscripts

We begin with the "M" in M-A-P-S, which will remind you that God has supernaturally preserved His Word through literally thousands of *manuscripts*. First, it should be noted that the New Testament has stronger manuscript support than any other work of classical literature—including Homer, Plato, Aristotle, Caesar, and Tacitus. There are presently more than five thousand copies of Greek manuscripts in existence[16] and as many as twenty thousand more translations in such languages as Latin, Coptic, and Syriac. The earliest manuscript fragments can be dated to within a hundred years after Christ's death and resurrection. The accumulation of fragments is now so large that one can piece together most of the New Testament from fragments that are dated within two centuries of Christ's death and resurrection.[17] This is amazing when you consider that only seven manuscript copies of Plato's *Dialogues* are in existence—and there is a thirteen-hundred-year gap that separates the earliest copy (eighth century A.D.) from the original writing (fifth century B.C.). Similarly, there are only 650 copies of Homer's *Iliad* (the bible of the ancient Greeks) in existence—and there is a one-thousand-year gap that separates the earliest copy (second century A.D.) from the original writing (eighth century B.C.).

Bart Ehrman, who chairs the department of Religious Studies at the University of North Carolina, Chapel Hill, has sought to negate the value of the manuscript evidence by arguing that "there are more differences among our manuscripts than there are words in the New Testament."[18] At first blush his argument seems to have credibility. A closer examination, however, demonstrates that it has no weight. Here's why.

Suppose you wrote an essay and asked five friends to produce a handwritten copy of it. Imagine further that each of them asked five friends to do the same. The first five would make mistakes, and those who copy the copies would make additional errors. By the fifth generation you would have approximately four thousand flawed manuscripts. Sounds pretty grim, right? But think with me for a moment. Your five friends made mistakes, but they didn't all make the same mistakes. If you compared the copies, you would find that one group contained the same mistakes, while the other four did not. This, of course, would make it easy to tell the copies from the original. Not only so, but most of the mistakes would be obvious—such as misspelled words or a missed conjunction. Even if you lost the original, as long as you had access to the copies, it would be a rather simple matter to reproduce the original piece. That's essentially the situation with the New Testament. We have thousands of copies that have been classified by scholars into groups and, thus, we can determine with great precision what the originals actually said. While it can be argued that there are differences in style and spelling among the various manuscripts, it cannot be credibly asserted that there are significant differences in substance.

What is true of the New Testament is true of the Old Testament as well. The Dead Sea Scrolls (100 B.C.) discovered in the late 1940s predate what was then the earliest extant text—Masoretic (A.D. 900)—by some one thousand years. In other words, there is a full millennium during which the text might well have been significantly altered. When the Masoretic text was compared to the Dead Sea Scrolls, differences in style and spelling were discovered but no significant difference in substance.

Furthermore, the reliability of Scripture is confirmed through the eyewitness credentials of its authors. Moses, for example, participated in and was an eyewitness to the remarkable events of the Egyptian captivity, the Exodus, the forty years in the desert, and Israel's final encampment before entering the promised land, all of which are accurately chronicled in the Old Testament. The New Testament has even stronger eyewitness authenticity. For example, Luke says that he gathered eyewitness testimony and "carefully investigated everything" (Luke 1:1–3). John writes, "That which was from the beginning, which we have heard, which we have seen with our eyes, which we have looked at and our hands have touched—this we proclaim concerning the Word of life" (1 John 1:1). Likewise, Peter reminded his readers that the disciples "did not follow cleverly invented stories" but "were eyewitnesses of [Jesus'] majesty" (2 Peter 1:16). These were eyewitnesses, mind you, who were willing to testify to the point of shedding their own blood.

Finally, secular historians—including Josephus (before A.D. 100), the Roman Tacitus (around A.D. 120), the Roman Suetonius (A.D. 110), and the Roman governor Pliny the Younger (A.D. 110)—confirm the many events, people, places, and customs chronicled in the New Testament. Early church leaders such as Irenaeus, Tertullian, and Clement of Rome—all writing before A.D. 250—also shed significant light on the historical accuracy of the New Testament. From such sources one can piece together highlights of the life of Christ independent of the Bible. As such, credible historians today concede that the Bible is a remarkable historical document.

A—Archaeology

As with the manuscript evidence, *archaeology* is a powerful witness to the accuracy of the New Testament documents. Over and over again, comprehensive archaeological fieldwork and careful biblical interpretation affirm the reliability of the Bible. It is telling when secular scholars must revise their biblical criticism in light of solid archaeological evidence.

One of the most well-known New Testament examples concerns the books

of Luke and Acts. A biblical skeptic, Sir William Ramsay, trained as an archaeologist, set out to disprove the historical reliability of this portion of the New
Testament. But through his painstaking Mediterranean archaeological trips, he
became converted as one after another, the historical allusions of Luke were
proved accurate.[19]

Furthermore, archaeologists in the last decade discovered a gold mine of
archaeological nuggets that provide a powerful counter to objections raised by
scholars against the biblical account of Christ's crucifixion and burial. In the
October 25, 1999, *U.S. News and World Report*, Jeffrey Sheler highlights the
significance of the recent discovery of the remains of a man crucified during the
first century. This discovery calls into question the scholarship of liberals who
contend that Jesus was tied rather than nailed to the cross and that His corpse
was likely thrown into a shallow grave and eaten by wild dogs rather than
entombed. The following is Sheler's account:

> Explorers found the skeletal remains of a crucified man in a burial cave at
> Giva'at ha-Mitvar, near the Nablus road outside of Jerusalem. It was a
> momentous discovery: While the Romans were known to have crucified
> thousands of alleged traitors, rebels, robbers, and deserters in the two cen-
> turies straddling the turn of the era, never before had the remains of a
> crucifixion victim been recovered. An initial analysis of the remains found
> that their condition dramatically corroborated the Bible's description of the
> Roman method of execution.
>
> The bones were preserved in a stone burial box called an ossuary and
> appeared to be those of a man about 5 feet, 5 inches tall and 24 to 28 years
> old. His open arms had been nailed to the crossbar, in the manner similar
> to that shown in crucifixion paintings. The knees had been doubled up and
> turned sideways, and a single large iron nail had been driven through both
> heels. The nail—still lodged in the heel bone of one foot, though the execu-
> tioners had removed the body from the cross after death—was found bent,
> apparently having hit a knot in the wood. The shin bones seem to have
> been broken, corroborating what the Gospel of John suggests was normal
> practice in Roman crucifixions.[20]

Finally, recent archaeological finds have also corroborated biblical details
surrounding the trial that led to the fatal torment of Jesus Christ—including

Pilate, who ordered Christ's crucifixion, as well as the burial grounds of Caiaphas the high priest, who presided over the religious trials of Christ. As noted by Sheler, in 1990 a burial chamber dating back to the first century was discovered two miles south of Temple Mount. "Inside, archaeologists found 12 limestone ossuaries. One contained the bones of a 60-year-old man and bore the inscription *Yehosef bar Qayafa*—'Joseph, son of Caiaphas.'" Experts believe these remains are probably those of Caiaphas the high priest of Jerusalem, who, according to the Gospels, ordered the arrest of Jesus, interrogated Him, and handed Him over to Pontius Pilate for execution.[21]

Regarding Pontius Pilate, Sheler notes that excavations at the seaside ruins of Caesarea Maritima—the ancient seat of the Roman government in Judea—uncovered a first-century inscription that confirmed that Pilate was the Roman ruler at the time of Christ's crucifixion. Archaeologists working at the Herodian theater found a plaque inscribed with the Latin words *Tiberieum . . . [Pon]tius Pilatus . . . [praef]ectus Juda[ea]e*. "According to experts, the complete inscription would have read, 'Pontius Pilate, the Prefect of Judea, has dedicated to the people of Caesarea a temple in honor of Tiberias.' The discovery of the so-called Pilate Stone has been widely acclaimed as a significant affirmation of biblical history because, in short, it confirms that the man depicted in the Gospels as Judea's Roman governor had precisely the responsibilities and authority that the Gospel writers ascribe to him."[22] Truly, with every turn of the archaeologist's spade we continue to see evidence for the trustworthiness of the Scriptures.

Indeed, you can use the *shaft* of the archaeologist's spade as a means by which to remember that what is discovered in the soil corresponds to that which is detailed in the Scriptures.

The "S" in S-H-A-F-T will serve to remind you of the archaeological discovery in 1896 of a *slab* or *stele*, variously referred to as the *Merneptah* or *Israel stele*. This discovery is hugely significant in countering skeptics who argue that the biblical account of the Exodus is pure mythology. The seven-foot black granite stele is inscribed in part with the words *"Israel is desolated, its seed is not."* The stele not only lends credence to the fact that, in accord with Scripture, Israel was a significant people group, but also, as noted by the eminent ancient historian Dr. Paul Maier, "This is the earliest reference to Israel in non-biblical sources and demonstrates that as of c. 1230 B.C. the Hebrews were already living in the Promised Land."[23]

The "H" reminds us of *Hittites*. Prior to the early twentieth century, the

Hittites were thought to be part and parcel of biblical mythology. However, in 1906, archaeologists unearthed the ruins of Hattusas, the chief city of the ancient Hittites. As such, we now have evidence to corroborate the biblical references to a Hittite empire that prospered from c. 1800 B.C. to c. 1200 B.C.

The "A" in S-H-A-F-T stands for the *Assyrians*. The Assyrians, like the Hittites, were thought to be a mythological people group. As such, Sargon, Assurbanipal, and Sennacherib were all considered to be kings of a mythological kingdom. That is, until the nineteenth century when Layard the great Assyriologist —an Indiana Jones if ever there was one—uncovered the ruins of Nineveh, the capital of the Assyrian empire on the plains of Northern Iraq.

The "F" represents the word *flood*. The notion of a great deluge was not merely relegated to a biblical account. It was impregnated on the collective consciousness of the ancient world. As such, the Sumerians, the Babylonians, and the Greeks all chronicled accounts of a primordial deluge. The Babylonian epic of Gilgamesh, which contains a corrupted version of the Flood story—replete with a less-than-seaworthy cube-shaped ark and an insufficient fourteen-day downpour—nonetheless lends credibility to the real McCoy.

The "T" in the acronym S-H-A-F-T will serve to remind you of a *tunnel* that is today as it was described almost three millennia ago in 2 Chronicles 32:30. King Hezekiah (721–686 B.C.), bracing for a siege by the Assyrian Sennacherib, cut this tunnel through solid rock in order to channel water from the Gihon Spring to the Pool of Siloam inside the walls of Jerusalem. An archaeological inscription in the museum of Istanbul bears eloquent testimony to this remarkable historical reality.[24]

P—Prophecy

The "P" in the acronym M-A-P-S represents one of the most powerful proofs to the divine origins of the biblical text. The book of Daniel is a classic case in point. In the midst of the sixth-century B.C. Babylonian captivity, YHWH reveals through Daniel His present and eternal purposes for Israel and the world. Daniel accurately predicts the progression of kingdoms from Babylon through the Median and Persian empires to the further persecution and suffering of the Jews under Antiochus IV Epiphanes, including the Syrian despot's desecration of the Jerusalem temple, his untimely death, and freedom for the Jews under Judas Maccabeus in 165 B.C.

Moreover, the book of Daniel prophetically looks forward to the coming of Messiah. As prophesied by Jeremiah, Jerusalem would experience a partial restoration after seventy years of exile (Jeremiah 29:10); however, as revealed through the angel Gabriel, the return from exile was merely a type of the anti-typical freedom that would be experienced through Judas Maccabeus, which itself was typological of ultimate restoration through Jesus the Messiah. As such, the seventy-sevens of Daniel encompass ten Jubilee eras and represent the extended exile of the Jews that would end in the fullness of time—the quintessential Jubilee—when the people of God would experience ultimate redemption and restoration, not in a holy city turned harlot city, but in a holy Christ.

Furthermore, Christ, who came in the fullness of time, looked back at the "abomination that causes desolation, spoken of through the prophet Daniel" as the basis for prophesying that the temple that had been desecrated by the forces of Antiochus would ultimately be destroyed by the forces of Antichrist. "At that time," said Jesus, "the sign of the Son of Man will appear in the sky, and all the nations of the earth will mourn. They will see the Son of Man coming on the clouds of the sky, with power and great glory" (Matthew 24:30). So as to leave no doubt regarding the time of His coming, Jesus said, "I tell you the truth, *this generation* will certainly not pass away until all these things have happened. Heaven and earth will pass away, but my words will never pass away" (vv. 34–35, emphasis added).

Skeptics and infidels have seized upon these words to designate Christ a false prophet. Had they understood the language of the Bible, however, they may not have been as quick to wag their fingers at the Master. While they are correct in dismissing the grammatical gyrations of Faith teachers who routinely attempt to absolve Christ of false prophesy by suggesting that when Jesus said "*this* generation" He really meant "*that* generation" (i.e., the generation alive at His second coming), they are incorrect in assuming that Jesus was predicting the time of His second coming.

When Jesus said, "they will see the Son of Man *coming* on the clouds of the sky, with power and great glory," He was using language that anyone familiar with the Old Testament would readily grasp. Like Daniel, Isaiah, Ezekiel, and a host of prophets before Him, Jesus employed the language of "clouds" to warn His disciples of judgment that would befall Jerusalem within a generation.

Using final consummation language to characterize a near-future event, the Master prophesied, "At that time the sign of the Son of Man will appear in the sky, and all the nations of the earth will mourn. They will see the Son of Man coming on the clouds of the sky, with power and great glory" (Matthew 24:30). Far from predicting His second coming, Jesus was telling His disciples that those who witnessed Jerusalem's destruction would likewise see His vindication and exaltation as Israel's rightful king.

In the Olivet Discourse, Jesus took the quintessential Jewish nightmare and extended it to cosmic proportions. In the fullness of time, what Jesus declared desolate was desolated by Roman infidels. They destroyed the temple fortress and ended the daily sacrifice. This time, the blood that desolated the sacred altar flowed not from the carcasses of unclean pigs but from the corpses of unbelieving Pharisees. This time, the Holy of Holies was not merely desecrated by the defiling statue of a pagan god but was manifestly destroyed by the pathetic greed of despoiling soldiers. This time, no Judas Maccabaeus intervened. Within a generation, the temple was not just desecrated; it was destroyed! "Not one stone here," said Jesus, "will be left on another; every one will be thrown down" (Matthew 24:2). A generation later, when the disciples saw "Jerusalem being surrounded by armies" they *knew* "its desolation" was near (Luke 21:20). Thus, as Jesus had instructed, they *fled to the mountains* (Matthew 24:16; Luke 21:21).

Finally, since Christ is not only the quintessential prophet but the culminating theme of the Old Testament, it should not surprise us that prophecies regarding Him outnumber all others. Many of these prophecies would have been impossible for Jesus to deliberately conspire to fulfill—such as His descent from Abraham, Isaac, and Jacob (Genesis 12:3; 17:19); His birth in Bethlehem (Micah 5:2); His crucifixion with criminals (Isaiah 53:12); the piercing of His hands and feet on the cross (Psalm 22:16); the soldiers' gambling for His clothes (Psalm 22:18); the piercing of His side and the fact that His bones were not broken at His death (Zechariah 12:10; Psalm 34:20); and His burial among the rich (Isaiah 53:9). Not only so, but the Christ who walked through the doorway of Old Testament prophecy made the ultimate prediction: *"Destroy this temple, and I will raise it again in three days* . . . After he was raised from the dead, his disciples recalled what he had said. Then they believed the Scripture and the words that Jesus had spoken" (John 2:19, 22, emphasis added). Predictive prophecy is a principle of biblical reliability that reaches even hard-boiled skeptics!

S—Scriptural Synergy

Simply stated, the principle of Scriptural Synergy means that the whole of Scripture is greater than the sum of its individual passages. We cannot comprehend the Bible as a whole without comprehending its individual parts. And we cannot comprehend its individual parts without comprehending the Bible as a whole. Individual passages of Scripture are synergistic rather than deflective with respect to the whole of Scripture. In other words, it is synergistic and harmonious. Indeed, the Bible is a collection of sixty-six books, written by forty different human authors in three different languages (Hebrew, Aramaic, and Greek) over a period of fifteen hundred years, on thousands of different subjects, yet it is unified and consistent throughout. How is that possible? The individual writers had no idea that their message would eventually be assembled into one Book, yet each work fits perfectly into place with a unique purpose as a synergistic component of the whole. The synergistic harmony of the Bible is a powerful testimony and an enduring reminder that God has spoken—that these are His words. Clearly, the principle of Scriptural Synergy is a powerful indicator of the trustworthiness of Scripture.

The next time someone denies the reliability of the Bible, just remember the acronym M-A-P-S, and you will be ready to give "the reason for the hope that you have" (1 Peter 3:15). *M*anuscripts, *A*rchaeology, *P*rophecy, and *S*criptural Synergy not only chart a secure course through the turnpikes of skepticism but also demonstrate conclusively that the Bible is divine rather than merely human in origin.

Appendix C

THE THREE UNIVERSAL CREEDS

The Apostles' Creed

I believe in God the Father Almighty, Maker of heaven and earth. And in Jesus Christ, His only Son, our Lord; who was conceived by the Holy Ghost, born of the Virgin Mary; suffered under Pontius Pilate, was crucified, dead, and buried; He descended into hell; the third day He rose again from the dead; He ascended into heaven, and sitteth on the right hand of God the Father Almighty; from thence He shall come to judge the quick and the dead.

I believe in the Holy Ghost; the holy Catholic Church, the communion of saints; the forgiveness of sins; the resurrection of the body; and the life everlasting. Amen.

The Nicene Creed

I believe in one God, the Father Almighty, Maker of heaven and earth, and of all things visible and invisible.

And in one Lord Jesus Christ, the only-begotten Son of God, begotten of the Father before all worlds, God of God, Light of Light, very God of very God, begotten, not made, being of one substance with the Father; by whom all things were made; who for us men, and for our salvation, came down from heaven, and was incarnate by the Holy Ghost of the Virgin Mary, and was made man, and was crucified also for us under Pontius Pilate; He suffered and was buried; and the third day He rose again according to the Scriptures; and ascended into heaven, and sitteth on the right hand of the Father; and He shall come again with glory to judge the quick and the dead; whose kingdom shall have no end.

And I believe in the Holy Ghost, the Lord and Giver of life, who proceedeth from the Father and the Son; who with the Father and the Son together is worshiped and glorified; who spoke by the Prophets.

And I believe in one holy Catholic and Apostolic Church.

I acknowledge one Baptism for the remission of sins; and I look for the resurrection of the dead, and the life of the world to come. Amen.

The Creed of Athanasius, written against the Arians

Whosoever will be saved, before all things it is necessary that he hold the Catholic faith.

Which faith except everyone do keep whole and undefiled, without doubt he shall perish everlastingly.

And the Catholic faith is this, that we worship one God in Trinity, and Trinity in Unity;

Neither confounding the Persons, nor dividing the Substance.

For there is one Person of the Father, another of the Son, and another of the Holy Ghost.

But the Godhead of the Father, of the Son, and of the Holy Ghost is all one: the glory equal, the majesty coeternal.

Such as the Father is, such is the Son, and such is the Holy Ghost.

The Father uncreate, the Son uncreate, and the Holy Ghost uncreate.

The Father incomprehensible, the Son incomprehensible, and the Holy Ghost incomprehensible.

The Father eternal, the Son eternal, and the Holy Ghost eternal.

And yet they are not three Eternals, but one Eternal.

As there are not three Uncreated nor three Incomprehensibles, but one Uncreated and one Incomprehensible.

So likewise the Father is almighty, the Son almighty, and the Holy Ghost almighty.

And yet they are not three Almighties, but one Almighty.

So the Father is God, the Son is God, and the Holy Ghost is God.

And yet they are not three Gods, but one God.

So likewise the Father is Lord, the Son Lord, and the Holy Ghost Lord.

And yet not three Lords, but one Lord.

For like as we are compelled by the Christian verity to acknowledge every Person by Himself to be God and Lord,

So are we forbidden by the catholic religion to say, There be three Gods, or three Lords.

The Father is made of none; neither created nor begotten.

The Son is of the Father alone: not made, nor created, but begotten.

The Holy Ghost is of the Father and of the Son: neither made, nor created, nor begotten, but proceeding.

So there is one Father, not three Fathers; one Son, not three Sons; one Holy Ghost, not three Holy Ghosts.

And in this Trinity none is before or after other; none is greater or less than another;

But the whole three Persons are coeternal together, and coequal: so that in all things, as is aforesaid, the Unity in Trinity and the Trinity in Unity is to be worshiped.

He, therefore, that will be saved must thus think of the Trinity.

Furthermore, it is necessary to everlasting salvation that he also believe faithfully the incarnation of our Lord Jesus Christ.

For the right faith is, that we believe and confess that our Lord Jesus Christ, the Son of God, is God and Man.

God of the Substance of the Father, begotten before the worlds; and Man of the substance of His mother, born in the world;

Perfect God and perfect Man, of a reasonable soul and human flesh subsisting.

Equal to the Father as touching His Godhead, and inferior to the Father as touching His manhood;

Who, although He be God and Man, yet He is not two, but one Christ:

One, not by conversion of the Godhead into flesh, but by taking the manhood into God;

One altogether; not by confusion of Substance, but by unity of Person.

For as the reasonable soul and flesh is one man, so God and Man is one Christ;

Who suffered for our salvation; descended into hell, rose again the third day from the dead;

He ascended into heaven; He sitteth on the right hand of the Father, God Almighty; from whence He shall come to judge the quick and the dead.

At whose coming all men shall rise again with their bodies, and shall give an account of their own works.

And they that have done good shall go into life everlasting; and they that have done evil, into everlasting fire.

This is the catholic faith; which except a man believe faithfully and firmly, he cannot be saved.*

---

* Concordia Triglotta, 33–35.

SCRIPTURE INDEX

SUBJECT INDEX

BIBLIOGRAPHY

Adler, Margot, *Drawing Down the Moon* (Boston: Beacon Press, 1986 rev.).

Aland, Kurt, ed., *Synopsis of the Four Gospels* ([New York]: United Bible Societies, 6th rev., 1983).

Allman, John, W., "Revival Prays to Raise an Infant from the Dead," *The Pensecola News Journal* (20 September 1998),

Amundsen, Darrel W., *The Anguish and Agonies of Charles Spurgeon, Christian History*, 10:1 (1991), 22–25.

Anastasios, Archimandrite, President of Ecclesiastical Court Jaffa, Greek Orthodox Patriarchate Certificate of baptism of Issa Nabil Benedictos [Christopher N. Hinn], son of Costandi Hin and Clemence Salameh, born in Jaffa, 20 May 1954, baptized in Jaffa, 19 October 1957, signed by Secretary L. Hanna (9 July 1968).

Arbitron, Top 20 Syndicated Religious Programs [May 1992], Religious Broadcasting (October 1992), 38.

———, Top 20 Syndicated Religious Programs [July 1992], Religious Broadcasting (December 1992), 34.

Archer, Gleason L., Jr., *Encyclopedia of Bible Difficulties* (Grand Rapids: Zondervan, 1982).

Archer, John, "PrimeTime Lies?" *Charisma & Christian Life*, 17:7 (February 1992), 30–31.

Armstrong, Herbert W., *Mystery of the Ages* (Pasadena, CA: Worldwide Church of God, 1985).

Armstrong, M., "She Trusted God to Save Her," *Woman's World* (27 October 1992).

Associated Press, "Despite TV Stations' Protests, Oral Roberts Won't Stop Life-or-Death Appeal for Funds," *Orange County Register* [Santa Ana, CA] (14 January 1987), A19.

———, "4 Killed When Balloon Hits Wires and Burns," *St. Louis Post-Dispatch* (16 December 1979), 14A.

——— (Tulsa, OK), "Guilt Prompts Tilton Worker to Quit," *Denton Record Chronicle* (16 December 1991).

———, "TV Ban Won't End Oral Roberts Vow of Cash or Death," *Toronto Star* (14 January 1987), L/11.

Autism Society of America, "What's Unique about Asperger's Disorder?" (http://www.autism-society.org/site/PageServer?pagename=life_aspergers), accessed 12 May 2008.

Avanzini, John, *Believer's Voice of Victory*, Trinity Broadcasting Network (20 January 1991).

———, *It's Not Working, Brother John!* (Tulsa: Harrison House, 1992).

———, *Praise the Lord: Praise-a-Thon*, Trinity Broadcasting Network (15 September 1988).

———, *Praise the Lord: Praise-a-Thon*, Trinity Broadcasting Network (April 1990).

———, *Praise the Lord: Praise-a-Thon*, Trinity Broadcasting Network (Spring 1990).

———, *Praise the Lord: Praise-a-Thon*, Trinity Broadcasting Network (5 November 1990).

———, *Praise the Lord: Praise-a-Thon*, Trinity Broadcasting Network (6 November 1990).

———, *Praise the Lord: Praise-a-Thon*, Trinity Broadcasting Network (April 1991).

———, *Praise the Lord: Praise-a-Thon*, Trinity Broadcasting Network (10 April 1992).

———, *Praise the Lord: Praise-a-Thon*, Trinity Broadcasting Network (7 July 1992).

———, *Praise the Lord: Praise-a-Thon*, Trinity Broadcasting Network (15 September 1988).

———, *Praise the Lord: Praise-a-Thon*, Trinity Broadcasting Network (1 August 1989).

———, *Was Jesus Poor?* videotape (Hurst, TX: His Image Ministries, n.d.).

Avanzini, John with Morris Cerullo, *The Endtime Manifestation of the Sons of God* (San Diego: Morris Cerullo World Evangelism, n.d.), audiotape 1.

Bakker, Jim, letter quoted in Terry Mattingly, "Prosperity Christian Sings a Different Tune," *Rocky Mountain News* (16 August 1992), 158.

Baradell, Scott, "Robert Tilton's Heart of Darkness," *Dallas Observer* (6 February 1992), 13ff.

———, "The Man Who Could Topple Tilton," *Dallas Observer* (19 March 1992).

———, "Under the Tilton Hearing Big Top," *Dallas Observer* (12 March 1992), 18–19.

Barbet, Pierre, *A Doctor at Calvary* (New York: P. J. Kenedy/Doubleday, 1953 Eng. transl. [French orig. 1950]).

Barbour, Bruce, Publisher, Thomas Nelson Publishers, G. Richard Fisher telephone interview (8 May 1992).

———, Publisher, Thomas Nelson Publishers, telephone interview by Hanegraaff (20 July 1992).

Barron, Bruce, *The Health and Wealth Gospel* (Downers Grove, IL: InterVarsity Press, 1987).

———, "Why Settle for Riches if You Can Be a God?" Updating the Word-Faith Controversy (paper presented to the Society for Pentecostal Studies, November 1988).

Bauer, Walter, William F. Arndt, and F. Wilbur Gingrich, *A Greek-English Lexicon of the New Testament and Other Early Christian Literature* (Chicago: University of Chicago Press, 1952 rev.) (1979 rev.).

Baudouin, Charles, *Suggestion and Autosuggestion* (London: George Allen and Unwin, 1954).

Beik, Stephen W. (Benny Hinn attorney), letter to Kurt Goedelman and G. Richard Fisher, Personal Freedom Outreach (PFO) (9 October 1992).

Bentley, Todd, "Encounter with Heaven," part 3, edited by Kathy Thorne, (http://www.sidroth.org/site/News2?abbr=art_&page=NewsArticle&id=6569&news_iv_ctrl=1054), accessed 8 July 2008.

————, *Journey into the Miraculous: Experiencing the Touch of the Supernatural God* (Shippensburg, PA: Destiny Image Publishers, 2008).

Berkhof, Louis, *Systematic Theology* (Grand Rapids: Eerdmans, 4th rev., 1949).

Berkow, Robert, MD, ed., *The Merck Manual* (Rahway, NJ: Merck, 16th rev. 1992).

Best, Paul, telephone interview by CRI-Canada (3, 14 September 1992).

Bickersteth, Edward H., *The Trinity* (Grand Rapids: Kregel, 1976).

Billheimer, Paul E., *Destined for the Throne* [TBN edition] (Fort Washington, PA: Christian Literature Crusade, 1988 reprint [1975]).

Blackwelder, Boyce W., *Light from the Greek New Testament* (Grand Rapids: Baker Book House, 1958).

Blizard, Paul R., "The Orlando Christian Center: Where you're only a visitor once," *Personal Freedom Outreach [PFO] Quarterly Journal*, 13:1 (January–March 1993), 8–9.

Blizzard, Roy, " The fact of the matter," *Through Their Eyes*, 2:1 (January 1987), 19.

Boa, Kenneth, and Larry Moody, *I'm Glad You Asked* (Wheaton, IL: Victor Books, 1982).

Bowman, Robert M., Jr., "A Summary Critique: Good Morning, Holy Spirit," *Christian Research Journal*, 13:4 (Spring 1991), 36–38.

Box, Terry, "Backers Think Tilton Will Endure," *Dallas Morning News* (16 February 1992), 1A, 12A–13A.

————, "Tax Appraiser Is Scrutinizing Tilton's Church," *Dallas Morning News* (22 March 1992), 1A, 10A.

Braden, Charles S., *Spirits in Rebellion: The Rise and Development of New Thought* (Dallas, TX: Southern Methodist University Press, 3rd ed. 1970 [1963]).

Brand, Paul, and Philip Yancey, *Healing: What Does God Promise?* (Portland, OR: Multnomah Press, 1984 [*Guideposts* reprint, Carmel, NY]).

Brayley, Manuel, telephone interview by CRI-Canada (13 September 1992).

Bromiley, Geoffrey W., ed., *Theological Dictionary of the New Testament* (Grand Rapids: Eerdmans/Paternoster Press, 1985).

Brown, Colin, gen. ed., *The New International Dictionary of New Testament Theology* (Grand Rapids: Zondervan, 1975 Eng. transl.).

Brown, Harold, O. J., *Heresies: Heresy and Orthodoxy in the History of the Church* (Peabody, MA: Hendrickson Publishers, 1998).

Bruce, Alexander B., "The Synoptic Gospels," in W. Robertson Nicoll, ed., *The Expositor's Greek Testament* (Grand Rapids: Eerdmans, 1979 reprint).

Bruce, F. F., *The Gospel of John* (Grand Rapids: Eerdmans, 1983).

Buckner, Jerry L., "The Man, His Ministry, and His Movement: Concerns About the Teachings of T. D. Jakes," *Christian Research Journal*, Vol. 22, No. 2 (1999).

Budge, E. A. Wallis, *From Fetish to God in Ancient Egypt* (London: Oxford University Press, 1934 [New York: Dover, 1988 reprint]).

————, *Osiris: The Egyptian Religion of Resurrection*, 2 vols. (London: Warner, 1911 [New York: University Books, 1961 reprint]).

Burgess, Stanley M., Gary B. McGee, and Patrick H. Alexander, eds., *Dictionary of Pentecostal and Charismatic Movements* (Grand Rapids: Regency/Zondervan, 1988).

Byrne, Rhonda, *The Secret* (New York: Atiria Books / Beyond Words, 2006).

Bynum, Juanita, *Praise the Lord: Praise-a-Thon 2002*, TBN (7 November 2003).

————, *Praise the Lord: Praise-a-Thon*, Trinity Broadcasting Network (5 November 2002).

————, *Praise the Lord: Praise-a-Thon*, Trinity Broadcasting Network (4 November 2002).

C. C. [name withheld for privacy], letter, 19 June 1992.

Cady, H. Emilie, *God a Present Help* (Lee's Summit, MO: Unity School of Christianity, 1938).

————, et al, *Foundations of Unity*, series 2 (Unity Village, MO: Unity, n.d.).

Capps, Charles, *Angels* (Tulsa: Harrison House, 1984 [1991, 6th printing]).

————, *Authority in Three Worlds* (Tulsa: Harrison House, 1982).

————, *Changing the Seen and Shaping the Unseen* (Tulsa: Harrison House, 1980), (1981 [1991, 11th ed.]).

357

———, *Dynamics of Faith & Confession* (Tulsa: Harrison House, 1987).

———, *God's Creative Power* (Tulsa: Harrison House, 1976 [1991, 27th ed.]).

———, *Kicking over Sacred Cows* (Tulsa: Harrison House, 1987).

———, *The Substance of Things* (Tulsa: Harrison House, 1990).

———, *The Tongue: A Creative Force* (Tulsa: Harrison House, 1976 [1991, 25th ed.]).

Carden, Paul, "Special Report: Tilton's Tottering TV Empire," *Christian Research Journal*, 15:1 (Summer 1992), 5.

Carson, Herbert M., "*The Epistles of Paul to the Colossians and Philemon* [Tyndale New Testament Commentaries] (Grand Rapids: Eerdmans, 1977).

Cerullo, Morris, A Word from God at the Deeper Life World Conference, *Deeper Life*, 22:2 (March 1982), 15.

———, *The Endtime Manifestation of the Sons of God* (San Diego: Morris Cerullo World Evangelism, n.d.), audiotape 1.

———, "From the Heart," *Victory* (January/February 1992), 6.

———, The Greatest Message in the World, *Deeper Life* 21:3 (April 1981), 8.

———, *The Miracle Book* [special charter ed.] (San Diego, CA: Morris Cerullo World Evangelism, 1984).

[Cerullo, Morris, World Evangelism], "God's faithful, anointed servant, Morris Cerullo" [brochure] (San Diego, CA: Morris Cerullo World Evangelism, n.d.).

[Cerullo, Morris, World Evangelism], *7 Point Outreach—World Evangelism and You* (San Diego, CA: Morris Cerullo World Evangelism, n.d.).

Chandler, Charles, "Q&A with preacher Todd Bentley," *Charlotte Observer*, 18 June 2008 (http://www.charlotte.com/345/story/676593.html), retrieved 19 June 19 2008.

Chironna, Mark, *Praise the Lord*, Trinity Broadcasting Network (10 February 2003).

Cho, Paul Yonggi, *The Fourth Dimension* [vol. 1] (So. Plainfield, NJ: Bridge Publishing, Inc., 1979).

———, *The Fourth Dimension*, [vol. 2] (So. Plainfield, NJ: Bridge Publishing, Inc., 1983).

"Cho Starts Newspaper," *Charisma & Christian Life*, 16:5 (Dec. 1990), 33.

Chopra, Deepak, *The Seven Spiritual Laws of Success: A Practical Guide to the Fulfillment of Your Dreams* (Amber-Allen Publishing/New World Library, 1995).

Christian Research Journal, 12:2 (Fall 1989), 27.

Cone, Marla, "Oral Roberts Stable After Heart Problem," *Los Angeles Times* (8 October 1992), B1, B9.

Copeland, Gloria, *Believer's Voice of Victory*, Trinity Broadcasting Network (25 October 1992).

———, *God's Will for You* (Fort Worth, TX: Kenneth Copeland Publications, 1972).

———, *God's Will Is Prosperity* (Tulsa: Harrison House, 1978).

———, "Paul's Thorn in the Flesh," *Believer's Voice of Victory*, 11:11 (November 1983), 5, 8.

———, *Praise the Lord: Praise-a-Thon*, Trinity Broadcasting Network, 5 November 1990.

Copeland, Kenneth, *The Abrahamic Covenant* (Fort Worth, TX: Kenneth Copeland Ministries, 1985), audiotape #01-4405.

———, *Believer's Voice of Victory*, Trinity Broadcasting Network (28 March 1991).

———, *Believer's Voice of Victory*, Trinity Broadcasting Network (21 April 1991), [originally delivered at Full Gospel Motorcycle Rally Association 1990 Rally, Eagle Mt. Lake, TX].

———, *Following the Faith of Abraham I* (Fort Worth, TX: Kenneth Copeland Ministries, 1989), audiotape #01-3001.

———, *The Force of Faith* (Fort Worth, TX: KCP Publications, 1989).

———, *The Force of Love* (Fort Worth, TX: Kenneth Copeland Ministries, 1987), audiotape #02-0028.

———, *Forces of the Re-created Human Spirit* (Fort Worth, TX: Kenneth Copeland Ministries, 1982).

———, "The Forgotten Power of Hope," *Believer's Voice of Victory*, 20:3 (March 1992), 2–3.

———, *Freedom from Fear* (Fort Worth, TX: KCP Publications, 1983).

———, *God's Covenants with Man II* (Fort Worth, TX: Kenneth Copeland Ministries, 1985), audiotape #01-4404.

———, *Healed: To Be or Not to Be* (Fort Worth, TX: Kenneth Copeland Ministries, 1979).

———, ed., *Holy Bible: Kenneth Copeland Reference Edition* (Fort Worth, TX: Kenneth Copeland Ministries, 1991).

———, *The Image of God in You* (Fort Worth, TX: Kenneth Copeland Ministries, n.d.), audiotape #01-1403.

———, *Inner Image of the Covenant* (Fort Worth, TX: Kenneth Copeland Ministries, 1985), audiotape #01-4406.

———, "Jesus Our Lord of Glory," *Believer's Voice of Victory* (April 1982), 3.

———, *The Laws of Prosperity* (Fort Worth, TX: Kenneth Copeland Publications, 1974). .

———, *Legal and Vital Aspects of Redemption* (Fort Worth, TX: Kenneth Copeland Ministries, 1985), audiotape #01-0403.

———, "Living to Give" [brochure] (Fort Worth, TX: Kenneth Copeland Ministries, n.d. [ca. 1988]).

———, *Our Covenant with God* (Fort Worth, TX: KCP Publications, 1987 reprint [1976]).

———, *The Power of the Tongue* (Fort Worth, TX: KCP Publications, 1980).

———, *Praise the Lord*, Trinity Broadcasting Network (5 February 1986).

———, *Praise the Lord*, Trinity Broadcasting Network (6 February 1986).

———, *Praise the Lord: Praise-a-Thon*, Trinity Broadcasting Network (1988).

———, *Praise the Lord: Praise-a-Thon*, Trinity Broadcasting Network (April 1988).

———, presentation at Melodyland Christian Center, Anaheim, CA (30 March 1983), audiotape.

———, "The Price of It All," *Believer's Voice of Victory* 19:9 (September 1991), 4–6.

———, "Question & Answer," *Believer's Voice of Victory*, 16:8 (August 1988), 8.

———, *Sensitivity of Heart* (Fort Worth, TX: KCP Publications, 1984).

———, Sermon tape supplied by Dave Hunt (n.d.).

———, *Spirit, Soul and Body 1* (Fort Worth, TX: Kenneth Copeland Ministries, 1985), audiotape #01-0601.

———, *Substitution and Identification* (Fort Worth, TX: Kenneth Copeland Ministries, 1989), audiotape #00-0202.

———, "Take Time to Pray," *Believer's Voice of Victory* 15:2 (February 1987), 9.

———, *The Troublemaker* (Fort Worth, TX: Kenneth Copeland Publications, n.d. [ca. 1970]).

———, *Walking in the Realm of the Miraculous* (Fort Worth, TX: Kenneth Copeland Ministries, 1979).

———, *Welcome to the Family* (Fort Worth, TX: Kenneth Copeland Ministries, 1979).

———, *What Happened from the Cross to the Throne* (Fort Worth, TX: Kenneth Copeland Ministries, 1990), audiotape #02-0017.

———, *Why All Are Not Healed* (Fort Worth, TX: Kenneth Copeland Ministries, 1990), audiotape #01-4001.

Covey, Stephen, *The 7 Habits of Highly Effective People* (New York: Simon & Schuster, 1990).

Crawford, Thomas J., *The Doctrine of Holy Scripture Respecting the Atonement* (Grand Rapids: Baker Book House, 1954).

Creflo Dollar Ministries, "Dr. Creflo A. Dollar Biography" (http://www.creflodollarministries.org/Public/AboutUs/Biography-Creflo-Dollar.aspx).

Crenshaw Christian Center staff member, CRI telephone interview (31 July 1992).

Crouch, Jan, *Behind the Scenes*, Trinity Broadcasting Network (12 March 1992).

———, *Praise the Lord*, Trinity Broadcasting Network (20 August 1987).

———, *Praise the Lord*, Trinity Broadcasting Network (5 February 1986).

———, *Praise the Lord*, Trinity Broadcasting Network (31 July 1992).

Crouch, Paul, *Behind the Scenes*, Trinity Broadcasting Network (12 March 1992).

———, letter to M. A. [name withheld for privacy], (28 August 1992).

———, letter to R. C. [name withheld for privacy], (22 January 1992).

———, *Praise the Lord: Praise-a-Thon*, Trinity Broadcasting Network (April 1990).

———, *Praise the Lord: Praise-a-Thon*, Trinity Broadcasting Network (6 November 1990).

———, *Praise the Lord: Praise-a-Thon*, Trinity Broadcasting Network (2 April 1991).

———, *Praise the Lord*, Trinity Broadcasting Network (28 March 2001).

———, *Praise the Lord*, Trinity Broadcasting Network (5 February 1986).

———, *Praise the Lord*, Trinity Broadcasting Network (18 February 1986, rebroadcast on 6 August 1991).

———, *Praise the Lord*, Trinity Broadcasting Network (7 July 1986).

———, *Praise the Lord*, Trinity Broadcasting Network (5 September 1991).

———, *Praise the Lord*, Trinity Broadcasting Network (21 July 1992).

———, *Praise the Lord*, Trinity Broadcasting Network (31 July 1992).

———, *Praise the Lord*, Trinity Broadcasting Network (6 October 1992).

———, *Praise the Lord*, Trinity Broadcasting Network (23 October 1992).

———, *Praise the Lord*, Trinity Broadcasting Network (2 April 1991).

———, *Praise the Lord* [TBN newsletter] 19:7 (July 1992), [1].

———, *Praise the Lord* [TBN newsletter] 19:8 (August 1992).

———, *Praise the Lord* [TBN newsletter] 19:11 (November 1992).

Crouch, Paul and Benny Hinn, *Praise the Lord: Praise-a-Thon*, Trinity Broadcasting Network (November 1990).

Cuneo, Michael W., *American Exorcism* (New York: Doubleday, 2001).

D. B. [name withheld for privacy], letter, 13 July 1992.

Dager, Albert James, "Special Report: Benny Hinn Pros & Cons," *Media Spotlight* (May 1992).

Dake, Finis J., ed., *Dake's Annotated Reference Bible* (Lawrenceville, GA: Dake Bible Sales, 1963).

Dake, Finis J., *God's Plan for Man* (Lawrenceville, GA: Dake Bible Sales, 1949 [1977 reprint]).

Darrach, Brad, "Masking His Biblical Teaching in Theatrics, Pastor Fred Price Gets His Message Across Swimmingly," *People* (10 October 1983), 48, 53.

Dart, John, "Huge FaithDome in L.A.," *Los Angeles Times* (9 September 1989), Part II, 9–10.

Dart, John, "Scholarly Black Pastor Has a Burgeoning Flock," *Los Angeles Times* (7 December 1981), 6–8.

DeArteaga, William, *Past Life Visions: A Christian Exploration* (New York: Seabury Press, 1983).

———, *Quenching the Spirit* (Lake Mary, FL: Creation House, 1992).

Dembski, William A., "First-Person: Neither faith nor healing," *Baptist Press News*, 11 July 2008 (http://www.bpnews.net/bpnews.asp?id=28460), retrieved 11 July 2008.

Dollar, Creflo, *Creflo Dollar Crusade*, Trinity Broadcasting Network (9 February 1999).

———, *Creflo Dollar Ministries: World Changers*, Trinity Broadcasting Network (23 May 2002).

———, *Creflo Dollar Ministries: World Changers*, Trinity Broadcasting Network (15 September 2002).

———, *Creflo Dollar Ministries: World Changers*, Trinity Broadcasting Network (8 December 2002).

———, *Expanding Your Faith*, tape series, tape 3.

———, *Our Equality with God Through Righteousness*, video series (7 January 2001).

———, *Our Equality with God Through Righteousness*, video series (21 May 2001).

———, *Praise the Lord*, Trinity Broadcasting Network (23 August 2001).

———, *Praise the Lord*, Trinity Broadcasting Network (20 July 1999).

———, *Praise the Lord: Praise-a-Thon*, Trinity Broadcasting Network (6 April 2000).

———, "The First Begotten Son" (http://www.creflodollarministries.org/public/bible/article.aspx?id=18&version=printer).

———, *The Miracle of Debt Release* audiotape series, (College Park, GA: Creflo Dollar Ministries, 2000).

———, "The Just Shall Live by Faith," *Changing Your World*, TBN (20 September 1998).

Dorst, Karen MacIntire, telephone interview by CRI-Canada (23 August 1992).

Duplantis, Jesse, *Kenneth Copeland Ministries*, Trinity Broadcasting Network, 1 May 1995.

———, *Praise the Lord*, Trinity Broadcasting Network (8 January 2003).

———, *Praise the Lord*, Trinity Broadcasting Network (11 July 2003).

———, *Praise the Lord: Praise-a-Thon*, Trinity Broadcasting Network (6 November 2002).

Duriez, Colin, *AD 33: The Year That Changed the World* (Downers Grove, IL: InterVarsity Press, 2006).

Eddy, Mary Baker, *Science and Health with Key to the Scriptures* (Boston: First Church of Christ, Scientist, 1971 reprint [1875]).

Edgerton, Franklin, *The Beginnings of Indian Philosophy* (London: George Allen & Unwin, 1963).

Enroth, Ronald, *What Is a Cult? A Guide to Cults and New Religions* (Downers Grove, IL: InterVarsity Press, 1983).

Enroth, Ronald, ed., *Evangelizing the Cults* (Ann Arbor, MI: Servant Publications, 1990).

Enroth, Ronald M., and J. Gordon Melton, *Why Cults Succeed Where the Church Fails* (Elgin, IL: Brethren Press, 1985).

Erickson, Millard J., *Christian Theology* (Grand Rapids: Baker Book House, 1988).

Evans, D. W., and John Grimshaw, *Journal of Discourses* (London: Horace S. Eldredge, 1871 [reprint 1966]).

Ever Increasing Faith, "FAQ-Crenshaw Christian Center" (http://www.crenshawchristiancenter.net/ecomm/index.php?option=com_content&task=view&id=36&Itemid=49), accessed 15 July 2008.

Farah, Charles, "A Critical Analysis: The Roots and Fruits of Faith-Formula Theology" (unpublished paper for Soc. for Pentecostal Studies, November 1980).

———, *From the Pinnacle of the Temple* (Plainfield, NJ: Logos, 1978).

Fear Is the Master (Hemet, CA: Jeremiah Films, 1987).

Fee, Gordon D., *The Disease of the Health & Wealth Gospels* (Beverly, MA: Frontline Publishing, 1985).

Fillmore, Charles, *Prosperity* (Lee's Summit, MO: Unity Books, 1967 reprint [1936]).

Fisher, G. Richard, "Editorial: A History Lesson for Benny Hinn," *Personal Freedom Outreach [PFO] Quarterly Journal*, 12:4 (October–December 1992), 2, 9–10.

Fisher, G. Richard, with Stephen F. Cannon and M. Kurt Goedelman, "Benny Hinn's Anointing: Heaven Sent or Borrowed?" *Personal Freedom Outreach [PFO] Quarterly Journal* 12:3 (July–September 1992), 1, 10–14.

Fisher, G. Richard, telephone interview by CRI (9 October 1992).

Fisher, G. Richard, Paul R. Blizard, and Kurt Goedelman, "Benny Hinn: Mr. Confusion: The Demystification of the Miracle Man," *Personal Freedom Outreach [PFO] Quarterly Journal*, 13:1 (January–March 1993), 5–12.

Frame, Randy, "Best-Selling Author Admits Mistakes, Vows Changes," *Christianity Today* (28 October 1991), 44–45.

———, "Same Old Benny Hinn, Critics Say," *Christianity Today*, 36:11 (5 October 1992), 52–54.

———, telephone interview by CRI (3 September 1992).

———, telephone interview with Hanegraaff, 3 September 1992.

Fresh Fire Ministries, "Todd Bentley" (http://www.freshfire.ca/index.php?Id=101&pid=8&pid=8), retrieved 5 July 2008.

Friedrich, Gerhard, ed. (transl. ed. Geoffrey W. Bromiley), *Theological Dictionary of the New Testament* (Grand Rapids: Eerdmans, 1968 Eng. transl.) (1974 ed.).

Gaebelein, Frank E., ed., *The Expositor's Bible Commentary* [vol. 9] (Grand Rapids: Zondervan, 1981).

Garfield, Ken, "Faith Healer from Florida Draws Crowds, and Questions," *Charlotte Observer* (15 October 1992), 1C.

Geisler, Norman, and J. Yutaka Amano, *The Reincarnation Sensation* (Wheaton, IL: Tyndale House Publishers, 1986).

Germain, Annabeth, telephone interview by Hanegraaff (21 October 1992).

Gish, Duane T., *Evolution: The Challenge of the Fossil Record* (El Cajon, CA: Creation-Life Publishers, 1991).

God's Bountiful Double Portion, *The Word of Faith*, 26:1 (December 1992).

God TV, "Personal Message from Rory & Wendy Concerning Lakeland" (http://us.god.tv/ Groups/1000034309/God_TV/Lakeland_News_Update/Lakeland_News_Update.aspx), accessed 30 September 2009.

——— "Florida Healing Outpouring, 7 June 2008."

———, "Florida Healing Outpouring, July 11, 2008" (http://www.god.tv/revival_god, also posted at http://www.god.tv/god?region=tb).

Gohr, Glenn W., and Frederick K. C. Price, in Stanley M. Burgess, Gary B. McGee, and Patrick H. Alexander, eds., *Dictionary of Pentecostal and Charismatic Movements* (Grand Rapids: Regency/ Zondervan, 1988), 727.

Goldman, Ari L., "Religion Notes," *New York Times* [Nat. Ed.] (21 November 1992), 8.

Good, Joseph, *Difficult Verses* (Port Arthur, TX: Hatikva Ministries, April 1990), audiotape #5.

Goppelt, Leonhard, *Typos: The Typological Interpretation of the Old Testament in the New*, trans. by Donald H. Madvid, forward by Earl Ellis (Grand Rapids: Wm. B. Eerdmans Publishing Co., 1982).

Grant, Cincilla, "'Holy Water' Triggers Healing Revival" *Charisma*, (June 1996).

Gregorios, Archimandrite, President of the Greek Orthodox Patriarchate Ecclesiastical Court, Certificate (26 January 1967), no. 56, vol. 67, Jaffa.

H. C. [name withheld for privacy], letter, ca. 6 August 1991.

Hagee, John, *Beginning of the End: The Assassination of Yitzhak Rabin and the Coming Antichrist* (Nashville: Thomas Nelson, Inc., 1996).

———, *In Defense of Israel* (Lake Mary, FL.: Front Line, 2007).

———, *The Seven Secrets: Unlocking Genuine Greatness* (Lake Mary, FL: Charisma House, 2004).

———, *Should Christians Support Israel?* (San Antonio, TX: Dominon, 1987).

———, *John Hagee Today*, Trinity Broadcasting Network (16 July 2007).

———, *John Hagee Today*, Trinity Broadcasting Network (31 October 2003).

———, *Praise the Lord*, Trinity Broadcasting Network (8 January 2003).

———, *Praise the Lord*, Trinity Broadcasting Network (29 March 2001).

———, *Praise the Lord: Praise-a-Thon 2002*, Trinity Broadcasting Network (5 November 2002).

Hagin, Kenneth E., Jr., *The Answer for Oppression* [Tulsa: Kenneth Hagin Ministries, 1983).

———, *Blueprint for Building Strong Faith* (Tulsa: Kenneth Hagin Ministries, 1980).

———, *Faith Worketh by Love* (Tulsa: Kenneth Hagin Ministries, 1979).

———, letter to the author (4 January 1991).

———, "Trend Toward Faith Movement," *Charisma & Christian Life* (August 1985), 67–70.

Hagin, Kenneth E. (Sr.), letter to H. Robert Cowles, Executive Vice President of Christian Publications, Inc. (28 February 1984).

———, *Authority of the Believer* (Tulsa: Kenneth Hagin Ministries, 1967).

———, *Believer's Authority* (Tulsa: Kenneth Hagin Ministries, 2nd rev. 1991).

———, *Bible Faith Study Course* (Tulsa: Hagin Evangelistic Assoc., n.d. [ca. 1966]).

———, *Casting Your Cares Upon the Lord* (Tulsa: Kenneth Hagin Ministries, 1981).

———, *Classic Sermons: The Word of Faith 25th Anniversary 1968–1992 Commemorative Edition* (Tulsa: Kenneth Hagin Ministries, 1992).

———, *Demons and How to Deal with Them* (Tulsa: Kenneth Hagin Evangelistic Assoc., 1976; Kenneth Hagin Ministries, 2nd rev. 1983).

———, *El Shaddai* (Tulsa: Kenneth Hagin Ministries, 1980).

———, *Exceedingly Growing Faith* (Tulsa: Kenneth Hagin Ministries, 1983 [2nd ed. 1990]).

———, *Faith Food for Spring* (Tulsa: Kenneth Hagin Ministries, 1978).

———, *The Glory of God* (Tulsa: Kenneth Hagin Ministries, 1987).

———, "God's Best Belongs to You!" *The Word of Faith*, 26:1 (December 1992).

———, *God's Medicine* (Tulsa: Kenneth Hagin Ministries, 1977).

———, *Having Faith in Your Faith* (Tulsa: Kenneth Hagin Ministries, 1980 [1988 reprint]).

———, "Healing: The Father's Provision," *The Word of Faith* (August 1977).

———, *How God Taught Me About Prosperity* (Tulsa: Kenneth Hagin Ministries, 1985).

———, *How Jesus Obtained His Name* (Tulsa: Kenneth Hagin Ministries, n.d.), audiotape #44H01.

———, *How to Write Your Own Ticket with God* (Tulsa: Kenneth Hagin Ministries, 1979).

———, *How You Can Be Led by the Spirit of God* (Tulsa: Kenneth Hagin Ministries, 1978).

———, *The Human Spirit* (Tulsa: Kenneth Hagin Ministries, 1974).

———, *I Believe in Visions* (Old Tappan, NJ: Spire Books/Revell, 1972).

———, *I Went to Hell* (Tulsa: Kenneth Hagin Ministries, 1982).

———, "The Incarnation," *The Word of Faith*, 13:12 (December 1980), 14.

———, *The Interceding Christian* (Tulsa: Kenneth Hagin Ministries, 1978 printing).

———, *The Key to Scriptural Healing* (Tulsa: Kenneth Hagin Evangelistic Assoc., 1977) (1984 rev. ed.).

———, *Knowing What Belongs to Us* (Tulsa: Kenneth Hagin Ministries, 1989).

———, "Made Alive," *The Word of Faith* (April 1982), 3.

———, *Ministering to the Oppressed* (Tulsa: Kenneth Hagin Evangelistic Assoc., 7th ed. 1977).

———, *Must Christians Suffer?* (Tulsa: Kenneth Hagin Ministries, 1982).

———, *The Name of Jesus* (Tulsa: Kenneth Hagin Ministries, 1979, 1981).

———, *Obedience in Finances* (Tulsa: Kenneth Hagin Ministries, 1983).

———, *The Real Faith* (Tulsa: Kenneth Hagin Ministries, 1970 [1982 reprint]).

———, *Right and Wrong Thinking for Christians* (Tulsa: Kenneth Hagin Ministries, 1966).

———, *Seven Steps for Judging Prophecy* (Tulsa: Kenneth Hagin Ministries, 1982).

———, *Seven Things You Should Know About Divine Healing* (Tulsa: Kenneth Hagin Ministries, 1979).

———, *Three Big Words* (Tulsa: Kenneth Hagin Ministries, 1983).

———, *Understanding How to Fight the Good Fight of Faith* (Tulsa: Kenneth Hagin Ministries, 1987).

———, *What Faith Is* (Tulsa: Kenneth Hagin Ministries, 1983 rev.; 1966 orig. ed.).

———, *What to Do When Faith Seems Weak & Victory Lost* (Tulsa: Kenneth Hagin Ministries, 1979).

———, *Why Do People Fall Under the Power?* (Tulsa: Kenneth Hagin Ministries, 1981).

————, *Words* (Tulsa: Kenneth Hagin Ministries, 1979).

————, *Zoe: The God-Kind of Life* (Tulsa: Kenneth Hagin Ministries, 1981; 1989).

[Hagin Ministries], *Faith Library Catalog* (Tulsa: Kenneth Hagin Ministries, 1991).

————, "Faith Seminar of the Air," radio station listings in *The Word of Faith* 25:6 (June 1992), 18–19.

————, "Graduation 92: A Gateway to the Nations!" *The Word of Faith* 25:7 (July 1992), 8ff.

————, "RHEMA's First Russian Graduate!" *The Word of Faith* 25:7 (July 1992), 10–11.

Hanegraaff, Hendrik (Hank), certified letter to Bruce Barbour, Thomas Nelson Publishers (28 July 1992).

————, "A Summary Critique: The Anointing [by] Benny Hinn," *Christian Research Journal*, 15:2 (Fall 1992), 38.

————, CRI Perspective: Binding and Loosing (Irvine, CA: CRI, n.d. [1991]), order no. CP-0610.

————, *The Apocalypse Code: Find Out What the Bible REALLY Says about the End Times . . . and Why It Matters Today* (Nashville: Thomas Nelson, Inc., 2007).

————, *The Legacy Study Bible* (Nashville: Thomas Nelson, Inc., 2007).

————, letter from L. E. [name withheld for privacy], 31 August 1992.

————, letter to Paul Crouch (6 December 1991).

————, MAPS to chart our course to biblical reliability (San Juan Capistrano, CA: Memory Dynamics, 1993).

————, *Personal Witness Training: Your Handle on the Great Commission* (San Juan Capistrano, CA: Memory Dynamics, 1993).

————, Testimony of a Former Skeptic, Acts & Facts: Impact no. 202 (April 1990).

————, *The F-A-C-E That Demonstrates the Farce of Evolution* (San Juan Capistrano, CA: Memory Dynamics, 1993).

————, *The F-E-A-T That Demonstrates the Fact of the Resurrection* (San Juan Capistrano, CA: Memory Dynamics, 1993).

"Happy Church Buys Shopping Mall," *Charisma & Christian Life*, 15:12 (July 1990), 26.

Harrell, David Edwin, Jr., *Oral Roberts: An American Life* (Bloomington, IN: Indiana Univ. Press, 1985).

Harris, R. Laird, Gleason L. Archer, Jr., and Bruce K. Waltke, eds., *Theological Wordbook of the Old Testament*, 2 vols. (Chicago: Moody Press, 1981).

Hayes, Norvel, *Praise the Lord*, Trinity Broadcasting Network (13 November 1990).

————, presentation at East Coast Believer's Convention, 24 May 1992, audiotape.

Hays, Pat, "Betty Price Speaks at 1991 Wisdom from Above Luncheon," *Ever Increasing Faith Messenger*, 13:1 (Winter 1992), 12–13.

————, "Farewell Old Sanctuary, Welcome Kenneth E. Hagin Auditorium!" *Ever Increasing Faith Messenger*, 11:2 (Spring 1990), 13.

Helm, Leslie, "Religious Battle Taking Shape in Foothills of Mt. Fuji," *Los Angeles Times* (16 December 1991), A21.

Hexham, Irving, and Karla Poewe, *Understanding Cults and New Religions* (Grand Rapids: Eerdmans, 1986).

Hickey, Marilyn, *Breakthroughs to Faith* (Denver: Marilyn Hickey Ministries, n.d.), audiotape #1105.

————, *Claim Your Miracles* (Denver: Marilyn Hickey Ministries, n.d.), audiotape #186.

————, direct-mail letter, undated (ca. 1992).

————, direct-mail letter, undated (ca. December 1988).

————, *Today with Marilyn*, Trinity Broadcasting Network (11 April 1991).

Hickey Ministries, direct-mail piece (n.d. [1992]).

————, direct-mail piece (n.d.).

Higher Ground Always Abounding Assemblies, Inc., "Church Register" (http://www.highergroundaaa.com/listing.htm), accessed 29 September 2008.

Hinn, Benny *The Anointing* (Nashville: Thomas Nelson, Inc., 7th ed. 1992).

————, *Double Portion Anointing*, part 3 (Orlando, FL: Orlando Christian Center, n.d.), audiotape #A031791-3, aired on TBN (7 April 1991).

————, *Good Morning, Holy Spirit*, draft manuscript (ca. September 1989).

————, *Good Morning, Holy Spirit* (Nashville: Thomas Nelson, Inc., 7th ed. 1990).

————, letter to Hanegraaff with medical records (4 September 1992).

————, letter to S. R. [name withheld for privacy], 14 September 1992.

————, "Miracle Invasion," Anaheim, California, Convention Center, 22 November 1991.

——, *Our Position in Christ*, part 1 (Orlando, FL: Orlando Christian Center, 1991), videotape #TV-254.

——, *Our Position in Christ #5: An Heir of God* (Orlando, FL: Orlando Christian Center, 1990), audiotape #A031190-5.

——, *Our Position in Christ #2: The Word Made Flesh* (Orlando, FL: Orlando Christian Center, 1991), audiotape #A031190-2.

——, personal interviews by Hanegraaff and CRI Vice President-Research Robert Lyle (21 August 1992).

——, Personal testimony, audiotape, recorded at Orlando Christian Center (19 July 1987).

——, Benny Hinn (15 December 1990), *The Person of Jesus* (delivered during Orlando Christian Center's Sunday morning service on 2 December 1990), comprises part 4 of Hinn's six-part series *The Revelation of Jesus* (Orlando: Orlando Christian Center, 1991), videotape #TV-292.

——, *Praise the Lord: Praise-a-Thon*, Trinity Broadcasting Network (1 April 2003).

——, *Praise the Lord: Praise-a-Thon*, Trinity Broadcasting Network (6 November 1990).

——, *Praise the Lord: Praise-a-Thon*, Trinity Broadcasting Network (8 November 1990).

——, *Praise the Lord: Praise-a-Thon*, Trinity Broadcasting Network (April 1991).

——, *Praise the Lord: Praise-a-Thon*, Trinity Broadcasting Network (2 April 1991).

——, *Praise the Lord*, Trinity Broadcasting Network (3 October 1991).

——, *Praise the Lord*, Trinity Broadcasting Network (26 December 1991).

——, *Praise the Lord*, Trinity Broadcasting Network (16 April 1992).

——, *Praise the Lord*, Trinity Broadcasting Network (17 April 1992).

——, *Praise the Lord*, Trinity Broadcasting Network (8 October 1992).

——, *Praise the Lord*, Trinity Broadcasting Network (23 October 1992).

——, presentation at World Charismatic Conference, Melodyland Christian Center, Anaheim, California, 7 August 1992, CRI audiotape.

——, Benny Hinn (13 October 1990).

——, Benny Hinn (20 October 1990).

——, Benny Hinn (3 November 1990).

——, Benny Hinn (15 December 1991), from *The Revelation of Jesus, Part 4: The Person of Jesus* (Orlando, FL: Orlando Christian Center, 1991), videotape #TV-292.

——, Benny Hinn (8 June 1992).

——, Benny Hinn (29 June 1992).

——, Benny Hinn (6 July 1992).

——, *The Person of Jesus* [delivered during Orlando Christian Center's Sunday morning service on 2 December 1991]: *The Revelation of Jesus*, Part 4 (Orlando, FL: Orlando Christian Center, 1991), videotape #TV-292.

——, "Prophecy for the '90s," Orlando Christian Center (1 January 1990), tape.

——, *"Rise and be healed!"* (Orlando, FL: Celebration Publishers, 1991).

——, sermon at Miracle Invasion Rally, Anaheim [California] Convention Center (22 November 1991).

——, sermon at Orlando Christian Center (31 December 1989).

——, telephone interview by Hanegraaff (19 August 1992).

——, telephone interview by Randy Frame, *Christianity Today* (3 September 1992).

——, telephone interview by Renee Hooley Munshi, freelance reporter for *Bookstore Journal* (26 August 1992).

——, videotaped sermon (3 November 1990).

Hinn, Christopher N., telephone interview by Hanegraaff (30 September 1992).

Hinn Ministries/Orlando Christian Center spokesman Steve, telephone interview by G. Richard Fisher (PFO) (21 April 1992).

Hinn, Mrs. E., CRI telephone interview (27 July 1992).

Hollinger, Dennis, "Enjoying God Forever: An Historical/Sociological Profile of the Health and Wealth Gospel," *Trinity Journal* 9:2 (Fall 1988), 145–48.

Holmes, Ernest, *Creative Mind and Success* (New York: Dodd, Mead & Co., 1967 rev. [1919]).

——, *The Science of Mind* (New York: Dodd, Mead & Co., 1938 rev.).

Horton, Michael, ed., *The Agony of Deceit* (Chicago: Moody Press, 1990).

Howard-Browne, Rodney, *Flowing in the Holy Ghost* (Louisville, KY.: RHBEA Publications, 1991).

Hughes, Phillip E., *Paul's Second Epistle to the Corinthians* [Ned B. Stonehouse, ed., *The New International Commentary on the New Testament*] (Grand Rapids: Eerdmans, 1962).

Hunt, Rev. Garth, telephone interview by CRI-Canada (13 September 1992).

Hutchinson, Steve and Michelle (O'Connor) Hutchinson, telephone interviews by CRI-Canada (30 August 1992).

Hunter, Bob, "Christianity Still in Crisis: A Word of Faith Update," *Christian Research Journal*, Vol. 30, No. 3 (2007).

Jakes, Bishop T. D., "My Views on the Godhead: Jakes Responds to *Christianity Today* Article, Apologetics Journal Criticizes Jakes," *Christianity Today* (1 February 2000), www.christianitytoday.com/ct/2000/februaryweb-only/13.0b.html, retrieved 1 August 2008.

————, *Potter's House*, Trinity Broadcasting Network (20 June 1999).

————, *Potter's House*, Trinity Broadcasting Network (23 February 2004).

————, *Potter's House*, Trinity Broadcasting Network (3 December 2004).

————, *Potter's House*, Trinity Broadcasting Network (7 June 2004).

————, *Praise the Lord: Praise-a-Thon*, Trinity Broadcasting Network (12 November 2001).

————, *Praise the Lord: Praise-a-Thon*, Trinity Broadcasting Network (5 November 2003).

————, *Praise the Lord: Praise-a-Thon*, Trinity Broadcasting Network (5 November 2001).

————, "MegaCare 1," *The Potter's Touch*, Lightsource.com, iTunes Podcast (17 August 2008).

Jeffrey, Steve, Michael Ovey and Andrew Sach, *Pierced for Our Transgressions: Rediscovering the Glory of Penal Substitution* (Wheaton: IL: Crossway Books, 2007).

Jeffreys, Mary Ann, "Sayings of Spurgeon," *Christian History*, 10:1 (1991).

Jenkins-Bryant, Flo, "We've Come This Far by Faith! And It's Time to Rejoice!!!" *Ever Increasing Faith Messenger*, 11:1 (Winter 1990), 8.

Jones, Jim, "Tilton Ministry Still Strong Despite Layoffs, Assistant Says," *Fort Worth Star-Telegram* (23 November 1992).

————, "The Undercover Thorn in Robert Tilton," *Fort Worth Star-Telegram* (26 January 1992), 1A, 20A.

Jones, R. Tudor, *The Great Reformation* (Downers Grove, IL: InterVarsity Press, 1985).

Juedes, John P., "George M. Lamsa: Christian Scholar or Cultic Torchbearer?" *Christian Research Journal* 12:2 (Fall 1989), 8–14.

Keener, Craig S., *The IVP Bible Background Commentary: New Testament* (Downers Grove, IL: InterVarsity Press, 1993).

Kelly, J. N. D., *Early Christian Doctrines* (San Francisco: Harper & Row, 1978 rev.).

Kenyon, E. W., *The Blood Covenant* (Lynnwood, WA: Kenyon's Gospel Publishing Society, 1969).

————, *The Father and His Family*, 17th ed. (Lynnwood, WA: Kenyon's Gospel Publishing Society, 1964).

————, *The Hidden Man*, 5th ed. (Kenyon's Gospel Publishing Society, 1970).

————, *The Two Kinds of Faith: Faith's Secret Revealed* (Lynwood, WA: Kenyon's Gospel Publishing Society, 1942 [1969 reprint]).

————, *What Happened from the Cross to the Throne*, 12th ed. (Lynnwood, WA: Kenyon's Gospel Publishing Society, 1969).

Kinnebrew, James M., *The Charismatic Doctrine of Positive Confession: A Historical, Exegetical, and Theological Critique* (doctoral dissertation, Mid-America Baptist Theological Seminary, September 1988 [Ann Arbor, MI: University Microfilms, 1992 reprint]).

L. E. [name withheld for privacy], letter, 25 August 1992.

Lamsa, George M., transl., *Holy Bible: From the Ancient Eastern Text* (New York: A.J. Holman, 1933 [San Francisco: Harper & Row, 1984, reprint]).

Larsen, David L., "The Gospel of Greed Versus the Gospel of Grace," *Trinity Journal* 9:2 (Fall 1988), 211–20.

Latourette, Kenneth Scott, *A History of Christianity* (New York: Harper & Row, 1975 rev.).

Lee, Christopher, "Tilton's Wife Defends Ministry, Blasts TV Exposé of Husband," *Dallas Morning News* (25 November 1991), 1A, 12A.

Lenski, R. C. H., *The Interpretation of the Epistles of St. Peter, St. John and St. Jude* (Minneapolis: Augsburg Publishing House, 1966).

Lewis, C. S., *Mere Christianity*, 22d pr. (New York: Macmillan Publishing Co., 1976).

Lewis, Gordon R., *Confronting the Cults* (Grand Rapids: Baker Book House, 1975).

Liddell, Henry George, and Robert Scott (rev. Henry Stuart Jones), *A Greek-English Lexicon* (Oxford, Eng.: Oxford Univ. Press, 1968 rev.).

Life Christian University Web site, "Questions," http://www.lcus.edu/questions.htm, accessed 5 July 2008.

Lightfoot, John B., *St. Paul's Epistles to the Colossians and to Philemon* (Peabody, MA: Hendrickson, 1981).

Lockman Foundation, *The Amplified Bible* (Grand Rapids: Zondervan, 1965).

Lockwood, David, telephone interview by G. Richard Fisher (PFO) (26 July 1992).

Lubenow, Marvin L., *Bones of Contention* (Grand Rapids: Baker Book House, 1992).

MacArthur, John, *Charismatic Chaos* (Grand Rapids: Zondervan Publishing House, 1992).

MacLean, Mike and Anne, telephone interviews by CRI-Canada (13 September 1992).

MacLean, Mike, telephone interview by G. Richard Fisher (PFO) (10 November 1992).

MacMillan, John A., *The Authority of the Believer* (Harrisburg, PA: Christian Publications, 1980 reprint [1932]).

Marks, Robert W., *The Story of Hypnotism* (New York: Prentice-Hall, 1947).

Marrie, Deborah, "Locked in Their Own World," *Charisma Magazine* (http://www.charismamag.com/display.php?id=9219).

Marshall, Alfred, *NASB-NIV Parallel New Testament in Greek and English with Interlinear Translation* (Grand Rapids: Regency/Zondervan, 1986).

Martin, Walter, *The Errors of Positive Confession* (Christian Research Institute, n.d.), audiotape #C-100.

———, *Healing: Does God Always Heal?* (Christian Research Institute, n.d.), audiotape #C-95.

———, *The Health and Wealth Cult* (San Juan Capistrano, CA: Christian Research Institute, n.d.), audiotape #C-152.

———, *The Kingdom of the Cults* (Minneapolis: Bethany House Publishers, 1985 rev.).

———, *The Warnings of God* (Kenneth Copeland's False Prophecy) (San Juan Capistrano, CA: CRI, 1987), audiotape #C-210.

———, "You Shall Be as God," in Michael Horton, ed., *The Agony of Deceit* (Chicago: Moody Press, 1990).

Martinez, Sylvia, "Tilton Sues ABC News, PrimeTime," *Dallas Morning News* (11 November 1992), 29A, 33A.

Mattingly, Terry, "'Prosperity Christian' sings a different tune," *Rocky Mountain News* (16 August 1992), 158.

Mattox, Kent, Orlando Christian Center, telephone interview by Renee Hooley Munshi, for *Bookstore Journal* (1 September 1992).

McAlister, Rev. Jim, telephone interview by CRI-Canada (30 August 1992).

McAteer, Michael, "Debunkers Put No Faith in Healer's Miracles," *Toronto Star* (24 September 1992), A2.

McConkie, Bruce R., *Mormon Doctrine* (Salt Lake City: Bookcraft, 2nd ed. 1974 reprint [1966]).

McConnell, Daniel R., *A Different Gospel* (Peabody, MA: Hendrickson Publishers, 1988).

———, "The Kenyon Connection: A Theological and Historical Analysis of the Cultic Origins of the Faith Movement," master's thesis, Oral Roberts University, 1982.

Melton, J. Gordon, *Encyclopedic Handbook of Cults in America* (New York: Garland Publishing, Inc., 1986).

———, *The Encyclopedia of American Religions* (Detroit: Gale Research Inc., 3rd rev. 1989).

Mérat, Pierre, MD, "Critical Study: Anatomy and Physiology of the Shroud," *The Catholic Counter-Reformation in the XXth Century*, no. 218 (April 1989), 1–6.

Metzger, Bruce M., *A Textual Commentary on the Greek New Testament* (London & New York: United Bible Societies, 1975 rev.).

Meyer, Joyce, "About Joyce," Joyce Meyer Ministries (http://www.joycemeyer.org/AboutUs/AboutJoyce), accessed 5 July 2008.

———, *Approval Addiction: Overcoming Your Need to Please Everyone* (New York: FaithWords, 2005).

———, *Eight Ways to Keep the Devil Under Your Feet* (New York: Warner Faith, 2002).

———, *Enjoying Everyday Life*, Trinity Broadcasting Network (16 July 2004).

———, *Enjoying Everyday Life*, Trinity Broadcasting Network (21 August 2008).

———, *From the Cross to the Throne*, audiocassette (St. Louis: Life Christian Center, n. d).

———, "Practical Steps to Understanding and Experiencing Healing" (http://www.joycemeyer.org/ourMinistries/Magazine/0703/Healing+and+wholeness.htm), retrieved 24 September 2008.

———, *Praise the Lord: Praise-a-Thon*, Trinity Broadcasting Network, (3 November 2003).

———, radio interview by Todd Wilken, *Issues Etc.*, KFOU, 23 May 2005.

————, *The Most Important Decision You Will Ever Make: A Complete and Thorough Understanding of What It Means to Be Born Again* (Fenton, MO: Life in the Word, 1991).

————, *The Word, the Name, the Blood* (Tulsa: Harrison House, Inc., 1995).

————, *Trophies of God's Grace* (Fenton, MO: Joyce Meyer Ministries, 1991), tape.

————, "Violent Christians in a Violent Society: Interrupting Satan's Plan: Releasing the Supernatural Power of God through Prayer," tape 3, San Jose, CA (19 July 2001).

————, *Witchcraft & Related Spirits*, part 1 (n.d.), audiotape.

Michel, Otto, Faith, in Colin Brown, gen. ed., *The New International Dictionary of New Testament Theology* (Grand Rapids: Zondervan, 1975 Eng. transl.).

Miller, Elliot, "T. D. Jakes Responds to the Journal," *Christian Research Journal*, Vol. 22, No. 3 (1999).

Mikkelson, Barbara and David P. Mikkelson, "Deadly Imaginings" (http://www.snopes.com/horrors/gruesome/freezer.asp).

Miller, Elliot, *Healing: Does God Always Heal?* (San Juan Capistrano, CA: CRI, 1979).

Moberg, David O., *The Church as a Social Institution* [Englewood Cliffs: Prentice-Hall, Inc., 1962).

Monteros, Laura, "The Rebirth of Morris Cerullo," *Los Angeles Herald-Examiner* (18 November 1978).

Morphew, Clark, "What's to Become of Oral Roberts' City of Faith?" *St. Paul Pioneer Press* (27 June 1992) reprinted in *The Christian News* (20 July 1992).

Morris, Leon, *The Apostolic Preaching of the Cross*, 3rd ed., (Grand Rapids: Wm. B. Eerdmans Publishing Company, 1986).

Munroe, Myles, *Praise the Lord*, TBN (3 March 2003).

————, *Praise the Lord*, Trinity Broadcasting Network (23 February 2000).

————, *Praise the Lord*, Trinity Broadcasting Network (11 December 2000).

Munshi, Renee Hooley, "Benny Hinn: An Enigma," draft article for *Bookstore Journal* faxed to CRI and Hinn Ministries (31 August 1992).

————, "Benny Hinn: An Enigma," revised draft article for *Bookstore Journal* faxed to CRI and Hinn Ministries (2 September 1992).

————, telephone interview with CRI (1 September 1992).

National & International Religion Report, 1:18 (21 September 1987), 4.

Neuman, H. Terris, "An Analysis of the Sources of the Charismatic Teaching of Positive Confession" (unpublished paper, Wheaton Graduate School, 1980).

————, "Cultic Origins of Word-Faith Theology Within the Charismatic Movement," *PNEUMA: The Journal of the Society for Pentecostal Studies*, 12:1 (Spring 1990), 3–55.

New World Translation, *The Christian Research Newsletter*, 3:3 (1990), 5.

Niebuhr, Gustav, and Laurie Goodstein, "The Preachers: A Special Report; New Wave of Evangelists Vying for National Pulpit," *The New York Times*, 1 January 1999, http://query.nytimes.com/gst/fullpage.html?res=9E03EEDE1E3FF932A35752C0A96F958260.

Nicoll, W. Robertson, ed., *The Expositor's Greek Testament* (Grand Rapids: Eerdmans, 1979 reprint).

Noss, John B., *Man's Religion* (New York: Macmillan, 4th ed. 1969).

Ogata, Mamoru Billy, "A Comparison Between Paul Yonggi Cho's Church (Korea), and the Soka Gakkai (Japan)," [Appendix A] in *Ogata, A Comparative Study of Church Growth in Korea and Japan with Special Application to Japan* (Fuller Theological Seminary, thesis, 1984).

Onken, Brian, *The Atonement of Christ and the Faith Message*, Foreword 7:1 (1984), 11–12.

Orange County Register (24 January 1992), O6.

Osborn, T. L., and Daisy, *She & He Photo-Book: Go For It!* (Tulsa: Osborn Foundation, 1983).

Osborn, T. L., *Faith Digest*, XXII:E, 34–77.

Osteen, Joel, *Become a Better You: 7 Keys to Improving Your Everyday Life* (New York: Free Press, 2007).

————, *Discover the Champion in You*, Trinity Broadcasting Network (3 May 2004).

————, *Discover the Champion in You*, Trinity Broadcasting Network (26 April 2004).

————, Easter service message at Lakewood Church, Sermon #CS_002 - 4-23-00, 23 April 2000 (http://www.lakewood.cc/sermons/cs_002.htm) transcript archived online at http://web.archive.org/web/20040408215244/ and http://www.lakewood.cc/sermons/cs_002.htm, retrieved 1 August 2008.

————, *Your Best Life Now: 7 Steps to Living at Your Full Potential* (New York: Warner Faith, 2004).

————, *The 6th Sense. Faith* (Houston, TX: John Osteen Publications, 1980).

Parsley, Rod, *Ancient Wells Living Water* (Lake Mary, FL: Creation House Press, 2003).

————, *Breakthrough with Rod Parsley*, Trinity Broadcasting Network (27 March 2002).

————, *Breakthrough with Rod Parsley*, Trinity Broadcasting Network (6 April 2000).

————, *Praise the Lord*, Trinity Broadcasting Network (12 June 2003).

————, *Praise the Lord*, Trinity Broadcasting Network (7 August 2003).

————, *Praise the Lord: Dominion Camp Meeting*, Trinity Broadcasting Network (6 July 1999).

————, *Praise the Lord: Praise-a-Thon*, Trinity Broadcasting Network (3 April 2003).

————, *Praise the Lord: Praise-a-Thon*, Trinity Broadcasting Network (7 November 2003).

————, *Praise the Lord: Praise-a-Thon*, Trinity Broadcasting Network (9 November 2000).

Paulk, Earl, *Satan Unmasked* (Atlanta: K Dimension Publishers, 1984).

Peck, M. Scott, *The Road Less Traveled* (New York: Simon & Schuster, 1978).

Peel, Robert, *Christian Science* (New York: Henry Holt, 5th ed. 1959).

Pinsky, Mark I., "FCC Reviewing Trinity's Minority Subsidiary," *Los Angeles Times* (29 September 1991), B7.

————, "He Wished Death on Foes: Theologians Fault Prayer by Crouch," *Los Angeles Times* [Orange County ed.] (16 February 1989), II-1, II-10.

Piper, John, *Desiring God* (Portland, OR: Multnomah Press, 1986). Gene Polino, personal interviews by Hanegraaff and CRI Vice-President-Research Robert Lyle (21 August 1992).

Polino, Gene, telephone interview by Renee Hooley Munshi, freelance reporter for *Bookstore Journal* (1 September 1992).

Poynter, Mrs. Jim, telephone interview by CRI-Canada (13 September 1992).

Price, Betty, "A Praise Report," *Ever Increasing Faith Messenger*, 12:3 (Summer 1991).

————, "Health Update: Then and Now from Betty Price," *Ever Increasing Faith Messenger*, 13:4 (Fall 1992), 5.

————, "Radio Interview: An Intimate Look at Betty Price," *Ever Increasing Faith Messenger*, 8:1 (January 1987), 8.

Price, Frederick K. C., *Ever Increasing Faith Messenger* (June 1980), 7.

————, *Ever Increasing Faith*, Trinity Broadcasting Network (1 May 1992), audiotape #PR11.

————, *Ever Increasing Faith*, Trinity Broadcasting Network (16 November 1990).

————, *Ever Increasing Faith*, Trinity Broadcasting Network (23 November 1990).

————, *Ever Increasing Faith*, Trinity Broadcasting Network (9 December 1990), available from Crenshaw Christian Center (audiotape #CR-A2).

————, *Ever Increasing Faith*, Trinity Broadcasting Network (29 March 1992).

————, *Ever Increasing Faith*, Trinity Broadcasting Network (1 May 1992), audiotape #PR11.

————, *Ever Increasing Faith*, Trinity Broadcasting Network (3 May 1992).

————, *Faith, Foolishness, or Presumption?* (Tulsa: Harrison House, 1979).

————, *How Faith Works* (Tulsa: Harrison House, 1976).

————, *Identification #3* (Los Angeles: Ever Increasing Faith Ministries, 1980), audiotape #FP545.

————, *Identification #8* (Los Angeles: Ever Increasing Faith Ministries, 1980), audiotape #FP550.

————, *Identification #9* (Los Angeles: Ever Increasing Faith Ministries, 1980), audiotape #FP551.

————, *Is God Glorified Through Sickness?* (Los Angeles: Crenshaw Christian Center, n.d.), audiotape #FP605.

————, *Is Healing for All?* (Tulsa: Harrison House, 1976).

————, letter to B. G. [name withheld for privacy] (14 October 1992).

————, "Name It and Claim It! What Saith the WORD?" *Ever Increasing Faith Messenger*, 10:3 (Summer 1989), 2.

————, *Paul's Thorn #1* (Los Angeles: Ever Increasing Faith Ministries, 1980), audiotape #FP606.

————, *Petition Prayer, or the Prayer of Faith* (Los Angeles: Ever Increasing Faith Ministries, 1991).

————, *Praise the Lord*, Trinity Broadcasting Network (21 September 1990).

————, *Prosperity on God's Terms* (Tulsa: Harrison House, 1990).

————, *What Every Believer Should Know About Prayer* (Los Angeles: Ever Increasing Faith Ministries, 1990).

Pusey, Allen, "Florida Couple Sues Tilton Organization: Suit Says Story Misrepresented, Funds Misused," *Dallas Morning News*, 14 November 1992.

Pusey, Allen and Howard Swindle, "Tilton Bankrolled 83 TV License Bids, Source and Files Say," *Dallas Morning News* (12 July 1992), 1A, 29A.

Pynkoski, Paul, telephone interview by CRI-Canada (14 September 1992).

Quimby, Phineas, ed., *H. W. Dresser, The Quimby Manuscripts* (New Hyde Park, NY: University Books, 1961 [1859 orig.]).

Ramm, Bernard, *Protestant Biblical Interpretation* (Grand Rapids: Baker Book House, 1978).

Reed, David A., *Jehovah's Witnesses Answered Verse-By-Verse* (Grand Rapids: Baker Book House, 1986).

[Religious News Service], "TV Preachers Seen as Beggars: Public Dislikes Evangelists' Onscreen Methods, Professor Says," *Dallas Morning News* (21 November 1992).

Reston, James, Jr., and Noah Adams, "Father Cares: The Last of Jonestown," program on National Public Radio (23 April 1981).

Reymond, Robert L., *Jesus, Divine Messiah* (Phillipsburg, NJ: Presbyterian and Reformed Publishing, 1990).

Rhodes, Ron, "Esotericism and Biblical Interpretation," *Christian Research Journal* 14:3 (Winter 1992), 28–31.

Richardson, James T., *The Brainwashing/Deprogramming Controversy: Sociological, Psychological, Legal and Historical Perspectives* (Toronto: Edwin Mellen Press, 1983).

Riss, Richard M. and Kenneth Copeland, in *Dictionary of Pentecostal & Charismatic Movements*, 226.

Robert, Risa, "Tilton Sent Dead Man Personal Mail," *Tulsa Tribune*, 27 February 1992, 7A.

Roberts, Oral, ed., *Daily Blessing: A Guide to Seed-Faith Living*, 24:1 (January–February–March 1982).

Roberts, Oral, *A Daily Guide to Miracles: And Successful Living Through SEED-FAITH* (Tulsa: Pinoak Publications, 1975).

———, direct-mail letter, undated (ca. 1 January 1985).

———, direct-mail letter, undated (ca. 1 March 1987).

———, "God's Mandate to Me," *Abundant Life* (March/April 1987), 3.

———, *How I Learned Jesus Was Not Poor* (Altamonte Springs, FL: Creation House, 1989).

———, *101 Questions and Answers* (Tulsa: Oral Roberts, 1968).

———, *Oral Roberts' Best Sermons and Stories* (Tulsa: Oral Roberts, 1956).

———, *Praise the Lord*, Trinity Broadcasting Network (6 October 1992).

———, presentation at World Charismatic Conference, Melodyland Conference Center, Anaheim, CA, 7 August 1992, tape recording by CRI.

Roberts, Oral and Richard, direct-mail letter (August 1984).

Roberts, Patti, with Sherry Andrews, *Ashes to Gold* (Waco, TX: Word Books, 1983).

Roberts, Richard, direct-mail letter, undated (ca. 1 January 1987).

Robertson, Archibald Thomas, *A Grammar of the Greek New Testament in the Light of Historical Research* (Nashville: Broadman Press, 1934).

———, *Word Pictures in the New Testament* (Nashville: Broadman Press, 1930).

Robertson, Archibald Thomas, and W. Hersey Davis, *A New Short Grammar of the Greek Testament* (Grand Rapids: Baker Book House, 1979 reprint [10th rev. 1933]).

Robertson, Pat, *The 700 Club*, CBN (26 August 2004).

Robinson, Stephen E., *Are Mormons Christians?* (Salt Lake City: Bookcraft, 1991).

Rossiter, Don, telephone interview by CRI-Canada (13 September 1992).

Rowe, Sean, "Second Coming," *Dallas Observer*, 6 November 1997, online at http://www.dallasobserver.com/1997-11-06/news/second-coming, retrieved 1 August 2008.

S. C. [name withheld for privacy], letter (25 September 1991).

Sailhamer, John, H., *Expositor's Bible Commentary*, vol. 2, ed. Frank E. Gaebelein (Grand Rapids: Zondervan Publishing House, 1990).

Sarles, Ken L., "A Theological Evaluation of the Prosperity Gospel," *Bibliotheca Sacra* 143:572 (October–December 1986), 338.

Savelle, Jerry, *The Authority of the Believer, in Word Study Bible* (Tulsa: Harrison House, 1990), 1141.

———, *Framing Your World with the Word of God* [parts 1–2] (Fort Worth, TX: Jerry Savelle Evangelistic Assn., n.d.), audiotape #SS-36.

———, *If Satan Can't Steal Your Joy* (Tulsa: Harrison House, 1982).

Schaff, Philip, *The Creeds of Christendom* (Grand Rapids: Baker Book House, 1985).

———, *History of the Christian Church* (New York: n.p., 1888 [reprint n.p.: AP & A, n.d.]).

Schultze, Quentin J., *Televangelism and American Culture* (Grand Rapids: Baker Book House, 1991).

Shelley, Bruce, *Church History in Plain Language*, updated 2nd edition (Dallas, TX: Word Publishing, 1995).

Simmons, Dale H., "A Theological and Historical Analysis of Kenneth E. Hagin's Claim to Be a Prophet," master's thesis, Oral Roberts University, 1985.

Simpson, Preston, MD, medical analysis report (28 October 1992).

———, telephone interviews by CRI (6 and 23 October 1992).

Sire, James W., *Scripture Twisting* (Downers Grove, IL: InterVarsity Press, 1980).

Smith, Joseph, "The King Follett Discourse," in Joseph Fielding Smith, ed., *Teachings of the Prophet Joseph Smith* (Salt Lake City: Deseret Book Co., 21st ed. 1972).

Smith, Joseph Fielding, in Bruce R. McConkie, ed., *Doctrines of Salvation* (Salt Lake City: Bookcraft, 1975 [1954]).

Snow, Shauna, "Turner's Pro-Choice Film Creates a Stir," *Los Angeles Times*, 15 July 1989, Calendar, part 5; page 1; column 4, Entertainment Desk.

"Special Report: Campmeeting '83," *The Word of Faith*, 16:10 (October 1983), 3–11.

Sproul, R. C., *Knowing Scripture* (Downers Grove, IL: InterVarsity Press, 1977).

Spurgeon, Charles Haddon, "A Sermon from a Rush," in Metropolitan Tabernacle Pulpit, 63 vols. (Pasadena, TX: Pilgrim Publiclations, 1989).

St. Pierre, Nancy, "Judge Rejects Tilton Bid for Restraining Order," *Dallas Morning News* (15 May 1992), 1A, 8A.

———, "Judge Rejects Tilton's Suit Against Foes," *Dallas Morning News* (25 June 1992), 29A, 32A.

———, "Man Sifted Tilton's Trash for Evidence," *Dallas Morning News* (6 March 1992), 1A, 6A.

———, "2nd Widow Sues Tilton over Letters," *Dallas Morning News* (18 March 1992), 28A.

———, "Tilton's Lawyer Has Key Role," *Dallas Morning News* (17 February 1992), 1A, 14A.

———, "Tilton's Wife Tells of Finances," *Dallas Morning News* (5 March 1992), 1A, 7A.

———, "U.S. Court Judge Criticizes Morales in Tilton Inquiry," *Dallas Morning News* (19 March 1992), 1A, 13A.

Stevenson, Kenneth E., and Gary R. Habermas, *The Shroud and the Controversy* (Nashville: Thomas Nelson, Inc., 1990).

Stott, John R. W., *The Cross of Christ* (Leicester: IVP, 1986).

Strang, Stephen, "The Ever Increasing Faith of Fred Price," *Charisma & Christian Life* (May 1985), 23.

Strang, Stephen, Marilyn Sweitzer Hickey, in *Dictionary of Pentecostal & Charismatic Movements*, 389.

Strang, Steve, "The Long-Term Effects of Revival," Strang Report, 22 May 2008, online at http://www.strangreport.com/2008_05_01_archive.html.

Stott, John R. W., *The Cross of Christ* (Leicester: InterVarsity Press, 1986).

Swindle, Howard, "Tilton Letters to Dead Man Prompt Widow to File Suit," *Dallas Morning News* (28 February 1992), 1A, 18A.

Swindle, Howard, and Allen Pusey, "Tilton Ends Syndication of His Sunday Services," *Dallas Morning News* (13 August 1992), 1A, 28A.

Swindoll, Charles R., *Growing Strong in the Seasons of Life* (Portland, OR: Multnomah Press, 1983).

Synan, H. Vinson, Capps, and Charles Emmitt, in *Dictionary of Pentecostal & Charismatic Movements* (1988), 107.

Synan, Vinson, "The Faith of Kenneth Hagin," *Charisma & Christian Faith*, 15:11 (June 1990), 68.

Talmage, James E., *Jesus the Christ* (Salt Lake City: Deseret Book Co., 1969).

Tasker, R. V. G., The Second Epistle of Paul to the Corinthians [*Tyndale New Testament Commentaries*] (Eerdmans, 1977 reprint [1958]).

Tenney, Merrill C., The Gospel of John, in Frank E. Gaebelein, ed., *The Expositor's Bible Commentary* [vol. 9] (Grand Rapids: Zondervan, 1981).

Thayer, Joseph Henry, *The New Thayer's Greek-English Lexicon of the New Testament* (Peabody, MA: Hendrickson, 1981 rev. [1889 rev.]).

Thomas, Larry, *No Laughing Matter* (Excelsior Springs, MO: Double Crown, 1995).

Thomas, Mike, "The Power and the Glory," *Florida* [weekly magazine of *Orlando Sentinel*] (24 November 1991), 12–18.

"Tilton Cuts Back," *Dallas Morning News* (22 November 1992).

Tilton Ministries, "PrimeTime Lies," program broadcast in place of Robert Tilton's regular *Success-N-Life* television program (18 August 1992).

Tilton, Robert, direct-mail letter with enclosures (1990).

———, *Success-N-Life* television program (18 October 1990).

———, *Success-N-Life* television program (27 December 1990).

———, *Success-N-Life* television program (18 July 1991).

———, *Success-N-Life* television program (22 November 1991).

———, *Success-N-Life* television program (n.d. [ca. 1991]), video on file at CRI.

Time magazine (17 September 2001).

Tolle, Eckhart, *A New Earth: Awakening to Your Life's Purpose* (New York: Penguine, 2005).

Torrey, Reuben A., *The Power of Prayer* (Grand Rapids: Zondervan Publishing House, 19th ed. 1981).

Treat, Casey, *Renewing the Mind* (Seattle, WA: Casey Treat Ministries, 1985).

Tregelles, Samuel P., transl., *Gesenius Hebrew and Chaldee Lexicon to the Old Testament Scriptures* (Grand Rapids: Eerdmans, 1976 reprint [1857]).

Tribbe, Frank C., *Portrait of Jesus?* (New York: Stein & Day, 1983).

Trinity Foundation release, "Does Word of Faith=Wheel of Fortune?" (9 December 1991).

———, "Tons of Tilton Prayer Requests Discovered in Recycle Center" (9 December 1991).

Troeltsch, Ernst, transl. Olive Wyon, *The Social Teaching of the Christian Churches*, 2 vols. (London: George Allen and Unwin, 1931).

Trump, Donald, interview by Larry King, *Larry King Live*, CNN, 26 November 2007.

Turner, Nigel, *Grammatical Insights into the New Testament* (Edinburgh: T. & T. Clark, 1977).

Unger, Merrill, rev. Gary N. Larson, *The New Unger's Bible Handbook* (Chicago: Moody Press, 1984).

Van Biema, David, "Spirit Raiser," *Time*, 17 September 2001, online at http://www.time.com/time/printout/0,8816,1000836,00.html, retrieved 16 July 2008.

Van Gorden, Kurt, "The Unity School of Christianity," in Ronald Enroth, ed., *Evangelizing the Cults* (Ann Arbor, MI: Servant Publications, 1990).

Vaughan, Curtis, and Virtus E. Gideon, *A Greek Grammar of the New Testament* (Nashville, TN: Broadman Press, 1979).

Villanueva, Eric, "Viewpoint: Territorial Spirits and Spiritual Warfare: A Biblical Perspective," *Christian Research Journal*, 15:1 (Summer 1992).

Vine, W. E., *An Expository Dictionary of New Testament Words* (Old Tappan, NJ: Revell, 1966 reprint).

Vitale, Joe, interview by Larry King, *Larry King Live*, CNN, 8 March 2007.

Wagner, C. Peter, School of World Missions, Fuller Theological Seminary, CRI telephone interview (30 July 1992).

Walker, Ken, "The Preacher Who Tells It Like It Is," *Charisma* (November 1998).

Watson, Merv and Merla, telephone interviews by CRI-Canada (30 August 1992).

Watt, G. D., ed., *Journal of Discourses* (Liverpool, England: F. D. Richards, 1855).

What the Mormons Think of Christ (Salt Lake City: Deseret News Press, n.d.).

White, Paula, "Paula's Life Story," Paula White Ministries (www.paulawhite.org/content/view/115/88888970), retrieved 19 June 2008.

———, "Follow God's Principles 'To Have it All,'" Paula White Ministries (http://www.paulawhite.org/content/view/213/88888897), retrieved 19 June 2008.

———, "Understanding the Power of Words over Your Money," Paula White Ministries (http://www.paulawhite.org/content/view/172/88888897), retrieved 19 June 2008.

———, *Praise the Lord*, Trinity Broadcasting Network (10 June 2003).

———, *Praise the Lord*, Trinity Broadcasting Network (6 February 2004).

———, *Praise the Lord: Praise-a-Thon*, Trinity Broadcasting Network (5 April 2005).

———, *Praise the Lord: Praise-a-Thon*, Trinity Broadcasting Network (3 November 2003).

White, Russ, "Congregation Keeps the Faith with Spellbinding Benny Hinn," *Orlando Sentinel* (11 October 1987), F-6.

Wilckens, U., "hysteros", etc., in Geoffrey W. Bromiley, ed., *Theological Dictionary of the New Testament* [abridged ed.] (Grand Rapids: Eerdmans/Paternoster Press, 1985), 1240–41.

Wilson, Bryan, *Religious Sects*, World University Library Series (Englewood, NJ: McGraw-Hill, 1970).

Wilson, Dwight J. and Paul Yonggi Cho, in *Dictionary of Pentecostal & Charismatic Movements* (1988), 161.

Wilson, Ian, *The Mysterious Shroud* (Garden City, NY: Doubleday, 1986).

Wilson, Ron, Executive Director, Evangelical Press Association, CRI telephone interview (24 July 1992).

Winfrey, Oprah, "One Week Later: The Huge Reaction to *The Secret*," *The Oprah Winfrey Show* (16 February 2007).

Woodward, Kenneth L., and Lynda Wright, "The T Stands for Troubled," *Newsweek*, 99:13 (30 March 1992), 60.

Word Study Bible (Tulsa: Harrison House, 1990).

Wright, N. T., *The Resurrection of the Son of God* (Minneapolis, MN: Augsburg Fortress Press, 2003).

Yancey, Philip and Tim Stafford, *The Student Bible* (Grand Rapids: Zondervan, 1986).

Yesterday, Today, and Tomorrow: 15 Years of Covering the Earth with the Word, Outpouring, 15:1 (special edition), [3].

Yinger, J. Milton, *Religion, Society and the Individual* (New York: The Macmillan Company, 4th printing 1962 [1957]).

Yogi, Maharishi Mahesh, *Meditations of Maharishi Mahesh Yogi* (New York: Bantam, 1968).

YouTube, "Bentley- Receive Resurrection Power—Lakeland Florida," (http://www.youtube.com/watch?v=u1DGXFg7cKY), accessed 9 September 2008.

———, "Che Ahn—Prophetic Wave" (http://www.youtube.com/watch?v=lIAuD_OEcUs), accessed 10 September 2008.

———, "Exploding tumor!!!" (http://www.youtube.com/watch?v=QAgLVFx_yh8), accessed 5 July 2008.

———, "Florida Outpouring – Resurrection #16" (http://www.youtube.com/watch?v=Mf6ewKmSMWU), retrieved 15 July 2008.

———, "Todd Bentley—The Visitation" (http://www.youtube.com/watch?v=2ApnwQXW6Ns), accessed 5 July 2008.

———, "Winds of Change Seems Much the Same" (http://www.youtube.com/watch?v=TuqwjUyb9io), accessed 5 June 2008.

———, "WORST ASSAULT at Todd Bentley Raging Revival part 3" (http://www.youtube.com/watch?v=DUTCWLoD4-4), accessed 5 July 2008.

———, "Jesse Duplantis: Making Your Dreams Come True - CBN.com" (http://www.youtube.com/watch?v=FlosLSf6RCA), posted 21 July 2008, accessed 26 September 2008.

———, "Joyce Meyer-Little Gods" (http://www.youtube.com/watch?v=7Y4eVu2oxP8), accessed 12 July 2007.

"Yonggi Cho Changes His Name," *Charisma & Christian Life*, 18:4 (November 1992).

Young, Brigham, "Discourse," *Deseret News* [Salt Lake City] (18 June 1873), 308.

———, "The Gospel: The One-Man Power," discourse delivered 24 July 1870, reported by D. W. Evans and John Grimshaw, *Journal of Discourses* (London: Horace S. Eldredge, 1871 [reprint 1966]).

———, *Journal of Discourses* 13:271 (24 July 1890).

———, sermon (9 April 1852), in G. D. Watt, ed., *Journal of Discourses* (Liverpool, Eng.: F. D. Richards, 1855), 1:50.

Zoe College, Jacksonville, Florida, advertisement, *Charisma & Christian Life* (May 1992), 82.

NOTES

Preface

1. Acts 20:30–31.
2. John W. Allman, "Revival Prays to Raise an Infant from the Dead," *The Pensacola News Journal*, 20 September 1998.

Introduction

1. Joel Osteen, *Your Best Life Now: 7 Steps to Living at Your Full Potential* (New York: Warner Faith, 2004), 129.
2. Rhonda Byrne, *The Secret* (New York: Atria Books/Beyond Words, 2006), ix.
3. Byrne's *The Secret* is the official companion book to the film *The Secret,* Extended Edition (TS Production LLC, 2006), DVD. As of this writing, *The Secret* has been on the *New York Times* bestseller hardcover advice list for fifty-eight weeks—currently it is number one (http://www.nytimes.com/pages/books/bestseller/index.html, accessed 25 February 2008).
4. Oprah Winfrey, "One Week Later: The Huge Reaction to *The Secret,*" *The Oprah Winfrey Show,* 16 February 2007, emphasis added.
5. Byrne, *The Secret,* 4.
6. Ibid., 15.
7. Ibid., 47.
8. Ibid., 47ff. Though Byrne claims that the "Creative Process used in *The Secret*" is taken from the New Testament, she does not actually cite a biblical passage. Presumably she has in mind, though completely out of context, Jesus' Sermon on the Mount, in which He teaches, "Ask and it will be given to you; seek and you will find; knock and the door will be opened to you. For everyone who asks receives; he who seeks finds; and to him who knocks, the door will be opened" (Matthew 7:7–8).
9. Ibid., 61, emphasis in original.
10. Ibid., 62.
11. Ibid., 59, emphasis in original.
12. Ibid., 28, emphasis added.
13. Joe Vitale in an interview with Larry King, *Larry King Live,* CNN, 8 March 2007, emphasis added.
14. Byrne, *The Secret,* 36.
15. Ibid., 46.
16. Joel Osteen, *Your Best Life Now,* 129.
17. Joel Osteen, *Become a Better You: 7 Keys to Improving Your Life Every Day* (New York: Free Press, 2007), inside back cover.
18. Ibid., 115.
19. Joel Osteen, *Discover the Champion in You,* Trinity Broadcasting Network, 3 May 2004.
20. Osteen, *Your Best Life Now,* 148–49.
21. Ibid., 151.
22. Osteen, *Become a Better You,* 111.
23. Ibid., 113, emphasis added. In reality, while Sarai and Sarah are two forms of the *same* name meaning "princess," the change draws attention to the name's meaning, which becomes especially evident in the original Hebrew alliteration (see John H. Sailhamer, *Genesis,* in Frank E. Gaebelein, gen. ed., *The Expositor's Bible Commentary, Volume 2* [Grand Rapids: Zondervan, 1990], 139, 141).
24. Ibid., 112.
25. Ibid., 111.
26. Ibid., 112, emphasis added. Osteen wrenches Romans 4:17b out of context; the verse actually reads, "He [Abraham] is our father in the sight of God, in whom he believed—the God who gives life to the dead and calls things that are not as though they were."
27. Ibid., 114.
28. Ibid., 114.
29. Ibid., 60.

30. Ibid., 61.

31. *Larry King Live*, CNN, 26 November 2007.

32. *Time* magazine cover, 17 September 2001.

33. Crouch's heated words—"To hell with you! Get out of my life. Get out of my way. Quit blocking God's bridges. I'm tired of this. Oh, hallelujah! . . . Get out of God's way. Quit blocking God's bridges, or God's gonna shoot you if I don't! . . . Don't even call me if you want to argue doctrine, if you want to straighten somebody out over here, if you want to criticize Ken Copeland for his preaching on faith, or Dad Hagin. Get out of my life! I don't want to even talk to you or hear you! I don't want to see your ugly face! Get out of my face, in Jesus' name."—were aired during *Praise-a-Thon*, Trinity Broadcasting Network, 2 April 1991.

34. Benny Hinn, *Praise the Lord*, Trinity Broadcasting Network, 23 October 1992.

35. Benny Hinn, Presentation at World Charismatic Conference, Melodyland Christian Center, Anaheim, CA, 7 August 1992.

36. Benny Hinn, *Praise the Lord: Praise-a-Thon*, Trinity Broadcasting Network, 8 November 1990.

37. See Shauna Snow, "Turner's Pro-Choice Film Creates a Stir," *Los Angeles Times*, 15 July 1989, Calendar, part 5; page 1; column 4, Entertainment Desk.

38. Byrne, *The Secret*, 109.

Part One: *Turning Truth into Mythology*

1. Kenneth Copeland: "Heaven has a north and a south and an east and a west. Consequently, it must be a planet" (*Spirit, Soul and Body I* [Fort Worth, TX: Kenneth Copeland Ministries, 1985] audiotape #01-0601, side 1).

2. Kenneth Copeland in ibid: "Now God is not some creature that stands twenty-eight feet tall, and He's got hands, you know, as big as basketballs. That's not the kind of creature He is . . . He's very much like you and me. Can you conceive that? Not hardly in the mind, but your heart can. Your heart can. A Being, a Being that stands somewhere around six-two to six-three, that weighs somewhere in the neighborhood of a couple of hundred pounds, little better, [and] has a [hand]span nine inches across."

   Kenneth Hagin: "And I said, 'Why, Alton, God weighs more than 250 pounds'" (*Exceedingly Growing Faith* [Tulsa: Kenneth Hagin Ministries, 1983 (2nd ed. 1990)] 15).

   In another context, Kenneth Hagin said that God's Son is a bit shorter and lighter: "As I looked to see who it was, I saw Jesus . . . I saw Him. He had on a white robe. He wore roman sandals . . . He seemed to be about 5 feet 11 inches tall. He looked to weigh about 180 pounds" (*How You Can Be Led by the Spirit of God* [Tulsa: Kenneth Hagin Ministries, 1978] 29–30).

3. Charles Capps: "God filled His words with faith to cause the things He said to come into manifestation. There was an image inside Him. He expressed it in words" (*The Substance of Things* [Tulsa: Harrison House, 1990] 19).

4. Kenneth Copeland: "Faith is a power force. It is a tangible force. It is a conductive force" (*The Force of Faith* [Fort Worth, TX: KCP Publications, 1989], 10).

   Creflo Dollar: "Now, God used faith substance to make everything that He made . . . in every one of those words they were filled with faith substance, because words are nothing but containers . . . Every time God speaks, He can't help but to speak words that are filled with faith . . . God's guts are called faith stuff . . . Everything in Him is faith . . . What's in His heart is faith . . . If you were to cut God open you'd see nothing but faith. Every time He opens His mouth now, He automatically fills those words with His faith material" ("The Just Shall Live by Faith," *Changing Your World*, Trinity Broadcasting Network, 20 September 1998).

5. Charles Capps: "Faith is the substance, the raw material . . . Faith is the substance that God used to create the universe, and He transported that faith with His words . . . Faith is the substance of things, but you can't see faith. Faith is a spiritual force" (*Changing the Seen & Shaping the Unseen* [Tulsa: Harrison House, 1980], 14–15).

6. Jerry Savelle: "Well, just because the Bible says that God framed the world with things that were not seen, that does not mean that He framed this world out of nothing. It simply means that He framed the world out of something that you could not see. In other words, He didn't go out here and pick up something—a few raw materials—and then sling a world together. No, the raw material or the

substance that God used to frame this world was His faith and His Word—His faith and His Word . . . The way that He created the world was, first of all, He conceived something on the inside of Him. He conceived; He had an image; He had a picture. God doesn't just sling things into existence without first of all conceiving it first" (*Framing Your World with the Word of God*, part 2 [Fort Worth, TX: Jerry Savelle Evangelistic Association, Inc., n.d.], audiotape #SS-36, side 1).

7. Kenneth Copeland: "You don't think earth was first, do you? Huh? Well, you don't think that God made man in His image, and then made earth in some other image? There is not anything under this whole sun that's new. Are you hearing what I'm saying? This is all a copy. It's a copy of home. It's a copy of the Mother Planet. Where God lives, He made a little one just like His and put us on it" (*Following the Faith of Abraham I* [Kenneth Copeland Ministries, 1989], audiotape #01-3001, side 1).

8. Charles Capps: "He framed the world with His words. You can't build without substance. He took words—faith-filled words were God's substance. Here, essentially, is what God did. God filled His words with faith. He used His words as containers to hold His faith and contain that spiritual force and transport it out there into the vast darkness by saying '*Light be!*' That's the way God transported His faith causing creation and transformation" (*Dynamics of Faith & Confession* [Harrison House, 1987], 28–29.)

9. Charles Capps: "God said, *Let us make man in our image after our likeness*. The word *likeness* in the original Hebrew means "an exact duplication in kind" . . . *Adam was an exact duplication of God's kind!*" (*Authority in Three Worlds* [Harrison House, 1982], 15–16 [emphasis in original]).

   Creflo Dollar: "If the Godhead gets together and say let us make man then what are they producing? . . . They're producing gods . . . You are gods because you came from God and you are gods, you're not just human. The only human part about you is this physical body that you live in" (*World Changers*, 15 September 2002).

   T. D. Jakes: "We were made out of God. When God created Adam, He created him from the dust of the earth. He put His mouth on him; blew in him the breath of life. He became a living soul. God said, "I wanted to see what I looked like, so I made you to be in My image. You have My DNA. You are created out of Me. You are a derivative of Me. You are My picture in the Earth" ("MegaCare 1," *The Potter's Touch*, Lightsource.com, iTunes Podcast, 17 August 2008).

10. Paul Crouch, speaking to Kenneth Copeland, said: "Somebody said—I don't know who said it—but they claim that you Faith teachers declare that we are gods. You're a god. I'm a god. Small 'g' now, but we are the gods of this world . . . Well, are you a god—small 'g'?" To this, Jan Crouch, referring to Copeland, enthusiastically exclaimed: "He's gonna say, 'Yes.' I love it" (*Praise the Lord*, Trinity Broadcasting Network, 5 February 1986).

11. Paul Crouch: "He [God] doesn't even draw a distinction between Himself and us . . . You know what else that's settled, then, tonight? This hue and cry and controversy that has been spawned by the devil to try and bring dissension within the body of Christ that we are gods. I am a little god! . . . I have His name. I'm one with Him. I'm in covenant relation. I am a little god! Critics, be gone!" (*Praise the Lord*, Trinity Broadcasting Network, 7 July 1986).

   Joyce Meyer: "If you as a human being have a baby, you call it a human kind. If cattle have another cattle, they call it cattle-kind. I mean, what's God supposed to call us? Doesn't the Bible say we're created in His image? Now, you understand, I'm not saying you are God with a capital 'G'" (YouTube, "Joyce Meyer—Little Gods" (http://www.youtube.com/watch?v=7Y4eVu2oxP8), accessed 12 July 2007).

12. Kenneth Copeland: "God *spoke* Adam into existence in authority with words (Gen. 1:26, 28). These words struck Adam's body in the face. His body and God were exactly the same size" (*Holy Bible: Kenneth Copeland Reference Edition* [Kenneth Copeland Ministries, 1991], 45 [emphasis in original]).

13. Kenneth Copeland: "God's reason for creating Adam was his desire to reproduce himself. I mean a reproduction of himself, and in the garden of Eden he did just that. He was not a little like God. He was not almost like God. He was not subordinate to God, even . . . Adam is as much like God as you could get, just the same as Jesus . . . Adam, in the garden of Eden, was God manifested in the flesh" (*Following the Faith of Abraham I*, audiotape, side 1).

   Creflo Dollar: "Philippians chapter 2 and in Philippians chapter 2, I want you to look at verse 5; (laughs) look at this now, verse 5: let this mind be in you; a better way to say that is let this attitude be in you. Let this mind, let this attitude be in you which was also in Christ Jesus. So now what mind, what attitude is it that you want me to make sure that this same attitude is in me; what is this way of thinking? What is this, it'll move me even into confidence that you want me have here. Verse 6, here it is: who being in the form of God thought it not robbery to be equal with God. Let this attitude that was in Jesus be in you. Let this way of thinking that was in Jesus be in you. Let this confidence that was in Jesus be in you. Jesus didn't think it was robbery. He didn't think it was a dishonor. He didn't; he didn't think it was. Oh, you ought not think that way? No, he said, let this attitude, let this way of thinking be in you, who being in the form of God thought it not robbery to be equal with God. Now, if I'm to take what he said here and put it on, then my whole attitude should be, I have equality with God. That's my way of thinking.

"Now, somebody says, well, it's hard to think that way. Well, keep saying it, *I have equality with God.* Talk yourself into it; you've talked yourself into other things. Talk yourself into this attitude. Talk yourself into this way of thinking. Talk yourself into it until you build a confidence on the inside of you that I have equality with God.

"Now, when the guy says, the storm is coming over; get ready; it's gonna blow your house down; you go out on the porch because you have this way of thinking on the inside you, and you say peace be still; you will not cause any destruction on this property. Let this mind be in you that was in Christ Jesus. And then he moves down, on to verse 15, says why: that you may be blameless and harmless, the sons of God without rebuke in the midst of a crooked and perverse nation among whom you shine as lights in the world. This is God's desire that we shine as light. He says, notice, he says, we're not going to shine as lights until we change the way we think. We're not going to shine as lights 'til we accept our equality with God. We're not gonna shine as lights until we stop thinking that being equal with God is a dishonor and a robbery. He says, but when we take hold of this way of thinking in this crooked and perverse generation, he says we will shine as lights, and now we will be the reflection of God in this earth. He is light. God is light, and He says now we can shine in this world like He shines and truly be a reflection of God in this earth" (*World Changers* Internet broadcast, 23 May 2002).

14. Kenneth E. Hagin: "Originally, God made the earth and the fullness thereof, giving Adam dominion over all the works of His hands. In other words, Adam was the god of this world" (*The Believer's Authority*, 2nd ed. [Tulsa: Kenneth Hagin Ministries, 1991], 19).

15. Frederick K. C. Price: "God can't do anything in this earth realm except what we, the body of Christ, allow Him to do. Now, that statement is so—that's so—that's so foreign and so contrary to tradition that, like I said, if they could get their hands on me right now, most evangelicals would burn me at the stake and dismember me and feed me to the crocodiles, because they'll consider that statement to be just heresy" (*Ever Increasing Faith*, Trinity Broadcasting Network, 1 May 1992 [audiotape #PR11]).

Myles Munroe: "I'm going to say it again! Prayer is man giving God authority, or God license, to interfere in the affairs of man. In fact, God—I'm going to take a deep breath because some of you religious people aren't going to understand me—Are you ready? God cannot do anything in the earth without a human's permission!" (*Praise the Lord*, Trinity Broadcasting Network, 23 February 2000).

Rod Parsley: "Why does God say, 'Ask of Me'? Why does He say that? *Because He can't do it on His own! He can't get what He wants on His own because He placed you in authority on this earth*" (*Praise the Lord*, Trinity Broadcasting Network, 7 August 2003 [emphasis added]).

Creflo Dollar: "Who do you think you are, going around commanding God around? Well, that's what the Bible said to do in the book of Isaiah. Command ye me!" (*Expanding Your Faith* tape series, tape 3).

16. Benny Hinn: "Adam was a super being when God created him. I don't know whether people know this but he was the first superman that really ever lived. First of all, the Scriptures declare clearly that he had dominion over the fowls of the air, the fish of the sea—which means he used to fly. Of course, how can he have dominion over the birds and not be able to do what they do? The word 'dominion' in the Hebrew clearly declares that if you have dominion over a subject, that you do everything that subject does. In other words, that subject, if it does something you cannot do, you don't have dominion over it. I'll prove it further. Adam not only flew; he flew to space. He was—with one thought he would be on the moon" (*Praise the Lord*, Trinity Broadcasting Network, 26 December 1991).

17. Kenneth Copeland: "Adam was made in the image of God. He was as much female as he was male. He was exactly like God. Then God separated him and removed the female part. Woman means 'man with the womb.' Eve had as much authority as Adam did as long as they stayed together" (*Sensitivity of Heart* [Fort Worth, TX: KCP Publications, 1984], 23).

18. Kenneth E. Hagin: "Adam committed high treason and sold out to Satan, and Satan, through Adam, became the god of this world. Adam didn't have the moral right to commit treason, but he had the legal right to do so" (*The Believer's Authority*, 19).

    Joyce Meyer: "Through listening to Satan rather than God, Adam surrendered to him the authority to rule the earth that God had originally given to man . . . The devil said, 'All dominion and authority over the earth has been turned over to me, and it is mine.' Adam had been given a lease to the earth by God, and he turned it over to Satan. In 2 Corinthians 4:4 we read that Satan is the god of this world, or we might say, the god of this world system" (*The Word, The Name, The Blood* (Tulsa: Harrison House, Inc., 1995) 100–101).

19. Kenneth E. Hagin: "God came down in the cool of the day in the garden of Eden to commune and fellowship with him [Adam], as He had in the past. And He couldn't find him. He called out to him, 'Adam, where art thou?' And he said, 'I hid myself.' Why? Because of sin. Because, first, sin separates you from God. Secondly, by sinning, by listening to the devil, he took upon himself the nature of the devil into his spirit being" (*How Jesus Obtained His Name* [Kenneth Hagin Ministries, n.d.], audiotape #44H01, side 2).

20. E. W. Kenyon: "Man [i.e., Adam] was actually Born Again when he sinned. That is, he was born of the Devil. He became a partaker of Satanic Nature" (*The Father and His Family*, 17th ed. [Lynnwood, WA: Kenyon's Gospel Publishing Society, 1964], 48).

21. Benny Hinn: "He [the Holy Spirit] says, 'God's original plan is that the woman was to bring forth children out of her side' . . . Adam gave birth to his wife out of his side. It was sin that turned the thing around . . . And it was sin that transformed her flesh and her body. When God took the woman out of man, He closed up his rib. But she was created identically as him. In other words, she was created with an opening in her side, and children were supposed to be born. And I get that from the very fact that you'll never see birth spiritually, except from the side" (*Our Position In Christ #5: An Heir of God* [Orlando, FL: Orlando Christian Center, 1990], audiotape #A031190-5, side 2]).

22. E. W. Kenyon: "Adam evidently had a legal right to transfer this dominion and authority into the hands of the enemy. God has been obliged through the long period of human history to recognize Satan's legal standing, and legal right and authority, and on this ground, and this only, can we understand the legal side of the Plan of Redemption . . . Adam had legally transferred to him [Satan] the Authority with which God had invested him" (*The Father and His Family*, 38–39).

23. Kenneth Copeland: "God had no avenue of lasting faith or moving in the earth. He had to have covenant with somebody . . . He had to be invited in, in other words, or He couldn't come . . . God is on the outside looking in. In order to have any say so in the earth, He's gonna have to be in agreement with a man here" (*God's Covenants with Man II* [Kenneth Copeland Ministries, 1985], audiotape #01-4404, side 1).

24. Kenneth Copeland: "I was shocked when I found out who the biggest failure in the Bible actually is . . . The biggest one is God . . . I mean, He lost His top-ranking, most anointed angel; the first man He ever created; the first woman He ever created; the whole earth and all the fullness therein; a third of the angels, at least—that's a big loss, man . . . Now, the reason you don't think of God as a failure is He never said He's a failure. And you're not a failure till you say you're one" (*Praise the Lord: Praise-a-Thon*, Trinity Broadcasting Network, April 1988).

25. Frederick K. C. Price: "Adam, as I said, gave it [the earth] away to the serpent, to the devil. As a result of it, he got his behind kicked out of the garden. He went out of Eden, out of the garden. He began to wander around, and he has troubles from day one. Now God was out of the business. God was out of the earth realm. God had no more stock in this earth realm. No more. None at all. Nothing He could do. Not a thing in the world He could do . . . The only way God could get back into this earth realm, He had to have an invitation. Ha-hah! He had to have an invitation. And so, God looked around—saw different men, saw Noah, saw different ones. He gave them a few instructions. They did what He said. So and so and so and so. But, finally, He got to a point where He had His plan ready for operation. And He saw a man named Abraham" (*Ever Increasing Faith*, Trinity Broadcasting Network, 1 May 1992 [audiotape #PR11]).

26. E. W. Kenyon: "[A]s soon as they [the parties of the covenant] cut the covenant, they are recognized as blood brothers by others, and they are called the blood brothers . . . God and Abraham had

entered the Covenant . . . God cut the Covenant with Abraham" (*The Blood Covenant* [Kenyon's Gospel Publishing Society, 1969], 14, 16).

27. Charles Capps: "In this [Abraham's Covenant], God is establishing some legal entry into the earth, and He is giving Abraham access to Himself . . . This Covenant gave God legal entry into the earth through Abraham . . . Until that time God was, to a certain extent, still on the outside looking in. He needed a legal entry through man so that He could destroy the works of the Devil who was running rampant on earth . . . Abraham was God's avenue of entry into the earth" (*Authority in Three Worlds*, 60–61).

28. Kenneth Copeland: "Once that [Abrahamic] covenant was established, God began to release His Word into the earth. He began to paint a picture of a Redeemer, a man who would be the manifestation of His Word in the earth" (*The Power of the Tongue* [KCP Publications, 1980], 9).

29. Kenneth Copeland: "So before Jesus came to the earth, God spoke His Word and then spoke His Word again. How many times did He say the Messiah was coming? It was prophesied over hundreds, even thousands, of years. He kept saying, 'He is coming. He is coming.' The circumstances in the earth made it look as if there was no way He could accomplish it; but He just kept saying it. He would not be moved by what He saw . . . God would not relent" (*The Power of the Tongue*, 9–10).

30. Kenneth Copeland: "The angels spoke the words of the covenant to her [Mary]. She pondered them in her heart, and those words became the seed. And the Spirit of God hovered over her and generated that seed, which was the Word that the angel spoke to her. And there was conceived in her, the Bible says, a holy thing. The Word literally became flesh" (*The Abrahamic Covenant* [Kenneth Copeland Ministries, 1985], audiotape #01-4405, side 2).

31. Benny Hinn: "The Bible says the prophets spoke the Word not knowing what they were saying. But 4,000 years passed when the <u>Word</u> became a human being and walked and talked and moved. The spoken Word became a human being. The spoken Word became flesh. The spoken Word got legs on, arms, eyes, hair, a body. And He was no longer saying, 'Thus saith the Lord.' He was saying, 'I say unto you.' The Word that was spoken through the lip [*sic*] of prophets was now walking on the seashore of Galilee (*Benny Hinn*, Trinity Broadcasting Network, 15 December 1990 [emphasis in original]). This message, entitled "The Person of Jesus" (delivered during Orlando Christian Center's Sunday morning service on 2 December 1991), comprises part four of Hinn's six-part series, *The Revelation of Jesus* (Orlando Christian Center, 1991), videotape #TV-292).

32. John Avanzini: "Jesus had a nice house, a big house—big enough to have company stay the night with Him at the house. Let me show you His house. Go over to John the first chapter and I'll show you His house . . . Now, child of God, that's a house big enough to have company stay the night in. There's His house" (*Believer's Voice of Victory*, Trinity Broadcasting Network, 20 January 1991).

John Hagee: "John 1:38 says that Jesus turned to those who were following and said, 'Come with me,' and they said, 'Where dwellest thou?' He said, 'Come and see,' and Jesus took the crowd home with Him to stay in His house. That meant it was a big house" (John Hagee, *Praise the Lord: Praise-a-Thon*, Trinity Broadcasting Network, 5 November 2002).

33. John Avanzini: "Jesus was handling big money because that treasurer He had was a thief. Now you can't tell me that a ministry with a treasurer that's a thief can operate on a few pennies. It took big money to operate that ministry because Judas was stealing out of that bag" (*Praise the Lord*, Trinity Broadcasting Network, 15 September 1988).

34. John Avanzini: "John 19 tells us that Jesus wore designer clothes. Well, what else you gonna call it? Designer clothes—that's blasphemy. No, that's what we call them today. I mean, you didn't get the stuff He wore off the rack. It wasn't a one-size-fits-all deal. No, this was custom stuff. It was the kind of a garment that kings and rich merchants wore. Kings and rich merchants wore that garment" (*Believer's Voice of Victory*, Trinity Broadcasting Network, 20 January 1991).

John Hagee: "Jesus had a seamless robe so valuable that Roman soldiers gambled for it at the cross. It was a designer robe" (*The Seven Secrets: Unlocking Genuine Greatness* [Lake Mary, FL: Charisma House, 2004], 232).

35. Frederick K. C. Price: "The Bible says that He [Jesus] had a treasurer—a treasury (they called it "the bag"); that they had one man who was the treasurer, named Judas Iscariot, and the rascal was stealing out of the bag for three and a half years, and nobody knew that he was stealing. You know why? Because there was so much in it, He couldn't tell. Nobody could tell that anything was missing. If He had three oranges in the bottom of the bag and he stole two of them, don't tell me He wouldn't

know that some was missing. Beside that, if Jesus didn't have anything, what do you need a treasury for? A treasury is for surplus. It's not for that which you're spending. It's only for surplus—to hold it until you need to spend it. Therefore, He must have had a whole lot that needed to be held in advance that He wasn't spending. So He must have had more than He was living on (*Ever Increasing Faith*, Trinity Broadcasting Network, 23 November 1990).

John Hagee: "When you have to have a secretary-treasurer to carry the excess money, you're not poor" (*The Seven Secrets*, 232).

36. Charles Capps: "Notice that when Jesus said, 'I have finished the work' [John 17:4], we know that He had <u>not</u> finished the work. But I want you to catch something in the way He prayed and the way He talked—<u>He spoke the end results</u>. He never spoke what <u>was</u>. He never admitted death or defeat . . . Jesus was speaking the end results in His prayer to the Father" (*Authority in Three Worlds*, 258–59 [emphasis in original]).

37. John Avanzini: "You don't think these apostles didn't walk around with money? I mean, they had money. I just thank God that I saw this and gave up the denominational line and got on God's line before I starved me and all my family to death. Go to Acts 24. I mean, you don't think there wasn't money in this Paul's life? . . . Paul had the kind of money that people, that government officials, would block up justice to try to get a bribe out of old Paul" (*Believer's Voice of Victory*, Trinity Broadcasting Network, 20 January 1991).

38. Kenneth Copeland (through whom Jesus allegedly delivered the following prophecy): "They crucified Me [Jesus] for claiming that I was God. But I didn't claim I was God; I just claimed I walked with Him [the Father] and that He was in Me" ("Take Time to Pray," *Believer's Voice of Victory* 15, 2 [February 1987]:9).

39. E. W. Kenyon: "Jesus was conceived without sin. His body was not mortal. His body did not become mortal until the Father laid our sin nature upon Him when He hung on the cross. The moment that He became sin, His body became mortal, only then could He die. When this happened, spiritual death, the nature of Satan, took possession of His Spirit . . . He was to partake of Spiritual Death, the nature of the Adversary . . . Jesus knew that the moment had come, and He was to be made Sin. He must partake of that dread nature of the Adversary. His body would become mortal. Satan would become His master . . . He [Jesus] had been lifted up as a serpent. Serpent is Satan. Jesus knew He was going to be lifted up, united with the Adversary" (*What Happened from the Cross to the Throne* [Lynwood, WA: Kenyon's Gospel Publishing Society, 1969], 20, 33, 44–45).

40. Benny Hinn: "I'm going to be led by the Holy Ghost today. Is that all right with you? . . . God came from heaven, became a man, made man into little gods, went back to heaven as a man. He faces the Father as a man. I face devils as the son of God. Do you see what I'm talking about? You say, 'Benny, am I a little god?' You're a son of God, aren't you? You're a child of God, aren't you? You're a daughter of God, aren't you? What else are you? Quit your nonsense! What else are you? If you say, 'I am,' you're saying I'm a part of Him, right? Is He God? Are you His offspring? Are you His children? You can't be human! You can't! You can't! God didn't give birth to flesh. He gave birth to a new creation. And the new creation is not flesh and blood and bone, for no flesh and blood would inherit heaven. Did you hear what I said? Some of you didn't really hear what I said. You said, 'Well, that's heresy.' No, that's your crazy brain saying that" (*Our Position in Christ #2: The Word Made Flesh* [Orlando Christian Center, 1991], audiotape #A031190-2, side 2).

41. Benny Hinn: "When you were born again, the Word was made flesh in you. And you became flesh of His flesh and bone of His bone. Don't tell me you have Jesus. You <u>are</u> everything He was and everything He is and ever He shall be . . . It [the new man] says, 'I am as He is.' That's what it says. As He is, so are we in this world. Jesus said, 'Go in my name; go in my stead.' Don't say, 'I have.' Say, 'I am, I am, I am, I am, I am.' That's why you never ever, ever, ever ought to say, 'I'm sick.' How can you be sick if you're the new creation? Say, 'I'm healed!' Don't say, 'I'm a sinner.' The new creature is no sinner. I'm the righteousness of God in Christ" (Ibid.).

42. Frederick K. C. Price: "Do you think that the punishment for our sin was to die on a cross? If that were the case, the two thieves could have paid your price. No, the punishment was to go into hell itself and to serve time in hell separated from God . . . Satan and all the demons of hell thought that they had Him bound. And they threw a net over Jesus and they dragged Him down to the very pit of hell itself to serve our sentence" (*Ever Increasing Faith Messenger* [June 1980],

7; quoted in D. R. McConnell, *A Different Gospel* [Peabody, MA: Hendrickson Publishers, 1988], 120).

Joyce Meyer: "You cannot go to heaven unless you believe with all your heart that Jesus took your place in hell" (*The Most Important Decision You Will Ever Make* [Fenton, MO: Life in the Word, 1991], 37).

43. Charles Capps: "The sinless son of God became as a serpent that He might swallow up all evil . . . If you will behold what happened when the sin offering was made and the fact that Jesus became a serpent upon the pole, it will change your life . . . Jesus died spiritually, not for any of His own sin! He became the serpent on the pole, the snake on the ground, in the Old Testament type" (*Authority in Three Worlds*, 177, 166–67).

44. Paul E. Billheimer: "The Father turned Him over, not only to the agony and death of Calvary, but to the satanic torturers of His pure spirit as part of the just desert of the sin of all the race. As long as Christ was 'the essence of sin' he was at Satan's mercy in that place of torment . . . While Christ identified with sin, Satan and the hosts of hell ruled over Him as over any lost sinner. During that seemingly endless age in the nether abyss of death, Satan did with Him as he would, and all hell was 'in carnival'" (*Destined for the Throne*, special edition for Trinity Broadcasting Network [Fort Washington, PA: Christian Literature Crusade, 1988 (orig. 1975)], 84).

45. Charles Capps: "If there's any part of hell Jesus did not suffer, you'll have to suffer it. But, thank God, Jesus suffered it all, for you! In the place of the wicked dead, all the demons of hell and Satan rejoiced over the prize. The corridors of hell were filled with joy. 'We've done it! We've captured the Son of God! We'll no longer be in the pit of the damned! The earth and all that is therein is ours! Forever it will be ours!' Rejoicing in hell had never been so great as it was that day. But it was short-lived" (*Authority in Three Worlds*, 143 [emphasis in original]).

46. Kenneth Copeland: "Satan didn't realize He [Jesus] is in there [hell] illegally . . . This man had not sinned. This man has not fallen out of the covenant of God, and He had the promise of God for deliverance. And Satan fell into the trap. He took Him into hell illegally. He carried Him in there [when] He did not sin" (*What Happened from the Cross to the Throne* [Kenneth Copeland Ministries, 1990], audiotape #02-0017, side 2).

47. Charles Capps: "When Jesus was in the pit of hell, in that terrible torment, no doubt the Devil and his emissaries gathered around to see the annihilation of God's Son. But in the corridors of hell, there came a great voice from heaven: 'Turn Him loose! He's there illegally!' And all of hell became paralyzed" (*Authority in Three Worlds*, 143).

48. Kenneth Copeland: "He [Jesus] is suffering all that there is to suffer. There is no suffering left apart from Him. His emaciated, poured out, little wormy spirit is down in the bottom of that thing [hell]. And the devil thinks he's got Him destroyed" (*Believer's Voice of Victory*, Trinity Broadcasting Network, 21 April 1991. This message was originally delivered at the Full Gospel Motorcycle Rally Association 1990 Rally at Eagle Mt. Lake, Texas).

49. Kenneth Copeland: "That Word of the living God went down into that pit of destruction and charged the spirit of Jesus with resurrection power! Suddenly His twisted, death-wracked spirit began to fill out and come back to life. He began to look like something the devil had never seen before" ("The Price of It All," *Believer's Voice of Victory* 19, 9 [September 1991]:4).

Creflo Dollar: "When you accepted Jesus as your Lord and Savior, you became born again. That simply means that your spirit was transformed from a state of spiritual death to life in a split second of time. But have you ever considered that Jesus went through the exact same thing? Often, *in the midst of our religious views of Him, we forget that He was actually the first person to ever become born again*" ("The First Begotten Son," emphasis added [http://www.creflodollarministries.org/public/bible/article.aspx?id=18&version=printer]).

50. Kenneth Copeland: "He [Jesus] was literally being reborn before the devil's very eyes. He began to flex His spiritual muscles . . . Jesus was born again—the firstborn from the dead the Word calls Him—and He whipped the devil in his own backyard. He took everything he had away from him. He took his keys and his authority away from him" (Ibid., 4–6).

51. Kenneth E. Hagin: "Every man who has been born again is an incarnation and Christianity is a miracle. The believer is as much an incarnation as was Jesus of Nazareth" ("The Incarnation," *The Word of Faith* 13, 12 [December 1980]:14; cf. E. W. Kenyon, *The Father and His Family*, 100).

52. Frederick K. C. Price: "The whole point is I'm trying to get you to see—to get you out of this malaise of thinking that Jesus and the disciples were poor and then relating that to you—thinking that you, as a child of God, have to follow Jesus. The Bible says that He has left us an example that we should follow His steps. That's the reason why I drive a Rolls Royce. I'm following Jesus' steps" (*Ever Increasing Faith*, Trinity Broadcasting Network, 9 December 1990).

53. Benny Hinn: "When you say, 'I am a Christian,' you are saying, 'I am mashiach' in the Hebrew. I am a little messiah walking on earth, in other words. That is a shocking revelation . . . May I say it like this? You are a little god on earth running around" (*Praise the Lord: Praise-a-Thon*, Trinity Broadcasting Network, 6 November 1990).

54. Frederick K. C. Price: "When I first got saved they didn't tell me I could do anything. What they told me to do was that whenever I prayed I should always say, "The will of the Lord be done." Now, doesn't that sound humble? It does. Sounds like humility; it's really stupidity. I mean, you know, really, we insult God. I mean, we really do insult our heavenly Father. We do; we really insult Him without even realizing it. If you have to say, "If it be thy will" or "Thy will be done"—if you have to say that, then you're calling God a fool because He's the One that told us to ask . . . If God's gonna give me what He wants me to have, then it doesn't matter what I ask. I'm only gonna get what God wants me to have. So that's an insult to God's intelligence" (*Ever Increasing Faith*, Trinity Broadcasting Network, 16 November 1990).

55. Kenneth Copeland: "As a believer, you have a right to make commands in the name of Jesus. Each time you stand on the Word, you are commanding God to a certain extent because it is His Word" (*Our Covenant with God* [KCP Publications, 1987], 32).

56. Jerry Savelle: "You mean to tell me I can talk my world into existence? You certainly can. That's how you got the one you're living in now. You talked it in there . . . You talked that one in there, the one you're living in right now, brother. You can't blame it on nobody else. Your words got it there. You framed it. Somebody says, 'You mean the world that I'm living in right now originated by the words of my mouth?' They certainly did because the Bible says you are snared by the words of your mouth; you are taken by your words. Amen? (*Framing Your World with the Word of God,* part 1, audiotape #SS-36, side 1).

 Joel Osteen: "I want to speak to you today about the importance of speaking faith-filled words over your life. Words are like seeds. They have creative power. When we speak something out we give life to what we're saying. It's just like we're planting that seed. And if we say it long enough eventually we're going to reap a harvest" (*Discover the Champion in You*, 3 May 2004).

 Joyce Meyer: "Words are containers for power. They carry creative or destructive power, positive or negative power. And so we need to be speaking right things over our lives and about our futures if we expect to have good things happen. Because what you say today is what you'll probably end up having tomorrow" (*Enjoying Everyday Life*, Trinity Broadcasting Network, 16 July 2002).

 T. D. Jakes: "If the power of life and death is in the tongue and you can have whatever you say," it's time for you to "Declare it! Speak it! Confess it! Get your list out!" (*The Potter's House*, 3 December 2001).

 Paula White: "Oh come on, Paula . . . are you actually saying that just because my mouth says it, that makes it true? Well I am here to tell you, yes, that's just what I am saying: *Your words create your world*" ("Understanding the Power of Words Over Your Money," Paula White Ministries, emphasis in the original [http://www.paulawhite.org/content/view/172/88888897/]).

Chapter 1: Cult or Cultic?

1. J. Milton Yinger, *Religion, Society and the Individual* (New York: The Macmillan Company, 1962 [orig. 1957]), 154. Most modern sociological studies involved with the classification of religious groups have built on Ernst Troeltsch, *The Social Teaching of the Christian Churches*, trans. by Olive Wyon (London: George Allen and Unwin, 1931), 2 vols. Troeltsch, in turn, "acknowledged the stimulation of [sociologist Max] Weber in developing his concepts" (David O. Moberg, *The Church as a Social Institution* [Englewood Cliffs, NJ: Prentice-Hall, Inc., 1962), 76 n. 4.

 Another sociologist, John Lofland, comments that "cults are 'little groups' which break off from the 'conventional consensus and espouse very different views of the real, the possible, and the moral'" (quoted in Ronald Enroth, "What Is a Cult?" in *A Guide to Cults and New Religions* [Downers Grove,

IL: InterVarsity Press, 1983], 14). James T. Richardson, meanwhile, defines a cult as "'a group that has beliefs and/or practices that are counter to those of the dominant culture,' adding that these 'beliefs and practices may also be in opposition to those of a subculture'" (quoted in Irving Hexham and Karla Poewe, *Understanding Cults and New Religions* [Grand Rapids: Wm. B. Eerdmans Publishing Co., 1986], 6). See also James T. Richardson, *The Brainwashing/Deprogramming Controversy: Sociological, Psychological, Legal and Historical Perspectives* (Toronto: Edwin Mellen Press, 1983); and Bryan Wilson, *Religious Sects*, World University Library Series (Englewood, NJ: McGraw-Hill, 1970), cited in Hexham and Poewe, ibid.

2. J. Gordon Melton, *Encyclopedic Handbook of Cults in America* (New York: Garland Publishing, Inc., 1986), 5.

3. An interesting discussion in this area can be found in Ronald M. Enroth and J. Gordon Melton, *Why Cults Succeed Where the Church Fails* (Elgin, IL: Brethren Press, 1985), 11–19.

4. Gordon R. Lewis, *Confronting the Cults* (Grand Rapids: Baker Book House, 1975), 4.

5. Walter Martin, *The Kingdom of the Cults*, rev. ed. (Minneapolis, MN: Bethany House Publishers, 1985), 11.

6. For an excellent corrective, see James W. Sire, *Scripture Twisting* (InterVarsity Press, 1980).

7. See Martin, *The Kingdom of the Cults*, 18–24.

8. Referring to the International Convention of Faith Churches and Ministers (ICFCM), some have pointed out that there is an active move to form a distinct Faith denomination. However, as of late, the enterprise seems to have lost its momentum. See D. R. McConnell, *A Different Gospel* (Peabody, MA: Hendrickson Publishers, 1988) 84–87; cf. J. Gordon Melton, *The Encyclopedia of American Religions*, 3rd ed. (Detroit: Gale Research Inc., 1989), 377–78.

9. A discussion of essential Christian doctrine can be found in chapter 29 of this book.

10. For a fuller treatment of this subject, see Harold O. J. Brown, *Heresies: Heresy and Orthodoxy in the History of the Church* (Peabody, MA: Hendrickson Publishers, 1998).

Chapter 2: Charismatic or Cultic?

1. The origin of this maxim is uncertain. Although it is popularly attributed to Augustine, its earliest documentable appearance seems to be in a tract written about 1627 by a Lutheran scholar named Rupertus Meldenius (see James J. O'Donnell, "A common quotation from 'Augustine'?" (http://ccat.sas.upenn.edu/jod/augustine/quote.html, retrieved 1 October 2008).

2. For the purposes of this book, I will not draw the distinction commonly made between Pentecostals and charismatics. I believe that to do so in this setting would be to invite confusion since my goal, at this point, is to clarify the controversy between those who hold to the perpetuity of spiritual gifts (charismatics) and those who do not (noncharismatics), with reference to the Faith movement.

3. Walter Martin, *The Health and Wealth Cult* (San Juan Capistrano, CA: Christian Research Institute, n.d.), audiotape #C-152; *The Errors of Positive Confession* (Christian Research Institute, n.d.), audiotape #C-100; *Healing: Does God Always Heal?* (Christian Research Institute, n.d.), audiotape #C-95.

4. Gordon Fee, *The Disease of the Health and Wealth Gospels* (Beverly, MA: Frontline Publishing, 1985).

5. D. R. McConnell, *A Different Gospel* (Peabody, MA: Hendrickson Publishers, 1988).

6. Charles Farah, *From the Pinnacle of the Temple* (Plainfield, NJ: Logos, 1978); and "A Critical Analysis: The 'Roots' and 'Fruits' of Faith-Formula Theology" (paper presented at the Society for Pentecostal Studies, November 1980).

7. Elliot Miller, *Healing: Does God Always Heal?* (San Juan Capistrano, CA: Christian Research Institute, 1979).

8. H. Terris Neuman, *An Analysis of the Sources of the Charismatic Teaching of "Positive Confession"* (unpublished paper, Wheaton Graduate School, 1980); and "Cultic Origins of Word-Faith Theology Within the Charismatic Movement," *PNEUMA: The Journal of the Society for Pentecostal Studies* 12, 1 (Spring 1990):32–55. Neuman also lists a number of articles and papers by members of the Assembly of God that critique the Faith movement (p. 52, n. 154).

9. Dale H. Simmons, "A Theological and Historical Analysis of Kenneth E. Hagin's Claim to Be a Prophet," master's thesis, Oral Roberts University, 1985.

10. See Bruce Barron, *The Health and Wealth Gospel* (Downers Grove, IL: InterVarsity Press, 1987), 23.

Chapter 3: Cast of Characters

1. Matthew 7:22–23.

2. See, for example, Phineas P. Quimby, quoted in Horatio W. Dresser, *The Quimby Manuscripts* (New Hyde Park, NY: University Books, Inc. 1969 [orig. 1921]), 32–35, 61, 165, 186, 279, 295. Quimby's writings in this book were taken from his manuscripts dating between 1846 and 1865. Note the striking parallel in Kenneth Hagin's remark: "It makes a great deal of difference what one thinks. I believe that is why many people are sick, even though they are prayed for by everyone in the country. They get in every healing line and still never receive healing. The reason they are not getting healed is that they are thinking wrong" (Kenneth E. Hagin, *Right and Wrong Thinking* [Tulsa: Kenneth Hagin Ministries, 1978], 19).

3. New Thought writer Warren Felt Evans (1817–1889) is one such example. See Charles S. Braden, *Spirits in Rebellion* (Dallas: Southern Methodist University Press, 1970), 121–23.

4. See, for example, Claude Bristol, *The Magic of Believing* (New York: Prentice-Hall, Inc., 1948), 122; H. Emilie Cady, *Lessons in Truth* (Unity Village, MO: Unity Books, n.d.), 41:9; 43:17; 45:25; 46:31; 48:40–42; 51:6; 52:9; 53:11; 55:22; 57:32; Mary Baker Eddy, *Science and Health with Key to the Scriptures* (Boston: The First Church of Christ, Scientist, 1971 [orig. 1875]), 376:21–27; Charles Fillmore, *Prosperity* (Lee's Summit, MO: Unity Books, 1967), 103–4; and Ernest Holmes, *How to Use the Science of Mind* (New York: Dodd, Mead and Co., 1950), 39–45.

5. Rhonda Byrne, *The Secret* (New York: Atria Books/Beyond Words, 2006), 9. Prentice Mulford, an early New Thought practitioner, wrote a book titled *Thoughts Are Things* (1889).

6. Ibid., 25.

7. Warren Felt Evans, *Mental Medicine: A Treatise on Medical Psychology*, 15th ed. (Boston: H. H. Carter & Co., 1885 [orig. 1873]), 152; quoted in *Braden, Spirits in Rebellion*, 121.

8. Warren Felt Evans, *Esoteric Christianity and Mental Therapeutics* (Boston: H. H. Carter & Karrick, 1886), 152, emphasis in original; quoted in Braden, *Spirits in Rebellion*, 122–23.

9. Cady, *Lessons in Truth*, 56:30; cf. Holmes, *How to Use the Science of Mind*, 72, 78.

10. Cady, ibid., 52:8.

11. For a fine historical treatment of the healing revivalists, see David Edwin Harrell Jr., *All Things Are Possible: The Healing and Charismatic Revivals in Modern America* (Bloomington, IN: Indiana University Press, 1975). It should be pointed out that a number of the healing revivalists' unsound teachings and practices were previously spread by their predecessors—most notably John Alexander Dowie, Maria B. Woodworth-Etter, Smith Wigglesworth, F. F. Bosworth, and Thomas Wyatt.

12. Osborn's indebtedness to both Kenyon and Faith healer F. F. Bosworth (another "Kenyonite") is mentioned in T. L. Osborn, *Healing the Sick*, 23rd ed. (Tulsa: Osborn Foundation, 1959), 6, 203, 205; cf. Richard M. Riss, "Kenyon, Essek William," *Dictionary of Pentecostal and Charismatic Movements*, ed. by Stanley Burges, Gary B. McGee, and Patrick H. Alexander (Grand Rapids: Regency/Zondervan, 1988), 517; and Don Gossett and E.W. Kenyon, *The Power of the Positive Confession of God's Word*, 2d pr. (Blaine, WA: Don & Joyce Gossett, 1979), 3.

    On Osborn's teaching regarding the "little gods" doctrine, see T. L. Osborn, *You Are God's Best!* special Trinity Broadcasting Network edition (Santa Ana, CA: Trinity Broadcasting Network, n.d.), 30–31, 93–94, 122. Osborn has also stated, "He [referring to God] came down in human flesh, and we call him William Branham" (Tommy L. Osborn, *A Tribute to William Marrion Branham* [Bartow, FL: Spoken Word Outreach Center, Inc., n.d.], 18; cf. 11, 13, 17; also see *Praise the Lord*, Trinity Broadcasting Network, 19 June 1989).

13. William Marrion Branham, *Revelation Chapter Four #3* (Throne of Mercy and Judgment) (Jeffersonville, IN: Voice of God Recordings, Inc., 1961), audiotape #61-0108, side 2; cf. William Marrion Branham, *Footprints on the Sands of Time: The Autobiography of William Marrion Branham*, Part Two (Jeffersonville, IN: Spoken Word Publications, 1975), 606–07.

14. Benny Hinn, *Praise the Lord*, Trinity Broadcasting Network, 12 April 1991.

15. Benny Hinn, *Double Portion Anointing*, part 3 (Orlando Christian Center, n.d.), audiotape #A031791-3, sides 1 and 2. This sermon was also aired on TBN (7 April 1991).

16. Benny Hinn, *Praise the Lord*, Trinity Broadcasting Network, 16 April 1992.

17. Quoted in Russell Chandler, "Talked with Jesus, Evangelist Says," *The Los Angeles Times* (3 February 1983), 3, 16.

18. Clark Morphew, "What's to become of Oral Roberts' City of Faith?" *St. Paul Pioneer Press* (27 June 1992); reprinted in *The Christian News* (20 July 1992), 2.

19. A. A. Allen, *The Secret to Scriptural Financial Success* (Miracle Valley, AZ: A.A. Allen Publications, 1953); quoted in Harrell, *All Things Are Possible*, 75.

20. A. A. Allen, "Miracle Oil Flows at Camp Meeting," *Miracle Magazine* (June 1967):6–7; quoted in Harrell, *All Things Are Possible*, 200.

21. Reported in "New Revival Tent Dedicated in Philadelphia," *Miracle Magazine* (September 1967):15; quoted in Harrell, *All Things Are Possible*, 200.

22. See Harrell, *All Things Are Possible*, 199.

23. Harrell, *All Things Are Possible*, 70–71.

24. Ibid., 202. One writer describes Allen's cause of death as "cirrhosis" of the liver (see Gary L. Ward, "Allen, Asa Alonzo," in J. Gordon Melton, *Religious Leaders of America* [Detroit, MI: Gale Research, 1991], 9).

Essek William Kenyon

25. E. W. Kenyon, *The Father and His Family* (Lynnwood, WA: Kenyon's Gospel Publishing Society, 1964), 118.

26. E. W. Kenyon, *The Hidden Man*, 5th ed. (Lynnwood, WA: Kenyon's Gospel Publishing Society, 1970), 98.

27. Notable works include Charles Farah, "A Critical Analysis: The 'Roots' and 'Fruits' of Faith-Formula Theology" (paper presented at the Society for Pentecostal Studies, November 1980); James M. Kinnebrew, "The Charismatic Doctrine of Positive Confession: A Historical, Exegetical, and Theological Critique," doctoral dissertation, Mid-America Baptist Theological Seminary, 1988; D. R. McConnell, "The Kenyon Connection: A Theological and Historical Analysis of the Cultic Origins of the Faith Movement," master's thesis, Oral Roberts University, 1982, and "A Different Gospel" (Peabody, MA: Hendrickson Publishers, Inc., 1988); H. Terris Neuman, "An Analysis of the Sources of the Charismatic Teaching of Positive Confession" (unpublished paper, Wheaton Graduate School, 1980); "Cultic Origins of Word-Faith Theology Within the Charismatic Movement" (*Pneuma: The Journal of the Society for Pentecostal Studies*, 12, 1, Spring 1990:3–55); and Dale H. Simmons, "A Theological and Historical Analysis of Kenneth E. Hagin's Claim to Be a Prophet," master's thesis, Oral Roberts University, 1985. Cf. also William DeArteaga, *Quenching the Spirit*; Joe McIntyre, *E. W. Kenyon and His Message of Faith: The True Story* (Lake Mary, Florida: Creation House, 1997).

28. See McConnell, *A Different Gospel*, 35–43.

29. See chapter 2, endnote 9, 386; see also ibid., 23.

30. McConnell, *A Different Gospel*, 23, 28 note 23.

31. Ibid., 23, 33.

32. Kenyon, *The Father and His Family*, 118.

33. Kenneth E. Hagin, *Zoe: The God-Kind of Life* (Tulsa: Kenneth Hagin Ministries, Inc., 1989), 35–36, 41.

Kenneth E. Hagin

34. Ibid., 35.

35. Vinson Synan, "The Faith of Kenneth Hagin," *Charisma & Christian Faith*, 15:11 (June 1990), 68.

36. Ibid.

37. The demonic entity was described as "an evil spirit" (Hagin, *I Believe in Visions* [Old Tappan, NJ: Spire Books; Old Tappan, NJ: Revell, 1972], 80); as "an evil spirit that looked like a monkey" (*Zoe*, 47; *Visions*, 80); and as "an evil spirit that looked like a little monkey or elf" (*The Believer's Authority*, 29).

38. Hagin claims to have seen a "demon monkey" on another occasion, when it was oppressing a woman with cancer: "I saw a demon or an evil spirit hanging on to her body from the outside. It was like a little monkey hanging onto a tree limb. It looked like pictures we've seen of little elves" (*Ministering to the Oppressed* [Tulsa: Kenneth Hagin Evangelistic Association, 7th pr. 1977], 23). A pastor told Hagin of seeing a similar entity oppressing his church: "There sitting above the ceiling on a rafter was a spirit that looked like a big ape or baboon" (*The Interceding Christian* [Tulsa: Kenneth Hagin Ministries, 1978], 17).

39. "Now understand," explains Hagin, "'that' doesn't just include the demon; it included the dark cloud that shut off the vision of Jesus and heaven. It included communication that didn't get through—prayers, or whatever" (See Hagin, *Zoe*, 49).

40. Hagin, *I Believe in Visions*, 81.

41. Ibid.

42. Ibid.

43. Hagin, *Zoe*, 57. Hagin also says euphemistically that he received "the left foot of fellowship" from the Baptists (Kenneth E. Hagin, *Casting Your Cares upon the Lord* [Tulsa: Kenneth Hagin Ministries, 1981], 13; Kenneth E. Hagin, *Seven Things You Should Know About Divine Healing* [Tulsa: Kenneth Hagin Ministries, 1979], 21; Kenneth E. Hagin, *What to Do When Faith Seems Weak & Victory Lost* [Tulsa: Kenneth Hagin Ministries, 1979], 47).

44. Kenneth Hagin Jr., *Faith Worketh by Love* (Tulsa: Kenneth Hagin Ministries, 1979), 21, emphasis added.

45. H. Vinson Synan, "Capps, Charles Emmitt," *Dictionary of Pentecostal & Charismatic Movements*, ed. by Stanley M. Burgess, Gary B. McGee, and Patrick H. Alexander (Grand Rapids: Regency/Zondervan, 1988), 107; Russ White, "Congregation Keeps the Faith with Spellbinding Benny Hinn," *Orlando Sentinel* (11 October 1987), F6.

46. Kenneth Hagin, *Faith Seminar of the Air*; radio station listings in *The Word of Faith*, 25, 6 (June 1992):18–19. Additionally, Hagin's son, Kenneth Jr., has his own separate weekly radio program, *Rhema Radio Church*.

47. "Graduation 92—A Gateway to the Nations!" *The Word of Faith* 25, 7 (July 1992):8; "RHEMA's First Russian Graduate!" ibid., 10–11.

48. Kenneth Hagin Jr., "Trend Toward Faith Movement," *Charisma & Christian Life* (August 1985), 67–70, cited in Kinnebrew, "The Charismatic Doctrine of Positive Confession," 16 and note 20; cf. discrepant figures in Bruce Barron, *The Health and Wealth Gospel* (Downers Grove, IL: InterVarsity Press, 1987), 55.

49. According to Ron Wilson, Executive Director of the Evangelical Press Association, *The Word of Faith* magazine has a circulation total of 396,259 (CRI telephone interview on 24 July 1992).

50. Hagin, *Classic Sermons: Word of Faith 25th Anniversary 1968–92 Commemorative Edition* (Tulsa: Kenneth Hagin Ministries, 1992), Preface [ix]. According to Hagin's October 1990 Ministry Partner letter, more than forty thousand cassette tapes are duplicated and mailed every month; according to Hagin's *Classic Sermons* (112), some forty thousand to fifty thousand tapes are sent out monthly now.

51. "Faith Library Catalog" (Tulsa: Kenneth Hagin Ministries, 1991).

52. Synan, "The Faith of Kenneth Hagin," 63.

53. Hagin, *I Believe in Visions*, 14–16.

54. See, for example, Kenneth E. Hagin, *I Went to Hell* (Tulsa: Kenneth Hagin Ministries, 1982), 5, 9, 14, 18, 23. Hagin attempts to cite still other biblical precedents for his own experience (*Exceedingly Growing Faith*, 36). Hagin refers to Paul's description of a journey by someone (most commentators believe Paul was referring to himself) to the third heaven, in which Paul states that he did not know whether this vision occurred in or out of the body and that only God knows which it was (2 Corinthians 12:1–4). But Hagin clearly describes himself as knowing that he was out of his body, despite his clever statement, "I know what Paul meant when he said that he didn't know if he was in the body, or out of the body" (*Exceedingly*, 36)—a statement that does not actually say Hagin was incapable of telling whether he was in or out of his body, only that Hagin knew how Paul must have felt, that he could sympathize.

Hagin, in fact, describes his exact locations outside of his "partially paralyzed" body lying on his sickbed with his heart stopped (*Visions*, 12; *Exceedingly*, 35): "I knew I was outside of my body. I could see my family in the room" (*Hell*, 5). "I knew I was out of my body . . . I came up head first to the porch outside that south bedroom. Just for a second I knew that I was standing up on the porch. Then I went right through the wall. I seemed to leap inside my body. Back inside my body, I could contact the physical again" (*Exceedingly*, 35–37 [emphasis added]). "I came back into that room just as real as at any other time" (*Visions*, 12). In another deathbed experience soon after, Hagin writes: "I had the same sensation I'd had before . . . As I leaped out of my body and left it, I began to ascend . . . When I got up to about where the roof of the house should have been,

approximately 16 feet above the bed, my ascent stopped and I seemed to stand there. I was
fully conscious and knew everything that was going on. Looking back into the room, I saw
my body lying on the bed and my mother stooped over it holding my hand in hers"
(*Exceedingly*, 37).

55. Hagin, *I Believe in Visions*, 12–16; also *I Went to Hell*, 14; and *The Name of Jesus* (Tulsa: Kenneth
Hagin Ministries, 1981), 68. McConnell calls this Hagin's "out-of-body descent into hell"
(McConnell, 74 n. 2). Other Faith teachers who have reported out-of-body experiences include
Benny Hinn, Norvel Hayes, and Kenneth Copeland.

The ancient Egyptians believed that the human soul or spirit exits and enters through the mouth:
E. A. Wallis Budge, *Osiris: The Egyptian Religion of Resurrection*, 2 vols. (London: Warner, 1911
[New York: University Books, 1961 reprint]), 1:399; cf. 1:333; 2:128; Budge, *From Fetish to God in
Ancient Egypt* (London: Oxford University Press, 1934 [New York: Dover, 1988 reprint]), 331–33.

56. Hagin, *I Believe in Visions*, 5.

57. Kenneth E. Hagin, *The Glory of God* (Tulsa: Kenneth Hagin Ministries, 1987), 13–15.

58. Ibid., 16.

59. Hagin, *I Believe in Visions*, 51.

60. Ibid., 50.

61. See Henry George Liddell and Robert Scott (rev. Henry Stuart Jones), *A Greek-English Lexicon*
(Oxford, England: Oxford University Press, 1968 rev. ed.), 1983b–84a, "cheir" items I.1, II.6.c,
III.1; Gerhard Friedrich, ed., transl. Geoffrey W. Bromiley, *Theological Dictionary of the New
Testament* (Grand Rapids: Wm. B. Eerdmans Publishing Co., 1974), 9:424–25, 430, items A.1.a. and
fn. 4, C.1.b.; and Walter Bauer, William F. Arndt, and F. Wilbur Gingrich, *A Greek-English Lexicon
of the New Testament* (Chicago: University of Chicago Press, 1979 rev. ed.), 880a. See also Kenneth
E. Stevenson and Gary R. Habermas, *The Shroud and the Controversy* (Nashville: Thomas Nelson,
Inc., 1990), 152.

62. Dr. Pierre Barbet was the chief surgeon at St. Joseph's Hospital in Paris. He performed experiments
on cadavers in the 1930s that showed that crucifixion by nails through the palms could not have
supported the weight of the body on the cross. The nails would have ripped through the flesh. See
Pierre Barbet, *A Doctor at Calvary*, Eng. transl. (New York: P. J. Kennedy and Doubleday, 1953
[French orig. 1950]), 17, 20; and Frank C. Tribbe, *Portrait of Jesus?* (New York: Stein & Day, 1983), 80, 99–104.

Interestingly, an actual crucifixion victim of the Roman destruction of Jerusalem in A.D. 70,
named Yohanon ben ha-Galgol, was excavated by Israeli archaeologists in a New Testament–era
cemetery just outside Jerusalem in 1968. Yohanon was crucified with a nail through the radius and
ulna bones of the forearm, as evidenced by grinding found on the inside of the radius bone at the
wrist end (Wilson, 32–33; and Tribbe, 86–87).

Barbet's experiments with cadavers have recently been repeated and confirmed by Paris orthopedic
surgeon Dr. Pierre Merat ("Critical Study: Anatomy and Physiology of the Shroud," *The Catholic
Counter-Reformation in the XXth Century*, no. 218 [April 1989], 3–4).

63. "Special Report: Campmeeting '83," *The Word of Faith*, 16, 10 (October 1983):3.

64. Hagin, *I Believe in Visions*, 115.

65. Ibid., 115.

66. Kenneth E. Hagin, *Why Do People Fall Under the Power?* (Tulsa: Kenneth Hagin Ministries, 1981),
10.

67. Ibid., 11–12.

68. Benny Hinn: "They call it the ministry, my foot. You know, I've looked for one verse in the Bible.
I just can't seem to find it. One verse that says if you don't like them, kill them. I really wish I
could find it. But there's nowhere in the Bible it says it. Ladies and gentlemen, don't attack God's
servants. Don't publicly attack them by name. You can make statements, general statements.
Nobody cares about that. We all do that. There's nothing wrong with it. But don't mention
people's names on your radio program and your TV program, thinking you're doing God a service.
You're not. You stink, frankly . . . You know, Paul [Crouch], it angers me to no end. There's no
power but judgment. No life but death. Quit it! I'm sorry. I'm not exactly the normal kind of guy,
you know. I'm from Israel. Sometimes I wish God would give me a Holy Ghost machine gun. I'd

blow your head off" (*Praise the Lord: Praise-a-Thon* program, Trinity Broadcasting Network, 8 November 1990).

69. See Randy Frame, "Best-Selling Author Admits Mistakes, Vows Changes," *Christianity Today* (28 October 1991), 44.

70. Benny Hinn, sermon delivered during "Miracle Invasion Rally" at the Anaheim [CA] Convention Center (22 November 1991).

71. Paul Crouch, *Praise the Lord: Praise-a-Thon*, Trinity Broadcasting Network, 2 April 1991.

72. Kenneth Copeland, *Why All Are Not Healed* (Fort Worth, TX: Kenneth Copeland Ministries, 1990), audiotape #01-4001, side 1.

Kenneth Copeland

73. Kenneth Copeland, *Praise the Lord: Praise-a-Thon* program, Trinity Broadcasting Network, April 1988.

74. Barron, *The Health and Wealth Gospel*, 56–57; see also Kenneth Hagin Jr., *Faith Worketh by Love*, 21.

75. Barron, *Health & Wealth Gospel*, 183, note 59.

76. Richard M. Riss, "Copeland, Kenneth," *Dictionary of Pentecostal & Charismatic Movements*, 226; cf. Gloria Copeland, *God's Will for You* (Fort Worth, TX: Kenneth Copeland Publications, 1972), xii.

77. Kenneth Copeland, *Living to Give* [brochure] (Fort Worth, TX: Kenneth Copeland Ministries, n.d. [ca. 1988]), 4.

78. Ibid., 5–6.

79. Kenneth Copeland, *Walking in the Realm of the Miraculous* (Fort Worth, TX: Kenneth Copeland Ministries, 1979), 8.

80. Ibid., [8], emphasis in original.

81. Kenneth Copeland, *Following the Faith of Abraham I* (Fort Worth, TX: Kenneth Copeland Ministries, 1989), audiotape #01-3001, side 1; compare also Finis J. Dake, *Dake's Annotated Reference Bible* (Lawrenceville, GA: Dake Bible Sales, 1963), OT p. 388 col. 1b, 467 col. 1f.

82. Brigham Young, "Discourse . . . June 8th, 1873," *Deseret News* [Salt Lake City] (18 June 1873), 308; Brigham Young, sermon, 9 April 1852; G. D. Watt, ed., *Journal of Discourses* (Liverpool, England: F. D. Richards, 1855), 1:50.

83. Kenneth Copeland, *Spirit, Soul and Body I* (Fort Worth, TX: Kenneth Copeland Ministries, 1985), audiotape #01-0601, side 1.

84. Joseph Smith, "The King Follett Sermon" (7 April 1844), *History of the Church* 8th pr. (Salt Lake City: Deseret Book Co., 1975), 6:305; Joseph Smith, "The King Follett Discourse," *Teachings of the Prophet Joseph Smith*, 21st pr., in Joseph Fielding Smith, ed. (Salt Lake City: Deseret Book Co., 1972), 345.

85. Copeland, *Following the Faith of Abraham I*, side 1.

86. Joseph Smith, *History of the Church of Jesus Christ of Latter-day Saints*, Vol. 6 (Salt Lake City: Deseret Book Company, 1978), 305–6.

87. Copeland, *Following the Faith of Abraham I*.

88. Copeland, *Praise the Lord: Praise-a-Thon*, Trinity Broadcasting Network, April 1988.

89. Copeland, *Holy Bible: Kenneth Copeland Reference Edition* (Fort Worth, TX: Kenneth Copeland Ministries, 1991), 129, emphasis in original.

90. Copeland, *Believer's Voice of Victory*, Trinity Broadcasting Network, 21 April 1991.

91. Kenneth Copeland, *Inner Image of the Covenant* (Fort Worth, TX: Kenneth Copeland Ministries, 1985), audiotape #01-4406, side 2.

92. Ibid.

93. Ibid.

94. Kenneth Copeland, *Believer's Voice of Victory*, Trinity Broadcasting Network, 28 March 1991.

95. Copeland, *Inner Image of the Covenant*, audiotape, side 2.

96. Gloria Copeland, "Paul's Thorn in the Flesh," *Believer's Voice of Victory* 11:11 (November 1983), 5:8.

97. United States Senator Chuck Grassley of Iowa, "Letter to Kenneth and Gloria Copeland" (http://grassley.senate.gov/public/releases/2007/110620076.pdf, accessed 15 July 2008).

98. Baird Helgeson and Michelle Bearden, "Senator Set to Intensify Investigation of Ministries, *Tampa Tribune*, 8 February 2008 (http://www2.tbo.com/content/2008/feb/08/na-senator-set-to-intensify-investigation-of-minis, accessed 15 July 2008).

99. Benny Hinn, *Benny Hinn*, Trinity Broadcasting Network, 8 June 1992.

Benny Hinn

100. Benny Hinn, *Our Position in Christ #2: The Word Made Flesh* (Orlando, FL: Orlando Christian Center, 1991), audiotape #A031190-2, side 2.

101. Benny Hinn, *The Anointing* (Nashville: Thomas Nelson, Inc., 1992), 98, cited in Hank Hanegraaff, *Counterfeit Revival: Looking for God in All the Wrong Places*, expanded and updated (Nashville: Thomas Nelson, Inc., 2001), 189.

102. G. Richard Fisher, Stephen F. Cannon, and M. Kurt Goedelman, "Benny Hinn's Anointing: Heaven Sent or Borrowed?" *The Quarterly Journal, Personal Freedom Outreach* 12, 3 (July–September 1992):12, cited in Hanegraaff, *Counterfeit Revival*, 189.

103. Benny Hinn, *Praise the Lord*, Trinity Broadcasting Network, 8 July 1996, audiotape.

104. Hinn, *The Anointing*, 86, 94.

105. Ibid., 94–95.

106. White, "Congregation Keeps the Faith," F6: "Hinn claims that . . . he helped heal even those who have AIDS . . . He doesn't say whom he has healed or present documented proof." See also Mike Thomas, "The Power and the Glory," 12; Michael McAteer, "Debunkers Put No Faith in Healer's 'Miracles,' *Toronto Star*, 24 September 1992, A2; cf. Hinn's "hundreds of verified healings," *Anointing*, 94–95.

107. Mike Thomas, "The Power and the Glory," 12. Hinn and his spokesman/personal aide, Gene Polino, Administrator of Orlando Christian Center, later denied that Susan Smith documents healings for the church, asserting that she merely works in the video department and that Kent Mattox does the miracle documentation instead (Benny Hinn and Gene Polino meeting with CRI President Hanegraaff and Vice President, Research, Robert Lyle, 21 August 1992; Gene Polino interview by Renee Munshi, freelance reporter for *Bookstore Journal*, 1 September 1992; CRI interview with Munshi, 1 September 1992; Renee Munshi, "Benny Hinn: An Enigma," revised draft article faxed to CRI and Hinn Ministries, 2 September 1992).

    However, on September 4, 1992, Hinn provided CRI some medical records allegedly documenting three of his healing miracles, and among them were standardized forms used by the Hinn ministries for recording information in interviews with people thought to have been healed. Susan Smith's name appears on the form as the interviewer (the exact role stated by *Florida* magazine in the first place and admitted by Polino to Munshi). Thus Smith does appear to help document miracles for Hinn's ministry.

108. "But despite all the thousands of miracles claimed by Hinn, the church seems hard pressed to come up with any that would convince a serious skeptic . . . [Susan] Smith also said there was a documented AIDS cure, but when pressed for details, she later said the final tests weren't in yet," according to Mike Thomas in "The Power and the Glory," *Florida*, 12. No such test results proving the AIDS cure were forthcoming nearly a year later when Hinn talked about the subject, and he sounded as though he was only then starting to investigate for the first time: "Hinn said he does not know if there is documentation that authenticates the healing of people with AIDS but promised a 'thorough search' to see if such documentation exists" (McAteer, "Debunkers Put No Faith in Healer's Miracles," A2).

    Medical records and other documents enclosed with cover letter from Benny Hinn, 4 September 1992.

109. Benny Hinn, *Lord, I Need A Miracle* (Nashville: Thomas Nelson, Inc., 1993), 61, 77, 80, 82, 85–86.

110. Ibid., 79, 96.

111. Ibid., 60–62.

112. Ibid., 72–73.

113. Ibid., 99–102.

114. Ibid., vii.

115. Preston Simpson, MD, medical analysis report, 28 October 1992; CRI telephone interviews with Dr. Preston Simpson, 6 and 23 October 1992. Although Hinn's medical documentation assistant or "pastor for followup," Kent Mattox, claims he has compiled "proof" of Hinn's healings from the records of physicians who have conducted "*before-and-after examinations*," Dr. Simpson found there were virtually no before-miracle medical records to make a "before-and-after" comparison (Mattox interview by Renee Munshi for *Bookstore Journal*, 1 September 1992; CRI interview with Munshi, 1

September 1992; Munshi, "Benny Hinn: An Enigma," revised draft article [2 September 1992]).

"We do not know whether this man was cured by a miracle or by standard surgical treatment," according to Simpson, medical analysis, 28 October 1992. Cf. CRI telephone interviews with Dr. Simpson, 6 and 23 October 1992. It is also unclear whether the tumor started diminishing in size before or after the Hinn Miracle Crusade.

116. Hinn, *Lord I Need a Miracle*, viii.
117. Simpson, medical analysis, 28 October 1992. For the effects of lupus, see Robert Berkow, ed., *The Merck Manual*, 15th rev. ed. (Rahway, NJ: Merck, 1987), 1276–77.
118. This case involves a three-inch tumor that invaded the lower spinal vertebrae and caused two of them to fracture and collapse. The net result was that the forty-year-old woman in question apparently was unable to walk, but the medical records provided do not explicitly document this fact. Nearly two years into the case, her doctors did not seem to know what diagnoses or tests had been run previously or what treatments had been given. It is not even clear from the records provided whether the tumor was cancerous or caused by a viral or bacterial infection. One medical report (dated 30 December 1991) suggested polio or TB infections as possible causes, yet this was nearly *two years* after some form of cancer was supposedly first diagnosed on January 19, 1990 (seemingly in the lymphatic system). Although it is unclear from the records exactly when the spinal tumor was discovered, surely it should have been diagnosed as cancerous or not after the November 19, 1991, spinal X-rays mentioned in the incomplete records provided by Hinn. (There is no actual radiology report for that date. The X-rays are mentioned in later reports.) (Medical records supplied to CRI by Benny Hinn, 4 September 1992.)
119. Radiology report, 2 July 1992.
120. The Hinn Miracle Crusade was on May 14, 1992, in Tulsa, Oklahoma, but the tumor was still present at the examination on July 2, 1992.
121. Even the apparent exception of the two-stage healing of the blind man in Mark 8:22–25 constituted an acted-out parable that illustrated the sluggish spiritual awakening of the disciples (see vv. 27ff).
122. For a full-orbed discussion on the subtle power of suggestion, see chapter 25, Hanegraaff, *Counterfeit Revival*.
123. Benny Hinn, *Our Position in Christ # 5: An Heir of God* (Orlando, FL: Orlando Christian Center, 1990), audiotape # A031190-5, side 2, cited in Hank Hanegraaff, *Christianity in Crisis* (Eugene, OR: Harvest House, 1993), 380.
124. Hinn, *Double Portion Anointing*, part 3 (Orlando, FL: Orlando Christian Center, n.d.), audiotape #A031791-3, sides 1 and 2; aired on TBN, 7 April 1991.
125. Benny Hinn, sermon delivered at Orlando Christian Center, 31 December 1989; partial transcript in Albert James Dager, "Special Report: Benny Hinn Pros & Cons," *Media Spotlight* (May 1992).
126. Cf. Ken Garfield, "Faith Healer from Florida Draws Crowds, and Questions," *Charlotte Observer* (15 October 1992), 1C (1 million-plus copies of *Good Morning, Holy Spirit*); Randy Frame, "Same Old Benny Hinn, Critics Say," *Christianity Today*, 36:11 (5 October 1992):54 (1.7 million copies of both books combined).
127. Benny Hinn, *Good Morning, Holy Spirit* (Nashville: Thomas Nelson, Inc., 1990), 56.
128. Ibid., 42.
129. This account of Hinn's Oshawa sermon of December 7, 1974, is taken from Hinn, *Anointing*, 23–27; and Hinn, *Good Morning, Holy Spirit*, 44–46.
130. Hinn, *Anointing*, 26.
131. Ibid., 27.
132. See the author's detailed book review, "*The Anointing* by Benny Hinn," *Christian Research Journal*, 15, 2 (Fall 1992):38.
133. Hinn, *Anointing*, 31.
134. Ibid., 79.
135. Ibid., 177–78.
136. Benny Hinn, *Praise the Lord*, Trinity Broadcasting Network, 8 November 1990.
137. Randy Frame, "Best-Selling Author Admits Mistakes, Vows Changes," *Christianity Today* (28 October 1991), 44–45.
138. Ibid.

139. Ibid.

140. Hinn, "Miracle Invasion," Anaheim, California, Convention Center (22 November 1991). Hinn was responding to the previous night's ABC *PrimeTime Live* exposé of Robert Tilton, Larry Lea, and W. V. Grant, but he seemed oblivious to the bad timing of making dire threats on the anniversary of a presidential assassination.

141. White, "Congregation Keeps the Faith," F-6.

142. *Benny Hinn*, Trinity Broadcasting Network, 8 June 1992.

143. Ibid., 29 June 1992.

144. Ibid., 6 July 1992.

145. Hinn, *Praise the Lord*, Trinity Broadcasting Network, 19 October 1999.

146. Benny Hinn, *Prophecy for the '90s*, Orlando Christian Center," audiotape, 1 January 1990.

147. Ibid.

148. Benny Hinn, Orlando Christian Center, 10 October 1993.

149. Benny Hinn, "This is Your Day," 29 March 2000.

150. Benny Hinn, *Praise the Lord: Praise-a-Thon*, Trinity Broadcasting Network, 2 April 2000.

151. Ibid.

152. Rita Elkins, "Meditating on Maitreya," *Florida Today*, 12 March 2000, People, 1.

Joel Osteen

153. Joel Osteen, *Your Best Life Now: 7 Steps to Living at Your Full Potential* (New York: Warner Faith, 2004), 129.

154. Osteen writes, "In 2003, *Forbes* magazine named Lakewood Church 'the largest church in America,' with twenty-five thousand people attending each weekend. And we're still growing!" (Ibid., 217.)

155. Patrick Rogers and Vickie Bane, "Joel Osteen Counts His Blessings," *People*, 17 December 2007, 96.

156. Osteen, *Your Best Life Now*, 149.

157. See John 5:1–15, specifically verses 8–9.

158. Osteen, *Your Best Life Now*, 211.

159. Ibid., 212.

160. Ibid., 227.

161. Joel Osteen, Easter service message at Lakewood Church, Sermon #CS_002 - 4-23-00, 23 April 2000, transcript formerly online at http://www.lakewood.cc/sermons/cs_002.htm, emphasis added; transcript archived online at http://web.archive.org/web/20040408215244/http://www.lakewood.cc/sermons/cs_002.htm, retrieved 1 November 2008. Cf. Joel Osteen, Easter service message 2004 on *Discover the Champion in You* program, Trinity Broadcasting Network, 26 April 2004.

162. Ibid.

163. Ibid.

164. See John R. W. Stott, *The Cross of Christ* (Leicester: IVP, 1986), 179–81; Leon Morris, *The Apostolic Preaching of the Cross*, 3rd ed. (Grand Rapids: Wm. B. Eerdmans Publishing Co., 1984), 112–28. Also, "Some have argued, largely on the basis of this verse [Leviticus 17:11], that 'blood' in Scripture signifies life rather than death. However, in all of the Old Testament sacrifices, blood is obtained by killing an animal, and the life spoken of in Lev. 17:11 is that 'which ceases to exist when the blood is poured out'" (Steve Jeffrey, Michael Ovey, Andrew Sach, *Pierced for Our Transgressions: Rediscovering the Glory of Penal Substitution* [Wheaton: IL: Crossway Books, 2007], 45, n. 23.

165. Joel Osteen, *Discover the Champion in You* program, Trinity Broadcasting Network, 3 May 2004.

166. Osteen, *Become a Better You*, 63.

167. Ibid., 63–64.

168. Ibid., 64.

169. Osteen, *Your Best Life Now*, 7–8.

170. Ibid., 8–9.

171. Osteen, *Become a Better You*, 26.

172. Ibid., 63.

173. Byrne, *The Secret*, 60.

Joyce Meyer

174. Joyce Meyer, *The Most Important Decision You Will Ever Make: A Complete and Thorough Understanding of What It Means to Be Born Again* (Fenton, MO: Life in the Word, 1991), 37.

175. http://www.joycemeyer.org/AboutUs/AboutJoyce, accessed 5 July 2008.

176. Ibid.

177. Life Christian University Web site, "Questions," at http://www.lcus.edu/questions.htm, accessed 5 July 2008.

178. Joyce Meyer, *Eight Ways to Keep the Devil Under Your Feet* (New York: Warner Faith, 2002), 27.

179. Ibid., 28.

180. Ibid., 30.

181. Meyer, "Interrupting Satan's Plan: Releasing the Supernatural Power of God Through Prayer," tape 3 of the series titled, "Violent Christians in a Violent Society," recorded in San Jose, California, 19 July 2001.

182. Elsewhere, in a chapter titled "Watch Your Mouth," Meyer writes, "Words are containers for power. They carry either creative power or destructive power." (Meyer, *Eight Ways*, 87–88).

183. See Meyer, *Eight Ways*.

184. Ibid., 95.

185. Ibid., 151.

186. For example, concerning near accidents in a fast-food restaurant parking lot, Meyer writes, "'I rebuke the spirit of accidents, in the name of Jesus!' I believe there are certain powers and principalities over certain areas. Those close calls were attacks from the devil!"

187. Joyce Meyer, *Trophies of God's Grace,* part 1 (Fenton, MO: Joyce Meyer Ministries, 1991), audiotape.

188. See, for example, Ezekiel 18:2–4, 20.

189. Meyer, *The Most Important Decision You Will Ever Make: A Complete and Thorough Understanding of What It Means to Be Born Again* (Tulsa: Harrison House, 1996), 41.

190. Ibid., 42 (emphasis in original).

191. Meyer, *The Most Important Decision You Will Ever Make* (1991), 37. In the 1996 edition, Meyer deleted the words "in hell" from this particular passage; but two paragraphs earlier, within the same context, she retained (as in her 1991 edition) the line "So they put Him—that is, His body—in a grave, and His spirit went to hell because that is where we deserved to go." And within the same chapter, titled "What Should You Believe?" still within the same context, Meyer writes, "Believe that Jesus did what the Bible says . . . He was in the grave three days. During that time, He entered hell, where you and I deserved to go (legally) because of our sin. He paid the price there . . . *Jesus paid* on the cross and went to hell in my place . . . Jesus went to hell for *you*. He paid for *your* sins . . . When the bill was paid and all our debt completely cancelled, the Father raised Him from the dead. But until that happened, He was alone for three days satisfying the courts of justice and conquering the hosts of hell" (41, 43, 44, emphasis in original).

192. Meyer, *The Most Important Decision You Will Ever Make* (1996), 43.

193. Ken Walker, "The Preacher Who Tells It Like It Is," *Charisma*, November 1998, 55.

194. See Todd Wilken interview with Joyce Meyer, *Issues Etc.*, KFUO Radio, 23 May 2005.

195. Joyce Meyer, *From the Cross to the Throne*, audiocassette (St. Louis: Life Christian Center, n.d.).

196. Ibid., emphasis added.

197. Luther described a Christian as "simultaneously righteous and sinner" (Simul Iustus et Peccator), especially on the basis of Romans 4.

198. Joyce Meyer, *Enjoying Everyday Life*, 16 July 2002.

199. YouTube, "Joyce Meyer—Little Gods" (http://www.youtube.com/watch?v=7Y4eVu2oxP8), accessed 12 July 2007.

200. Joyce Meyer, "Witchcraft & Related Spirits" (part 1), n.d.

John Hagee

201. John Hagee, *Should Christians Support Israel?* (San Antonio, TX: Dominon, 1987), 124–25, emphasis in original.

202. John Hagee, *Praise-a-Thon 2002*, Trinity Broadcasting Network, 5 November 2002.

203. Hagee, *The Seven Secrets: Unlocking Genuine Greatness* (Lake Mary, FL: Charisma House, 2004), 232.

204. Ibid.

205. Cf. Merrill C. Tenney, *The Expositor's Bible Commentary*, vol. 9, ed. Frank E. Gaebelein (Grand Rapids: Zondervan, 1981), 181.

206. Hagee, *The Seven Secrets*, 231–32.

207. Cf. Craig S. Keener, *The IVP Bible Background Commentary: New Testament* (Downers Grove, IL: InterVarsity Press, 1993), 162.

208. Hagee, *The Seven Secrets*, 41.

209. Ibid., 122–23.

210. Cf. Barbara and David P. Mikkelson, "Deadly Imaginings," http://www.snopes.com/horrors/gruesome/freezer.asp, retrieved 30 September 2008.

211 Hagee, *The Seven Secrets*, 39.

212. Ibid., 52.

213. Ibid., 205–9.

214. Ibid., 219.

215. Hagee, *Should Christians Support Israel?* 1, 73.

216. Ibid., 124–25, emphasis in original.

217. Ibid., 125, capitalization in original; cf. John Hagee, *In Defense of Israel* (Lake Mary, FL: Front Line, 2007), 132ff; also, in a video promotion, Hagee states, "*In Defense of Israel* will shake Christian theology. It scripturally proves that the Jewish people, as a whole, did not reject Jesus as Messiah. It will also prove that Jesus did not come to earth to be the Messiah . . . Since Jesus refused, by word and deed, to claim to be the Messiah, how can the Jews be blamed for rejecting what was never offered?" video online at http://www.youtube.com/watch?v=m8khCJTDD44, retrieved 1 August 2008.

218. Ibid., 67–68 passim; cf. 69, 72.

Creflo Dollar

219. Creflo Dollar, *Creflo Dollar Ministries: World Changers*, Trinity Broadcasting Network, 15 September 2002.

220. Creflo Dollar Ministries, "Dr. Creflo A. Dollar Biography" (http://www.creflodollarministries.org/Public/AboutUs/Biography-Creflo-Dollar.aspx).

221. *Creflo Dollar Ministries: World Changers*, Trinity Broadcasting Network, 8 December 2002.

222. Ibid.

223. Ibid.

224. *Praise the Lord*, Trinity Broadcasting Network, 23 August 2001.

225. *Creflo Dollar Ministries: World Changers*, Trinity Broadcasting Network, 15 September 2002.

226. Ibid., 23 May 2002.

227. Creflo Dollar, *Expanding Your Faith*, tape series, tape 3.

228. Ibid., tape series.

29. Creflo Dollar, *The Miracle of Debt Release* audiotape series, apparently from 1999, but tape is copyrighted 2000; *Bible Answer Man*, 5 July 2002.

30. Creflo Dollar, *Our Equality with God Through Righteousness*, video series, 7 January 2001.

31. Creflo Dollar, *Praise the Lord*, Trinity Broadcasting Network, 20 July 1999.

T. D. Jakes

232. T. D. Jakes, *Potter's House*, Trinity Broadcasting Network, 7 June 2004.

233. T. D. Jakes, *Potter's House*, Trinity Broadcasting Network, 23 February 2004.

234. T. D. Jakes, *Praise the Lord: Praise-a-Thon*, Trinity Broadcasting Network, 5 November 2003.

235. T. D. Jakes, *Praise the Lord: Praise-a-Thon*, Trinity Broadcasting Network, 12 November 2001, emphasis added.

236. See http://www.highergroundaaa.com/listing.htm, retrieved 1 August 2008.

237. Gustav Niebuhr and Laurie Goodstein, "The Preachers: A Special Report: New Wave of Evangelists Vying for National Pulpit," *The New York Times*, 1 January 1999, archived online at www.nytimes.com.

238. Jerry L. Buckner, "The Man, His Ministry, and His Movement: Concerns About the Teachings of T. D. Jakes," *Christian Research Journal*, vol. 22, no. 2 (1999), online at www.equip.org; Bob Hunter, "Christianity Still in Crisis: A Word of Faith Update," *Christian Research Journal*, vol. 30, no. 3

(2007), online at www.equip.org. See also Elliot Miller, "T. D. Jakes Responds to the Journal," *Christian Research Journal*, vol. 22, no. 3 (1999), online at www.equip.org.

239. David Van Biema, "Spirit Raiser," *Time*, 17 September 2001, online at http://www.time.com/time/printout/0,8816,1000836,00.html, retrieved 16 July 2008.

240. T. D. Jakes, *The Potter's House*, Trinity Broadcasting Network, 7 June 2004.

241. T. D. Jakes, *The Potter's House*, Trinity Broadcasting Network, 3 December 2001.

242. Ibid.

243. T. D. Jakes, *The Potter's House*, Trinity Broadcasting Network, 7 June 2004.

244. See Elliot Miller, "T. D. Jakes Responds to the Journal," *Christian Research Journal*, vol. 22, no. 3 (1999), online at www.equip.org.

245. T. D. Jakes, "My Views on the Godhead: Jakes Responds to *Christianity Today* Article, Apologetics Journal Criticizes Jakes," christianitytoday.com, 1 February 2000 (http://www.christianitytoday.com/ct/2000/februaryweb-only/13.0b.html, retrieved 1 August 2008).

246. T. D. Jakes, *The Potter's House*, Trinity Broadcasting Network, 20 June 1999.

Rod Parsley

247. Rod Parsley, *Ancient Wells, Living Water* (Lake Mary, FL: Creation House Press, 2003), 130.

248. Rod Parsley, *Praise the Lord*, Trinity Broadcasting Network, 7 August 2003.

249. Rod Parsley, *Breakthrough with Rod Parsley*, Trinity Broadcasting Network, 27 March 2002.

250. Rod Parsley, *Praise the Lord: Praise-a Thon*, Trinity Broadcasting Network, 9 November 2000. On another occasion, Parsley declared, "Healing and prosperity are not a promise, they are an accomplished fact. It's already done. What we've got to learn is how to get heaven out of heaven and in your living room. That's what we need—a little bit of heaven. I said, that's what we need—a little bit of heaven. God's got streets made out of the stuff and we run around thinking we're doing something because we've got a little piece of it on our finger. Let me explain something to you: if God hadn't wanted to break the tentacles of lack off of you, He shouldn't have. God already made up His mind, you heretic hunter! He can't change His mind. He said He takes pleasure in the prosperity of His servants" (*Praise the Lord: Praise-a-Thon*, Trinity Broadcasting Network, 7 November 2003).

251. Rod Parsley, *Praise the Lord*, Trinity Broadcasting Network, 12 June 2003.

252. Ibid.

253. Rod Parsley, *Praise the Lord: Dominion Camp Meeting*, Trinity Broadcasting Network, 6 July 1999.

254. Michael W. Cuneo, *American Exorcism* (New York: Doubleday, 2001), xiii.

255. Rod Parsley, *Praise the Lord: Praise-a-Thon*, Trinity Broadcasting Network, 3 April 2003; *Praise the Lord*, Trinity Broadcasting Network, 10 December 2001.

256. Parsley, *Ancient Wells, Living Water* (Lake Mary, FL: Creation House Press, 2003), 129–30.

257. Ibid., 130.

258. Deborah Marrie, "Locked in Their Own World," *Charisma Magazine*, online at http://www.charismamag.com/display.php?id=9219, retrieved 30 September 2008. Asperger's syndrome is a developmental disorder. The *American Psychiatric Association's Diagnostic and Statistical Manual of Mental Disorders (DSM-IV)* categorizes Asperger's as a separate disorder from autism; however, some mental health professionals consider Asperger's to be a less severe form of autism (Autism Society of America, "What's Unique about Asperger's Disorder?" http://www.autism-society.org/site/PageServer?pagename=life_aspergers, retrieved 30 September 2008).

Frederick K. C. Price

259. Frederick K. C. Price, *Ever Increasing Faith Messenger* (June 1980), 7; quoted in McConnell, *A Different Gospel*, 120.

260. Frederick K. C. Price, *Is Healing for All?* (Tulsa: Harrison House, 1976), 20.

261. Frederick Price, *Faith, Foolishness, or Presumption?* (Tulsa: Harrison House, 1979), 88.

262. Betty Price, "A Praise Report," *Ever Increasing Faith Messenger* 12, 3 (Summer 1991); Pat Hays, "Betty Price Speaks at 1991 'Wisdom from Above' Luncheon," ibid., 13, 1 (Winter 1992):12–13.

263. Quoted in McConnell, *A Different Gospel*, 4.

264. "FAQ-Crenshaw Christian Center," Ever Increasing Faith Ministries, http://www.crenshawchristiancenter.net/ecomm/index.php?option=com_content&task=view&id=36&Itemid=4,

accessed 15 July 2008. Earlier editions of *Christianity in Crisis* reported 16,000 members (cf. John Dart, "Huge 'FaithDome' in L.A.," *Los Angeles Times* [9 September 1989], Part II, 9–10; cf. Glenn W. Gohr, "Price, Frederick K. C.," *Dictionary of Pentecostal & Charismatic Movements*, 727).

265. Stephen Strang, "The Ever Increasing Faith of Fred Price," *Charisma & Christian Life* (May 1985), 23; cf. Gohr, "Price, Frederick K. C.," 727.

266. See Strang, "The Ever Increasing Faith of Fred Price," 24–25; Gohr, "Price," *Dictionary of Pentecostal & Charismatic Movements*, 727; Brad Darrach, "Masking His Biblical Teaching in Theatrics, Pastor Fred Price Gets His Message Across Swimmingly," *People* (10 October 1983), 48, 53; John Dart, "Scholarly Black Pastor Has a Burgeoning Flock," *Los Angeles Times* (7 December 1981), 6–8.

267. "Special Report: Campmeeting '83," *The Word of Faith* 16, 10 (October 1983), 11b.

268. Strang, "The Ever Increasing Faith of Fred Price," 25; Dart, "Scholarly Black Pastor Has a Burgeoning Flock," 8.

269. Frederick K. C. Price, "Name It and Claim It! What Saith the WORD? . . . ", *Ever Increasing Faith Messenger* 10, 3 (Summer 1989):2, capitalization in original.

270. Flo Jenkins-Bryant, "We've Come This Far by Faith! . . . and It's Time to Rejoice!!!" *Ever Increasing Faith Messenger* 11, 1 (Winter 1990):8.

271. Frederick K. C. Price, *Ever Increasing Faith*, Trinity Broadcasting Network, 9 December 1990, available from Crenshaw Christian Center (audiotape #CR-A2).

272. Price, *Ever Increasing Faith*, Trinity Broadcasting Network, 16 November 1990.

273. Price, *Ever Increasing Faith*, Trinity Broadcasting Network, 3 May 1992.

274. Frederick K. C. Price, *Identification #3* (Inglewood, CA: Ever Increasing Faith Ministries, 1980), audiotape #FP545, side 1.

275. Frederick K. C. Price, *Ever Increasing Faith Messenger* (June 1980), 7; quoted in McConnell, *A Different Gospel*, 120.

276. Frederick Price, *Ever Increasing Faith*, Trinity Broadcasting Network, 23 November 1990.

277. Ibid.

John Avanzini

278. John Avanzini, *Praise the Lord: Praise-a-Thon*, Trinity Broadcasting Network, 15 September 1988.

279. John Avanzini, *Believer's Voice of Victory*, Trinity Broadcasting Network, 20 January 1991.

280. The Greek word in the passage, *chiton*, is properly defined as a "*tunic, shirt*, a garment worn next to the skin, and by both sexes" (see Walter Bauer, William F. Arndt, and F. Wilbur Gingrich, *A Greek-English Lexicon of the New Testament* and Other Early Christian Literature, rev. ed. [Chicago: University of Chicago Press, 1952], 890b, emphasis in original); cf. F. F. Bruce, *The Gospel of John* (Grand Rapids: Wm. B. Eerdmans Publishing Co., 1983), 370; and Merrill C. Tenney, "The Gospel of John," ed. by Frank E. Gaebelein, in *The Expositor's Bible Commentary* (Grand Rapids: Zondervan, 1981), 9:81.

281. Avanzini, *Believer's Voice of Victory*, Trinity Broadcasting Network, 20 January 1991.

282. John Avanzini, *Praise the Lord*, Trinity Broadcasting Network, 1 August 1989.

283. Avanzini, *Praise the Lord: Praise-a-Thon*, Trinity Broadcasting Network, April 1991.

284. John Avanzini, *It's Not Working, Brother John!* (Tulsa: Harrison House, 1992).

285. Avanzini, *Praise the Lord: Praise-a-Thon*, Trinity Broadcasting Network, 1 November 1990.

286. Avanzini, *Praise the Lord: Praise-a-Thon*, Trinity Broadcasting Network, 9 April 1992.

287. Benny Hinn, *Praise the Lord: Praise-a-Thon*, Trinity Broadcasting Network, 6 November 1990.

Robert Tilton

288. Scott Baradell, "Robert Tilton's Heart of Darkness," *Dallas Observer*, 6 February 1992, 19–20.

289. Ibid., 13, 18.

290. Ibid., 18.

291. Ibid., 19–20.

292. Ibid., 13, 18, 19–20.

293. Ibid., 13.

294. Howard Swindle and Allen Pusey, "Tilton Ends Syndication of His Sunday Services," *Dallas Morning News* (13 August 1992), 1A, 28A; Terry Box, "Backers Think Tilton Will Endure" (16 February

1992), 1A, 12A–13A; Jim Jones, "The Undercover Thorn in Robert Tilton," *Fort Worth Star-Telegram* (26 January 1992), 1A, 20A.

295. Tilton's Arbitron ratings dropped 39 percent following the ABC television exposé in November 1991. (See Allen Pusey and Howard Swindle, "Tilton Bankrolled '83 TV License Bid, Source and Files Say" [12 July 1992], 1A, 29A.)

296. Nancy St. Pierre, "Tilton's Wife Tells of Finances," *Dallas Morning News* (5 March 1992), 1A, 7A; Terry Box, "Tax Appraiser Is Scrutinizing Tilton's Church" (22 March 1992), 1A; see similar estimates of Tilton's ministry income in Trinity Foundation release, "Does Word of Faith = Wheel of Fortune?" (9 December 1991); Box, "Backers Think Tilton Will Endure," 1A, 12A–13A.

297. "Guilt prompts Tilton worker to quit" [Associated Press report from Tulsa, OK] *Denton [Texas] Record Chronicle* (16 December 1991). On July 9, 1992, ABC *PrimeTime Live* interviewed two close assistants of Tilton who have come forward since the first report. Brenda Reynolds said she had been the nanny to the Tiltons' children for six years. When she tried to bring prayer request letters from the garage into the house for Tilton to pray over them, she said Tilton told her to throw them away. "I know for a fact he didn't pray over them, and I took them to the trash myself," said Reynolds.

Associated Press reported in December 1991 that an assistant manager of a paper-recycling plant in Tulsa had found thousands of prayer requests sent to Tilton. (See John Archer, "PrimeTime Lies?" *Charisma & Christian Life*, 17, 7 [February 1992]:30–31.) Another account states that a CNN camera crew found "tons" of requests in a recycling bin in Tulsa. (See Trinity Foundation release, "Tons of Tilton Prayer Requests Discovered in Recycle Center" [9 December 1991].)

Televangelist-watchdog Ole Anthony, president of the Trinity Foundation in Dallas, testified at a federal court hearing that he, too, found evidently unanswered prayer requests in trash bins outside Tulsa businesses. Anthony said he turned the evidence over to the Texas attorney general in November 1991. (See Nancy St. Pierre, "Man Sifted Tilton's Trash for Evidence," *Dallas Morning News* [6 March 1992], 1A, 6A.)

Tilton has always denied publicly he threw away unread prayer requests but admitted in a videotaped court deposition for the Texas attorney general's office in March 1992—made public by ABC over Tilton's objections—that he did not pray over every letter but prayed over computer printout lists of some letters. What did he do with these letters? "I threw them away," said Tilton.

298. *PrimeTime Lies*, broadcast in place of Robert Tilton's regular *Success-N-Life* television program (18 August 1992).

The ABC charges against Tilton were not very convincingly rebutted in Tilton's response. For example, the rebuttal video tried to portray the Tiltons' former housekeeper/nanny, Brenda Reynolds, as somehow not in the position to have knowledge of Tilton throwing away unread prayer-request letters stored in the family home where she worked for six years.

Tilton has sued ABC News, its *PrimeTime Live* show anchor Diane Sawyer, and others for libel (Sylvia Martinez, "Tilton Sues ABC News, 'PrimeTime,'" *Dallas Morning News* [11 November 1992], 29A, 33A).

299. Robert Tilton, *Success-N-Life* television program, 22 November 1991.

300. Ibid.; Tilton has also alleged that the dumpster full of prayer requests found by ABC was actually planted by enemies to discredit him. (See Christopher Lee, "Tilton's Wife Defends Ministry, Blasts TV Exposé of Husband," *Dallas Morning News* [25 November 1991], 1A, 12A.) Excerpts from Tilton's televised replies about "ink poisoning" and the "stolen and planted" letters were aired on ABC's *PrimeTime Live* update, July 9, 1992.

301. Ibid.; Tilton quoted Jim Moore, president of Response Media, which processes Tilton ministry's mail, as saying his employees became ill due to an allergy to a certain type of yellow ink. None of Moore's employees evidently reported getting "strokes in the brain" or having to undergo plastic surgery as Tilton claimed for himself.

302. Sean Rowe, "Second Coming," *Dallas Observer*, 6 November 1997, online at http://www.dallasobserver.com/1997-11-06/news/second-coming, retrieved 1 August 2008.

Marilyn Hickey

303. Marilyn Hickey, *Claim Your Miracles* (Denver: Marilyn Hickey Ministries, n.d.), audiotape #186, side 2.

304. Marilyn Hickey Ministries, direct-mail piece (n.d. [ca. 1992]), emphasis in original.

305. Ibid.

306. Hickey, *Claim Your Miracles*, side 2.

307. Hickey, *Today with Marilyn*, Trinity Broadcasting Network, 11 April 1991.

308. Hickey, *Breakthroughs to Faith*, audiotape (Denver: Marilyn Hickey Ministries, n.d.) 1105, side 2.

309. Hickey, *Claim Your Miracles*, side 1.

310. Ibid., side 2.

Charles Capps

311. Charles Capps, *Dynamics of Faith & Confession* (Tulsa: Harrison House, 1987), 86–87; cf. Charles Capps, *Authority in Three Worlds* (Tulsa: Harrison House, 1982), 76, 85.

312. Charles Capps, *The Tongue—A Creative Force* (Tulsa: Harrison House, 1976), 91.

313. Capps, *Dynamics of Faith*, 86–87; cf. Capps, *Authority in Three Worlds*, 76, 85.

314. Ibid., 83, emphasis added; cf. Capps, *Dynamics of Faith*, 88; Capps, *The Tongue*, 19.

315. Capps, *Dynamics of Faith*, 79–80.

316. See McConnell, 4. Capps claims that Kenneth Hagin's book *Right and Wrong Thinking* was responsible for his move into positive confession. "It went off inside me like a bombshell," says Capps. "I knew instantly that this was truth" (Capps, *The Tongue*, 66).

317. Charles Capps, *The Substance of Things* (Tulsa: Harrison House, 1990), 41–42.

318. Ibid., 42.

Jerry Savelle

319. Jerry Savelle, *Framing Your World with the Word of God*, part 2 (Fort Worth, TX: Jerry Savelle Evangelistic Association, Inc., n.d.), audiotape #SS-36, side 1.

320. See his http://profile.myspace.com/index.cfm?fuseaction=user.viewprofile&friendid=83173745.

321. Kenneth Copeland, *Spirit, Soul and Body I* (Fort Worth, TX: Kenneth Copeland Ministries, 1985), audiotape #01-0601, side 1.

322. Savelle, *Framing Your World with the Word of God*, part 2, side 1.

323. Ibid.

324. Ibid., side 2.

325. Ibid., side 1.

Morris Cerullo

326. Morris Cerullo, *The Endtime Manifestation of the Sons of God* (San Diego: Morris Cerullo World Evangelism, Inc., n.d.), audiotape 1, sides 1 and 2.

327. Morris Cerullo, *The Miracle Book* [special charter ed.] (San Diego, CA: Morris Cerullo World Evangelism, 1984), ix.

328. "God's Faithful, Anointed Servant, Morris Cerullo" [brochure] (San Diego, CA: Morris Cerullo World Evangelism, n.d.).

329. *7 Point Outreach—World Evangelism and You* (San Diego: Morris Cerullo World Evangelism, n.d.), [4].

330. Cerullo, *Miracle Book*, xi.

331. *7 Point Outreach*, [4].

332. Cerullo, *Miracle Book*, xi.

333. Ibid.

334. Ibid., xii.

335. "God's Faithful, Anointed Servant, Morris Cerullo."

336. Cerullo, *Miracle Book*, x.

337. Morris Cerullo, "Few Are Chosen," *Deeper Life* 21: 5 (June 1981), 2.

338. Cerullo, *The Endtime Manifestation of the Sons of God*, sides 1 and 2.

339. "God's Faithful, Anointed Servant, Morris Cerullo."

340. Laura Monteros, "The Rebirth of Morris Cerullo," *Los Angeles Herald-Examiner*, 18 November 1978.

341. Morris Cerullo, "From the Heart," *Victory* (January/February 1992), 6, emphasis in original.

Paul Crouch

342. Paul Crouch, *Praise the Lord: Praise-a-Thon* program, Trinity Broadcasting Network, 2 April 1991.

343. Mark Pinsky, "FCC Reviewing Trinity's Minority Subsidiary," *Los Angeles Times* (29 September 1991), B7.

344. So Trinity Broadcasting Network claims, as of April 2008, online at http://www.tbn.org/index.php/7 .html?nid=254, accessed 16 July 2008; cf. differing details at TBN's "About Us" page, http://www .tbn.org/index.php/3.html, accessed 16 July 2008.

345. Paul Crouch, *Praise the Lord* [TBN newsletter] 19, 7 (July 1992):[1], capitalization in original.

346. Many of today's most well-known Faith and prosperity preachers have their own programs on TBN, including Kenneth Copeland, Frederick K. C. Price, Benny Hinn, Marilyn Hickey, John Avanzini, Dwight Thompson, T. L. Osborn, and Oral and Richard Roberts.

347. John Avanzini, *Praise the Lord: Praise-a-Thon*, Trinity Broadcasting Network, 6 November 1990.

348. *Praise the Lord: Praise-a-Thon*, Trinity Broadcasting Network, 7 November 2003.

349. *Praise the Lord: Praise-a-Thon*, Trinity Broadcasting Network, 4 November 2002.

350. Roy Blizzard has appeared on the *Praise the Lord* program and had his own weekly show, *Treasures of the Jewish World*, sponsored by Trinity Broadcasting Network. On Blizzard's anti-Trinitarian stance, see Roy Blizzard, "The fact of the matter . . .," *Through Their Eyes* 2, 1 (January 1987):19.

351. Joseph Good is a frequent guest on the *Praise the Lord* program and has two weekly shows, *Footsteps of the Messiah* and *Ancient Israel*, sponsored by Trinity Broadcasting Network. On Good's denial of Christ's deity during His incarnation and after the Resurrection, see Joseph Good, *Difficult Verses* (Port Arthur, TX: Hatikva Ministries, April 1990), audiotape #5.

352. Paul Crouch, *Praise the Lord*, Trinity Broadcasting Network, 5 September 1991.

353. Paul Crouch, *Praise the Lord: Praise-a-Thon*, Trinity Broadcasting Network, 2 April 1991.

354. Paul Crouch, *Praise the Lord: Praise-a-Thon*, Trinity Broadcasting Network, April 1990.

355. Paul Crouch, *Praise the Lord: Praise-a-Thon*, 2 April 1991.

356. Paul Crouch, *Praise the Lord*, Trinity Broadcasting Network, 31 July 1992.

357. Paul Crouch, *Praise the Lord*, Trinity Broadcasting Network, 18 February 1986 (rebroadcast 6 August 1991).

Juanita Bynum

358. Juanita Bynum, *Praise the Lord: Praise-a-Thon*, Trinity Broadcasting Network, 5 November 2002.

359. Ibid.

360. Juanita Bynum, *Praise the Lord*, Trinity Broadcasting Network, 28 March 2001.

361. Bynum, *Praise the Lord: Praise-a-Thon*, 5 November 2002.

Paula White

362. Paula White, *Praise the Lord: Praise-a-Thon*, Trinity Broadcasting Network, 3 November 2003.

363. Paula White Ministries, "Paula's Life Story" (www.paulawhite.org/content/view/115/88888970/), retrieved 19 June 2008.

364. Paula White Ministries, "Follow God's Principles 'To Have it All,'" http://www.paulawhite.org/ content/view/213/88888897/, retrieved 19 June 2008.

365. White, *Praise the Lord: Praise-a-Thon*, 3 November 2003.

366. Ibid.

367. White, *Praise the Lord: Praise-a-Thon*, Trinity Broadcasting Network, 5 April 2005.

368. Paula White Ministries, "Understanding the Power of Words over Your Money," http://www .paulawhite.org/content/view/172/88888897, 19 June 2008.

369. White, *Praise the Lord*, Trinity Broadcasting Network, 6 February 2004.

370. White, *Praise the Lord*, Trinity Broadcasting Network, 10 June 2003.

Todd Bentley

371. Todd Bentley, *Journey into the Miraculous: Experiencing the Touch of the Supernatural God* (Shippensburg, PA: Destiny Image Publishers, 2008), 239.

372. Steve Strang, "The Long-Term Effects of Revival," Strang Report, 22 May 2008, online at http:// www.strangreport.com/2008_05_01_archive.html.

373. Che Ahn, undated video on YouTube at http://www.youtube.com/watch?v=lIAuD_OEcUs, accessed 10 September 2008.

374. Fresh Fire Ministries Web site at http://www.freshfire.ca/index.php?Id=101&pid=8&pid=8, retrieved 5 July 2008.

375. Bentley, *Journey into the Miraculous*, 83.

376. Ibid., 86.

377. Ibid., 97–98.

378. Ibid., 109.

379. Ibid., 109.

380. Ibid., 113.

381. Ibid., 112.

382. Ibid., 112–13.

383. Ibid., 117.

384. Ibid., 133.

385. Ibid., 223.

386. Ibid., 232–33.

387. Ibid., 239.

388. Ibid., 240.

389. Ibid., 242.

390. Todd Bentley, video posted 3 February 2008, online at http://www.youtube.com/watch?v=2ApnwQXW6Ns, accessed 5 June 2008.

391. See God TV archived broadcast, 7 June 2008.

392. Todd Bentley, edited by Kathy Thorne, "Encounter with Heaven," part 3, posted online at http://www.sidroth.org/site/News2?abbr=art_&page=NewsArticle&id=6569&news_iv_ctrl=1054, accessed 8 July 2008.

393. Ibid.

394. Bentley, *Journey into the Miraculous*, 168.

395. See Hinn, *Good Morning, Holy Spirit*, 26, 42.

396. Bentley, *Journey into the Miraculous*, 86.

397. Stanley M. Burgess and Eduard M. Van Der Maas, eds., *The New International Dictionary of Pentecostal and Charismatic Movements*, revised and expanded edition (Grand Rapids: Zondervan, 2002), 441.

398. Todd Bentley, video posted 27 April 2008, online at http://www.youtube.com/watch?v=TuqwjUyb9io, accessed 5 June 2008.

399. Rodney Howard-Browne, *Flowing in the Holy Ghost* (Louisville, KY.: RHBEA Publications, 1991), 54.

400. See video montage of Todd Bentley, posted 3 June 2008, online at http://www.youtube.com/watch?v=QAgLVFx_yh8, accessed 5 July 2008.

401. Howard-Browne, *Flowing in the Holy Ghost*, 53–54.

402. Todd Bentley, video posted 26 June 2008, online at http://www.youtube.com/watch?v=DUTCWLoD4-4, accessed 5 July 2008.

403. See Charles Chandler, "Q & A with preacher Todd Bentley," *Charlotte Observer*, 18 June 2008, online at http://www.charlotte.com/345/story/676593.html, retrieved 19 June 2008; "Florida Outpouring—Resurrection #16," video posted online at http://www.youtube.com/watch?v=Mf6ewKmSMWU, 31 May 2008, retrieved 15 July 2008.

404. In the video clip, "Florida Outpouring—Resurrection #16," Bentley claims that he has received "thousands and thousands" of testimonies of healings and he is preparing to turn the medical reports and documentation of these healings over to the media.

405. See http://www.god.tv/revival_god, archived broadcast of 11 July 2008.

406. William A. Dembski, "First-Person: Neither faith nor healing," *Baptist Press News*, posted 11 July 2008, online at http://www.bpnews.net/bpnews.asp?id=28460, retrieved 11 July 2008.

407. Larry Thomas, *No Laughing Matter* (Excelsior Springs, MO: Double Crown, 1995), 48.

408. The coined term *evangelastic* is a combination of *evangelistic* and *elastic*, and in this context means Counterfeit Revivalists habitually stretch the truth beyond recognition.

409. Cincilla Grant, "'Holy Water' Triggers Healing Revival," *Charisma*, June, 1996: 21–23.

410. Robert W. Marks, *The Story of Hypnotism* (New York: Prentice-Hall, 1947), 150.

411. Ibid., 190.

412. Ibid., 191.

413. Charles Baudouin, *Suggestion and Autosuggestion* (London: George Allen and Unwin, 1954), 80.

414. Marks, *The Story of Hypnotism*, 193.

415. Ibid., 195.

416. Baudouin, *Suggestion and Autosuggestion*, 82.

Chapter 4: Charting the Course

1. Kenneth Copeland, *Holy Bible: Kenneth Copeland Reference Edition* (Fort Worth, TX: Kenneth Copeland Ministries, 1991), 129, emphasis in original.

2. Frederick K. C. Price, *Ever Increasing Faith Messenger* (June 1980), 7; quoted in D. R. McConnell, *A Different Gospel* (Peabody, MA: Hendrickson Publishers, 1988), 120.

3. Kenneth Copeland, *Believer's Voice of Victory*, 21 April 1991. This message was originally delivered at the Full Gospel Motorcycle Rally Association 1990 Rally at Eagle Mt. Lake, Texas.

4. Kenneth Copeland, *Walking in the Realm of the Miraculous* (Fort Worth, TX: Kenneth Copeland Ministries, 1979), 77.

5. Kenneth E. Hagin, "The Incarnation," *The Word of Faith* 13, 12 (December 1980):14.

6. Kenneth Copeland, *God's Covenant with Man II* (Fort Worth, TX: Kenneth Copeland Ministries, 1985), audiotape #01-4404, side 2.

7. Benny Hinn, *"Rise and be healed!"* (Orlando, FL: Celebration Publishers, 1991), 62.

8. Ibid., 47–48.

Part Two: *Faith in Faith*

1. Ephesians 6:16.

2. Marilyn Hickey, *Claim Your Miracles* (Denver: Marilyn Hickey Ministries, n.d.), audiotape #186, side 2.

3. T. D. Jakes, *The Potter's House*, Trinity Broadcasting Network, 23 February 2004.

Chapter 5: Force of Faith

1. Joyce Meyer, Joyce Meyer Ministries broadcast, Trinity Broadcasting Network, 16 July 2002. Elsewhere, in a chapter titled "Watch Your Mouth," Meyer writes, "Words are containers for power. They carry either creative power or destructive power" (Joyce Meyer, *Eight Ways to Keep the Devil Under Your Feet* [New York: Warner Faith, 2002], 87–88).

2. Kenneth Copeland, *The Force of Faith* (Fort Worth, TX: KCP Publications, 1989), 10.

3. Kenneth Copeland, *The Laws of Prosperity* (Fort Worth, TX: Kenneth Copeland Publications, 1974), 19.

4. Kenneth Copeland, *Forces of the Re-created Human Spirit* (Fort Worth, TX: Kenneth Copeland Ministries, 1982), 8.

5. Kenneth Copeland, *Spirit, Soul and Body I* (Fort Worth, TX: Kenneth Copeland Ministries, 1985), audiotape #01-0601, side 1.

6. Kenneth Copeland, *Freedom from Fear* (Fort Worth, TX: Kenneth Copeland Ministries, 1980), 11–12.

7. Ibid.; cf. Copeland, *The Force of Faith*, 11.

8. Charles Capps, *The Tongue—A Creative Force* (Tulsa: Harrison House, 1976), 92.

9. Copeland, *Forces of the Re-created Human Spirit*, 15; cf. 14.

10. Kenneth Copeland, *The Power of the Tongue* (Fort Worth, TX: KCP Publications, 1980), 4.

11. Ibid.

12. E. W. Kenyon, *Two Kinds of Faith*, 14th ed. (Lynnwood, WA: Kenyon's Gospel Publishing Society, 1969), 20.

13. Byrne, *The Secret*, 4.

14. Ibid., 15.

15. Ron Rhodes, *The Counterfeit Christ of the New Age Movement* (Grand Rapids: Baker Book House, 1990), 149.

16. See D. R. McConnell, *A Different Gospel* (Peabody, MA: Hendrickson Publishers, 1988), 3–12.
17. Creflo Dollar, "The Just Shall Live By Faith," *Changing Your World*, Trinity Broadcasting Network, 20 September 1998.
18. Jerry Savelle, *Framing Your World with the Word of God*, part 2 (Fort Worth, TX: Jerry Savelle Evangelistic Assn., n.d.), audiotape #SS-36, side 1.
19. Savelle, *Framing Your World with the Word of God*, part 1, side 1.
20. Charles Capps, *Authority in Three Worlds* (Tulsa: Harrison House, 1982), 24, emphasis in original.
21. Robert Tilton, *Success-N-Life* television program (18 October 1990).
22. Kenneth Copeland, *Authority of the Believer II* (Fort Worth, TX: Kenneth Copeland Ministries, 1987), audiotape #01-0302, side 1.
23. See, for example, Kenneth E. Hagin, *Having Faith in Your Faith* (Tulsa: Kenneth Hagin Ministries, 1988).
24. *The Analytical Greek Lexicon* (Grand Rapids: Zondervan Publishing House, 1970 [Orig. London: Samuel Bagster & Sons, 1852; rev. ed. 1860]), 419, col. 1.
25. Louis Berkhof, *Systematic Theology*, 4th rev. ed. (Grand Rapids: Wm. B. Eerdmans Publishing Co., 1949), 500.
26. Osteen, *Become a Better You*, 112, emphasis added. Osteen wrenches Romans 4:17b out of context; the verse actually reads, "He [Abraham] is our father in the sight of God, in whom he believed—the God who gives life to the dead and calls things that are not as though they were."
27. Joyce Meyer, *Enjoying Everyday Life*, Trinity Broadcasting Network, 21 August 2008.

Chapter 6: Formula of Faith

1. Rhonda Byrne, *The Secret* (New York: Atria Books/Beyond Words, 2006), 47ff.
2. E. W. Kenyon, *The Two Kinds of Faith: Faith's Secret Revealed* (Lynnwood, WA: Kenyon's Gospel Publishing Society, 1942), 67.
3. Kenneth E. Hagin, *Having Faith in Your Faith* (Tulsa: Kenneth Hagin Ministries, 1988), 4.
4. Ibid., 5.
5. Ibid., 4–5, emphasis in original. Hagin and the other Faith teachers almost always point to this passage to "prove" that Jesus taught His disciples to have faith in their faith so that whatsoever they believe and say will come to pass. That notion, however, is utterly false. The context of the passage makes it clear that we are to place our faith in God and His awesome power, rather than our own frail human devices (v. 22; cf. chapter 9, "The Faith of God"). Moreover, according to Jesus' own words here, it is *God*, not the believer, who brings about the end results. Thus Jesus says, "It will be done *for* you" (NIV), not "*you* will do it;" "believe that you have *received* it" (NIV), not "believe that you have *taken* it." And this will only happen when we *pray*; that is, when we *ask God*, who answers those requests that are in accordance with His will (1 John 5:14). It is not some substance called faith, but God Himself who ultimately determines which "mountains are thrown into the sea"; He is also the One who carries out the task. If we are to observe the teaching of Scripture, our faith is to be in *God*, not in our faith or in our words.

   Hagin also points to the healing of the woman suffering from a hemorrhage (Mark 5:25–34; see Hagin, *How to Write Your Own Ticket with God* [Tulsa: Kenneth Hagin Ministries, 1979], 7–8, 11–16) to bolster his "faith in faith" error. Yet the careful Bible reader will recognize that the object of the woman's faith—which was responsible for her healing (v. 34)—was not her own faith, but Christ (v. 28); why else would she be determined to get to Him if she really believed that exercising faith in her faith would cure her? She received healing not because she had faith in her faith but because she had *faith in Christ* (vv. 27–29). One commentator writes: "When Jesus attributes the woman's restoration to her faith, i.e., her trust and confidence in Jesus, he does not make her faith the *causa efficiens* [or "efficient cause"], but only the *causa instrumentalis* [or "instrumental cause"] . . . the hand that receives the gift" (R. C. H. Lenski, *The Interpretation of St. Mark's Gospel* [Minneapolis, MN: Augsburg Publishing House, 1964], 225).
6. Hagin, *How to Write Your Own Ticket with God*, 2–3. This booklet has been incorporated as chapter 6 of Kenneth E. Hagin, *Exceedingly Growing Faith*, 2d ed. (Tulsa: Kenneth Hagin Ministries, 1988), 73–74.
7. Hagin, *How to Write Your Own Ticket with God*, 3.

8. Ibid., 5.

9. Ibid., emphasis deleted.

10. Ibid., 6.

11. Ibid., 6–8 passim.

12. Ibid., 11.

13. Ibid., 12.

14. Ibid., 17.

15. Ibid., 18, emphasis in original.

16. Ibid., 19, emphasis deleted.

17. Ibid., 20.

18. Ibid., 20.

19. Ibid., 21.

20. Ibid., 23, emphasis in original.

21. Charles Capps, *The Tongue—A Creative Force* (Tulsa: Harrison House, 1976), 91.

22. Norvel Hayes, *Praise the Lord*, Trinity Broadcasting Network, 13 November 1990.

23. Paul's use of strong language is also found in such verses as Galatians 5:12 and 1 Timothy 4:1–2.

24. Other instances where Jesus issued harsh condemnations of false teachers can be found in the following passages: Matthew 3:7; 6:2, 5, 16; 7:5; 12:34; 22:18; 23:13–19, 23–29; Luke 3:7; 6:42; 11:39–52; 12:1, 56; John 8:44.

25. Kenneth Copeland, *Inner Image of the Covenant* (Fort Worth, TX: Kenneth Copeland Ministries, 1985), audiotape #01-4406, side 2.

26. Kenneth Copeland, "The Forgotten Power of Hope (part II)," *Believer's Voice of Victory*, 20, 3 (March 1992):2–3.

27. Copeland, *Inner Image of the Covenant*, audiotape side 2.

28. Ibid.

29. Ibid.

30. The Church Universal and Triumphant is one New Age group that greatly emphasizes "the scientific use of the mantra or the dynamic decree of the Word," otherwise known as "the exercise of God's power according to the spoken Word" (Mark and Elizabeth Clare Prophet, *The Lost Teachings of Jesus 2: Mysteries of the Higher Self* [Livingston, MT: Summit University Press, 1988], 144, 207; cf. 103. Also see Mark L. Prophet, *The Soulless One* [Corwin Springs, MT: Summit Publications, 1981 (orig. 1965)], 34).

31. Copeland, *Inner Image of the Covenant*, audiotape, side 2.

32. Ibid.

33. Kenneth Copeland, *Believer's Voice of Victory*, Trinity Broadcasting Network, 28 March 1991.

34. Paul Yonggi Cho, *The Fourth Dimension*, vols. 1 and 2 (South Plainfield, NJ: Bridge Publishing, 1979, 1983).

35. Cho, *The Fourth Dimension*, vol. 1 (1979), 36–43, 64; vol. 2 (1983), 38–39.

36. Ibid., vol. 1, 64.

37. Ibid., vol. 1, 37.

38. Ibid., vol. 1, 18. This quote does not appear in the second version, vol. 2, 30.

39. Ibid., vol. 2, 30. This comment does not appear in the first version (see volume 1, 18–19, for first part of the interview) until the end of the question session (vol. 1, 20).

40. Ibid., vol. 2, 30–31. In the first version, the question is phrased differently, and the three choices are "Asian, Caucasian, or Black?" (vol. 1, 19).

41. Ibid., vol. 2, 30. Cf. vol. 1, 19: "Number three: do you want your husband slim and nice looking, or just pleasantly plump?" "I want to have him skinny." The profession is asked as Question No. 5 in the first story.

42. Ibid., vol. 1, 20–21; vol. 2, 30–31.

43. Ibid., vol. 1, 35.

44. Ibid., 65.

45. Ibid., vol. 2, 68.

46. Ibid., vol. 1, ch. 3, "The Creative Power of the Spoken Word," 67–86, passim, e.g., emphasis added: "So men, by exploring their spiritual sphere of the fourth dimension through the development of

concentrated visions and dreams in their imaginations, can brood over and *incubate* the third dimension, influencing and changing it. This is what the Holy Spirit taught me" (39–40); "you have the fourth dimension in your heart, and it . . . has *dominion over the three material dimensions* . . . Through dominion in the fourth dimension—the realm of faith—you can give order to your circumstances and situations . . . give beauty to the ugly and chaotic, and healing to the hurt and suffering" (66); "*use the spoken word*: to create the power to have a successful personal life" (71–72); "Then God spoke, '. . . Don't just beg and beg for what you need. *Give the word* . . . As I did when creating the world, *speak* forth. Say "let there be light," or say, "let there be firmament," (73–74); "through the fourth dimension I can incubate the third dimension, and *correct it*" (78); "the *spoken* word has powerful creativity" (87).

47. Rather than teach their followers to walk by the power of the Holy Spirit, a number of Faith teachers encourage them to tap into the same "power source" used by metaphysical practitioners, New Agers, Yogis, Soka Gakkai Buddhists, and other assorted occultists. Sadly enough, it seems that they are doing so because their methods supposedly work. Yet if the methods used by occult groups are indeed able to produce miraculous results, then these methods should give Christians even greater pause. After all, any supernatural power that energizes anti-Christian groups cannot be of God (cf. Matthew 12:22–28; Deuteronomy 13:1–5). And if the source is not divine, then it can only derive from fallen humanity (in which case it is merely a delusion) or fallen angels (in which case it is demonic) or some combination of the two. Despite such obvious dangers, the Faith teachers persist in promoting such practices.

48. Benny Hinn, *Praise the Lord*, Trinity Broadcasting Network, 1 June 1989. Hinn's story seems odd in light of the fact that Wiccans (or witches) generally hold all forms of life to be sacred, due for the most part to their pantheistic worldview (all is God). As such, Wiccans typically stand in opposition to rituals, activities, and practices that are harmful to nature in general and animals in particular.

49. See, for example, Capps, *The Tongue—A Creative Force*, 127–28; and Kenneth Copeland, *The Power of the Tongue* (Fort Worth, TX: Kenneth Copeland Ministries, 1980), 3.

50. In one sense it may be said that Proverbs 18:21 has a special relevance to Solomon (see heading in Proverbs 10), as he is the one who penned it. The verse may therefore be legitimately interpreted as an allusion to Solomon's power to pronounce death or life (condemnation or pardon) over his subjects. Others see this text as Solomon's advice to his successor, who would one day take over his father's responsibility. Still another possible way to look at the passage is to consider how our spoken words affect another person's feelings (12:18, 25; 16:24), self-image (29:5), and convictions (10:21; 11:9), as well as our own and other people's attitudes toward that person (18:8). There can be no denying that what people say often affects outlooks and perceptions, which in turn may alter intervening and subsequent circumstances; yet nowhere does the Bible teach that humans can speak things into existence (see James Kinnebrew, "The Charismatic Doctrine of Positive Confession: A Historical, Exegetical, and Theological Critique," doctoral dissertation, Mid-America Baptist Seminary, 1988, 185–88; and Derek Kidner, *The Proverbs: An Introduction and Commentary*, from the *Tyndale Old Testament Commentary* series, ed. by D. J. Wiseman [Downers Grove, IL: InterVarsity Press, 1964], 15:46–47).

The Faith teachers are also fond of quoting the latter portion of Romans 4:17 (". . . even God, who quickeneth the dead, and calleth those things which be not as though they were" [KJV]) in claiming that human speech literally contains the power of creation. However, as is obvious, this verse is a direct reference to God. Applying the passage to humanity, whether redeemed or not, diminishes the sheer magnificence and immensity of God's power. To suggest that believers are capable of performing such acts of creation is tantamount to exalting humanity to godhood, which is clearly unbiblical. There is, after all, only one God, who alone is capable of calling whatever He chooses into existence (Isaiah 43:10; 44:6, 24). "Calling into existence" is the literary terminology chosen by the Scripture writers to express what we creatures can never personally accomplish—namely, the creation of something from nothing. "God's voice" does not serve as the substance for material things. Rather, "God's voice" represents His ability or authority to create from nothing.

51. Capps, *The Tongue—A Creative Force*, 67, emphasis in original.

52. Frederick K. C. Price, "Prayer: Do You Know What Prayer Is . . . and How to Pray?" *The Word Study Bible* (Tulsa: Harrison House, 1990), 1178.

53. Creflo Dollar, *Creflo Dollar Crusade*, Trinity Broadcasting Network, 9 February 1999.

54. Ibid.

55. Todd Bentley, "Bentley–Receive Resurrection Power—Lakeland Florida," (http://www.youtube.com/watch?v=u1DGXFg7cKY), 6 June 2008, accessed 9 September 2008.

56. Joel Osteen, *Discover the Champion in You*, 3 May 2004, emphasis added.

Chapter 7: Faith of God

1. Creflo Dollar, "The Just Shall Live by Faith," *Changing Your World*, Trinity Broadcasting Network, 20 September 1998.

2. Kenneth Copeland, *The Force of Faith* (Fort Worth, TX: KCP Publications, 1989), 14.

3. Kenneth Copeland, *Spirit, Soul and Body I* (Fort Worth, TX: Kenneth Copeland Ministries, 1985), audiotape #01-0601, side 1.

4. Kenneth Copeland, *Praise the Lord: Praise-a-Thon*, Trinity Broadcasting Network, April 1988.

5. Frederick K. C. Price, *Ever Increasing Faith*, Trinity Broadcasting Network (1 May 1992), audiotape #PR11; Kenneth Copeland, *God's Covenants with Man II* (Fort Worth, TX: Kenneth Copeland Ministries, 1985), audiotape #01-4404, side 1; Charles Capps, *Authority in Three Worlds* (Tulsa: Harrison House, 1982), 60–61; Kenneth E. Hagin, *Zoe: The God-Kind of Life* (Tulsa: Kenneth Hagin Ministries, 1989), 49; Hagin, *I Believe in Visions* (Old Tappan, NJ: Spire Books/Fleming H. Revell Co., 1972), 81; Paul Yonggi Cho, *The Fourth Dimension* (South Plainfield, NJ: Bridge Publishing, 1979), vol. 1, 83.

6. Richard N. Ostling, "Religion: Power, Glory and Politics," *Time* 127, 7 (17 February 1986):69; cited in D. R. McConnell, *A Different Gospel* (Peabody, MA: Hendrickson Publishers, 1988), 95–96 note 6.

7. Kenneth Copeland, *Holy Bible: Kenneth Copeland Reference Edition* (Fort Worth, TX: Kenneth Copeland Ministries, 1991), NT, 68,

8. Charles Capps, *God's Creative Power* (Tulsa: Harrison House, 1976), 2–3, emphasis in original.

9. Frederick K. C. Price, *How Faith Works* (Tulsa: Harrison House, 1976), 95.

10. Kenneth Hagin, *Bible Faith Study Course* (Tulsa: Hagin Evangelistic Assoc., n.d. [ca. 1966]), 88.

11. Alfred Marshall, *NASB-NIV Parallel New Testament in Greek and English with Interlinear Translation* (Grand Rapids: Regency/Zondervan, 1986), 139.

12. Archibald Thomas Robertson, *Word Pictures in the New Testament* (Nashville: Broadman Press, 1930), 1:361.

13. A. T. Robertson and W. Hersey Davis, *A New Short Grammar of the Greek Testament*, 10th rev. ed. (Grand Rapids: Baker Book House, 1979 [orig. 1933]), 227–28, emphasis added. See also A. T. Robertson, *A Grammar of the Greek New Testament in the Light of Historical Research* (Nashville: Broadman Press, 1934), 500, "we rightly translate 'have faith *in* God,'" emphasis added).

14. According to renowned Greek scholars Walter Bauer, William F. Arndt, and F. Wilbur Gingrich, Mark 11:22 is an *objective genitive* and is to be translated as "faith *in* God" (*A Greek-English Lexicon of the New Testament and Other Early Christian Literature*, rev. ed. ([Chicago: Univ. of Chicago Press, 1979], 357, emphasis added). Nigel Turner concludes that the genitive "have the faith *of* God" in Mark 11:22 is objective and "surely must mean 'have faith *in* God' (*Grammatical Insights into the New Testament* [Edinburgh: T. & T. Clark, 1977], 110, emphasis in original). Likewise, Curtis Vaughan and Virtus E. Gideon, *A Greek Grammar of the New Testament* (Nashville: Broadman Press, 1979), 35. For further confirmation, see: Kurt Aland, ed., *Synopsis of the Four Gospels*, 6th rev. ed. (New York: United Bible Societies, 1983), 240 ("Have faith *in* God," emphasis added); Bruce M. Metzger, *A Textual Commentary on the Greek New Testament*, rev. ed. (London and New York: United Bible Societies, 1975), 109, fn. 1 ("faith *in* God," emphasis added); Joseph Henry Thayer, *The New Thayer's Greek-English Lexicon of the New Testament*, rev. ed. (Peabody, MA: Hendrickson, 1981 [orig. 1889]), 514a ("to trust *in* God," emphasis added); Alexander B. Bruce, "The Synoptic Gospels," *The Expositor's Greek Testament*, ed. by W. Robertson Nicoll (Grand Rapids: Wm. B. Eerdmans Publishing Co., 1979), 1:419, fn. vv. 20–25 ("faith *in* God," emphasis in the original); Otto Michel, "Faith," *The New International Dictionary of New Testament Theology*, ed. by Colin Brown (Grand Rapids: Zondervan, 1975 Eng. transl.), 1:600 ("to have faith *in* God," emphasis added). See also Gerhard Friedrich, ed. (transl.-ed. Geoffrey W. Bromiley), *Theological Dictionary of the New Testament* (Grand Rapids: Wm. B. Eerdmans Publishing Co., 1968 Eng. transl.), 6:204 and fn. 230 (*pistin* in Mark 11:22 is objective genitive).

Even the one possible dissenter, Boyce W. Blackwelder, who considers that Mark 11:22 could either be objective or subjective genitive, nevertheless explains that this does not mean that God personally has faith but merely that faith is "divinely imparted" to us (*Light from the Greek New Testament* [Grand Rapids: Baker Book House, 1958], 146).

15. This information was included in an advertisement for Zoe College, Jacksonville, Florida, taken from *Charisma* (May 1992), 82.

16. Kenneth Copeland, *Freedom from Fear* (Fort Worth, TX: KCP Publications, 1983), 11.

17. Ibid., 12, emphasis in original.

18. Kenneth Copeland, *The Power of the Tongue* (Fort Worth, TX: KCP Publications, 1980), 9.

19. Capps, *Authority in Three Worlds*, 80.

20. Ibid., 82, emphasis added.

21. Ibid., 83.

22. Ibid., 85.

23. Copeland, *The Force of Faith*, 14.

24. Frederick K. C. Price, *Praise the Lord*, Trinity Broadcasting Network, 21 September 1990.

25. Kenneth E. Hagin, *The Name of Jesus* (Tulsa: Kenneth Hagin Ministries, 1981), 16, emphasis in original.

26. Creflo Dollar, "The Just Shall Live by Faith," *Changing Your World*, Trinity Broadcasting Network, 20 September 1998.

27. Mark Chironna, *Praise the Lord*, Trinity Broadcasting Network, 10 February 2003.

Chapter 8: Faith Hall of Fame

1. Joyce Meyer, *Approval Addiction: Overcoming Your Need to Please Everyone* (New York: Faith Words, 2005), 9–10.

2. Benny Hinn, *Benny Hinn*, Trinity Broadcasting Network, 3 November 1990.

3. For further injunctions against adding words to Scripture, see Deuteronomy 4:2; 12:32; Galatians 3:15; Revelation 22:18.

4. Benny Hinn, *Benny Hinn*, Trinity Broadcasting Network, 3 November 1990.

5. Kenneth Copeland, sermon recorded at Melodyland Christian Center (Anaheim, CA) (30 March 1983).

6. Charles Capps, *Kicking over Sacred Cows* (Tulsa: Harrison House, 1987), 37–63.

7. Jerry Savelle, *Framing Your World with the Word of God*, part 1 (Fort Worth, TX: Jerry Savelle Evangelistic Assn., n.d.), audiotape #SS-36, side 1.

8. Paul and Jan Crouch, *Behind the Scenes*, Trinity Broadcasting Network, 12 March 1992.

9. Hinn, along with other Faith teachers, almost always cites Job 3:25 KJV ("For the thing which I greatly feared is come upon me, and that which I was afraid of is come unto me") to demonstrate the devastating impact of "negative confessions." He teaches that Job called down calamity upon himself by setting in motion the force of fear via his negative confession.

   Such an interpretation ignores the fact that Job's lamentation comes *after* his trials (1:6–2:13), not before. His lament was a *product* of his suffering, not its *cause*. At no time before his trials is Job said to have uttered a negative confession—a necessity, according to Faith theology, if the force of fear is to be released. Even after Job had suffered two major trials, the Bible asserts that "in all this, Job did not sin in what he said" (2:10). And do not forget that God judged Job to be "blameless and upright" after he had suffered his first calamity—hardly an apt description for someone who supposedly had unleashed forces hostile to God. In fact, that God chose Job above all others to be tested says much for the man's character, integrity, and devotion to God (Job 1:1, 8).

   Still, Job was certainly not sinless. He was part of a cursed creation, imperfect and beset with the frailties of fallen humanity. His misfortunes prompted him to lament his birth (chapter 3); to vacillate between desiring God to crush him (6:8–9) and to heal him (7:7–10); to blame God for tormenting him (13:21, 25) and treating him unjustly (9:21–24); to question God's treatment of him (chapter 10); to occasionally perceive God as his enemy (7:20; 10:16–17; 16:9); and to virtually demand to have his case presented before God (13:13–19). For these reasons, God rebuked Job (38–42). *But Job was rebuked for challenging God's wisdom and sovereignty and for acting out of ignorance (38:2) and presumption (40:8)—not for speaking "negative confessions."*

   And don't miss the fact that Job repents! This is why God says to Job's friends in 42:7, "You have not spoken of me what is right, *as my servant Job has*" (emphasis added). No, Job was not perfect;

404

but the book that bears his name makes it clear that, in his day, he was the most righteous man alive on the planet.

10. Benny Hinn, *Benny Hinn*, Trinity Broadcasting Network, 3 November 1990.

11. Meyer, *Approval Addiction*, 9–10.

12. John Hagee, *The Seven Secrets* (Lake Mary Fl: Charisma House, 2004), 39–41.

13. N. T. Wright, *The Resurrection of the Son of God* (Minneapolis: Fortress Press, 2003), 664.

14. Early church tradition associates Thomas with Parthia and India (see, for example, Acts of Thomas); cf. Bruce Shelley, *Church History in Plain Language*, updated 2nd edition (Dallas, TX: Word Publishing, 1995), 30; and Colin Duriez, *AD 33: The Year That Changed the World* (Downers Grove, IL: InterVarsity Press, 2006), 156–57.

Part Three: *Little Gods*

1. Psalm 82:6–7.

2. I first heard a version of this illustration from D. James Kennedy at Coral Ridge Presbyterian Church, Fort Lauderdale, Florida.

3. Eckhart Tolle, *A New Earth: Awakening to Your Life's Purpose* (New York: Plume, 2005), 57.

4. Deepak Chopra, *The Seven Spiritual Laws of Success: A Practical Guide to the Fulfillment of Your Dreams* (Amber-Allen Publishing/New World Library, 1995), 3.

Chapter 9 Deification of Man

1. Myles Munroe, *Praise the Lord*, Trinity Broadcasting Network, 23 February 2000.

2. M. Scott Peck, *The Road Less Traveled* (New York: Simon & Schuster, 1978), 270.

3. Margot Adler, *Drawing Down the Moon*, rev. ed. (Boston: Beacon Press, 1986), 25.

4. Bhagwan Shree Rajneesh, quoted in *Fear Is the Master* (Hemet, CA: Jeremiah Films, 1987).

5. Maharishi Mahesh Yogi, *Meditations of Maharishi Mahesh Yogi* (New York: Bantam, 1968), 178; quoted in James W. Sire, *Scripture Twisting* (Downers Grove, IL: InterVarsity Press, 1980), 34.

6. Jim Jones, quoted in James Reston Jr. and Noah Adams, "Father Cares: The Last of Jonestown," aired on National Public Radio (23 April 1981).

7. Kenneth E. Hagin, *Zoe: The God-Kind of Life* (Tulsa: Kenneth Hagin Ministries, Inc., 1989), 35–36, 41, emphasis in original.

8. Kenneth Copeland, *Following the Faith of Abraham I* (Fort Worth, TX: Kenneth Copeland Ministries, 1989), tape #01-3001, side 1.

9. John Avanzini with Morris Cerullo, *The Endtime Manifestation of the Sons of God* (San Diego: Morris Cerullo World Evangelism, n.d.), audiotape 1, side 2.

10. Morris Cerullo, *The Endtime Manifestation of the Sons of God*, (San Diego: Morris Cerullo World Evangelism, n.d.), audiotape 1, sides 1 and 2.

11. Creflo Dollar, World Changers Internet broadcast, 15 September 2002.

12. Creflo Dollar, World Changers Internet broadcast, 23 May 2002.

13. YouTube, "Joyce Meyer—Little Gods" (http://www.youtube.com/watch?v=7Y4eVu2oxP8), accessed 12 July 2007.

14. Charles Capps, *Authority in Three Worlds* (Tulsa: Harrison House, 1982), 16, emphasis in original.

15. Herbert W. Armstrong, *Mystery of the Ages* (Pasadena, CA: Worldwide Church of God, 1985), 37, 85, emphasis added.

16. Stephen E. Robinson, *Are Mormons Christians?* (Salt Lake City: Bookcraft, 1991), 63.

17. Kenneth Copeland, *The Force of Love* (Fort Worth, TX: Kenneth Copeland Ministries, 1987), audiotape #02-0028, side 1.

18. Benny Hinn, *Praise the Lord: Praise-a-Thon*, Trinity Broadcasting Network, 6 November 1990.

19. J. N. D. Kelly, *Early Christian Doctrines*, rev. ed. (San Francisco: Harper & Row, 1978), 352, 378, 391, 397, 486.

20. On New Thought, see Charles S. Braden, *Spirits in Rebellion: The Rise and Development of New Thought*, 3rd ed. (Dallas, TX: Southern Methodist University Press, 1970 [orig. 1963]), 10, 13, 38, 71–75, 103–09, 134–36, 151, 198–99. On Christian Science, see Mary Baker Eddy, *Science and Health with Key to the Scriptures* (Boston: First Church of Christ, Scientist, 1971 [orig. 1875]), 109–11, 113–14, 116–17, 119–20, 127, 129, 139, 591; cf. Robert Peel, *Christian Science*, 5th ed.

(New York: Henry Holt, 1959), 121–22. On Unity, see H. Emilie Cady et al, *Foundations of Unity*, series 2 (Unity Village, MO: Unity, n.d.), 1:32–36, 41, 50–51; Cady, *God a Present Help* (Lee's Summit, MO: Unity School of Christianity, 1938), 52–53, quoted in Kurt Van Gorden, "The Unity School of Christianity," *Evangelizing the Cults*, ed. by Ronald Enroth (Ann Arbor, MI: Servant Publications, 1990), 148, 190, note 23. On Religious Science, see Ernest Holmes, *The Science of Mind*, rev. ed. (New York: Dodd, Mead & Co., 1938), 98, 100, 362.

21. Henotheism (the belief that ascribes supreme power and devotes worship solely to one god without denying the existence of other gods) can be considered a subcategory of polytheism (the belief in the existence of more than one god). It is often used in discussions of early Hinduism: "Either the particular god of the moment is made to absorb all the others, who are declared to be manifestations of him [a trend toward pantheism]; or else, he is given attributes which in strict logic could only be given to a sole monotheistic deity" (Franklin Edgerton, *The Beginnings of Indian Philosophy* [London: George Allen & Unwin, 1963], 18ff, quoted in John B. Noss, *Man's Religion*, 4th ed. [New York: Macmillan, 1969]), 94.

22. Paul Crouch, *Praise the Lord*, Trinity Broadcasting Network, 7 July 1986.

23. The Mormon Scriptures teach both that there is only one God (e.g., 2 Nephi 31:21; Mosiah 15:1–5; Alma 11:26–31; cf. Ether 3:14) and that many gods exist (e.g., Abraham 3:15; 4:3, 10, 25; 5:8).

24. YouTube, "Joyce Meyer—Little Gods" (http://www.youtube.com/watch?v=7Y4eVu2oxP8), accessed 12 July 2007.

25. Earl Paulk, *Satan Unmasked* (Atlanta: K Dimension Publishers, 1984), 96.

26. Frederick Buechner, quoted in Philip Yancey and Tim Stafford, *The Student Bible* (Grand Rapids: Zondervan, 1986), 482.

27. Paul Crouch and Benny Hinn, *Praise the Lord: Praise-a-Thon*, Trinity Broadcasting Network, November 1990.

28. Kenneth Copeland, *Praise the Lord*, Trinity Broadcasting Network, 5 February 1986.

29. Capps, *Authority in Three Worlds*, 15–16; and Jerry Savelle, "The Authority of the Believer," *The Word Study Bible* (Tulsa: Harrison House, 1990), 1141.

30. R. Laird Harris, Gleason L. Archer Jr., and Bruce K. Waltke, eds., *Theological Wordbook of the Old Testament*, 2 vols. (Chicago: Moody Press, 1981), 1:192, emphasis added.

31. Cf. James M. Kinnebrew, "The Charismatic Doctrine of Positive Confession: A Historical, Exegetical, and Theological Critique," doctoral dissertation, Mid-America Baptist Seminary, 1988, 157: "To give the root word, '*dama*,' the meaning that Capps has assigned to it is to make nonsense of many biblical passages. Such a definition would make the psalmist a bird (Psalm 102:7), the neck of the Shulamite a tower (Song of Solomon 4:4), and the armies of God a mere cloud (Ezekiel 38:9)."

32. See also Job chapters 9; 10; 14; 34:20; Psalms 90; 102:11–12; 103:15; Isaiah 40:6–8; James 1:10–11; 1 Peter 1:24–25.

33. See also Jeremiah 32:17; Matthew 19:26; Mark 10:27; Luke 1:37; 18:27.

34. See also 2 Corinthians 12:9; Hebrews 4:15; Job 23.

35. See also Job 11:7–12; 21:22; 36:22–33; 37:5–24; 38:4.

36. See also Psalm 139:7–12; Ephesians 1:23; 4:10; Colossians 3:11.

37. See also Job 23; 37:23; 38–41.

38. Millard J. Erickson, *Christian Theology* (Grand Rapids: Baker Book House, 1988), 510.

39. Ibid., 514.

40. Benny Hinn, *Praise the Lord*, Trinity Broadcasting Network, 26 December 1991. Hinn seems to have derived this idea from Finis J. Dake, *Dake's Annotated Reference Bible* (Lawrenceville, GA: Dake Bible Sales, 1963), Old Testament 1, col. 4 (note on Genesis 1:26), 619, col. 1, note 2; and Dake, *God's Plan for Man* (Lawrenceville, GA: Dake Bible Sales, 1977 [orig. 1949]), 35.

41. Brigham Young, "The Gospel—The One-Man Power" discourse delivered 24 July 1870, reported by D. W. Evans and John Grimshaw, *Journal of Discourses* (London: Horace S. Eldredge, 1966 [orig. 1871]), 13:271.

42. See also Hebrew *mashal* (Psalm 8:6). Harris, Archer, and Waltke, *Theological Wordbook of the Old Testament*, 1:534, 2:833; and Samuel P. Tregelles, transl., *Gesenius' Hebrew and Chaldee Lexicon to the Old Testament Scriptures* (Grand Rapids: Wm. B. Eerdmans Publishing Co., 1976 [orig. 1857]), 517b, 758a.

43. Joyce Meyer, "Joyce Meyer—Little Gods," video online at http://www.youtube.com/watch?v=7Y4eVu2oxP8, accessed 30 January 2008.

44. Myles Munroe, *Praise the Lord*, Trinity Broadcasting Network, 11 December 2000. Says Munroe: "Two things that you must take note here. First, God created man in His own image. The word 'image' means character, nature, moral, spiritual character. Then 'likeness' means 'to function like.' So God created you as a creature, the spirit being, to be just like Him in nature. Means you are naturally like God. You have the same nature as God Himself. That's what the word 'image' means. You have the essence and the characteristics of God. Then 'likeness' means you function like God. That means, how does God function? The same way you function. You want to know how you're supposed to live, you study God. How does God function? He functions by speaking until things come into being. In other words, your voice, your lips are the most powerful force you have because whatever man speaks comes to pass. You have the same gift that God has to create things with your words. I would dare say that you'll become exactly what you've been saying. That's exactly what you are. You've been saying it, and you've become it because you create your own world the same way God creates His. He speaks, and things happen; you speak, and they happen. That's why you be careful what you hear because if you hear something, you end up saying it, and then it happens to you too. So it's important for you to note that God created you to be like Him and to act like Him."

45. Myles Munro, *Praise the Lord*, Trinity Broadcasting Network, 23 February 2000.

46. Jesse Duplantis, audio recording, Trinity Broadcasting Network, c. March 2000.

Chapter 10: Demotion of God

1. Rod Parsley, *Praise the Lord*, Trinity Broadcasting Network, 7 August 2003.

2. T. D. Jakes, "MegaCare 1," *The Potter's Touch*, Lightsource.com, iTunes Podcast, 17 August 2008.

3. Creflo Dollar, *Our Equality with God Through Righteousness* video series, 21 May 2001.

4. Kenneth Copeland, *Spirit, Soul and Body I* (Fort Worth, TX: Kenneth Copeland Ministries, 1985), audiotape #01-0601, side 1. Some have suggested that Copeland may have simply been referring to Jesus in this statement. However, this creates yet another huge problem—namely, that Jesus had a body prior to His incarnation. Although Jesus *appeared* in the Old Testament in what are appropriately referred to as theophanies (appearances of God), He always did so for the purpose of communicating with men; and in the context of Copeland's sermon, men had not yet been created. For further discussion about theophanies, see Ron Rhodes, *Christ Before the Manger* (Grand Rapids: Baker Book House, 1992), 79–91.

5. Jerry Savelle, *Framing Your World with the Word of God*, part 2 (Fort Worth, TX: Jerry Savelle Evangelistic Association, Inc., n.d.), audiotape #SS-36, side 1.

6. Morris Cerullo, *The Miracle Book* (San Diego, CA: Cerullo World Evangelism, Inc., 1984), x–xi.

7. Benny Hinn and Jan Crouch, *Praise the Lord*, Trinity Broadcasting Network, 3 October 1991.

8. Benny Hinn, *Benny Hinn*, Trinity Broadcasting Network, 3 October 1990.

9. Randy Frame, "Best-Selling Author Admits Mistakes, Vows Changes," *Christianity Today* (28 October 1991), 44–45. Hinn resumed teaching that both the Father and the Holy Spirit have bodies (on TBN's October 3, 1991, *Praise the Lord* program) shortly after his supposed change of heart as related in his interview with *Christianity Today*. The interview was conducted one month before the article's October 28 release date. Cf. Randy Frame, "Same Old Benny Hinn, Critics Say," *Christianity Today* (5 October 1992), 53.

10. Ibid.

11. Benny Hinn, *Praise the Lord*, Trinity Broadcasting Network (23 October 1992). Cf. Hinn, *Good Morning, Holy Spirit* (Nashville: Thomas Nelson, Inc., 1990), 72, 82–84.

12. For a biblical and historical discussion on the doctrine of the Trinity, see E. Calvin Beisner, *God in Three Persons* (Wheaton, IL: Tyndale House Publishers, 1984); and Edward H. Bickersteth, *The Trinity* (Grand Rapids: Kregel, 1976).

13. In the case of the Faith teachers' claim that God possesses a literal body—whether some form of physical body or a spirit body—the error is indeed a serious one. For as has already been pointed out, the doctrine itself implies that the Trinity is actually composed of three separate beings. Conversely, the Bible teaches there are three Persons in one Being called God (Deuteronomy 6:4).

Additionally, since God, according to these Faith teachers, has a body, His presence would be confined to the area occupied by His body. And since God's body supposedly has definite dimensions (e.g., a measurable hand span, height, and weight), it would mean God cannot truly be at those places that are not currently occupied by His body. In other words, the Faith God cannot be omnipresent. Scripture, on the other hand, presents a God who transcends all such limitations. The one true God is everywhere present in all His fullness: "'Am I only a God nearby,' declares the LORD, 'and not a God far away? Can anyone hide in secret places so that I cannot see him?' declares the LORD. 'Do not I fill the heaven and earth?' declares the LORD" (Jeremiah 23:23–24; cf. Psalm 139:7–10; Matthew 28:20; Ephesians 1:23; 4:10; Colossians 3:11).

Copeland apparently reasoned that a God with a physical body needs a physical habitat. So he conveniently transforms heaven into a planet. "Heaven has a north and a south and an east and a west," begins Copeland. "Consequently, it must be a planet." He also says the earth is really "a copy of the mother planet where God lives." How Copeland could squeeze God on any planet is hard to fathom, especially since Solomon pointed out that heaven itself cannot contain God (1 Kings 8:27).

It seems that the Faith teachers have arrived at their physical God by erroneously taking verses that figuratively describe God in human (anthropomorphic) terms and reading them literally. Thus, God is made out to be a spirit being with a body, complete with eyes and eyelids (Psalm 11:4), ears (Psalm 18:6), nostrils (Psalm 18:8), a mouth (Numbers 12:8), hands and fingers (Psalm 8:3–6), and feet (Exodus 24:10). Yet if these verses were meant to be taken literally, it would also have to be concluded that God has feathers and wings as well (Psalm 91:4)—an obvious absurdity.

The simple fact is that such anthropomorphic descriptions were used primarily to help us understand and relate to our Maker. They were never intended to convey the notion that God possesses physical features like His human creation. The Creator is, after all, "God, and not man" (Hosea 11:9). Jesus made it clear that God is *spirit* (John 4:24), not a spirit being with a body (cf. Deuteronomy 4:12).

Some may try to point to Christ as proof of God having a body. However, all such appeals fail on at least two counts. First, the vast majority of verses cited by such proponents occur in the Old Testament, during a time before Christ took human form (John 1:14; cf. 1 John 4:2; 2 John 7). Second, and even more importantly, the Lord Jesus is not only fully God but also fully man. He is the God-man. His physical attributes are due not to His deity but to His humanity (Romans 8:3; Philippians 2:7).

14. Kenneth Copeland, *Praise the Lord: Praise-a-Thon*, Trinity Broadcasting Network, April 1988.

15. Kenneth Copeland, *Our Covenant with God* (Fort Worth, TX: KCP Publications, 1987), 8–11 passim.

16. Rod Parsley, *Praise the Lord*, Trinity Broadcasting Network, 7 August 2003.

17. Myles Munroe, *Praise the Lord*, Trinity Broadcasting Network, 3 March 2003.

Chapter 11: Deification of Satan

1. Kenneth Copeland, *Image of God in You III* (Fort Worth, TX: Kenneth Copeland Ministries, 1989), audiotape #01-1403, side 1.

2. C. S. Lewis, *Mere Christianity*, 22nd pr. (New York: Macmillan Publishing Co., 1976), 48.

3. Kenneth Copeland, *The Force of Faith* (Fort Worth, TX: KCP Publications, 1989), 11.

4. Benny Hinn, *Our Position in Christ #2: The Word Made Flesh* (Orlando: Orlando Christian Center, 1991), videotape #255, emphasis added. See also Hinn's claim that believers are "little messiahs" or "little gods" on TBN's *Praise the Lord: Praise-a-Thon* (6 November 1990).

5. Ibid.

6. Kenneth Copeland, *Praise the Lord: Praise-a-Thon*, Trinity Broadcasting Network, April 1988.

7. Copeland, *Image of God in You III*, side 1.

8. Joyce Meyer, *The Word, The Name, The Blood* (Tulsa: Harrison House, Inc., 1995), 100–1.

9. Charles Capps, *Authority in Three Worlds* (Tulsa: Harrison House, 1982), 50–51, emphasis added.

10. Kenneth Copeland, *What Happened from the Cross to the Throne* (Fort Worth, TX: Kenneth Copeland Ministries, 1990), audiotape #02-0017.

11. Bentley, *Journey into the Miraculous*, 97–98.

12. Ibid., 109.

13. Rory and Wendy Alec, "Personal Message from Rory and Wendy Concerning Lakeland" Eblast, 25 September 2008, online at http://www.god.tv/lakeland080925, retrieved 26 September 2008, capitalization in original.

14. *John Hagee Today*, Trinity Broadcasting Network, 16 July 2007, emphasis added. Lest this outburst be considered a mere slip of the tongue, Hagee provides graphic details regarding the Antichrist's death, departure from his body, and resurrection in a book titled *Beginning of the End: The Assassination of Yitzhak Rabin and the Coming Antichrist* (Nashville: Thomas Nelson, Inc., 1996). In this book, Hagee has the Antichrist descending to the place of the dead (*Sheol*), making a deal with the devil, and then ascending from death and the grave. Here's how he puts it: "Just as Satan took Jesus up into a mountain, showing Him all the kingdoms of the world and offering them as a reward, I believe that Satan may take the Antichrist into the depths of the Abyss and offers him the kingdoms of the world. And while Jesus refused to bow down to Satan, the Antichrist will gladly bow to Satan and worship him. In return for this worship, Satan reanimates the Antichrist, infusing him to the very core of his being with wickedness, rage and ruthlessness . . . When the Antichrist ascends from Sheol, his mortal wound miraculously healed, he will fully unveil his worldwide religion. And from this foundation, he will then implement the world-wide system of commerce that becomes the leverage he uses to force the nations of the world to submit to his political control. But first he will capture the imagination and confidence of the world through his miraculous recovery . . . To the satanically blinded world of the Tribulation, the Antichrist's healing will look exactly like the death and resurrection of Jesus Christ—except in this instance they will see it happen with their own eyes on CNN" (168–69).

Chapter 12: Demotion of Christ

1. Kenneth Copeland, *Substitution and Identification* (Fort Worth, TX: Kenneth Copeland Ministries, 1989), audiotape #00-0202, side 2.
2. Creflo Dollar, *Creflo Dollar Ministries: World Changers*, 8 December 2002.
3. Ibid.
4. Ibid.
5. Kenneth Copeland, "Take Time to Pray," *Believer's Voice of Victory* 15, 2 (February 1987):9.
6. Kenneth Copeland, "Question & Answer," *Believer's Voice of Victory* 16, 8 (August 1988):8, emphasis in original.
7. Benny Hinn, *Good Morning, Holy Spirit* (Nashville: Thomas Nelson, Inc., 1990), 135–36, emphasis added. In the seventh printing, certain unannounced changes were made in the text in response to criticism from CRI so that the passage now reads (changes emphasized): "And let me add this: Had the Holy Spirit not been with Jesus, He *may have likely sinned*. That's right. It was the Holy Spirit *who* was the power that kept Him pure. He was not only sent from heaven, but He was called the Son of Man—and as such He was capable of sinning . . . Without the Holy Ghost, Jesus *may* have never made it." The "Can you imagine . . ." sentence was deleted entirely. But even with the changes, Christ is still made out to depend on the Holy Spirit to keep Him from sinning, thus denying Christ the sinlessness that is an essential attribute of God.
8. For the significance of the title "Son of Man" in Daniel, see Gleason L. Archer Jr., *Encyclopedia of Bible Difficulties* (Grand Rapids: Zondervan, 1982), 322–24; and Robert L. Reymond, *Jesus, Divine Messiah* (Phillipsburg, NJ: Presbyterian and Reformed Publishing, 1990), 52–61.
9. Copeland, *Substitution and Identification*, side 2.
10. Kenneth Copeland, *The Incarnation* (Fort Worth, TX: Kenneth Copeland Ministries, 1985), audiotape #01-0402, side 1, emphasis in original. We should note that while Copeland, in this tape, speaks of Jesus as the God-man, his statement, "He cannot be a God," clearly indicates otherwise.
11. Charles Capps, *Authority in Three Worlds* (Tulsa: Harrison House, 1982), 189.
12. Charles Capps, *Dynamics of Faith & Confession* (Tulsa: Harrison House, 1987), 86.
13. Kenneth Copeland, *The Image of God in You III* (Fort Worth, TX: Kenneth Copeland Ministries, 1989), audiotape #01-1403, side 2.
14. Ibid.
15. Kenneth Copeland, *Christianity, a Series of Decisions* (Fort Worth: Kenneth Copeland Ministries, n.d.), audiotape, #01-0406, side 2.

Part Four: *Atonement Atrocities*

1. 1 John 2:2.

2. According to a number of Faith teachers, God was able to get a foothold back on the earth after arranging a deal with Abraham. However, according to this peculiar theology, it was not until God caught Satan committing an "illegal move" that He was able to regain control of the universe (see pages 184 to 186—[the first couple pages of chapter 15, "Rebirth in Hell"]). This highly unusual view stands in marked contrast to the historical ransom theory as set forth by such figures as Origen, Gregory of Nyssa, Augustine, and Anselm (see Millard J. Erickson, *Christian Theology* [Grand Rapids: Baker Book House, 1988], 792–96, 821–22).

Chapter 13: Re-creation on the Cross
1. Kenneth E. Hagin, *The Name of Jesus* (Tulsa: Kenneth Hagin Ministries, 1981), 31.
2. Kenneth Copeland, *What Happened from the Cross to the Throne* (Fort Worth, TX: Kenneth Copeland Ministries, 1990), audiotape #02-0017, side 1.
3. Benny Hinn, *Benny Hinn*, Trinity Broadcasting Network, 15 December 1990 (emphasis in original). This message, titled *The Person of Jesus* (delivered during Orlando Christian Center's Sunday morning service on December 2, 1990), comprises part four of Hinn's six-part series, *The Revelation of Jesus* (Orlando: Orlando Christian Center, 1991), videotape #TV-292. Although Hinn was quoted in October 1991 by *Christianity Today* as confessing he "no longer believe[s] the Faith message," it was not long before Hinn was back on the air teaching, once again, the Faith doctrines of prosperity (*Praise the Lord*, Trinity Broadcasting Network [17 April 1992]) and guaranteed healing (*Praise the Lord*, Trinity Broadcasting Network [26 December 1991 and 16 April 1992]). To what degree Hinn has "returned" to the Faith camp remains uncertain, though his favorable allusions to both Oral Roberts and Kenneth Hagin (in the programs mentioned) indicate disturbing tendencies.
4. Hagin, *The Name of Jesus*, 31, emphasis in original. What is particularly disturbing in Hagin's case is that when he was confronted by the ramifications of this blasphemous notion, he denied ever having taught it. In a written response addressed to me by Kenneth Hagin Jr. (who has now succeeded Hagin Sr. as president of Kenneth Hagin Ministries), I was informed the following: "We don't agree with much of the doctrine currently being taught in 'word-faith' circles and haven't *ever* taught many of the doctrines now being circulated . . . It is very frustrating to us to be quoted on the same page with some of these ministers and connected with them as though we believed the same things they are teaching . . . In many, many cases this is just not true, as I think the enclosed questions and answers will indicate" (personal letter to the author, 4 January 1991).
    In the enclosure referred to, Hagin accuses people like myself of jumping "to their own conclusions" and denies the teaching "that Jesus took on Satan's nature or submitted to his lordship."
    It becomes very confusing indeed when someone denies the very thing he affirms. Although I would love to give Hagin the benefit of the doubt, investigation reveals that not only has he *distorted doctrine*, but he has also *distorted his record* in an effort to avoid the criticisms generated by his blasphemous remarks.
5. Frederick K. C. Price, *Identification #3* (Inglewood, CA: Ever Increasing Faith Ministries, 1980), audiotape #FP545, side 1.
6. Glenn W. Gohr, "Price, Frederick K. C.," *Dictionary of Pentecostal and Charismatic Movements*, eds. Stanley M. Burgess, Gary B. McGee, and Patrick H. Alexander (Grand Rapids: Regency/Zondervan, 1988), 727.
7. See James E. Talmage, *Jesus the Christ* (Salt Lake City: Deseret Book Co., 1969), 613–14. Cf. "What the Mormons Think of Christ," pamphlet (Salt Lake City: Deseret New Press, n.d.), 31–32; and Joseph Fielding Smith, *Doctrines of Salvation*, compiled by Bruce R. McConkie (Salt Lake City: Bookcraft, 1975 [orig. 1954]), 1:121–38, especially p. 130.
8. Copeland, *What Happened from the Cross to the Throne*, side 2.
9. For more on this point, see Brian Onken, "The Atonement of Christ and the 'Faith' Message," *Forward* 7, 1 (1984):11–12.
10. Thomas J. Crawford, *The Doctrine of Holy Scripture Respecting the Atonement* (Grand Rapids: Baker Book House, 1954), v; quoted in Onken, "The Atonement," 12.
11. Phillip E. Hughes, *Paul's Second Epistle to the Corinthians*, from *The New International Commentary on the New Testament* series, ed. by Ned B. Stonehouse (Grand Rapids: Wm. B. Eerdmans Publishing Co., 1962), 213–14. For similar comments, see R. V. G. Tasker, *The Second Epistle of Paul to the*

Corinthians, from the *Tyndale New Testament Commentaries* series (Wm. B. Eerdmans Publishing Co., 1977 [orig. 1958]), 90–91.

12. Joyce Meyer, *The Most Important Decision You Will Ever Make* (Fenton, MO: Life in the Word, 1991), 37. In the 1996 edition, Meyer deleted the words "in hell" from this particular passage; but two paragraphs earlier, within the same context, she retained (as in her 1991 edition) the line, "So they put Him—that is, His body—in a grave, and His spirit went to hell because that is where we deserved to go." And within the same chapter, titled "What Should You Believe?" still within the same context, Meyer writes, "Believe that Jesus did what the Bible says . . . He was in the grave three days. During that time, He entered hell, where you and I deserved to go (legally) because of our sin. He paid the price there . . . *Jesus paid* on the cross and went to hell in my place . . . Jesus went to hell for *you*. He paid for *your* sins . . . When the bill was paid and all our debt completely cancelled, the Father raised Him from the dead. But until that happened, He was alone for three days satisfying the courts of justice and conquering the hosts of hell" (Joyce Meyer, *The Most Important Decision You Will Ever Make* [Tulsa: Harrison House, 1996], 41, 43–44, emphasis in original).

13. Noted Bible scholar Merrill C. Tenney says of this passage: "The use of the perfect tense in 'It is finished' (*tetelestai*) signifies full completion of Jesus' work and the establishment of a basis for faith. Nothing further needed to be done. Jesus' act was voluntary and confident, for he had discharged perfectly the Father's purpose and was leaving the scene of his human struggle" ("The Gospel of John" from *The Expositor's Bible Commentary* series, gen. ed. Frank E. Gaebelein [Grand Rapids: Regency/Zondervan, 1981], 9:184).

14. Joel Osteen, Easter service message at Lakewood Church, Sermon #CS_002 - 4-23-00, 23 April 2000, emphasis added; transcript formerly online at http://www.lakewood.cc/sermons/cs_002.htm; transcript archived online at http://web.archive.org/web/20040408215244/http://www.lakewood.cc/sermons/cs_002.htm, retrieved 1 August 2008. Cf. Joel Osteen, Easter service message 2004, *Discover the Champion in You*, Trinity Broadcasting Network, 26 April 2004.

Chapter 14: Redemption in Hell

1. Frederick K. C. Price, *Ever Increasing Faith Messenger* (June 1980), 7; quoted in D. R. McConnell, *A Different Gospel* (Peabody, MA: Hendrickson Publishers, 1988), 120.

2. Joel Osteen, Easter service message at Lakewood Church, Sermon #CS_002 - 4-23-00, 23 April 2000, transcript formerly online at http://www.lakewood.cc/sermons/cs_002.htm; transcript archived online at http://web.archive.org/web/20040408215244, retrieved 1 November 2008. On another occasion, Osteen said, "A little over 2,000 years ago a Baby was born in a manger. He went about bringing hope and healing everywhere He went. Yet, for some reason, the world hated Him. Finally they nailed Him on the cross and they thought that was the end of it. But that was only the beginning. For three days Jesus fought with the enemy. It was the battle of the ages. Light versus darkness, good versus evil. But thank God Satan was no match for Jesus. The Bible says that Jesus crushed Satan's head and He forever, once and for all, defeated and dethroned our eternal enemy. The good news is the grave couldn't hold Jesus in. They put Him on the tomb on Friday afternoon but on Sunday morning He came out. He said 'I am He that lives and was dead; and, behold, I am alive forevermore.' And He said, by the way, one more thing: 'I've got the keys to death and hell.' Friends, God has already been down our path. He's already conquered death, hell, and the grave for *every one* of us. Now we don't have to be afraid." (Joel Osteen, *Discover the Champion in You*, Trinity Broadcasting Network, 26 April 2004).

3. Joel Osteen, Sermon #CS_002 - 4-23-00.

4. See John R. W. Stott, *The Cross of Christ* (Leicester: IVP, 1986), 179–81; Leon Morris, *The Apostolic Preaching of the Cross*, 3rd ed. (Grand Rapids: Wm. B. Eerdmans Publishing Co., 1984), 112–28. Also, "Some have argued, largely on the basis of this verse [Leviticus 17:11], that 'blood' in Scripture signifies life rather than death. However, in all of the Old Testament sacrifices, blood is obtained by killing an animal, and the life spoken of in Lev. 17:11 is that 'which ceases to exist when the blood is poured out'" (Steve Jeffrey, Michael Ovey, Andrew Sach, *Pierced for Our Transgressions: Rediscovering the Glory of Penal Substitution* [Wheaton: IL: Crossway Books, 2007], 45, n. 23).

5. Joyce Meyer, *The Most Important Decision You Will Ever Make* (Fenton, MO: Life in the Word, 1991), 37. See Chapter 13, note 12.

6. Robert Tilton, *Success-N-Life* television program, 18 July 1991.

7. Price, *Ever Increasing Faith Messenger*, 120.

8. Kenneth E. Hagin, "How Jesus Obtained His Name" (Tulsa: Kenneth Hagin Ministries, n.d.), tape #44H01, side 1. Also, see Hagin's article "Made Alive," *The Word of Faith* 15, 4 (April 1982):3, where he writes: "Jesus died as our Substitute. He who knew no sin was made to be sin. He took upon Himself our sin nature. And He died—He was separated and cut off from God. He went down into the prison house of suffering in our place. He was there three days and nights."

9. Kenneth Copeland, "Jesus—Our Lord of Glory," *Believer's Voice of Victory* 10, 4 (April 1982):3.

10. Paul E. Billheimer, *Destined for the Throne*, special edition for TBN (Fort Washington, PA: Christian Literature Crusade, 1988 [orig. 1975]), 83–84, emphasis in original; quoted at length by Jan Crouch during the *Praise the Lord* program on TBN (20 August 1987).

11. Philip Schaff, *The Creeds of Christendom* (Grand Rapids: Baker Book House, 1985), 45–46, 69.

12. Strangely enough, some Faith teachers use the same line of argumentation employed by Jehovah's Witnesses to try to get around this point—namely, by claiming that the word "today" indicates *when* Jesus uttered His statement to the thief, not when the thief would be with the Lord in paradise (see, for example, E. W. Kenyon, *What Happened from the Cross to the Throne*, 12th ed. [Lynnwood, WA: Kenyon's Gospel Publishing Society, 1969], 60). For a solid biblical response, see David A. Reed, *Jehovah's Witnesses Answered Verse-By-Verse* (Baker, 1986), 67–69.

 I understand the terms to convey distinct ideas. In simple terms, *hades* is the Greek equivalent for the Hebrew word *sheol*. It is depicted as the place of disembodied spirits or souls. The Bible in passages such as Luke 16 portrays it as containing two distinct areas. One area is a place of torment for the wicked; the other is a place of conscious bliss for the righteous (referred to as "paradise" or "Abraham's bosom"). Both are but a foretaste of what is to come.

 The unrighteous in hades await the day of judgment when they will stand before God and receive final sentencing. Then death and hades will be thrown into the lake of fire, which is the second death (Revelation 20:14). It is this lake of fire which Scripture refers to as hell or gehenna—the future place of punishment in the eternal state.

 The notion that Jesus went to hades is in part derived from 1 Peter 3:18–20. On the basis of this passage the Church Fathers held that Jesus proclaimed victory to those in hades while the Reformers held that Christ by His Spirit spoke through Noah to the people of His day. The pretext that Jesus was tormented or finished the work of redemption in hades is completely foreign to both historical orthodoxy as well as the text of Scripture.

13. Joyce Meyer, *The Most Important Decision You Will Ever Make: A Complete and Thorough Understanding of What It Means to Be Born Again* (Tulsa: Harrison House, 1996), 41, emphasis added.

14. Ibid., 42, emphasis in original.

Chapter 15: Rebirth in Hell

1. Creflo A. Dollar, "The First Begotten Son," online at http://www.creflodollarministries.org/public/bible/article.aspx?id=18, retrieved 10 September 2008, emphasis added.

2. Kenneth Copeland, *Walking in the Realm of the Miraculous* (Fort Worth, TX: Kenneth Copeland Ministries, 1979), 77.

3. Kenneth Copeland, *What Happened from the Cross to the Throne* (Fort Worth, TX: Kenneth Copeland Ministries, 1990), audiotape #02-0017, side 2.

4. Kenneth Copeland, *Believer's Voice of Victory*, 21 April 1991. This message was originally delivered at the Full Gospel Motorcycle Rally Association 1990 Rally at Eagle Mountain Lake, Texas.

5. Kenneth Copeland, "The Price of It All," *Believer's Voice of Victory* 19, 9 (September 1991):4–6.

6. Charles Capps, *Authority in Three Worlds* (Tulsa: Harrison House, 1982), 212–13, emphasis in original.

7. Kenneth E. Hagin, *The Name of Jesus* (Tulsa: Harrison House, 1981), 29.

8. Joyce Meyer, *The Most Important Decision You Will Ever Make* (Tulsa: Harrison House, 1996), 41–42, emphasis in original.

9. The term *firstborn* in Romans 8:29 has also received similar mistreatment from the Faith teachers. See, for example, Frederick K. C. Price, "Identification #8" (Los Angeles: Ever Increasing Faith Ministries, 1980), tape #FP550, side 1.

10. For additional discussions on this point, see J. B. Lightfoot, *St. Paul's Epistles to the Colossians and to Philemon* (Peabody, MA: Hendrickson Publishers, Inc., 1981), 156–58; cf. 146–47; and Herbert M. Carson, *The Epistles of Paul to the Colossians and Philemon*, from the *Tyndale New Testament Commentaries* series (Grand Rapids: Wm. B. Eerdmans Publishing Co., 1977), 43–44.

11. Paul E. Billheimer, *Destined for the Throne*, special edition for TBN (Fort Washington, PA: Christian Literature Crusade, 1988 [orig. 1975]), 86; quoted at length by Jan Crouch during the *Praise the Lord* program on TBN (20 August 1987).

12. See, for example, R. C. H. Lenski, *The Interpretation of the Epistles of St. Peter, St. John and St. Jude* (Minneapolis, MN: Augsburg Publishing House, 1966), 159.

13. Kenneth Copeland, *Substitution and Identification* (Fort Worth, TX: Kenneth Copeland Ministries, 1989), audiotape #00-0202, side 2.

14. Benny Hinn, *Our Position In Christ*, part 1 (Orlando, FL: Orlando Christian Center, 1991), videotape #TV-254.

15. Dollar, "The First Begotten Son," emphasis added.

Chapter 16: Reincarnation

1. Kenneth E. Hagin, "The Incarnation," *The Word of Faith* 13, 12 (December 1980):14.

2. Paul Crouch, *Praise the Lord: Praise-a-Thon*, Trinity Broadcasting Network, 6 November 1990.

3. Hagin, "The Incarnation." Hagin's entire article was taken almost word for word from the first half of a chapter titled "The Incarnation or the Humanity and Deity of Jesus," in E. W. Kenyon's book *The Father and His Family* (Lynnwood, WA: Kenyon's Gospel Publishing Society, 1964), 97–101.

4. See for example, Bruce R. McConkie, *Mormon Doctrine*, 2nd ed. (Salt Lake City: Bookcraft, 1974 [orig. 1966]), 216–17, 278, 282, 590, 750–51.

5. Morris Cerullo, *The Endtime Manifestation of the Sons of God* (San Diego: Morris Cerullo World Evangelism, Inc., n.d.), audiotape 1, sides 1 and 2.

6. Creflo Dollar, "The First Begotten Son" online at http://www.creflodollarministries.org/Public/Bible/Article.aspx?id=18, accessed 10 September 2008.

7. Benny Hinn, Trinity Broadcasting Network, 1 November 1990. Says Hinn: "When you say 'I am saved,' what are you saying? You're saying, 'I am a Christian.' What does that word mean? It means I am anointed. You know what the word 'anointed' means? It means 'Christ.' When you say, 'I am a Christian' you're saying, 'I am *meshiac*' in the Hebrew. 'I am a little messiah walking on earth,' in other words. That's a shocking revelation. We are not, we are not having, we don't have a part of Him running around in our stomach feeling goose bumps, okay. His Spirit and our spirit-man are one, united. There's no separation. It's impossible. The new creation is created after God in righteousness and true holiness. The new man is after God. Like God, Godlike, complete in Christ Jesus. The new creation is just like God. May I say it like this? You are a little God on earth running around.'"

Part Five: *Wealth and Want*

1. Proverbs 30:8–9.

2. "Turn Your Eyes Upon Jesus," music and lyrics by Helen H. Lemmel, *Glad Songs* (British National Sunday School Union, 1922).

Chapter 17: Cultural Conformity

1. Frederick K. C. Price, *Ever Increasing Faith*, Trinity Broadcasting Network, 9 December 1990.

2. Jesse Duplantis, *Praise the Lord*, Trinity Broadcasting Network, 11 July 2003.

3. Quentin J. Schultze, *Televangelism and American Culture* (Grand Rapids: Baker Book House, 1991), 132–33. Cf. Dennis Hollinger, "Enjoying God Forever: An Historical/Sociological Profile of *The Health and Wealth Gospel*," *Trinity Journal* 9, 2 (Fall 1988): 145–48.

4. Jesse Duplantis, *The 700 Club*, Christian Broadcasting Network, n.d., video segment online at http://www.godtube.com/view_video.php?viewkey=9cf573517f2152303a3e, accessed 30 September 2008; also online at YouTube, "Jesse Duplantis: Making Your Dreams Come True-CBN.com" (http://www.youtube.com/watch?v=FlosLSf6RCA), posted 21 July 2008, accessed 26 September 2008.

5. John Hagee, *Praise the Lord*, Trinity Broadcasting Network, 29 March 2001.

6. See Part One: *Turning Truth into Mythology*, notes 32–35.

7. *Praise the Lord: Praise-a-Thon*, Trinity Broadcasting Network, 5 November 2002.

8. John Hagee, *The Seven Secrets: Unlocking Genuine Greatness* (Lake Mary, FL: Charisma House, 2004), 232.

9. Cf. Merrill C. Tenney, *The Expositor's Bible Commentary*, vol. 9, ed. Frank E. Gaebelein (Grand Rapids: Zondervan, 1981), 181.

10. John Avanzini, *Was Jesus Poor?* videotape (Hurst, TX: His Image Ministries, n.d.).

11. Frederick K. C. Price, *Ever Increasing Faith*, Trinity Broadcasting Network, 9 December 1990.

12. Avanzini, *Was Jesus Poor?*

13. John Avanzini, *Praise the Lord*, Trinity Broadcasting Network, 1 August 1989.

14. John Hagee, *Praise the Lord*, Trinity Broadcasting Network, 8 January 2003.

15. John Avanzini, *Believer's Voice of Victory*, Trinity Broadcasting Network, 20 January 1991.

16. For a brief yet forceful critique of materialism within Christianity today, see David L. Larsen, "The Gospel of Greed Versus the Gospel of Grace," *Trinity Journal* 9, 2 (Fall 1988):211–20.

17. T. L. and Daisy Osborn, *She & He Photo-Book—Go for It!* (Tulsa: Osborn Foundation, 1983), 62.

18. Ibid., 65, capitalization in original.

19. Frederick K. C. Price, *Faith, Foolishness, or Presumption?* (Tulsa: Harrison House, 1979), 34.

20. Frederick K. C. Price, *Ever Increasing Faith*, Trinity Broadcasting Network, 29 March 1992.

21. Patti Roberts with Sherry Andrews, *Ashes to Gold* (Waco, TX: Word Books, 1983), 110–11.

22. Rod Parsley, *Breakthrough with Rod Parsley*, Trinity Broadcasting Network, 27 March 2002.

23. Joel Osteen, *Your Best Life Now: 7 Steps to Living at Your Full Potential* (New York: Warner Faith, 2004), 7–8.

24. Creflo Dollar, *Praise the Lord: Praise-a-Thon*, Trinity Broadcasting Network, 6 April 2000.

25. John Hagee, *Praise the Lord*, Trinity Broadcasting Network, 8 January 2003.

26. Jesse Duplantis, *Praise the Lord: Praise-a-Thon*, Trinity Broadcasting Network, 6 November 2002.

27. T. D. Jakes, *Praise the Lord: Praise-a-Thon*, Trinity Broadcasting Network, 5 November 2003.

28. T. D. Jakes, *Praise the Lord: Praise-a-Thon*, Trinity Broadcasting Network, 12 November 2001, emphasis added.

Chapter 18: Cons and Cover-Ups

1. Juanita Bynum, *Praise the Lord: Praise-a-Thon*, Trinity Broadcasting Network, 7 November 2003.

2. Philip Schaff, *History of the Christian Church*, 8 vols. (n.p.: AP & A, n.d. [reprint ca. 1888]), 7:69.

3. Ibid., 72.

4. Ibid., 73–74.

5. Ibid., 73.

6. Ibid., 75.

7. Ibid., 78.

8. Quote collated from Kenneth Scott Latourette, *A History of Christianity*, rev. ed., 2 vols. (New York: Harper & Row, 1975), 2:717; and R. Tudor Jones, *The Great Reformation* (Downers Grove, IL: InterVarsity Press, 1985), 44. For additional bibliographic data and discussion of variant renderings, see Schaff, *History of the Christian Church*, 7:139, 141.

9. Patti Roberts with Sherry Andrews, *Ashes to Gold* (Waco, TX: Word Books, 1983), 121.

10. Oral Roberts, *A Daily Guide to Miracles* (Tulsa: Pinoak Publications, 1975), 63, capitalization in original.

11. David Lane, president and general manager of WFAA-TV in Dallas, quoted in Associated Press dispatch from Tulsa, Oklahoma, printed as: "TV Ban Won't End Oral Roberts' Vow of 'Cash or Death,'" *Toronto Star* (14 January 1987), A11; and "Despite TV Stations' Protests, Oral Roberts Won't Stop Life-or-Death Appeal for Funds," *Orange County [California] Register* (14 January 1987), A19.

12. Ibid.

13. Oral Roberts, direct-mail letter, undated (ca. 1 March 1987). For the "end of March" deadline, see Oral Roberts, "God's Mandate to Me," *Abundant Life* 41, 2 (March/April 1987):3.

14. Oral Roberts letter (ca. 1 March 1987), 2.

15. Ibid., 4.

16. Richard Roberts, direct-mail letter, undated (ca. 1 January 1987), 1–3 passim. Oral Roberts's sixty-ninth birthday was on January 24, 1987.

17. Ibid., capitalization in original.

18. Oral Roberts, direct-mail letter, undated (ca. 1 January 1985?), 1–2, emphasis in original.

19. Ibid., 1.

20. Ibid., 2, capitalization in original.

21. Ibid., 3, capitalization in original.

22. Ibid., 1, 3, capitalization in original.

23. Ibid., 2, capitalization in original.

24. Oral Roberts, presentation at the World Charismatic Conference, Melodyland Christian Center, Anaheim, CA (7 August 1992), audiotape excerpt on file at Christian Research Institute, emphasis added.

25. See Charles Fillmore, *Prosperity* (Lee's Summit, MO: Unity Books, 1967 [orig. 1936]).

26. The item referred to here is a poem, presented as the day's devotional that was previously published in *Unity Magazine*. R. H. Grenville, "Whatever Good," *Daily Blessing: A Guide to Seed-Faith Living*, 24, 1 (January–February–March 1982); 46.

27. Gloria Copeland, *God's Will Is Prosperity* (Tulsa: Harrison House, 1978), 54.

28. Ibid.

29. *Praise the Lord: Praise-a-Thon*, Trinity Broadcasting Network, 5 November 1990.

30. Ibid.

31. Ibid.

32. Ibid.

33. Ibid.

34. Ibid.

35. Paul Crouch, *Praise the Lord*, Trinity Broadcasting Network, 21 July 1992.

36. Oral Roberts, *Oral Roberts' Best Sermons and Stories* (Tulsa: Oral Roberts, 1956), 46; *101 Questions and Answers* (Tulsa: Oral Roberts, 1968), 18; quoted in David Edwin Harrell, Jr., *Oral Roberts: An American Life* (Bloomington, IN: Indiana University Press, 1985), 451, 604, note 110.

37. Robert Tilton, direct-mail letter with enclosures (1990), 6.

38. Ibid, emphasis in original.

39. Ibid., 5–6.

40. Ibid., 2–3, capitalization and emphasis in original.

41. Ibid., 4.

42. Marilyn Hickey, direct-mail letter, undated (ca. December 1988), 4, emphasis in original.

43. Oral and Richard Roberts, direct-mail letter (August 1984), 2–3.

44. Ibid., 3.

45. Ibid., capitalization in original.

46. Ibid.

47. Ibid., 4, capitalization in original.

48. Ibid., capitalization in original.

49. Ibid.

50. Ibid.

51. Oral Roberts, *A Daily Guide to Miracles*, 64.

52. Ibid., 66.

53. Ibid., 68.

54. Ibid., 65.

55. Marilyn Hickey, direct-mail letter, undated (ca. 1992?), 3.

56. John Avanzini, *It's Not Working, Brother John!* (Tulsa: Harrison House, 1992), 13, emphasis in original.

57. Subtitle of Avanzini's book (ibid.).

58. Ibid., 45–53.

59. Ibid., 49–52; also see previous chapter on "Cultural Conformity."

60. Ibid., 52 (footnote).

61. Ibid., 141–42, capitalization in original.

62. Ibid., 142.

63. Ibid., 145, capitalization in original.

64. Ibid., 143.

65. Ernest Holmes, *Creative Mind and Success*, rev. ed. (New York: Dodd, Mead & Co., 1967 [orig. 1919]), 84.

66. Avanzini, *It's Not Working, Brother John!*, 213, back cover.

67. Ibid., 124, 122, emphasis in original.

68. Ibid., 122, emphasis in original.

69. Ibid., 123, emphasis in original.

70. Joyce Meyer, *Praise the Lord: Praise-a-Thon*, Trinity Broadcasting Network, 3 November 2003.

71. Rod Parsley, *Praise the Lord: Praise-a-Thon*, Trinity Broadcasting Network, 3 April 2003.

72. Benny Hinn, *Praise the Lord: Praise-a-Thon*, Trinity Broadcasting Network, 1 April 2003.

73. Juanita Bynum, *Praise the Lord: Praise-a-Thon*, Trinity Broadcasting Network, 4 November 2002.

74. Ibid.

75. Bynum, "Praise-a-Thon 2003," *Praise the Lord*, Trinity Broadcasting Network, 7 November 2003.

76. Paula White, *Praise the Lord: Praise-a-Thon*, Trinity Broadcasting Network, 3 November 2003.

77. White, *Praise the Lord: Praise-a-Thon*, Trinity Broadcasting Network, 5 April 2005.

78. White, *Praise the Lord: Praise-a-Thon*, Trinity Broadcasting Network, 3 November 2003.

79. White, *Praise the Lord: Praise-a-Thon*, Trinity Broadcasting Network, 5 April 2008.

Chapter 19: Covenant-Contract

1. John Hagee, *Praise the Lord*, Trinity Broadcasting Network, 8 January 2003.

2. Kenneth Copeland, *Our Covenant with God* (Fort Worth, TX: KCP Publications, 1987), 10.

3. Benny Hinn, sermon at the World Charismatic Conference, Melodyland Conference Center, Anaheim, CA (7 August 1992), audiotape excerpt on file at Christian Research Institute.

4. Kenneth Copeland, *God's Covenant with Man II* (Fort Worth, TX: Kenneth Copeland Ministries, 1985), audiotape #01-4404, side 2.

5. E. W. Kenyon, *The Blood Covenant* (Lynnwood, WA: Kenyon's Gospel Publishing Society, 1969), 14, 16.

6. The Faith movement clearly promotes a view of covenants, which better fits the description of contracts than the biblical idea of covenants. Consider these key features that distinguish covenants from contracts (adapted from Elmer A. Martens, *God's Design: A Focus on Old Testament Theology* [Grand Rapids: Baker Book House, 1981], 72–73):

    1. Contracts are *thing-oriented* (focusing largely on the benefits to which each party is entitled), whereas covenants are *person-oriented* (arising out of a desire to form an intimate relationship, one party to another).

    2. Contracts arise from a *mutual agreement* between two parties (thereby involving some form of *negotiation*), whereas covenants are initiated by the *stronger party* (who offers nonnegotiable help, not of necessity, but out of grace or as a gift).

    3. Contracts have conditions that are *performance-oriented* (focusing on the fulfillment of certain terms), whereas covenants stipulate obligations in terms of *personal loyalty*.

    The divine covenants discussed in the Old Testament (i.e., between God and humanity) are comprised of elements that are strikingly similar to those found in suzerainty treaties of the ancient Near East. In light of this fact, one may well contend that the Faith teaching of "covenant-contracts" has been proven false by the archaeological and historical records. (On the relationship between ancient Near Eastern suzerainty treaties and Old Testament covenants, see William Dyrness, *Themes in Old Testament Theology* [Downers Grove, IL: InterVarsity Press, 1979], 114–16; the classic treatment on this subject is George E. Mendenhall, "Covenant Forms in Israelite Tradition," *The Biblical Archaeologist* 17, 3 [September 1954]: 50–76.)

7. Kenneth Copeland, *Christianity, A Series of Decisions* (Fort Worth, TX: Kenneth Copeland Ministries, 1985), audiotape #01-0406, side 2; *Origin of the Blood Covenant* (Fort Worth, TX: Kenneth Copeland Ministries, 1985), audiotape #01-4401, side 2.

8. Charles Capps, *Authority in Three Worlds* (Tulsa: Harrison House, 1982), 66, emphasis in original.

9. Kenneth Copeland, *The Power of the Tongue* (Fort Worth, TX: KCP Publications, 1980), 10.

10. Kenneth Copeland, *The Laws of Prosperity* (Fort Worth, TX: Kenneth Copeland Publications, 1974), 51, emphasis in original.

11. Frederick K. C. Price, *Prosperity on God's Terms* (Tulsa: Harrison House, 1990), 36–37, emphasis in original.

12. Copeland, *The Laws of Prosperity*, 50–51. Copeland is here referring to Galatians 3:13–14 to argue that Jesus has redeemed all Christians from the curse of the law (which the Faith teachers wrongly associate with the curses listed in Deuteronomy 28) and has procured for them the material blessings of Abraham. However, the context of the passage militates against any such interpretation, as the discussion involves spiritual redemption and not earthly riches.

   The message of Galatians 3 is straightforward and simple: fallen humanity can achieve a right standing with God only through faith in Christ. God's law demands nothing short of perfection; hence it becomes a curse for those who attempt to attain a righteous standing by striving to fulfill it through sheer human effort (vv. 10–12). Sinful humanity is wholly incapable of coming close to meeting such high standards (v. 3). The good news is that Christ redeemed the elect from that curse by His perfect obedience and sacrifice to the Father. Our faith or trust in Christ's finished work is credited as righteousness and justifies us before God (vv. 26–28), which is precisely the blessing Abraham received (vv. 6–9).

   The Faith teachers diminish the infinite value and worth of Christ's sacrifice by falsely asserting that He died so that we may pamper ourselves in material indulgences. Far from concerning itself with such triflings, Galatians 3 calls attention to the grace of God, who, knowing that we could never be righteous in His sight through our own works, offered the supreme sacrifice so that we might be reconciled to Him.

13. Robert Tilton, *Success-N-Life* television program, 27 December 1990.

14. John Hagee, *Praise the Lord*, Trinity Broadcasting Network, 29 March 2001.

15. Jim Bakker, quoted in Terry Mattingly, "'Prosperity Christian' Sings a Different Tune," *Rocky Mountain News* (16 August 1992), 158.

16. Ibid.

17. John Hagee, *Praise the Lord*, Trinity Broadcasting Network, 8 January 2003.

18. Paraphrased from Charles H. Spurgeon, "A Sermon from a Rush" [commenting on Job 8:11–13, sermon 651 of sermons preached during 1865] in *Metropolitan Tabernacle Pulpit*, 63 vols. (Pasadena, TX: Pilgrim Publications, 1989), 11:537.

Chapter 20: Context, Context, Context

1. John Hagee, *In Defense of Israel* (Lake Mary, FL: Front Line, 2007), 136. Hagee emphatically concludes, "The Jews did not reject Jesus as Messiah" (132).

2. John Hagee, *Should Christians Support Israel?* (San Antonio, TX: Dominion, 1987), 67-68 passim; cf. 69, 72.

3. Paul Crouch, *Praise the Lord: Praise-a-Thon*, Trinity Broadcasting Network, 2 April 1991.

4. Ibid. Other opponents of orthodox Christianity have also received a warm welcome on TBN. Anti-Trinitarians who have been given a platform include Roy Blizzard, Joseph Good, and at least one minister from the United Pentecostal Church (UPC). William DeArteaga, who wrote a book advocating a form of "Christian" reincarnation (*Past Life Visions: A Christian Exploration* [New York: Seabury Press, 1983]; cf. Norman Geisler and J. Yutaka Amano, *The Reincarnation Sensation* [Wheaton, IL: Tyndale House Publishers, 1986], 52–53), has also appeared on TBN to promote his latest book dealing with the Charismatic movement and the Faith controversy. Although DeArteaga has claimed that he has since abandoned his metaphysical ideas, it is uncertain whether this includes his views regarding reincarnation (cf. *Quenching the Spirit* [Lake Mary, FL: Creation House, 1992], 13, 279, note 25).

5. Ibid.

6. For a discussion on this topic, see Ron Rhodes, "Esotericism and Biblical Interpretation," *Christian Research Journal* 14, 3 (Winter 1992):28–31.

7. For a short list of helpful aids and resources, see R. C. Sproul, *Knowing Scripture* (Downers Grove, IL: InterVarsity Press, 1977), 123–25.; Gordon D. Fee and Douglas Stuart, *How to Read the Bible for All It's Worth*, 3rd ed. (Grand Rapids: Zondervan, 2003), 265–75.

8. John Avanzini, *Praise the Lord: Praise-a-Thon*, Trinity Broadcasting Network, 5 November 1990.

9. Walter Bauer, William F. Arndt, F. Wilbur Gingrich, *A Greek-English Lexicon of the New Testament*

and Other Early Christian Literature, 4th rev. and aug. ed. (Chicago: The University of Chicago Press, 1957), 857a; U. Wilckens, "hysterema, hysteresis," *Theological Dictionary of the New Testament*, abridged in one vol. and ed. by Geoffrey W. Bromiley (Grand Rapids: Eerdmans/Paternoster Press, 1985), 1241; W. E. Vine, *An Expository Dictionary of New Testament Words* (Old Tappan, NJ: Fleming H. Revell Co., 1966), 196.

10. *The Legacy Study Bible* (Nashville: Thomas Nelson, Inc., 2007) and *The Apocalypse Code: Find Out What the Bible REALLY Says About the End Times . . . and Why It Matters Today* (Nashville: Thomas Nelson, Inc., 2007)—available through Christian Research Institute at www.equip.org.

11. Oral Roberts, *A Daily Guide to Miracles* (Tulsa: Pinoak Press, 1975), 36–38 passim.

12. Gordon D. Fee, *The Disease of the Health and Wealth Gospels* (Beverly, MA: Frontline Publishing, 1985), 6, emphasis in original.

13. Twentieth-century German biblical scholar Leonhard Goppelt has noted in this regard that "for our understanding of the OT, typology provides a framework that is determined not only by the NT but also by the OT itself; one that unites the two Testaments with one another and that facilitates the understanding of each by pointing to the other" (Leonhard Goppelt, 237). And, as Earl Ellis explains, "The NT's understanding and exposition of the OT lies at the heart of its theology, and it is primarily expressed within the framework of a typological interpretation" (E. Earl Ellis from the foreword to Leonhard Goppelt, Donald H. Madvid, transl., *Typos: The Typological Interpretation of the Old Testament in the New* (Grand Rapids: Wm. B. Eerdmans Publishing Co., 1982), xx.

14. Joel Osteen, Sermon #CS_002 - 4-23-00.

15. See John R. W. Stott, *The Cross of Christ* (Leicester: IVP, 1986), 179–81; Leon Morris, *The Apostalic Preaching of the Cross*, 3rd ed. (Grand Rapids: Wm. B. Eerdmans Publishing Co., 1984), 112–28. Also, "Some have argued, largely on the basis of this verse [Leviticus 17:11], that 'blood' in Scripture signifies life rather than death. However, in all of the Old Testament sacrifices, blood is obtained by killing an animal, and the life spoken of in Lev. 17:11 is that 'which ceases to exist when the blood is poured out'" (Steve Jeffrey, Michael Ovey, Andrew Sach, *Pierced for Our Transgressions: Rediscovering the Glory of Penal Substitution* [Wheaton: IL: Crossway Books, 2007], 45, n. 23.

16. John Piper, *Desiring God* (Portland, OR: Multnomah Press, 1986), 163, 167.

Part Six: *Sickness and Suffering*

1. Job: 13:15 KJV.

2. Paraphrasing Job 8:6 (Bildad the Shuhite); 11:4–6, 14–15 (Zophar the Naamathite); 15:5–6; 22:5–7, 9, 23 (Eliphaz the Temanite). Elihu the son of Barachel the Buzite was not described as a "friend" of Job's, but he, too, attacked Job for alleged sin (Job 34:37). Some Faith commentators try to twist these passages around to argue that since God seemingly did not condemn Elihu at the end, but only Job's three "friends" (Job 42:7–8; cf. 2:11), this means that Elihu's charges against Job still stand. This argument fails because God not only condemned the three friends but also added repeatedly that they had "not spoken of me what is right, *as my servant Job has*" (Job 42:7–8, emphasis added). Thus, regardless of the reason for omitting reference to Elihu at the end of the book, Job was still upheld by God Himself as having told the truth, obviously including Job's many statements that he had not sinned against God.

3. Frederick K. C. Price, *Is Healing for All?* (Tulsa: Harrison House, 1976), 20.

4. Betty Price, "A Praise Report," *Ever Increasing Faith Messenger*, 12:3 (Summer 1991); see also Pat Hays, "Betty Price Speaks at 1991 'Wisdom from Above' Luncheon," *Ever Increasing Faith Messenger*, 13:1 (Winter 1992), 12–13; and Betty Price, "Health Update . . . then . . . and . . . now from Betty Price," *Ever Increasing Faith Messenger*, 13:4 (Fall 1992), 5.

5. Kenneth Hagin: "I've been able to live for nearly sixty years without having a headache. I didn't say headache symptoms never tried to attack me. I said I haven't had a headache in nearly sixty years because when a symptom came, I demanded that it leave in Jesus' Name, and it left! . . . When you exercise your authority by faith in the Name of Jesus, sickness or disease must go!" (*Classic Sermons: Word of Faith 25th Anniversary 1968–1992 Commemorative Edition* [Tulsa: Kenneth Hagin Ministries, 1992], 159). "I have not had one sick day in 45 years. I did not say that the devil hadn't attacked me. But before the day is out, I am healed" (*The Name of Jesus* [Tulsa: Kenneth Hagin Ministries, 1979], 133). In the early days, Hagin was not so sure he was always healed by the end of

the day: "Perhaps the next day it [the healing] has not yet materialized, but we have to walk by faith and hold fast to our confession" (*Right and Wrong Thinking* [Tulsa: Kenneth Hagin Ministries, 1966], 21.) Later, Hagin was not only sure he had always been healed by the end of the day, but that it in fact took no more than one and a half hours (Kenneth E. Hagin, *Seven Things You Should Know About Divine Healing* [Tulsa: Kenneth Hagin Ministries, 1979], 68). Now, Hagin maintained that he had been healed "within just a few seconds," evidently referring to a 1942 instance of heart trouble (Hagin, "God's Best Belongs to You!" *The Word of Faith*, 26:1 [December 1992], 5c).

On Hagin's "no headache" since 1933/1934 comment, see Kenneth E. Hagin, sermon at the "All Faith's Crusade," Anaheim [CA] Convention Center (21 March 1991); and Hagin, *Name of Jesus* (Tulsa: Kenneth Hagin Ministries, 1981), 44. "Forty-five years have come and gone, and I haven't had a headache. Not one. The last headache I can actually remember having was in August 1933. I haven't had a headache, and I'm not expecting to have one. But if I had a headache, I wouldn't tell anybody. And if somebody asked me how I was feeling, I would say, 'I'm fine, thank you'" (Kenneth E. Hagin, *Words* [Tulsa: Kenneth Hagin Ministries, 1979], 6–7).

Hagin claims he was healed of his "deformed heart," "paralysis," and "incurable blood disease." In case he missed something, he declared his "healing from the top of my head to the soles of my feet" on August 7, 1934, so that "every symptom of distress, deficiency and physical wrongness was driven out of my body," perpetually. "I'm still healed after 49 years," Hagin said. (Kenneth E. Hagin, *Exceedingly Growing Faith*, 2nd rev. ed. [Tulsa: Kenneth Hagin Ministries, 1990], 48–49, 82–83.) See also Kenneth E. Hagin, *Understanding How to Fight the Good Fight of Faith* (Tulsa: Kenneth Hagin Ministries, 1987), 6; Kenneth E. Hagin, *What Faith Is*, rev. ed. (Tulsa: Kenneth Hagin Ministries, 1983), 18–19; Kenneth E. Hagin, *How to Write Your Own Ticket with God* (Tulsa: Kenneth Hagin Ministries, 1979), 16–17; Kenneth E. Hagin, *Faith Food for Spring* (Tulsa: Kenneth Hagin Ministries, 1978), 9; Kenneth E. Hagin, *I Believe in Visions* (Old Tappan, NJ: Revell, 1972), 27–30 (apparently his healing occurred on Tuesday of the "second week" of August 1934, or August 7, which was not the same date as the "second Tuesday" that month [August 14]). Elsewhere Hagin gives various dates, such as "6 days before my 17th birthday [20 August 1934]," which would be August 14, the "second Tuesday of August 1934" (Kenneth E. Hagin, *El Shaddai* [Tulsa: Kenneth Hagin Ministries, 1980], 24–25). But see Kenneth E. Hagin, *How You Can Be Led by the Spirit of God* (Tulsa: Kenneth Hagin Ministries, 1978), 87 (healing on a "Thursday" in August 1934). In still another place, Hagin claims his healing was on "August 8, 1934," which was a Wednesday (Kenneth E. Hagin, *Zoe: The God-Kind of Life* [Tulsa: Kenneth Hagin Ministries, 1981], 13). The blood disease may have been a form of hemolytic anemia (Hagin, *How You Can Be Led*, 88).

6. Hagin suffered heart-crisis episodes in 1939, 1942, 1949, and 1973:

1. Ca. May 1939: "I attended a Full Gospel convention . . . As I sat in the service, I began to have sharp pains around my heart. It seemed to quiver and stop. It even felt as if my breath were being cut off" (Hagin, *Right and Wrong Thinking*, 20–21).

2. 1942: "While pastoring a church in East Texas, I had a battle in my body . . . I didn't tell anyone about it. I just told the Lord and believed He would heal me. Then I stood my ground. There were some trying moments in the nighttime when it seemed as if I wouldn't make it . . . I had fought this battle for about six weeks . . . I had been fighting this battle for a long time" (Kenneth E. Hagin, *Authority of the Believer* [Tulsa: Kenneth Hagin Ministries, 1967], 9). "In the nighttime I would be awakened with alarming heart symptoms . . . I battled that thing for about six weeks" (Kenneth E. Hagin, *The Believer's Authority*, 2d rev. ed. [Tulsa: Kenneth Hagin Ministries, 1991], 8). "I had a battle with symptoms in my body . . . At times it looked like I wasn't going to make it" (Kenneth E. Hagin, *Faith Food for Spring* [Tulsa: Kenneth Hagin Ministries, 1978], 29).

This is apparently the same incident as the following: "The heart symptoms did come back on me . . . I struggled with it in the nighttime . . . 'Yes, I've got heart symptoms. In fact, if it gets any worse, I don't know what I'm going to do' (*The Name of Jesus*, 138). "Some alarming heart symptoms tried to come back on me . . . I knew that these symptoms could mean death, but I never budged an inch. I didn't discuss it with anyone. The devil kept telling me, 'You are not going to make it. You're going to die . . .' I . . . took my Bible and put it on the floor and put both my feet on it" (Kenneth E. Hagin, *The Real Faith* [Tulsa: Kenneth Hagin Ministries, 1982], 27). "I remember many years ago after I was healed, physical symptoms came back . . . The devil said to me, '. . . You're going to die . . . !' . . . I laid my Bible on the floor and literally stood on it" (Kenneth E. Hagin, "God's Best," *The Word of Faith* [December 1992], 5c).

3. July 10, 1949: "I was planning to preach at a church in East Texas . . . and I attended a men's Bible class before the service. I was sitting on a bench and suddenly my heart stopped, and I pitched over on the floor on my face. I fell right at the pastor's feet. He picked me up, and my heart began to race. You couldn't detect the beating. It felt like something shaking like a bowl full of gelatin . . . They told me later, 'We knew you were dead.' I was cold all over and white as a sheet. Death was upon my brow" (Kenneth E. Hagin, *Must Christians Suffer?* [Tulsa: Kenneth Hagin Ministries, 1982], 38). "Sitting in [Sunday school] class my heart suddenly stopped beating. I fell from my seat to the floor. Then my heart started beating erratically with a rapid pulse . . . When some ministers . . . felt my pulse they said, 'We cannot distinguish a beat—all we can feel is a flutter.' It seemed to me as if it were racing two or three hundred times a minute . . . I became as cold as ice all over . . . I knew when death came over me . . . [I] nearly died" (Kenneth E. Hagin, *The Human Spirit* [Tulsa: Kenneth Hagin Ministries, 1974], 24–25).

4. 1973 heart episode: "[Hagin] had a heart attack and like to died. God told him, says, 'You gonna die at the age of fifty-five [1972–73] if you don't start prophesying' . . . It come real close of costing Kenneth Hagin his whole life . . . That was the year before Rhema was started [in 1974]" (Norvel Hayes, presentation at the East Coast Believers' Convention [24 May 1982], audiotape). Possibly this is the same incident described by Hagin in 1978: "I was awakened at 1:30 A.M., several years ago, with severe symptoms in my heart and chest. I knew something about them because I'd been bedfast and expected to die with a heart condition as a teenager" (*Faith Food for Spring*, 89). In 1989 Hagin added some details about this occurrence: "I was holding a meeting in Pasadena, Texas. After one of the evening meetings, I had just gotten off to sleep, when I was awakened about 1:30 in the morning with severe heart pains. It seemed as if the incurable heart disease I'd had as a teenager had come back on me . . . I lay in bed that night with severe heart pain gripping me" (Kenneth E. Hagin, *Knowing What Belongs to Us* [Tulsa: Kenneth Hagin Ministries, 1989], 13–14).

5. No date: "Twice in my life it seemed that death had come and fastened itself upon me. Both times I just started laughing." One of the incidents I've already described (Pasadena, Texas, no date; Hagin, *Knowing What Belongs to Us*, 13).

6. Possible heart condition for three days, no date: "One time when I was attending a convention, I was having physical problems. I didn't say anything to my wife, but I couldn't sleep. Three nights I got down by the bed praying, but my healing would not come into manifestation. The symptoms would not leave me" (Kenneth E. Hagin, *Three Big Words* [Tulsa: Kenneth Hagin Ministries, 1983], 24).

7. One-night episode, no date: "A number of years ago, just before bedtime I was troubled with physical symptoms of alarming proportions . . . I got into bed, but these symptoms only grew worse. I continued to praise God for healing and finally managed to fall asleep. Almost immediately I was awakened with these symptoms. I finally said, 'Lord, I just don't know how much longer I can take this' . . . Awakened by serious symptoms for the third time, I heard in my spirit the words, 'Consider not' . . . My struggle was with appropriating physical healing in my body as alarming symptoms persisted . . . Symptoms and pain persisted" (Kenneth E. Hagin, *The Key to Scriptural Healing* [Tulsa: Kenneth Hagin Evangelistic Assoc., 1977], 27–28, [1984 rev.], 25–26).

7. Hagin, "God's Best," 5c.
8. "God's Bountiful Double Portion," *The Word of Faith* (December 1992), 10b–c.
9. Bruce Barron, *The Health and Wealth Gospel* (Downers Grove, IL: InterVarsity Press, 1987), 14–34.
10. Marla Cone, "Oral Roberts Stable After Heart Problem," *The Los Angeles Times* (8 October 1992), B1, B9; Oral Roberts and Paul Crouch on *Praise the Lord* show on TBN (6 October 1992). When Crouch laid hands on Roberts to minister to Roberts's chest pains, the latter exclaimed, "I feel the healing power of Jesus!" and said it felt like an "electric current." Less than four hours later, while visiting a home in Newport Beach, Roberts felt more pains and was hospitalized at Hoag Presbyterian Memorial Hospital (also in Newport Beach), shortly after midnight. Subsequent articles report that Roberts's heart attack was "near fatal" ("Evangelist Has Tests," *The Orange County [CA] Register* [16 December 1992], A-7) and resulted in the evangelist receiving a

pacemaker ("Roberts Out of Hospital," *The Orange County [CA] Register* [21 December 1992], A-30).

Paul Crouch's heart trouble: "Just this week . . . Paul [Crouch] just had the awfullest heart pains for two days. Just the awfullest heart pains. His heart would beat and stop, and stop and flutter and go and pain and pain and pain" (Jan Crouch, *Praise the Lord*, Trinity Broadcasting Network [31 July 1992]).

11. Letter from L. E. [name withheld for privacy] (25 August 1992).

12. Letter from D. B. [name withheld for privacy] (13 July 1992).

Chapter 21: Symptoms and Sickness

1. Jesse Duplantis, *Praise the Lord*, Trinity Broadcasting Network, 8 January 2003.

2. Kenneth Copeland, *The Troublemaker* (Fort Worth, TX: Kenneth Copeland Publications, n.d. [ca. 1970]), 6.

3. Kenneth Copeland, *Healed . . . to Be or Not to Be* (Fort Worth, TX: Kenneth Copeland Ministries, 1979), 25.

4. Ibid., 31–32, emphasis in original.

5. Benny Hinn, *"Rise and be healed!"* (Orlando, FL: Celebration Publishers, 1991), 44.

6. Ibid., 14.

7. Ibid., 32, emphasis in original.

8. Ibid., 65, emphasis in original.

9. Jerry Savelle, *If Satan Can't Steal Your Joy* (Tulsa: Harrison House, 1982), 9.

10. Ibid., 9–10, emphasis in original.

11. Ibid., 10–11, emphasis in original.

12. "I also have successfully resisted the flu all these years," claimed Hagin. "The longest any symptoms ever stayed was an hour and a half. Generally speaking, we Christians do not do that [resist illness]. At the first little *symptom of flu* that shows up (a headache or whatever) we will say, 'Oh, yes, I've got it'" (*Seven Things You Should Know about Divine Healing* [Tulsa: Kenneth Hagin Ministries, 1979], 68, emphasis added). "Someone asked, 'Brother Hagin, are you ever sick?' 'No'" (Kenneth E. Hagin, *God's Medicine* [Tulsa: Kenneth Hagin Ministries, 1977], 17).

Hagin once declared during a 1957 flu epidemic, "This epidemic doesn't worry me. I will never have the Asian flu" (*Understanding How to Fight the Good Fight* [Tulsa: Kenneth Hagin Ministries, 1987], 119). In another version Hagin asserts, "I'll *never* [Hagin's emphasis] have the Asian flu" (*El Shaddai* [Tulsa: Kenneth Hagin Ministries, 1980], 35–36). See also Hagin's son's report of the incident (Kenneth E. Hagin Jr., *Blueprint for Building Strong Faith* [Tulsa: Kenneth Hagin Ministries, 1980], 27). Hagin's son mentioned that his own young son (senior Hagin's grandson) was "diagnosed as having a brain tumor that required immediate surgery," but there is no mention of any faith healing whatsoever (Kenneth E. Hagin Jr., *The Answer for Oppression* [Tulsa: Kenneth Hagin Ministries, 1983], 14–16, 23).

However, during another flu epidemic in Texas in 1960, Hagin admits: "Everyone [*sic*] of those symptoms passed over my body in the night time, but I never told a person" (*Bible Faith Study Course* [Tulsa: Hagin Evangelistic Assoc., n.d. (ca. 1966)], 6). Elsewhere Hagin admits, "At times when I've had symptoms of a cold, some have said to me, 'Oh, you're getting a cold.' I say, 'No, I don't have a cold, and I'm not going to have one' (*Understanding How to Fight*, 129).

Jesus supposedly told Hagin in January 1950: "Sometimes even while you were preaching any symptoms you had would disappear" (Kenneth E. Hagin, *How God Taught Me About Prosperity* [Tulsa: Kenneth Hagin Ministries, 1985], 11).

13. Frederick K. C. Price, *Faith, Foolishness, or Presumption?* (Tulsa: Harrison House, 1979), 76–77.

14. Kenneth Copeland, "West Coast Believer's Convention," recorded in Anaheim, CA, 13 June 1991, emphasis added.

15. Kenneth E. Hagin, *Right and Wrong Thinking* (Tulsa: Kenneth Hagin Ministries, 1966), 20–21, emphasis added.

16. Ibid., 21.

17. Ibid.

18. Paul Brand and Philip Yancey, *Healing: What Does God Promise?* (Portland, OR: Multnomah Press, 1984 [*Guideposts* reprint, Carmel, NY]), 7.

19. Ibid.

20. Mary Baker Eddy, *Science and Health with Key to the Scriptures* (Boston: First Church of Christ, Scientist, 1971 [orig. 1875]), 390.

21. Phineas Quimby, *The Quimby Manuscripts*, ed. by Horatio W. Dresser (New Hyde Park, NY: University Books, 1961 [orig. 1859]), 186.

22. Hagin, *Right and Wrong Thinking*, 19, 24.

23. Kenneth Copeland, *Walking in the Realm of the Miraculous* (Fort Worth, TX: Kenneth Copeland Ministries, 1979), 37.

24. Price, *Faith, Foolishness*, 93. Also see Frederick K. C. Price, *How Faith Works* (Tulsa: Harrison House, 1976), 92–93, quoted in D. R. McConnell, *A Different Gospel* (Peabody, MA: Hendrickson Publishers, 1988), 154, 167, note 31.

25. Price, *Faith, Foolishness*, 88.

26. Hagin, "Healing: The Father's Provision," *The Word of Faith* (August 1977), 9; quoted in McConnell, *A Different Gospel*, 157, 168, note 41.

27. Hinn, *"Rise and be healed!"* 64.

28. Paul Crouch letter to M. A. [name withheld for privacy], 28 August 1992, emphasis added.

29. Copeland, *Healed . . . to Be*, 12.

30. Ibid., 12–13.

31. For additional treatment of the Faith movement's misuse of Isaiah 53:5 and other verses, see Elliot Miller, *Healing: Does God Always Heal?* (San Juan Capistrano: CRI, 1979), 3–5.

32. *Bible Answer Man*, 17 September 2008.

33. Joyce Meyer, "Practical Steps to Understanding and Experiencing Healing," online at http://www.joycemeyer.org/ourMinistries/Magazine/0703/Healing+and+wholeness.htm, retrieved 24 September 2008 (capitalization in original).

34. Jesse Duplantis, *Praise the Lord*, Trinity Broadcasting Network, 8 January 2003.

35. See 1 Peter 2:18–25, especially verse 24.

36. Kenneth Hagin Ministries, www.rhema.org/latestupdate, archived at http://web.archive.org/web/20030920042803rn_3/www.rhema.org/latestupdate.cfm, retrieved 1 October 2008; Kelly Kurt, "Rev. Kenneth E. Hagin, founder of international ministries dies," Associated Press, 19 September 2003.

Chapter 22: Satan and Sickness

1. Kenneth E. Hagin, *Faith Food for Spring* (Tulsa: Kenneth Hagin Ministries, 1978), 72–73, 79, emphasis in original.

2. Kenneth Copeland, *The Power of the Tongue* (Fort Worth, TX: Kenneth Copeland Ministries, 1980), 20, emphasis in original.

3. Ibid., 30.

4. Ibid., 23–24, emphasis in original.

5. Finis J. Dake, *God's Plan for Man* (Lawrenceville, GA: Dake Bible Sales, 1977 [orig. 1949]), 241.

6. Frederick K. C. Price, *Faith, Foolishness, or Presumption?* (Tulsa: Harrison House, 1979), 88, 94.

7. Frederick K. C. Price, *Is Healing for All?* (Tulsa: Harrison House, 1976), 113, emphasis in original.

8. Kenneth E. Hagin, *I Believe in Visions* (Old Tappan, NJ: Spire Books/Revell, 1972), 65.

9. Ibid., 67.

10. Robert Tilton, *Success-N-Life* television program (ca. 1991), video on file at Christian Research Institute.

11. Matthew, in context, is saying that when church members sin and repent, the church must "loose" or restore them to fellowship; but when they cannot, they should "bind" or remove them. (See Hendrik H. Hanegraaff, "CRI Perspective: 'Binding and Loosing' [Irvine, CA: CRI, 1991], order no. CP-0610; Eric Villanueva, "Territorial Spirits and Spiritual Warfare: A Biblical Perspective," *Christian Research Journal*, 15:1 [Summer 1992], 39).

12. An infectious disease, especially caused by a fungus.

13. Kenneth E. Hagin, *Faith Food for Spring* (Tulsa: Kenneth Hagin Ministries, 1978), 72–73, 79, emphasis in original.

14. Frederick K. C. Price, *How Faith Works* (Tulsa: Harrison House, 1976), 23.

15. Frederick K. C. Price, *Is God Glorified Through Sickness?* (Los Angeles: Crenshaw Christian Center, n.d.), audiotape #FP605, emphasis added.

16. Todd Bentley, video posted 26 June 2008, online at http://www.youtube.com/watch?v=DUTCWLoD4-4, accessed 5 July 2008.

17. Joyce Meyer, *Approval Addiction: Overcoming Your Need to Please Everyone* (New York: Faith Words, 2005), 9–10.

18. Joyce Meyer, *Eight Ways to Keep the Devil Under Your Feet* (New York: Warner Faith, 2002), 27.

19. Ibid., 28.

20. Osteen, *Your Best Life Now*, 149.

21. Gloria Copeland, *Believer's Voice of Victory*, Trinity Broadcasting Network, 25 October 1992.

Chapter 23: Sin and Sickness

1. Kenneth Copeland, *The Troublemaker* (Fort Worth, TX: Kenneth Copeland Publications, n.d.), 12.

2. Letter from S. C. [name withheld for privacy] (25 September 1991), 2.

3. Letter from H. C. [name withheld for privacy] (ca. 6 August 1991).

4. Letter from C. C. [name withheld for privacy] (19 June 1992).

5. Kenneth Copeland, presentation at Melodyland Christian Center, Anaheim, California (30 March 1983), emphasis in original.

6. Frederick K. C. Price, *How Faith Works* (Tulsa: Harrison House, 1976), 77.

7. Frederick K. C. Price, *Paul's Thorn #1* (Los Angeles: Ever Increasing Faith Ministries, 1980), audiotape #FP606, side 2. See also Price's statement, "Paul was a man who was prone to brag and boast" (*Is Healing for All?* [Tulsa: Harrison House, 1976], 12).

8. It is even more obvious in the original Greek than it is in English that Paul was *given* a thorn in the flesh, as opposed to giving it to himself. In Greek, the passive verb (*edothe*) is used to make it clear that Paul was the *recipient of the giving*. In other wo rds, the giving came from somewhere else. If the Holy Spirit had intended to indicate that Paul's own sin was responsible for his sickness or affliction, the middle voice (*edoto*) would have been used.

9. Gordon D. Fee, *The Disease of the Health and Wealth Gospels* (Beverly, MA: Frontline Publishing, 1985), 28–30, emphasis in original.

10. Jesse Duplantis, "What is Christianity, part 1," *Jesse Duplantis Ministries* webcast, 1 June 2002, www.jdm.org/media/weeklyarchive.html.

11. Benny Hinn, *"Rise and be healed!"* (Orlando, FL: Celebration Publishers, 1991), 62.

12. Kenneth Copeland, *The Troublemaker* (Fort Worth, TX: Kenneth Copeland Publications, n.d.), 12.

13. Mary Ann Jeffreys, "Sayings of Spurgeon," *Christian History* 10, 1 (1991):12a.

14. Price, *Is Healing for All?* 14–15.

15. George M. Lamsa, *Holy Bible: From the Ancient Eastern Text* (New York: A.J. Holman, 1933 [San Francisco: Harper & Row, n.d., 1984 reprint]), 1065a.

16. See John P. Juedes, "George M. Lamsa: Christian Scholar or Cultic Torchbearer?" *Christian Research Journal* 12, 2 (Fall 1989):8–14.

17. Price, *Is Healing for All?* 15 (footnote).

18. Kenneth Copeland, *The Power of the Tongue* (Fort Worth, TX: Kenneth Copeland Ministries, 1980), 22.

19. Kenneth Copeland, *Welcome to the Family* (Fort Worth, TX: Kenneth Copeland Ministries, 1979), 25, emphasis in original.

20. Rod Parsley, *Ancient Wells, Living Water* (Lake Mary, FL: Creation House Press, 2003), 129.

21. Joyce Meyer, *Trophies of God's Grace*, part 1 (Fenton, MO: Joyce Meyer Ministries, 1991), audiotape.

22. John Hagee, *John Hagee Today*, Trinity Broadcasting Network, 31 October 2003.

23. Ibid., emphasis added.

24. Pat Roberson, *The 700 Club*, Christian Broadcasting Network, 26 August 2004.

25. Darrel W. Amundsen, "The Anguish and Agonies of Charles Spurgeon," *Christian History* 10, 1 (1991):22–25 at 25b-c.

Chapter 24: Sovereignty and Sickness

1. Rod Parsley, *Ancient Wells, Living Water: God Invites You to Come and Drink* (Lake Mary, FL: Charisma House, 2003), 128–29.

2. Benny Hinn, *"Rise and be healed!"* (Orlando, FL: Celebration Publishers, 1991), 47–48.

3. Frederick K. C. Price, *Ever Increasing Faith*, Trinity Broadcasting Network, 16 November 1990.

4. Matthew 26:42; Mark 14:36; Luke 22:42; John 4:34; 5:30; 6:38; Acts 18:21; 1 Corinthians 4:19; Hebrews 10:7; Psalms 40:8; 143:10.

5. Gordon D. Fee, *The Disease of the Health and Wealth Gospels* (Beverly, MA: Frontline Publishers, 1991), 22.

6. Parsley, *Ancient Wells, Living Water*, 130.

7. Ibid.

8. Ibid., 128–29.

9. See Deborah Marrie, "Locked in Their Own World," *Charisma*, July 2004, online at http://www.charismamag.com/display.php?id=9219, retrieved 29 September 2008; Rod Parsley, *Silent No More* (Lake Mary, FL: Charisma House, 2005).

Part Seven: *Back to Basics*

1. John 12:24.

2. Associated Press release, "4 Killed When Balloon Hits Wires and Burns," *St. Louis Post-Dispatch* (16 December 1979), 14A.

Chapter 25: A=Amen

1. Revelation 3:14.

2. Frederick K. C. Price, *Ever Increasing Faith*, Trinity Broadcasting Network, 16 November 1990.

3. Frederick K. C. Price, "What Every Believer Should Know about Prayer," pamphlet (Los Angeles: Ever Increasing Faith Ministries, 1990), [4]. In light of the fact that the Faith teachers promote the error that "confession brings possession," their dim view of adding "Thy will be done" to prayer is not too surprising. Their system, implicitly if not explicitly, opposes the biblical teaching of submitting prayer petitions to the will of God. After all, petitions in prayer are *requests* that are subject to God's will, while confessions in Faith theology are outright *demands* supposedly guaranteed by God to bring each individual's personal desires into being. As Price's role model wrote: "I have found that the most effective way to pray can be when you demand your rights. That's the way I pray: 'I demand my rights!'" (Kenneth E. Hagin, *The Believer's Authority*, 2nd ed. [Tulsa: Kenneth Hagin Ministries, 1984], 22).

4. Frederick K. C. Price, "Petition Prayer, or the Prayer of Faith," pamphlet (Los Angeles: Ever Increasing Faith Ministries, 1991), [1], emphasis in original.

5. Price, "What Every Believer Should Know about Prayer," [4].

6. Frederick K. C. Price, letter to B. G. [name withheld for privacy] (14 October 1992), emphasis added.

7. Price, "Petition Prayer, or the Prayer of Faith," [1], capitalization in original.

8. Ibid., [3], capitalization in original.

9. Ibid., [4], capitalization and emphasis in original.

10. R. A. Torrey, *The Power of Prayer* (Grand Rapids: Zondervan, 1981) 123–24, emphasis in original.

Chapter 26: B=Bible

1. 2 Timothy 3:16–17.

2. Charles R. Swindoll, *Seasons of Life* (Portland, OR: Multnomah Press, 1983), 53, emphasis in original.

3. A number of Faith teachers have seized upon this verse and twisted it to justify their grossly unbiblical doctrine of wealth and prosperity. However, the context of the passage (and the entire book, for that matter) does not allow for any such interpretation. The prosperity and success mentioned in verse 8 pertain to Joshua's conquest of Canaan. God's command to remember and meditate upon the Book of the Law was given to bolster the Israelites' strength and courage as they prepared to do battle in Canaan (cf. verses 6–7). It served to remind them that God would be with them wherever they went (verse 9). As one observer rightly noted, "Joshua was a general, not a banker; financial prosperity is simply not in view here" (Ken L. Sarles, "A Theological Evaluation of the Prosperity Gospel," *Bibliotheca Sacra* 143, 572 [October–December 1986]:338).

4. Cited in Bernard Ramm, *Protestant Biblical Interpretation* (Grand Rapids: Baker Book House, 1978),

14. We should note that many if not all the Faith teachers bank on "new revelations" comparable to Scripture. Benny Hinn on one occasion made the following remark: "Don't think OCC [Orlando Christian Center] is here to repeat something you heard for the last fifty years.

"If God called me to repeat things you heard, I shouldn't be here. If *we quit giving you new revelations, we're dead.*" He then proceeded to tell his congregation and the larger viewing audience that Jesus was simply the product of God's positive confession. (See Hinn, *Benny Hinn*, Trinity Broadcasting Network [15 December 1991], from *The Revelation of Jesus*, Part 4: *The Person of Jesus* [Orlando, FL: Orlando Christian Center, 1991], videotape #TV-292, emphasis added).

5. Walter M. Martin, *The Kingdom of the Cults*, rev. ed. (Minneapolis: Bethany House, 1985), 67–125; "The New World Translation," *Christian Research Newsletter* 3, 3 (1990):5.

6. John P. Juedes, "George M. Lamsa: Christian Scholar or Cultic Torchbearer?" *Christian Research Journal* 12, 2 (Fall 1989):8–14.

7. Finis J. Dake, ed., *Dake's Annotated Reference Bible* (Lawrenceville, GA: Dake Bible Sales, 1963), NT pp. 96 col. 1, 97 cols. 1–2, emphasis in original; OT pp. 388 col. 1b, 467 col. 1f.

8. Ibid., NT p. 1 col. 1a.

Chapter 27: C=Church

1. Acts 2:42.

2. I believe I first heard a version of this illustration from D. James Kennedy.

Chapter 28: D=Defense

1. 1 Peter 3:15–16.

2. Paul Crouch, *Praise the Lord: Praise-a-Thon*, Trinity Broadcasting Network, 10 November 1987.

3. John Avanzini, *Praise the Lord: Praise-a-Thon*, Trinity Broadcasting Network, 5 November 1990.

4. Henry M. Morris and Gary E. Parker, *What Is Creation Science?* rev. (El Cajon, CA: Master Books, 1987), 154–57.

5. See Duane T. Gish, *Evolution: The Challenge of the Fossil Record* (El Cajon, CA: Creation-Life Publishers, 1991), 180–84; and Marvin L. Lubenow, *Bones of Contention* (Grand Rapids: Baker Book House, 1992), 86–120.

Chapter 29: E=Essentials

1. 1 Timothy 4:16.

2. Paul Crouch, *Praise the Lord*, Trinity Broadcasting Network, 5 September 1991.

3. Although the Athanasian Creed bears the name of Athanasius, the great fourth-century Trinitarian defender of the faith, most scholars today do not believe this creed was written by Athanasius, although they do affirm its universal acceptance by the church.

4. The statistical illustration is pertinent even though it is not meant to convey that everyone who is evangelized will become a believer.

Epilogue

1. Creflo Dollar, *Praise the Lord*, Trinity Broadcasting Network, 26 June 2001.

2. Jerry Savelle, *Framing Your World with the Word of God*, part 1 (Fort Worth, TX: Jerry Savelle Evangelistic Association, n.d.), audiotape #SS-36, side 1.

3. Benny Hinn, *Praise the Lord: Praise-a-Thon*, Trinity Broadcasting Network, 2 April 1991.

4. Although Bakker's current theology leaves much to be desired, his remarks in this letter from prison were refreshing to say the least.

Appendix B: Apologetics: The Defense of the Faith

1. Colin Patterson, personal letter to Luther Sunderland, 10 April 1979, quoted in Luther D. Sunderland, *Darwin's Enigma* 4th ed. (Santee, CA: Master Books, 1988), 89.

2. See Henry M. Morris and Gary E. Parker, *What Is Creation Science?* rev. ed. (El Cajon, CA: Master Books, 1987), 148.

3. Ibid., 150.

4. Adapted from Ken Boa, *I'm Glad You Asked* (Wheaton, IL: Victor Books, 1982), 36.

5. See Gary Habermas, *The Historical Jesus: Ancient Evidence for the Life of Christ* (Joplin, MO: College Press Publishing Co., 1996), 143–70 (esp. 158); Paul Copan, ed., *Will the Real Jesus Please Stand Up? A Debate between William Lane Craig and John Dominic Crossan* (Grand Rapids: Baker Books, 1998), 26–27.

6. Gary Habermas, *The Historical Jesus: Ancient Evidence for the Life of Christ* (Joplin, MS: College Press Publishing Co., 1996), 71.

7. William Lane Craig, "Did Jesus Rise from the Dead?" in Michael J. Wilkins and J. P. Moreland, gen. eds., *Jesus Under Fire* (Grand Rapids: Zondervan Publishing House, 1995), 147–48; Paul Copan, ed., *Will the Real Jesus Please Stand Up? A Debate between William Lane Craig and John Dominic Crossan* (Grand Rapids: Baker Books, 1998), 26–27.

8. Craig, "Did Jesus Rise from the Dead?" in Wilkins and Moreland, *Jesus Under Fire*, 152. See Matthew 28:13.

9. See Habermas, *The Historical Jesus*, 205–6.

10. William Lane Craig, *Reasonable Faith: Christian Truth and Apologetics*, rev. ed. (Wheaton, IL: Crossway Books, 1994), 276.

11. C. H. Dodd, "The Appearances of the Risen Christ: A Study in the Form Criticism of the Gospels," in *More New Testament Studies* (Manchester: University of Manchester, 1968), 128, as quoted in William Lane Craig, *Reasonable Faith: Christian Truth and Apologetics*, revised edition (Wheaton, IL: Crossway Books, 1994), 282.

12. Habermas, *The Historical Jesus*, 154; cf. Craig L. Blomberg, "Where Do We Start Studying Jesus?" in Wilkins and Moreland, gen. eds., *Jesus Under Fire*, 42–43.

13. See William Lane Craig, *Reasonable Faith: Christian Truth and Apologetics*, rev. ed. (Wheaton, IL: Crossway Books, 1994), 285.

14. Norman Perrin, *The Resurrection According to Matthew, Mark, and Luke* (Philadephia: Fortress, 1977), 80, as quoted by William Lane Craig in Paul Copan, ed. *Will the Real Jesus Please Stand Up? A Debate between William Lane Craig and John Dominic Crossan* (Grand Rapids: Baker Book House, 1998), 28.

15. Simon Greenleaf, *The Testimony of the Evangelists: The Gospels Examined by the Rules of Evidence* (Grand Rapids: Kregel Classics, 1995; originally published 1874), 31–32.

16. The New Testament was originally written in Greek. Nearly all of these extant Greek manuscripts predate the invention of the printing press, and some eight hundred predate A.D. 1000. Lee Strobel, interviewing Dr. Bruce Metzger of Princeton Theological Seminary, writes: "'While papyrus manuscripts represent the earliest copies of the New Testament, there are also ancient copies written on parchment, which was made from the skins of cattle, sheep, goats and antelope.

'We have what are called *uncial* manuscripts, which are written in all-capital Greek letters,' Metzger explained. 'Today we have 306 of these, several dating back as early as the third century. The most important are *Codex Sinaiticus*, which is the only complete New Testament in uncial letters, and *Codex Vaticanus*, which is not quite complete. Both date to about A.D. 350.

'A new style of writing, more cursive in nature, emerged in roughly A.D. 800. It's called *minuscule*, and we have 2,856 of these manuscripts. Then there are also lexionaries, which contain New Testament Scripture in the sequence it was to be read in the early churches at appropriate times during the year. A total of 2,403 of these have been cataloged. That puts the grand total of Greek manuscripts at 5,664.'" (Lee Strobel, *The Case for Christ* [Grand Rapids: Zondervan, 1998], 62–63).

The acronym L-U-M-P can be used as a memory aid so as not to *lump* all manuscripts together—Lexionaries, Uncial, Miniscule, and Papyrus.

17. See Philip Wesley Comfort, "Texts and Manuscripts of the New Testament," in Philip Wesley Comfort, ed., *The Origin of the Bible* (Wheaton: Tyndale House Publishers, 2003), 198–205.

18. Bart D. Ehrman, *Misquoting Jesus: The Story Behind Who Changed the Bible and Why* (New York: HarperSanFrancisco, 2005), 10.

19. See William M Ramsay, *The Bearing of Recent Discovery on the Trustworthiness of the New Testament*, repr. ed. (Grand Rapids: Baker, 1953); *St. Paul the Traveler and the Roman Citizen* (Grand Rapids: Baker Book House, 1962).

20. Jeffrey L. Sheler, "Is the Bible True?" *U. S. News and World Report*, 25 October 1999, 58; reprinted from Jeffrey L. Sheler, *Is the Bible True?* (San Francisco: HarperSanFrancisco, 1999).

21. Ibid., 58–59.

22. Ibid., 59. Sheler discusses other archaeological and historical insights of recent years, including the House of David inscription at Dan, which affirms the historicity of King David (54–58).
23. Paul L. Maier, "Archaeology: Biblical Ally or Adversary?" *Christian Research Journal*, 27, no. 2 (2004), online at www.equip.org.
24. See Maier, "Archaeology: Biblical Ally or Adversary?"

CONTACT CHRISTIAN RESEARCH INSTITUTE

By Mail

CRI United States
P.O. Box 8500
Charlotte, NC 28271-8500

CRI Canada
56051 Airways P.O.
Calgary, Alberta T2E 8K5

By Phone

U. S. 24–hour Toll–Free Customer Service: 1 (888) 7000-CRI
Fax: (704) 887-8299

Canada Toll-Free Credit Card Line: 1 (800) 665-5851
Canada Customer Service: (403) 571-6363

On the Internet

www.equip.org

During the *Bible Answer Man* Broadcast
Call in your questions toll free in the United States and Canada:
1 (888) ASK HANK (275-4265),
Monday through Friday, 5:50 p.m. to 7:00 p.m. Eastern Time

For a list of stations airing the *Bible Answer Man*
or to listen to the broadcast via the internet
Log on to our Web site at *www.equip.org*

If you would like Hank to speak in your church or in your area
Contact Paul Young at (704) 887-8222